W9-CRW-039

Patterns of
World History

Brief Edition

Volume I: To 1600

USED

Peter von Sivers
University of Utah

Charles A. Desnoyers
La Salle University

George B. Stow
La Salle University

New York   Oxford
OXFORD UNIVERSITY PRESS

Oxford University Press is a department of the University of Oxford. It furthers the University's
objective of excellence in research, scholarship, and education by publishing worldwide.

Oxford   New York
Auckland   Cape Town   Dar es Salaam   Hong Kong   Karachi
Kuala Lumpur   Madrid   Melbourne   Mexico City   Nairobi
New Delhi   Shanghai   Taipei   Toronto

With offices in
Argentina   Austria   Brazil   Chile   Czech Republic   France   Greece
Guatemala   Hungary   Italy   Japan   Poland   Portugal   Singapore
South Korea   Switzerland   Thailand   Turkey   Ukraine   Vietnam

Copyright © 2013 by Oxford University Press.

For titles covered by Section 112 of the US Higher Education Opportunity
Act, please visit www.oup.com/us/he for the latest information about
pricing and alternate formats.

Published by Oxford University Press.
198 Madison Avenue, New York, New York, 10016
http://www.oup.com

Oxford is a registered trademark of Oxford University Press.

All rights reserved. No part of this publication may be reproduced,
stored in a retrieval system, or transmitted, in any form or by any means,
electronic, mechanical, photocopying, recording, or otherwise,
without the prior permission of Oxford University Press.

Library of Congress Cataloging-in-Publication Data
Von Sivers, Peter.
  Patterns of world history, brief edition / Peter von Sivers, Charles A. Desnoyers, George Stow.
    v. cm.
  Includes bibliographical references and index.
  Contents: v. 1. To 1600 — v. 2. Since 1400.
    ISBN 978-0-19-994374-6 (combined v.: acid-free paper) — ISBN 978-0-19-994375-3
(v. 1: acid-free paper) — ISBN 978-0-19-994376-0 (v. 2: acid-free paper) 1. World history—
Textbooks. I. Desnoyers, Charles, 1952– II. Stow, George B. III. Title.
  D21.V66 2013
  909—dc23   2011031148

Printing number: 9 8 7 6 5 4 3 2 1
Printed in the United States of America
on acid-free paper

Coniugi Judithae dilectissimae
—Peter von Sivers

To all my students over the years, who have taught me at least as much as I've taught them; and most of all to my wife, Jacki, beloved in all things, but especially in her infinite patience and fortitude in seeing me through the writing of this book.

—Charles A. Desnoyers

For Susan and our children, Meredith and Jonathan.

—George B. Stow

—*I hear and I forget; I see and I remember; I do and I understand*
(Chinese proverb) 我听见我忘记；我看见我记住；我做我了解

Brief Contents

Contents

PART ONE

From Human Origins to Early Agricultural Centers

PREHISTORY–600 BCE   2

> **Features:**
> **Patterns Up Close:**
> Symbolic Thinking   24

> **Features:**
> **Patterns Up Close:**
> Babylonian Law Codes   42

Chapter 4
5000–481 BCE

Agrarian Centers and the Mandate of Heaven in Ancient China

Chapter 5
30,000–600 BCE

Origins Apart: The Americas and Oceania

PART TWO

The Age of Empires and Visionaries

600 BCE – 600 CE   138

Chapter 6
600 BCE–600 CE

Chiefdoms and Early States in Africa and the Americas   140

Features:

Patterns Up Close:
The Mayan Ball
Game   160

Chapter 7
550 BCE–600 CE

Persia, Greece, and Rome   168

Features:

Patterns Up Close:
The Plague of
Justinian   182

Chapter 8
600 BCE–600 CE

Empires and Visionaries in India   200

Features:

Patterns Up Close:
The Global Trade of
Indian Pepper   220

Chapter 9
722 BCE–618 CE

China: Imperial Unification and Perfecting the Moral Order   228

Features:

Patterns Up Close:
The Stirrup   240

Chapter 13
550–1500 CE

Religious Civilizations Interacting: Korea, Japan, and Vietnam

Chapter 14
600–1450 CE

Patterns of State Formation in Africa

Features:

Patterns Up Close:
Human Sacrifice and
Propaganda   428

PART FOUR

Interactions Across the Globe

Features:

Patterns Up Close:
Shipbuilding   442

Chapter 18
1500–1800

Maps

Studying with Maps

MAPS

World history cannot be fully understood without a clear comprehension of the chronologies and parameters within which different empires, states, and peoples have changed over time. Maps facilitate this understanding by illuminating the significance of time, space, and geography in shaping the patterns of world history.

Projection

A map *projection* portrays all or part of the earth, which is spherical, on a flat surface. All maps, therefore, include some distortion. The projections in *Patterns of World History* show the earth at global, continental, regional, and local scales.

Topography

Many maps in *Patterns of World History* show *relief*—the contours of the land. Topography is an important element in studying maps because the physical terrain has played a critical role in shaping human history.

Scale Bar

Every map in *Patterns of World History* includes a *scale* that shows distances in both miles and kilometers and, in some instances, in feet as well.

Map Key

Maps use symbols to show the location of features and to convey information. Each symbol is explained in the map *key*.

Global Locator

Many of the maps in *Patterns of World History* include *global locators* that show the area being depicted in a larger context.

The Inca Empire ca. 1525 CE

Inca expansion

- To 1438
- Under Pachacuti, 1438–1463
- Under Pachacuti and Tupac Yupanqui, 1463–1471
- Under Tupac Yupanqui, 1471–1493
- Under Huayna Capac, 1493–1525
- Imperial boundary
- Boundary between the four quarters of the empire
- Inca road
- ☐ Imperial capital
- ○ Major Inca administrative center
- **PERU** Modern-day country

Preface

Since the publication of *Patterns of World History* in December 2011, the response to its approach, comprehensiveness, and utility by instructors working in the field has been extraordinarily gratifying to those of us involved in its development. The diversity of schools that have adopted the book—from community colleges to state universities to small liberal arts schools—suggests to us that its central premise of exploring *patterns* in world history is both adaptable in a variety of pedagogical environments and congenial to a wide body of instructors. Indeed, from the responses to the book we have received thus far, we expect that the level of writing, timeliness and completeness of the material, and analytical approach will serve it well as the discipline of world history continues to mature.

Among the recent developments in the instructional field, one marked trend has been toward shorter texts. At a time when the daunting proliferation of electronic media and networking tools has altered the instructional landscape forever, teachers and professors are increasingly turning to the "brief book" as a more accessible base from which to structure their courses. In fact, of the many comments and suggestions we have received to date, requests for a brief version of our text have been among the most prominent. We are therefore pleased to offer *Patterns of World History* in this "brief book" edition, in the hope that it will become a valuable part of the world historian's instructional repertory. As with the longer format of *Patterns*, the brief book comes with a full array of supporting online and hard copy features and services—though with fewer illustrations and without the document boxes, Concept Maps, and Review and Respond features of the large volumes. Needless to say, the core elements of the book—the central concept of *patterns*, the structure of *origins, interactions, and adaptations,* the opening vignettes and "Patterns Up Close" feature—have all been retained. As a final note, we wish to thank all those involved in reviewing and preparing this edition; whatever errors or omissions that remain are strictly ours.

One of the hallmarks of our species is that we are historical creatures. We strive to remember the past in innumerable ways for an endless array of purposes: for cultural transmission, for moral instruction, for record keeping, to minimize risk in attempting new enterprises, to improve society or individuals, to tell entertaining or satisfying stories of ourselves. You, your family, your town or city, state, province, or country all have histories, all of them used in an endless variety of ways. As the historian G. R. Elton (1921–1994) put it, history is the only living laboratory we have of human behavior. So how is one to make sense of this bewildering, unending stream of information—especially if, as Elton would have it, the "experiments" in the "laboratory" are running and evaluating themselves?

Our approach in this book is, as the title suggests, to look for patterns in world history. We should say at the outset that we do not mean to select certain categories into which we attempt to stuff the historical events we choose to emphasize; nor do we claim that all world history is reducible to such patterns; nor do we mean to suggest that the nature of the patterns determines the outcome of historical events. We see them instead as broad, flexible, organizational frameworks around which to build the structure of a world history in such a way that the enormous sweep and content of the past can be viewed in a comprehensible narrative, with sound analysis and ample scope for debate and discussion. In this sense, we view them much like the role of armatures in clay sculptures, giving support and structure to the final figure but not necessarily preordaining its ultimate shape.

Take, for example, the role of innovation, in the broadest sense, in world history. The quest for the new and better has always been an animating spirit within the human saga—from the first wheel to the latest smart phone. Certainly, all such innovations, whether they are technological, intellectual, social, political, and so on, are vital to an understanding of human history. Our approach is to highlight the patterns we find in the development of such innovations as a way of taking a step back to make sense of them and the way that they foster change. Take the history of something from our recent past, e-mail, for example: Although electronic technology had advanced to the point in the 1960s where messages could be sent by computer, they could be sent and received only by operators using the same "server," as we would say today. What was needed, therefore, was a new system whereby messages could be sent and received by multiple servers in remote locations. The young engineer Ray Tomlinson (b. 1941), well versed in an early form of computer communication known as "ARPANET," which the American military used to share classified documents, concluded that, given the correct linkage, computers in far-flung locations could "talk" to each other. He worked out the missing piece in the form of the simple "@" sign, which he said "was used to indicate that the user was 'at' some other host rather than being local." Thus, the text message—and the e-mail address format we use today—originated through Tomlinson's interactions with other people and by means of his adapting other technologies available to him; these were then expanded exponentially by millions of others interacting with Tomlinson's breakthrough. This is but one recent example of the unfolding of a pattern of innovation; world history is full of them, and tracing their stories, effects, and implications comprises the heart of this book.

From its origins, human culture grew through interactions and adaptations on all the continents except Antarctica. A voluminous scholarship on all regions of the world has thus been accumulated, which those working in the field have to attempt to master if their explanations and arguments are to sound even remotely persuasive. The sheer volume and complexity of the sources, however, mean that even the knowledge and expertise of the best scholars are going to be incomplete. Moreover, the humility with which all historians must approach their material contains within it the realization that no historical explanation is ever fully satisfactory or final: As a driving force in the historical process, creative human agency moves this process into directions that are never fully predictable.

As we enter the second decade of the twenty-first century, world historians have long since left behind the "West plus the rest" approach that marked the field's early years, together with economic and geographical reductionism, in the search for a new balance between comprehensive cultural and institutional examinations, on the one hand, and those highlighting human agency, on the other. All too often, however, this is reflected in texts that seek broad coverage at the expense of analysis, thus resulting in a kind of "world history-lite." Our aim is therefore to simplify the study of the world—to make it accessible to the student—without making world history itself simplistic.

World History and Patterns of World History

Patterns of World History thus comes to the teaching of world history from the perspective of the relationship between continuity and change. What we advocate in this book is a distinct intellectual framework for this relationship and the role of innovation and historical change through patterns of origins, interactions, and adaptations, or as we like to call it, O-I-A. Each small or large technical or cultural innovation originated in one geographical center or independently in several different centers. As people in the centers interacted with their neighbors, the neighbors adapted to, and in many cases were transformed by, the innovations. By "adaptation" we include the entire spectrum of human responses, ranging from outright rejection to creative borrowing and, at times, forced acceptance.

Small technical innovations often went through the pattern of origin, interaction, and adaptation across the world without arousing much attention, even though they had major consequences. For example, the horse collar, which originated in ninth-century China and allowed for the replacement of oxen with stronger horses, gradually improved the productivity of agriculture in eleventh-century western Europe. More sweeping intellectual–cultural innovations, by contrast, such as the spread of universal religions like Buddhism, Christianity, and Islam and the rise of science, have often had profound consequences—in some cases leading to conflicts lasting centuries—and affect us even today.

Sometimes change was effected by commodities that to us seem rather ordinary. Take sugar, for example: It originated in southeast Asia and was traded and grown in the Mediterranean, where its cultivation on plantations created the model for expansion into the vast slave system of the Atlantic basin from the fifteenth through the nineteenth centuries, forever altering the histories of four continents. What would our diets look like today without sugar? Its history continues to unfold as we debate its merits and health risks and it supports huge multinational agribusinesses. Or take a more obscure commodity: opium. Opium had been used medicinally for centuries in regions all over the world. But the advent of tobacco traded from the Americas to the Philippines to China created an environment in which the drug would be smoked for the first time. Enterprising rogue British merchants, eager to find a way to crack closed Chinese markets for other goods, began to smuggle it in from India. The market grew, the price went down, addiction spread, and Britain and China ultimately went to war over China's attempts to eliminate the traffic. Here, we have an example of an item generating interactions on a worldwide scale, with impacts on everything from politics to economics, culture, and even the environment. The legacies of the trade still weigh heavily on two of the rising powers of the twenty-first century: China and India. And opium and its derivatives, like morphine and heroin, continue to bring relief and suffering on a colossal scale to hundreds of millions of people.

What, then, do we gain by studying world history through the use of such patterns? First, if we consider innovation to be a driving force of history, it helps to satisfy an intrinsic human curiosity about origins—our own and others. Perhaps more importantly, seeing patterns of various kinds in historical development brings to light connections and linkages among peoples, cultures, and regions—as in the examples—that might not otherwise present themselves.

Second, such patterns can also reveal differences among cultures that other approaches to world history tend to neglect. For example, the differences between the civilizations of the Eastern and Western Hemispheres are generally highlighted in world history texts, but the broad commonalities of human groups creating agriculturally based cities and states in widely separated areas also show deep parallels in their patterns of origins, interactions, and adaptations: Such comparisons are at the center of our approach.

Third, this kind of analysis offers insights into how an individual innovation was subsequently developed and diffused across space and time—that is, the patterns by which the new eventually becomes a necessity in our daily lives. Through all of this we gain a deeper appreciation of the unfolding of global history from its origins in small, isolated areas to the vast networks of global interconnectedness in our present world—that is, how a tsunami in Japan can affect everything from early warning systems in coastal areas of distant countries to fluctuations in international bond and currency markets.

Finally, our use of a broad-based understanding of continuity, change, and innovation allows us to restore culture in all its individual and institutionalized aspects—spiritual, artistic, intellectual, scientific—to its rightful place alongside technology, environment, politics, and socioeconomic conditions. That is, understanding innovation in this way allows this text to help illuminate the full range of human ingenuity over time and space in a comprehensive, evenhanded, and open-ended fashion.

It is widely agreed that world history is more than simply the sum of all national histories. Likewise, *Patterns*

of World History is more than an unbroken sequence of dates, battles, rulers, and their activities; and it is more than the study of isolated stories of change over time. Rather, in this textbook we endeavor to present in a clear and engaging way how world history "works." Instead of merely offering a narrative history of the appearance of this or that innovation, we present an analysis of the process by which an innovation in one part of the world is diffused and carried to the rest of the globe. Instead of focusing on the memorization of people, places, and events, we strive to present important facts in context and draw meaningful connections, analyzing whatever patterns we find and drawing conclusions where we can. In short, we seek to examine the interlocking mechanisms and animating forces of world history, without neglecting the human agency behind them.

Patterns of Change and Six Periods of World History

For the convenience of instructors teaching a course over two 15-week semesters, we have limited the book to 31 chapters. For the sake of continuity and to accommodate the many different ways schools divide the midpoint of their world history sequence, Chapters 15–18 overlap in both volumes; in Volume 2, Chapter 15 is given as a "prelude" to Part 4. Those using a trimester system will also find divisions made in convenient places, with Chapter 10 coming at the beginning of Part 3 and Chapter 22 at the beginning of Part 5. Finally, for those schools that offer a modern world history course that begins at approximately 1750, a volume is available that includes only the final two parts of the book.

Similarly, we have attempted to create a text that is adaptable to both chronological and thematic styles of instruction. We divide the history of the world into six major time periods and recognize for each period one or two main patterns of innovation, their spread through interaction, and their adoption by others. Obviously, lesser patterns are identified as well, many of which are of more limited regional interactive and adaptive impact. We wish to stress again that these are broad categories of analysis and that there is nothing reductive or deterministic in our aims or choices. Nevertheless, we believe the patterns we have chosen help to make the historical process more intelligible, providing a series of lenses that can help to focus the otherwise confusing facts and disparate details that comprise world history.

Part 1 (Prehistory–600 BCE): Origins of human civilization—tool making and symbol creating—in Africa as well as the origins of agriculture, urbanism, and state formation in the three agrarian centers of the Middle East, India, and China.

Part 2 (600 BCE–600 CE): Emergence of the axial age thinkers and their visions of a transcendent god or first principle in Eurasia; elevation of these visions to the status of state religions in empires, in the process forming multiethnic and multilinguistic polities.

Part 3 (600–1450): Disintegration of classical empires and formation of religious civilizations in Eurasia, with the emergence of religiously unified regions divided by commonwealths of multiple states.

Part 4 (1450–1750): Rise of new empires; interaction, both hostile and peaceful, among the religious civilizations and new empires across all continents of the world. Origins of the New Science in Europe, based on the use of mathematics for the investigation of nature.

Part 5 (1750–1900): Origins of scientific–industrial "modernity," simultaneous with the emergence of constitutional and ethnic nation-states, in the West (Europe and North America); interaction of the West with Asia and Africa, resulting in complex adaptations, both coerced as well as voluntary, on the part of the latter.

Part 6 (1900–Present): Division of early Western modernity into the three competing visions: communism, fascism, and capitalism. After two horrific world wars and the triumph of nation-state formation across the world, capitalism remains as the last surviving version of modernity. Capitalism is then reinvigorated through the "dot.com revolution," in which increasingly sophisticated software, Internet applications, and electronic communication devices lead to increasing use of social networking media in popularizing both "traditional" religious and cultural ideas and constitutional nationalism in authoritarian states.

Chapter Organization and Structure

Each part of the book addresses the role of change and innovation on a broad scale during a particular time and/or region, and each chapter contains different levels of exploration to examine the principal features of particular cultural or national areas and how each affects, and is affected by, the patterns of origins, interactions, and adaptations:

- *Geography and the Environment*: As we saw in the opening of this preface, the relationship between human beings and the geography and environment of the places they inhabit is among the most basic factors in understanding human societies. In Japan, for example, earthquakes and tsunamis have always been seen as part of the natural condition of things. Indeed, "tsunami" is a Japanese word with the tragically evocative meaning of "harbor wave." In this chapter segment, therefore, the topics under investigation involve the natural environment of a particular region and the general conditions affecting change and innovation. Climatic conditions, earthquakes, tsunamis, volcanic eruptions, outbreaks of disease, and so forth all have obvious effects on how humans react to the challenge of survival. The initial portions of chapters introducing new regions for study therefore include environmental and geographical overviews, which are revisited and expanded in later chapters as necessary. The larger issues of how decisive the impact of geography on the development of human societies is—as in the commonly asked question "Is geography destiny?"—are also examined here.
- *Political Developments*: In this segment, we ponder such questions as how rulers and their supporters wield political and military power. How do different political traditions develop in different areas? How do states expand, and why? How do different political arrangements attempt to strike a balance between the rulers and the ruled? How and why are political innovations transmitted to other societies? Why do societies accept or reject such innovations from the outside? Are there discernable patterns in the development of kingdoms or empires or nation-states?

• *Economic and Social Developments*: The relationship between economics and the structures and workings of societies has long been regarded as crucial by historians and social scientists. But what, if any, patterns emerge in how these relationships develop and function among different cultures? This segment explores such questions as the following: What role does economics play in the dynamics of change and continuity? What, for example, happens in agrarian societies when merchant classes develop? How does the accumulation of wealth lead to social hierarchy? What forms do these hierarchies take? How do societies formally and informally try to regulate wealth and poverty? How are economic conditions reflected in family life and gender relations? Are there patterns that reflect the varying social positions of men and women that are characteristic of certain economic and social institutions? How are these in turn affected by different cultural practices?

• *Intellectual, Religious, and Cultural Aspects*: Finally, we consider it vital to include an examination dealing in some depth with the way people understood their existence and life during each period. Clearly, intellectual innovation—the generation of new ideas—lies at the heart of the changes we have singled out as pivotal in the patterns of origins, interactions, and adaptations that form the heart of this text. Beyond this, those areas concerned with the search for and construction of meaning—particularly religion, the arts, philosophy, and science—not only reflect shifting perspectives but also, in many cases, play a leading role in determining the course of events within each form of society. For example, the shift to the use of mathematics as a foundation of the "scientific revolution" contributed mightily to the rationalism and empiricism of the Enlightenment—and hence to the development of the modernity that we find ourselves in today. All of these facets of intellectual life are, in turn, manifested in new perspectives and representations in the cultural life of a society.

Features

• **Seeing Patterns/Thinking Through Patterns:** Successful history teachers often employ recursive, even reiterative, techniques in the classroom

to help students more clearly perceive patterns. In a similar fashion, "Seeing Patterns" and "Thinking Through Patterns" use a question–discussion format in each chapter to pose several broad questions ("Seeing Patterns") as advance organizers for key themes, which are then matched up with short essays at the end ("Thinking Through Patterns") that examine these same questions in a sophisticated yet student-friendly fashion. Designed to foster discussion, instructors who have class-tested *Patterns of World History* report that "Thinking Through Patterns" also serve as excellent models for writing short essays.

• **Patterns Up Close:** Since students frequently better apprehend macro-level patterns when they see their contours brought into sharper relief, "Patterns Up Close" essays in each chapter highlight a particular innovation that demonstrates origins, interactions, and adaptations in action. Spanning technological, social, political, intellectual, economic, and environmental developments, the "Patterns Up Close" essays combine text, visuals, and graphics to consider everything from the pepper trade to the guillotine to rock and roll.

• **Marginal Glossary:** To avoid the necessity of having to flip pages back and forth, definitions of words that the reader may not know, as well as definitions of key terms, are set directly in the margin at the point where they are first introduced.

Today, more than ever, students and instructors are confronted by a vast welter of information on every conceivable subject. Beyond the ever-expanding print media, the Internet and the Web have opened hitherto unimaginable amounts of data to us. Despite such unprecedented access, however, all of us are too frequently overwhelmed by this undifferentiated—and all too often indigestible—mass. Nowhere is this more true than in world history, by definition the field within the historical profession with the broadest scope. Therefore, we think that an effort at synthesis—of narrative and analysis structured around a clear, accessible, widely applicable theme—is needed, an effort that seeks to explain critical patterns of the world's past behind the billions of bits of information accessible at the stroke of a key on a computer keyboard. We hope this text, in tracing the lines of transformative ideas and things that left their patterns deeply imprinted into the canvas of world history, will provide such a synthesis.

Additional Learning Resources for *Patterns of World History*

- **Instructor's Resource Manual:** Includes, for each chapter, a detailed chapter outline, suggested lecture topics, learning objectives, map quizzes, geography exercises, classroom activities, "Patterns Up Close" activities, "Seeing Patterns and Making Connections" activities, "Concept Map" exercises, biographical sketches, a correlation guide for the list of assets on the Instructor's Resource DVD, as well as suggested Web resources and digital media files. Also includes, for each chapter, approximately 40 multiple-choice, short-answer, true-or-false, and fill-in-the-blank as well as approximately 10 essay questions.
- **Instructor's Resource DVD:** Includes Power-Point slides and JPEG and PDF files for all the maps and photos in the text, an additional 400 map files from *The Oxford Atlas of World History*, as well as approximately 250 additional Power-Point-based slides organized by theme and topic. Also includes approximately 1,500 questions that can be customized by the instructor.
- **Sources in Patterns of World History: Volume 1: To 1600:** Includes approximately 100 text and visual sources in world history, organized to match the chapter organization of *Patterns of World History*. Each source is accompanied by a headnote and reading questions.
- **Sources in Patterns of World History: Volume 2: Since 1400:** Includes approximately 100 text and visual sources in world history, organized by the chapter organization of *Patterns of World History*. Each source is accompanied by a headnote and reading questions.
- **Mapping Patterns of World History, Volume 1: To 1600:** Includes approximately 50 full-color maps, each accompanied by a brief headnote, as well as Concept Map exercises.
- **Mapping Patterns of World History, Volume 2: Since 1400:** Includes approximately 50 full-color maps, each accompanied by a brief headnote, as well as Concept Map exercises.
- **Companion Website (www.oup.com/us/vonsivers):** Includes quizzes, flashcards, map exercises, documents, interactive Concept Map exercises, and links to YouTube videos.
- **E-book for Patterns of World History:** An e-book is available for purchase at www.coursesmart.com.

Bundling Options

Patterns of World History can be bundled at a significant discount with any of the titles in the popular Very Short Introductions or Oxford World's Classics series, as well as other titles from the Higher Education division world history catalog (www.oup.com/us/catalog/he). Please contact your OUP representative for details.

Acknowledgments

Throughout the course of writing, revising, and preparing *Patterns of World History* for publication we have benefited from the guidance and professionalism accorded us by all levels of the staff at Oxford University Press. John Challice, vice president and publisher, had faith in the inherent worth of our project from the outset and provided the initial impetus to move forward. In the early stages of the editorial process, Brian Wheel and Frederick Speers provided helpful critiques and advice, saving us from textual infelicities; Meg Botteon later added a final polish. Lauren Aylward carried out the thankless task of assembling the manuscript and did so with generosity and good cheer. Picture researcher Francelle Carapetyan diligently tracked down every photo request despite the sometimes sketchy sources we provided, Leslie Anglin copyedited the manuscript with meticulous attention to detail, and Shelby Peak steered us through the intricacies of production with the stoicism of a saint.

Most of all, we owe a special debt of gratitude to Charles Cavaliere, our editor. Charles took on the daunting task of directing the literary enterprise at a critical point in the book's career. He pushed this project to its successful completion, accelerated its schedule, and used a combination of flattery and hard-nosed tactics to make sure we stayed the course. His greatest contribution, however, is in the way he refined our original vision for the book with several important adjustments that clarified its latent possibilities. From the maps to the photos to the special features, Charles's high standards and concern for detail are evident on every page.

Developing a book like *Patterns of World History* is an ambitious project, a collaborative venture in which authors and editors benefit from the feedback provided by a team of outside readers and consultants. We gratefully acknowledge the advice that the many reviewers, focus group participants, and class testers (including their students) shared with us along the way. We tried to implement all of the excellent suggestions. Of course, any errors of fact or interpretation that remain are solely our own.

Reviewers

Stephanie Ballenger, Central Washington University

Alan Baumler, Indiana University of Pennsylvania

Robert Blackey, California State University

Robert Bond, San Diego Mesa College

Mauricio Borrero, St. John's University

Linda Bregstein-Scherr, Mercer County Community College

Scott Breuninger, University of South Dakota

Paul Brians, Washington State University

Gayle K. Brunelle, California State University-Fullerton

James De Lorenzi, City University of New York, John Jay College

Jennifer Kolpacoff Deane, University of Minnesota-Morris

Andrew D. Devenney, Grand Valley State University

Francis A. Dutra, University of California, Santa Barbara

Jeffrey Dym, Sacramento State University

Jennifer C. Edwards, Manhattan College

Lisa M. Edwards, University of Massachusetts-Lowell

Charles T. Evans, Northern Virginia Community College

Christopher Ferguson, Auburn University

Scott Fritz, Western New Mexico State University

Arturo Giraldez, University of the Pacific

Candace Gregory-Abbott, California State University-Sacramento

Derek Heng, Ohio State University

Eric Hetherington, New Jersey Institute of Technology

Laura J. Hilton, Muskingum University

Elizabeth J. Houseman, State University of New York-Brockport

Hung-yok Ip, Oregon State University

Geoffrey Jensen, University of Arkansas

Roger E. Kanet, University of Miami

Kelly Kennington, Auburn University

Amelia M. Kiddle, University of Arizona

Frederic Krome, University of Cincinnati-Clermont College

Mark W. Lentz, University of Louisiana, Lafayette

Heather Lucas, Georgia Perimeter College

Susan Mattern, University of Georgia

Susan A. Maurer, Nassau Community College

Jason McCollom, University of Arkansas

Douglas T. McGetchin, Florida Atlantic University

Stephen Morillo, Wabash College

Carolyn Neel, Arkansas Tech University

Kenneth J. Orosz, Buffalo State College

Alice K. Pate, Columbus State University

Patrick M. Patterson, Honolulu Community College

Daniel Pope, University of Oregon

G. David Price, Santa Fe College

Michael Redman, University of Louisville

Leah Renold, Texas State University

Jeremy Rich, Middle Tennessee State University

Jason Ripper, Everett Community College

Chad Ross, East Carolina University

Nana Yaw B. Sapong, Southern Illinois University-Carbondale

Daniel Sarefield, Fitchburg State College

Claire Schen, State University of New York, Buffalo

Robert C. Schwaller, University of North Carolina-Charlotte

George Sochan, Bowie State University

Ramya Sreenivasan, State University of New York, Buffalo

John Stanley, Kutztown University

Vladimir Steffel, Ohio State University

Anthony J. Steinhoff, University of Tennessee-
  Chattanooga

Micheal Tarver, Arkansas Tech University

Shane Tomashot, Georgia State University

Kate Transchel, California State University-Chico

Melanie Tubbs, Arkansas Tech University

Andrew Wackerfuss, Georgetown University

Evan R. Ward, Brigham Young University

Joseph K. S. Yick, Texas State University-San Marcos

Please let us know your experiences with *Patterns of World History, Brief Edition*, so that we may improve it in future editions. We welcome your comments and suggestions.

Peter von Sivers
pv4910@xmission.com

Charles A. Desnoyers
desnoyer@lasalle.edu

George B. Stow
gbsgeorge@aol.com

Note on Dates and Spellings

In keeping with widespread practice among world historians, we use "BCE" and "CE" to date events and the phrase "years ago" to describe developments from the remote past.

The transliteration of Middle Eastern words has been adjusted as much as possible to the English alphabet. Therefore, long vowels are not emphasized. The consonants specific to Arabic (alif, dhal, ha, sad, dad, ta, za, ayn, ghayn, and qaf) are either not indicated (except for ayn in the middle of words) or rendered with common English letters. A similar procedure is followed for Farsi. Turkish words follow the alphabet reform of 1929, which adds the following letters to the Western alphabet or modifies their pronunciation: c (pronounced "j"), ç (pronounced "tsh"), ğ (not pronounced, lengthening of preceding vowel), ı ("i" without dot, pronunciation close to short e), i/İ ("i" with dot, including in caps), ö (no English equivalent), ş ("sh"), and ü (no English equivalent). The spelling of common Middle Eastern and Islamic terms follows daily press usage (which, however, is not completely uniform). Examples are "al-Qaeda," "Quran," and "sharia."

The system used in rendering the sounds of Mandarin Chinese—the northern Chinese dialect that has become in effect the national spoken language in China and Taiwan—into English in this book is *hanyu pinyin*, usually given as simply *pinyin*. This is the official Romanization system of the People's Republic of China and has also become the standard outside of Taiwan, Republic of China. Most syllables are pronounced as they would be in English, with the exception of the letter q, which is given an aspirated "ch" sound; ch itself has a less aspirated "ch" sound. *Zh* carries a hard "j" and j, a soft, English-style "j." Some syllables also are pronounced—particularly in the regions around Beijing—with a retroflex r so that the syllable *shi*, for example, carries a pronunciation closer to "shir." Finally, the letter r in the *pinyin* system has no direct English equivalent, but an approximation may be had by combining the sounds of "r" and "j."

Japanese terms have been Romanized according to a modification of the Hepburn system. The letter g is always hard; vowels are handled as they are in Italian—e, for example, carries a sound like "ay." We have not, however, included diacritical markings to indicate long vowel sounds in u or o. Where necessary, these have been indicated in the pronunciation guides.

For Korean terms, we have used a variation of the McCune-Reischauer system, which remains the standard Romanization scheme for Korean words used in English academic writing, but eliminated any diacritical markings. Here again, the vowel sounds are pronounced more or less like those of Italian and the consonants, like those of English.

For Vietnamese words, we have used standard renditions based on the modern Quoc Ngu ("national language") system in use in Vietnam today. The system was developed by Jesuit missionaries and is based on the Portuguese alphabet. Once more, we have avoided diacritical marks, and the reader should follow the pronunciation guides for approximations of Vietnamese terms.

Latin American terms (Spanish, Nahua, or Quechua) generally follow local usage, including accents, except where they are Anglicized, per the *Oxford English Dictionary*. Thus, the Spanish-Quechua word "Tiahuanacu" becomes the Anglicized word "Tiwanaku."

We use the terms "Native American" and "Indian" interchangeably to refer to the peoples of the Americas in the pre-Columbian period and "Amerindian" in our coverage of Latin America since independence.

In keeping with widely recognized practice among paleontologists and other scholars of the deep past, we use the term "hominins" in Chapter 1 to emphasize their greater remoteness from apes and proximity to modern humans.

Phonetic spellings often follow the first appearance of a non-English word whose pronunciation may be unclear to the reader. We have followed the rules for capitalization per *The Chicago Manual of Style*.

About the Authors

Peter von Sivers is associate professor of Middle Eastern history at the University of Utah. He has previously taught at UCLA, Northwestern University, the University of Paris VII (Vincennes), and the University of Munich. He has also served as chair, Joint Committee of the Near and Middle East, Social Science Research Council, New York, 1982–1985; editor, *International Journal of Middle East Studies*, 1985–1989; member, Board of Directors, Middle East Studies Association of North America, 1987–1990; and chair, SAT II World History Test Development Committee of the Educational Testing Service, Princeton, NJ, 1991–1994. His publications include *Caliphate, Kingdom, and Decline: The Political Theory of Ibn Khaldun*, several edited books, and three dozen peer-reviewed chapters and articles on Middle Eastern and North African history, as well as world history. He received his Dr. Phil. from the University of Munich.

Charles A. Desnoyers is associate professor of history and director of Asian studies at La Salle University, Philadelphia. He is also past director of the Greater Philadelphia Asian Studies Consortium and president (2011–2012) of the Mid-Atlantic Region Association for Asian Studies. His scholarly publications include *A Journey to the East: Li Gui's "A New Account of a Trip Around the Globe"* (University of Michigan Press, 2004) and former coeditor of the World History Association's *Bulletin*.

George B. Stow is professor of history and director of the graduate program in history at La Salle University, Philadelphia. His teaching experience embraces a variety of undergraduate and graduate courses in ancient Greece and Rome, medieval England, and world history; and for excellence in teaching he has been awarded the Lindback Distinguished Teaching Award. Professor Stow is a member of the Medieval Academy of America and a Fellow of the Royal Historical Society. He is the recipient of a National Defense Education Act Title IV Fellowship, a Woodrow Wilson Foundation Fellowship, and research grants from the American Philosophical Society and La Salle University. His publications include a critical edition of a fourteenth-century monastic chronicle, *Historia Vitae et Regni Ricardi Secundi* (University of Pennsylvania Press), as well as numerous articles and reviews in scholarly journals including *Speculum*, *The English Historical Review*, the *Journal of Medieval History*, the *American Historical Review*, and several others. He received his PhD from the University of Illinois.

Patterns of World History

Brief Edition

PART ONE

From Human Origins to Early Agricultural Centers

PREHISTORY–600 BCE

World history is the discipline that tells us what humans had in common as they evolved both materially and mentally from prehistory to the present. When we study these common patterns, we find that the first period of world history (prehistory–600 BCE) can be subdivided into three wide-ranging phases, which we will discuss very broadly in this part opening essay. We will return to these same patterns as they develop—and discover new, more complex patterns—in Chapters 1–5.

The Origins of Modern Humanity

The first phase (6.5 million years ago–8500 BCE) began with the origins and evolution of humanity in Africa. After about 5.5 million years, around 80,000–70,000 BCE, groups of modern humans left Africa and began carrying their civilization of stone tools, shell jewelry, figurines, carvings, rock paintings, and shamanism across the entire world.

Technologically, the modern humans who left Africa had already acquired the skills to make tools from stone, bone, and wood. Mentally, they were also creating artifacts to which they attributed symbolic meaning, such as seashell necklaces and stone surfaces incised with geometric figures. The tools and artifacts of our earliest ancestors were obviously far less sophisticated than ours today. But they nevertheless defined a fully human civilization that spread across the globe—until the last ice age (32,000–12,000 years ago) put a stop to much of their interactions. Separated by impenetrable ice or desert barriers and existing without much contact for thousands of years, modern human groups developed their own distinct regional technologies and cultures.

Wherever our forager forebears were, they organized themselves into larger tribal societies with shared initiation rites and shamans who mediated the material and spiritual worlds. Even the stone tools, jewelry, figurines, and rock images displayed remarkable similarities across this region. In short, African-originated material technology and mental culture dominated the world.

Origins, Interactions, and Adaptations

7 million years ago
Toumaï, Oldest Possibly Hominin Fossil to Date

15,500 years ago
Earliest Archaeological Evidence of Humans in the Americas

200,000 years ago
Homo sapiens, or Modern Human, Emerges in East Africa

11500 BCE
End of Last Ice Age

The Origins of Agricultural Centers

The second phase (8500–3300 BCE) began once the global climate normalized, after the "great thaw," when agricultural centers originated in the Middle East, south and east Asia, and the Americas. In the Middle East, foragers resumed their migratory patterns, carrying their languages into regions opened up by receding glaciers and deserts. Between 8500 and 7000 BCE, foragers settled in permanent villages situated below mountain ranges, where seasonal runoff water supported rich forests and meadows. They grew skilled in the collection of plant seeds, which they developed, through selective breeding, into domesticated wheat, barley, rice, millet, and corn. They also captured young animals and domesticated them in their houses for their meat, milk, and hair.

Some of the early hill farmers moved into river valleys and deltas, where they expanded irrigation systems, supporting the rise of cities and kingdoms. The first agrarian-urban centers of the Middle East, India, China, and the Americas originated in irrigated river valleys between 3500 and 2500 BCE. Structured societies emerged in which kings, claiming divine mandates, and administrative and military ruling classes governed craftspeople and farmers.

The Origins of Empires

In the third phase, people outside the Eurasian agrarian centers adapted to agriculture through interaction with the agrarian-urban centers (3300–600 BCE). Steppe peoples, who controlled the mines containing the raw materials for making bronze alloys, used their horses and bronze weapons to migrate to, conquer, or establish new, distant kingdoms. Through their migrations or conquests, the nomadic steppe peoples of Europe and central Asia connected the three agrarian centers of the Middle East, India, and China. A pattern was established whereby the three centers were continuously adapting to each other's technological and cultural achievements, with steppe nomads functioning as their intermediaries.

From 1100 BCE onward the three Asian agrarian centers gradually replaced bronze with a cheaper metal, iron, as the principal material for weapons and tools. As a result, political and military competitiveness among kingdoms escalated dramatically. The first empires—that is, assemblages of conquered kingdoms under a king-of-kings or emperor—appeared, for example, the Neo-Assyrian Empire in the Middle East. Meanwhile, in some regions of the more sparsely populated continents of Africa and the Americas, agrarian centers grew more slowly, from villages to towns and, in a few places, even small kingdoms.

Thinking Like a World Historian

▶ What is the best way to describe the three early phases of world history?

▶ Why and how do we differentiate "modern" humans from earlier ancestors?

▶ What adaptations were necessary to improve agriculture? How did improvements in agriculture affect the development of society?

▶ What adaptations changed the methods of early warfare? How did developments in warfare affect regional interactions among civilizations?

▶ How did regional interactions with agricultural centers give rise to early kingdoms?

9500 BCE
Beginnings of Agriculture in Fertile Crescent

ca. 7000 BCE
First Evidence of Rice Cultivation in Yangzi Valley

3000 BCE–200 CE
Lapita Cultural Complex in Western Pacific

ca. 2700 BCE
First American City at Caral-Supé in Peru

2500–1700 BCE
Flourishing of Harappan Culture Along Indus River Valley, India

1766–1122 BCE
Traditional Dates for the Shang Dynasty

1650 BCE
Hittite Empire; Beginnings of Iron Smelting

750 BCE
City-States in Greece and Ionia

Chapter 1 PREHISTORY-10,000 BCE
The African Origins of Humanity

SAHARA

AFRICA

Great Rift Valley

■ Modern rain forest
■ Ancient rain forest

When Donald Johanson awoke in his tent on the morning of November 30, 1974, he felt that this was the day on which something "terrific" might happen. He and Tom Gray got into their Land Rover and drove for about a half hour to "locality 162" at Hadar in the Afar desert of Ethiopia in northeastern Africa. Once there, the two men walked about, checking the ground carefully for fossils of human predecessors. Members of the expedition had gone over the ground twice before but failed to find anything beyond animal bones.

After 2 hours of fruitless searching, with the temperature now soaring to 110 degrees Fahrenheit, the two took a final glance at a gully the team had visited not long before. Amid the heat waves shimmering off of the baking ground, Johanson found himself squinting at something out of place and called out, "That's a bit of a [hominin] arm." With growing excitement, he and Gray began to locate other bones nearby. "An unbelievable, impermissible thought flickered through my mind," Johanson remembered. "Suppose all these fitted together? Could they be parts of a single, extremely primitive skeleton? No such skeleton had ever been found—anywhere." The two raced back to the camp, sharing their excitement with the other scientists and local Afar workers. When night fell and the camp was rocking with joy, a tape recorder was belting out the Beatles' song "Lucy in the Sky with Diamonds"; so fossil Hadar AL 288-1, dated to 3.2 million years ago, became known ever after as "Lucy."

ABOVE: Satellite view southward across the African Rift Valley.

Today, a quarter-century later, Lucy is neither the oldest nor the most significant skeleton ever found. She remains the most famous, however. Many of the local people in Afar still think of Lucy as the ancestor of all humankind. Cafés in Ethiopia carry the name "Lossy" in her honor. Her image has appeared on stamps, and her name is a staple in crossword puzzles. For many people Lucy—the petite female buried for 3.2 million years in a sand bank on the edge of a former lake or stream—is all they know about human origins.

The story of Lucy provides our entry into the study of the origins and evolution of humankind. In the course of millions of years of interactions between cooling climates, more differentiated environments, and genetic changes favoring larger brains, splits among hominin lineages produced early human lines that could fashion at first simple, and later more sophisticated, stone tools. From among other lineages back in Africa, finally the line of anatomically and intellectually modern humans evolved that fashioned cultural artifacts, such as jewelry, geometrical figures cut into stone, and rock drawings. Once more, humans left Africa and settled the world, not only Eurasia but also Australia and the Americas. For the first time in the history of life on earth, a single species was no longer completely bound to the forces of evolution and its interplay between environment and genetics. These first modern humans had become *cultural beings*, by means of which they had acquired a measure of freedom from evolution: Instead of nature writing their history, they could create their own human history—the world history you are about to enter with this book.

The Origins of Humanity

Becoming human was a long and arduous journey. In the interactions between climate, environment, and genes, every evolutionary step had to build successively on every preceding one so that *anatomically*, as well as *intellectually*, fully evolved modern humans could emerge in Africa about 100,000 years ago. Nothing in this journey was predetermined, but it was also not accidental, given what we know about the genetic architecture of human DNA. It is open-ended, as is the human history which followed the emergence of modern humans. Both evolution and history display recognizable patterns, but these patterns neither were preprogrammed nor occurred by happenstance—they included both predictable and spontaneous occurrences resulting from the constraints and opportunities offered by the interaction of climate, environment, and genes. As we will see throughout this book, however, history equally depends on human agency and its resulting actions. Human prehistory is significant for us today because, thanks to much work done by archaeologists and anthropologists, we are beginning to recognize the complexity of all that had to happen on our evolutionary path to make us fully human: to reach the point where we could become the active creators of our world.

Hominins: No Longer Apes but Not Yet Human

Modern humans are the descendants of long lines of early human-like primates called **hominins**, which in the distant past lived in East Africa. The line of hominins split from that of the apes sometime around 7 million years ago, but the fossil record is still

Seeing Patterns

▶ What made it possible for *Homo sapiens* to survive in a dangerous environment? Why is it difficult to imagine life as a prehistoric forager?

▶ Where did humans go when they left Africa, and what kinds of lives did they establish for themselves in the areas where they settled? Which were the most important social patterns that evolved, and how were the humans impacted by the worsening Ice Age?

▶ How did humans express their experience of sharing their life force with animals? How do we know that this experience was important to them?

Hominins: Forerunners of humans after genetically splitting from the chimpanzees.

5

too poor to allow definite conclusions. Equally unclear is the parentage among the twenty or so species of hominins coming thereafter, which paleoanthropologists (as the archaeologists and researchers of fossils are called) have discovered so far. The fog begins to lift only around 2 million years ago, with the emergence of *Homo erectus*, the first hominin that left Africa and was adaptable to many new environments in Eurasia. It thus took some 4 million years of dead ends as well as environmentally more adaptable forerunners of humans to pave the way for the human species to emerge.

Many historians view the *pre*history of humans as a field belonging to archaeologists and anthropologists. For these historians, *history* begins only with the rise of the first cities in which scribes created written documents. This view is unfortunate since historians routinely take the findings of scholars in other disciplines, such as archaeology, anthropology, climatology, geography, medicine, and sociology, into consideration when they write histories on topics after about 3500 BCE. Since written records, furthermore, are highly unreliable documents—subject to manipulation by human hand subsequent to their original production—historians regularly take recourse in the more reliable findings of other disciplines wherever they can. Indeed, in the twenty-first century historians with broad visions have pleaded persuasively for eliminating the artificial distinction between prehistory and history. They speak instead—as the medieval cultural historian Daniel Lord Smail does—of the "deep history" of humanity.

Who Are Our Ancestors?   The specific environmental and genetic interactions favorable for the split between the ape and hominin lines are poorly understood. We know that changes in the climate between warm and cool cycles played a part, which were reflected in the African rain forest advancing and retreating. At present, the find of the 6–7 million-year-old skull of Toumaï, discovered in 2001 in Chad, then still covered by rain forest, is the only specimen close to the ape–hominin split.

Human Origins. Donald Johanson with Lucy.

But whether Toumaï is from before or after this split is still hotly debated among scholars. Without additional bones, the solitary Toumaï skull remains tantalizingly ambiguous.

In 2000, a Kenyan–British–French team unearthed a variety of bones of five individuals belonging to the species *Orrorin tugenensis*, dating to 6 million years ago in what was then the edge of a rain forest in western Kenya that had shrunk during a cooling period. Scholars consider the orrorins to be perhaps the first hominins because of their anatomical differences from apes and dental characteristics similar to modern humans. Unfortunately, no skull bones were found to allow any conclusions about brain size. Orrorins lived in trees, where they walked upright on branches with relatively short legs and swung from tree to tree by their arms. They were also able to walk upright on the ground for short distances. They walked upright but only marginally so.

A much larger fossil record is that of the **australopiths**. These hominins date to 3.9–3.0 million years ago and were widespread, ranging from Ethiopia to South Africa (see Map 1.1). We are fairly certain of these date ranges and regional distributions because of a couple of key paleoanthropological finds, which have been widely publicized: (1) a set of fossilized footprints uncovered in Kenya and (2) an almost complete skeleton found in Ethiopia, which has become known as "Lucy" (see the vignette at the beginning of the chapter). The footprints reveal how much better the australopiths were as bipedalists, but they were still also very much at home in the rain forest. Paleoanthropologists are agreed that the orrorins and australopiths were not related but disagree on everything else, especially on their role as human ancestors. At present, there are many branches but no trunk yet of the hominin tree.

Australopiths: Prehuman species that existed before those classed under the genus *Homo*.

Bipedalism and Environmental Adaptability　Improved **bipedalism** became a key evolutionary advantage to hominins. Walking on two feet is more energy-efficient than knuckle-walking and frees the arms to do something else. Being upright exposes a smaller body surface to the sun, a factor important for venturing out from the rain forest into the woodlands and savanna, that is, the more open forests and the grassland with tree stands. Partaking of the plant resources available in these three natural environments made hominins gradually more flexible than apes, which were limited to their rain forest habitat. On the one hand, the rain forest abounded with fruits and nuts; but on the other hand, the woodlands offered grasses and seeds. From the fossil record, it appears that by around 2.4 million years ago, hominins were able to move about in the two environments of the rain forest and savanna.

While all of our hominin ancestors shared basic traits, their lines were about to become much more varied, primarily because of the new and different environments

Bipedalism: The first human characteristic of hominins, specifically, the ability to walk for short periods or distances on their hind legs, although knuckle-walking and tree climbing continued to be practiced.

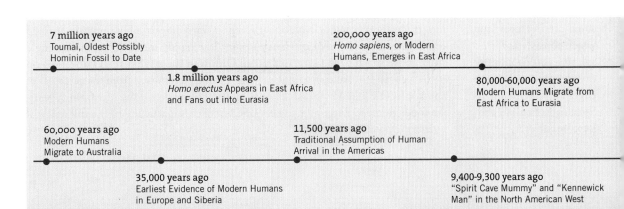

7 million years ago
Toumaï, Oldest Possibly Hominin Fossil to Date

200,000 years ago
Homo sapiens, or Modern Humans, Emerges in East Africa

1.8 million years ago
Homo erectus Appears in East Africa and Fans out into Eurasia

80,000-60,000 years ago
Modern Humans Migrate from East Africa to Eurasia

60,000 years ago
Modern Humans Migrate to Australia

11,500 years ago
Traditional Assumption of Human Arrival in the Americas

35,000 years ago
Earliest Evidence of Modern Humans in Europe and Siberia

9,400-9,300 years ago
"Spirit Cave Mummy" and "Kennewick Man" in the North American West

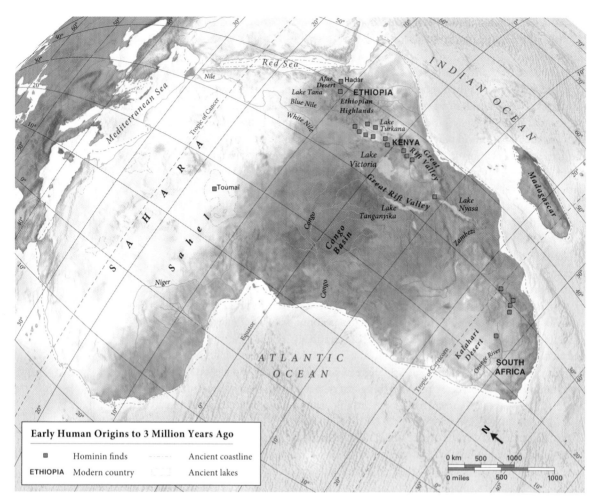

MAP 1.1 **Early Human Origins to 3 Million Years Ago.**

with which each group interacted. In some, brain sizes did not increase much; others reached the volume of half of modern human brains. Indeed, early hominin adaptations to the changing world would later give rise to diverse human cultures; and, as we will see, such different human cultures would, in turn, have a profound effect on our human evolution. This pattern of early human adaptation and cultural diversity is of great importance to historical study because it gives the earliest indications of how humans differentiated themselves—and how they became who we are today.

On the Threshold of Humanity   As they moved more and more easily around in their forest and savanna habitats, about 2.4 million years ago some hominins made another major evolutionary step forward. Improved brainpower enabled one of the new lines, that of *Homo habilis* ("the handy human"), to make simple stone tools: sharp-edged scrapers, called **Oldowan** tools (after the Oldovai region in the Kenyan Rift Valley), with which meat could be removed from the carcasses of animals freshly killed by beasts of prey. *H. habilis* broadened the diet from vegetarian foods to meat. Early humans became omnivores, partaking of the full range of nutrition available in nature.

Oldowan: The earliest stone-carving technique, which consisted of splitting a stone into two, thereby producing sharp edges on both fragments. See also **Acheulian** and **Levallois**.

The making of stone tools marks the beginning of the **Paleolithic**, or Old Stone Age, in prehistory, which lasted until about 11,600 years ago. During this time early humans, and later fully evolved humans, made increasingly varied and refined stone tools. Another cool, dry spell about 1.8 million years ago made mobility even more important. Scientists identify the early humans who adapted to the greater demands of mobility with long legs and comparatively shorter arms as *H. erectus* (Latin, "upright human"; in Africa called *H. ergaster* ["workman"]). These humans no longer lived in trees, were fully stabilized on their feet, and became regular long-distance walkers adapted to the demands of rain forest, savanna, and now also steppe habitats. They mastered the control of fire, apparently collecting it from lightning-caused wildfires, first in Africa, possibly 1.5–1.4 million years ago, as announced in 2004 on the basis of finds in South Africa and Kenya. Small groups of perhaps two dozen early humans, so scholars assume, huddled around fires in what must have been early camps at cave entrances or rock overhangs. *H. erectus* brain size was about 75 percent of that of the fully evolved *H. sapiens*, and thus, the lines of early humans had become quite distinct from hominins.

The increased mobility and brain volume had their consequences. Soon after 1.8 million years ago, groups of the *H. erectus* line walked across the Suez land passage in the northeast that connected the African continent with southwest Asia. Once in southwest Asia, these groups quickly scattered in all directions (Map 1.2).

Paleolithic: Old Stone Age, 2.5 million–11,500 years ago.

MAP 1.2 **Human Migration out of Africa.**

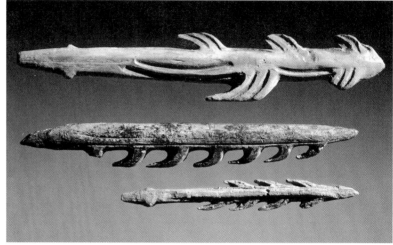

Early Human Toolkit. The preferred materials for Acheulian axes were obsidian, chert, or flint. The stone scraper on the right shows the Levallois technique in which the edges of a stone are trimmed and flaked. Harpoons like the ones shown at the top right were made from reindeer antlers. On the left is a spear thrower from France that dates to about 12,000 BCE. Spear throwers gave hunters the ability to propel their missiles with surer aim. Note the horse-shaped handle.

Acheulian: A technique which consisted of flaking a hard piece of rock (preferably flint, chert, or obsidian) on both sides into a triangle-shaped hand axe, with cutting edges, a hand-held side, and a point.

The dating of fossils from the country of Georgia in the Caucasus and Java in southeast Asia, as well as stone tools in India, to 1.8–1.6 million years ago demonstrates the relative speed of this dispersion and adaptation to new environments.

Early humans are also well documented in east Asia. The oldest fossil bones, found in 2001 at Nuangjou [New-ahng-JOE] in northern China and in 2010 at Denisova Cave in southern Siberia, point to the presence of early humans in east Asia as early as 1.66 and 1 million years ago, respectively. Fossil finds in Korea and Japan indicate the arrival of *H. erectus* at the southeastern end of Asia around 500,000 years ago. In Spain, the 2007 discovery of a tooth from *H. erectus* documents the presence of this early human from 1.2 million years onward in Europe, the northernmost region it apparently was able to adapt to. Thus, we have ample documentation that this line of early humans settled in a considerable variety of habitats in Africa and Eurasia.

In addition to being an accomplished walker, *H. erectus* was the creator of vastly improved stone tools. Instead of the simple Oldowan stones with sharp edges, around 1.8–1.6 million years ago, *H. erectus* created the new **Acheulian** [ah-SHOI-lee-yan] stone technology. (This technology appeared first in East Africa, although it was named after St. Acheul, a suburb of Amiens in northern France where finds were made in the nineteenth century.) Acheulian tools were oval or pear-shaped hand axes cut with the help of hammer stones from larger cores, or they were one or more flakes split from cores. When the edges of these hand axes became dull, *H. erectus* split further, smaller flakes away to resharpen the edges. A simple visual examination of Oldowan and Acheulian tools reveals how much the manual skills of early humans advanced in about a million years.

H. erectus showed considerable staying power, thriving in most places until around 350,000 years ago and on the island of Java in southeast Asia until perhaps 27,000 years ago. Strong disagreements exist among scholars whether this early human type spawned intellectually more developed successors, died out, or was absorbed by interbreeding with successor lineages arriving from outside Asia. Therefore, it is unclear how these early humans in Africa and Asia are related to each other.

Flores "Hobbits"   The discovery of *Homo floresiensis* is a startling case of *H. erectus'* longevity. In 2003, an Australian–Indonesian archaeological team unearthed a skull and assorted bones belonging to 13 early humans in a cave on the Indonesian island of Flores. These tiny humans measured only 3 feet high and had brains no larger than those of chimpanzees or australopiths. Archaeologists dated them to ca. 38,000–12,000 years ago and identified them as descendants of *H. erectus*.

Popularly known as "hobbits"—after the tiny characters in J. R. R. Tolkien's *Lord of the Rings*—these miniature people pose intriguing questions. Were *H. erectus'* descendants capable of crossing the ocean? What caused them to shrink? Did they die out after 12,000 years ago? Hobbits were evidently early builders of rafts since Flores was an island from at least 1 million years ago. Some of their tools were pre-Acheulian, but others were more advanced than the ones of *H. erectus* since the hobbits hunted, using spears and spear points. Isolation might have contributed to their shrinking, like it did to the elephants, also documented through fossils. Other species, such as reptiles, however, developed gigantism; and it is far from clear why the Flores animals and early humans mutated into one or the other genetic variation.

Human Adaptations: From Africa to Eurasia and Australia

H. ergaster, the African version of *H. erectus*, was the ancestor of *H. sapiens* ("the wise human"), the species of modern humans. Scholars are far from agreed, however, as to how many intermediate lineages can be assumed to have existed between then and now. When *H. sapiens* arrived, however, two characteristics distinguished this human being from its less evolved forerunners: (1) rapidly developing *technical skills* and (2) *cultural creativity*. These two characteristics represent a fundamental transformation of humans that placed them on a path toward liberation from the determinism of nature. The timing and extent of this liberation are still debated by scientists, but world historians generally assume that when *H. sapiens* created a recognizable culture in Africa, it became at least partially the free creator of a new direction in natural history.

The African Origins of Human Culture

H. sapiens appeared around 280,000 years ago in East Africa. (The Latin term "*Homo sapiens*," meaning "wise man," will be used interchangeably with "modern human" in the remainder of this chapter.) The oldest specimen discovered so far is a fossil discovered in 1967 in Ethiopia and dated in 2005 to 195,000 years ago. The archaeological record documenting modern humans is still spotty, but the 17 African sites containing bone and skull remnants of *H. sapiens* as well as a half-dozen sites with human artifacts allow for at least one important conclusion: *H. sapiens*, in a process of gradual development in Africa, became physically and intellectually fully human, endowed with the basics of culture. While humans continued to remain subject to the natural interaction between environment and genes, requiring constant updates in adaptation, culture gave them the freedom to accept and reject—a completely new dimension largely independent from nature.

Livelihood   Early humans, as discussed earlier, did not hunt; they scavenged meat from carcasses with the help of stone scrapers. Early spears made of sharpened sticks for hunting animals are some 400,000 years old, belonging to the elusive post-*H. erectus* lineages. Really effective spears had to await *H. sapiens* as the creator of the much refined new stone-working technique, the **Levallois** [le-val-WAH], derived from the name of a suburb of Paris, France, where in the nineteenth century the first spear points were found. With this technique, a craftsperson chipped off small flakes from the edges of a prepared stone core and then hammered a larger flake—flat on the bottom, domed on the top, and sharpened by the small flakes around the edge—from the center of the core, leaving a more or less deep indentation in the spent core. These center flakes could be as large as hand axes and meat cutters or as small as spear points. The appearance of spear points and increasingly large numbers of animal bones in the archaeological sites was an indicator that *H. sapiens* was emerging as an efficient hunter of animals. The hunt, requiring strength as well as endurance, tended to be the province of males—and remained a prestige occupation for much of human history. But it provided no more than a supplement to *H. sapiens'* nutrition.

The combination of the male-dominated hunt with the communal gathering of vegetal foods defines what is called "forager society." Foraging, sometimes called "hunting and gathering," was the dominant pattern of human history for the longest period, several hundred thousand years. It is also the most spottily documented period, requiring for its understanding a combination of archaeology with the anthropological insights gained from observation of surviving foraging societies in the nineteenth and twentieth centuries. Thus, the descriptions of such societies we offer are unavoidably somewhat speculative.

H. sapiens continued to live in sheltered places provided by cave entrances and rock overhangs, the source of the popular stereotype of the "caveman." But there were also campsites with hut-like shelters made from branches. Clothing consisted of skins and furs acquired through hunting and slung around the body. Hearths, in which *H. sapiens* could build fire at will, served as places for the roasting of meat or the provision of warmth during cold nights. Anthropological studies suggest that extended families congregated around the hearths to groom each other or give each other comfort and companionship. In the vicinity of the campsite, a dozen or so dispersed families were in touch with one another, forming a clan, among which sexual partners were chosen.

Around 120,000 years ago, food gathering and preparation in the camps appear to have become considerably more varied. *H. sapiens* began to include shellfish collected on the beach in their diets. A little later, humans began catching fish on the coasts and in the lakes and rivers of Africa, using tools carved from bone, such as hooks and barbed points mounted on spears. With the help of grindstones, men and women pulverized hard seeds for consumption or storage. Plaster-lined storage pits appeared in the camps, as did separate refuse dumps. And as the settlements became more numerous, trade networks sprang up, providing toolmakers with obsidian mined as far as 200 miles away. Obsidian is a glass-like hard rock found near

Levallois: A stone technique where stone workers first shaped a hard rock into a cylinder or cone.

volcanoes and therefore relatively rare, so it was much sought after. We may also see this initial period of trade as marking the beginning of thousands of years of increasing human *interaction*—a process vital to the transferring of cultural and technological innovation among human groups.

Gender Relations   A central element in human culture is the relationship between men and women. Unfortunately, archaeology is unable to reveal anything decisive about this relationship in Paleolithic forager society. Obviously, the roles of men and women were less specialized among foragers than in agrarian–urban society: Males and females spent most of their time collecting and preparing vegetal foods together, and the male-dominated hunt was a supplemental occupation. But how much these occupations furthered a male–female balance or allowed for one of the two genders to become dominant is not easy to determine.

With the rise of the feminist movement in the 1970s, scholars revived the idea, popular in the nineteenth century, of an early female-centered society. Marija Gimbutas (1921–1994), a Lithuania-born archaeologist, published several books on what she assumed was a "matristic" society in Russia prior to 4500 BCE. This society, so she asserted, was egalitarian, peaceful, and goddess-oriented. It was by this time agrarian, but by implication matristic culture was assumed to have had deep roots in the preceding forager stage of human life. In her view, aggressive, war-like male dominance came about only with the rise of horseback-riding herders from the southern Russian steppes who were bent on conquest. Other anthropologists, instead, assumed that male dominance began at about the same time that warring kingdoms emerged in the Middle East. War captives became slaves and elaborate hierarchies emerged in which women, in turn, found themselves relegated to inferior positions. However the origins of patriarchy are explained, there is little controversy over its connection with agrarian–urban life. What came before, however, and was prevalent during the Paleolithic forager period of human history is impossible to determine one way or the other. While patriarchy was part and parcel of the agrarian–urban pattern, what we know of the preceding forager society so far does not indicate a prevalence of matriarchy. In African Paleolithic forager society, females and males differed in their functions but not so decisively that the one or the other could easily become dominant.

Creation of Symbols   Parallel to the development of foraging, hunting, and beginning gender roles, there were also first signs of a development of *H. sapiens'* mental life. Activity in the camps expanded from the craftsmanship of tools to that of non-utilitarian objects. This expansion was perhaps the decisive step with which *H. sapiens* left the worlds of animals, hominins, and early humans behind and became truly modern. Around 135,000 years ago, humans in what is today Morocco in northwest Africa took seashells and fragments of ostrich eggshell, perforated them, and strung them on leather strips as pendants and necklaces. The significance of this step cannot be overemphasized. By themselves, seashells and ostrich eggshells are natural objects of no particular distinction, but as jewelry they have the unique meaning of beauty for their wearer: In the form of jewelry they are *symbols*, which are clearly distinct from tools. Jewelry is more than the material it is made of; its beauty gives it its distinction and makes it a symbol of whatever human emotions it is designed to express. *H. sapiens* was the first and only being that did not think only in the concrete, practical terms of tool-making but also in *abstract* symbolic terms by using something to express something else, such as jewelry for feelings. This vital transformation may be seen as the root of the human capacity to conceptualize and, with it, the foundation of art, religion, philosophy, science, and all other intellectual pursuits.

Archaeological examples for the emergence of abstract symbolic thinking in Africa are not yet very numerous. But taken together they powerfully suggest an intellectual modernity emerging to match the anatomical modernity of African *H. sapiens*. From about 90,000 years ago, for example, we begin to see grave sites, indicators of reflection on the significance of life, death, ancestral dignity, and generational continuity. Humans added jewelry as the preferred grave gift, suggesting the contemplation of an afterlife or spirit world. Another example of symbolic thought may be seen in a rock formation inside a cave, discovered in Botswana in 2006, which had been carved and shaped into the head of a python, complete with scales, an eye, and a mouth, some 77,000 years ago. With this example, we

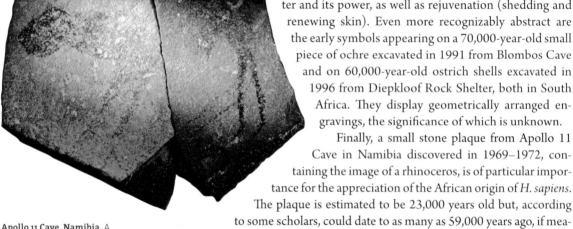

come close to encountering one of the most enduring (religious) symbols, the snake or dragon, signifying water and its power, as well as rejuvenation (shedding and renewing skin). Even more recognizably abstract are the early symbols appearing on a 70,000-year-old small piece of ochre excavated in 1991 from Blombos Cave and on 60,000-year-old ostrich shells excavated in 1996 from Diepkloof Rock Shelter, both in South Africa. They display geometrically arranged engravings, the significance of which is unknown.

Finally, a small stone plaque from Apollo 11 Cave in Namibia discovered in 1969–1972, containing the image of a rhinoceros, is of particular importance for the appreciation of the African origin of *H. sapiens*. The plaque is estimated to be 23,000 years old but, according to some scholars, could date to as many as 59,000 years ago, if measured by the age of strata found on top of the plaque. If the latter age is true, this would be humanity's oldest pictorial representation found to date.

Apollo 11 Cave, Namibia. A rhinoceros depicted on a stone slab, from about 59,000–23,000 years ago, making it contemporary with Australian and European rock art. Together with the Blombos Cave ochre, this artwork is evidence of early humans' ability to create symbols.

Collectively, these examples can be taken as a confirmation of *H. sapiens* not only as a technically versatile toolmaker but also as the one animal capable of creating symbols that signify something other than the materials from which they were made. Much of what we will see later in this book as the wonderfully varied cultures of the world will ultimately spring from these sources (see "Patterns up Close" on pages 23–24).

Migration from Africa   Once the *H. sapiens* lineage was fully equipped with practical skills and the foundations of culture, it was adaptable to almost any environment. Genetic research suggests that the first groups of modern humans left Africa between 80,000 and 60,000 years ago. Many scholars assume that these first groups left Africa for Asia by crossing the straits between Ethiopia and Yemen and between Oman and Iran. The members of this group, so it is thought, drifted like beachcombers along the coast, making their way to India, Malaysia, and Indonesia perhaps about 77,000 years ago. Some of their descendants seemed to have just kept on moving, reaching China about 70,000 years ago, sailing to Australia

60,000 years ago, and crossing from Korea over a then existing land bridge to Japan about 30,000 years ago. Eventually, modern humans from south Asia migrated northwestward to Europe and northeastward to Siberia, where they arrived around 35,000 years ago. The Siberian groups then made their way to Alaska in North America 16,000 years ago, completing the journey around the world in 70,000 years (see Map 1.2).

Migration from South Asia to Australia

The migration of human groups from south Asia to Australia deserves a closer look within the context of foraging society as the basic mode of human social organization. Australia was the only large world region where foraging remained dominant until the modern scientific–industrial age and, therefore, could be studied almost until today. During the geological beginnings of the earth, Australia was part of a vast land mass, called "Sahul." It comprised what is now New Guinea, Australia, and Tasmania and was connected to Antarctica and the Americas. About 100 million years ago Sahul separated and began moving slowly toward Asia. It never connected with Eurasia however, and deep sea channels always kept Sahul separated from the north.

Geography and Migration   About 4–5 million years ago, Sahul had moved far enough northward to encourage the emergence of a variety of geographical zones. In the north (today's New Guinea and far northern Australia), rain forest covered the landscape. In the east (today's eastern Australia), various mixtures of forest, bush, and grassland evolved. The center and most of the west of the continent (today's central and western Australia) developed a mixture of deserts, lakes, steppes, and grassland. The south (today's southeastern Australia and Tasmania) became temperate, with an almost South African or Mediterranean climate. Small pockets of mountain vegetation came into existence only in what are today the central parts of eastern Australia and southern Tasmania. Sahul displayed geological formations and climate zones corresponding to those of Africa south of the Sahara. These geographical environments would become the homes to modern humans, who came originally from Africa and had adapted to life in south Asia.

During an ice age 70,000–60,000 years ago, south Asia and most of the northern islands of Indonesia were connected by land bridges. Farther south, island chains where one could travel by boat without losing sight of land encouraged the idea of further travel. Inevitably, the mariners reached a point where land was no longer visible on the horizon. About 60,000 years ago, the distance from the island of Timor to Australia was 65 miles. Scholars have speculated that smoke rising from lightning-produced brush fires in the south could have suggested to some enterprising mariners that there was land beyond the horizon. Whatever motivated them to take to the sea, they evidently succeeded in crossing it.

Settlement of the Continent   As *H. sapiens* groups arrived on the Australian continent, presumably in the northwest, they fanned out eastward and southward, slowly populating it. The descendants of the original settlers became known in our own time as **Aboriginals**. Bringing their African and south Asian foraging customs with them, the settlers hunted the Australian animals and gathered what was edible of its plant life. Australia's animals, as they are today, were very different from those

Aboriginals: The original settlers of Australia, who arrived some 60,000 years before European settlers at the end of the eighteenth century CE.

in Africa and south Asia: On account of the continent's early separation from South America as well as its relatively small size, its game animals were largely marsupials, carrying their newborns in protective pouches during the weaning phase. Unlike in Africa and Eurasia, with their profusion of dangerous animals, there were few marsupial predator species to threaten these first humans. The Aboriginal peoples gradually hunted the large marsupial species to extinction, and by about 16,000 years ago, only small animals were left to hunt.

As elsewhere in foraging societies, men were the hunters. They used spears and spear throwers—short sticks with a curve or hook on the end to extend the length of the thrower's arm and give additional power to the flight of the spear—but not bows and arrows, which were introduced in Eurasia and Africa after 60,000 years ago, too late for these settlers to take with them on their journey to Australia. In southern Australia, eel was a major protein staple. Men trapped this fish in rivers and human-made river basins, using nets made of bulrush fiber. In Tasmania the main meat source was the seal. Once the large marsupials were gone, hunting became a highly diversified set of activities for the Aborigines.

Women, and secondarily men, were responsible for gathering vegetal foods. The basic staples were wild millet and rice. The main fruits and vegetables were the solanum [sow-LAH-noom], a tomato-like fruit rich in vitamin C; the yam daisy, a sweet, milky tuber with yellow, daisy-like flowers; and the quandong [KWAN-dong] fruit, also abounding in vitamin C, which was collected from trees and then dried. Women used grindstones to prepare hard seeds and vegetables, such as pine nuts, flax, and acacia seeds, as well as bracken (large fern) and bindweed (family of vines). Yam, taro, and banana, shared with New Guinea until 8,000 years ago when the land bridge was submerged by the sea, thrived only in the northeast. Eucalyptus, a native of Australia found nearly everywhere, served for firewood in the stone-built hearths. People also used fire as a hunting tool and to promote revegetation. Controlled grass and brush fires drove animals in the desired direction where strategically positioned hunting parties could slaughter them. Forest fires were used to synchronize more closely the production and harvest of nuts and fruits on trees, thereby increasing the efficiency of harvests. Over time, the Aborigines developed a keen sense of how to exploit nature efficiently, while consciously setting about preserving it.

Australia was less rich in grasses suitable for grain collection than southwest Asia. For example, Australia had only two types of grain; in southwest Asia, there were around 40 types of grain. Thus, it should come as no surprise that foraging remained the dominant mode of subsistence, even if people stayed in their camps for long periods of time before moving them. Only in the south, where eel trapping was the main form of livelihood, did permanent villages appear, similar in many ways to their counterparts in late forager Africa, Europe, North America, and Japan. Aborigines thus remained closely adapted to the basic, relatively modest patterns of forager livelihood until the first English settlers arrived at the end of the eighteenth century CE.

Social Structures and Cultural Expressions   Since modern-day Aborigines have remained faithful to their traditional forms of life, a great deal about their social structures and organization is known. Australian anthropologists have collected a wealth of data, observing forager culture as it existed in the nineteenth and early twentieth centuries. Unfortunately, today foraging is disappearing before our eyes at an accelerated rate. But the existing literature contains much that is rooted in the distant past, even though, of course, the Aborigines changed in the course of world history just like humans on all other continents.

According to this literature, in the traditional Aboriginal society of the nineteenth century or earlier marriages were *monogamous*, that is, they consisted of a husband and wife. Men who not only were successful hunters but also became wealthy through trade could acquire additional wives. Families that camped together and assisted each other in hunting and food gathering formed *clans*, which were units in which all families considered themselves to be descendants of a common ancestor. Groups of clans formed a tribe of between 500 and 1,500 members. Generally, tribes were too large to camp or move about together. They were, rather, loose associations of clans living miles apart but from which they selected their marriage partners. Marriages took place between members of one group of clans and members of another group of clans. Tribes met collectively once a year at one of the sacred places of their land to celebrate shared rituals and ceremonies.

The Dreamtime   Despite this loose social organization, tribal members considered themselves trustees of clearly marked parcels of ancestral land. Typical markers were identifiable features of the landscape, such as rocks, rivers, or trees. Myths and *taboos*—things or practices that were forbidden—surrounded both land and markers. Tribespeople venerated them through rituals, ceremonies, dances, and recounting the myths. Respected elders, who commanded a particularly high degree of regard, presided over the rituals. An elder was venerated when he had a large number of sons, family alliances, and valuable artifacts acquired through trade. The most esteemed elders possessed a deep knowledge of the tribe's past in the **Dreamtime**, the name given to the ancient period in which the tribe's past was embedded.

More specifically, the Dreamtime consisted of the stories, customs, and laws which defined the tribe in its original, perfect state at the time of creation. Elders acquired access to this time through trance states, requiring many years of initiation, training, and practice. Their knowledge of the Dreamtime, it was believed, gave them access to creation's hidden powers, enabling them to read other people's minds, recognize their secret concerns, and heal illnesses. Elders, however, did not possess a monopoly over knowledge of nature's hidden powers. All members of the clan, it was assumed, had access to the tribe's sacred heritage and could use it, to varying degrees, to practice magic, experiment with sorcery, or cast spells.

Aboriginal elders never were able to wield political power through armed force within their own tribes. Since there was no agriculture and, therefore, no agricultural surplus and since trade did not evolve beyond the exchange of obsidian, tools, and weapons, elders could not acquire enough wealth to pay fighters. Only on the continent's northern coast was there a modest trade in local pearls for knives, pottery, cloth, sails, and canoes from Timor; but it too did not make for the rise of powerful chiefdoms. Aboriginal society thus remained "stateless" in the sense of possessing no administrative institutions. Elders in positions of authority used persuasion, not force, to keep the peace.

Australian Rock Art   How much the Dreamtime involved rock paintings, existing in large numbers in Australia, is unfortunately not known. Rock art is the

Dreamtime: In the Australian Dreamtime, the shaman constructs an imaginary reality of the tribe's origins and roots, going back to the imaginary time when the world was created and the creator devised all customs, rituals, and myths.

Australian Shaman. A Shaman in a trance from a rock carving 40,000–20,000 years ago. This "Bradshaw" figure is usually interpreted as showing movements and communication with the spirits of animate nature.

one form of cultural expression where historical change in the otherwise slow-paced Aboriginal culture is evident: Contemporary Aborigines are unable to interpret the meaning of early rock paintings, which archaeologists were able to date. There are many more recent rock paintings, but they are very different in content and style from the earlier ones. Changing climatic conditions leading to different migration patterns are presumably responsible for modern Aboriginals losing their familiarity with the rich culture of ancient Australian rock art.

The best-known Australian rock paintings are the so-called Bradshaw paintings in the Kimberley Region in northwest Australia, which probably date to a period of 30,000–20,000 years ago. Between two ice ages, this region had a fairly even year-round climate with sufficient rainfall to support foraging and, hence, the presence of human groups practicing rock art. At present, scholars work with a classification of the Bradshaw paintings into two major stylistic periods, beginning with (1) indentations, grooves, and animals and followed by (2) elongated human figures with tassels or sashes, fruits and vegetables resembling human figures, as well as clothes pin figures and stick figures.

The two periods are very difficult to date since so far none of the places where they have been found have yielded any material that could be reliably carbon-dated. Only one Bradshaw painting has been dated so far as at least 17,500 years old, thanks to a wasp nest on top of it that contained sand grains suitable for thermoluminescent dating. The painting could be much older, of course, depending on when the wasp settled on it. Scholars generally assume that the proliferation of Bradshaws was roughly contemporary with the efflorescence of European rock art.

The striking parallelism between Australian and European rock art demonstrates that humans did not have to interact to express themselves culturally in similar ways. Similar forager patterns could evolve without mutual contact. The fact that a great proliferation of paintings occurred simultaneously in Australia and Europe at a later stage of forager culture leads to the conclusion that none of the human groups migrating away from Africa was privileged over any other. This cultural parity among foragers needs to be kept in mind as we turn to African *H. sapiens* migrating to Europe.

Migration from South Asia to Europe

There was a gap of at least 30,000 years between groups of modern humans leaving Africa (80,000–60,000 years ago) and migrating to Europe (35,000 years ago). Scholars assume that these humans settled first in south Asia before their descendants fanned out to Europe as well as east Asia. Little is known about the migratory path these descendants chose as they walked across the Middle East to Europe. It is generally assumed that they moved from the Black Sea up the valley of the Danube River since the oldest archaeological findings stem from sites near the upper reaches of the river (see Map 1.2).

Two Human Species   When *H. sapiens* arrived in Europe around 35,000 years ago, this region was already settled by another human species, that of the

Neanderthals [Nay-AN-der-tall, after a valley in northwest Germany where the first specimen was found in the nineteenth century]. This species is assumed to have descended from successors of *H. erectus* in Africa half a million years ago, although the exact line of descent is unclear. Neanderthals are the best-documented Paleolithic fossil humans in Europe and western Asia, with over 600 finds. The fossils range in age from 230,000 to 24,000 years ago and are widely distributed geographically between western Europe, the Altai Mountains in eastern Asia, and the Middle East. *H. sapiens*—or **Cro-Magnon** [Crow-man-YON, after the name of the cave in southwestern France where, in the nineteenth century, European *H. sapiens* bones were first found]—was clearly an intruder in an inhabited, if still sparsely settled, human landscape.

Neanderthals were smaller and more heavily boned than modern humans. In their forager livelihood, the two species were very similar, although Neanderthals buried their dead without the gifts of jewelry and, later, sprinklings of red ochre, a symbol of lifeblood, which modern humans included. The stone and bone toolkits of the two were also alike, but whether Neanderthals created paintings, as in Tito Bustillo Cave, Spain, depends on dating methods employed. Paleoanthropologists assume that Neanderthals were able to talk in a rudimentary way but did not yet possess the throat structures of *H. sapiens*. The two species overlapped for about 11,000 years. In 2010, the Swedish-born paleogeneticist Svante Pääbo and his Leipzig, Germany, team completed an analysis of the Neanderthal DNA (through bones from Croatian Neanderthals, from which they first removed microbial contamination) and found that there was interbreeding. Thus, the Neanderthals were absorbed into the modern human genome.

Figurines and Rock Paintings

H. sapiens' cultural creativity, which had burst forth in Africa, continued after the migration into Europe. There are some 700 open-air sites with small figurines and caves with rock paintings and engravings. Presently, the oldest known artifact is a small ivory figurine of a mammoth, found in 2007 in Vogelherd Cave in southwestern Germany and dating to the time of *H. sapiens'* arrival in western Europe 35,000 years ago. Two slightly younger, equally small ivory statuettes of humans with lion heads, one of them apparently dancing, were also found in southwestern Germany. The mammoth legs have unpolished holes, leading to the speculation that this artifact was sown to garments. Other figurines might have been worn as pendants.

Several thousand years later, an entire class of female figurines, some thin and delicate and others bulging and coarse, called "Venuses," appeared all over western Europe. These figurines were made of stone or bone and one of them, unearthed in the Czech Republic, was formed of fired clay ca. 26,000 years ago. The creation of the first ceramic pieces was thus a Paleolithic invention, even though the regular production of pottery appeared some 17,000 years later in agrarian society. All figurines were small, fitting comfortably into the palm of a hand, and therefore easily transportable. The bulging Venuses have been interpreted as fertility goddesses, indicating an early matriarchy; but this interpretation is questionable, given the great variety of female and male figurines of the Venus type. Other scholars view these figurines as dolls for children in the camps or as representatives of relatives or ancestors in camp rituals. Hard proof, however, is still outstanding.

The great majority of rock paintings in Europe show animals, alone or in herds, at rest or in motion, either chasing or fleeing other beasts, or locked in conflict with

Mythical Imagery. Two lion-headed figurines, one apparently dancing, described by the excavator, archaeologist Nicholas Conard, as a "depiction of mythical imagery." The ca. 32,000-year-old figurines were found in two caves in southwestern Germany.

each other. The oldest paintings to date are of animals that humans were familiar with in nature, such as reindeer, horses, cattle, bulls, bison, mammoths, rhinoceroses, lions, and owls. Dating to 30,000 years ago, they were discovered in 1994 in Chauvet [show-VAY] Cave in southern France. One intriguing image in this cave depicts the head and torso of a bison and the legs of a human. A similarly intriguing image from 13,000 years ago, found in the Trois-Frères [Troah-FRAIR] cave in southwestern France, is "the sorcerer," an upright being with human hands and legs but also equipped with reindeer ears and antlers, a bird face, a fox tail, and a phallus. These hybrid beings are rare, however, in comparison to the many types of large mammals on which the painters concentrated.

Hunting scenes and depictions of humans are also rare. The best known, at Lascaux [Las-COE] in southwestern France and dated to 17,000 years ago, is that of an injured bull charging its hunter, who is depicted as a stick figure with a phallus. By contrast, a set of 15,000-year-old engravings on slabs used to cover the floor of La Marche [La-MARSH] Cave in west-central France shows expertly executed, realistic sketches of young and old males and females, dressed in boots, robes, and hats. These sketches could easily be modern cartoons: They demonstrate that there is little that separates contemporary humans from those who lived 15,000 years ago.

Modern chemical analyses have shown that the rock painters knew how to grind and mix minerals to make different colors. They mixed charcoal and manganese dioxide to outline their paintings in black. To add color, they used other ground minerals, such as hematite for red, mixed in various, finely graded proportions. Painters carefully sketched the images before filling them in with paint and shading the figures. They often used protrusions in the rock walls to enhance three-dimensionality and augment the technique of shading. In many images, frontal and lateral views are combined. One image depicts a bison with six legs, evidently simulating its swift motion. Thus, the thematic diversity of images had its complement in technical versatility.

Venus Figurine. Excavated at Dolni Vestonice, Czech Republic, in 1986, 25,000 years old. This is the oldest known figurine made of fired clay. Many more broken figurines were found near the kiln. They perhaps represented family members during rituals and, as bearers of their spirits, had to be destroyed at the end of the rituals so as to end their influence.

Lascaux Cave, France. This 17,000 year-old image shows a human, perhaps injured, under attack by a bison.

The main places with rock art are halls and domes deep inside the often miles-long caves. The complete darkness was illuminated with torches and grease-filled bowls with wicks. Flutes, made of swan bones, and stalagmites, tapped as percussion instruments, testify to the presence not only of painters but also of musicians. To judge by the extant footprints, teenagers as well as adults, men as well as women assembled inside the caves. Modern scholars, such as the South African archaeologist J. David Lewis-Williams, speculate that the caves were places for rituals, perhaps even shamanic assemblies, in which elders, in trance, entered a spiritual world shared with all living beings. Hints of the human mind reflecting on such a shared spiritual world can perhaps be found in the hybrid lionman, bisonman, and sorcerer figurines and rock images mentioned previously. The Australian Bradshaw figures, apparently showing swaying shamans, may similarly point in the direction of such a reflection. It is possible to recognize in the Paleolithic artifacts the roots of *animism*, that is, the idea of a shared life force in the world, which later became prominent in Africa and the Americas (see "Patterns Up Close" on pp. 24–25).

Animism. The meaning of this cave drawing from Trois-Frères, France—known as the "Little Sorcerer"—continues to baffle. The figure combines traits of a deer, an owl, a fox, and a human. It could be a hunter stalking prey. The morphing of animal and human qualities characterizes much Ice Age art.

The Ice Age Crisis and Human Migration to the Americas

In the course of its natural history, the earth has traversed many ice ages. Modern humans experienced two. The first one, 70,000–60,000 years ago, created land bridges that enabled humans to traverse much of the Indonesian archipelago on foot and travel the rest of the distance by boat to Australia. This ice age was comparatively mild and short-lived, in contrast to the last ice age of the world's history, 25,000–13,500 years ago, which severely tested the flora and fauna on all continents. Humans, although suffering through it, exploited it for one major achievement: their migration from Siberia to the Americas.

The Ice Age
Toward its end, the Paleolithic era turned into one of the climatically most inhospitable periods in world history. Large parts of the world either descended into a deep freeze or became bone dry. The northern zone of Eurasia, from England to Siberia, changed into a desolate wasteland, partially covered with gigantic ice sheets. The central zone, from southern France to Mongolia, consisted of tundra (frozen earth) in the winter and semiarid steppe in the summer. The southern zone, from Iberia (today's Spain and Portugal) to southern China, was temperate but semidry, with grasslands and pockets of woodlands. In Africa and Australia, the rain forest was reduced to a few areas in central Africa and the northern tip of Australia, leaving the rest of the continents largely exposed to drought. The northern Sahara and southern Kalahari in Africa as well as the interior of Australia were giant deserts, cutting deep into what were once rich savannas and rain forest. Life for modern humans in Eurasia, Africa, and Australia during this ice age was an arduous struggle for daily survival (see Map 1.3).

Difficult Living Conditions   Signs of stress and even desperation testify to the harsh conditions of the Ice Age. For example, human bone remnants from a number of ancient campsites in modern-day Russia display signs of malnutrition and disease. Because of the difficult conditions, humans abandoned the northern European

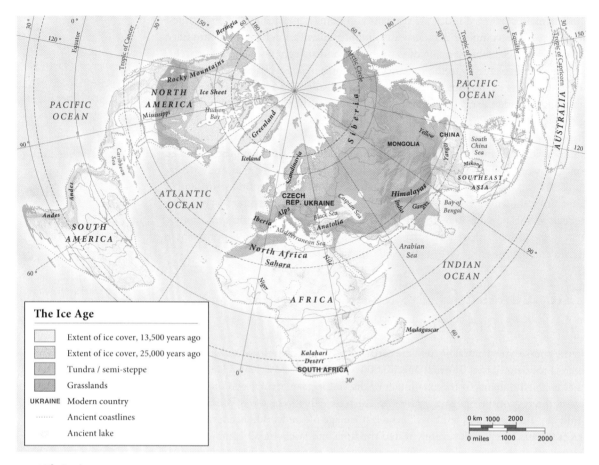

MAP 1.3 **The Ice Age.**

and Russian plains, which remained uninhabited for 15 millennia. Central European settlements were hemmed in between Scandinavian and Alpine glaciers. In an important development, humans domesticated the dog sometime around 15,000 years ago, probably to help in hunting increasingly rare large animals (mammoth, rhinoceros, and giant deer), which were also suffering under environmental stress. Unfortunately, overhunting became an additional factor in the drastic reduction in the numbers of large animals. Ultimately, most of these huge beasts died out around 6,000–4,000 years ago, forcing humans to go after smaller game.

Although life was not easy, *H. sapiens* possessed the technological and mental resources to survive even the worst climate conditions. The modern humans had at their disposal a great variety of implements for catching fish, snaring birds, and hunting animals, including harpoons, fishhooks, and darts made of bone, fishnets, and bird traps. Boomerangs, invented independently and in parallel with their development in Australia, were also used for hunting larger fowl. Wooden handles attached to large stone axe heads increased the efficiency of cutting meat or wood. In a situation of increasingly disappearing large animals, *H. sapiens* became efficient at hunting larger numbers of small animals.

Human mobility increased substantially. Canoes took the form of dugouts or were constructed of bone and wood frames covered with skins. As a result of innovations like the canoe, the range for trading expanded. Baltic *amber* (fossilized resin from fir trees, prized for making jewelry) was found 600 miles away in southern Europe, and Mediterranean shells were carried by traders to the Ukraine, 800 miles away in the northeast. Modern humans dressed themselves warmly, wearing hooded fur coats stitched together with bone needles, using thin leather strips, as evidenced by figurines discovered in Siberia. An imprint left on kiln-fired clay, found in the Czech Republic, indicates that humans also began to weave woolen cloth on looms, another historical first. No doubt, *H. sapiens* groups were decimated by the impact of the Ice Age, but groups of hearty survivors were still tenaciously hanging on when the world warmed up again and became wetter around 14,500 years ago.

The Beringia Land Bridge   During the coldest time in the Ice Age around 19,000 years ago, sea levels dropped by 450 feet, increasing the land mass of the continents by about 100 miles in all directions and exposing land bridges connecting Indonesia to Malaysia, Japan to Korea, and Asia to North America. The land connecting Asia and North America between Siberia and Alaska was Beringia, a large land mass of some half a million square miles.

Most of Siberia was covered with ice, but southern Beringia and Alaska consisted of ice-free tundra. Mammoths and other large, hairy herd animals roamed the land. Whether there was ever a human presence on Beringia is unknown since today the land is submerged by the sea. But there are traces of human presence in both eastern Siberia and Alaska, dating from the Ice Age thawing stage some 16,500–12,500 years ago. In eastern Siberia these traces include the foundations of small houses, hearths, flaked stone points for spear shafts, and a pit containing amber beads and stone pendants for jewelry. In Alaska, archaeologists have found stone tools and spear points. Around 11,500 BCE the warming climate caused the sea to start rising again, covering Beringia with water and cutting off the humans in Alaska from those in Siberia. But by that time, *H. sapiens*, adapting to the changing world of the Ice Age, had successfully migrated from Eurasia to the Americas.

Migration to the Americas

During the coldest time in the Ice Age, a gigantic ice sheet covered North America, preventing the humans in Alaska from migrating south. Around 11,500 BCE, however, it is thought that the glacier split in what is today the Canadian province of Alberta, creating a narrow passageway that made a human pathway from Alaska possible. If there was a migration, it must have occurred soon after the passageway opened. Since many of the thousands of spear points that have been found all over North America south of the ice sheet—the so-called Clovis points (see Chapter 5)—go as far back as 11,000 BCE, there were about 500 years for humans to move from Alaska to North America. Traditionally, scholars have thought it plausible that it was at this time that humans settled the Americas.

Multiple Migrations   In the 1990s and early 2000s, however, a number of spear points and human settlements older than 11,000 BCE were discovered in unanticipated places. Sites at Monte Verde in Chile, Meadowcroft in Pennsylvania, Topper in South Carolina, Cactus Hill in Virginia, Buttermilk Creek in Texas, Taíma Taíma [Ta-EE-ma] in Venezuela, Santana de Riacho [Ree-AT-sho], and Lapa do Boquete [Bo-KE-te] in Brazil have been reliably dated to 16,000–14,000

Symbolic Thinking

As demonstrated in this chapter, the crucial element that separates *Homo sapiens* from earlier hominins is evidence of what might be called "modern behavior," exemplified by the capacity for symbolic thinking. But what is symbolic thinking? A useful definition offered by archaeologists is the ability to conceptualize images by thinking abstractly; that is, to create symbols out of everyday materials. This unique ability in turn lies at the very foundation of the creation of art, language, and communication. The question is, however, When—and where—did symbolic thinking first appear in the long historical development of humankind?

Until very recently, it was commonplace to point to the stunning cave paintings of southwestern Europe as proof-positive of the earliest expressions of symbolic thinking. Routinely referred to as a "cultural explosion," it was thought these images represented a sudden creative outburst produced by modern *H. sapiens*, who arrived in Europe around 35,000 years ago. The paintings of Chauvet, for example, dated to 30,000 years ago, depict a wide range of animals, including deer, bison, horses, lions, and more exotic creatures like rhinoceroses, leopards, and even an owl. The caves at Lascaux (17,000 years ago) and Altamira (16,500 years ago) present similar images. Taken together, these magnificent cave murals present superb examples of representational art produced by Stone Age artists utilizing sophisticated tools, paints, and techniques such as shadowing and coloration to depict realistic images.

The Human Mind. Ochre from Blombos Cave, 1991, South Africa. The ochre is 70,000 years old. The incisions are the earliest evidence of geometrical conceptualizations beginning to form in the minds of modern humans, representing culture in the sense of religion, the arts, philosophy, and the sciences.

1 cm

years ago. The effect of the new research has been that the arrival of humans prior to 11,000 BCE is no longer mere speculation but is fast becoming the scientific consensus (see Map 1.4).

Long-distance ocean travel in ancient times was perhaps less difficult than has been previously assumed. After all, *H. sapiens* had already traveled by boat from Indonesia to Australia 60,000 years ago. Could modern humans have followed the Canadian coastline and sailed down to Washington State about 16,000 years ago? Proof for such a journey would, unfortunately, be difficult to come by since the coastline was some 50 miles farther out in the Pacific than it is today and any settlement traces would now be submerged below sea level. In the absence of underwater archaeology so far, nothing is known about such settlements.

Indeed, a number of small groups could have successfully sailed from Siberia, Japan, or even Sahul at various times prior to the appearance of the Beringian land bridge during the Ice Age or even earlier. Recent linguistic studies, using mathematical models for the development of language families, conclude that the Americas may have been inhabited for as long as 40,000–30,000 years. These models are based on the assumption that the nearly 200 contemporary Native American languages would have required this range of years to diversify, starting from a stock of three or more original languages.

Scientists examining the mitochondrial DNA of contemporary Native Americans have identified four circum-Pacific groups as ancestors migrating as early as

Archaeological discoveries during the 1990s, however, have pushed back the origins of symbolic thinking among *H. sapiens* to a much earlier age—and to a non-European origin. The stunning artifact found at Blombos Cave in southern Africa, dated at around 70,000 years ago, clearly indicates the ability of early *H. sapiens* artists to express thoughts in abstract symbols. According to the Blombos excavation director, Christopher Henshilwood, these intricate designs "could have been interpreted by those people as having meaning that would have been understood by others"; that is, they represent a form of visual communication.

The discoveries at Blombos and other sites in Africa suggest that early expressions of symbolic thinking originated in southern Africa 40,000–30,000 years earlier than in Europe. They also attest not only to a quantum leap in the intellectual development of *H. sapiens* over earlier hominins but also to the development of "modern behavior" in *H. sapiens* before this human being migrated out of Africa into Eurasia. In the final analysis, the foundations for the more detailed representational and technically developed cave paintings of France, Spain, and Australia derived from concepts originally conceived in the minds of early African *H. sapiens*.

Questions

- Are there any similarities between the earliest evidence to date of symbolic thinking in Africa and the much later cave paintings in Europe? If so, what does this say about early human culture and society?

- Will it ever be possible to fully comprehend how early humans imagined their world?

40,000 years ago to the Americas. Mitochondrial DNA relating to a fifth group, discovered in 1997 and found in 3 percent of Native Americans, however, has thrown a curve into this genetic research: It seems to identify a European or Central Asian ancestral group. As we have seen a number of times already, however, in the world of the archaeological, linguistic, and genetic science there is rarely a last word.

Some 80 skulls, skeletons, and bones unearthed in Brazil during the 1980s and 1990s were similarly discovered to be ethnically diverse. The ages of these fossils, established by radiocarbon dating, ranged between 12,800 and 9,000 years. Moreover, complex measurements of the skulls determined that many of the fossils were more closely related to aboriginal Ainu in Japan, Polynesians on a number of Pacific islands, and Aborigines in Australia than to today's Native Americans. The only conclusion to be drawn from these scientific examinations in North and South America was that isolated communities of early, non-Native American settlers populated the Americas until around 8000 BCE, when these settler groups finally merged into a single Native American population.

Americans Prior to Native Americans   Among these early and surprisingly diverse remains, two North American fossil specimens have attracted special attention. The first is the "Spirit Cave mummy," discovered near Reno, Nevada, in 1940, whose true age of 9,400 years was not determined until 1994. The second

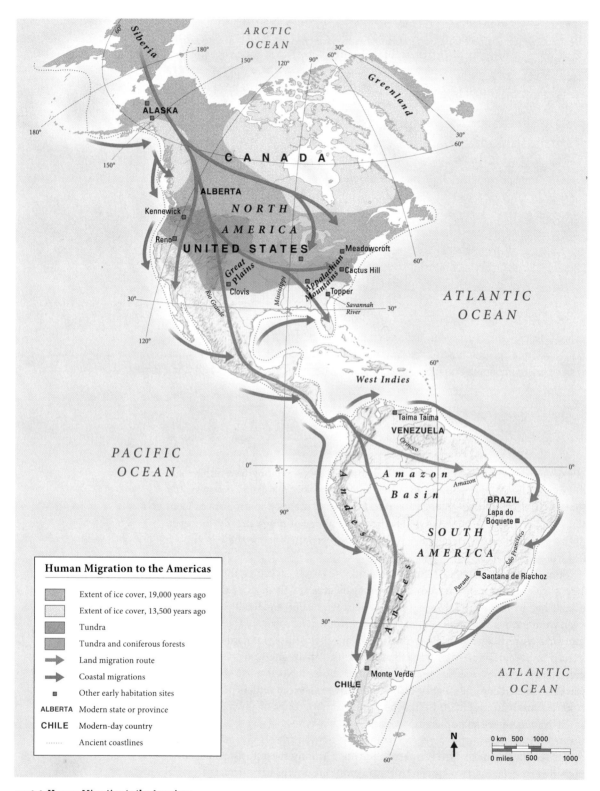

MAP **1.4** **Human Migration to the Americas.**

set of remains is that of "Kennewick man," discovered accidentally in Washington State in 1996 and dated to 9,300 years ago. On the basis of the anatomical features of both fossils, paleoanthropologists determined that they were of Ainu descent, that is, originating from the first inhabitants of Japan. The Spirit Cave mummy was a man about 45 years old when he died, from fever following dental abscesses. His spine was deformed, and as an adult, he must have lived with considerable back pain. A year before his death, he had suffered skull and wrist fractures, but both were healed when he died. Earlier in his life he was an active forager, but later on he depended on the care of his group, which actually fed him his last meal of fish. The group buried him in a cave, laying him on his side in a flexed position, which was typical also among the foragers in Africa, Australia, and Europe. Dry weather mummified his head and right shoulder and preserved the rest of his bones and clothes, including his moccasins and the bulrush mat in which he was wrapped. No doubt, we will learn much more about him once scholars have carried out a more detailed study.

Reconstruction of the Facial Features of Kennewick Man (9,300 Years Ago).

By contrast, Kennewick man, also resembling the Ainu of Japan, was tall and robust when he died. He was in good health throughout his youth and died also at the age of about 45 years. Similar to the Spirit Cave mummy, however, he suffered several major, even brutal external injuries. His forehead, left elbow, and a number of ribs showed signs of healed-over fractures. His worst wound came from a spear, which had been thrust into his pelvis, leaving a fragment of the spear point in his bone, which produced periodically a festering, debilitating bone wound that might have contributed to his death.

The study of humans of ethnically diverse backgrounds in the Americas both before and after Clovis is still in its infancy, and much will have to be learned before definitive conclusions can be drawn about who migrated when to the Americas. At present, all that can be said is that small groups trickled in at various times, from about 40,000 years ago, and that a uniform Native American population emerged only after 8000 BCE.

Putting It All Together

The time it took from Toumaï to the first modern humans in East Africa was slightly less than 7 million years. Another 100,000 years elapsed before modern humans peopled the earth, down to Clovis and the transition to agriculture in the Fertile Crescent of the Middle East. From there, in another 10,000 years we reached our own time. The proportions are staggering: The history from Clovis and the Fertile Crescent to the present is a mere 0.02 percent of the time from Toumaï to the present and 4 percent from the first *H. sapiens* fossil to the present. Practically the entire time we needed to become genetically human is buried in the "deep history" mentioned at the beginning of this chapter.

Nearly as deeply buried is the process during which we began to carve out the space for culture, which we possess within the frameworks of our genes and the environment. Realizing how long these genetic and cultural time spans of prehistory are is what matters for us today: The 10,000 years of history from the shift of forager to agrarian–urban and eventually scientific–industrial society represent a breathtakingly short time of development yet one that is so overwhelmingly complex that we have great difficulty understanding it. When we step back from this frenetically paced world history of the past 10,000 years and consider the much slower deep history of humanity, we become aware that, had it not been for this slow, tortuous, and often dead-end incubation, we would never have been able to sustain the speed of the later history of which we are the current product.

The principal reason for the slow pace of deep history was the conscious effort of foragers to limit population growth as well as the size of their groups. Women as well as men, constantly on the move in search for food, had a strong interest in having few children and weaning them for several years so as to extend birth spacing. Of course, Paleolithic populations grew over the course of the millennia; otherwise, there would not have been a pattern shift from foraging to agrarian–urban life. Thus, even though the culture of foraging sought to inhibit population growth, this culture was not so rigid that people under climatologically and environmentally benign circumstances were not open to material and cultural change. It was under these circumstances at the end of the Ice Age 13,500 years ago that humans in some parts of the world gradually abandoned foraging and began adapting to agriculture.

▶ For additional resources, including maps, primary sources, visuals, and quizzes, please go to www.oup.com/us/vonsivers. Please see the Further Resources section at the back of the book for additional readings and suggested websites.

Thinking Through Patterns

▶ **What made it possible for *Homo sapiens* to survive in a dangerous environment? Why is it difficult to imagine life as a prehistoric forager?**

We are twice removed from the world of foragers: After foraging came farming, which is also difficult to understand because today's pattern of life is part of scientific–industrial civilization. Even those among us who practice wilderness survival still have a lifeline to modern civilization (cell phones, GPS, etc.). *H. sapiens* foragers in prehistory, by contrast, relied on their stone tools, bows and arrows, rock shelters, clan members, and unsurpassed knowledge of animals, berry bushes, fruit and nut trees, mushroom patches, and grass fields to guide them through their daily lives. Collecting vegetables, catching fish, and killing the occasional animal did not take as much of an effort as farming later did; and foragers had more leisure time than farmers engaged in the annual agricultural cycle.

After modern humans left East Africa, probably in several waves between 80,000 and 60,000 years ago, in all likelihood they first went to northern India, before fanning out in all directions to Australia, Siberia, and Europe. They encountered *H. erectus* and successors, such as Neanderthals, and interbred with the latter. The modern humans who settled in Australia remained foragers because the African flora did not include grasses that could be cultivated through selective breeding into grains. From the complex tribal societies into which they evolved, we can see that forager life could acquire a differentiated culture, expressed in the so-called Dreamtime. However, when the Ice Age hit, forager clans and tribes had to retreat southward and adapt to the harsh environmental conditions. Foremost among the adaptations were the abilities to make protective woolen clothing and build boats with which to travel to more favorable places.

▶ **Where did humans go when they left Africa, and how did they establish themselves in the areas where they settled? How did they adapt to the worsening Ice Age?**

▶ **How did humans express their experience of sharing their life force with animals? How do we know that this experience was important to them?**

We can glimpse the interior lives of early humans through the figurines and cave paintings which they left behind. These artifacts have given rise to speculations about *H. sapiens'* culture, which are impossible to verify but, at a minimum, demonstrate to us the keen awareness about the difference between the natural world and the companionship that humans and other animals as living beings experienced. Prehistoric humans made a clear distinction between the things seen and unseen, that is, the animals as they are encountered in nature and the life force or motivating spirit which they share with humans.

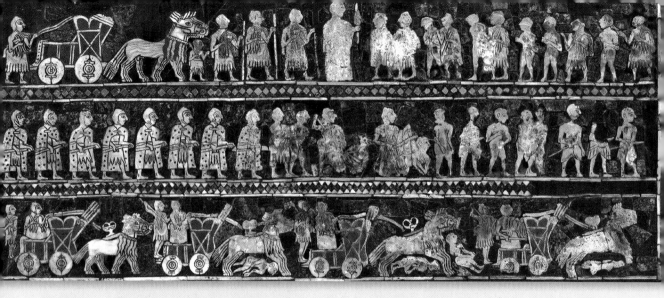

Chapter 2 11,500-600 BCE

Agrarian–Urban Centers of the Middle East and Eastern Mediterranean

She was the first writer in world history we know by name. The high priestess Enheduanna [En-hay-doo-AN-nah] lived at the end of the third millennium BCE and was a daughter of Sargon of Akkad, ruler of Mesopotamia's first recorded kingdom. Amazingly, her writings are still available today in translation. Her best-known poem, "The Exaltation of Inanna," was written after a rebel leader had deposed Enheduanna as high priestess. In the poem Enheduanna sadly wonders why Inanna (also known as Ishtar), the goddess of love, fertility, and war, has abandoned her: She has fulfilled all rituals and sacrifices, and yet she is exiled from her goddess! Imploring Inanna to take her back into her good graces, Enheduanna marshals all her poetic powers.

After reciting prayerful poems night and day, Enheduanna finally succeeded. Inanna accepted her priestess' appeals and the rightful ruler returned Enheduanna to her temple position.

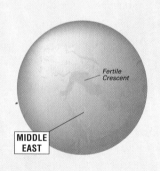

Fertile
Crescent

MIDDLE
EAST

ABOVE: The Standard of Ur (c. 2500 BCE), an inlaid wooden box depicting a Sumerian army.

The end of the third millennium BCE, when Enheduanna lived, was a time when **agrarian–urban society**, with its villages and cities, had become well established in several different areas. Foragers had pioneered agriculture and village settlements during a long period of 5,000 years in the Fertile Crescent of the Middle East, a region particularly favored by climate, vegetation, and animal populations. Once these early inhabitants had become farmers, they began interacting with foragers in the marshes of the Mesopotamian river delta, where—with the help of river water conducted via canals to the fields for irrigation—the groups merged. This combined population used the bountiful harvests for the foundation of cities in which craftspeople, priests and priestesses, merchants, kings, and rebels mingled, creating the fundamentals of the urban amenities of contemporary civilization: comfortable houses, places of worship, administrative centers, public archives, taverns, workshops, and markets. Many of these urban achievements are still crucial to our lives today. This chapter will trace the origins of farming, villages, cities, kingdoms, and empires in the Middle East, the first of the agrarian–urban centers in world history.

Agrarian Origins in the Fertile Crescent, ca. 11,500–1500 BCE

The movement from foraging to agriculture—one of the most pivotal patterns in world history—was a slow process covering several millennia. During this time, farmers built villages, in which they worked small garden-like plots and depended on annual rains for the growth of their crops. Farming gathered momentum as people mastered increasingly complex methods of irrigation. Farmers began to settle in the two great river valleys of the Tigris–Euphrates [You-FRAY-teez], in present-day Turkey, Syria, and Iraq, and of the Nile in Egypt. In these valleys, irrigation using river water allowed for larger plots and bigger harvests. Nutrient-rich river silt from the regular floods made the fields even more fertile and provided for often considerable surpluses of grain. These surpluses allowed populations to build cities and states, with ruling institutions composed of kings, advisors, armies, and bureaucracies.

Sedentary Foragers and Foraging Farmers

The region of the Middle East and the eastern Mediterranean stretches over portions of three continents—eastern Europe, southwestern Asia, and northeastern Africa. Historically, this region has always formed a single geographical unit within which there was extensive circulation of goods and ideas, although it did not constitute a single cultural zone. After the rise of the political institution of the empire, from about 1100 BCE, areas in the Middle East and the eastern Mediterranean were often also in competition with each other.

Geography and Environment   To understand how people in the Middle East and eastern Mediterranean adopted farming and settlement, we need to look first at the geography of the region. The western half includes Thrace and Greece in the north, together with numerous islands in the Aegean Sea, a branch of the Mediterranean Sea. The terrain on the mainland as well as the islands is mostly mountainous, covered with forests or brushwood. To the east, adjacent to Thrace

Seeing Patterns

▶ What are the main factors that enabled the transition from foraging to farming?

▶ Where did the pattern of agricultural life first emerge and why?

▶ How did the creation of agrarian–urban society—what we commonly call "civilization"—make for an entirely new pattern of world history?

Agrarian–urban society: A type of society characterized by intensive agriculture and people living in cities, towns, and villages.

and Greece, lies Anatolia, which comprises most of modern Turkey. Anatolia is a peninsula consisting of a central high plain which is ringed by mountain chains and traversed by rivers.

South of Anatolia and lying on the eastern shore of the Mediterranean Sea is the Levant (from French for "rising sun"), encompassing modern Syria, Lebanon, Israel, and Palestine. Along the coastline is a mountain chain reaching from Mount Lebanon in the north to the hill country of Palestine in the south. Mount Lebanon was covered at the time with huge cedars, of which only remnants survive today. The Levant, the Taurus Mountains of southeastern Anatolia, and the Zagros Mountains of southwestern Iran are often referred to as the "Fertile Crescent," to indicate the birthplace of agriculture (Map 2.1).

To the east of the mountain chain extends the Syrian steppe, which gradually gives way to the Arabian Desert. South of the Levant on the African continent are Egypt and Nubia (today's northern Sudan) on both sides of the Nile River. Both are largely covered by desert but bisected by the fertile Nile valley. This valley is wide and swampy in Sudan and narrow in Egypt, except for the Fayyum Depression and the Nile's Mediterranean delta. In the center of the Middle East are three smaller regions:

• Persia (modern-day Iran), stretching from the Caspian Sea southward to the Persian Gulf
• Mesopotamia, "the land between the rivers" of the Euphrates and Tigris in present-day Iraq and Kuwait
• the Arabian Peninsula, modern Saudi Arabia, the United Arab Emirates, Qatar, Oman, and Yemen

Recent historical climate research has established that between the end of the Ice Age (around 11,500 BCE) and 4000 BCE monsoon rain patterns extended farther west

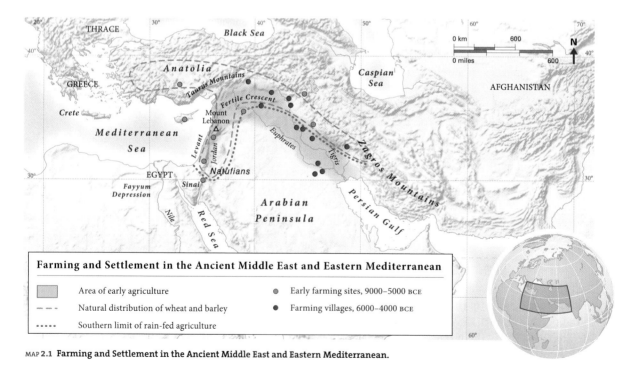

Farming and Settlement in the Ancient Middle East and Eastern Mediterranean

▨ Area of early agriculture	● Early farming sites, 9000–5000 BCE
– – – Natural distribution of wheat and barley	● Farming villages, 6000–4000 BCE
····· Southern limit of rain-fed agriculture	

MAP 2.1 **Farming and Settlement in the Ancient Middle East and Eastern Mediterranean.**

than they do today. Monsoon rain currently forms in the summer in South Africa and moves northeastward along East Africa before moving to India and China. When the monsoon still covered the Middle East, from the Mediterranean coast to the Persian Gulf, verdant vegetation covered land that is desert today. At present, only the highlands of Yemen and mountain rings around the central salt desert of Iran receive enough rain to sustain agriculture. At the eastern end of the Middle East is Afghanistan, a country with steppe plains and high mountains bordering on India—like the Fertile Crescent and Mesopotamia. It was also a center of early **agrarian society**.

Agrarian society: At a minimum, people engaged in farming cereal grains on rain-fed or irrigated fields and breeding sheep and cattle.

The Natufians   The richness of the Fertile Crescent in plants and animals during the early centuries after the end of the Ice Age seems to have encouraged settlement. Foragers found everything they wanted within a radius of a few miles: wild grains, legumes such as lentils and chickpeas, and game. Nature replenished its ample resources year after year. Semipermanent hamlets, forming the Natufian culture (11,500–9500 BCE), arose in the Jordan and upper Euphrates valleys.

Each hamlet of the Natufians, consisting of about 60 inhabitants, contained a few semicircular pit houses made up of a stone foundation, posts, thatched walls, and a thatched roof. Sometimes their homes would even become their final resting places—the Natufians buried their dead underneath the floors of abandoned houses or along the edges of settlements. Some graves contained ornaments, and at least two persons have been found buried with their dogs. Later Natufians often removed the skulls of their ancestors—whether before or after the burial of the body is unknown—and venerated them in altar niches in their houses. Thus began an important ancestral cult that spread across the Middle East and lasted for several millennia.

Early Natufian Decorated Skull, from El-Wad. Note the simulation of hair on top of the skull. Eyes were simulated through inlaid semiprecious stones. During 11500–5700 BCE Middle Easterners practiced ancestor cults, with the deceased buried underneath house floors and separated heads often decorated and kept in house niches.

To gather food, the Natufians went out into the woods with baskets and obsidian-bladed sickles. Wild cereal grains had evolved over the millennia so that their seeds scattered easily upon ripening, furthering the growth of new crops. Gatherers carefully tapped plants whose seeds had not yet scattered and collected the grains in baskets. Back in the hamlets, the grain was ground with pestles on grindstones. Storage seems to have been minimal, limited to portable containers, such as baskets. The abundant food supply, however, did not last. A near-glacial cold and dry period from 10,900 to 9600 BCE, called the "Younger Dryas" (named after a cold-resistant mountain flower), caused wild cereal stands to wither and game animals to drift away to warmer climes. Most of the sedentary foragers deserted their hamlets and returned to a fully migratory life of foraging. The short-lived, semisettled culture of the Natufians collapsed.

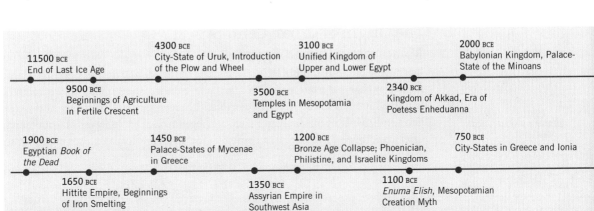

11500 BCE End of Last Ice Age	4300 BCE City-State of Uruk, Introduction of the Plow and Wheel	3100 BCE Unified Kingdom of Upper and Lower Egypt	2000 BCE Babylonian Kingdom, Palace- State of the Minoans
9500 BCE Beginnings of Agriculture in Fertile Crescent	3500 BCE Temples in Mesopotamia and Egypt	2340 BCE Kingdom of Akkad, Era of Poetess Enheduanna	
1900 BCE Egyptian *Book of* *the Dead*	1450 BCE Palace-States of Mycenae in Greece	1200 BCE Bronze Age Collapse; Phoenician, Philistine, and Israelite Kingdoms	750 BCE City-States in Greece and Ionia
1650 BCE Hittite Empire, Beginnings of Iron Smelting	1350 BCE Assyrian Empire in Southwest Asia	1100 BCE *Enuma Elish*, Mesopotamian Creation Myth	

Neolithic Age: Period from ca. 9600 to 4500 BCE when stone tools were adapted to the requirements of agriculture, through the making of sickles and spades.

In the few hamlets that survived, people turned to storing grain in plastered pits or stone silos in order to cope with the harsher winters. In spring, they planted some of their stored grain to thicken the sparse wild grain stands. When warmer and more humid weather returned, a new era began, the **Neolithic**, or New Stone Age. Scholars use this designation for the period from about 9600 to 4500 BCE in the Middle East because it was characterized by polished stone implements (spades and sickles), the introduction of agriculture, animal domestication, sun-dried bricks, plaster, and pottery—in short, most of the key elements of agrarian society.

Selective Breeding of Grain and Domestic Animals   Climatically, the Neolithic Age began with a metaphorical bang. Within just a few generations, summer temperatures increased by an extraordinary 7 degrees. Thereafter, temperatures continued to rise, at a more modest rate, for another 2,000 years. In this balmy climate, both old and newly established hamlets expanded quickly into villages of around 300–500 inhabitants. People continued to collect grain but also began to plant fields. In the early summer, they waited for the moment when the great majority of the grain was still in its ears. Through selective breeding, they gradually weeded out early-ripening varieties and began harvesting fields in which all grain ripened at the same time. The kernels of these first wheat and barley varieties were still small, and it took until about 7000 BCE in the Middle East before farmers had bred the large-grained wheat and barley of today.

Parallel to the selective breeding of grain, farmers also domesticated *pulses*—the edible seeds of pod-bearing plants—beginning with chickpeas and lentils. Pulses had the advantage of helping with the refertilization of the grain fields: Pods, stalks, and roots contain nitrogen needed by all plants to grow. Farmers continued to hunt, but they also captured young wild goats and sheep and through selective breeding accustomed them to live with humans in their houses and pens: the first domestication of livestock. For two millennia, this kind of early farming remained essentially garden farming, with hand-held implements, such as digging sticks, spades, and sickles.

The original agriculture—the cultivation of grain and pulses and the domestication of goats and sheep—relied on annual rains in the Fertile Crescent and became more widespread when farmers tapped creeks for the irrigation of their fields during dry months. Inhabitants of this region discovered the benefits of rotating their crops and driving goats and sheep over the stubble of harvested grain fields, using the animals' droppings for refertilization and leaving the fields fallow for a year. Around 6500 BCE, these peoples added cattle, pigs, donkeys (domesticated first in Nubia), and pottery (clay vessels fired in kilns) to their farms. For the first time in world history, the epic transition from foraging to farming had been completed.

The Origin of Urban Centers in Mesopotamia and Egypt

During the fifth millennium BCE, the climate of the Middle East and eastern Mediterranean changed from monsoon rains falling during the summer to wet winters and dry summers in the west and north and general dryness prevailing in the east and south. Most of the Arabian Peninsula began to dry up. In lower Mesopotamia, drier conditions forced settlers coming from upstream to pay closer attention to

FIRST AGRARIAN-URBAN CENTERS

irrigation. All of these changes would contribute to the rise of the first agrarian–urban centers founded along rivers—in the Middle East, Egypt, the Indus valley in the Indian subcontinent, and later, the Yellow River valley in China.

Euphrates and Nile Floods   The Tigris River in eastern Mesopotamia, with its turbulent waters and high banks, did not lend itself early on to the construction of irrigation canals. The Euphrates River in western Mesopotamia, however, flowed more tranquilly and closer to the surface of the land, providing favorable conditions for irrigated farming. At its lower end, in present-day Iraq, the Euphrates united with the Tigris and dispersed out into swampland, lagoons, and marshes, which supported a rich plant and animal life. It was here that the first farmers, coming from central and northern Mesopotamia, settled, establishing the Ubaid culture of villages (6000–4000 BCE).

The annual snowmelt in the mountains of northeastern Anatolia caused the Euphrates and Tigris to carry often devastating deluges of water down into the plain. The floods arrived in early spring just as the first grain was ready for harvest, forcing the farmers into heroic efforts to keep the ripening grain fields from being inundated by water. On the other hand, the spring floods helped prepare the fields for the growing of smaller crops, such as chickpeas, peas, lentils, millet, and animal fodder. The floods also softened hardened soils and sometimes leached them of salt deposits. Thus, in spite of some drawbacks, irrigated farming in lower Mesopotamia, with its more predictable water supplies, was more abundant and reliable than was the more irregular rain-fed agriculture in the Taurus–Zagros–Levant region to the north.

The Egyptian Nile originates in regions of East Africa where the rains hit during the early summer. Much of this rain is collected in Lake Victoria, from where the White Nile flows northward. In the Sudan it unites with the Blue Nile, which carries water and fertile silt from the rains down from the Ethiopian mountains. The Nile usually begins to swell in July, crests in August–September, and recedes during October. For the Neolithic inhabitants of Egypt these late-summer and fall floods created conditions quite different from those of lower Mesopotamia, which depended on the spring floods.

In Egypt, the floods coincided with the growing season of winter barley and wheat. Silt carried by the Nile fertilized the fields every year, prior to planting. Because of the steeper descent in both the long valley and short delta of the Nile, the water table was lower and the danger of salt rising to the surface was less than in Mesopotamia, where over time large areas became infertile. The first agricultural settlements appeared in the Fayyum [Fay-YOOM], a swampy depression off the Nile southwest of modern Cairo, around 5200 BCE. By about 3500 BCE, agriculture had spread south along the Nile and north into the delta.

Early Towns   Between 5500 and 3500 BCE, villages in lower Mesopotamia and Upper Egypt developed into towns. They were composed of a few thousand inhabitants, with markets where farmers exchanged surplus food staples and traders offered goods not produced locally. The Mesopotamian towns administered themselves through local **assemblies**, in Sumerian called *puhrum* [POOH-room]. All male adults came together at these assemblies to decide on communal matters such as mutual help during the planting and harvesting seasons, the digging of canals, punishments for criminal acts by townspeople, and relations with other towns and

Assembly: Gathering of either all inhabitants or the most influential persons in a town; later, in cities, assemblies and kings made communal decisions on important fiscal or juridical matters.

Sharecroppers: Farmers who received seed, animals, and tools from landowners in exchange for up to two-thirds of their harvest.

Nomads: People whose livelihood was based on the herding of animals, such as sheep, goats, cattle, horses, and camels; moving with their animals from pasture to pasture according to the seasons, they lived in tent camps.

villages. For nearly two millennia towns in this region regulated their irrigated agriculture through communal cooperation (see Map 2.2).

In Mesopotamian and Egyptian towns an irrigated field produced about twice as much wheat or barley as did a rain-fed field. Indeed, irrigation made it possible for townspeople to accumulate an agricultural surplus that protected them against famines and allowed for population increases. Some people accumulated more grain than others, and the first social distinctions along the lines of wealth appeared. Gradually, wealthy families became owners of land beyond their family properties. **Sharecroppers** who worked these lands were perhaps previously landowners who had fallen into debt and now paid rent (in the form of grain) to the new landowners. Other landless farmers left agriculture altogether and became **nomads**, breeding *onagers* (ancestors of donkeys), sheep, and goats on steppe lands unsuited for agriculture. Wealthy landowners appropriated the places of ritual and sacrifice in the villages and towns and constructed elaborate temples, mansions, workshops, and granaries.

Eventually, the landowning priestly families stopped not only farming their own land but also making tools, pottery, cloth, and leather goods, turning the production of these goods over to specialized craftspeople, such as toolmakers (for stone, bone, or wood tools), potters, weavers, or cobblers, and paying them with grain rations. The landowners employed traders who traveled to other areas with crafts (pottery, cloth, leather goods), trading them for raw materials. Mesopotamian merchants traveled with cloth and tools to villages and towns in the Zagros Mountains and returned with timber, stone, obsidian, and copper. Egyptian villagers traded textiles with villagers in the Sinai Peninsula in return for copper and with Nubian villagers in return for gold.

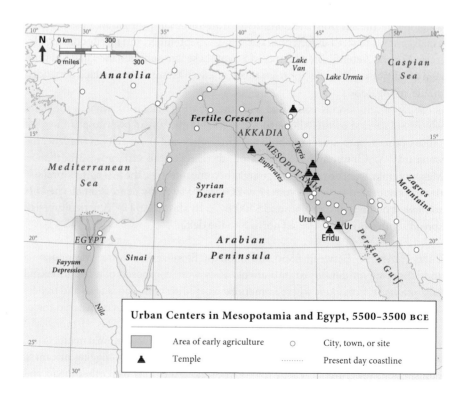

MAP **2.2 Urban Centers in Mesopotamia and Egypt, 5500–3500 BCE.**

Around 4300 BCE, some mountain people in the region had mastered the crafts of mining and smelting copper. This metal was too soft to replace obsidian, but the many other uses to which it was put have led scholars to mark the middle of the fifth millennium BCE as the moment when the Neolithic, or New Stone, Age of polished stone tools came to an end and the *Chalcolithic*, or Copper, Age began.

The Temple at Eridu. Artist's reconstruction of the temple at Eridu. Note the immense platform supporting the temple and the sacred enclosure, which measured 200 square yards.

Temples   In the course of the fifth millennium BCE, wealthy landowners gained control over the communal grain stores and clan shrines and enlarged these into town shrines. In Eridu, the shrine, originally a mud brick structure with an offering table for sacrifices, grew over the millennia through a dozen superimpositions into a monumental temple. Adjacent to the early temples were kilns, granaries, workshops, breweries, and administrative buildings. The wealthy landowners, presiding over the temples as priests, were responsible for the administration of all aspects of cult ritual in the temples, as well as the provision of labor in the temple fields, which included the digging and cleaning of irrigation canals; the planting, harvesting, transporting, and storing of crops; and the pasturing, stabling, and breeding of animals.

In Upper Egypt, landowner-priests presided over the construction of the first temples around 3500 BCE, together with elegantly embellished tombs for themselves. The decorations in both temples and tombs depict boats, animals, and humans. One such painting shows a leader carrying out an expedition on the Nile upstream to Nubia, returning with gold, ebony, and diorite (black rock for statues) to create elaborate ornaments for his temple and tomb. Unfortunately, the sparse archaeological record in Egypt at this point presents few details concerning the transition from village to town.

The World's First Cities   In contrast to a town, a **city** (or **city-state**, if the surrounding villages are included) is defined as a place of more than 5,000 inhabitants, with a number of nonfarming inhabitants, such as craftspeople, merchants, and administrators. The latter lived on the food they received in exchange for their own handiwork, such as pottery, textiles, and traded goods. To keep order in such a large place where many people did not know each other, the dominant landowner-priest created a personal entourage of armed men, wielding police power. The first place in Mesopotamia to fit the definition of a city was Uruk, founded near Eridu around 4300 BCE. Within a millennium, it was a city of 50,000–80,000 inhabitants with a mixture of palaces, multistory administrative buildings, workshops, residences, palace estates, and villages clustered around the city with both large and small individual farms.

The people of Uruk were important pioneers of technical and intellectual innovations. It was here that the first known plow was found. Mesopotamian plows were sophisticated wooden constructions with seeder funnels on top and pulled by pairs of oxen or donkeys. Plowing and controlled sowing allowed for much larger

City, city-state: A place of more than 5,000 inhabitants with nonfarming inhabitants (craftspeople, merchants, administrators), markets, and a city leader capable of compelling obedience to his decisions by force.

harvests. Uruk craftspeople introduced the potter's wheel, which accelerated and made more precise the manufacture of earthenware and ceramics. The sizes of jars, pots, and bowls gradually became standardized, simplifying the storage of grain and its distribution in the cities.

At the same time, two- and four-wheeled carts pulled by oxen expedited the transportation of large quantities of grain from the fields to the city. The grain was made into bread, to conveniently feed the populace, and beer, which became the safe, potable, and easily storable drink of choice among urban dwellers. By some estimates, more than 40 percent of Mesopotamia's grain was committed to beer production, and archaeologists have unearthed numerous recipes for the brew.

Another particularly serviceable invention was bronze, the world's first *alloy*— that is, a blending of two or more metals in the smelting process. Bronze is an alloy of copper and arsenic or tin, producing a hard, although relatively expensive, metal that could be used in tools and weapons. Bronze became so useful in the Middle East and eastern Mediterranean during the following centuries that it replaced stone and copper implements for all but a few purposes in daily life, leading historians to refer to this as the *Bronze Age* (in the Middle East from 3300 to 1200 BCE). Bronze became one of the hallmarks of agrarian–urban life as its use spread or was independently developed in other places in Eurasia.

Cuneiform Writing   The administrators in the bureaucracy, who were responsible for the accounting and distribution of grain, animals, ceramics, textiles, and imported raw materials, greatly simplified their complicated tasks around 3450 BCE by inventing a system of writing. Scribes wrote in cuneiform [Kyoo-NEE-uh-form] (from the Latin, meaning "wedge-shaped") script on clay tablets, using signs denoting objects and sounds from the spoken language. Small stone or clay tokens indicating different types of grain or goods on baskets or containers had been ubiquitous in the Middle East since the late Paleolithic. These tokens with a variety of engraved or imprinted signs might have been precursors of cuneiform writing. Historians are still researching and arguing these points. However the debate is eventually settled, it is obvious that writing was a major expansion of the conceptual horizon of humankind that reached back to the first flaked stones, ornaments, figurines, and cave paintings in the Paleolithic. For the first time, scribes could not only write down the languages they spoke but also clarify for future generations the meaning of the sculpted and painted artifacts which would otherwise have been mute witnesses of history. With the advent of writing, record keeping, communication, increasingly abstract thought, and, for the first time, history could all be recorded.

Kingdoms in Mesopotamia, Egypt, and Crete

With the introduction of the plow and increasing numbers of metal tools, city leaders greatly expanded their landholdings. They employed large groups of laborers to cut canals through riverbanks onto virgin lands. Vast new areas of lowlands, situated at some distance from riverbanks, became available for farming. Portions of this land served as overflow basins for floodwaters, to protect the ripening grain fields. Craftspeople invented lifting devices to channel water from the canals into small fields or gardens. As a result of this field and irrigation expansion, the grain surpluses of both temples and villages increased enormously.

Kingship in Mesopotamia   A consequence of the expansion of agriculture was the rise of nearly two dozen cities in lower and central Mesopotamia. As cities expanded and multiplied, the uncultivated buffer lands which had formerly separated them disappeared. People drew borders, quarreled over access to water, made deals to share it, and both negotiated and fought over the ownership of wandering livestock.

When it became impossible to contain conflicts and wars broke out, city dwellers built walls and recruited military forces from among their young population. The commanders, often of modest origins, used their military positions to acquire wealth and demanded to be recognized as leaders. They disputed authority with the priests, who had been the traditional heads of villages and towns. Depending on circumstances, the Mesopotamian city assemblies chose their leaders from either the self-made or the priestly leaders, calling the former "great man" (*lugal*) and the latter "king" (*en*).

Cuneiform Script. Scribes impressed the syllables on the wet clay with a scalpel-like writing instrument.

Once in power, a royal leader sought to make his position independent from the assemblies and impose dynastic or family rule on the city. To set himself apart from his assembly colleagues, he claimed divine or sacred sanction for his kingship. The King List of 2125 BCE, in which the reigns of all early kings in lower Mesopotamia were coordinated, begins with "after the kingship descended from heaven, the kingship was in Eridu." In other words, the kings argued that as divinely ordained rulers they no longer needed the consensus of the assemblies for their power or that of their sons and grandsons. The earliest king known by name and attested in the archaeological record was Enmebaragesi [En-me-ba-ra-GAY-see] of Kish, who reigned around 2500 BCE. Later kings are known for all the nearly two dozen cities of Mesopotamia.

Akkadia and Babylonia   During the 2000s BCE, these Mesopotamian cities began competing against each other for military supremacy. The first royal dynasty to bring them together in a unified territorial state or kingdom—numbering about 2 million inhabitants—was that of Akkadia (ca. 2340–2150 BCE). Sargon, the first major king (r. 2334–2279 BCE), commanded several thousand foot soldiers armed with bronze helmets, leather coats, spears, and battle-axes. Sargon's grandson, Naram-Sin, added the Zagros Mountains and Syria to the Akkadian kingdom and claimed to be the "king of the four (world) shores." He considered his state to be an open-ended kingdom stretching in all four directions and limited only by the sea which surrounded the earth. Naram-Sin was the first king to conceive of a grand imperial design which would lead to the unification of the ethnically, linguistically, and religiously diverse peoples of the Middle East, with or without their consent. However, he did not possess yet the military means to embark on large-scale conquests and **empire** building. The Hittites and Assyrians a millennium and a half later would be the first to reach that milestone (see Map 2.3).

Empire: Large multiethnic, multilinguistic, multireligious state consisting of a conquering kingdom and several defeated kingdoms.

A later major Mesopotamian kingdom was Babylonia. Its best-known king was Hammurabi (1792–1750 BCE), who ordered the engraving of the entire code of Babylonian law onto a 7-foot slab of basalt. Like so many rulers in Mesopotamia and, indeed, in cultures around the world, Hammurabi saw himself as the executor of a stern, divinely sanctioned law that punished evildoers and rewarded the righteous. By today's standards, Hammurabi's laws were harsh, threatening severe punishments for crimes against

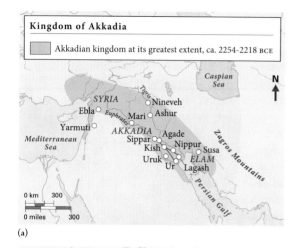

(a)

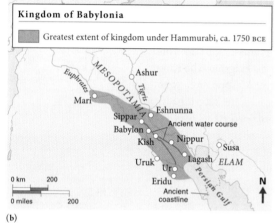

(b)

MAP 2.3 (a) **The Akkadian Kingdom.** (b) **Kingdom of Babylonia.**

property, land, and commerce. For example, tavern owners who overcharged customers or who failed to notify the police of the presence of criminals on their property were to be drowned. Priestesses caught in taverns were to be burned to death. The law of Mesopotamia was no longer the customary law of villages and towns but the royal writ, divinely ordained and backed by military force (see "Patterns Up Close" on pp. 42–43).

Patriarchy   The pattern of state formation from villages to kingdoms contained in itself another pattern crucial in the development of society in the Middle East and beyond: the increasingly pronounced patriarchal structure of society. As we have seen in Chapter 1, the archaeological evidence does not allow many conclusions concerning gender functions in Paleolithic society. The Lascaux image of the injured bull charging its hunter, who is depicted as a stick figure with a phallus, is a rare exception. The gathering and preparation of vegetal food was an occupation that required communal cooperation among all and probably more than balanced the special occupation of males in the hunt. The Neolithic rise of agriculture does not seem to have changed much in these largely unstructured gender relations.

The wars among the city-states and kingdoms were important events in the creation of new patterns of gender relations. Large numbers of war captives, providing cheap labor as slaves in temple households and wealthy residences, gave the priestly and self-made kings a decisive edge in beginning the restructuring of agrarian–urban society. A ruling class emerged, composed of dynastic families who collaborated with other landowning and priestly families. One rank below the ruling class were the merchants and craftspeople, who formed a hierarchy among themselves, with merchants and jewelry makers at the top and tanners—because of the unpleasant odor of their manufacturing processes—in the lower ranks. At the bottom of this increasingly structured, hierarchical society were slaves and other marginal urban groups, such as day laborers and prostitutes.

The formation of hierarchical social structures did not stop with the rise of social classes. As we shall see in later chapters, men assumed legal power over women on all levels of society in nearly every agrarian–urban culture. At first, the patriarchy was still relatively mild. In the ruling classes of Mesopotamia, female members held high positions as priestesses, queen consorts, and in a few cases even queens but only as extensions of male dynastic rule. Enheduanna, in the vignette at the beginning of this chapter, was an example of a highborn woman unhappily dependent on the decisions of the male members of her family.

In New Kingdom Egypt (1550–1070 BCE), princesses had the same rights of divine descent as princes. Sisters and brothers or half-brothers sometimes married each other, reinforcing the concept that their lineage was divine and pure, containing no mortal blood. A famous example is Hatshepsut [Hat-SHEP-soot], who was married to her half-brother. She was a strong-willed woman who became "king" (the title of "queen" did not exist) after the death of her husband, ruling for over two decades (r. ca. 1479–1457 BCE), before a son from one of her former husband's concubines succeeded her. In later millennia, after empires formed, noble women disappeared from their male-dependent public positions and lived in secluded areas of the palaces. Men tightened the law, relegating women to inferior family positions. Patriarchy was thus a product not of agrarian but of urban society in city-states and kingdoms of Mesopotamia and, a little later, Egypt.

Egyptian Kingdoms   In Egypt, the first city was Hierankopolis [Hee-ran-KO-po-lis], funded around 3000 BCE. Smaller cities dotted the river downstream to the delta. As in Mesopotamia, the rulers of cities began to develop into small-scale kings. Among the first of these we know by name were Menes, Narmer, and Aha. Whoever among these three was the first pharaoh (king, from Egyptian *Pr-aa*, "great house"), he unified all Egyptian lands—stretching from Upper Egypt down the Nile to the delta—and established the first dynasty of Egypt's Early Dynastic Period (ca. 3100–2613 BCE), choosing Memphis, near modern Cairo, as his capital. At first, lesser rulers continued their reigns in the other cities. They even rebelled against the pharaoh from time to time. Therefore, the early policies of the Egyptian kings were focused almost exclusively on the unification of Egypt. Since it was not easy to subjugate the lesser rulers in a country of some 650 miles in length, unification was a protracted process.

The first king claimed divine birth from Egypt's founder god, Horus, the falcon-headed deity. As god on earth, the king upheld the divine order (*ma'at* [Ma-AHT]) of justice and peace for all. For their part, the inhabitants of his kingdom were no more than humble servants whose duty was to provide for the king's earthly and heavenly life by paying him taxes and constructing an opulent palace and tomb for him. Of course, in practice this royal supremacy was far from complete. Even during times of strong centralization there were always some powerful figures—provincial landowners and governors, for example—who held title

Egyptian Hieroglyphs, Luxor, Valley of the Kings; Carved into the Wall and Colored.

to their properties in their own names and collected rents from the farmers working on these properties. As in Mesopotamia, the claim of the kings to divine sanction or even divinity did not keep rivals from bidding for supreme power.

Hieroglyphs, Bureaucracy, and Pyramids   As with cuneiform in Mesopotamia, the Egyptian kings were greatly aided in the process of unification by the introduction of a system of accounting and writing. Around 3500–3200 BCE, administrators and scribes developed *hieroglyphic* writing in Egypt. In this system, formalized pictures symbolizing objects and syllables were used to represent words. Hieroglyphic writing was limited to royal inscriptions; *hieratic*, a less elaborate version, was the writing used in bureaucratic documents. The writing material used in Egypt was papyrus, which was more expensive but less cumbersome than the Mesopotamian clay tablets. Papyrus was made from a special kind of Egyptian reed, the core of which was cut into strips, laid out crosswise, and pressed into textured

Patterns Up Close | Babylonian Law Codes

Stele with Hammurabi's Law.

In addition to the invention of cuneiform writing and the use of the wheel, the Babylonians in lower Mesopotamia produced the earliest known collections of written laws. Because of their formal, written nature, these law codes differed from earlier oral and customary law, common to all early cultures. When did these laws originate, how did they develop across time, and what was their influence on later ages?

The origin and evolution of the legal tradition are intertwined with developments associated with the complexity of urban life. In order to sustain sufficient agricultural production, people devised an intricate system of irrigation and drainage canals, along with dikes and dams, to control the often unpredictable flooding of the Tigris and Euphrates Rivers. All of this necessitated not only extensive planning and maintenance but also the allotment of plots of land, some closer and others farther from water sources. In addition, the emergence of complex political, economic, and social relationships—fraught with disputes and inequalities—called for the establishment of a set of centrally administered rules and regulations in order to provide for conflict resolution as well as retribution for wrongdoing.

Across a span of nearly 500 years from the earliest codification of King Urukagina of Lagash in ca. 2350 BCE to the monumental code of Hammurabi in 1750 BCE, law developed through a successive series of increasingly comprehensive and refined legal codes consistent with developing complexities of urban expansion. Consequently, evolving law codes address correspondingly wider audiences, they cover a broader spectrum of social classes, and they present more complex examples of potential infractions as well as more nuanced resolutions. Most legal codes open with a prologue, which is followed by a body of laws, and close with an epilogue. In terms of format, Sumerian laws follow the format of "if this, then that" regarding violations and ensuing punishments, and punishments are meted out with reference to social status. Finally, they pay growing attention to the importance of irrigation, with more and more references to the maintenance of river dikes and irrigation canals, along with harsh consequences for not doing so.

The law code of Hammurabi, king of Babylon (r. 1792–1750 BCE), represents the first complete written and well-organized code of law. An amalgamation of

sheets. First documented around 2700 BCE, papyrus became a major export item in the following millennium.

In addition to aiding in communication, writing—as it did in Mesopotamia—lent itself to a larger and more efficient bureaucracy in Egypt. At the beginning of the Old Kingdom (ca. 2613–2160 BCE), heavy Nile flooding enabled the Egyptian kings to expand agriculture on their lands. The royal palace and temple became large, elaborately hierarchical organizations in which everything was minutely regulated, including the food rations distributed to the palace administrators, priests, craftspeople, and laborers. Using arithmetic manuals, scribes calculated the quantities of bread, beer, and meat rations to be distributed; of timber for the shipyards; and of flax for the linen-weaving workshops. For unused fractions of rations a credit system evolved whereby earlier Sumerian precepts, the code exceeds them in its extensions and embellishments; whereas earlier codifications list around 40 laws, those of Hammurabi number fully 282. Like earlier models, the code acknowledges distinctions in social hierarchies along with inequalities among them but goes beyond them in addressing more social classes and grouping the classes according to relative wealth and social standing. Also, like previous collections, the code is broken down into several categories, including issues related to property and family law; but here again it covers many more possible scenarios as ways to close previous loopholes.

Unlike its Sumerian predecessors, however, the code departs significantly when it comes to retribution in that it calls for more extreme punishments according to the principle of *lex talionis* ("an eye for an eye"). Thus, "If a man put out the eye of another man, his eye shall be put out." Further, the importance of maintaining irrigation systems is consistent with earlier themes but in more nuanced terms: "If any one open his ditches to water his crop, but is careless, and the water flood the field of his neighbor, then he shall pay his neighbor [grain] for his loss."

The long-term influence of Sumerian and Babylonian legal codes—particularly Hammurabi's code—extends far beyond ancient Mesopotamia. Many of its concepts and precepts served as predecessors of Hittite, Egyptian, and Assyrian laws. Instances of its influence appear in the development of biblical law, and striking similarities to the notion of *lex talionis* are found in ancient Jewish law. The code was carried westward across the Mediterranean, where many of its principles found their way into Roman law, especially the organized codification of civil cases.

Questions

- What do the first law codes tell us about ancient Sumerian and Babylonian societies?

- Are the legacies of these first law codes still evident in modern Western legal practice today?

officials traded among themselves what strongly resembled "futures" on a modern commodity market. In its complexity, the Egyptian bureaucratic system of the Old Kingdom easily surpassed that of lower Mesopotamia during the contemporary Akkadian period (see Map 2.4).

The most astounding bureaucratic achievement of the Old Kingdom was Pharaoh Khufu's (r. 2589–2566 BCE) construction of a pyramid near modern Cairo as a funerary monument for himself. (Two smaller pyramids in the vicinity served as tombs for the bodies of later pharaohs.) Under orders of the stern and even cruel Khufu, stone workers quarried local limestone from the cliffs behind the right bank of the Nile for the central portion of each of the pyramids. Finer, less brittle casing stones came from quarries upstream on the Nile. Ramparts of chipped stone and other debris, as well

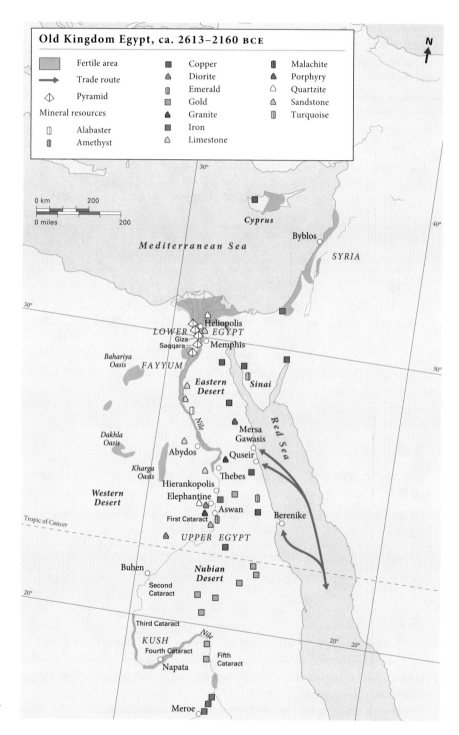

MAP **2.4 Old Kingdom Egypt, ca.**
2613–2160 BCE.

as sledges, rollers, and heavy levers made of timber, helped laborers move the stone blocks into place, as much as 479 feet high. After the completion of the pyramid, the construction machinery was dismantled, and today sand covers what were once the workers' camps.

The workforce, perhaps as many as 10,000 laborers, consisted of farmers who were working off their annual 1-month labor service owed to the king. A special labor office made sure that the withdrawal of groups of laborers from the villages was staggered in such a way that regular field labor was disrupted as little as possible. Foremen administered the groups of laborers. Other officials provided rations for them in their camps. Although the workers were strictly supervised, we know that they also occasionally went on strike. Labor unrest, however, could easily be suppressed by the Egyptian army, which was composed of up to 20,000 soldiers, mostly Nubian archers.

The pharaohs of the Middle Kingdom (ca. 2040–1750 BCE) were more modest builders and focused instead on large-scale agricultural projects, the mining of metals in Sinai, and long-distance trade. During Amenemhet III's long reign (r. ca. 1843–1796 BCE), Egypt reached the peak of its internal development. Workers transferred from Syria drained the Fayyum Depression and created irrigated fields similar to those found around many cities in Mesopotamia. Merchants developed close relations with other merchants in the Levant, from where they imported cedar wood for ships, roofs, and coffins. Egyptian exports consisted of jewelry and art objects made of gold. In the Sinai Peninsula Egyptian miners dug for copper and turquoise. In the desert valleys of Nubia they quarried diorite and mined gold and copper. By the end of Amenemhet's reign, the kingdom numbered about 1 million inhabitants and was a formidable power, even more impressive than the Old Kingdom with its pyramids.

The Minoan Kingdom   After farming had spread from the Levant to Anatolia, seafarers carried the practice westward around 6500 BCE to Greece and the Aegean islands. The first large islands where they settled were Cyprus and Crete. The latter island is about 170 miles long and about 35 miles wide at its widest point. Over the millennia, some of the early villages of Crete grew into towns, and by around 2000 BCE small states with kings, spacious palaces, and surrounding villages were flourishing. The dominant **palace-state** was that of the Minoans (named after its founder, King Minos), a polity with as many as 12,000 inhabitants in the sprawling palace and a few villages outside.

Palace-state: A city or fortified palace with surrounding villages.

The Minoan kingdom was centered on a palace with hundreds of rooms, including vast storage spaces for food and cisterns for the collection of water. Among the palace personnel were scribes who used a pictorial-syllabic script on clay tablets similar to the writing and recording systems of Mesopotamia. Unfortunately, this script, called by scholars *Linear A*, has thus far not been deciphered. In the villages, farmers produced grain, olive oil, wine, and honey. Royal merchants traded these products for obsidian, copper, and tin from Greece, Anatolia, and Cyprus. Craftspeople made pottery, bronze vessels, and jewelry for the palace as well as for export to Egypt, Syria, and Mesopotamia. Minoans were skilled boat builders who constructed oceangoing vessels, some as long as 100 feet, and powered by both sails and rowers. Minoan Crete was closely related to its older neighbors, from whom it had creatively borrowed—but it had also created its own independent trade and seafaring traditions.

Minoan Island of Thera, Akrotiri Palace, ca. 1550 BCE. Mural depicting a flotilla of Minoan aristocracy on a visiting tour.

Interactions Among Multiethnic and Multireligious Empires, ca. 1500–600 BCE

From around 1700 to 1000 BCE, society in the Middle East and the Mediterranean changed in important ways. Chariot warfare, iron tools, and iron weapons were developed and refined. Agriculture spread from the original core of Syria, Mesopotamia, and Egypt to the periphery in Greece, central Anatolia, central Asia, and Arabia. The peoples in this peripheral area adapted the basic agricultural methods acquired from the core area but also introduced contributions of their own, especially military and transport technologies. On the basis of these contributions, conquerors built large empires in which a small, ethnically defined ruling class ruled over collections of other ethnic groups, speaking a multiplicity of languages and sacrificing to a multiplicity of gods.

The Hittite and Assyrian Empires, 1600–600 BCE

Agriculture spread from the Middle East to foragers in Western Europe and Central Asia. Villagers in Central Asia, known as "Proto-Indo-Europeans," domesticated the horse and used it for pulling chariots. Later, Indo-Europeans migrated with their horses and chariots to the Middle East, India, and Western Europe, where they settled as ruling classes among the indigenous villagers.

Horses and Chariots from Central Asia   The spread of agriculture into Europe and central Asia had major consequences for the Middle East and the eastern Mediterranean. Shortly after 3000 BCE, in the region around the Ural Mountains in central Asia, local Indo-European villagers domesticated the horse, using it for its meat and for transporting heavy loads. Around 2000 BCE, after villages in the southern Ural Mountains had been transformed into towns through trade, town leaders emerged who were equipped with horse-drawn chariots, as well as with composite bows, made of a combination of grooved wood and horn carefully glued together. With a length of 4 feet and a range of 150 yards, this bow was much more powerful than the existing simpler and shorter bows dating back to the Paleolithic. A chariot could accommodate two to three warriors, one to guide the horses with leather reins and bronze bits and the others to shoot arrows with the composite bow. Around 1700 BCE, both chariot and composite bow made their entry into the Middle East and eastern Mediterranean. They contributed to a major transformation of the kingdoms that had hitherto relied solely on foot soldiers.

The Hittite Empire   The first rulers in the Middle East to make use of chariots and composite bows for their military were the Hittites (1650–1182 BCE), Indo-Europeans settling in central Anatolia. This area, one of the richest mining regions in the Middle East, had large iron deposits. Iron was a by-product of copper smelting but was initially considered useless since it manifested itself in the form of "bloom iron," a spongy substance with an abundance of ore impurities. Only after prolonged forging, that is, of hammering during which the bloom iron had to be kept red hot, were smiths able to remove the impurities. By around 1500 BCE, smiths in Anatolia had fully mastered the art of iron making. The Hittites incorporated iron into their chariot armies, in the form of swords, helmets, and protective armor. The combination of these military elements gave the Hittites an early advantage, which they used to become the pioneers of a new type of conquering polity—the multilinguistic, multiethnic, and multireligious empire that was not regionally confined like the kingdom. At its peak, the Hittite Empire stretched from Anatolia to northern Syria, comprising peoples of many languages and religions (see Map 2.5).

To distinguish themselves from ordinary kingdoms, the Hittite kings called themselves "great kings." In their capital, Hattusa, they ruled with an assembly (*panku*) of their principal administrators, recruited from the aristocracy. When they set out on campaign to conquer rival kingdoms, they left the lesser, conquered kings in their positions as provincial rulers. The core of Hittite armies consisted of a nobility of highly trained, disciplined, and mobile chariot warriors. Mercenary foot soldiers, acting as skirmishers, protected the chariots from direct attacks by enemy infantry. These skirmishers were enrolled from among mountaineers, herders, and nomads for the duration of campaigns.

In the conquered lands, the "great kings" placed nobles in strategic garrisons to keep the local, non-Hittite rulers in check. Since the imperial warehouses held

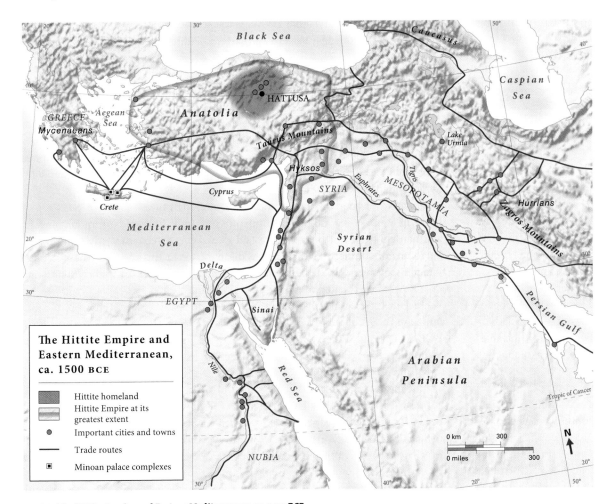

MAP **2.5 The Hittite Empire and Eastern Mediterranean ca. 1500 BCE.**

King Tutankhamen [Tut-an-KHAM-un] (1336–1327 BCE) of Egypt in Full Battle Regalia. The king, accompanied by skirmishers (*far left*), is aiming at deer in a herd fleeing from his galloping horses.

limited amounts of foodstuffs, the nobility received land grants, using the rents they extracted from the towns and villages for their livelihood. This Hittite system of employing both its nobility and local rulers was to become the model of organization for all subsequent Middle Eastern and eastern Mediterranean empires.

Imperial Egypt   During the New Kingdom (1550–1070 BCE), the Egyptians vigorously pushed their border with the Hittites as far north as possible, building garrisons and collecting tributes from a number of coastal cities in southern Syria (modern Palestine). The Egyptians eventually clashed with the Hittites at Qadesh [KAH-desh] in northern Syria (1274 BCE), where they engaged in the largest chariot battle ever fought in the Middle East. Neither side prevailed, and the two empires decided to curb their imperialism and coexist diplomatically with each other, with Syria divided between them.

A short time later, this coexistence was shattered by invasions of the "Sea People" from the Aegean Sea. Originally a mixture of former foot soldiers, mountaineers, and herders from northern Greece had raided the Mycenaean [My-sen-EE-yan] kingdoms of southern Greece, as we discuss later in this chapter. These people, joined by survivors of the collapsing kingdoms, took to the sea (hence their name "Sea People") and sailed to the wealthy kingdoms of the Levant. One group of Sea People, the Ahhiyawa [Ahi-YA-wah], in Greek "Achaians" [A-KAY-ans], presumably remnants of one of the Mycenaean kingdoms, destroyed the Hittite Empire in 1207 BCE, reducing it to a few small fragments. The Egyptian Empire lost southern Syria to another set of seafaring invaders, the Pelesets [PE-le-sets] (Philistines or Palestinians), and retreated to Sinai, abandoning its imperial ambitions.

The invasions by Sea People triggered the so-called **Bronze Age collapse** of ca. 1200 BCE with which the **Iron Age** in the Middle East and eastern Mediterranean began. The collapse is explained as a crisis in which the overextended early empires of the Hittites and Egyptians were unable to sustain the enormous expenses required for chariot warfare. With the decline in the numbers of chariots, large numbers of skirmishers became jobless. Scholars assume that most of the destruction and diminishment of these early kingdoms was due to marauding or migrating skirmishers like the Ahhiyawa and Pelesets who were unemployed.

Bronze Age collapse: Around 1200 BCE, resulting from the collapse of the Hittite Empire and the weakening of the Egyptian New Kingdom; chariot warfare had become unsustainable in these early kingdoms.

Iron Age: Around 1500–1200 BCE, smiths were able to produce sufficiently high temperatures to smelter iron bloom, a mixture of iron and a variety of impurities.

The Assyrians   Emerging after the Bronze Age collapse, the Assyrians (ca. 1350–607 BCE) founded a new empire, which was also based on rain-fed agriculture, much like the Hittite Empire. Its capital was Assur, a city founded in upper Mesopotamia around 2000 BCE on an island in the Tigris River. Originally, Assur's farming base was too limited to support territorial conquests. Instead, its inhabitants enriched themselves through trade. They built trading outposts as far away as central Anatolia and exchanged textiles for timber, copper, tin, and silver, much of which they sold to the Babylonians in the south. In the fourteenth century BCE, the Assyrian kings began to use Assur's commercial riches to finance their first large-scale conquests.

The Assyrians expanded into both the Zagros Mountains and Syria, reaching the borders of the Hittite Empire and claiming equal status with them. The great king of the Hittites, however, haughtily rejected the upstart's claim: "On what account should I write to you about brotherhood? Were you and I born from the same mother?" Stopped at the Hittite borders, Assyrian troops turned southeastward and expanded into lower Mesopotamia. Here, they occupied Babylon for a short period, humiliating their wealthy neighbors by carrying away the statue of the city god.

After some severe military setbacks, during which Assyria was reduced to its upper Mesopotamian center, ambitious kings renewed Assyrian expansion, creating Neo-Assyria (New Assyria), which lasted from 934 to 607 BCE. They embarked on conquests as had no other kings before them, systematically and ruthlessly conquering the lands around them. The core of the Neo-Assyrian armies consisted of small chariot forces and larger regiments of a new type of warrior—horsemen, chosen from among the nobility. These horsemen rode without stirrup on saddlecloths and fought using bows and arrows. The conquered peoples were forced to contribute soldiers to the Assyrian infantry, thus replenishing and multiplying the ranks of the largest and most expendable forces. Iron swords, iron-tipped lances, full-length scale armor (iron platelets sewn on leather shirts), and iron helmets were now common and helped the Assyrians to become the most formidable empire builders of their day.

In fact, the Assyrians were among the most ruthless campaigners in recorded history. They destroyed temples, razed cities, and forcibly deported the defeated inhabitants of entire provinces to other parts of the empire. Scholars have estimated that hundreds of thousands of deportees, the men among them often in chains, had to walk hundreds of miles through the countryside before being settled in new villages. At the peak of their conquests (745–609 BCE), the Assyrian rulers became the first to unify all of the Middle East, a dream first expressed by King Naram-Sin of Akkad centuries earlier. This same accomplishment would be repeated many more times in years to come (see Map 2.6).

Small Kingdoms on the Imperial Margins, 1600–600 BCE

Syria was a region between the Hittite (or later, Assyrian) Empire in the north and the Egyptian Empire in the south. The dominant form of political organization in these regions was the city-state under a royal dynasty. These city-states were located on the coast and had harbors, a number of surrounding villages, and a larger hinterland of independent villages in the hills and mountains. In northern Syria, the city-states were those of the Phoenicians; in southern Syria, they were those of the

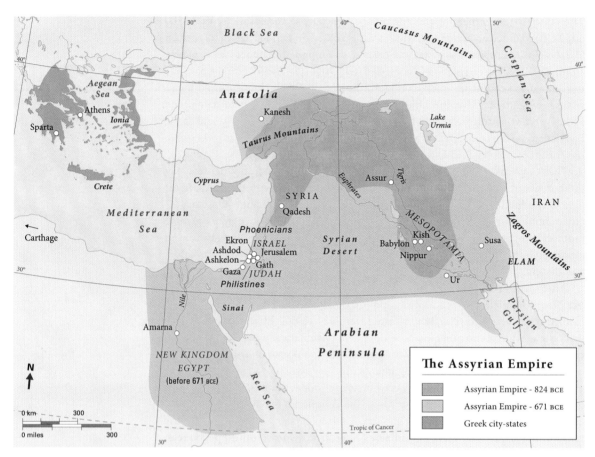

MAP 2.6 **The Assyrian Empire.**

Pelesets on the coast and the Israelites in the hills. In the eastern Mediterranean, outside the military reach of the Hittite and Assyrian Empires but in commercial contact with them, were the Mycenaean palace-states and early Greek city-states.

The Phoenicians   The people known in Greek as "Phoenicians" and by the Egyptians as "Canaanites" held the city-states of Byblos (modern Jubeil [Joo-BALE]), Sidon, and Tyre (ca. 1600–300 BCE), each with a population of several tens of thousands. The Phoenicians also controlled the slopes of Mount Lebanon, with its famous cedars. These valuable trees, together with timber from Anatolia, were much sought after in the Middle East and eastern Mediterranean as construction material for buildings and ships. No less important was a species of sea snail collected on the beaches, from which a highly valued purple textile dye was extracted. The surrounding villages produced barley and wheat for the cities as well as olive oil, wine, dried fruits, and nuts for export. Urban craftspeople made ceramics, textiles, leather goods, jewelry, and metalware with distinctive Phoenician designs, destined for sale abroad. More than any other territorial states in the Middle East, the Phoenician city-states were engaged in trade.

Phoenicians as traders appear in the historical record from 2500 BCE onward. During ca. 1600–1200 BCE, the Phoenicians and Mycenaeans shared the sea trade of the eastern Mediterranean, transporting their own goods as well as metals, timber, and stone. On land, they preferred paying tribute and occasionally putting their fleets at the service of Hittite or Egyptian imperial overlords. When the Mycenaean kingdoms and Hittite Empire collapsed and the Egyptians withdrew around 1200 BCE under the onslaught of the Sea People, the Phoenicians seized their chance. Systematically expanding their reach in the Mediterranean, they established trade outposts on islands and along the Mediterranean coast as far west as modern Morocco and Spain.

In addition to founding numerous ports and outposts around the Mediterranean (one of which, Carthage, would later become a powerful empire on its own), the Phoenicians acquired world-historical importance through their introduction of the letter alphabet. People in Syria had been familiar with the Mesopotamian cuneiform and Egyptian hieroglyphic writing systems for centuries. Both systems were complicated, however, and required many years of training to learn. From rock inscriptions discovered in 1998 in Egypt it appears that Phoenician (or Syrian) merchants began experimenting around 1900–1800 BCE with a much simplified writing system. In this system letters replaced the traditional signs and syllables, with each letter standing for a spoken consonant. Subsequently, in various parts of Syria, fully developed alphabets with letters for about 30 spoken consonants appeared (the vowels were not written). The Phoenician alphabet of ca. 1200 BCE was the most widely used, becoming the ancestor of all alphabetical scripts.

The Pelesets and Israelites

During its imperial phase (ca. 1550–1200 BCE), Egypt controlled the Palestinian towns of Gaza, Ashkelon, Ashdod, Gath, and Ekron. Occasionally, the Egyptian kings aided their governors in these towns by carrying out punitive campaigns. After one such campaign, a defeated people in southern Syria was "stripped bare, wholly lacking seed," as an Egyptian inscription of 1207 BCE recorded. The name used in the inscription for this people was "Israel," the first time this name appeared in the records. "Israel" seems to refer to some sort of tribal alliance among Canaanite villagers and herders in the hills.

When the Pelesets, or Philistines, took over southern Syria and Egypt withdrew a short time later, agriculture and trade quickly recovered from heavy Egyptian taxation. The coastal Philistines established garrisons among the Israelites in order to secure trade routes through the highlands and along the Jordan valley. In response, as is recorded in the Hebrew Bible (the Old Testament in Christian usage), a military leader named Saul and a number of tribal leaders recruited a military force that began a war of liberation against the Philistines. According to this scripture, Saul was killed during the early stages of the war and his successor, David, completed the liberation, establishing himself as king in Jerusalem shortly after 1000 BCE.

According to the Hebrew Bible, Jerusalem was a town on top of a mountain spur in southern Syria. David's son Solomon is said to have greatly enlarged the town, constructing a palace, the famous temple, and administrative buildings. To date, archaeologists have found few traces of Solomon's constructions except a few foundation walls and terraces on the eastern slope of present-day Jerusalem. Moreover, they have not even been able to confirm the rise of Jerusalem from village to city level. For historians, therefore, the biblical account, like that of many ancient texts, is perhaps best understood not as history but as a religious foundation story, demonstrating God's providence.

According to the Hebrew Bible, the two states that emerged after Solomon, Israel in the north (930–722 BCE) and Judah in the south (930–587 BCE), enjoyed only short periods of independence from the coastal Philistines. The empire of Assyria and its successor, Neo-Babylonia (626–539 BCE), conquered the two kingdoms in the sixth century BCE. Thousands of members of the two royal families, priests, scribes, landowners, and craftspeople had to resettle in other parts of Syria or in Mesopotamia. The Philistines, together with people in the Syrian steppes (collectively called "Arabs"), suffered similar fates of defeat and deportation. In their place, Anatolian and Iranian populations settled in Syria. The final wave of Israelite deportations, under the Neo-Babylonians in 597–582 BCE, became the infamous "Babylonian captivity" (*gola*) mourned by several prophets in the Hebrew Bible.

The Mycenaeans and Early Greeks   Parallel to the Phoenicians, Pelesets, and Israelites in Syria, the Mycenaeans arose in Greece and the eastern Mediterranean during the middle of the second millennium BCE. After the adaptation to farming, demand for specialized agricultural products (such as olive oil, wine, dried fruits, and nuts) among the villages had advanced sufficiently to result in the emergence of towns and cities which traded in these goods as well as in copper and bronze wares. Around 1700 BCE, in Attica and the Peloponnesus, two peninsulas with relatively large plains suitable for agriculture, leaders built forts as refuges in times of war for their fellow villagers. The best known among these forts were Mycenae, Tiryns, Pylos, Sparta, and Athens.

Two centuries later, the forts evolved into palaces with warrior lords and kings, as well as administrative offices, surrounded by clusters of villages. In these palace-states, scribes introduced a new, cuneiform-derived script which, contrary to the Linear A of the Minoans, has been deciphered. This *Linear B* script provides us with invaluable information for understanding early Greek culture. About 1450 BCE, chariot and bronze weapon–equipped Mycenaean warriors sailed to Minoan Crete and conquered the island. For about two and a half centuries the Mycenaeans were the major seafaring power in the eastern Mediterranean, establishing trading outposts in competition with the Phoenicians.

The Mycenaean palace-states were short-lived. When an earthquake hit around 1250 BCE, the walls of many palaces collapsed. Former mercenaries (skirmishers in the chariot armies of the Hittites) joined by herders from northern Greece raided the weakened Mycenaean palace-states. A century later most palaces had disappeared, together with their administrators, scribes, and archives. The descendants of the kings, however, managed to salvage some wealth, as evidenced by their tombs. Iron swords and jewelry found in these tombs were of Phoenician origin and indicate that some sea trade continued even after the destruction of the Mycenaean states.

A general recovery in Greece began during the eighth century BCE. Trade in agricultural goods such as grain, olive oil, and honey was revived in new market outposts in Anatolia, Syria, and Egypt. The Anatolian craft of ironworking spread to Greece. Literacy returned as the Greeks adopted the Phoenician alphabet, adding vowels to the existing consonants to create the Greek alphabet. The population increased, often so quickly that many people were unable to find employment. After 750 BCE, many unemployed or adventurous Greeks seeking new challenges emigrated to the Anatolian west coast or as far as Italy and the Black Sea to colonize the land and establish new cities. As they developed into city-states of their own, the settlements on the Anatolian coast became known collectively as "Ionia."

The distinctive mark of these new cities was the absence of palaces. Instead, a sacred precinct in a city's center served as an open space for general assemblies.

Contained within this space were a temple and administrative buildings with porches supported by rows of pillars. The construction techniques and styles for these temples and pillars came from Egypt. Farmers in villages outside the city walls produced grain, vegetables, olive oil, and wine for the urban dwellers. A city with surrounding villages formed a city-state, or *polis*. Each of these new city-states administered its own internal and external affairs, although they also formed alliances or pursued hostilities with each other.

Initially, kings from among the landowning families were responsible for the administration of the city-states. Their forerunners had been the warrior lords and the landowning families of the post-Mycenaean period and made up what the Greeks called the "aristocracy" of the states. During the period 750–600 BCE, conflict often broke out between the aristocracy and the common folk—merchants, traders, craftspeople, and free farmers—over the distribution of wealth in the growing cities. Some aristocrats exploited these tensions and allied themselves with groups of commoners. Once allied, these aristocrats assumed power as tyrants, who attempted to create family dynasties. Many of the would-be dynasts sponsored festivals, public work projects, and artists; but their popularity rarely lasted beyond the sons who succeeded them.

Other aristocrats opposed the tyrants and agreed to power sharing with the commoners. Through trade, many commoners were becoming wealthier than the aristocrats. Both aristocrats and commoners served as foot soldiers in the city-states' defense forces. These armies relied not on charioteers but on foot soldiers, who were heavily armed with shields, lances, and swords, all made of iron. Their battle order was the *phalanx*, that is, a block of eight or more rows of soldiers marching forward shoulder to shoulder, the shield held in the left hand of each man helping to guard the man to his left, while in his right hand he held a lance or pike.

In the narrow valleys and defiles of Greece and Ionia these bristling "hedgehog" formations were nearly impossible to break with archers, infantry, or cavalry—if each man held his position and the men in the back moved up to take the place of those who fell. In these phalanxes it was not individual aristocratic valor that counted but the courageous willingness of each citizen-soldier to support and protect the other. Thus, as many ordinary city dwellers became the military equals of the aristocracy in the crucible of battle, they quite naturally began to demand an equal share of political power in times of peace.

Political reformers in the sixth century BCE gave commoners their first basic political rights. The best-known reforms were those introduced in Athens and Sparta, the city-states with the largest agricultural territories. In Athens, aristocratic rule was replaced with political rights distributed according to levels of property ownership. The poorest class had the right to participate in the citizen assembly (*ekklesia*), cast votes, and sit on juries; the wealthier classes could run for a variety of leadership and temple offices. A written law code curbed arbitrariness. With these assemblies, the Greek city-states continued the Mesopotamian and Hittite systems of assemblies discussed earlier. Whether the Greeks developed their assemblies independently or adopted them from their predecessors is not known. What can be argued, however, is whether the idea of political participation is deeply rooted in the region of the Middle East and the eastern Mediterranean. In Greece, and later Rome, these traditions would evolve into the ancestral forms of many of the political institutions we live under today, particularly **republican** and **democratic** offices.

Republicanism: A system of government in which, in the place of kings, the people are sovereign, electing representatives to executive and legislative offices.

Democracy: A system of government in which most or all of the people elect representatives and in some cases decide on important issues themselves.

In Sparta, the traditional rule by two co-equal kings was held in check through a newly created board of five officers elected annually from among the popular assembly. These officers were responsible for the administration of day-to-day affairs in Sparta. The assembly was made up of all landowners wealthy enough to live in town because of the revenue they collected from their legally indentured (unfree) tenant farmers in the surrounding villages. These political reforms, however, did not prevent new tyrants from rising up in periodic takeover attempts. Thus, in the middle of the first millennium BCE Greeks were still struggling to find a consistent direction for their political development.

Religious Experience and Cultural Achievements

By around 5500 BCE, when agriculture had replaced foraging, many human groups began to move from animism to polytheism as their new form of religion. In *animism*, people experience an awe and reverence toward the creatures and forces of the natural world. However, there is no indication in the available archaeological record that people identified these creatures and forces with particular deities. With the rise of cities and the development of writing, these forces received names. *Polytheism* is the general term used to denote religions of personified forces in nature. Artists depicted and sculpted the deities as well as the rulers who derived their mandates from these gods. Writers recorded myths and hymns exploring the relationship between humans and gods. Administrators, responsible for constructing architectural monuments, calculating the calendar, and assessing the taxes laid the foundations of the mathematical and physical sciences. Since many of the religious and cultural achievements were expressed in writing, we can evaluate them today with far better understanding than the culture of the foragers and early farmers.

Shrine. Reconstruction of a household shrine from Çatal Hüyük, Turkey, with the ox or bull heads implanted in the walls.

Toward Polytheism   The creators of the Paleolithic rock paintings in Africa, Europe, and Australia (discussed in Chapter 1) have left us few hints of their spiritual preoccupations in their world full of dangerous animals. The depictions of "lionman," "bisonman," and "sorcerer" are but a few examples where the human and animal worlds are merged, presumably with people in the cave rituals experiencing this merger, with the purpose of influencing the animal world. In the Neolithic transition period from foraging to agriculture, the principal change was the transfer of ritual from caves to aboveground sanctuaries and towns.

An example of the transfer to a sanctuary was Göbekli Tepe in southern Anatolia, a place where foragers came together for rituals during 9000–6000 BCE. Excavations begun in 1995 are still in progress, but a rich imagery of animals, mostly in the form of reliefs, has already been unearthed. It shows that animism was still in force, even if the venue was no longer a cave. The oldest example documenting the transfer of ritual from the cave to the town is Çatal Hüyük [Tsha-TAL Hoo-YOOK] (7500–5700 BCE) in southern Anatolia, excavated in the 1960s and 1990s.

At its height, the town had 5,000 inhabitants, who lived in densely packed houses accessible only from the top with ladders. The inhabitants farmed fields outside of town, using irrigation water from the Taurus Mountains, and hunted extensively. Probably communal rooms in town contained a concentration of artifacts, among which Venus-type figurines and reliefs and wall paintings of animals, especially of *aurochs* (ancestors of bulls), are prominent. The imagery is reminiscent of that of the Paleolithic foragers, but the emergence of urban places of ritual indicates that humans were far along in the transition from nature to civilization.

In Ubaid Mesopotamia (6000–4000 BCE), urban places of ritual evolved into temples. These temples contained figurines of the hybrid human–animal as well as the Venus type of exaggerated female form. Urban dwellers then took the decisive steps of transition from animism to polytheism in the period 3500–2500 BCE when writing developed and kings ruled cities.

This connection between writing, kingship, and gods is crucial for an understanding of polytheism and religion in general: Prior to 3500 BCE, religion was an impersonal and nameless animism; thereafter, it was the polytheism of kings with often colorful personalities, told in myths and epics. Writing made it possible to record the names of individuals, kings viewed themselves as the guarantors of urban life, and gods were the powers that endowed kings with the authority to prevent urban life from slipping back into preurban culture. In the cities, people were no longer in awe of wild animals, as they had been during forager days. But they were still in awe of nature's powers, as they had been during the earlier Neolithic village life, when nature could be benevolent through bounty and fertility as well as wrathful through floods, storms, droughts, or blights.

Polytheism began when kings became individuals—through adopting patron deities—and associated the awe-inspiring natural powers and phenomena with these deities. Perhaps polytheism evolved the other way around: Villagers created rituals to please the awe-inspiring anonymous forces of nature, and after the introduction of writing and kingship, these forces became deities. Either way, the rise of polytheism depended crucially on writing and kingship.

Mesopotamian and Egyptian Literature

Among the earliest writings in the world exploring religious themes are the *Epic of Gilgamesh* and the myth of *Enuma Elish*. These had their origins in third-millennium BCE Mesopotamia but were not recorded for another millennium. The first is the story of Gilgamesh, who was a mythical king in early Sumer. Gilgamesh, according to the epic, ruled Uruk and built its walls. Like the Chinese sage kings we will meet in Chapter 4, he fought many battles and carried out heroic deeds in both this world and the underworld but failed in his ultimate quest to find immortality. In the end, Gilgamesh could not escape the fate of all mortals and had to suffer death as well.

The myth of *Enuma Elish* (named after its first line, which means "when on high . . .") tells the story of creation when nothing existed but Father Abzu (the Depth or Abyss) and Mother Tiamat (Ocean) and their numerous children, who were the city gods of Mesopotamia. The raucous behavior of his children enraged Abzu. He tried to kill them but was instead murdered by one of them. Tiamat [Tee-ya-MAT] and her second husband continued the violent domestic battle, finally driving the children away. Marduk [MAR-dook], alone among the children, eventually returned and slaughtered both his mother and stepfather. He split Tiamat's body into two halves, which became heaven and earth. From the blood of the stepfather he made humankind, whom he predestined to serve the gods. One senses how the unknown authors of this text struggle with the question of power in nature—at times benevolent and at times violent, always unpredictable, even as one sacrifices to please it.

The Egyptian version of the creation myth, like those of the Mesopotamians, also begins with an original ocean. In the Egyptian telling, an island arose from the depth of this ocean. The ruler of this island was the creator god Atum, who contained all the qualities of nature in himself. He created things in pairs, one after the other, beginning with air and water and finishing his handiwork with the male and female of the human race. This Egyptian creation myth is more explicit than its Mesopotamian cousin about the infinity of the original "depth" and "ocean," out of which earth and heaven were created. It is also far less violent, a reflection of the more gradual and harmonious growth of the Egyptian kingdom and empire.

Greek Literature   The earliest Greek literature dates to the eighth century BCE. The period 750–600 BCE was a time of close cultural contact between the rising Greek city-states and Neo-Assyria, which dominated Syria and Anatolia. Not surprisingly, therefore, the Assyrian versions of the Mesopotamian epic and creation myths, *Gilgamesh* and *Enuma Elish*, made their way to the Greeks, where they were incorporated into Greek culture.

This incorporation was the work of two gifted writers, Homer (fl. ca. 730 BCE) and Hesiod (fl. ca. 700 BCE), both from Greek city-states in Anatolia. Homer composed two epics in the form of extended poems, the tragedy *Iliad* and the narrative legend *Odyssey*. Hesiod's *Theogony* begins with "Chaos, the Abyss," out of which the earth, or Gaia, came into being. The rest of the *Theogony* is devoted to telling the stories of some 300 divinities descended from Chaos and Gaia. Three of the first four generations of deities destroyed each other violently. The fourth, the Olympians, became the present pantheon of gods, with Zeus as the patriarch.

As in Mesopotamia and Egypt, seasonal festivals were of great importance in Greece. In contrast to Mesopotamia and Egypt, however, Greek city culture encouraged personal artistic expression. Given the increasing participation of commoners in the state, festivals in Greece became occasions for writing songs and poems whose authors were remembered by name. Festivals often had poetry contests, and Hesiod appears as the earliest winner of such a contest. In the following century, a writer who acquired fame outside the poetry contest circuit was Sappho. She was the instructor of female initiation groups in one of the city-states on the island of Lesbos. Her poetry reflects the experience of erotic experimentation among adolescent girls which was part of their preparation for marriage.

Sculptures and Paintings   Mesopotamian and Egyptian rulers wanted to impress those who observed them as severe, powerful, and pious persons. Early Mesopotamian kings had massive statues made of themselves, showing them posed in prayer. In Egypt, compact, block-like royals stand freely or sit impassively on their thrones. Statues in both regions often have wide, oversized eyes that stare sternly at the viewer. On many half-sculptures carved into stone, larger-than-life-size kings with bulging muscles trample victoriously over diminutive enemies. In all these sculptures the primary objective of the artists was not photographic realism but a rendering of the gulf between gods and kings, on the one hand, and subjects, on the other.

Wall paintings were highly popular among Mesopotamians, Egyptians, and Minoans. Unfortunately, in the humidity of lower Mesopotamia, few such paintings survived. By contrast, in the dry climate of Egypt (except for the delta) a large number still exist. Paintings filled the interior of tombs, illustrating scenes from their owners' lives. The painters' point was not only to show their royal features but also to draw them from all angles: Looking at the images from the perspective of eternal life, the kings should be able to see themselves in all their earthly aspects simultaneously. Accordingly, face, arms, and legs were painted in profile; eyes, shoulders, and upper body appear frontally; and the waist was half frontal but turned to reveal the navel. Later, as more nonroyal people built tombs for themselves, the complex multiangled royal perspective gave way to a simpler, single-angle realism.

The Greek arts began in the Minoan and Mycenaean city-states. Minoan wall paintings, stylistically related to those of the Egyptian New Kingdom (1550–1070 BCE), show realistic scenes with vegetation, birds, dolphins, and bulls. The art of Mycenae is mostly known to us from small sculptures, masks, drinking vessels, and jewelry found in the tombs of royal warriors. Through their close contact with the Assyrians, the Greeks in their growing city-states (during the period ca. 750–600 BCE) learned not only about Mesopotamian literature but also about their arts. Winged and fighting animals, as well as muscular gods and heroes, appear in vase paintings. Egypt was the inspiration for the development of sculptures, which initially were block-like, wide-eyed, and stylized. Gradually, however, with the decline of the aristocracy, stylized representation was replaced by realism. By the 500s BCE, the heavy and stern-looking kings were succeeded by well-proportioned, smoothly muscled, and slightly smiling figures depicted as one would encounter them in the market.

Egyptian Statue (*left*) and Early Greek (*right*) Adaptation. The Egyptian influence on the Greek cities is striking. Here, we have a visual example of the pattern of origins, interaction, and adaptation. The Greek example is a creative adaptation of an Egyptian-originated model.

Scientific Beginnings   In both Mesopotamia and Egypt, conceptualization of reality advanced substantially from Old and New Stone Age imagery. For the first time we get glimpses of humans constructing abstract ideas, without recourse to the senses—for example, in mathematics. Mathematical calculations, such as addition and subtraction, began in Mesopotamia even before the first writing system was introduced.

Subsequently, scribes developed tables for multiplication and division, squares, cubes, roots, cube roots, and reciprocal and exponential functions. They calculated numerical approximations for the roots of 2 and 3. Exercise texts from the Old Babylonian period (ca. 2000–1600 BCE) pose such problems as "Beyond the ditch I made a dike, one cubit per cubit is the inclination of this dike. What is the base, the top and the height of it? And what is its circumference?" Babylonian mathematical interests focused primarily on the roots of algebra. Scribes also laid the foundations for geometry and astronomy by devising the system of 60 degrees for arcs, angles, and time—all still in use today.

In Egypt, the *Rhind Mathematical Papyrus* (ca. 1550 BCE) is an early handbook of geometrical and algebraic questions typically used by scribes and administrators. It teaches the apprentice scribe how to calculate the volume of rectangles, triangles, and pyramids and how to measure the slopes of angles. Algebraic operations are illustrated through examples such as "[animal] fat [worth] ten gallons [of grain] is issued for one year; what is its share per day?" As in Mesopotamia, Egyptian mathematics implicitly employed important mathematical principles without yet stating them explicitly.

The *Kahun* (ca. 1825 BCE) and *Edwin Smith* (ca. 1534 BCE) *Papyri* are the best-known texts on the applied science of medicine. They cover diagnosis, prescriptions, and surgery. A few examples illustrate ancient Egyptian medical standards. Headache is diagnosed as "half-head," which the Greeks translated as "*hemi-krania*," from which our English word "migraine" is derived. Prescriptions for treating stiffness of limbs, pregnancy, birth complications, and childhood diseases, as well as advice on birth control and abortion, recommend mixtures of homeopathic herbs and elements. Surgeons received advice on how to use copper knives for male and female circumcision and needles for stitching up wounds. During their work, physicians were encouraged to repeat magic healing formulas that encouraged their patients to use their own self-healing powers.

Putting It All Together

The beginning of the agrarian age in the Middle East and eastern Mediterranean was marked by agricultural surpluses, especially in irrigated areas. Depending on the size of the surplus, a pattern of state formation became visible along which city-states, kingdoms, and empires emerged in the various areas of the region. The central concern of the rulers in these small and large states was establishing and maintaining their authority, which included the use of military force—something not always easy to justify, especially when trade and ruling class cooperation were also important. Therefore, the rulers appealed to gods, that is, personalized forces in nature stronger than rulers. The will of these forces was conceived as being expressed in the law code of each state. Gods were lawgivers, and their law possessed divine authority; thus, rulers became the executers of the god-given law.

Although "divine," the rulers' mandate was never absolute. Popular or aristocratic assemblies from preroyal times of tribal or clan organization survived stubbornly or were revived in the Greek *poleis*. Although the Hittite and Assyrian kings succeeded in marginalizing these assemblies during periods of empire building, the divine mandate was not exclusively theirs and they had to share power, if only to a limited degree. It is important to note that this tradition of assemblies, which we often associate solely with Greece, is widespread in the Middle East. This awareness is necessary to understand the period after 600 BCE when individuals arose with messages of personal salvation and announced that it was not simply fate or misfortune to live and die under these often harsh imperial powers. Instead, they insisted that the destiny of humanity *transcended* these all too human institutions.

▶ For additional resources, including maps, primary sources, visuals, and quizzes, please go to www.oup.com/us/vonsivers. Please see the Further Resources section at the back of the book for additional readings and suggested websites.

Thinking Through Patterns

▶ **What are the main factors that enabled the transition from foraging to farming?**

One crucial factor in this pattern was the environment of the Taurus–Zagros–Levant region, the Fertile Crescent. Adequate rainfall, abundant edible plants suitable for domestication, and several animals that proved useful and easy to domesticate characterized the region. But had it not been for human beings mastering irrigation, such a transition might have remained confined to small microclimatic regions. Populations in the great riverine agricultural areas in Mesopotamia and Egypt (and, as we will see in the following chapters, India and China) took as their task the mastery of the fertility of river valleys and the use of reliable river water for irrigation, rather than relying on rainfall. Here was a system adaptable to a variety of climates, as witnessed by the fact that these four early agricultural civilizations arose in dry climates watered by large river systems.

▶ **Where did the pattern of agrarian life first emerge and why?**

While scholars still debate the absolute origins of the domestication of plants and animals, most are in agreement that the Fertile Crescent is central to this process. Here, experimentation with local grains, leaf plants, and pulses during the Neolithic helped humans develop more reliable and better-yielding crops, which were then traded regionally and, through regional trade, further afield. The climatic zones of Eurasia were especially well suited to this because of the long east–west axis. Animals like sheep, goats, and cattle were similarly found over wide areas and were easy to trade, which led to the sharing of information about raising livestock. Another important factor was that as populations grew from the stability of food production by agriculture, groups split off and started their own communities, carrying the new techniques with them. Thus, by about 5000 BCE, the basic techniques and species of Eurasian and North African domestication were well established.

▶ **How did the creation of agrarian–urban society—what we commonly call "civilization"—make for an entirely new pattern of world history?**

The ability of humans to create large food surpluses encouraged a considerable degree of settlement. Such stability enabled the nonproducing part of the population to occupy themselves with creating nonagricultural things—buildings, religious centers, defensive works, dwellings. As these elements of villages and towns grew and became more complex, they allowed the cumulative knowledge and production of human beings to enlarge in these sites. In short, cities created an entirely new kind of society with elaborate class hierarchies built on power and efficiency. Rivalry and competition among cities required ever more powerful defenses to protect the people, their wealth, and their trade. From this period, the patterns of urban life and of state formation were established, patterns we readily recognize today as our own.

Chapter 3 3000-600 BCE
Shifting Agrarian Centers in India

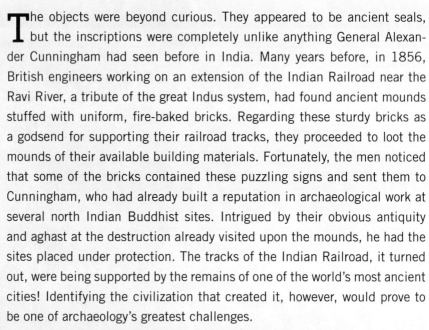

The objects were beyond curious. They appeared to be ancient seals, but the inscriptions were completely unlike anything General Alexander Cunningham had seen before in India. Many years before, in 1856, British engineers working on an extension of the Indian Railroad near the Ravi River, a tribute of the great Indus system, had found ancient mounds stuffed with uniform, fire-baked bricks. Regarding these sturdy bricks as a godsend for supporting their railroad tracks, they proceeded to loot the mounds of their available building materials. Fortunately, the men noticed that some of the bricks contained these puzzling signs and sent them to Cunningham, who had already built a reputation in archaeological work at several north Indian Buddhist sites. Intrigued by their obvious antiquity and aghast at the destruction already visited upon the mounds, he had the sites placed under protection. The tracks of the Indian Railroad, it turned out, were being supported by the remains of one of the world's most ancient cities! Identifying the civilization that created it, however, would prove to be one of archaeology's greatest challenges.

It was well into the next century before scholars really began to understand the place of this "lost city" of Harappa—the center of one of the world's oldest and most mysterious societies. And although a full program of archaeological investigation has been under way at Harappa and dozens of similar sites throughout the Indus valley since the 1920s, some of the most basic questions about this society remain to be answered. For

ABOVE: The Ruins of Mohenjo-Daro.

example, how did their writing system—comprised of the symbols carved on the seals first brought to Cunningham—work? Moreover, unlike other early civilizations that endured for thousands of years, Harappan society was relatively short-lived, lasting perhaps 600 years before vanishing almost entirely. Why did it disappear? And while scholars believe the structures of Harappan village life set many of the patterns for later Indian rural society, exactly how did these structures develop over the intervening generations? Indeed, how and why did urban societies reemerge later along the Ganges River, setting so many of the patterns of south Asian history? In short, what were the fundamental patterns that marked these founding cultures, and how did these patterns change the lives of the peoples in the region and come to be adopted and adapted by them?

One important pattern marking the history of northern India, like that of Mesopotamia, lies in regular rhythms of migration and invasion, interchanges of innovation, assimilation of peoples, and the expansion of ideas. In contrast to the long history of political unification in Egypt or China, all of India did not experience rule by a single regime until the nineteenth century CE. Yet, considerable cultural and religious unity had already been created thousands of years earlier under the influence of newly emerging states along the Ganges River. The ability to maintain this cultural continuity while creating social systems with the flexibility to manage innovation from outside has marked India to the present day. Among their most significant achievements, the social, philosophical, and political challenges facing these early Ganges states resulted in some of the world's most important religious movements: Hinduism, Jainism, and the most widespread and influential religious movement in Asia, Buddhism.

The Vanished Origins of Harappa, 3000–1500 BCE

Since the first intensive archaeological work of the 1920s, the sites of the Indus valley have been imbued with all the romance of "lost civilizations." Unlike Egypt (see Chapter 2), where the patterns of society remained remarkably stable for thousands of years, or Mesopotamia, which spawned a succession of states and empires, the cities of the Indus valley flourished for less than 1,000 years—from about 2500–1700 BCE—before vanishing almost without a trace. Anchored by two major cities—Harappa [Hah-RAP-uh] in the north and Mohenjo-Daro [Moe-hen-joe DAH-roe] in the southwest—and extending from the upper Ganges River to the Arabian Sea, a dense network of small cities, towns, and villages marked by a remarkable consistency of architecture and artifact occupied the largest cultural area of the third millennium BCE: twice the size of the Old Kingdom of Egypt and four times that of the empire of Sargon in Mesopotamia. Trade with southwest Asia and Egypt extended Harappan influence even farther.

Seeing Patterns

▶ Who were the Harappans? Where did they come from? What evidence exists for their origins?

▶ What explanations have been offered for the collapse of Harappan society? How well do the rival theories hold up, given what scholars and archaeologists have discovered?

▶ How can we know about the newcomers to northern India? What sources exist for historians to examine?

▶ What patterns can we see evolving in the Ganges River states that will mark the subsequent development of Indian civilization?

Yet, this "Harappan" or "Indus valley," culture, as archaeologists have named it, remains by far the most mysterious of the early centers of agriculturally supported urban society. The sophistication and precision of its urban planning, the standardization of weights and measures, and the attention to cleanliness and comfort all suggest an elaborate system of social organization; yet we know virtually nothing of its arrangement. Scholars have labored for nearly a century to unlock the secrets of the Harappan pictographic symbols, yet they remain mostly undeciphered. Most tantalizing of all is the fundamental question: Why, as the new mode of urban society gathered momentum elsewhere, did the inhabitants of this one abandon their cities and slip beneath the surface of the historical record? To look at what we can and do know about these mysterious people, we must start with the geography of the Indus and its region.

The Region and People

Geographers refer to the region encompassed by the modern states of India, Pakistan, and Bangladesh as a *subcontinent*—a large, distinct area of land somewhat smaller than a continent. While the region is attached to the Eurasian landmass, it is almost completely cut off from it by some of the most forbidding physical barriers on earth. The lower two-thirds of India form a vast peninsula surrounded on three sides by the Arabian Sea, the Indian Ocean, and the Bay of Bengal. To the north of the bay, extending from Bangladesh through the Indian province of Assam to the north and east and deep into Myanmar (formerly Burma), are continuous ranges of heavily forested mountains. Some of the world's highest annual rainfall totals—over 100 inches—are regularly recorded here.

Forming the northeastern border of the subcontinent above the rain belt is the "roof of the world," the Himalayan Mountains. These meet another set of formidable peaks, the Hindu Kush, which extends into Pakistan and with the Sulaiman and Kirthar ranges marks the northwestern border of the region. Access to the Indian peninsula by land is thus limited to a handful of mountain passes through the Himalayas and the more substantial Khyber and Bolan Passes of the northwest. Historically, these have been the main avenues of trade, migration, and, frequently, invasion (see Map 3.1).

Topography: The physical features— mountains, rivers, deserts, swamps, etc.— of a region.

The Monsoon System   Surrounded by water and framed by high mountains, India's internal **topography** also has a considerable influence on its climate. The Deccan Plateau, Vindhya Range, and other internal highland areas tend to both trap tropical moisture against the west coast and funnel it toward the region drained by the Ganges River in the northeast. The moisture itself comes from the summer winds of the monsoon system, a term derived from the Arabic word *mausim*, for "season." The winds carry moisture generated from the heat of southern Africa as it flows southwest to the northeast over the Indian Ocean from June through October and govern the climatic cycles of southeastern Asia, Indonesia, and southern China as well as India. In the winter months the winds reverse direction and pull hot, dry air down from central Asia. During this dry season, rainfall is scant or nonexistent over large areas of south Asia.

The extremes of the monsoon cycle, as well as its regularity, exert a powerful influence on Asian agriculture. This is particularly so in India, where the monsoon rainfall amounts differ widely from region to region. Because even minor variations

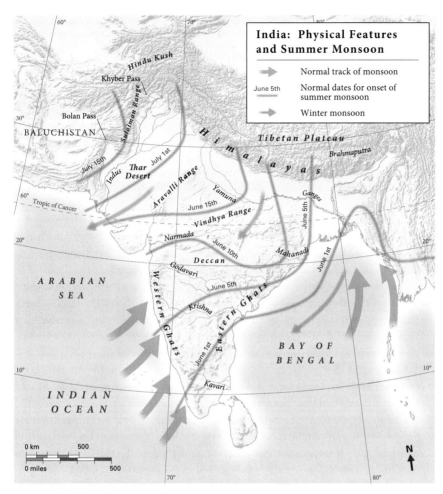

MAP **3.1** India: Physical Features and Summer Monsoon.

in the timing of the cycle or the volume of rain may spell potential flood or famine, the arrival of the monsoon is even today greeted with nervous anticipation. Generally speaking, the subcontinent becomes drier as one moves farther north and west until one reaches the Thar, or Great Indian, Desert and the plain of Sind, the site of some of the hottest temperatures ever recorded on earth—nearly 130 degrees Fahrenheit. It is this arid region bordered by mountains and watered by the Indus River system that saw the rise of the first Indian cities.

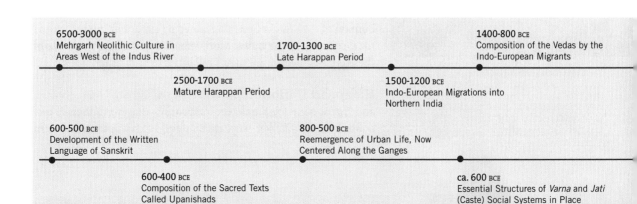

As the Greek historian Herodotus called Egypt "the gift of the Nile," so too, as archaeologists have noted, should Harappan civilization be called the "gift of the Indus." A vast river system composed of seven main branches in ancient times, the Indus' slow, meandering course has for millennia left behind rich deposits of fertile soil, by some estimates twice as much as the Nile. Moreover, like the Yellow River in China, the constant buildup of silt in the riverbed periodically caused the water to overflow its banks and change course—dangerous for those living close by but an effective means of spreading soil over a wide area.

Mehrgarh Culture   Researchers have found a number of Neolithic sites near the river, one of the most productive being Mehrgarh [MARE-gar], located near a strategic mountain pass in Baluchistan. Scholars have dated the Mehrgarh culture to about 6000 BCE, making it perhaps the oldest on the Indian subcontinent. Like the inhabitants of the Fertile Crescent, villagers in Neolithic Baluchistan raised wheat and barley and domesticated sheep, goats, and cattle. As long ago as 5500 BCE pottery was being produced in the area. Also dating from this period are the crafting and trading of fine *lapis lazuli* (an opaque, dark blue gemstone) beadware, or "microbeads," later a coveted item among Harappan luxury goods. Significantly, even the earliest Baluchistani dwellings are made of mud brick, a technique that with greater scope and sophistication became a hallmark of the Harappan cityscape. For all of these reasons, some archaeologists have viewed Mehrgarh culture as a possible precursor to Harappa.

Scholars agree that by about 3000 BCE a culture of villages and towns with elaborate trade networks, sophisticated pottery, and a substantial array of domesticated plants and animals had long been established in the hills of Baluchistan adjacent to the Indus and its western tributaries. Attracted, most likely, by the comparative ease of growing staple crops in the reliably fertile river valleys, the inhabitants of these hill sites extended their settlements eastward sometime before 2600 BCE and began a rapid phase of consolidation, which culminated in the region's first cities.

Adapting to Urban Life in the Indus Valley

By about 2300 BCE the two major cities of Harappa and Mohenjo-Daro—separated by 350 miles—marked the poles of a system of small cities, towns, and villages sprawled across an area estimated to be between 650,000 and 850,000 square miles (see Map 3.2). At its height, the city of Harappa had a population of over 40,000—comparable to that of the largest Mesopotamian cities of the period—and its defensive walls measured 3.5 miles in circumference. The location of these cities on a floodplain, moreover, dictated that they be built on enormous artificial hills to protect them from damage during times that the rivers overflowed their banks. Mohenjo-Daro, for example, with an estimated 3,000 dwellings and a population of about 41,000, was built on two 40-foot mounds separated by a channel 200 yards wide for easy access to the Indus. More remarkable than the sheer size of these cities, however, are their similarities to each other.

The Great Bath at Mohenjo-Daro. This mysterious structure suggests linkages to both the individual Harappan dwellings' inside shower/bath areas and later practices of bathing in rivers such as the Ganges. What conclusions would you draw from its size, structure, and position in the city?

Harappan Uniformity   While all the cities of Mesopotamia and Egypt contained architectural features that make them a recognizable part of their respective cultures, Harappan cities seem

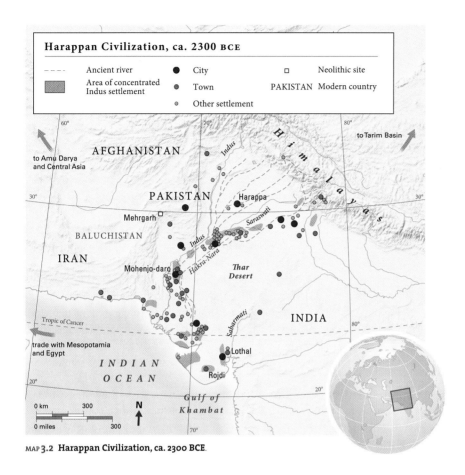

MAP **3.2 Harappan Civilization, ca. 2300 BCE**.

almost to have been designed by the same hand. Harappa and Mohenjo-Daro, as well as several smaller cities and numerous towns, are laid out according to a rigorously surveyed and meticulously planned grid, with major thoroughfares running on north/south and east/west axes and squares, public buildings, temples, and markets at regular, convenient locations. The larger streets are paved with brick and remarkably straight. They are laid out according to standard widths, and most have drains and gutters connected to what may be the most elaborate urban sewer system of ancient times (see Map 3.3).

This uniformity appears to have extended into the personal realm as well. Houses of several stories were made of brick and plastered with gypsum, their floor plans strikingly similar even at widely spaced sites. Many had brick-lined indoor wells and primitive toilets emptying into terra-cotta **cesspits** whose overflow connected to the city's drains and sewers. Nearly all dwellings had a bathing room reminiscent of a modern shower stall, complete with a waterproof floor and drain system to direct the water into channels in the street. Inside the dwellings, a staggering array of wheel-turned, mass-produced clay pots, jars, cooking vessels, copper- and bronzeware, and even toys have been found at various sites.

Cesspits: Deep holes or trenches used to deposit human waste and refuse; in the case of Harappa, they were flushed with water into city sewers and drains, ultimately leading to the adjacent river.

The Harappan Diet

The rich alluvial soil of the region supported a wide variety of fruits, vegetables, and grains. Wheat and barley were staple crops, but peas,

MAP **3.3** **Mohenjo-Daro.**

melons, figs, and sesame were also produced. The recovery of cotton seeds and small patches of cloth and fishing line at Mohenjo-Daro suggests that the Harappans may also have been the first people to raise cotton for use in clothing. Cattle appear to have been the chief domestic animals, and indications of the large herds kept in some areas imply that they were seen as signs of wealth. It is not clear, however, whether they were used principally for food and milk or as work animals, as were water buffaloes. Whatever the case, some scholars see in their importance at this early time the origins of the later stereotype of the Indian "sacred cow."

Sheep and pigs were also widespread and appear to have been an important part of the Harappan diet. Seal carvings and figurines suggest that the Harappans were sophisticated dog breeders, with some of the animals wearing what appear to be collars and a variety of different sizes and snout and tail configurations depicted. It is also thought that the chicken was first domesticated here in Neolithic times. Rice, which figures so prominently in later Indian agriculture, may have also been grown but, because of the relatively arid climate, does not appear to have been a staple.

Harappan Identity and Government   But who were they? Even today, evidence concerning the identity of the Harappans is obscure and contradictory. Everyday items and statuary offer few clues. Samples of symbols, most of which are found on what are believed to be merchant seals, were once believed to hold some tenuous links to a "Proto-Dravidian" language group distantly related to that of some modern south Indian peoples. Scholars have also suggested that the Harappans may have been an eastern branch of a people called "Proto-Mediterraneans," who ranged widely across southwest Asia. Complicating the matter further, archaeologists have identified an urban society designated as the "Bactria-Margiana Archaeological Complex" (BMAC) to the northwest of the Indus valley culture that shares some technological features with the Harappans but thus far no other obvious connections beyond some evidence of trade. Such findings are thus intriguing, but the uniqueness of Harappan urban life argues against any theory of simple cultural diffusion.

As with other early urban cultures, there appears to have been a close relationship among the religious, political, and social spheres of Harappan society. Nevertheless, the clues, while suggestive, again yield little that is definitive. For example, the replication of city plans and architecture throughout such a wide area might indicate the kind of strong central authority and bureaucratic control typically found in a kingdom or empire. Yet, we know virtually nothing of how it might have been organized. Moreover, some departures from the otherwise rigorous uniformity of previous sites found in recent work at Rojdi [ROEJ-dee] have led scholars to amend this picture in favor of one of overall unity marked by discernable regional styles. This modified view, along with findings that suggest that a number of pockets of Harappan culture survived the collapse of the cities by many centuries, would, in light of the apparent self-sufficiency of these areas, seem to work against theories of highly centralized control.

Harappan Trade The ability to mass-produce a vast array of articles implies specialization, regulation, and an occupation-based class system. Moreover, elaborate port facilities suggest the prominence of a merchant class with overseas connections. Mesopotamian records from about 2300 BCE tell of a people called "Meluha" [MUH-loo-hah], now believed to be the Harappans, who carried on extensive seaborne trade and maintained colonies of merchants in several of their cities.

Harappan seals have been found at Ur in Mesopotamia, and there is evidence of Harappan merchandise being traded as far away as Egypt and central Asia. Because of the apparent occupational specialization of the Harappans, some scholars have theorized that they may have belonged to *guilds*, organizations whose members all pursue the same trade or craft. However, the plainness and uniformity of Harappan dwellings, in contrast to the pervasiveness of their amenities—generous living quarters, indoor plumbing, and so forth—defy any easy generalizations about class structure.

The Horned God. The figure on this seal found at Mohenjo-Daro may be a depiction of a Harappan deity. Its cross-legged "lotus" position and multiple faces prompted archaeologist Sir John Marshall to theorize in the 1930s that it was an early version of the Hindu god Shiva. More recently, scholars have moved away from this claim, noting that mention of Shiva does not occur for another 1,000 years during the Vedic years. Above the figure is a typically short sample of the pictographic Harappan script.

The Harappans appear to have maintained complex trade networks both within their cultural sphere and outside of it. Fortified border settlements, evidently trading posts, extended their influence to the borders of modern Iran and as far north as the Amu Darya, or Oxus River, the region of the BMAC. Curiously, however, we see virtually no evidence of foreign trade goods in the Indus cities, suggesting perhaps tight government control over outside influences. As we have seen, a surprising variety of agricultural products and craft specialties were also created for both internal commerce and overseas export.

In addition to bulk foodstuffs such as grain, the Mesopotamian records of the Meluha note that their merchants dealt in beadwork, lapis lazuli, pearls, rare woods, cotton cloth, and dog and cat figurines. Due in part to our inability to decipher the Harappan symbols, we know much less about their imports, though foodstuffs, oils,

Building Foundations and Street Layout at Lothal. The precision of Indus urban planning and execution is evident in this photograph of a residential area in Lothal.

Dockyard at Lothal. While some scholars maintain that this structure was a holding tank or reservoir, the current consensus is that it was in fact a technologically advanced area for loading and unloading oceangoing ships. A sophisticated system of channels kept it flooded to the proper level, prevented overflow, and, with locks and gates, allowed access to the river and sea.

and cloth seem to be among them. The network of cities along the Indus also seems to have been pivotal in the long-distance trade of copper from Baluchistan and in the exchange of gold, silver, semiprecious stones, shells, and timber throughout an extensive area north and west into Afghanistan and east to central Asia. Harappan figurines have been found along a broad front of nomadic routes from the Tarim basin west.

Lothal   The complexity of these questions of trade and social organization may be seen quite vividly at Lothal [LOW-tall]. Located several miles up the Sabarmati River from the Gulf of Khambat (Cambay), Lothal was a large—perhaps the chief—Harappan seaport. Recent work has shown it to be not only a vital link in Harappan maritime trade in the Arabian Sea and points west but an important manufacturing center of various trade items as well.

Lothal's central structure is an enormous basin, approximately 120 feet long and 70 feet wide, which was once connected to an inlet of the river. Most researchers believe that this was a dock for oceangoing ships, though some contend instead that it was a reservoir for water storage. Nearby are a number of structures believed to have been warehouses, each with numerous cubicles marked with what appear to be the stamps and seals of various merchants.

But Lothal was also a famous regional craft center, with microbeads used for decorative craft items and jewelry as its chief product for internal trade and export. Indeed, scholars theorize that the city's site may have been chosen precisely because of its proximity to convenient sources of precious stones for bead making. The site, with the precise city planning and water systems typical of Harappan cities, is also notable for its numerous specialized pottery kilns and bead "factories," complete with worker housing. Yet, for all this wealth of artifacts, such questions as who the merchants or workers were, how they were organized and governed, what levels of mobility there might have been among different classes, and even precisely what those classes might have been remain elusive.

Harappan Religion   Clues about Harappan religion are equally tantalizing. The swastika, a symbol long associated with the cyclical nature of life in Indian and Buddhist art before its appropriation by the Nazis in the twentieth century, is first found in the cities of the Indus. Moreover, recent scholarship has suggested that the entire Harappan system of symbols, always assumed to be a form of writing, may instead be best understood as a form of religious shorthand for use in the multiethnic and multilingual Indus society. Figurines depicting cows, buffaloes, tigers, crocodiles, elephants, and animals from surrounding regions have also been found. Along with female figurines and **phallic stones**, these perhaps connote a type of fertility religion. Like many Neolithic and agrarian–urban cultures, the Harappans interred their dead with ornaments and pottery, and perhaps food. Such practices have led scholars to speculate that the Harappans may have believed in an afterlife.

The prominence of such combined dualities as male and female or plant and animal may imply a principal deity embodying a unity of opposites, perhaps

Phallic stones/phallic: Of or referring to the male sex organ; Indian religions use a host of phallic images, or *lingams*, in shrines, rituals, and festivals to symbolize the male, or active, forces of both natural and supernatural creation.

prefiguring later Indian religious conceptions. Likewise, the central importance of the Indus River and the considerable attention paid to personal bathing are believed to be symbolically linked with a great ritual bath in the center of Mohenjo-Daro, perhaps adding yet another ritual dimension to the picture. Here again, however, the details are obscure and, for the moment, the nature of Harappan religion remains an open question.

The Collapse of the Cities

Around 1900 BCE the major cities of Harappan society appear to have been in decline. Structures of inferior quality seem to have been constructed on top of earlier buildings, suggesting a drop in population with a consequent loss of maintenance and services. By 1700 BCE the great cities appear to have been all but abandoned, their people moving to smaller outlying towns and villages, many returning to farming or becoming herders.

Some recent interpretations of Harappan urban decline attribute it to ecological collapse. The surrounding land—overgrazed, stripped of trees, and reliant upon the river for fertilization—had reached the limits of its capacity to support large cities. Perhaps increased flooding or weather-related problems stretched these limits even further. Some scholars have proposed that increasing salt levels in the Indus played a role, perhaps as the result of diverting too much of its water for irrigation and supplying the cities; one study places part of the blame on earthquakes, which may have partially diverted the river's flow around 1700 BCE. We do know that the Hakra-Nara River was abruptly shunted into the Indus by the early eighteenth century BCE, resulting in a progressive drying up of its old watershed and increased flooding on the lower Indus.

Recent work at sites in the area south of the Indus valley indicate a longer period of survival for some of the smaller late Harappan towns in the region. Nevertheless, by about 1500 BCE it appears that remnants of Indus civilization were to be found only within isolated regional cultures that blended Harappan influences with those of neighboring peoples. The expansion of Harappan village agriculture to the east and south, however, continued. Indeed, the firm base that had made Harappan urban life possible—the cultivation of regionally appropriate staple crops and domesticated animals by people organized in villages—might justly be called the foundation of Indian social history. In that sense, though its cities were long since abandoned, the culture that produced this pattern of world history can hardly be considered "lost." It would be centuries, however, before India again saw the rise of cities.

Interactions in Northern India, 1500–600 BCE

The "villains" of the Harappan collapse were long considered to be Indo-European migrants from the north who called themselves "Aryans" (Sanskrit, "the noble ones")—a term which, through a series of twisted associations and garbled history, Adolph Hitler later identified with Nazi Germany. Aryan tales recount their movement south and east through the Khyber Pass and across the Punjab between 1700 and 1400 BCE. Their accounts of epic battles had formerly been assumed to refer to their conquest of the Harappans. The earliest Aryan religious text, the *Rig-Veda* [Rig VAY-duh], refers to a short, dark-skinned people whom the Aryans contemptuously called *dasas*, or "the others," a term later used to denote servants or slaves. It also mentions conflicts with sedentary phallus-worshipping people living in cities and manning fortifications, which would certainly seem to describe the Harappans.

These works, however, were not written down until centuries after the events may have occurred, and whether their references date from the mid-second millennium BCE or were added later on is still not resolved. Moreover, while battles undoubtedly did occur, long periods of peaceful migration and settlement appear to have taken place as well. Perhaps the most significant problem, however, is that the Harappan cities appear to have been largely abandoned by the time the Aryans arrived on the scene.

In addition, the relative lack of Aryan artifacts; conflicts of interpretation between archaeologists, classical scholars, and linguists; and a growing body of scholarship by Indian researchers have produced in recent years a comprehensive questioning of the narrative of the role of Aryan migration altogether. Indeed, some scholars have suggested that long-held assumptions about the Aryans grew out of nineteenth-century beliefs of European superiority supported by the British occupation of India. Their contention is that the roots of Vedic society came not with invaders from the north but from peoples already long established in Punjab and, later, along the Ganges River. Since the debate has loomed increasingly large in revisiting broad currents of Indian history and identity, it most likely will remain unresolved for some time to come.

The Vedic World, 1750–800 BCE

Most scholars still assign a prominent, if not predominant, role to the Aryans. Their homeland is unknown, though some scholars believe it to be in the area around the Caspian Sea. Groups of nomadic peoples speaking a set of languages that linguists have designated "Proto-Indo-European" appear to have migrated along a broad front into Asia Minor, the eastern Mediterranean, Iran, and deep into central Asia, as evidenced by the recent find of the Tarim basin mummies. In all these areas they proved to be important catalysts in the diffusion of such technologies as iron working and the horse and chariot.

Indo-European Origins Their ancestors had already played an extensive role in the spreading of items and ideas throughout Eurasia long before the Aryans arrived in India. Indeed, recent European scholarship has suggested that their presence predated the Neolithic settlement of the continent. More recently, branches are believed to have migrated east and west across the continent from perhaps 4000 to 2500 BCE. In the course of their travels they were active agents in collecting, refining, and spreading a host of Bronze Age technologies. They are believed to have been the people who introduced the domestication of the wild horses of the central Asian steppes on a wide scale, along with such items as bridles and weapons for use on horseback. Similarly, it seems likely that they were instrumental in moving the technology of the chariot along a wide front, ranging from the eastern European steppes to China. As we saw in Chapter 2, around 1000 BCE various Indo-European-descended groups, most prominently the Hittites, brought the techniques of iron making out of Anatolia, ultimately taking them as far as the western reaches of the Yellow River basin.

Scholars have long identified a Proto-Indo-European language these groups are believed to have spoken as the parent tongue of a family of languages that includes Latin, German, Greek, the Slavic languages, Celtic languages such as Gaelic, and what became the Indian literary language, Sanskrit. A number of words with common roots for certain basic objects or concepts may be found among these languages. Examples include *pater* (Latin), *Vater* (German), and *pitar* (Sanskrit) for "father"; *sept* (Latin) and *sapta* (Sanskrit) for "seven"; and the place names "Iran" and "Erin/Eire/Ireland" (from "Aryan"). The identification of the Indo-European family of languages with the peoples of northern Europe in the nineteenth century, particularly the Germans, prompted the Nazi appropriation of the term "Aryan" for those of Germanic ethnicity in the 1930s and 1940s. However, a new group of scholars has argued for a thesis of "Paleolithic continuity theory," in which these groups had already begun to differentiate linguistically by the beginning of the Neolithic period and were not involved in massive "invasions" on the continent from the fifth to the third millennium BCE.

The Vedas Scholars believe that sometime around 2000 BCE a linguistic group designated "Indo-Aryans" had already split off from the Indo-Iranian subgroup and began moving toward the passes leading to northern India. As noted earlier, however, the confusing written record, the lack of firm archaeological sites, and national politics have made this history extraordinarily difficult to unravel. Some scholars see the Indo-Aryans as emerging from the BMAC culture; others see them as engaging in wars within the BMAC against the indigenous settled inhabitants; still others see them as migrating into the Punjab long after the Harappan cites had been in decline. In this context, they view their accounts of great "battles" and storming "citadels" as in reality cattle raids and attacks on village corrals.

In any case, the migrants appear to have carried with them an oral tradition of epic poetry, hymns, prayers, and heavily allegorical myth and history that would be carefully cultivated and preserved until committed to writing after 600 BCE. The core works, composed from around 1400 to 800 BCE, are the religious hymns known as the Vedas ("knowledge" or "truths"). Like the *Iliad* and *Odyssey* for Homeric Greece, the Vedas are still the principal window through which we can glimpse the world of the Aryans in northern India.

The *Rig-Veda*, the earliest of the Vedas, is currently believed to have been composed between about 1400 and 900 BCE. Some scholars, however, have suggested that some of the references contained in it point to much more ancient indigenous origins for it. Its verses were customarily memorized and passed from generation to generation by Aryan priests and their successors until after 1400 CE. The oldest recorded poetry in any Indo-European language, the *Rig-Veda's* 1,028 verses provide an idealized and allegorical vision of a society led by hard fighting, lusty warrior chieftains and priests, and composed of herders, cultivators, artisans, and servants. These groups became the prototypes of the four early social divisions, or *varnas*—priests, warriors, merchants, and commoners (see Patterns Up Close). Material wealth and skill in battle were the most valued attributes of Aryan culture. This emphasis on struggle and daring is seen as evidence of a strongly *patriarchal*, or male-led, society with an elaborate hierarchy based on kinship and prowess.

Nearly a quarter of the verses of the *Rig-Veda* celebrate the exploits of the god Indra, who is portrayed as the embodiment of the Aryan heroic ideal. In the accompanying quotation, he battles the serpent demon Vritra and triumphantly releases the rivers it had bottled up.

Early North Indian Society and Economics

Though a nomadic people, the Aryans possessed a high degree of technical skill. Not only had they benefited from the diffusion of earlier Bronze Age crafts, but, as we have seen, they were also important agents in distributing these crafts throughout Eurasia. They were particularly proficient in weaponry, and their bronze spear tips, arrowheads, and blades, in addition to the mobility of their chariots and horseborne warriors, very likely gave them a pronounced advantage over those of the village communities they encountered. After the beginning of the first millennium BCE, they also helped spread the use of iron.

Excellent horsemen, the Aryans made extensive use of horse-drawn wagons and chariots in battle. The earliest Aryan migrants may have introduced the horse to northern India, and it is likely that they first brought the chariot to late Xia or early Shang China. Elaborate equipment such as bridles, yokes, and harnesses and other items related to the use of horses have been found at a number of sites. The horse was so potent a symbol of power and well-being in Aryan culture and religion that its sacrifice became the most sacred of all ceremonies.

Ranging across vast stretches of grassland, the Aryans carried much of their food supply with them in the form of domestic animals. As for the Harappans, cattle were the chief measure of wealth, thus continuing the centrality of the "sacred cow" to the Indian religious experience. As skilled cultivators as well as herdsmen, the Aryans adapted easily to a wide range of environments. Sheep and goats were also mainstays of their livestock, while milk and butter, particularly the clarified butter called "ghee" [gee, with a hard "g"], occupied a prominent place in their religious symbolism.

As a highly refined product of the cow, ghee came to signify a rain that was at once purifying and fruitful. Even today ghee is used in daily household rituals. In the *Rig-Veda*, it acquired *cosmological* significance. That is, it was seen as something that reveals the underlying meaning and structure of the universe. In the accompanying passage from the *Rig-Veda*, ghee symbolically binds heaven and earth.

As with so many aspects of the deeper Indian past, ghee provides tantalizing clues about ancient practices but still leaves the veil of everyday life tightly drawn.

Aryan Settlement of Northern India

While the Vedas provide a rich literary account of Aryan conceptions of society and religion, the history of the Aryan occupation of northern India is far more obscure. Evidence from assorted sites suggests that there was a prolonged period of migration and settlement in the northwest of the subcontinent marked by a gradual transition of the Aryans from a nomadic and pastoral life to a settled and agricultural one. As early as 1000 BCE, evidence of large towns appears in the area around present-day Delhi. An important catalyst in bringing about the conditions necessary for the reemergence of large cities, however, was the beginning of widespread rice cultivation in the newly opened lands to the east.

First domesticated in Neolithic southeast Asia and south-central China, rice proved well suited to the warm temperatures, monsoon rains, and high fertility of the Ganges basin once the adjoining forests had been cleared. Here, it seems evident that the introduction of iron tools such as plows and axes was instrumental in preparing the land. High yields and a climate warm enough to permit two crops per year helped ensure the surpluses necessary to support an increasingly dense network of villages, towns, and cities, sometimes called by archaeologists India's "second urbanization."

However, the meticulous, intensive labor required at every stage of the rice plant's growth cycle required many hands for its successful cultivation. The plants must be grown in shallow water of a carefully prescribed depth and must be transplanted before the grain is harvested. Hence, the elaborate infrastructure of rice culture—the dikes, drainage ditches, terraces, raised paths, and other items related to water control—demanded a high degree of cooperation and increasingly sophisticated social organization. From roughly 800 BCE, we can trace the development of strong agrarian-based states called *janapadas* [jah-nah-PAH-duhs] ("populated territories" or "clan [*jana*] territories") in northern and northeastern India.

Statecraft and the Ideology of Power, 800–600 BCE

By the sixth century BCE the *janapadas* had encompassed the entire Ganges valley and were leading the way toward a cultural, if not a military, conquest of the subcontinent. Supported by the growing agricultural wealth and trade of the region, their influence was crucial in spreading their increasingly elaborate religion steadily east and south. Sixteen large states, or *mahajanapadas* [MAH-hah-jah-nah-PAH-duhs], now dominated northern India from the Bay of Bengal to the foothills of the Himalayas. The four largest—Avanti, Vatsa, Kosala, and Magadha—grew increasingly powerful, rich, and contentious along the Ganges. Buoyed by large revenues from agricultural and trade taxes and supported by theories that accorded kingship an almost divine status, their respective quests for domination grew as they absorbed their weaker neighbors. In this respect, as we shall see in Chapter 4, these states shared much in common with their contemporaries, the states of Zhou China.

Centralization and Power Among the Ganges States
The growing power and prosperity of the larger states tended to push them toward increasing centralization so that their resources might be used to maximal effect in the struggle for domination and survival. The two wealthiest *mahajanapadas*, Magadha and Kosala, found the route to consolidation through centralized kingdoms supported by the Brahmans, or priests. By the sixth century BCE this combination of state power and religion had produced kings, or *maharajas* [mah-hah-RAH-juhs], who were accorded god-like stature and wielded power that was seen as both secular and divine. For example, a number of kings, with the sanction of the priestly class, conducted increasingly elaborate horse sacrifices. The king's horse, accompanied by soldiers and royal grooms, was first made to wander the kingdom for a year, during which all land within the borders of its travels was claimed by the ruler. Its sacrifice thus became not only a supremely important religious festival but also a reminder of the king's power.

Other large states retained systems of government in which power was more diffuse, often being ruled by councils of various sorts as opposed to kings; scholars sometimes refer to these states as "republics." The most powerful of the republics, the Vajjian Confederacy, was ruled by a chief whose authority was derived from a council made up of heads or representatives of the principal clans. The council members were in turn responsible to local assemblies of clan elders and notables.

Even among the republics, the general trend appears to have been that of growing economic prosperity coupled with fierce competition among all the states for domination and survival—requiring ever greater efficiency in collecting revenue and spending for defense—pushing them toward either monarchy or absorption. The Vajjian Confederacy, for example, was eventually absorbed by Magadha during its drive for empire in northern India.

Thus, by the sixth century BCE, these states, like the Greek *poleis* and the states of late Zhou China, found themselves embroiled in continual political crises. Alliances between the states were sought and abandoned as the situation warranted; attempts to create a balance of power repeatedly failed as the largest states relentlessly vied for control. Increasing sophistication in strategy, tactics, and military technology—now including iron weapons, massed cavalry, war elephants, and even giant bows—put a premium on manpower and revenue, thus giving the larger states further advantages. By the late fourth century BCE, when these armies faced the threat of invasion by the forces of Alexander the Great and his successor Seleucus, they would number in the hundreds of thousands of men.

The Ideology of Rulership   Warfare conducted by kings vested with god-like status raised a number of ethical and practical questions about the nature of kingship, the responsibilities of rulers to their subjects, and their role as agents of a universal order. For example, how should a ruler monitor the activities of his subjects? What are the bounds of behavior in terms of diplomacy, espionage, the conduct of conflict, and the long-term welfare of the kingdom? Under what conditions may the rules be broken? In short, how should the ideal ruler comport himself for the good of his kingdom, subjects, and himself in accordance with his divine mission?

The growing size, wealth, and power of the Ganges states made these questions increasingly important as all struggled to expand—or merely survive. By 600 BCE, all the Gangetic rulers were, roughly speaking, in the situation later described by the political strategist Kautilya [Kaw-TEEL-yuh] of Magadha in his grimly realistic, pioneering political treatise, the *Arthashastra* [Arrh-tah-SHAS-truh]. In this constant war of all against all, says Kautilya, the wise ruler understands that those who encircle him on all sides and "prevail in the territory adjacent to his are . . . known as the enemy." On the other hand, those who control the territory "that is separated from the conqueror's territory by one [namely, the enemy's territory] is the constituent known as friend." Hence, one's policy toward neighboring states should be opportunistic: Attack the weak, seek allies against the strong, bide one's time with equals, and practice duplicity wherever and whenever necessary. As we shall see, there are many parallels with late Zhou Chinese treatises such as Sun Zi's *Art of War*. The prime purpose of such action, however, must always be the welfare of one's subjects by means of the survival and prosperity of the state.

This grim vision of the evolving world of statecraft was tempered somewhat by the themes depicted in the epics, composed during the Vedic period, though committed to writing only in the third century BCE, of which the two most famous are the Mahabharata [Mah-hah-BAH-rah-tuh] and the Ramayana [Rah-muh-YAH-nuh]. Perhaps the world's longest poem—at 100,000 verses in 18 books, it is many times longer than the Bible—the Mahabharata centers on the struggles among the descendants of the king, Bharata, and especially on the conflicting obligations imposed on the individual by state, society, and religion. The sixth book, Bhagavad Gita [BAH-ghuh-vahd GHEE-tuh] (Song of the Lord), has been called the "Indian gospel" because of its concentration on the tense and intricate combination of ethics and action.

On the eve of a battle in which the enemy includes his relatives and former companions, Arjuna, the protagonist, agonizes over fighting against his family and friends. His charioteer—actually the god Krishna in disguise—reminds him of the need to fulfill his duty according to *dharma* [DAR-mah] (literally "that which is firm"). To act according to dharma means that a person must follow his or her prescribed role according to that individual's place in society and in the natural order. As a warrior and ruler,

Illustration from the Mahabharata. The stories of the Mahabharata remain the most popular entertainment in India today. In this 1598 CE painting, Arjuna confronts his relatives on the battlefield.

therefore, Arjuna cannot leave the field of battle because of his personal connections to his opponents. Krishna tells him that the higher law of dharma demands that he put aside his personal reservations and fulfill his larger obligation to fight and win. Hence, Arjuna is urged to perform his duty without attachment as the agent of forces that transcend the immediate ties of friends or family. Thus, if Arjuna forces himself to do his duty because it must be done, abandoning his attachment to the result—whatever it may be—then, according to Krishna, he is acting wisely and advancing the course of the universe.

By about 600 BCE, the largest of the northern Indian states, especially Magadha and Kosala, were attempting both to expand southward and to absorb their neighbors along the Ganges. In this volatile political environment, they developed ideologies of kingship and power based on a common understanding of the religious and cultural implications of the Vedas and a realistic appraisal of their respective political environments. At once supported and trapped by the idea of dharma as it relates to kingship, they would struggle for the next several centuries until Magadha incorporated the northern third of the subcontinent (see Map 3.4).

Indian Society, Culture, and Religion, 1500–600 BCE

The first chronicles of Indian history do not make their appearance until well after the beginning of the common era. Because of this, such documentary evidence as we have about social history, especially that of families or village organization, is found in religious and literary texts, law codes, and the collections of folktales and genealogies called the *Puranas* [Poor-AH-nuhs] ("legends"), which date from about 500 BCE.

Society and Family in Ancient India

While part of Indian religious thought was becoming increasingly concerned with the nature of the absolute and ways to connect with it, much of the rest dealt with the arrangement of society, law, and duty; the role of the family and its individual members; and relationships between men and women.

Dharma and Social Class   For example, the Bhagavad Gita contains numerous illustrations of the dilemmas that come from following one's dharma: duty in accordance with one's capabilities and the requirements of one's place in society.

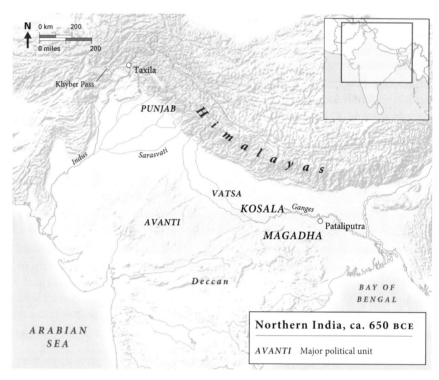

MAP 3.4 **Northern India, ca. 650 BCE.**

Krishna outlines these duties quite succinctly to Arjuna in the Bhagavad Gita in a set of passages that closely echo the structure of the *varnas*: "Tranquility, control, penance, purity, patience, and honesty, knowledge, judgment, and piety are intrinsic to the action of a priest," he notes, while "heroism, fiery energy, resolve, skill, refusal to retreat in battle, charity, and majesty in conduct are intrinsic to the action of the warrior." The activities that support the subsistence of society such as farming, herding cattle, and commerce "are intrinsic to the action of a commoner," while "action that is essentially service is intrinsic to the servant."

The great majority of Indians followed Krishna's last two sets of injunctions. Although one of the distinctive developments in the rise of the Gangetic states had been the rebirth of urban life in India, the village remained the center of the social world for perhaps 80–90 percent of the subcontinent's inhabitants—as it largely does to this day. Tending cattle and water buffalo and raising a variety of crops such as rice, wheat, barley, millet, and, as the southern areas were brought under the sway of the larger northern states, spices, medicinal herbs and barks, and forest products the villages were organized by clan and *jati*, or **caste** (see Patterns Up Close).

Caste: A system in which people's places in society—how they live, the work they do, and who they marry—are determined by heredity.

Though arranged according to a rigid hierarchy, the social system based on *jati* ("to be born," that is, "born into") functioned in many ways as a kind of extended family, each with its own clans, villages, local dialects, gods, laws, advisory councils, and craft and work specializations. Thus, as the organization of society became more complex—owing to the demands of increased size, trade, population diversity, and urbanization—the ritual importance of the four *varnas* of the nomadic Aryans was slowly giving way to the occupational emphasis of *jati* in the new agrarian–urban order.

As the system expanded south, it incorporated many local leaders, clan elders, and other notables into the higher castes. Sometimes entire villages were accorded their own castes on the basis of lineage or occupational specialty. At its peak, the number of castes and subcastes may have exceeded 3,000. As the various peoples of the subcontinent were brought into the structure, the older ritual and ethnic divisions of the early years of Aryan domination were slowly broken down even further, though their traces remain even to the present.

The all-pervasive force of dharma extended into the personal realm as well as that of politics. Behavior in village society and the family and even the possibilities for religious fulfillment hinged upon understanding and carrying out the demands of dharma. These demands, however, varied greatly according to an individual's social standing, gender, and place in the family.

Gender Roles: Men and Women in Society   The importance of family life in India is readily evident in religious scriptures and the law codes, or *smirti* [SCHMER-tee]. By 600 BCE, *artha* [AHR-tah], the pursuit of gain and subsistence was recognized as a moral course of action necessary to sustain family position and harmony. In addition to tending to the extensive ritual demands of daily life, the male householder of the upper caste was expected to "cast food on the ground for dogs, untouchables [the excluded castes], and crows." Moreover, according to the *smirti*, "Children, married daughters living in the father's house, old relatives, pregnant women, sick persons, and girls, as also guests and servants—only after having fed these should the householder and his wife eat the food that has remained." Thus, the male householder must be willing to habitually sacrifice his own needs for those of his family and dependents.

The position of women in the Indian family and in Indian society is more difficult to determine. At once partner and property, the center of the family, yet burdened with complex restrictions over education and marriage, adult women seem simultaneously to occupy several separated rungs in the hierarchies of family and society. Unswerving loyalty and devotion on the part of wives and daughters was demanded and highly prized. For example, a large part of the epic of the Ramayana, an allegorical account of the conquest of the peoples of the south, centers on the obsessive, though ultimately groundless, suspicion of the hero Rama [RAH-mah] about the faithfulness of his kidnapped wife, Sita. The reciprocal aspect of the demand for loyalty and devotion, as the Code of Manu advises, is that "regarding this as the highest dharma of all four classes, husbands . . . must strive to protect their wives." Thus, a great part of Rama's behavior toward Sita springs from his self-reproach over his failure to fulfill his most basic responsibility of protecting his wife. At the same time, Sita's loyalty to Rama makes her an exemplary model of dharma.

In household matters a wife should be engaged "in the collection and expenditure of . . . (the husband's) wealth, in cleanliness, in dharma, in cooking food for the family, and in looking after the necessities of the household." The position of women in this context, the code says, is "deserving of worship."

Coupled with this ideal of domesticity is a concept of women and women's sexuality as simultaneously compelling and threatening. The idea of kama, as encapsulated in the later *Kama Sutra*, included the enjoyment of a wide variety of sexual pleasures by men and women as part of a balanced social and religious life. Much Indian literature, both sacred and secular, as well as motifs, symbols, and statuary

Patterns Up Close | The Caste System

More than any other agrarian states, the *janapadas* developed an interlocking social order based on ethnicity and occupation. As the Aryans settled into northern India, the relatively fluid divisions of their nomadic society became more firmly defined according to ritual position and occupational status as the four *varnas* ("colors" or "complexions"): the first three for priests, warriors, and commoners, respectively, and a fourth that included both servants and laborers. The origin of the *varnas*, according to the *Rig-Veda*, lay in the seminal sacrifice of the cosmic being Purusha, which gave form to the universe: His mouth became the brahmans or priests; his arms became the kshatriyas [kuh-SHA-tree-yahs] kings and warriors; his two thighs the vaishyas [vy-SHEE-yahs], or merchants; and from his two feet the shudra, or peasants, servants, and laborers.

The newcomers' task of establishing and maintaining themselves as an elite class over the indigenous peoples meant that the system had to be expanded to accommodate all but with tight restrictions placed on social mobility. Thus, intermarriage was forbidden between Aryans and *dasas*, the term used for non-Aryans, and the latter were incorporated into the peasant/laborer/servant *varna*. By the sixth century BCE it appears that divisions between Aryans and non-Aryans that might have originally been based on skin color were giving way to ones based on occupation. An elaborate *jati*, or caste system—a term mistakenly derived from the Portuguese word *casta*, for "breed" or "race," later given to these social arrangements—was already developing.

Based on the original divisions of the four *varnas*, each caste was theoretically divisible into an infinite number of subcastes finely graded according to hereditary occupations. A new category of "excluded" castes—the so-called untouchables—was added, comprising people whose occupations were considered ritually unclean:

Brahman

Kshatriya

Vaishya

Shudra

associated with shrines and temples, graphically celebrates the union of male and female as the conduit for the primal creative force of the universe. Female beauty is identified with beneficial natural phenomena.

Later on, during the period of Classical Hinduism, numerous temples will have carvings depicting men and women in all phases of sexual activity, and even today small local temples feature phallic stones—representing the male member—which worshipers periodically anoint with milk and flowers.

In contrast to this concept of truth and purity arising from naked innocence was the idea that the material world in general, and sexuality as its most enticing aspect, could divert a person from fulfilling his or her dharma. As such, it poses a threat to the social and natural order if not properly controlled. The close relationship between society and religion in this regard provided considerable latitude for men to explore ways of going "beyond" the material and sexual world by engaging in solitary, often celibate, religious practices. On the other hand, it also bolstered the idea butchers, refuse collectors, privy cleaners, leather workers, and those involved with tending to the dead. The excluded castes also came to include "outcasts," people who for various offenses had "lost caste" and were therefore placed on the fringes of society. Perhaps a lingering vestige of early Aryan attempts at ethnic segregation, stringent prohibitions were imposed on sexual relations between *shudras* and members of the castes within the first three "twice born" (Aryan) *varnas*—so called because they alone were permitted to undergo the ceremony of the "sacred thread" and be "reborn" as initiates to the mysteries of the Vedic scriptures.

1805 French Lithograph of Indian Funeral (top) and Upper-Caste Dress (bottom).

The evolving *jati* system, with its precarious balance of flexibility and stability, expanded southward as the Ganges River states pushed farther and farther into these areas. Eventually, it incorporated villages, clans, and sometimes even entire tribal groups into their own *jatis*. Though highly restricted in terms of social mobility, these arrangements guaranteed a prescribed place for everyone in society, with at least a minimal degree of mutual support. Moreover, the idea of movement between castes became a vital part of Indian religious traditions through the doctrines of continual rebirth and the transmigration of souls. Thus, the evolving Indian innovation in response to the problem of incorporating a staggering multiplicity of ethnic, linguistic, and religious groups into its expanding culture was to create a space in society for each, while ensuring stability by restricting the social mobility of individuals and encouraging good behavior through the hope of a higher place in the next life. The fact that the system continues today despite its dissolution by the Indian government is testimony to its tenacious cultural roots and long-standing social utility.

Questions

- How is the caste system a cultural adaptation?
- How does the persistence of the caste system today demonstrate its social utility?

that a woman without the protection of a husband or family was a danger to herself and a source of temptation to others. For both men and women, independence from the social system of family, clan, or caste—unless channeled into an approved religious or social practice—was subject to severe sanction. But, because of the concept that the family was the foundation of society as a whole and the place of women was at the center of family life, the burdens of supporting the system and the penalties for failing to do so fell far more heavily on women than on men.

Cultural Interactions to 600 BCE

The social system of *varna* and *jati* held together as the religion of the Vedas expanded into the diverse body of beliefs, practices, and philosophy that would later be referred to by outsiders as "Hinduism." The term is derived from the Persian word *hindu*, taken from the Sanskrit *sindu*, or "rivers," in reference to the inhabitants of the Indus valley.

Gods and Priests   Though principally the embodiments or controllers of natural forces, the gods had human personalities as well. Indra, for example, was a swashbuckling warrior with a taste for *soma*, an intoxicating drink used in religious rituals. Varuna was the regulator of cosmic affairs and the lawgiver. Agni encompassed all the forces of light, sun, and fire and was, in a sense, the messenger of the gods, carrying the sacrifices of humans to the other deities.

As the members of the most important and respected *varna*, the prestige of the Brahmans (priests) grew as they monopolized the performance of ever more elaborate rituals and sacrifices. The priests carefully maintained the oral tradition of the Vedas, taking extreme care to pass on the exact formulas of the old rituals, while also creating new, increasingly elaborate ones centered on the needs of a more sedentary, agrarian people. The growing emphasis on the precise details of various rituals, as codified in the Vedic commentaries called Brahmanas, spurred the development of education among the men of the upper castes. By the sixth century BCE, the major works of the Vedic and Brahmanic oral tradition were being committed to writing in Sanskrit, from this time forward the sacred language of Indian scriptures.

Toward New Religious Directions   At the same time, this trend contributed to an increasing *formalism* within the Vedic-Brahmanic tradition: the belief that only the precise observance of all the proper forms of ritual behavior—prayers, sacrifices, daily and seasonal ceremonies—could ensure their effectiveness. Since the formulas for these rituals were for the most part accessible only to the "twice-born" or upper varnas, a small percentage of the population, and considered the special province of the Brahmans, there was considerable social and religious exclusiveness attached to the tradition as well.

A movement away from this restrictive formalism was already apparent by 600 BCE. Instead of appeasing the gods through the precise performance of ritual as a means of ensuring the cosmic order, some in the upper varnas began seeking the forces behind that order and trying to achieve communion with them. Two paths within the Vedic-Brahmanic tradition became discernible in this regard.

One path was *asceticism*, that is, full or partial renunciation of the material world, which, because of its impermanence, was seen as an impediment to a deeper understanding of reality. The Vedic tradition had long held a special reverence for hermits and those who fled society in order to purify themselves. The many schools of ascetic practice held that the multiple distractions of making a living, raising a family, and even the body itself hindered the quest for one's spiritual essence. These schools developed a variety of strategies for uncovering the unchanging, and thus real, "self" removed from a world where everything is impermanent and, hence, illusory.

Asceticism. For millennia great respect has been accorded those who withdraw from the lure of the material world and seek the unchanging within. Here, a modern "world renouncer," or *sannyasi*, is shown.

The practices of certain schools of *yoga* ("discipline"), for example, were based on the belief that mastery of the body allowed the adept to leave the restrictions of the material world and achieve communion with this inner self. Since the body, as part of the physical world, is subject to constant change, the discipline of postures, breathing, and meditation allows the practitioner to go beyond its limitations and find that which is unchanging within.

The other emerging path to a deeper spiritual reality was scriptural. Between the seventh and fifth centuries—though perhaps from as early as 800 BCE—a diverse group of writings called the Upanishads [Oo-PAHN-ee-shahds] ("secret knowledge") marked a dynamic new direction within the Vedic tradition. The Upanishads represented the Vedanta, "the end," or "fulfillment" of the Vedas, in which the hidden symbolism was revealed, layer by layer, and apparent inconsistencies were reconciled. While different levels of understanding the "true" principles of the Vedas were to be expected of those with limited access to the scriptures, a slavish reliance on the formal aspects of sacrifice was clearly subject to criticism.

The material world was increasingly regarded as extraneous as well. The individual "self" (*atman*) was ultimately to become identified with the cosmic "essence" (*brahman*—note that this usage is different from the same term used to describe the priestly *varna*).

Karma-Samsara Though the full impact of these trends would be felt only in succeeding centuries, speculation about the nature of individual and universal "essence" was already beginning to be reflected more broadly in culture and society. The elaboration of the idea of caste and its accompanying obligations carried with it the development of karma-samsara, the transmigration of souls and reincarnation. Though few references to these concepts are found in the Vedas, by the sixth century BCE the two ideas appear to have been widely accepted. The concept of a nonmaterial essence or "soul" carrying with it the residue of one's deeds—*karma*—is coupled with the idea of the rebirth of the soul into a new body—*samsara*. The fidelity with which a person pursues his or her dharma within the context of the caste system ensures an advance in caste in

Bathing in the Ganges at Varanasi. The sacred character of rivers in the Indian religious experience may go back all the way to the Harappans. As the multiple religious traditions we know as Hinduism developed in the Ganges valley, that river assumed a position of central importance in terms of ritual purification. Here, bathers are shown on the *ghats*—steps built on the riverbank—of the city of Varanasi, also known as Benares, site of some of Hinduism's holiest shrines.

the next life. Ultimately, the doctrine provided for *moksha*—release from the karmic cycle and the achievement of a state of complete understanding in this world—for those who are fully able to grasp the principles of atman–brahman and dharma.

Putting It All Together

In the Indus valley, as we have already seen in Egypt and Mesopotamia, a critical mass of factors required for the transition to agrarian-based cities had come together some time around 2500 BCE. Yet, our inability to decipher the symbols of the Harappans has proven to be a powerful impediment to our understanding of how their society worked and, equally important, why it fell. We are accustomed to thinking of history as a series of thresholds through which human societies pass in linear, progressive fashion—from forager society to agrarian to urban society, for example—without any substantial backtracking. And yet, there are the Harappans, who, for whatever reason, abandoned their splendid cities for, we must suppose, village agriculture or life in the forest.

Invasion by mobile nomads had formerly been seen as the cause, and this pattern of struggle between the settled and the nomadic will continue in various parts of the world for thousands of years. For the Harappans, however, the coming of the nomadic Indo-Europeans may not actually have had much of an impact, making the questions of interaction and adaptation that much more intriguing.

In India, the interruption in urban life lasted nearly 1,000 years. When cities again arose, they were centered hundreds of miles from the old, now forgotten Harappan sites. Instead of the apparent uniformity of the earlier society, the new one was to be marked by the struggle of individual states for advantage and supremacy. Yet, although these Gangetic states lacked political unity, their cultural and religious similarity remained an important factor throughout Indian history. Their unique innovation of the *jati* system was to act like a great flexible mold within which Indian society was increasingly cast into ever more complex sections.

Not surprisingly, this unsettled period of interaction and adaptation for the Gangetic societies was marked by widespread questioning of social, political, and religious arrangements. In the India of 600 BCE, the beginnings of an important redirection of the Vedic tradition were already under way through the speculations of the earliest Upanishads, which mark a pivotal development in the history of abstract religious and philosophical conceptualization. Moreover, amid the rich diversity of ascetic religious experience, some were shortly to map the direction of entirely new religious paths. One of these, Buddhism, may be seen as perhaps the first avowedly *universal* religious system and, thus, the beginning of a vitally important new pattern of world history.

▶ For additional resources, including maps, primary sources, visuals, and quizzes, please go to www.oup.com/us/vonsivers. Please see the Further Resources section at the back of the book for additional readings and suggested websites.

Thinking Through Patterns

▶ **Who were the Harappans? Where did they come from? What evidence exists for their origins?**

The riddle of the origins of the Harappans has been ongoing for close to 100 years. Most scholars believe their ancestors had been in the Indus region or nearby Baluchistan for millennia. Some also see them as perhaps related to extremely ancient peoples inhabiting the region around modern Kerala. Clues for this include archaic chants still practiced in Kerala that contain words that are believed to be so ancient that no one knows their meaning anymore. Carbon-14 dating, linguistic tracking, DNA surveys, and sedimentary analysis of ruins have all enhanced our understanding. One large impediment, however, remains: deciphering Harappan script—or, as we noted in this chapter, even judging whether the symbols the Harappans left behind are in fact a form of writing. Thus, a powerful analytic tool for understanding any civilization, the literary record, remains elusive.

Why do civilizations rise and fall? This is a key question for archaeologists and historians. Collapse can come from predictable causes—war, famine, ecological degradation—or random ones like earthquakes or volcanic eruptions. For the Harappans, the literary record of the Indo-Europeans long suggested that they conquered the Harappans, but it seems in conflict with more recent discoveries about the flooding patterns of the Indus, the sedimentary analysis of building and rebuilding of structures, and salinization levels at various points in the river. As is most often the case, historians generally expect to find no single *sufficient cause*—one that by itself led to the collapse—but rather a number of *necessary causes*—those that contributed but were not capable of causing the collapse all by themselves.

▶ **What explanations have been offered for the collapse of Harappan society? How well do the rival theories hold up, given what scholars and archaeologists have discovered?**

▶ **How can we know about newcomers to northern India? What sources exist for historians to examine?**

Another ongoing debate revolves around the identity and nature of the newcomers into northern India. Here, as noted in the previous discussion, the literary record of the Vedas, particularly the oldest, the *Rig-Veda*, appears in conflict with much of the archaeological evidence. While the Vedas are quite clear about where the newcomers ended up, they are tantalizingly vague about where they originated. Indo-European-speaking peoples ranged widely across Eurasia, which we can tell from the kinds of technologies moving from different regions of the continent that we know are associated with them: horse equipment, chariots, iron. But because they left little in the way of archaeological sites, piecing together their story from their material culture is extremely challenging. For the moment, much of the most productive work is being done through DNA collecting and gene tracing of the area's modern inhabitants, as well as increasingly refined linguistic techniques of *glottochronology*—the tracing of language change over time and space.

Since one of our primary tasks in this text is to help you look for patterns surrounding origins, interactions, and adaptations, the question arises about the nature of patterns we see evolving among the early north Indian states. Not all these states were monarchies, but the religious aura of the monarchs and its relationship to the first stirrings of what will become Hinduism is striking. The permeation of society by religion is certainly a pattern that continues to this day, as is the desire for transcending the bounds of the material world by a variety of ascetic or scholarly methods. The most pervasive pattern lies in the development of the caste system as the basic social structure of society, which tenaciously endures even today in the face of a constitutional ban.

▶ **What patterns can we see evolving in the Ganges River states that will mark the subsequent development of Indian civilization?**

Chapter 4 5000-481 BCE

Agrarian Centers and the Mandate of Heaven in Ancient China

Thousands of miles east of Harappa and several centuries after its decline, the twenty-first Shang king, Wu Ding, prepared to commune with his ancestors in the hope of gaining some insight into the childbearing prospects of his pregnant wife, Fu (Lady) Hao. Fu Hao, his favorite (and most powerful) wife, had come from a noble family outside the Shang capital of Yin, near the modern city of Anyang in northern China. Well educated and highly capable as an administrator, Fu Hao had even on occasion led Shang armies in the field. Now she was entrusted with what Wu Ding and his court considered to be the most important duty of all: continuing the line of Shang kings into the future. For the Shang kings believed that the past, present, and future rulers of their line formed an unbroken continuum, with the deceased existing in a spirit realm accessible to the living by ritual divination. Therefore, Wu Ding, whose concern for Fu Hao and her unborn child was paramount, sought the advice of the ancestors about her condition and that of her child to come. Wu Ding and his chief diviner, Que [Chway], scratched their questions into a cleaned and dried shoulder blade of an ox and held it over heat. The diviner then tapped it carefully

ABOVE: Skeleton and Shang War Chariot, Anyang, China.

with a bronze rod and attempted to read the meaning of the cracks as they appeared in the hot bone.

Que's reading of the cracks was "It is bad; it will be a girl." Although this was considered disappointing for ensuring an heir, Fu Hao remained Wu Ding's most beloved wife until her death. Indeed, after she died, the despondent king frequently sought her advice through the oracle bones on matters of state and private affairs. Fortunately for us, her tomb is one of the most completely preserved from the Shang era. Like the vast caches of oracle bones uncovered over the years, it tells us a great deal about society and gender, economics and trade, and the origins and interactions of Chinese states among themselves and with neighboring peoples.

Like Harappa along the Indus, the Shang state had developed from a process of growth and consolidation among the Late Neolithic settlements along China's Yellow River. But the Harappans and the Shang had begun very different paths to the present. Harappa and the other cities of the Indus, as we have seen, all but disappeared, their influence detectable only within the deepest currents of later Indian society. In contrast, the foundations laid by the Shang and subsequent dynasties developing in China's Yellow River valley remained vital into the twentieth-first century and profoundly influenced east and southeast Asia. The history of India was one of infusion and synthesis, of cycles of partial political unity punctuated by long stretches of fragmentation. The political and cultural experience of China, however, was marked by relatively little outside influence and thousands of years of centralized rule. Moreover, for the great majority of its history, China would be perhaps the world's greatest exporter of ideas and goods.

Seeing Patterns

▶ How did the interplay of environment and climate help to influence the earliest patterns of Chinese civilization? How do historians address the question of whether "geography is destiny" in this case?

▶ What can the remains of Neolithic Chinese settlements tell us about the continuities and disruptions of Chinese history?

▶ How did the Zhou concept of the Mandate of Heaven operate?

The Origins of Yellow River Cultures, 5000–1766 BCE

The sun beyond the mountain glows,
The Yellow River seaward flows,
If you want an even better sight,
Ascend an even greater height.
"Climbing 'Stork Pavilion,'" Wang Zhihuan (648–742 CE)

An observer at the site of the "Stork Pavilion" of poet Wang Zhihuan's reverie could justly claim to have gazed upon the heartland of Chinese history. Situated on a high bluff at Yongji in the south of the modern province of Shanxi, the pavilion marked a celebrated scenic spot commanding a view of the Yellow River as it approaches its great bend to the east. Here, it is joined by the Wei River from the west and rolls across the North China Plain in a leisurely but erratic manner for another 500 miles to the Bohai Gulf, an arm of the Yellow Sea.

Over the centuries, our observer might have witnessed the origins and development of some of China's first Neolithic cultures along the river. Sixty miles up the

Wei, he or she could have visited China's most famous Neolithic village at Banpo or one of dozens in between. Even today, on every side of the bend lie burial mounds from a wide selection of China's early village and town cultures. Nearby is the modern city of Xi'an [SHE-Ahn], the capital of no fewer than 13 Chinese regimes during its long history. And here, too, the richest and most famous site of all attracts visitors by the millions: the sprawling tomb complex of China's first emperor, Qin Shi Huangdi [Chin SHUHR Hwang-DEE], packed with thousands of life-sized terracotta soldiers in perfect ranks marching in timeless close-order drill.

Geography and Climate

While China's natural boundaries are perhaps less dramatic than those of India, they have had an equally profound effect on its history and society. As with India, the Himalayas and Pamirs along the southern border of Tibet mark one natural barrier. River systems such as the Amur and Ussuri in the north, the Salween in the southwest, and the Red in Vietnam have also represented past borders, though not impermeable ones. The northern and western deserts—the Gobi, Ordos, and Taklamakan—have also served as natural boundaries that frequently passed in and out of the hands of successive Chinese dynasties as their emperors sought to curb the incursions of nomads or control central Asian trade routes.

The chief effect of these features, however, has been to limit the principal avenues of outside interaction to the narrow corridor running west of Xi'an, south of Mongolia, and north of the modern province of Qinghai, spanning the route of the famous Silk Road. Like the Khyber Pass in India, this route has historically been the main avenue into China; unlike the Khyber, however, it has seldom been an invasion route for outsiders. The result of this has been that, on the one hand, the origins and early development of ancient China were more isolated than those of the other Eurasian centers of civilization. On the other hand, the absence of outside competitors facilitated both cultural and political unification.

While conditioned by many of the same factors found in India, China's climate is more varied. The area south of the Qin [Chin] Mountains marks the northern boundary of the region regulated by the monsoon, with warm temperatures and abundant summer rainfall. During the summer monsoon, rainfall amounts can range from about 40 inches per year in the eastern coastal city of Hangzhou [HAHNG-joe] to over 70 inches in the subtropical south. The suitability of the southern regions for rice cultivation, as with the Gangetic societies of India, resulted in rapid growth and high population density there. Above the monsoon line, temperatures and rainfall amounts are influenced more by the weather systems of the Eurasian interior. Thus, northern China is subject to blistering summers and frigid winters with sparse and unreliable precipitation.

One result of these conditions has been that China's population has historically been concentrated in the plains along the major river valleys and the coast. Three main river systems have remained the primary avenues of agriculture and commerce: the Pearl River (Zhujiang), in the south; the Yangzi [YAHNG-zuh] River (at 3,988 miles, it is the third longest in the world); and the Yellow River (Huanghe), where the most influential early Chinese societies developed (see Map 4.1).

The Yellow River   Rising in the highlands of Gansu and flowing north to the Ordos Desert, the Yellow River then turns south and east out of Inner Mongolia for

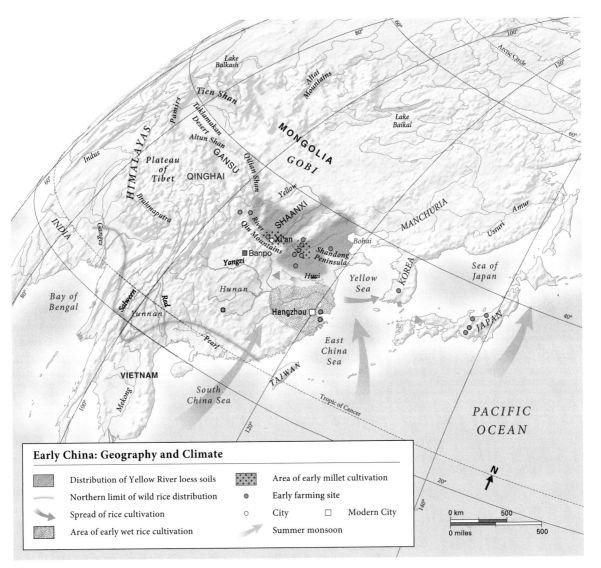

MAP **4.1 Early China: Geography and Climate.**

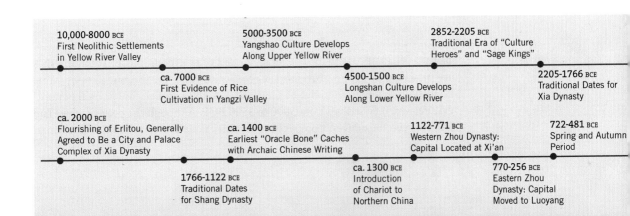

10,000-8000 BCE
First Neolithic Settlements
in Yellow River Valley

5000-3500 BCE
Yangshao Culture Develops
Along Upper Yellow River

2852-2205 BCE
Traditional Era of "Culture
Heroes" and "Sage Kings"

ca. 7000 BCE
First Evidence of Rice
Cultivation in Yangzi Valley

4500-1500 BCE
Longshan Culture Develops
Along Lower Yellow River

2205-1766 BCE
Traditional Dates for
Xia Dynasty

ca. 2000 BCE
Flourishing of Erlitou, Generally
Agreed to Be a City and Palace
Complex of Xia Dynasty

ca. 1400 BCE
Earliest "Oracle Bone" Caches
with Archaic Chinese Writing

1122-771 BCE
Western Zhou Dynasty:
Capital Located at Xi'an

722-481 BCE
Spring and Autumn
Period

1766-1122 BCE
Traditional Dates
for Shang Dynasty

ca. 1300 BCE
Introduction
of Chariot to
Northern China

770-256 BCE
Eastern Zhou
Dynasty: Capital
Moved to Luoyang

500 miles before making its bend to the east and the sea, a total distance of about 3,000 miles. The river gets its name as a result of the *loess*—a light, dry, mineral-rich soil deposited by centuries of strong winds—it picks up as it flows, giving it a yellowish tint. As with the Nile in Egypt, the rich, easily worked soil carried by the river has brought abundant agriculture to arid northern China; but like the Indus, the constant buildup of silt in the riverbed also causes it to overflow its banks, resulting in the devastation of fields and villages in its path through the North China Plain, the vast flatlands lining the river course on its final run to the sea.

"China's Sorrow"   This building up and bursting of natural levees, along with earthquakes and occasional human actions—such as the dynamiting of dikes during World War II to stop the Japanese invasion—have caused the Yellow River to change course 26 times during the last 3,000 years. Its mouth has shifted several times above and below the Shandong Peninsula, assuming its present course to the north following massive floods in 1854–1855. Not surprisingly, efforts to control the river have occupied a prominent place in the mythology, history, and political and social organization of the region from earliest times. For example, Yu, the supposed founder of the Xia dynasty, was said to have labored for decades to control the river's rampages. More recently, some scholars have pointed to the centralized bureaucratic structure of imperial China and suggested that it was dictated in part by the struggle for mastery of its waterways. Thus, despite its gift of fertility over the course of thousands of years, the Yellow River's unpredictable nature has prompted writers to sometimes refer to it as "China's sorrow."

The Origins of Neolithic Cultures

Between 50,000 and 20,000 years ago modern *Homo sapiens* had become established in eastern Eurasia. Human communities that produced small, refined stone implements such as arrowheads and knives ranged across north and central China from about 30,000 years ago, marking an extensive foraging culture. Within a few millennia of the last glacial retreat, settlements began to appear in northern China containing the first traces in the region of the transition from forager society to an agrarian one, based on agriculture and the domestication of animals.

Millet: A species of grass cultivated for its edible white seeds and as hay for animal feed.

Agriculture developed very quickly in China and included a wide variety of crops and livestock. Sites of rice cultivation in central China are, at 7000 BCE, among the earliest in the world, while several strains of **millet** were already being grown in the north. Recent work suggests that early strains of wheat and barley, perhaps diffused from areas around the Fertile Crescent, may also have been grown. Chickens, pigs, sheep, cattle, and dogs were also widely raised. Areas along the Yellow River contain some of the earliest agricultural villages in China and several *prototypical cultures*— those that pioneered techniques, institutions, or patterns of social organization widely copied in later years—emerged here and along the North China Plain over the next several thousand years.

Banpo Village   Perhaps the most studied of the thousands of Neolithic sites across China is Banpo [BAHN-paw] Village, located on the outskirts of Xi'an. Banpo village is representative of Yangshao [YAHNG-shaow], or "painted pottery," culture, which flourished from 5000 to 3500 BCE. Although the potter's wheel had not yet been introduced from western Eurasia, Yangshao communities like Banpo had sophisticated kilns that fired a wide variety of brightly painted storage pots, vases, etc. decorated with animal and geometric designs. The inhabitants of Yangshao villages also produced stone implements such as axes, chisels, and knives to support the community's hunting, farming, and fishing activities.

The perimeter of the Banpo settlement is surrounded by a defensive ditch, rather than the walls characteristic of later towns and cities, with 40 homes arranged around a rectangular central structure believed to be a clan meeting house or religious site. The homes were supported by vertical posts and had thatch roofs that, along with the walls, were plastered with mud and straw. The village contains a number of features that archaeologists believe to be early forms of certain long-standing patterns of rural life in northern China. For example, some of the huts contain raised clay beds with flues laid through them—an early version of the *kang* [kahng], the heated bed still found in older northern Chinese farming homes today. Also, silkworm cocoons and crude needles suggest the early development of silk weaving. Perhaps the most exciting finds, however, are the potsherds bearing stylized pictures of animals and geometric markings that some Chinese scholars have speculated may be ancestral forms of the Chinese written language.

Top: Interior View of Banpo Dwelling. *Bottom:* Circular Foundation Showing Postholes.

Longshan Culture   Settled life in villages and towns appears to have expanded greatly during the Longshan period, from about 4000 to 2000 BCE. Once thought to have grown out of Yangshao culture as it spread east to modern Shandong Province, the dates of the earliest distinct Longshan artifacts have now been pushed as far back as 4500 BCE. A later branch of Longshan culture based in what is now Henan [HEH-nahn] Province is also believed to have arisen around 2000 BCE, lasting until about 1500 BCE, when it was absorbed by the Shang dynasty.

Like their Yangshao counterparts, Longshan potters were highly skilled and pioneered forms and styles still favored by Chinese artisans today. The black-colored pottery associated with Longshan culture is particularly refined. Some of the pieces are so delicate and nearly transparent that they resemble the famous "eggshell porcelain" of later Chinese imperial pottery works. The introduction of the potter's wheel from the west in the mid-third millennium BCE—one of the earliest indications we have of late Neolithic Chinese interactions with other

Painted Pottery, or Yangshao, Earthenware Basin Found at Banpo Site. Contrast and compare this piece with the one from Longshan (p. 90). What similarities and differences can you spot?

Longshan (Black Pottery)
Culture Stemmed Beaker (*bei*),
Shandong, ca. 2000 BCE.

peoples—permitted unprecedented precision, while improved kilns—reaching firing temperatures in excess of 1,800 degrees Fahrenheit—and experimentation with kaolin clays began a long process of ceramic innovation that ultimately resulted in the first porcelain thousands of years later.

After 2000 BCE, the Longshan and other late Neolithic cultures were at a point where a transition to a society marked by large towns and even small cities supported by agriculture was becoming discernable. Towns of several thousand inhabitants have been uncovered, and a number of sites contain elaborate altars. The use of gold, copper, bronze, and jade in jewelry is also increasingly evident. Craft specialization and embryonic social classes are detectable.

Beyond the North China Plain   Given the subtropical environment of the regions below the Yangzi River basin in central China, it would be surprising if archaeologists did not find remains of flourishing cultures there as well. Until recently, however, such artifacts have been marginal and fragmentary. In addition to isolated sites on the western Yangzi River, a few close to modern Shanghai and Hangzhou, and at Dalongtan in Yunnan, the most extensive distinctive culture is that of Dapenkeng [DAH-pen-kehng], which flourished from 5000 to 2500 BCE. Artifacts including potsherds, arrowheads, and polished tools and axes indicate a sophisticated coastal and riverine society along an extensive corridor running from the borders of modern Vietnam along the south China coast to Fujian Province and, most strikingly, across the Taiwan Strait to the western coast of that island.

The vast reach of Dapenkeng culture and the similarity of its relatively sparse artifacts over a wide area suggest extensive interaction with peoples throughout the region. While the origins of this culture may be obscure, they do appear to be quite different from those of the north. Long and patient work by linguists has established this area as part of a Proto-Austronesian culture, one whose parent language is distinct from the Sino-Tibetan language group that contains the various Chinese dialects and that has strong links to the Austronesian speakers on modern Taiwan. This in turn has prompted scholars studying the origins of the Polynesian language family to search for possible links with these people on Taiwan and along the China coast.

Origins of Rice Cultivation   While the staple grain crops of the north included various strains of millet, with wheat and barley not coming into extensive cultivation until the Zhou period, the most far-reaching innovation in the regions south of the North China Plain was the development of widespread rice cultivation. Two sources have been cited as likely early centers of rice experimentation: southeast Asia and the area extending from China's modern province of Hunan to the coastal reaches of the Yangzi River, where rice grains have been dated to 7000 BCE. While we cannot know with precision which region played the more prominent role in spreading rice cultivation and techniques throughout China, we do know that southeast Asia remained an important source of new rice strains that allowed China's food production to keep pace with its population until well into the nineteenth century CE. Other food sources domesticated elsewhere making their appearance in Neolithic south China include chickens—perhaps obtained from south Asia via southeast Asia—and cattle, especially the water buffalo. Cattle, however, were raised primarily for farm work rather than consumption.

Toward a Chinese Culture   With these recent finds, the older view of Chinese civilization being the exclusive product of the Yellow River valley cultures, which then expanded to more distant areas, has undergone considerable modification. Instead, scholars now suggest that the area approximating modern China consisted around 3000 BCE of a collection of agrarian communities that remained distinct in their own right but whose interactions with each other began to contribute common cultural elements that ultimately became identified as "Chinese." Indeed, some scholars have adopted a view of China down through the end of the third millennium BCE as being not so far from the mythical period referred to by ancient writers as *wanguo* [WAHN-gwo]—the "ten thousand states."

Though scholars have filled in much of the picture of these ancient cultures, the precise time and duration of their transition to one marked by cities is still very much open to debate. Chinese chroniclers, however, drawing upon the world's largest and longest literary record, have long given pride of place in this regard to their first three dynasties: the Xia, Shang, and Zhou.

The Age of Myth and the Xia Dynasty, 2852–1766 BCE

The Chinese have been called the most historically minded people on earth. For thousands of years, the use of writing for purposes of record keeping has been of paramount importance and the written word itself was considered to have a kind of inner power. For millennia, the careful study, writing, and rewriting of history have been vital elements of individual self-cultivation as well as key mechanisms for political and social control (see "Patterns Up Close").

Among the earliest collections of Chinese writings we have are those of the *Shujing* [SHOO-jeeng]. Also known as the *Book of History* or *Classic of Documents*, the *Shujing* is a detailed compilation of ancient material purportedly from 2357 to 631 BCE. Though heavily encrusted with material of questionable reliability, it remains a principal documentary source for information about the people, places, and events of China's first three dynasties: the Xia [Sheah], Shang [Shahng], and Zhou [Joe]. In a surprising number of cases, its clues have helped to illuminate the archaeological evidence in recent attempts to establish the historical existence of the Xia dynasty.

Culture Heroes and Sage Kings   According to Chinese legend, mythical culture heroes and sage kings reigned from 2852 to 2205 BCE and introduced many of China's basic elements and institutions. Among the contributions attributed to the first culture hero, Fuxi, were medicine, divination, and, according to some stories, writing. His successor, Shen Nong was credited with developing agriculture. Fire and silkworm cultivation were said to have been introduced during the reign of Huangdi, the "Yellow Emperor," whose reign followed that of Shen Nong. The Yellow Emperor's rule was followed by that of the three sage kings—Yao, Shun, and Yu—who set the example for strong moral leadership and are credited with passing the role of leadership on to the land's most worthy men instead of to their own family members.

Between Myth and History   The *Shujing* acclaims Yu, the last sage king, as the tamer of the Yellow River. He is also traditionally considered to be the founder of the Xia dynasty in 2205 BCE. Because of the difficulty in establishing a clear archaeological record, however, Yu and his successors have largely remained suspended between myth and history.

Moreover, the character of the *Shujing* as a creation of later Zhou chroniclers—with a specific agenda of justifying Zhou rule—has cast a long shadow over events that allegedly took place over 1,500 years before. More generally, as the sole literary account we have of the period, it has naturally assumed a dominant and, most likely, misleading role as the master narrative of ancient Chinese history. Some scholars have even argued that the Xia were an invention of the Zhou. More recently, some have suggested that their rule was in fact a kind of Shang mythology. On the other hand, some, notably a group of Chinese archaeologists, have noted that the relative accuracy of the dates given in the *Shujing* for events in the Shang dynasty suggests a similar level of reliability for its accounts of the earlier Xia.

Recent archaeological work also has moved somewhat closer to confirming the historical existence of a widespread culture, if not yet a state, corresponding to the literary accounts of the Xia. Excavations at Erlitou [ARH-lee-toe] in southern Shaanxi Province in the 1950s and 1960s revealed that artifacts at the site fall within the traditional dates given for the existence of the Xia. In addition, artifacts, particularly early bronze ritual vessels virtually identical to those at Erlitou, appear widely throughout regions described in the *Shujing* as belonging to the Xia and, in some cases, considerably beyond it.

Xia Society   The small number of purported Xia sites makes it difficult to draw many firm conclusions about their society. Much of what we believe is based on the premise that the Xia was a transitional society, developing and elaborating the material culture of the late Longshan and Yangshao cultural periods. Of particular note in this transition are the growing importance of bronze casting, the increasingly complex symbols on pottery, and the widespread evidence of large-scale communal efforts at flood control, including dams, dikes, levees, and retention ponds.

As we have seen, the Yangshao and Longshan cultures stretched across a continuum from small hunting, fishing, and farming villages to substantial agriculturally supported towns. The Xia, however, though our picture of them is far from complete, appear to have reached the tipping point at which most of the hallmarks of urban society—what we commonly think of as "civilization"—began to appear. For example, the Erlitou excavation, dated to perhaps 2000 BCE, reveals a walled city of moderate size containing what is believed to be the foundation of China's first palace: a stamped-earth terrace extending over 100 yards on each side.

Moreover, the layout of the buildings within walled compounds dating from this time began to resemble that of later official residences. Beams supported by large wooden posts carry the weight of moderately sloped roofs with upturned ends, while "curtain walls"—which bear little or none of the structure's weight—are built between the posts of plastered brick or masonry. Most of the larger buildings are also built along a north–south axis with their courtyards and entrances facing south, an orientation favored even today by Chinese builders.

Literary evidence suggests that Xia leaders exercised a strong family- or clan-based rule, and the archaeological evidence seems to support this to a considerable degree. Evidence indicating the role of the elites as mediators with the spirit world, and particularly with the ancestors of Xia rulers, is also found in abundance at Erlitou. China's first bronze ritual vessels—wine beakers on tripod stands in shapes favored throughout subsequent Chinese history—as well as jade figurines, turquoise jewelry, the world's earliest lacquered wood items, and cowry shells—a medium of exchange monopolized by the Xia rulers—all testify to their leaders' religious and social roles. Moreover, foundations of workers' residences and workshops for copper and bronze casting have also been found. As with a number of Longshan sites, extensive cemeteries outside the city suggest the development of social classes in the number and kind of burial artifacts and the position and richness of elite plots.

Though the boundaries of Chinese history have been pushed back considerably by such work, the Xia remain, like their contemporaries the Harappans, an elusive, if not perhaps a "lost," civilization. Indeed, much of what we believe about them comes from interpretations extended back in time from the period of documented Shang dominance. Unlike the Xia, however, the written records and artifacts of the Shang dynasty offer a much more complete picture of East Asia's first Bronze Age society.

The Interactions of Shang and Zhou History and Politics, 1766–481 BCE

The Shang dynasty represents the first genuine flowering of urban society in east Asia. Though this development occurs somewhat later than in the other core areas of Egypt and the Mediterranean, southwest Asia, and the Indus valley, we nevertheless find here all of the attributes of such cultures elsewhere: a high degree of skill in metallurgy, a large and varied agricultural base, an increasingly centralized political and religious system, growing **social stratification**, a written language, and, of course, cities. In all of these areas the Shang made considerable contributions; in some, such as their spectacular bronzes and especially their system of written characters, they were startlingly original.

Social stratification: Groups or classes within a society arranged in a hierarchy, for example, peasants, merchants, officials, ministers, rulers.

The Shang Dynasty, 1766–1122 BCE

Unlike the idealized rule of the sage kings Yao, Shun, and Yu depicted in the *Shujing*, Shang social and political organization was kinship-based, with an emphasis on military power and efficiency of command. As in Mesopotamia, the advent of cities, with their vastly increased populations, now required rulers to wield greater power for defense and internal regulation, while at the same time appealing to an authority beyond human power for legitimacy. Thus, loyalty was pledged to the Shang king and his family. Members of the king's extended family controlled political and religious power, with more distant relatives acting as court officials.

Among the purported 31 Shang kings mentioned in literary records, succession often passed from uncle to nephew, though sometimes from elder brother to younger. Unlike the Aryan system of *varna*, there was no rigidly defined priestly class, though spirit mediums and diviners were widely used by Shang rulers—as we saw with Wu Ding—and exercised considerable influence at court. Local leaders who controlled walled cities and towns and their surrounding lands were employed by the ruling families as regional

Shang Weapon. A bronze ceremonial axe head with intricate decorative markings, from the 13th -11th centuries BCE.

officials, as were specially designated Shang allies, though the exact nature of these arrangements is not clearly understood.

Shang Armies and Expansion   Though small compared to the forces commanded by their successors, Shang rulers fielded the most powerful armies of east Asia in their day. One expeditionary force of the late thirteenth-century BCE king Wu Ding and his wife Fu Hao numbered more than 13,000 men and included both paid soldiers and local defense forces recruited from the larger walled towns. Excavations reveal that the armies were organized into companies of 100 men who wielded bronze-tipped spears and pikes topped with crescent-shaped axe heads and spear tips (see Map 4.2).

The Introduction of the Chariot   Another potent weapon used by the Shang was the chariot, possibly introduced to China through interaction with Indo-Europeans around 1300 to 1200 BCE, when these vehicles first make their appearance in Shang burial sites. Chariots seem to have been shortly preceded by the widespread introduction of the horse from the west, an innovation that had already revolutionized transport and warfare through much of Eurasia. Up to this point, the small Mongolian ponies native to the northern reaches of Shang lands seem to have attracted little interest, perhaps because of their limitations as transport and

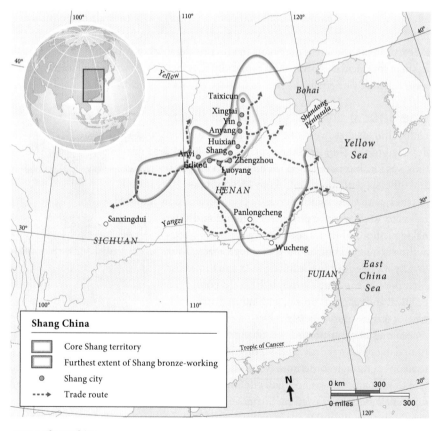

MAP **4.2 Shang China.**

Shang Chariot. Whether used for battle or state functions, Shang-era chariots were distinctive in their wide stance, roominess, and portability. The photograph shows a careful reconstruction of a Shang chariot with authentic bronze decorations and lacquered finish. Note the linchpins holding the wheels to the axles. These could be quickly removed for ease in changing wheels or breaking down the chariot in order carry its parts separately.

draught animals. The larger and faster steeds of central Asia and the western Eurasian steppes, however, were to remain important items of trade for the Chinese for thousands of years and were celebrated in painting, poetry, and song.

Shang chariots were pulled by two horses and generally held three men. Detachable wheels held by linchpins permitted easy storage and repair. Both charioteers and infantry wielded large composite bows—so called because they were made of wood, cattle horn, and sinew. The bows were curved away from the archer in their unstrung state for additional power. As with other ancient peoples, the combination of archers with the chariot gave Shang forces considerable striking power, especially when employed against slower and more unwieldy infantry formations.

Shang Politics and Foreign Relations   Because their prestige depended in large part on their military power and harmony with their ancestors, the Shang rulers constantly mounted campaigns for sacrifice—both material and human. Indeed, the archaeological evidence and oracle bone inscriptions suggest that the greater part of Shang foreign relations with **client states** and allies consisted of setting and enforcing levels of tribute and labor service. Shang kings, especially Wu Ding, continually led expeditions against settled peoples to the west, the most prominent of whom, the Zhou, based around modern Xi'an, were ultimately enlisted as allies and clients. Wu Ding's successors, such as Zu Geng [ZOO-gung] and Di Yin, met with less success however; and over time shifting coalitions of former allies and client states began to encroach on Shang lands. Significantly, even to the end of the Shang period, the interior lands of the state appear to have been considered secure enough to lack walls and other defensive structures around many major towns.

Client states: States that are dependent on or partially controlled by more powerful ones.

Shang Interactions   Throughout the span of roughly 1,200 years from the traditional beginnings of the Xia to the end of the Shang, interaction between the northern Chinese states and the other Eurasian civilizational cores seems to have been tenuous at best. The most direct links appear to have been through the trade and migrations of an ethnically and culturally diverse group of nomadic–pastoral peoples who ranged along a broad northern tier of Eurasia from the steppes of modern Ukraine to the area of modern Manchuria in the east. Though they left few traces, and early Chinese accounts use a haphazard collection of names for them, scholars have theorized that these nomads included both speakers of Altaic languages—the distant ancestors of the Mongols, Manchus, Huns, and Turks—and, perhaps more significantly at this point, the Indo-European peoples who played such an important role in spreading a host of ancient technologies throughout Eurasia.

Though direct mention of these nomadic peoples is almost completely absent from Shang records, a number of objects in Shang tombs carry clear signs of their foreign origins. For example, Fu Hao's tomb contains a number of bronze and jade objects—most significantly, bronze mirrors—that only later would come into widespread use in China. For their part, the Shang circulated local and foreign items such as bronze vessels, weapons, and jade throughout the region and beyond.

Many of these foreign items have been found as far south as northern Vietnam, and the peoples of surrounding areas acknowledged Shang predominance in wealth and culture. The picture is complicated somewhat by the recent work on cultures that show a connection to artifacts uncovered at Shang sites, and even at Erlitou, but have distinct—almost exotic—regional variations. The most intriguing example is that of the strange elongated figurines of Sanxingdui [SAN-shing-dway] in Sichuan [SIH-chwan], well out of Shang-dominated territory. On the whole, however, widespread recognition of Shang sophistication marks, with the ascendancy of the Zhou, an important example of a recurring pattern of world history, as well as that of China: conquerors on the cultural periphery interacting with and adapting to the culture of the conquered.

The Mandate of Heaven: The Zhou Dynasty to 481 BCE

Unlike the Xia and Shang dynasties, the nearly nine centuries of Zhou rule are extensively documented in such literary works as the *Zuo Zhuan* [ZWOA-jwan] (*The Commentaries of Mr. Zuo*), the *Chunqiu* [CHWUN-chew] (*Spring and Autumn Chronicles*), and later compilations such as the *Shiji* [SHIH-jee] (*Records of the Historian*) by the second-century BCE historian Sima Qian [Sihma-CHIEN] in addition to the *Shujing*.

Like the *Shujing*, these other Zhou records contain much of questionable value and uncertain origin. Nevertheless, they suggest both an ongoing quest for social, political, and moral order as well as institutional and intellectual experimentation on a grand scale. They also provide us, in the closing date of the *Spring and Autumn Chronicles* (481 BCE), with an important transition point with which to end this chapter. As we will see in Chapter 9, out of the increasingly fierce competition among the Zhou states for expansion and survival in the succeeding Warring States period (formally 403–256 BCE but used to encompass the entire era from 480 down to the creation of the Qin empire in 221 BCE) came China's greatest flowering of philosophical and political theory and ultimate unification into an empire that would last, with brief interruptions, for over 2,000 years.

The Mandate of Heaven   By the twelfth century BCE, it appears through the trend of oracle bone inscriptions that the size of the Shang state had shrunk considerably due to encroachment by peoples to the north and west. The oracle bones also suggest an increased concentration of power in the hands of the last Shang kings, a situation depicted in the literary record as coinciding with their dissolution and corruption. Against this backdrop, the state of Zhou to the west—which, as we have seen, had become a Shang dependency—began to take military action. The *Shujing* tells of the Zhou kings Wen, Wu, and Cheng and Cheng's regent, the Duke of Zhou, systematically pushing their holdings eastward from 1122 BCE, taking much of the Shang territory under their control. Sometime around 1045 BCE, Zhou forces captured and burned the last Shang capital and stronghold near Anyang. In doing so, the Zhou sought to portray their conquest as morally justified after an overlong interlude of Shang decadence (see Map 4.3).

Unlike the rise and fall of states in other areas, conquest by one of the three dynasties, as depicted in the literary record, did not mean exile, extinction, or enslavement for those defeated. On the contrary, the conquerors were shown as presenting their victories as acts of moral renewal for those they conquered by ridding them of oppressive or degenerate rulers and restoring leadership to the worthy. Although the attitudes of the common people toward such shifts of

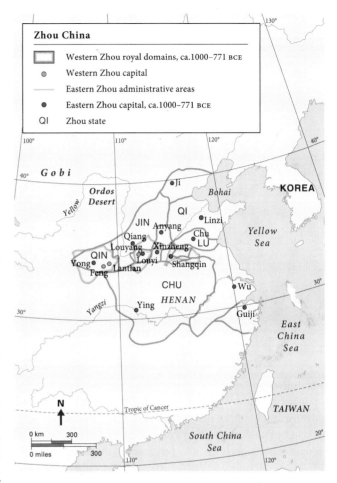

MAP **4.3 Zhou China.**

power remain unknown, the idealized speeches of the new rulers in the *Shujing*, for example, attempt to justify their actions and seek the cooperation of all classes in the new order.

As the compilers of this literary record, the Zhou sought to place themselves firmly within it. While it is unknown whether the practices they recorded had been widespread or newly invented by the conquerors, they provided the backdrop for one of China's most enduring historical and philosophical concepts: the Mandate of Heaven.

According to this idea, a dynasty's right to rule depends on the moral correctness of its rulers. Over time, dynasties grow weaker and tend to become corrupt as individual rulers give in to the temptations of court life or different factions seek to manipulate the throne. Under such conditions, rebellion from within or conquest by outside forces becomes morally justified. The success of such actions is then seen as proof that heaven's approval or "mandate" has been taken from the old rulers and bestowed on the insurgents, who may then legitimately found a new dynasty. Ultimately, however, the new dynasty, too, will decline. Thus, the fall of the Shang dynasty, as described in the *Shujing*, sprang from a loss of virtue, similar to that of the Xia, which had earlier resulted in Shang ascendancy. The idea of such a "dynastic cycle" operating as the driving force of history was later codified by court historians during the Han dynasty (202 BCE–220 CE).

Throughout Chinese history, these concepts not only allowed political renewal to take place internally but framed a remarkably durable system within which the Chinese and outside conquerors could interact and adapt themselves to each other in maintaining governmental and societal continuity.

Western Zhou and Eastern Zhou   By the end of the eleventh century BCE, nearly all of northern China as far south as the Yangzi River had come under Zhou rule. More precisely, a network of over 100 smaller territories was organized under Zhou control, marking the beginning of the Western Zhou era, which lasted until 771 BCE. Zhou rulers placed family, distinguished subjects, allies, and even some defeated Shang notables in leadership positions of these territories under a graded system of hereditary ranks. By the eighth century BCE, however, the more power-ful of these territories had begun to consolidate their holdings into states of their own. Though the states would continue to pledge their loyalty to the Zhou court, they increasingly worked toward promoting their own interests, which resulted in a weakening of Zhou political power. A half-century of war among court factions for ultimate rule, border struggles with nomadic peoples to the west and north, and a devastating earthquake further weakened Zhou power, resulting in the court being driven from its capital at Xi'an in 771 BCE and relocating to the east in Luoyang. This forced move began the Eastern Zhou period (770–256 BCE).

The Zhou in Decline   The Zhou system of decentralized government called *fengjian* [FUNG-jien], usually rendered as "**feudalism**," gave considerable auton-omy to its local rulers and was thus an important reason for the weakening of the Zhou central government and the strengthening of its dependent states. As these dependent states grew in power and their economies flourished, local rulers became less loyal to the Zhou leadership and some rulers even went as far as naming them-selves "king" (*wang*) of their own domains.

Feudalism: A system of decentralized government in which rule is held by landowners who owe obligations of loyalty and military service to their superiors and protection to those under them (we will see systems like this in Europe and Japan as well).

The prestige of the Zhou court was further weakened after its flight to Luoyang in 770. Continuing border problems with nomadic–pastoral peoples to the north and west around the Zhou home state and the relative isolation of its new capital drastically cut the flow of revenue from the dependent domains. This isolation was especially important since these states were in a period of tremendous economic expansion. Within a few generations of the inauguration of the Eastern Zhou in 770 BCE, Zhou control and power had significantly weakened in absolute as well as relative terms.

The Zhou decline is graphically described in the *Spring and Autumn Chronicles* and its accompanying work, *The Commentaries of Mr. Zuo*. Compiled in the Zhou state of Lu in the modern province of Shandong, these complementary works detail the maneuverings of states and individuals in northern China from 722 to 481 BCE. The world they depict is one in which repeated attempts at creating a stable political and social order among the 15 major Zhou states are frustrated by constantly shifting power dynamics and especially by the rise of dominant states on the Zhou periphery.

Hegemony: A system of state relations in which less powerful states directly or implicitly agree to defer to the lead of the most powerful state, which is, thus, the *hegemon*.

Early on, during the mid-seventh century, the most important of these states was Qi [Chee], which dominated northeast China and much of Shandong. By shrewd diplomacy and careful use of military power, Qi became the first "senior" or *ba* [bah] state in a system of **hegemony** in which the lesser Zhou states deferred to the *ba* state as the protector of the Zhou system. The successive *ba* states mounted alliances against non-Zhou states and attempted to regulate relations among those within the system. They also presided at conferences held from the mid-sixth century BCE aimed at regularizing trade and diplomacy among the states. Qi was succeeded by Jin, which reorganized the *ba* system and, in 579 BCE, sponsored a truce and disarmament conference among the Zhou states.

By the latter part of the sixth century, a rough balance of power among the four leading states of Jin, Chu [Choo] (the premier state of the southern periphery), Qi, and Qin (a rising force in the old Zhou homeland near Xi'an) held sway. While this system functioned for several decades, new powers on the peripheries, expansion into non-Zhou lands, and civil war in Jin ultimately precipitated the partition of Jin in 403 BCE, marking the formal opening of the Warring States period. By its close, Zhou itself had been absorbed by the combatants (in 256 BCE) and Qin would emerge as not just the dominant state but the creator of a unified empire in 221 BCE.

Economy, Society, and Family Adaptation in Ancient China

From Neolithic times, the Chinese economy has been based on agriculture. Even today, slightly more than half of the country's people are engaged in some variety of farm work. From early times as well, both the Yellow River states and those in the south of China outside of the control of the Shang and Zhou dynasties relied on a peasant subsistence economy based on family and clan landownership, with much of the local political power diffused to the thousands of villages dotting the landscape. While periodic concentration of landlord power and the problems of land-centered social relationships occupied Chinese rulers over the course of millennia, China, unlike some other agriculturally based societies, never developed an extensive system of slave labor.

Family life played a dominant role among all members of ancient Chinese society. Here, in a way parallel to trends in other agrarian kingdoms, the position of women in power among the elite eroded over time, a process that would be accelerated during the long interval of imperial rule. By the late Zhou period, the hierarchy of patriarchy and the growing influence of notions of *filial piety*—a model of behavior based on relationships among members of a family headed by the father—were on their way to becoming firmly established.

Shang Society

Though Shang leaders, like those of the Xia and Zhou, frequently moved their headquarters for political and military reasons, nearly all of their newly established capitals swiftly grew to proportions comparable to those developing in India and the Mediterranean.

Erligang   The capital city at Erligang [ARRH-lee-gahng] was characteristic of the late Xia or early Shang period. It had a defensive wall 4.5 miles in circumference, enclosing an urban center of about a square mile. The area within the walls was the province of the rulers, related families, diviners, and bronze casters and craftspeople in the direct service of the elites. Merchants and craftspeople involved in the manufacture of items other than bronze, jade, or ritual objects lived outside the city walls, as did peasants and slaves.

The life of the commoners in Erligang centered largely on communal agriculture. They tilled the soil with small plows, stone-tipped hoes, and assorted wooden implements, bronze being considered too valuable for use in agricultural tasks. They grew millet and vegetables as their staples and raised water buffalo, sheep in the more arid areas, chickens, and pigs. The pig, domesticated since at least Yangshao times, continued to be of central importance in the rural diet. Even today, the written character for "family" or "household" (家, *jia*) is represented by a character depicting a pig under a roof.

Social Class and Labor   Within the towns and villages immediately outside the larger cities, a more differentiated social structure was also developing, with artisans of various trades organized according to lineage. Many families and clans tended to pursue the same occupations for generations, and craft guilds and other organizations came to be dominated by family groups—such as potters and ceramics makers—as was the case later in imperial China. The constant warfare of Shang rulers and their increasing interest in monumental projects, for example, flood control along the Yellow River and its tributaries, all boosted the need for labor. Professional soldiers and local militia generally satisfied Shang military needs. Conscript labor, however, constituted an increasingly important part of the work force.

Interactions of Zhou Economy and Society

The large size of the territory claimed by the Zhou dynasty, and the enhanced trade that this expansion entailed, added to the wealth and power of all the rulers of its increasingly autonomous dependencies. The expansion of these dependencies to the Yangzi River basin brought much of east Asia's most productive farmland under some form of Zhou control and stimulated increased interaction with the inhabitants of the region.

Innovation and Adaptation in Agriculture   In the north, the introduction of the soybean from Manchuria, with its high protein content and ability to fix nitrogen in the soil, boosted crop yields and pushed growers to cultivate more marginal lands. The rotation of wheat and different varieties of millet allowed for more intensive farming. The use of more efficient ox-drawn plows and, from the fourth century BCE, iron-tipped tools as well as increasingly elaborate irrigation and water-conservancy efforts pushed yields even further. In the south, the Zhou dependencies, like the *janapadas* of India, developed rapidly as rice cultivation facilitated population growth. With the coming of intensive rice farming, the economic and demographic "center" of China moved steadily southward. By the middle of the sixth century BCE, the Zhou kingdoms taken together constituted the world's most populous, and perhaps richest, agriculturally based urban society.

Zhou Rural Society   The Zhou rulers devised a system of ranks for governing their dependencies based on the size of landholdings:

- *hou* [ho], the title given to rulers of the Zhou dependencies
- *qing* [ching], the chief functionaries of the *hou*
- *shi* [shihr], a general category for lower officials, eventually including talented commoners
- *shuren* [SHOO-ren], the remainder of the commoners

Members of the various ranks of the aristocracy were responsible for collecting taxes from their dependents and the *shuren* and were required to provide military service to those above in return for support and protection. Peasant cultivators worked their own lands, with the lands of the aristocracy often scattered in plots among those of the commoners.

The Well-Field System   In an attempt to untangle the more confusing aspects of this land arrangement, the Zhou were the first among many dynasties to attempt to impose a uniform system of land tenure in China. Later writers, most notably the philosopher Mencius, would look back nostalgically on the idealized *well-field system*—a method of land division said to have been devised by the Duke of Zhou. In this arrangement, each square *li* (one *li* is about one-third of a mile), consisting of 900 *mou* (each *mou* is approximately one-sixth of an acre) was divided into a grid of nine plots. Individual families would each work one of the eight outside plots while the middle one would be farmed in common for the taxes and rents owed the landowner or local officials. The term "well-field" comes from the Chinese character for "[water] well" (井, *jing*), which resembles a grid. Whether the system as idealized by Mencius was ever widely practiced is still a matter of debate among scholars. It did, however, remain the benchmark against which all subsequent attempts at land reform were measured, even into the twentieth century.

By the late 500s BCE, a substantial change had taken place in many of the Zhou states. The needs of individual governments to use the wealth of their states to support their militaries and developing bureaucracies prompted them to institute land taxes based on crop yields and, in some cases, commuting labor obligations to direct taxes payable in kind to the state. Depending on the state and the productivity of the land, these tended to vary from 10 to 20 percent of a family holding's yield. Then, as now, the taxes tended to affect the poor most.

The New Classes: Merchants and *Shi*   Further evidence for the decline of the Zhou feudal system is the rise of new classes. For the first time, the literary record now includes references to merchants. The growing power of this new class began, among other things, a long-term struggle with various governments for control of such vital commodities as salt and iron. It also marked the beginning of the perception of merchants as *usurpers*—a class with no ties to the land and thus no stake in the values of landholders or peasants—whose drive for profit from trafficking in the goods of others endangered the stability of Zhou social institutions. Accompanying the rise of a merchant class was the steady advance of a cash economy. The coining of money was becoming widespread by the late Zhou, including the round copper "cash" with the square middle hole—symbolically depicting heaven and earth—which remained almost unchanged for over 2,000 years.

Though often viewed with distaste by the landed aristocracy, merchants, with their wealth and expertise, were increasingly seen as resources to be tapped. Their rapid rise to economic prominence, however, meant that as a group their social position lay outside the traditional structures of agrarian life. Their independence and mobility, along with the steady growth of cities as centers of trade, helped spur political and economic centralization as the rulers of Zhou territories attempted to create more inclusive systems of administration. Direct taxation by the state, uniform law codes, and administrative restructuring were increasingly altering the old arrangement of mutual obligation between aristocratic landowners and dependent peasant farmers. Here, members of the new *shi* class—drawn from the lower aristocracy and wealthier commoners—who, like merchants, were divorced somewhat from the older structures of rural life, took on the role of bureaucrats and advisors. From the ranks of the *shi* would rise many of China's most famous thinkers, starting with Confucius; and the duties and proper conduct of the *shi* would come to occupy a prominent place in their writings from the late sixth century BCE on.

Central Asian Interactions   The growing wealth of north and central China spurred a dramatic increase in trade outside of the Zhou realm as well as among its constituent states, particularly in the south and along well-established routes into central Asia. As one measure of the extent of such interaction, scholars have pointed to silk threads appearing in the bindings of Egyptian mummies dated to 1000 BCE, in Greek gravesites several hundred years later, and even in central and northern European encampments from about 500 BCE. In this interchange, Zhou traders were increasingly helped by the carriers of the central Asian exchange.

By the sixth century BCE, a series of loosely related cultures along this northern front (called *Scythic* because of their broad cultural similarity to the peoples the Greeks called "Scythians") can be clearly discerned. These peoples appear to have taken Zhou goods much farther than originally thought, and scholars are only now beginning to realize the vast extent of their trade relations. What other goods besides silk may have been involved in such exchanges remains unknown, however, until the period of officially sanctioned and better recorded trade along the Silk Road began in the second century BCE.

Gender and the Family

While scholars have long explored the position of women and the family during China's imperial era, notably during the Song and Ming dynasties, serious study of gender roles in ancient China has only recently begun. One obvious reason for this is the relative scarcity of records during earlier times. Another is the development of women's instructional literature from roughly the first century BCE to the first century CE, a phenomenon that has provided modern scholars with an important focal point in charting a shift in perspectives of female "virtue" and proper behavior in the home and in public.

Elite Women of the Shang   In marked contrast to later Chinese court life, with its tightly proscribed etiquette and seclusion of wives and concubines from the avenues of power, elite women of the Shang often participated in political—and even military—affairs. As we saw in the opening of this chapter, one of the most complete Shang burial sites is that of Fu Hao, discovered in 1975. The most prominent of the 64 wives of Wu Ding, Fu Hao's burial artifacts—hundreds of bronzes, jade, and bone ornaments, as well as the sacrificial skeletons of sixteen people and six dogs—help bring to life a woman whose existence, though well established in written records, has otherwise been elusive.

The artifacts also shed light on a number of questions regarding Shang technology and material culture, court life, and especially the position of women among the aristocracy. For example, inscriptions on oracle bones in Fu Hao's tomb indicate that she wielded considerable power and influence even before becoming Wu Ding's principal wife. Prior to coming to court at the Shang capital of Yin sometime in the late thirteenth century BCE, she owned and managed a family estate nearby and was apparently well educated in a number of areas that would serve her well in palace life. She both supervised and conducted religious rituals at court and during military expeditions. As Wu Ding's chief confidant she advised him on political and military strategy and diplomacy. She even conducted her own military campaigns against Shang adversaries. The king apparently considered her so wise and beloved that after her death he frequently appealed to her for guidance through divination with oracle bones.

Artifacts Recovered from the Fu Hao Burial Site.

Women's Status in Transition   Elite women like Fu Hao appear to have shared a comparatively egalitarian status with male rulers, even to the point of leading armies and practicing divination. To the extent that such literature as the *Book of History* and the *Poetry Classic* of the early Zhou era address issues of women and power, women were still depicted as occupying important positions as mentors and advisors. Women's crafts such as spinning and weaving, and especially the different skills demanded in silk production, were highly regarded. In fact, there were government offices supervised and staffed by women to oversee silk and hemp cloth weaving.

The wives and concubines of rulers in many instances had their own sets of records and genealogies as well, an important asset among the powerful in this family-conscious society. Even by the late Zhou period, as one scholar notes, a "model" woman like Lady Ji of the state of Lu was able to instruct her son, the high official Wen Bo (Earl Wen), in the arts of government by comparing the roles of different officials to the proper arrangement of the components of a loom in the process of weaving. In this role of advisor, her virtue was much praised by subsequent thinkers.

Yet it was also true that by this time it was Wen Bo and not Lady Ji who actually held the reins of power. Late Zhou women might be well educated and highly capable, but they seldom ruled in their own right. In fact, the treaties hammered out during the Spring and Autumn period in many cases specifically barred women from involvement in state affairs. The same general trend may be glimpsed at other levels of society as well. The enormously complex web of family, clan, village, and class associations of the Zhou era reflects considerable respect for the wisdom and work of women; but these skills were increasingly seen as best exercised in the home instead of in the public sphere. The later development of state-sponsored Confucianism, with its preponderant emphasis on filial piety, ushered in a markedly secondary role for women.

Interactions of Religion, Culture, and Intellectual Life in Ancient China

In many respects, the evolution of Chinese religion follows a similar pattern to that of other agriculturally based urban societies. That is, like the gods of the early Mesopotamians, the first Chinese gods were local deities that inhabited a spirit world presided over by a ruling god. In China, the rulers' ancestors occupied the highest rungs of the spirit world and worship largely consisted of communication with them by various means. Religion was not separate from everyday life but permeated all aspects of it.

While they creatively adapted and adopted many other aspects of Shang culture, the Zhou era marked a turn toward a more abstract, impersonal, and universal concept of religion. In other words, Shangdi [SHANG-dee], the chief Shang deity—and other beings with superhuman powers but human-like personalities—began to give way to the more distant Zhou concept of "heaven" (*tian* [tien]) as the animating force of the universe. As in other religious traditions, there is a movement to go beyond the invocation of gods through proper sacrifice and divination rituals—*formalism*—in order to seek insight into the forces that control the universe. By the late Zhou era, this concept of heaven as the guiding cosmic force had become central to nearly every major Chinese religious and philosophical tradition.

Oracle Bones and Early Chinese Writing

Scholars agree that samples of Shang characters found on oracle bones are examples of China's earliest known writing, representing an entirely original system. One legend has it that the cultural hero Fuxi discovered writing from symbols etched on the back of a turtle, and indeed, the oracle bones themselves are mostly the undershells of turtles and the shoulder blades of oxen.

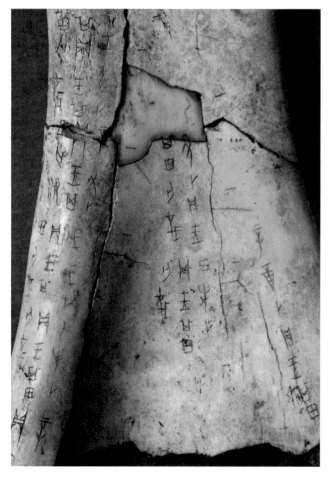

Shang Oracle Bone Inscription on Shoulder Blade of an Ox.

As we saw with Wu Ding in the opening of this chapter, those seeking guidance would have a diviner incise questions onto the bones. The bones were then heated and tapped with a rod, and the resulting cracks were interpreted as answers. Several thousand distinct symbols have been identified, and many are clearly ancient versions of modern Chinese characters. More importantly, the principles on which these symbols functioned as a form of writing had already moved away from those of other hieroglyphic or pictographic languages. Chinese characters became increasingly stylized and, after the Qin era (221–202 BCE), put into standard forms. But in most cases, these retained enough of their earlier character to be recognizable to later readers. Moreover, the political and religious significance of Shang and Zhou ritual vessels, which, in many cases, contained inscriptions in archaic characters, ensured that some knowledge of them would be preserved.

Shang Bronzes   While it now seems that, like the potter's wheel, some of the early bronze articles and weapons found at late Longshan sites may have come by way of trade routes from western Asia, bronze-casting techniques used in China quite likely diffused northward from southeast Asia at about the same time. The best evidence for this is that the "carved-clay" technique favored by Shang and Zhou casters—in which inner and outer molds of the object are made of clay and molten bronze is poured into the gap between them—is unique to China and radically different from the "lost wax" method of the peoples of western Eurasia. Shang and early Zhou ritual vessels themselves, with their richly stylized *taotie* [TAOW-tea-eh] motifs—fanciful abstract reliefs of real and mythical animals incorporated into the design—are utterly unlike anything outside of east Asia.

Shang Religion   The use of bronze vessels with their elaborately stylized *taotie* motifs constituted a central part of Shang religious ceremonies among the elites. Offerings of meats, grains (wheat, millet, and occasionally rice), as well as wine were a regular part of Shang ritual. Except for some limited references in later literature to offerings of wine and millet at local shrines and ancestral graves, we know little about the religious practices of Shang commoners. However, the growing number of artifacts and oracle bones found at the gravesites of elites and at the remains of royal palaces has considerably clarified the belief system of the rulers.

Ritual Vessel with *Taotie* Design Pattern.

The principal deity, Di or Shangdi, presided over the spirit world and governed both natural and human affairs. Shangdi was joined by the major ancestors of the dynastic line, deities believed to influence or control natural phenomena, and local gods appropriated from various Shang territories. The religious function of the Shang ruler, as it appears to have been for the Xia and would be for subsequent Chinese dynasties, was to act as the intermediary between the world of the spirits and that of humanity. Hence, rituals appear to have consisted largely of sacrifices to ancestors to assure their benevolence toward the living. As we have seen, the Shang sought the guidance of their ancestral spirits through divination on a wide variety of human affairs, such as royal marriages and military campaigns, and on such natural phenomena as droughts, floods, plantings, and harvests. Scholars theorize that many of the animals appearing as designs on ritual vessels represent messengers from the spirit world associated with divination.

As the Shang state grew more powerful and commanded more and more resources, the size and scope of the sacrifices also increased. Like the Xia, the Shang practiced human sacrifice. Excavations at both the early capital in the Erligang district of the modern city of Zhengzhou and later capitals near Anyang have yielded numerous sites containing headless skeletons. The evidence suggests that the death of a ruler was the occasion to slaughter hundreds of slaves, servants, and war captives, perhaps to serve the deceased in the spirit world.

Adaptations of Zhou Religion, Technology, and Culture

The Zhou, like other conquerors after them, sought to give legitimacy to their reign by adopting many of the forms of art and ritual practiced by the defeated Shang. As before, the ruler maintained his place as mediator between the human and divine

The Chinese Writing System

Of all the innovations commonly associated with China—paper, gunpowder, tea, the compass—perhaps the one with the longest-lasting impact was its unique writing system. Like many attempts at symbolic communication, such as those of the Egyptians, the Harappans, and, in the Americas, the Mayans, it was originally a system based on pictures. As with these other systems, the pictures became simplified and to some extent standardized for ease of interpretation. In its earliest form, for example, the Chinese character for the sun is a circle with a dot in the center. In its modern form it is still recognizable as 日.

Even in its archaic form, Chinese contained two basic types of characters: *pictographs*—pictures designating particular objects—and *ideographs*—pictures representing ideas—as well as some purely phonetic characters. Both types became increasingly elaborated and stylized, with the most basic characters acquiring phonetic components and compounds of simple characters formed to represent abstract expressions. For example, compounding the character 女, *nu* [neeu] (female or woman), with 子, *zi* [zuh] (child), created 好, *hao* [how] (good), an abstract expression symbolized quite concretely by a mother and child. Similarly, 女, *nu*, placed under the character for roof yielded the character, 安, *an* [ahhn], meaning peace or contentment. The characters for sun (日) and moon (月) placed together came to mean bright, 明.

The close association of the written language with early Chinese religious practices, court ceremonial functions, and self-cultivation and character development imbued it over the centuries with a kind of spiritual dimension not usually found among the written languages of other peoples. The patience and discipline demanded in learning the thousands of characters necessary for advanced literacy and the artistic possibilities embodied in the brush and ink traditionally used to write

worlds. But the Zhou also appear to have followed the trend toward more abstract religious ideas we have observed in other early civilizations.

Heaven   They introduced the concept of *tian*, "heaven," as a relatively neutral, impersonal controlling force of the universe, which eventually replaced the more approachable, human-like Shangdi. It was this more abstract heaven whose mandate gave the right to rule to all subsequent Chinese dynasties. Thus, throughout the long history of imperial China, the emperor retained the title of *Tianzi*, "son of heaven," as a symbol of his cosmic filial piety—his obligation to fulfill heaven's mandate as a son serves his father.

Iron Casting   Perhaps the most significant technological innovation introduced during the Zhou period was the use of iron. Late Shang and western Zhou tombs have contained iron objects of foreign origin, probably obtained from Indo-European peoples ranging across central Asia. By the seventh century BCE, basic technologies for mining and working iron are in evidence in western China. Significantly, it appears that the casting techniques of bronze production were adapted to this purpose. When them placed calligraphy at the top of Chinese aesthetic preferences. Thus, wherever written Chinese is used, skill at the three interrelated "excellences" of painting, poetry, and calligraphy is esteemed as the highest mode of self-expression.

The Chinese written language had a tremendous impact on the course of Asian history. While it requires extensive memorization compared to the phonetic languages of other cultures, it is remarkably adaptable as a writing system because the meaning of the characters is independent of their pronunciation. Thus, speakers of non-Chinese languages could attach their own pronunciations to the characters and, as long as they understood their structure and grammar, could use them to communicate. This versatility enabled Chinese to serve as the first written language not only for speakers of the Chinese family of dialects and languages on the Asian mainland but also for the Koreans, Japanese, and Vietnamese, whose spoken languages are totally unrelated to Chinese. The pattern of interaction and adaptation prompted by the acquisition of the written language allowed the vast body of Chinese literature, philosophy, religion, history, and political theory to tie the literate elites of these states together within a common cultural sphere. In this respect, it functioned in much the same way as Latin among the educated of Europe. Even today, despite the development of written vernacular languages in all these countries, the ability to read classical Chinese is still considered to be a mark of superior education. Moreover, the cultural heritage transmitted by Chinese characters continues to inform the worldviews of these societies.

Questions

- How did the pattern of interaction and adaptation that characterized the development of the Chinese writing system bring people together into a common cultural sphere?
- How does the impact of the Chinese writing system compare to the impact other writing systems have had in other parts of the world?

combined with the high-temperature technologies employed by Zhou potters, the Chinese produced the world's earliest cast iron. By the sixth century BCE, cast and wrought iron weapons, tools, and farm implements were in common use; and even some steel objects, including a sword, have been found. As in Gangetic India, they were instrumental in opening up new lands for cultivation and multiplying the deadliness of warfare.

Folk Culture: *The Book of Songs*   As noted in the previous section, we know relatively little about the lives of the common people during the period of the Xia, Shang, and Zhou dynasties. One of the few sources that does provide some clues is the *Shijing*, the *Poetry Classic*, sometimes called *The Book of Odes* or *The Book of Songs*. The subject matter covers a wide range of interest and emotion, from homely observations on the cycles of rural life to protests and cleverly veiled satire. It is believed that, in most cases, the verses were meant to be sung.

As historical source material as well as art, the *Shijing*'s songs and poems of the lives and loves, burdens and laments of peasants and soldiers, young wives and old men are still striking in their immediacy today.

Putting It All Together

The period from the first Neolithic settlements in the Yellow River valley to the birth of Confucius in 551 BCE witnessed the beginning of many of the foundations of the cultures of China and, through interaction with Chinese influences, east and southeast Asia. Like the other agricultural–urban cores in Mesopotamia, along the Nile, and in the Indus valley, the society that emerged in northern China was very much a product of its major river system. As early as 10,000 BCE, the Yellow River basin saw the rise of self-sufficient agricultural villages, marking the transition from forager to agrarian society. It was the early states that developed here that came to dominate the Chinese historical record. With the rise of the Xia dynasty late in the third millennium BCE, the first evidence of Chinese cities and the first people, places, and events traceable through later literary sources all make their appearance.

The Shang conquest of the Xia, traditionally held to be in 1766 BCE, marks the first flowering of China's "bronze age." The centering of political, military, and religious authority in one ruler; the development of a unique and versatile form of writing; the growth of cities; and the widespread use of bronze under the Shang in many ways run parallel to developments in the other early centers of civilization. In their casting techniques and design motifs of bronze ritual vessels and their system of writing, however, Shang contributions were original and long-lasting.

The theme of moral renewal came with the rise of the Zhou after 1122 BCE and was perhaps made retroactive by them as well. Nearly all of China from the Yangzi River basin north was incorporated into a decentralized governmental system centered on the Zhou court at Xi'an. But the growing power of the largest Zhou territories eventually eclipsed that of the court; and this began a prolonged era of struggle between the states. The increased wealth and power of rulers, aided by the drive of new social classes such as merchants and the *shi* to share in it, contributed to the breakdown of older feudal social patterns during the Spring and Autumn period from 722 to 481 BCE. Continual warfare stimulated both a drive for political consolidation and a questioning of the foundations of society. With the ideas of Confucius, to whom we turn at the beginning of Chapter 9, a radical direction in conceiving the nature and aims of society would soon take place. His ideas, adopted by a Chinese imperial system that would last over 2,000 years, would profoundly affect hundreds of millions of people inside and outside of China in the centuries to come.

▶ For additional resources, including maps, primary sources, visuals, and quizzes, please go to www.oup.com/us/vonsivers. Please see the Further Resources section at the back of the book for additional readings and suggested websites.

Thinking Through Patterns

> How did the interplay of environment and climate help to influence the earliest patterns of Chinese civilization? How do historians address the question of whether "geography is destiny" in this case?

The relationship of environment to the ways in which a particular culture lives is at once seemingly obvious and quite complex. In the case of northern China, the river both allows a large, reliably fertile area for cultivation to be maintained and restricts the ability to live too close to it because of flooding. Not surprisingly, the collective efforts of the early Chinese states to control the river proved central to the character of these states. But what kinds of larger conclusions can we draw? Some scholars in the past theorized that early civilizations based around rivers developed many similarities in their patterns of governing, such as centralization, bureaucracy, and elaborate labor regulations. But here, the key is in the details: How similar can we say Egypt is to Shang dynasty China? As for the larger question of geography and destiny, most historians would say that it is an important *conditional* factor, among many others, in determining how a civilization develops. But rarely can it be seen as *destiny*—as a *sufficient cause*.

Among other things, these remains can suggest the kinds of plants and animals that were domesticated, the kinds of shelters that housed people, how gender roles were assigned, how they handled their dead, and how they defended themselves. Many of these things are open to debate however. Chinese scholars in the People's Republic, for example, believed that such Neolithic villages were matriarchal and matrilineal; those from outside are less sure of the evidence for this. If true, the later switch to the strong patriarchal tradition represents an important change in the structure of Chinese families.

> What can the remains of Neolithic Chinese settlements tell us about the continuities and disruptions of Chinese history?

> How did the Zhou concept of the Mandate of Heaven operate?

The Mandate of Heaven, as we have seen, was at once a way for the Zhou to retrospectively legitimize their conquests and to create a precedent for future moral renewal. As part of a dynastic cycle, it set the fundamental pattern for the way the Chinese tended to view history. The rule of a particular dynasty was expected to advance in reform and expansion in its early stages, reach a comfortable point of harmony in its middle stages, and go into moral and material decline in its final stages. From that point, revolt breaks out and heaven transfers its mandate to a new dynasty—*if it succeeds.* If not, the rebels have committed the worst of crimes. There is a definite closed logic to this system: Heaven approves, so the rebels succeed; the rebels succeed because heaven approves. This pattern of dynastic cycle and heavenly mandate made China's historical experience—conveniently fitted to the theory—not only comprehensible but also predictable. Alert rulers constantly searched for signs that the mandate was in danger; the people themselves often speculated about portents or natural disasters as presaging dynastic change. Even China's modern rulers are heirs to this pattern: During human-made and natural disasters the Communist Party is even more alert to possible signs that the people are expecting a "dynastic" change.

Chapter 5 30,000-600 BCE

Origins Apart: The Americas and Oceania

North
America

Mesoamerica

Oceania   South
America

**THE AMERICAS
AND OCEANIA**

I n a dramatically understated press release from the Chicago Field Museum dated April 26, 2001, anthropological archaeologists Ruth Shady Solis, Jonathan Haas, and Winifred Creamer announced a stunning discovery in the archaeology of the Americas. The scientists had just finished conducting radiocarbon dating tests on plant fibers taken from site excavations of Caral, in the Supé valley in Peru. Though largely ignored for over a century, the site had recently stirred considerable interest because of its immense size (over 200 acres), monumental architecture—pyramids more than 60 feet high and nearly 500 feet square at the base—and evidence of early urban living. The test results, however, now demanded a complete retelling of the main narrative of the history of civilization in the Americas.

Because earlier evidence pointed toward a relatively late arrival for modern humans in the Americas and given the difficulty of domesticating staple grain plants—corn, for example, it was believed, took at least 1,000 years to breed into a useful food crop—the earliest known American civilizations had been assumed to be much more recent than their earliest Eurasian and African counterparts—until now, that is. For decades, discoveries in North and South America had strongly suggested that humans had migrated much earlier than previously thought, calling into question their puzzlingly swift occupation of the continents.

ABOVE: Ruins at the first Andean city site (c. 2700 BCE) at Caral-Supé.

But the Caral-Supé [Ka-RALL Soo-PAY] results, published in the journal *Science*, put the date of the materials tested at 2627 BCE, making the city as old as the pyramids of Egypt and the most ancient Mesopotamian cities. Indeed, work at nearby sites showed that they had been occupied by substantial villages for far longer, that the entire area was supported by elaborate irrigation works, and that Caral-Supé is only one of 18 similar urban sites in the Supé valley. Clearly, the human urge to create cities, monumental architecture, and religious sites ran deep enough to manifest itself thousands of miles away from other early models.

The Americas represent a vital counterpoint to the development of agrarian-based cities and states in Eurasia and Africa, which we have discussed in earlier chapters. In some ways, the parallels run very close:

- the development of urban centers as religious and trade centers
- the role of staple food surplus accumulation
- the kinds of buildings—pyramids, for example

Yet some of the differences in the civilizations provide enticing puzzles. For example, Caral-Supé appears to have been thriving long before ceramics turn up in Peru, an innovation that in all cases *predated* cities in Eurasia and Africa. In addition, although there is some evidence of record keeping by *khipu*, the much later system of knotted ropes used by the Incas, there is no writing—again, something the major Eurasian civilizations developed. Finally, as with later American civilizations, there is no evidence of the use of the wheel for transportation or mechanical work. Thus, in our search for patterns of world history, the Americas provide an entirely independent test case for examination and analysis.

- In Chapter 1, we examined the "big bang" of world history: the origins of human society in Africa and the first great pattern of human subsistence: foraging.
- In Chapter 2, we learned about the next great pattern of people moving from foraging to farming societies and some of the consequences that change brought.
- In Chapter 3, we explored how this pattern can be replayed and remixed in different ways—in some cases, like that of the Harappans, moving from an urban society back to village farming or foraging.
- In Chapter 4, we learned more about how civilizations become centralized, while at the same time how regional powers can challenge the forces of centralization.

In Chapter 5, we will see examples of all of these patterns but conditioned by the key variable of *separation*. How do we explain these similarities and differences appearing in societies separated by thousands of miles of ocean and with no evidence of contact? A vital part of our examination springs from interactions and adaptations. How did these take place thousands of miles away in the Americas and the islands of the Pacific? How do the critical elements of environment and culture play out in such societies separated from the intense contiguous contact among societies in Eurasia and Africa? How do they alter the patterns we have examined? How much

Seeing Patterns

▶ What do historians see as the advantages and disadvantages of the separation of the Americas from the societies of Eurasia and Africa?

▶ The wheel is often cited as the most basic human invention, yet large and sophisticated civilizations were able to flourish without this signal innovation. Why do you think it did not develop in the Americas?

▶ Why did no cities develop on the larger Pacific Islands?

more or less bearing do environment and culture have on the human societies on the thousands of islands of Oceania? How did the peoples interact with each other and adopt or reject certain innovations? Indeed, how "isolated" were they from each other and the societies of Asia, Australia, and the Americas? Finally, given the importance that we place on interaction and adaptation among peoples, what advantages and disadvantages did such separateness bring?

The Americas: Hunters and Foragers, 30,000–600 BCE

The remoteness of human beings on the American continents from the larger and more interconnected societies of Eurasia and Africa raises one of the key questions of world history: What would people do in places far removed from other human communities over long periods of time? The initial great migration out of Africa had equipped human beings with an assortment of tools, practices, and habits that collectively created an effective *foraging*—or hunting and gathering—type of society. As we read in Chapter 1, human foragers spread out to populate the earth in Eurasia and Australia, and the coming of humans to the Americas in many ways represented the final stage of their great migration from Africa.

The advances and retreats of the great ice sheets of the northern polar regions over the last 75,000 years allowed several possible opportunities for humans to migrate from the Eurasian landmass in search of game. Exactly when *Homo sapiens* began to move into these new lands, however, is at present a highly controversial question. Migration might have begun as early as 40,000–30,000 years ago, though only now has enough archaeological evidence accumulated to support dates before about 13,500 years ago. After this date, the number and range of humans multiplied rapidly on the two continents, forming small, highly mobile forager bands.

Yet, even at this stage, the migrants had begun to adapt the technology of spears, bows, and other hunting equipment to the big game of the new continent with astonishing swiftness. And as the success of their hunting began to reduce the populations of their favored game, a question arises for world historians: Would they now follow the same patterns by undergoing a Neolithic revolution and developing practices and institutions similar to those of humans in Eurasia and Africa?

It does indeed appear that they did. During the period from about 6000 to 4000 BCE, in what is today Mesoamerica (Mexico and Central America), and the Andes Mountains in South America in Ecuador and Peru, people began to settle in villages. They domesticated squash, beans, corn, and, somewhat later, potatoes and founded the first forms of agrarian society in the Americas. Separated by thousands of miles and vast bodies of water from the peoples of Eurasia and Africa, they were nevertheless traveling independently along the same crucial early pattern of world history: moving from foraging to farming and to settled life—until, ultimately, they built great cities, states, and empires. As we will see, however, there were also some important differences in their modes of subsistence and technology in the processes involved in the creation of these new societies.

The Environment

Next to Eurasia, the two continents comprising the Americas encompass the largest landmass on earth. From the perspective of Europe, they form the Western

Hemisphere, that is, the western "half" of the "sphere" or globe. Located north and south of the equator, the Americas are geographical mirror images of each other, sharing similar types of landscape and climate, though their shapes differ considerably.

The Americas' most prominent geographical feature is a contiguous spine of mountain ranges, or **cordilleras** [cor-dee-YEH-ras], near or along the entire western coast. Known as the Rocky Mountains in the north, these ranges become the Sierra Madre in the center and the Andes in the south. Water from these mountains feeds nearly all river systems, of which there are eight in the north and four in the south. Both continents also share low mountain systems along their eastern coasts. North and South America meet in Mesoamerica near the equator, with North America then reaching northward to the North Pole and South America extending southward almost to Antarctica. Thus, the climatic zones of both South and North America range from extreme cold to subtropical and tropical warmth.

Cordilleras: A continuous spine of mountain ranges near or along the entire western coast of the Americas.

Geographical Regions   North America consists of four main geographical regions:

- The Rocky Mountain region
- The Canadian Shield, which stretches from today's Canada to Greenland
- The Great Plains and central lowlands in the center of today's United States
- The Appalachian Mountains in the east and the broad coastal plain along the Atlantic Ocean

The four regions not only are distinct geographically but also vary considerably in precipitation and temperature. Historically, they have resulted in widely differing modes of subsistence and society among their inhabitants from the time of the first migrants through much of the history of present-day Canada, the United States, and Mexico, as well as among interior regions of all three countries.

Mesoamerica and South America form five distinct geographical regions:

- The Central American mainland and the Caribbean islands
- The Andes Mountain region along the west coast
- The Guyana Shield and Amazon basin in the northeast
- The Brazilian Shield and *Gran Chaco* in the east
- The Patagonian Shield, in the center of the continent's southern tip

Here, the size of the mountains and the extent of the rain forests dictated even greater regional separation than in North America until recent times.

During winters in North America, freezing winds from the Arctic blow south across the Canadian Shield into the central plains, or American Midwest. By

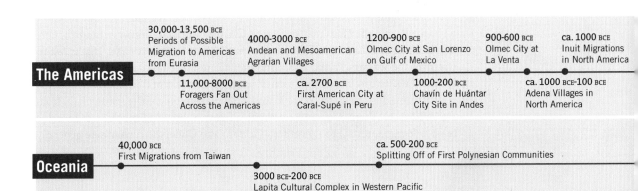

contrast, at the southern tip of South America, air currents are predominantly westerly and more moderate and do not push winter frost very far northward. Thus, apart from the southern tip at Cape Horn and Tierra del Fuego—the site of some of the world's most violent seas and frequent storms—snow and frost are mostly limited to the Andes. In North America, winter and summer temperatures vary greatly, except in Florida and southern California, as do precipitation levels, especially in the western half of the continent. Generally, the eastern and midwestern regions of North America receive regular rainfall throughout the year, while the western regions and lower Pacific coast tend to be drier, with occasional droughts, and intermittently subject to massive forest fires started by lightning strikes.

In Mesoamerica, the Caribbean, and the northern two-thirds of South America, temperatures and humidity levels tend to be relatively high. Large steppe and desert areas cover the western one-third of North America, while in South America deserts and steppes are more limited and mostly found along the northwestern coast and in the interior of the south. Prior to modern times, large forests covered the eastern two-thirds of North America and the northern half of South America.

Ocean Currents, Hurricanes, and El Niño   Like the monsoon system that wields so much influence in the agricultural life of India, China, the Indian Ocean, and western Pacific regions, large-scale weather events governed at least in part by the actions of ocean currents and continental weather systems have played historical roles in the Americas. Unlike the monsoon systems, however, their cycles have only recently come to be understood.

Running roughly parallel to the eastern coasts of northern South America and nearly all of North America, the Gulf Stream current of the Atlantic Ocean moves warm water from the south Atlantic along the Eastern Seaboard of the United States before heading northeast toward the European coast. There, it moderates the climate of northern Europe and the British Isles despite their high latitudes. In the Americas, the Gulf Stream's interactions with changing wind patterns in fall and winter in eastern North America frequently result in large storms called "nor'easters," a phenomenon first studied by the American scientist Benjamin Franklin.

More destructive is the frequency with which the Gulf Stream guides hurricanes into the Caribbean Sea and along the North American coast. The immense "heat pump" of the African interior and Sahara Desert continually spawns tropical disturbances in the eastern Atlantic, which gain strength over the warm waters there and the Caribbean as they move westward. Historically, the east–west winds that drive the tropical disturbances played a vital role in fostering the trans-Atlantic slave trade by making navigation swift and predictable. In the case of hurricanes, however, the storms are often picked up by the Gulf Stream, fed by its warm waters, and directed north from Cuba along the North American coast, where, in modern times, they have caused immense destruction in this heavily populated area.

In the Pacific, the Humboldt and Japan Currents work in a similar fashion, though, in relation to the direction of their waters in the Americas, in reverse. That is, warm waters of the western Pacific and along the Japanese Pacific coast move northward toward the Aleutian Islands and then down the west coast of the Americas. Like the Gulf Stream, this has a considerable moderating effect on climate, particularly from the coast of southern Alaska to northern California, home to much of the world's temperate rain forests. From northern California to Chile, the currents are generally cooler than the surrounding ocean and provide important fish and marine mammal habitats. For millennia, these supplied the peoples of the west coast with sustenance and allowed settled life with a minimum of agriculture.

The Pacific region is also home to the **El Niño** phenomenon, which, though little understood until recently, plays an immense role in global climatology. In cycles that vary from 3 to 8 years, large areas of abnormally warm water appear off the coasts of Peru and Chile (El Niño), which lowers barometric pressures there and raises them in the western Pacific. The results tend to vary but usually alter the jet stream patterns and cause abnormal rainfall and storm levels over large areas of the globe, particularly in the Americas. The reverse phenomenon, La Niña, occurs when the oceans in the region have large areas of abnormally cold water.

El Niño: A periodic reversal of the normal flow of currents in the Pacific, greatly altering weather patterns.

Human Migrations

As we saw in Chapter 1, one of the most hotly contested debates in modern archaeology is who exactly were the first people to appear in the Americas, and where did they come from? Part of the debate revolves around the authenticity of sites and the accuracy of techniques used to date them; part of it also arises from legal and political issues of who can claim to be the "first" Americans and have rights to the contents of such sites. Generally, however, scholars agree that the earliest period down to 7000 BCE is that of the *Paleoamericans*, whose remains indicate that they are from different areas in Asia, while later arrivals are classified as *Native Americans* (also often called *Amerindians*).

To give some idea of the scope of the problem, some scholars believe that the earliest immigrants might have been people similar to those migrating to Australia. Genetic evidence, however, suggests that later migrants came from southeast and northeast Asia. Complicating the picture even further, as we saw in Chapter 1, Kennewick man, discovered in 1996 on the banks of the Columbia River in Washington State and dated to ca. 9,300 years ago, has been determined to be genetically close to south Asians. Thus, the earliest populations of the Americas may have been far more ethnically diverse than had previously been supposed (see Map 5.1).

When the northeast Asians, the ancestors of the Native Americans of today, arrived is difficult to determine and one of the most contentious problems in American archaeology. Researchers working on Siberian sites have so far been unable to establish connections with the Alaskan sites that are assumed to be the places from which people migrated through the Alberta ice gap into North America around 13,500 years ago. What is known, however, is that these Alaskan immigrants, who formed initially only one group among many others, eventually around 7,000 years ago became the dominant population of "Native Americans."

Early Foragers   One of the ways in which scientists have attempted to track and date the migrations of early Americans is through their hunting technology. The earliest arrivals hunted with *stabbing spears*—weapons meant to be thrust into an animal's body or thrown from a very short distance. During the period from 11,000 to 8000 BCE, such spears were equipped with a stone point that was flat or "fluted" on both sides. These fluted sides allowed the spearhead to be inserted into a groove cut into one end of the spear and fastened there with a leather strip. As in Eurasia and Africa, the size and shape of spearheads and arrowheads provide valuable clues to regional variations in technology and, by tracking these, on migration patterns.

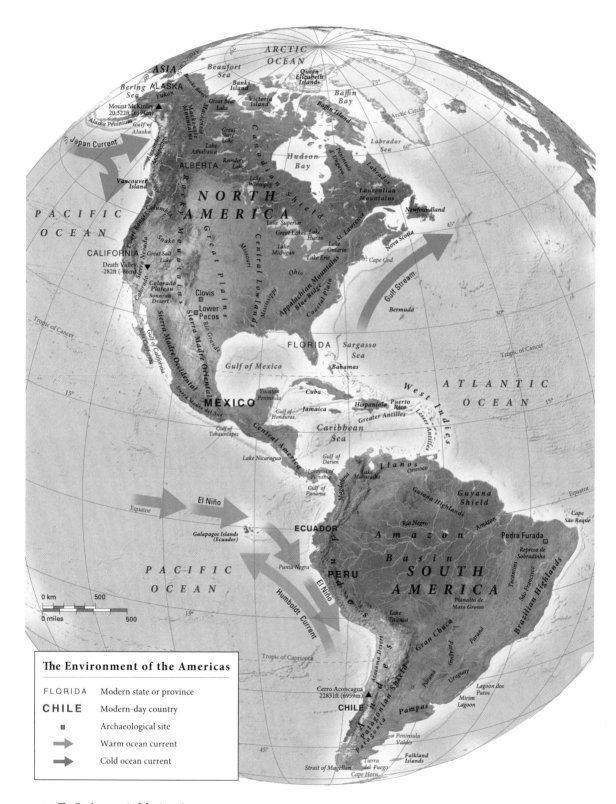

The Environment of the Americas

FLORIDA	Modern state or province
CHILE	Modern-day country
▪	Archaeological site
→	Warm ocean current
→	Cold ocean current

MAP **5.1 The Environment of the Americas.**

In North America, where the spearhead flutes were oval, they are known as "Clovis points," from the town in New Mexico near where scholars identified them for the first time in the 1930s. The pervasiveness of Clovis points in the north and a fishtail style of spear flutes in South America had suggested to scholars until very recently that their users were indeed the first migrants to the continents. It was also widely thought that their close dating and specialized use in big-game hunting indicated that these people had settled both continents within a few years of arriving and had, in short order, killed off most of the prehistoric big game such as mammoths, mastodons, ground sloths, and tapirs. The absence of Clovis points in Eurasia, and the presence of less sophisticated points and tools at the newly examined earlier sites (such as Buttermilk Creek in Texas), however, now seem to suggest that the Clovis people had already been here for some time. Indeed, these points might be seen as the first distinctively "American" innovations.

Like their counterparts we examined in Chapters 1 and 2, these early American settlers were hunters and gatherers, or *foragers*. They formed groups of extended families and lived in rock shelters, caves, and huts, moving whenever the food resources in a given territory were exhausted. Once a year, during the summer, extended families met to commemorate a common ancestor by sharing food and performing other rituals. Families held initiation ceremonies for adults, arranged marriages, and exchanged goods such as obsidian, copper, mica (a mineral that flakes off in transparent sheets), and seashells. Most of the time families stayed in their own territory, collecting wild foods such as grass seeds, roots, berries, mushrooms, fruits, and nuts.

As we have seen, the fluted spear points were designed specifically for hunting big game, such as mammoths, moose, and bison. Killing these animals would have required repeated stabbing, for which securely fastened points were necessary. The warming climate, however, favored the expansion of forests but was increasingly unfavorable to the survival of big mammal species. As big game became scarce, hunters shifted to smaller spear points and smaller game, such as antelope, deer, and rabbit. By about 8000 BCE most big mammal species were gone from the Americas.

Toward Settlements   As larger game became increasingly scarce, people in coastal areas began relying more on fish and shellfish and those in arid regions increased their collection of wild seeds and nuts. Hunters developed the spear thrower, a device for hurling smaller spears from a greater distance at elusive small animals. Obsidian, recovered from volcanic regions and traded over long distances, became the preferred material for spear points. Following a pattern similar to that of their distant relatives in Eurasia and Africa, humans in the Americas learned to grind, groove, and polish stone to make axes, mortars, pestles, and grindstones. Bone became an important material for spears, fishhooks, awls, needles, combs, and spatulas. Humans continued to live in rock shelters and caves, but now they began to construct huts made of poles and covered with skins or even more permanent wooden structures. These more permanent dwelling places appeared especially along the seacoasts, the Great Lakes, and large rivers, with plentiful resources of fish, shellfish, and waterfowl. The first domesticated animal, the dog, appeared, perhaps descended from the wolves picking through human **middens** or perhaps accompanying hunters migrating to the new continents. As bands of hunters and gatherers acquired more household goods, they became less inclined to move about over large

Midden: A refuse pile; archaeologists treasure such piles because a great deal can be learned about the material culture of a society by what the people threw out over long periods of time.

The White Shaman, Lower Pecos, Texas, ca. 2000 BCE. The practice of *shamanism*—the belief in the ability of certain individuals to communicate with spirits or inhabit the spirits of people or animals—appears to be a common feature of many widely diverse peoples. Many scholars believe that migrants from Asia carried these religious forms with them to the Americas because of the resemblance to practices among peoples in Siberia and other areas in northern Eurasia.

distances. As in Eurasia and Africa, they increasingly tended to stay close to favored long-term food sources and centers of ceremonial life.

Early Ceremonial Life   As did their contemporaries in north China, more sedentary foragers began to bury their dead in cemeteries, which soon became territorial centers. Hunter–gatherers in the Americas, like those on the other continents, buried their dead with gifts of ochre, symbolizing the color of life, and tools to help them in the life after death. Leaders of hunter–gatherer bands were often *shamans*, elders with spiritual powers that enabled them to deal with the forces of nature. By donning animal masks, playing music on flutes and drums, and engaging in ritual dance, shamans fell into ecstatic trances. During these trances they experienced themselves merging with powerful animals or other people, charming animals into submission, exorcising evils from humans, or healing afflictions. Leaders worked together with elders, forming councils for the administration of their settlements and hunting grounds.

Shaman-led ceremonies often took place in caves or overhangs, where people painted animals and humans on the rock walls. Probably the oldest paintings are those of Pedra Furada [PAY-drah Foo-RAH-dah] in northeastern Brazil, dating to about 8000 BCE. One of the most distinct paintings in the ceremonial vein is that of the so-called white shaman at Lower Pecos in Texas, dating to 2000 BCE. He is shown in a trance, leaving his body behind. His feet are feline, his arms are feathered, and he is surrounded during his spiritual journey by animals and humans, both dead (upside down) and alive (upright). Hunter–gatherers possessed

Pedra Furada, São Raimundo Nonato, Piauí, Brazil, ca. 8000 BCE. One of the earliest cave paintings in the Americas, and particularly striking because of its location in Brazil, this artwork perhaps depicts ceremonies related to warfare.

a complex culture, ranging from sophisticated gathering and hunting techniques and settlements ordered by elders to shamanic religious ceremonies.

Agriculture, Villages, and Urban Life

As we have seen in the preceding chapters, far-reaching changes accompanied human societies that made the transition from foraging to agriculture—from hunting and gathering to relying principally on domesticated plants and animals. The first major change we see associated with this momentous pattern is the ability to maintain large populations: to sustain villages, towns, and cities, developing increasingly complex societies with ever more diverse intellectual, cultural, and religious spheres. The second change is the opposite side of the coin: the potential for conflict and destruction on an unprecedented scale. Both of these changes grow from the Neolithic revolution (see Chapter 2). In the Americas, however, this grand pattern of world history appears to have begun somewhat later than in many areas of Eurasia and Africa.

The Neolithic Revolution in the New World

The most noteworthy first steps toward agriculture took place in central and southern Mexico in Mesoamerica and Ecuador and Peru in the Andes. Temperatures in these regions turned warmer after about 4000 BCE. Foragers shortened their annual migrations and extended existing patches of wild bean and **teosinte** [tay-oh-SIN-tay] (believed to be a wild grass precursor of maize) through purposeful planting. Careful harvesting and replanting, probably with obsidian-spiked sickles, led to early domesticated varieties of these plants, increasingly bearing larger kernels. Beans were domesticated first in Peru, and maize/corn followed somewhat later in southern Mexico. By about 3000 BCE, foragers in these regions had completed their transformation into farmers (see "Patterns Up Close").

Teosinte: a wild grass native to Mesoamerica, believed to be critical in the development of maize (corn).

Early Domestication of Plants and Animals   Humans in Mesoamerica and the Andes exchanged their domesticated species of beans and corn within their regions and began trading other domesticated staples as well. In Mesoamerica these included squash, manioc (a root), avocado, and chili pepper; in the Andes, quinoa (a seed), amaranth (an herb), potatoes, yams, tomatoes, and cotton. In time, these plants spread via trade throughout both regions wherever the climate and soil would support them.

The domestication of animals in the Americas, however, was more modest than that of plants. Unlike Eurasia and Africa, the majority of large mammals had died out after the last Ice Age, with the result that no draft, pack, or riding animals of sufficient size were left to be domesticated (see Figure 5.1). The Americas thus had no horses or cattle until they were brought by the Spanish in the sixteenth century CE as part of the so-called Columbian exchange of plants, animals, and diseases traveling both directions. The development of the wheel, so intimately connected with draft animals, with its nearly infinite uses on plows, chariots, carts, and other conveyances, never took place in the Americas, though some of the world's best roads were built through the Andes. The only animals suitable for domestication—besides the dog—were the llama, alpaca (both relations of the camel), guinea pig (a rodent), muscovy duck, turkey, and honeybee. The llama, whose capacity is limited to carrying about

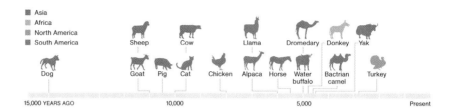

Figure 5.1 Comparative Timeline for Domestication of Animals.

60 pounds for 12 miles per day, was the only animal in pre-Columbian America to provide even modest transportation services. The wool of the alpaca, together with cotton, became an important textile fiber in the Andes. In the relative absence of domesticated animals raised for meat, hunting and fishing remained important methods of obtaining food (see Figure 5.1).

Early Settlements   Early agricultural settlements ranged in size from a few extended families to as many as 1,000 inhabitants. As in Neolithic China, the typical dwelling was a round, dome-shaped, wooden house with a sunken floor, stone foundation, and thatched roof. As in southwest Asia, some early American agrarian peoples mummified their dead by salting or smoking them before burial. Others buried their dead in midden piles on the outskirts of their villages or in the sand dunes along the beaches. Funeral gifts were modest, usually consisting only of the cotton clothes worn during life and a red mat—symbolizing the blood of life—wrapped around the body. In contrast to more transient hunter–gatherer settlements, agrarian villages became settled communities of the living and the dead.

Between 3000 and 2000 BCE, villagers in the lowlands along the Andes coast of Peru built rafts of balsa wood, which enabled them to fish farther from shore. They also pioneered the use of irrigation in the dozens of river deltas along the coast. With crop yields boosted by irrigation, the population of the villages increased to 2,000 or 3,000 inhabitants and the first signs of social stratification and distinctions in wealth appeared. Scholars have speculated that upstream families had more water and, thus, accumulated greater food reserves than downstream families. Under the leadership of upstream elders, inhabitants of several villages pooled their labor and built monumental plazas, platforms, and terraces in central locations in their settlements.

As had other societies making the agrarian transition, Mesoamerican and Andean societies also began producing pottery, which was used in the preparation and preservation of food. The earliest known pottery dates to about 3300–3200 BCE on the northern Andean coast; by 1800 BCE pottery making had spread throughout central and southern Mexico. Cotton textiles dating to about 3000 BCE have been found along the coasts of Ecuador and Peru. Richly colored pieces of cloth served as skirts and overcoats. Condors with outstretched wings, double-headed snakes, felines, and human figures were typical motifs on the textiles.

The Origins of Urban Life

As we saw in the opening vignette to this chapter, in 1994, archaeologists began excavating the ruins of a large, planned city covering over 200 acres at Caral in the Supé River river valley in Peru. Caral-Supé, was one of at least 18 sites of a culture that flourished in the valleys descending from the Andes to the coast. Researchers were stunned at the monumental stone architecture that included what appeared to be pyramid-shaped temples, plazas, a wide variety of dwellings of different sizes, and, perhaps most intriguing of all, a large amphitheater. As important as the initial survey of the sight turned out to be, its significance grew further in 2001 when carbon dating revealed the artifacts at the site to be from 2627 BCE, making this by far the oldest city in the Americas and contemporary with the early Mesopotamian cities and the Great Pyramid of Egypt. As Jonathan Haas, one of the scientists involved in the dating, noted, "This is a project that comes along once in a generation and offers opportunities rarely glimpsed in the field of archaeology."

Caral-Supé   Scholars now theorize that this city, like the similarly mysterious sites along the Indus, was part of a fairly large civilization supported by intensive agriculture and fishing, with extensive trading networks and an incipient class system. They have linked the Caral-Supé culture to the ruins at Aspero, on the Peruvian coast, which contain similar pyramids but had been previously covered by centuries of trash heaps. The varied climate, ranging from the coast through lowland plains and river valleys up to mountain highlands, produced pumpkins, squash, yams, corn, chilies, beans, and cotton, while the rivers and sea yielded a variety of edible aquatic life. The agriculture of the valley was supported by a highly complex and sophisticated irrigation system utilizing mountain runoff and directing water to individual plots (see Map 5.2).

Farmers were the largest social class, with merchants, administrators, and priests also in evidence, though it is not clear at this point exactly what constituted the hierarchy. Widely varying sizes of houses suggest disparities of wealth, and the proximity of some of the houses to pyramids seems to indicate a religious or bureaucratic

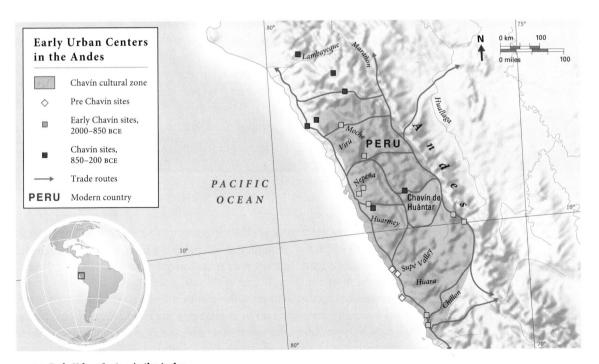

MAP **5.2 Early Urban Centers in the Andes.**

Patterns Up Close | The Origin of Corn

We have no idea who they were nor exactly where they might have lived nor even exactly when the momentous event took place. We do not know whether the idea occurred to a number of people simultaneously or to one lone experimenter. We assume, given the unprepossessing nature of the plant in question, the *teosinte* grass, that it did not suggest itself as a productive food crop, or even as edible, for quite some time. Yet, when these first bold people began to cultivate it, they were unknowingly taking part in one of the most momentous revolutions in world history: a completely independent chapter in the transition from foraging to agriculture and, ultimately, to agrarian-based urban civilization. The ultimate result of their work, maize, or corn, became the staple of the great Mesoamerican civilizations, sustained the early peoples of North America, and ultimately became the world's most versatile and widely grown food crop (see Map 5.3).

Various Types of Corn.

The site where we believe the event took place, somewhere in what is now southern Mexico, may have been inhabited by human beings for as few as 7,000 or 8,000 years. And it was here, perhaps 6,000–7,000 years ago, that they began the process of cultivating this unpromising grass into the grain that would shortly sustain vast numbers of people. Yet, to this day, plant geneticists are still not in agreement as to how this transition took place.

It was long assumed that *teosinte* was the sole ancestor of corn and that the process was one of painstaking selection and replanting. That is, people would inspect a group of plants and search for the ones with the largest and most numerous kernels and then plant them and repeat the process over many generations, hoping over time to select for those desirable qualities. Given the *teosinte* limit of eight rows of tiny seeds, it was assumed this process would take hundreds, perhaps thousands, of years. Yet, the short time between the known dates of early corn cultivation and the rise of corn-supported societies suggests that the transition was much faster. Because of this, scientists have recently theorized that corn is in fact

connection; but the exact nature of these remains the subject of speculation. Similarly, the uses to which the amphitheater was put can only be guessed, though pictures of musicians suggest that they were an important part of festivals held there.

Perhaps the most intriguing artifact of all is an intact khipu, a device of elaborate knotted ropes tied together in patterns that form a coded system of communication, a kind of writing system by means of knots. Since the khipu was also used by the Incas over 4,000 years later, it represents not only a direct connection between these two societies but one of the world's first, and oldest, systems of record keeping in continuous use.

the result of crossbreeding more than one species of plants.

The most promising results so far were presented by plant geneticist Mary Eubanks in 2004, who attempted to experimentally trace the origins of corn. Her experiments showed convincingly that *teosinte* was, in fact, an ancestor plant of modern corn but that it had at some point been bred with *gamagrass*, which contains key genes for multiplying and enlarging the kernels on each ear. Moreover, her work supported the work of other recent research that suggested that the plant had evolved very rapidly into a usable staple, perhaps in less than a century.

We have to assume that this momentous feat was accomplished by plan and experimentation, given its complexity. The result was one that permanently altered the agricultural patterns of world history, particularly over the last 300 years. Corn's versatility allows it to be cultivated on every habitable continent; in dry or moist, hot or cool climates; and often on land too marginal to support any other staple crop. It is widely used as human and animal food and helped to sustain population expansions in North America, Asia, and Europe. It spawned huge industries in such modern foodstuffs as syrup and oil and older ones like whiskey and beer. Most recently, and controversially, it has been touted as a biofuel. In short, this American innovation's uses are still unfolding as we wrestle with the problems of population, land use, and energy consumption.

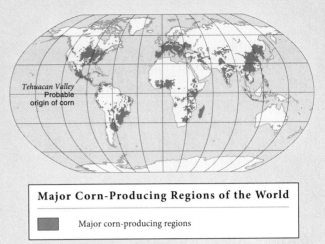

Major Corn-Producing Regions of the World

Major corn-producing regions

MAP **5.3** **Major Corn-Producing Regions of the World.**

Questions

- Why is the innovation of corn a "momentous revolution in world history"?
- Does the fact that this example of bioengineering occurred 6,000–7,000 years ago put today's debate on genetically modified foods into a new perspective?

Other Andean Cultures   Of smaller scale and a somewhat later period are the structures at El Paraíso, Peru, which date from about 2000 BCE. To construct these monuments, villagers built large rectangles of locally quarried rock and mud mortar. They filled the interior of the rectangle with rock rubble encased in large mesh bags, which may have been used to measure the amount of labor each villager contributed. Multichambered and multistoried buildings made of stone occupied some of the platforms. Steep staircases led from the lower plazas up to these buildings, which were plastered and painted in primary colors. Wooden beams supported the roofs.

Charcoal-filled pits in the building chambers indicate that some form of sacrifice took place there. The chambers were small, allowing access to no more than a few prominent villagers or shamans. The rest of the villagers assembled on upper and lower platforms according to their social status, to participate in religious functions and share communal feasts. Early sculptures dating to 1519 BCE depict ancestral warriors and suggest that villagers might also have come together for military displays.

Farmers in the Andean highlands also built ceremonial centers in their villages. As in the lowlands, these centers contained fire pits for sacrificial offerings. The buildings were, however, much smaller, with only one or two chambers, and stood on modest platforms. Highlanders, in addition to farming, engaged in long-distance trade, exchanging obsidian and cotton from the highlands for lowland pottery. Sometime around 1500 BCE, highlanders developed skills in metallurgy (perhaps including smelting), thus laying the foundation for the development of exquisitely crafted metalwork, including copper, gold, and silver.

Chavín de Huántar

While our understanding of the early Caral-Supé culture is still in its infancy, more extensive work on the later small highland city of Chavín de Huántar [Cha-VIN de Oo-WAN-tar] (ca. 1000–200 BCE) has yielded important insights into Andean cultural patterns. Situated in a valley high in the Andes Mountains on both banks of a tributary to the Marañón River, the modern town was connected by a bridge, which was destroyed in a landslide in 1945. A 3-day journey from both coast and rain forest and at an elevation of 10,000 feet, Chavín carried on an organized long-distance trade, built and graded roads, protected them with retaining walls, and cleared a number of mountain paths to facilitate travel. Residents of Chavín imported obsidian, used in the making of sharp tools, and metals and exported textiles, pottery, and gold and silver artifacts.

Chavín de Huántar, New Temple. Chavín is one of the best studied sites and over the years has yielded considerable information about town and small-city life in the ancient Americas.

Early Chavín was a small place of some 300 inhabitants, most of whom—including priest-rulers and craftspeople—were detached from agriculture. Another 700 full-time farmers and herders lived in outlying hamlets. Farmers grew potatoes, quinoa, and some corn on the slopes and valley floor, supplementing the rainfall with irrigation. Corn was used not only for making bread but also for brewing a type of beer, called *chicha*. On the higher grasslands, herders bred llamas and alpacas. The dried meat and wool of these animals contributed substantially to the village economy, as did the llamas' role as pack animals.

Chavín's ceremonial center consisted of U-shaped ramparts built on a plaza and lined with walls of cut and polished stone. The walls enclosed several partially interconnected underground complexes. Within the U was a round, sunken court accessible via staircase. A cross-shaped, centrally located chamber contained what is assumed to have been the center's main deity, a stone sculpture of a fanged, snarling feline creature, standing upright like a human, with one clawed paw extended upward and the other hanging down. The sculpture might have had a shamanic significance, symbolizing the priest's ability to assume the powers of a wild animal.

Other underground chambers were used for sacrificial offerings. Remnants of pottery once filled with the meat and bones of animals—as well as human bones—found in these chambers suggest animal and human sacrifices. An elaborate system of canals guided water through the underground chambers. Priest-rulers and the assembled villagers used the temple complex to offer sacrifices, observe open-air rituals, celebrate feasts, dance, and perform music.

By around 500 BCE, the population had grown to about 3,000 inhabitants. Artisans living in the town began to specialize in particular crafts. Craftspeople living in one section of town made beads and pendants from seashells, artisans in another section fabricated stone tools, and a third section of the town housed those who made leather goods. Whether these craftspeople had given up agricultural labor completely is not known. Homes for the wealthy were built of stone, while the less well-off lived in houses made of adobe. The rich dined on the meat of young llamas; poorer residents subsisted on the meat of decommissioned pack animals. Around the town, there must have been a number of villages with farmers producing enough food to feed the urban dwellers.

The increased population meant larger assemblies, which in turn required bigger platforms and a larger temple for more sacrifices. Laborers added a square, sunken court, a feature common to many Andean and Mesoamerican cities, and additional underground chambers, mostly for storage. By 400 BCE, Chavín had become the culturally dominant center of the region. Large numbers of travelers, traders, and pilgrims from the coast and rain forest visited the temple. Travelers made offerings of seashells, coca leaves, and textiles to the priests in return for receiving temple blessings, presumably for their health, welfare, and safe return. Residents of Chavín provided services for the visitors, such as lodging and meals. Craftspeople produced clothing, wall hangings, banners, and pottery in what were identifiable Chavín patterns, motifs, and styles. Archaeologists have found Chavín artifacts as far as 350 miles away.

Inhabitants of Chavín pioneered new techniques in the making of textiles and in metallurgy. Textile makers combined the wool from llamas with cotton to create a new blended cloth. They decorated it using new methods of dyeing and painting adapted to wool fibers. Goldsmiths devised new methods of soldering and alloying gold and silver to make large ornamental objects. Small objects, such as golden headbands, ear spools, beads, and pins, signified prestige and wealth. Gold artifacts found in the graves of the wealthy attest to the value residents of Chavín placed on gold.

Chavín came to a gradual end, perhaps declining as other centers began producing equivalent pottery, textiles, and gold jewelry and competing in trade. In any event, sometime after 500 BCE, archaeologists note a decisive trend toward militarization, with the emergence of fortified villages and forts. Possibly, the people of Chavín ultimately fell victim to a military attack. Sometime around 200 BCE,

Pectoral, Chavín de Huántar. The skillful working of gold was practiced by ancient Andean and Mesoamerican peoples, down to the Aztecs and Incas. Shown above is a pectoral—an ornament worn on a person's chest.

it appears that squatters invaded the largely deserted city, which subsequently fell into ruin.

The First Mesoamerican Settlements

In Mesoamerica, the first permanent villages appear to date from around 1800 BCE. The first ceremonial centers, the collaborative work of farmers from several villages, appeared along the Pacific coast of southern Mexico and Guatemala around 1500 BCE. As in the Andes, the ceremonial centers consisted of plazas, platforms, and terraces. Metallurgy, however, did not develop here for another millennium, and instead, craftspeople used jade for ornaments. (The Spanish believed that this green, translucent gemstone was useful in the treatment of kidney stones, *piedras de hijada*—hence the Anglicized word *jade* for the stone.) By around 1200 BCE, agrarian society throughout the Andes and Mesoamerica was characterized by ceremonial centers centrally located among several villages, monumental structures of plazas and platforms, and an emerging craftsmanship in the production of sacred ornaments.

Olmec Jade Mask. Like the Chinese, Mesoamerican peoples appear to have worked jade from very ancient times.

The Olmec   The first important Mesoamerican center was that of the Olmecs at San Lorenzo (1200–900 BCE), located on the Gulf of Mexico in hot, humid, and forested coastal lowlands. The name "Olmec" means "rubber people" in the language of the later Aztecs and refers to the rubber tree farming for which the area was later known. Farmers in these lowlands had to cut down the dense tropical rain forest with stone axes and burn it before they could plant corn. Once the riverbanks had been cleared, the silt deposited by floods during the rainy season and the rich soil created

Colossal Olmec Basalt Head. Among the most notable monumental statuary in the Americas are the giant heads sculpted from hard basalt by Olmec craftspeople. The one pictured here is from San Lorenzo, though exactly what its religious significance might be is as yet not known.

favorable agricultural conditions. As in Mesopotamia, Egypt, India, and China, the rivers here
proved marvelously productive. It is estimated
that farmers harvested as much as 3,200 pounds
of corn per acre from the riverbanks, a yield twice
as plentiful as that in the villages of the Mexican
valleys and highlands to the west. The high yield
allowed for the rise of wealthy ruling families,
who assumed a dominant position over small
farmers (see Map 5.4).

The ceremonial center of San Lorenzo was located on a plateau overlooking the surrounding
rain forest, villages, and fields. On this plateau,
archaeologists have so far unearthed some 60 terraced platforms, 20 ponds, countless basalt-lined
drainage troughs, and the foundations of dwellings for 1,000 inhabitants. These dwellings were
arranged around small family plazas. Among the
household goods found in the dwellings were
grindstones for preparing corn and tools for mak-

MAP **5.4 Olmec Civilization.**

ing beads and ear ornaments. The dense concentration of dwellings suggests that San
Lorenzo was an urban center, inhabited by priests, administrators, and craftspeople.
Based on estimates of crop yields in the area and the number of dwellings at the site,
scholars believe that this center was surrounded by some 10,000 small farmers dispersed in outlying villages and hamlets and producing the surplus food needed to feed
the urban center.

The priest-rulers of San Lorenzo engaged thousands of farmers as laborers to
construct the plateau and its terraced platforms. Laborers quarried blocks of basalt
from a mountain range 70 miles to the northwest of San Lorenzo. Large groups of
workers shouldered beams from which the basalt blocks, weighing 18 tons on average, hung in slings. They carried these blocks to the coast and shipped them to
San Lorenzo on rafts. There, sculptors fashioned the blocks into fierce-looking, hel-
meted heads, kneeling or sitting figures, and animal statues.

It is unknown whether these figures represented priest-rulers, gods, or divine beings. Olmec priest-rulers also commissioned sculptors to craft figurines
and masks of clay. Other craftspeople made figurines from jade and serpentine.
One jade figurine is that of a jaguar with a human body representing perhaps the
rain god. Like the legendary *werewolf*—a human being who is transformed into a
wolf when the moon is full—scholars have speculated that these figures might be
were-jaguars. That is, the figurine might indicate rituals in which priests possessed
shamanic powers shared with jaguars and other wild animals. Since jade and serpentine could be obtained only from areas some 200 miles away, San Lorenzo
appears not to have been an isolated urban center with surrounding villages but a
place with far-reaching trade connections.

La Venta   Around 900 BCE, a mysterious event took place that destroyed San
Lorenzo. Perhaps a religious calendar cycle was completed and a ruler ordered the
destruction of the urban center. Perhaps there was an internal uprising, with farmers

protesting their oppression by the ruling priests and administrators and then offering ritual atonement. Whatever occurred, the event left San Lorenzo's large stone sculptures mutilated and buried in carefully prepared graves, along with the sculptors' tools used in creating the images.

Following the fall of San Lorenzo, La Venta, 50 miles to the northeast, became the leading Olmec center. The first settlers at La Venta cleared the rain forest from a ridge on a swampy river island in the lowlands and then, like the Harappans on the Indus, graded the ridge to create a plateau. On the plateau they erected terraced platforms and a fluted, 100-foot-high earthen mound to establish an urban center. Burial sites at La Venta contained axes and figurines made of serpentine and jade as well as concave mirrors ground from hematite and other iron-bearing ores. Rulers' regalia included mirrors worn on the chest, but what significance these might have had is unknown.

Three of the burial sites at La Venta contained 485 pieces of serpentine carefully arranged to form a stylized jaguar face. Only two sites contained human remains as the extremely acid soil of La Venta dissolved most human bones. The burial gifts in the site included ochre, figurines, beads, ear ornaments, and awls made of jade. About 600 BCE La Venta ended under circumstances as mysterious as those that destroyed San Lorenzo. The next Olmec center was at Tres Zapotes, a more modest complex 70 miles to the northwest. Tres Zapotes endured from about 500 to 1 BCE, when it was eclipsed by new ceremonial centers in the highlands west of the Olmec lowlands.

Through their long-distance trade, the Olmecs left a strong cultural impact throughout Mesoamerica. Olmec traders, probably accompanied by armed escorts, obtained the obsidian needed for making stone-sculpting tools in Guatemala and jade from mines south of the Valley of Mexico and in Guatemala and Costa Rica. In exchange for these raw materials, the Olmecs exported cacao beans—from which chocolate is obtained—pottery, textiles, and jewelry. Along their trade routes, the Olmecs maintained settler outposts to supply the traders, mostly westward toward the Valley of Mexico, to which they exported their artistic styles.

Olmec Writing   In 2006 an announcement came that, like the work at Caral-Supé, redefined the archaeology of the Americas. Scientists at Cascajal in Veracruz, Mexico, found a large stone with what is currently believed to be Olmec writing on it. Dating to somewhere between 900 and 1100 BCE, it appears to be the oldest writing in the Americas. Moreover, it is unlike any of the later scripts of the Mayas or Aztecs and thus seems to have died out as a system with the decline of the Olmecs.

Like Egyptian hieroglyphics and Chinese Shang era scripts, the Olmec characters contain stylized representations of objects like fish, insects, and plants but also some that seem to have a phonetic component. Unfortunately, the samples contained on the Cascajal stone and a stone roller stamp dating from a few centuries later are simply too small to be deciphered. With the accumulation of other samples in the future it is hoped that the fragments of an Olmec literature may ultimately come to light. In the meantime, like the Linear A script of the Minoans and the seal figures of the Harappans, the Olmec figures present scholars with an important challenge in decoding the past.

Foraging and Farming Societies Outside the Andes and Mesoamerica

After 2000 BCE, many foragers in the forests, deserts, and tundras in North and South America had adopted agriculture as a full or partial mode of subsistence. While most societies in the Andes and Mesoamerica had become fully agrarian by around 2000 BCE, foraging groups in the places already mentioned continued to persist—in some places down to the present. Using stone tools, they hunted in the extreme north, slowly cleared the forests that covered the entire east and midwest of North America, irrigated and farmed arid areas of the southwest, and foraged and farmed in the Amazon basin of South America.

The Inuit   The Inuit [INN-ooh-it] from Siberia arrived in the far northern tundra of North America around 2000 BCE. For a long period the Inuit remained traditional hunter–gatherers, hunting mammals on land and fish in the rivers and sea. Much later, during the first millennium CE, they began hunting whales. As many as 20 sailors with paddles manned a boat built of walrus ribs and skin. In the summer, boats sailed the coastal seas for weeks at a time. When sailors spotted a bowhead whale, they shot a toggling harpoon into the animal. The head of the harpoon detached, burrowing into the skin of the animal. After many more harpoon shots and a long struggle, sailors killed the whale, hauled it ashore, and stored the fat and meat in ice. A whale carcass could feed a hamlet for an entire winter.

The Inuit lived in pit houses framed by whale ribs, covered with walrus skin, and piled over with sod. The entrances were long, dipped tunnels that trapped the cold air below the floor of the house. On winter hunts for seals and walruses, people built snow houses, or *igloos*, from ice blocks. During the summer, the Inuit moved from the often waterlogged pit houses to tents. Women were expert seamstresses, using caribou sinew and seal and caribou pelts to make warm and watertight pants, parkas, and boots. For transportation on snow and ice, the Inuit used dog teams to pull sleds made with bone runners. They traded mammal teeth and carved bone artifacts for timber and earthenware from the south. By 1000 CE the Inuit had expanded from the North American Arctic eastward, eventually reaching Greenland, where the Norse from Scandinavia had established their first settlement in 982 CE.

Adena and Hopewell   Agricultural villages appeared in the cleared forest areas of North America by the first millennium BCE. Village inhabitants planted sunflower, goosefoot, sump weed, and corn. The villagers of the Adena (1000–100 BCE) and Hopewell cultures (200 BCE–500 CE) pooled their labor to build

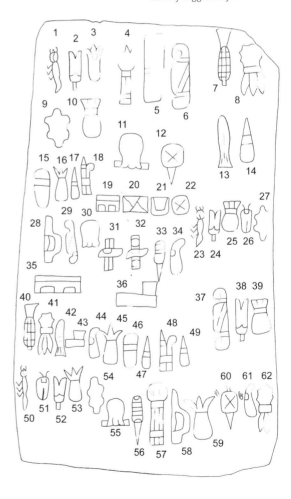

Cascajal Block. Currently the oldest example of writing found in the Americas, this sample dates from the Olmecs of the early first millennium BCE. Notice the stylized renderings of objects and placement horizontally, rather than vertically. What kinds of things do they suggest to you?

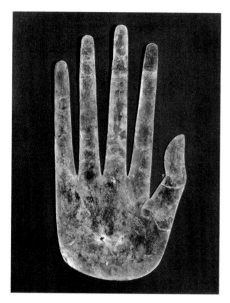

Hopewell Artwork. This delicately carved hand, made of mica, was excavated in Ohio. It was likely worn for public display.

ridges and mounds used in ceremonies and rituals. The phenomenon of mound building, a practice with very ancient roots, seems to have been widespread among peoples living in the east and midwest of North America. A small mound covering a child's grave found in Labrador is estimated to be some 7,500 years old. Others, much larger and more recent (about 4,500 years old), have been found in the lower Mississippi valley; some of these mounds are more than 20 feet high. In the case of the earthworks at Hopewell, large square and circular enclosures contained multiple mounds, tens of feet high, encompassing dozens of acres of land. Research from the mid-1990s suggests that some of the Hopewell settlements were also connected by roads up to 60 miles long, perhaps serving communal purposes of official visits and gift exchanges (see Map 5.5).

Amazonian Peoples   In the flood plains of the Amazonian rain forest in South America, agricultural villages also date to the first millennium BCE. The best-explored culture is that of Marajó, on a large

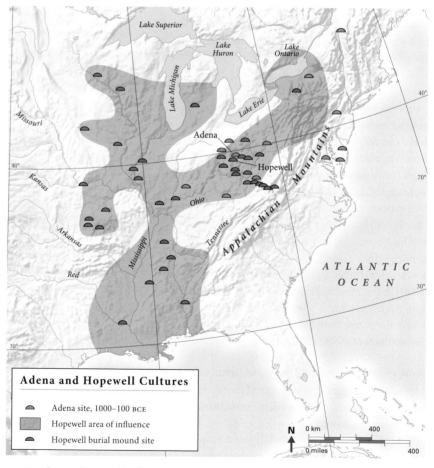

Adena and Hopewell Cultures

⬢ Adena site, 1000–100 BCE

▨ Hopewell area of influence

⬢ Hopewell burial mound site

MAP **5.5** Adena and Hopewell Cultures.

island in the mouth of the Amazon. At its height in ca. 500 BCE, the Marajó built large funeral mounds 30 feet high and 750 feet long. Depending on their social status, the dead were buried with modest grave gifts or in richly painted, jewelry-filled urns. The cultures of the flood plains in the upper Amazon drainage are still largely unexplored. For example, at an unknown date, the people of the Baures culture in today's Bolivia established a large hydraulic complex of canals, raised fields, moat-enclosed villages with sacred precincts, and causeways connecting the villages. The complexity of this culture left a strong impression on the Spanish missionaries who visited the area in the sixteenth century CE.

The Islands of the Caribbean   The earliest hunter–gatherer settlements in the rain forests of the Caribbean islands date to the fourth millennium BCE, but from where on the mainland these first settlers came is unknown. The first agricultural settlements appeared between 500 BCE and 500 CE, when migrants from the rain forests along the Orinoco River in the northeast of South America colonized the eastern Caribbean as far west as Hispaniola (today's Dominican Republic and Haiti). These people built villages and terraces on which they grew manioc. Their ceramics are in the shape of or painted to display a variety of animals, such as frogs, bats, and turtles, indicative of a shamanic religion. Beginning in eastern Hispaniola around 500 CE, villagers supported the emergence of the Taíno [Ta-EE-no] chieftain society that by ca. 1500 CE comprised nearly the entire Caribbean. Influenced by Mayan culture (see Chapter 6), some Taíno chiefs built ball courts and causeways. In their villages, the chiefs employed specialized craftspeople for the production of ceramics, cotton textiles, as well as stone and woodcarvings. Sailors using canoes traveled extensively to the mainland and among the islands in search of salt, jade, and metals. These travels connected the Taíno chiefdom society with Mesoamerican societies on the mainland.

The Origins of Pacific Island Migrations, 6000–600 BCE

If the early societies of the Americas show how the great patterns of world history can achieve striking variations in separation from other groups, the peopling of the thousands of islands of Oceania may be seen as an extreme case of the interaction of these patterns with culture and an environment apart. In prehistoric times, Asians traveled in multiple waves not only to the Americas but also to the islands of the Pacific and Indian Oceans (see Map 5.6).

The populating of Oceania must rank as one of humankind's greatest feats. Unlike the comparatively short distances involved in establishing human societies on the islands of the Caribbean or Mediterranean, vast amounts of ocean had to be routinely crossed between many of the island groups in the Pacific in order to settle them. Such trips were considered epic voyages as late as the eighteenth century CE. Yet, these early seafaring people settled island after island, traveling restlessly until they had discovered nearly every island of Oceania. As we saw in Chapter 4, their homeland appears to have been Taiwan and the Indonesian-Philippine archipelagos. Using computer-assisted linguistic analysis, modern scholars have now theorized that the people of Oceania are at least partially related to Taiwan's

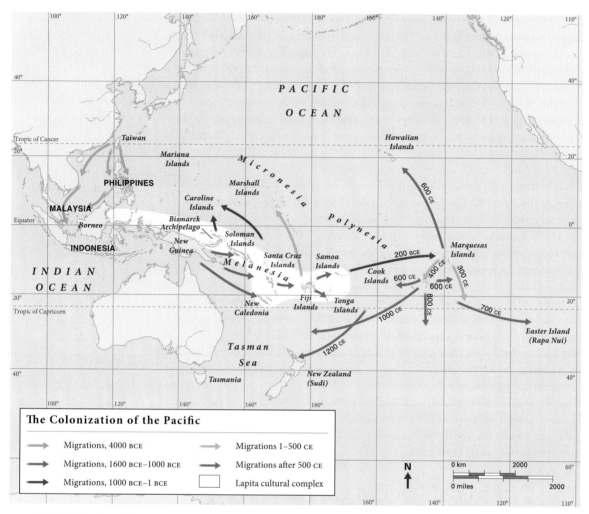

MAP 5.6 **The Colonization of the Pacific.**

aboriginal population (about half a million members today), mostly concentrated in the central mountains of Taiwan. About 6,000 years ago, the first seafaring people left Taiwan and, together with subsequent waves of emigrants, spread out in westerly and easterly directions. They settled in the Philippines, Indonesia, and the Malay Peninsula, bestowing their languages and ethnic identities on the aboriginal peoples of these lands.

In later times, descendants of these settlers, all speakers of languages belonging to the Austronesian family, spread farther into the Indian and Pacific Oceans. In the Indian Ocean, they sailed as far west as Madagascar, the island off the east coast of Africa, where they arrived around 200 CE and founded a number of chiefdoms. In the Pacific Ocean, they sailed to the Bismarck Archipelago, off the eastern coast of New Guinea. It was on this archipelago that settlers created the Lapita culture in ca. 1600 BCE, which was the homeland for the colonization of Oceania—that is, the islands of Polynesia, Micronesia, and parts of Melanesia. On the map, Oceania forms a huge triangle encompassing Hawaii, New Zealand, and Easter Island.

Lapita and Cultural Origins

By the fourth millennium BCE, a sophisticated system known as the Lapita Cultural Complex had already become well established. Named for a site on the island of New Caledonia, the Lapita culture was a system of kinship-based exchanges among the inhabitants of thousands of islands running from Borneo to the edge of Melanesia in the western Pacific. Of particular importance was obsidian, which, as in the Americas, was highly prized as a material for tools and weapons in the absence of workable metals. Another item in demand was a distinctive kind of pottery decorated with stamped patterns called Lapita Ware, after shards located at that site.

Environment and Long-Distance Navigation

By about 1600 BCE it appears that a number of factors had also come together to allow for decisive innovations in long-distance navigation over hundreds of miles of open sea as well as systematic colonization of otherwise uninhabitable islands. The development of ever larger and more sophisticated sail- and paddle-driven oceangoing canoes, stabilized with outriggers or double hulls, provided reliable craft for such journeys. An extensive, orally transmitted storehouse of navigational information—much of it still retained by Polynesian elders today—enabled sailors to set their courses by the sun and stars, retain elaborate mental maps of islands visited, read winds and currents, and take advantage of seasonal reverses in prevailing wind directions.

Bwaimas, **Papua New Guinea.** Some of the earliest known human attempts at agriculture took place in the highlands of Papua New Guinea perhaps 7000–9000 years ago. The introduction of yams several millennia later created an enduring staple crop, and their portability allowed their spread as they sustained seafarers throughout the Pacific.

Perhaps the most important development centered on supplying such voyages. Here, the cultivation of easily storable root crops, especially yams and taro, proved invaluable in sustaining long voyages. Among other staples circulated about the newly colonized islands were breadfruit, coconuts, and bananas, as well as such domesticated animals as pigs, chickens, and dogs, which entered the trade system from southeast Asia, the Philippines, and Indonesia. Over the centuries from 1600 to 100 BCE, Lapita sailors moved eastward and settled the islands of Vanuatu, Tonga, Fiji, and Samoa. Archaeologists believe that Fiji may be the ultimate source of the culture that sparked the next outward migration: that of the Polynesians.

Creating Polynesia

As populations grew, the primary mode of governmental and economic organization, the kinship-based chiefdom, became increasingly elaborated. On Tonga, the Society Islands, the Marquesas, and later the Hawaiian Islands, the power of local chiefs extended to nearby island systems. Even here, far removed from outside influences, the inclination of human societies toward centralization and its tension with smaller regional societies that we saw in Chapter 4 is apparent.

Conflict, Interaction, and Expansion   What effect such centralization and the increasingly intensified agriculture of staples in the more productive islands may have had on their inhabitants is uncertain. Up to a point, it may have made these societies more efficient as food producers. But the difficulties we have seen in other societies of sustaining large populations on limited amounts of land were undoubtedly intensified in an island society. Some researchers have theorized, for example, that environmental problems related to overpopulation may have developed in the Cook Islands and the Marquesas around 500 BCE and again in 200 BCE. Political disputes arising from the struggles between centralizing and decentralizing factions may have played a role as well. In any case, there seems to have been a break around 500 CE that resulted in the longest period of migration yet: to Hawaii around 600 CE, Easter Island (Rapa Nui) about 700 CE, and New Zealand by 1200 CE. In the cooler climates of Easter Island and New Zealand the introduction of the South American sweet potato—one of the rare examples of hypothetical Polynesian interaction with continental societies—allowed for a diversity of staple crops to support the population.

Later Interactions   By the time of the first European contact in the early sixteenth century CE, nearly every habitable island had been settled and some, Hawaii and New Zealand perhaps most dramatically, had populations of many hundreds of thousands. As we shall see in subsequent chapters, however, this vast achievement of exploration and colonization would soon be threatened by disease and a new breed of conquerors and colonists. Like the Amerindian cultures of the Americas, disease would reduce the populations in some of these islands by perhaps as much as 80 percent. The next three and a half centuries of European exploration of the Pacific would carry with them untold and, all too often, disastrously unforeseen consequences.

Polynesian Sea-Faring Canoe.
During the first millennium CE, Polynesian navigators struck out across hundreds and, in some cases, thousands of miles as they colonized far-flung island chains from Tahiti to New Zealand, Easter Island (Rapa Nui), and Hawaii. One reason for their success was an extensive astronomical lore and knowledge of winds and currents that allowed celestial navigation from memory over long distances. Another stemmed from advances in ship design as in the vessel pictured here.

Putting It All Together

Though separated from each other by thousands of miles of ocean and spawning radically different cultures, the Americas and Oceania share common patterns with each other as well as with the cultures of Eurasia and Africa. The first pattern that historians can see is that even in such widely separated areas human foraging communities at roughly the same time *independently began a process toward the development of agriculture and animal domestication.* While domestication of the first plants and animals and gathering into more settled village life began shortly after the last retreat of the glaciers in Eurasia, it came somewhat later in the Americas, perhaps because human groups were still rather scattered and few in number and could be sustained by large-game hunting. The many different types of plants available as food—especially legumes—were relatively high in protein, an important feature as large game became increasingly scarce. It is also the case that the plant that ultimately became a chief staple of the American societies, corn, required extensive experimentation before becoming domesticated in anything near its present form. Thus, it is only around 4000 BCE that we see its development and the beginning of its extensive domestication.

The second pattern we can see is *growth and sophistication of social structures and the development of the city and of monumental architecture for religious and political purposes.* Even in Oceania, where the critical population levels for cities were never reached, one finds the monoliths of Rapa Nui as evidence of this human pattern. In some cases, the types of structures—pyramids, terraces, and obelisks, for example—seem to follow an almost "universal" pattern, so much so that scholars still struggle to find evidence of contact among widely separated cultures where none appears to have existed.

Recent finds at the Caral-Supé sites show how rapidly the development of astonishingly sophisticated large cities took place once the threshold of plant and animal domestication was crossed. The accomplishments of the society that created Caral and the other sites uncovered so far, like those of the Indus valley, survived in the local practices of Andean peoples long after the cities themselves were abandoned. The settlements of the Olmecs on the southern gulf coast of Mexico, though coming somewhat later, were equally imposing in their architecture, the efficacy of their farming techniques and irrigation practices, the sophistication of their social structures, and, it now appears, their development of writing. Yet, it is also the case that people will not create all the aspects of "civilization" in the same ways and by the same means. One striking example of this is the use of the wheel. Rotation and cyclical motion appear to permeate the ritual lives of people all over the globe, yet the use of the wheel as a conveyance and as a basic concept of technology is not universal. Thus, as with so many human innovations, the intersection of need and opportunity led to a crucial breakthrough. Hence, despite the widespread use of ball courts employing spheres of rubber put through circular hoops as a central political and religious ceremony among Mesoamerican peoples and the enormous cyclical mathematical and time-keeping achievements of later peoples like the Mayas (and even the fact that we have evidence that American societies provided their children with toys that had wheels), the need and means for utilizing heavy-wheeled vehicles never occurred and, thus, never developed as it had in Eurasia and Africa.

In the case of Oceania, the peopling of the innumerable islands of the Pacific was inseparable from trade and cultural connections. Colonizing uninhabited islands could take place only when the plants and animals required could be brought along and provision could be made to trade for unavailable items. Thus, in terms of square mileage, the Lapita system was one of the world's largest trading spheres, stretching thousands of miles and including thousands of islands. Yet, for a variety of reasons—the necessities traded, the remoteness of the islands from other trade centers, the lack of connections to mainland Asia and the Americas, the unique seafaring skills of the island navigators—the peoples of Oceania remained separated from other such systems. Even here, as in the Americas, Eurasia, and Africa, we see yet another pattern emerging among the political behavior of human societies: *centralization and resistance to it*. As with other fundamental patterns of world history, we will see this one emerge repeatedly in a variety of guises as our story proceeds.

▶ For additional resources, including maps, primary sources, visuals, and quizzes, please go to www.oup.com/us/vonsivers. Please see the Further Resources section at the back of the book for additional readings and suggested websites.

Thinking Through Patterns

▶ **What do historians see as the advantages and disadvantages of the separate evolution of the Americas?**

Like the role of geography, this is a question that is often debated. For one thing, we can turn the question around and ask why we should consider the Americas as "isolated," rather than Eurasia and Africa. But it is also true that the societies were not as large or as ethnically diverse as their Eurasian counterparts. Historically, too, scholars still often view the two sets of continents as "old" and "new" and from that perspective view the Americas as "isolated." A big part of how one chooses to look at the question also revolves around how one sees the roles of invasion, infusion of innovation, and cultural competition. Some scholars have argued that the very shape of Eurasia allowed for the brisk dissemination of innovation along broad areas similarly situated in latitude. The Americas, by way of contrast, were more longitudinally oriented, making such diffusion more difficult. Some argue that the separateness of the Americas allowed them to hothouse distinctive cultural traits among their populations. Yet others argue that constant mixing of peoples and ideas accelerates innovation and, hence, "progress." One distinct disadvantage of isolation is that peoples become susceptible to diseases and biological changes suddenly inflicted on them. Thus, from the sixteenth to the early twentieth centuries CE, virulent epidemics of Eurasian and African diseases like smallpox devastated the peoples of the Americas when introduced. Though the Americas in all likelihood introduced syphilis in return, it did not cause nearly the devastation in Eurasia and Africa that the Old World diseases did in the New World.

While the Pacific Islanders had abundant access to food for immediate consumption, the islands themselves were generally too small to allow the accumulation of enough surplus food to free up the numbers of nonfarmers necessary to build and maintain a city. In addition, the islands themselves contained limited amounts of building materials and freshwater, while their isolation helped guard them against attack. Culturally, the islanders also had grown to *expect* that if their numbers outran the food supply, they could simply find another island to which the excess population could migrate.

▶ **Why did no cities develop on the larger Pacific Islands?**

▶ **The wheel is often cited as the most basic human invention, yet large and sophisticated civilizations were able to flourish without this signal innovation. Why do you think it did not develop in the Americas?**

Historians looking at this question tend to look at it in one of two ways: cultural or practical. Some cultural scholars see a lack of deep-seated affinities for circular motion in the belief systems of the American peoples as helping to prevent them from relating to the motion of the wheel in the way that Eurasian and African peoples did. Yet, American societies had toys with wheels on them, so they were not unaware of the concept of circular motion—indeed, far from it. The scholars favoring a practical or technological approach argue that the environment of the mountains close by seacoasts, rain forests, and dry, hilly regions was not conducive to bulk transport by wheeled vehicles and that the peoples there simply were never forced to look for more efficient means of transport.

PART TWO

The Age of Empires and Visionaries

600 BCE–600 CE

By the middle of the first millennium BCE, two major transformations changed the course of world history. First, kingdom formation, which had begun earlier in Eurasia, became a near universal pattern in the world, including sub-Saharan Africa and Meso-America. Second, visionaries emerged in Eurasia whose formulations of monotheism and monism laid the foundations of religious civilizations that eventually emerged in the Middle East, India, China, and adjacent regions after 600 CE.

Kingdoms and Empires

Sub-Saharan Africa and the Americas. Around 600 BCE, improvements in agricultural productivity made it possible for some chiefdoms to expand into kingdoms. In sub-Saharan Africa, the kingdoms were Meroë in the steppes of the middle Nile and Aksum in the highlands of Ethiopia; and in Meso-America, the kingdoms were those of the Maya in the Yucatán Peninsula and of Teotihuacán in the Mexican basin.

The Middle East and the Mediterranean. After the Hittites and Neo-Assyrians, around 600 BCE the Persian Achaemenids continued the pattern of empire-building. The Greeks resisted the Persians for a long time with their alternatives of city-states and elective offices. But eventually the Macedonian Greek Alexander the Great, his Hellenist successors, and the republican Romans in the western Mediterranean also adopted the imperial pattern, expanding into the Middle East. The Roman Empire competed with the two Persian successor empires of the Parthians and Sasanid for dominance of the region. The characteristic pattern of the Middle East and Mediterranean was competitive imperialism.

India and China. Intense political–military competition among small states ruled by a military class or royal dynasty led to the elimination of the weakest states and the consolidation of larger kingdoms in both India and China around 600 BCE. In contrast to the Middle East and Mediterranean, the pattern of India and China was that of rising and falling of single empires, followed by long periods of decentralization before the rise of new imperial dynasties that unified much or all of the region.

ca. 800 BCE
Earliest Evidence of Iron-Smelting in Sub-Saharan Africa

551–479 BCE
Traditional Date for Life of Confucius

550–331 BCE
Achaemenid Persia

ca. 427–347 BCE
Plato, Founder of the First Philosophical School, the Academy

Interaction in Eurasia and with Africa. Merchants in the kingdoms and empires of Eurasia and sub-Saharan Africa began to interact during the period 600 BCE–600 CE. They pioneered the sea routes to southern India, China, and eastern Africa and the land routes of the Silk Road through central Asia and the Sahara from northern to western Africa. Exchanges on these routes were not yet regular enough to lead to adaptations, for example, of technological inventions. But the trade whetted the appetites of rulers for luxury goods, such as spices, ointments, silks, and ceramics, stimulating the rise of merchant classes.

Visionaries and the Adoption of State Religions

Visionaries. At the height of the political–military competition among city-states, kingdoms, and empires around 700–500 BCE, individuals arose in Eurasia to proclaim new visions of reality. In the place of the polytheistic universe in which gods and humans mingled, they proclaimed a transcendent God or "first principle" beyond the universe. Their messages were not bound to the particular kingdoms or empires in which the visionaries lived but were addressed to anyone who would listen.

What difference did their new visions of reality make? For the first time in world history, individuals claimed to have discovered standards of truth and justice that were beyond the ever-changing circumstances of kingdoms and empires and their polytheistic pantheons. An unchanging God or first principle, so these individuals argued, was the measure for what was truthful and just on earth.

Empires and the Adoption of State Religions. In the centuries after the visionaries, small groups of followers popularized the messages of monotheism and monism. They formed priestly classes, churches, and/or schools. Interaction among groups of followers led to the adaptation of some monotheisms and monisms to each other. For example, Jews adopted elements from Zoroastrianism and Greek philosophy, Buddhists influenced Confucianism and Daoism, and a group of Jews founded the reform movement of Christianity and merged it with Greek philosophy.

As one might expect, kings and emperors sought to capitalize on the unifying forces they perceived in monotheism and monism. By 600 CE, monotheism or monism had become the dominant religion, philosophy, and/or ethics of the empires and kingdoms in Eurasia and parts of sub-Saharan Africa.

Previous chapters focused on the patterns of social and political formation, from foraging to agricultural villages, as well as towns and cities, and from there to kingdoms and empires. Now—after the adoption of state religions—kings, emperors, and religious officials laid the foundations for the formation of religious civilizations which, after 600 CE, evolved into social and cultural units that were geographically larger and more enduring than kingdoms and empires—lasting, in most cases, right to the present.

Thinking Like a World Historian

▶ What is the connection between food, population density, and patterns of social–political formation in world history, and why were sub-Saharan Africa and the Americas later in the development of these patterns?

▶ Which elements did the visionaries of ca. 700–500 BCE share in common, and what made their visions so decisive in the course of world history?

▶ What is the difference between kingdoms and empires, and how did empires change as a result of the adoption of state religions?

322–185 BCE
Most of India United for the First Time Under Mauryan Empire

196 BCE–284 CE
Early Roman Empire

250–900 CE
Classic Period of Maya Kingdoms

322–550 CE
Much of India Reunited Under Gupta Empire

221–206 BCE
First Chinese Empire Under Qin

100–750 CE
Moche Chiefdom in Northern Peru

300–600 CE
Kingdom of Aksum in Northeastern Sub-Saharan Africa

476 CE
End of Western Roman Empire

Chapter 6 600 BCE-600 CE

Chiefdoms and Early States in Africa and the Americas

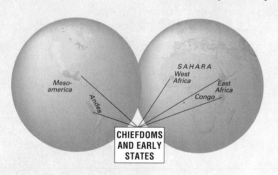

A humble stone carving in Oaxaca, southern Mexico, carbon-dated to about 600 BCE, is the earliest documentation for the existence of a 260-day divinatory calendar in Mesoamerica, which later played a central part in Mayan time reckoning and divination. Mexican archaeologists under the leadership of Alfonso Caso excavated the inscription in the 1930s, and an American archaeological team in the 1990s discovered perhaps an even earlier version of this calendar in Tabasco to the north of Oaxaca. Amazingly, this calendar system is still in use in southern Mexico, making it among the world's longest-lived methods of reckoning time. Similarly, an astronomical observatory in Kenya, carbon-dated to 300 BCE, is the earliest example of the so-called Borana lunar calendar of 354 days. It is still in use today among the Kushite herders of East Africa. Two American anthropologists, B. M. Lynch and L. H. Robbins, discovered this observatory in Namoratunga [Nah-mow-rah-TOON-ga], Kenya, during fieldwork in 1978. The two calendars not only attest to the cultural prowess of Mesoamerica and sub-Saharan East Africa during the period of 600 BCE–600 CE but, more important, are reminders of

ABOVE: The ruins of Meroitic pyramids at Jebel Barkal in modern Sudan.

the diversity and relativity of all calendar systems, including the modern Western one which dominates the world today.

Interest in time reckoning was not the only similarity between the Americas and sub-Saharan Africa. During the period 600 BCE–600 CE, these regions also resembled each other in terms of patterns of agricultural development, spread of villages, emergence of chiefdoms, and early rise of kingdoms. These institutions, results of regional interactions and adaptations, evolved more slowly than in the more populated Eurasia, where kingdoms and empires already proliferated prior to 600 BCE–600 CE. Since there was little contact between Eurasia and the Americas and much of sub-Saharan Africa it is all the more remarkable that the patterns of agriculture and life in villages, chiefdoms, and kingdoms were fairly consistent *within* world regions as much as *across* world regions. People did not need to be in contact with each other across the continents to build their cultures in similar ways. All they needed were sufficiently large populations for similar institutions to arise. Nevertheless, as we saw in Chapter 5, the isolated world regions, through their own internal interactions, adapted to a transition from foraging to agriculture. Indeed, as recent scholarship has revealed, urban centers like Caral-Supé appear to be of the same age as some of the earliest Old World sites.

In this chapter, we will see how, through continued internal interactions, sub-Saharan Africans and Americans blazed indigenous trails in pattern formation, from villages to **chiefdoms** and **kingdoms**. Sharing a common humanity with the Eurasians, they did not need the direct influence of those peoples to develop strikingly similar social and political patterns. The calendars of these two regions, while strikingly similar to Eurasian models in some respects, also illustrate both the adaptation of the concept to local needs as well as a striking sophistication.

Agriculture and Early African Kingdoms

Largely on account of its relative separation and lower population levels, sub-Saharan Africa (like the Americas and Oceania) transitioned from forager society to agrarian–urban society with its patterns of village, city-state, kingdom, and empire formation somewhat less rapidly or completely than Eurasia. However, north of sub-Saharan Africa inhabitants interacted with the Middle East and adapted to its agrarian patterns early on. They adopted village life, built cities, and created kingdoms (such as Kush and Nubia along the Nile) well before the period of 600 BCE–600 CE. After 600 CE, the kingdoms of Meroë [ME-ro-way] in the Nile valley and Aksum in the Ethiopian highlands flourished, while Africans farther south shifted from foraging to agriculture, villages, and chiefdoms. By 600 CE, urbanism had spread to West Africa and foraging had shrunk to pockets in the center and south of the continent.

Seeing Patterns

▶ How does comparing and contrasting sub-Saharan Africa with the Americas during 600 BCE–600 CE help in understanding the agrarian–urban patterns of social and political development across the world?

▶ Where did chiefdoms, cities, and kingdoms arise in sub-Saharan Africa and why? On which forms of agriculture, urbanization, and trade were they based?

▶ Which areas in the Americas saw the development of a corn- and potato-based agriculture that did not depend on the plow, the wheel, and iron making?

Chiefdom: An agricultural village or town of up to 1,000 inhabitants, in which people know each other, requiring a person of authority (an elder or the head of a large family) to keep order as a respected chief.

Kingdom: A city-state or territorial state in which a ruler, claiming a divine mandate and supported by a military force, keeps order and provides for the defense against outside attacks.

AFRICA, SHOWING SITES IN MAURITANIA 2000 BCE–600 BCE

Saharan Villages, Towns, and Kingdoms

For many millennia, the Sahara was relatively hospitable, with savannas and steppes, furthering the pattern shift from foraging to agriculture. But when the monsoon rains shifted eastward, during ca. 5000–3000 BCE, the desert expanded and savannas and steppes retreated southward. Agrarian life relocated to oases and the Nile River valley. In the northeast, the Kingdom of Meroë, successor of Napata, established its capital by the same name in the middle Nile basin, between the Nile and the western slopes of the northern Ethiopian highlands. The kingdom received its support from a sufficient, although not abundant, agricultural surplus produced with the help of annual Nile floods and irrigation.

Saharan Chiefdoms and Kingdoms

The earliest evidence of Africans shifting from foraging to agriculture comes from the area of the middle Nile around Khartoum, the capital of modern Sudan. Archaeological sites reveal a culture of raising cattle, cultivating sorghum, and shaping distinctive pottery. Sorghum tolerates a climate of less rainfall than wheat and barley, and it is possible that farmers along the middle Nile domesticated it locally, probably after becoming familiar with Middle Eastern farming. By the period between 4000 BCE and the first written records in Egypt in 3100 BCE, a substantial chiefdom of Nilo-Saharan speakers had emerged in northern Sudan, then called "Nubia" (from the Latinized Egyptian word *nebew* for "gold," which was found in a valley off the Nile). This chiefdom was based on farming, livestock raising, and trading of gold as well as rain-forest ivory and timber. Archaeologists have noted that even at this early date tombs in Nubia contained objects rivaling those of the Egyptians, including objects from southwest Asia and beyond. Moreover, Nubian military prowess emerged clearly in Egyptian records, with archers especially sought after as mercenaries. Indeed, the bow and arrow, both African inventions, gave their names to the state which the Egyptians called *Ta-Seti* [Tah-SAY-tee], the "Land of the Bow."

After 2500 BCE, a kingdom grew in wealth and power in Nubia, building a palace, large tombs, temples, and a wall around its capital city of Kerma, the first African city outside Egypt. During 1850–1400 BCE Kerma and Egypt were rivals for the control of Nile trade, with each conquering and ruling the other for periods of time until Egypt eventually destroyed Kerma and colonized Nubia for about half a millennium. Nubia regained autonomy early in the first millennium BCE, centered around the city of Napata, a new capital at some distance upstream on the Nile. Later, the Napatan kings liberated themselves from Egyptian control and even assumed the throne of their northern neighbor as the twenty-fifth dynasty (ca. 780–686 BCE). But when Assyria, the first empire to unify all of the Middle East, conquered Egypt, the defeated king retreated and relocated himself farther upstream at Meroë, south of the Nile bend in the border zone between the southern Sahara and savanna.

The Villages of Tichitt-Oualata

Contemporaneously with the Nubian kingdoms, villages emerged in the southeastern corner of today's Mauretania. As in Nubia, the climate in the western Sahara had changed during 5000–3000 BCE, away from the monsoon regime which since the end of the last Ice Age (12,500 BCE) had supported a steppe and savanna vegetation in what is desert today. As the monsoon patterns moved eastward, foragers retreated to shallow lakes and oases. They left behind a rich collection of cave paintings in the surrounding mountains dating to earlier times when the Sahara was still wet. During 3000–2000 BCE, these foragers—perhaps stimulated by the knowledge of Middle Eastern agriculture—domesticated pearl or bulrush millet, a type of grain requiring less water than wheat or barley to grow.

Archaeological evidence published by a British team in 2004 points to the emergence of a set of sizeable villages at Dhar Tichitt [Darr-tee-SHEET] and Dhar Oualata [Darr-wah-LAH-tah] in Mauretania around 2000 BCE, which flourished until 600 BCE. There, the team identified centers with large masonry structures. Corrals held herds of cattle, and granaries held large quantities of millet. Numerous tomb mounds, perhaps for the chiefs in the villages, held beads and copper jewelry. Furnaces contained remnants of charcoal and ore, evidence of craftspeople smelting copper that was mined in the nearby Saharan mountains. While it appears that the social structure was based on wealth in livestock, exactly how society was regulated, what nature of religious order it possessed, and which form of chiefly authority ruled are still unclear. One theory holds that the people eventually retreated farther south, together with the steppe and savanna, as the Sahara continued to dry out. As we shall see in Chapter 14, these migrants might have been the founders of the kingdom of ancient Ghana.

Meroë on the Middle Nile   The kings of Meroë [MAY-row-ay] were successors of the twenty-fifth Nubia-descended dynasty of Egypt, who, under Assyrian pressure, withdrew to the steppes of the middle Nile, about 100 miles north of present-day Khartoum. Here, they built their capital, Meroë. At that time, the flood plain to the south of the capital still received sufficient monsoon rainfall during the summer to support agriculture. In addition, the kings built large water reservoirs to supply the farmers. The latter grew the African cereals sorghum and millet, but archaeological finds also include barley and wheat, all of which were planted with the plow. Presumably, the kingdom financed itself for the most part from the agricultural surplus.

At its height, from the sixth through fourth centuries BCE, the city of Meroë encompassed 20,000 inhabitants and a substantial population lived in the provincial towns. Although the king was the recognized head of Meroë, the kingdom was largely decentralized. The provinces downstream and upstream along the Nile were largely autonomous, ruled by their own town chiefs who perhaps sent no more than annual presents to the capital. Outside the limited agricultural area, cattle nomads grazed their herds.

The difference in power between the kings and the chiefs was defined by the royal control over trade. Miners in the desert north of the capital produced iron ore and farmers south of the capital grew cotton, both of which were important for the urban crafts. Smiths and weavers in Meroë produced weapons, hoes, utensils, and

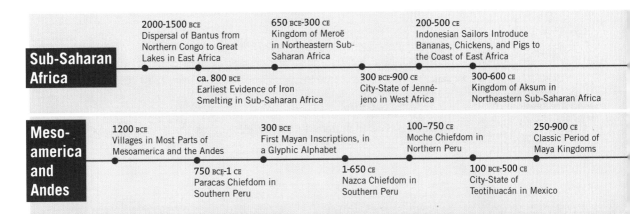

cloth, both for local consumption and for trade beyond the kingdom. Hunters in the south acquired ivory from elephants and feathers from ostriches hunted in the savanna. Traders carried these goods on donkey and camel caravans on the traditional trade route down the Nile to Egypt or across the Red Sea to Yemen by boat. In return, they brought back olive oil and wine from Egypt and frankincense and myrrh from Yemen (see Map 6.1).

From the kingdom's inception in the seventh century BCE, people in Meroë mined, smelted, and forged iron; they might have been the first to do so in sub-Saharan Africa. However, how and when the knowledge of smelting and forging iron began in sub-Saharan Africa has been a bone of contention among scholars. As is generally agreed, the craft of iron smelting evolved gradually in Hittite Anatolia during several centuries after 1500 BCE (see Chapter 2). To date, the possible spread of iron working skills from the Middle East to Africa has not been satisfactorily proved. But the independent origin of iron working in Africa has not been demonstrated conclusively either. Researchers such as Stanley Alpern and Jan Vansina, evaluating the evidence in the early 2000s, came to the conclusion that the earliest reliable carbon date for iron production is 839–782 BCE, in the savanna on the border between today's Central African Republic and Cameroon. If this date is correct, Meroë would have received the impetus for iron production from within sub-Saharan Africa.

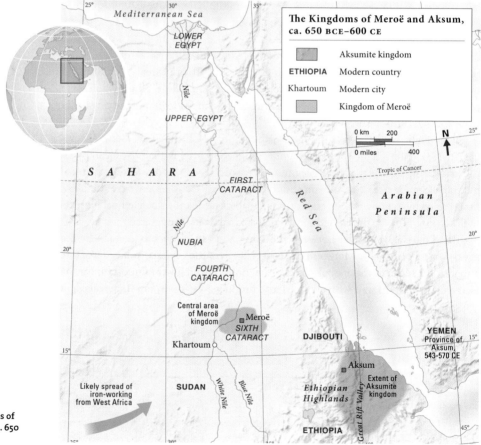

MAP 6.1 The Kingdoms of Meroë and Aksum, ca. 650 BCE–600 CE.

Meroë's Cultural Achievements   In Meroë, the kings adapted their Nubian–Egyptian heritage to the different regional circumstances of the steppe and savanna south of the Sahara. Their monuments acquired a distinct style, as is evidenced by their tombs, pyramids with flat tops, and pyramids with steep angles. Although the main temple and its priesthood remained in the north, the priests added native deities to the pantheon, such as the lion god Apedemek. Meanwhile, Egyptian hieroglyphics seem to have "evolved" into an alphabetic script, visible on many monuments, even though at present this script is still undecipherable.

In spite of its regional orientation, Meroë was well known to the outside world. Mediterranean travelers visited it quite frequently. In the early first century CE the kings of Meroë skirmished with Rome over border issues. And in the third century CE, when Meroë's power was already declining, Heliodorus of Emesa, a Hellenistic-Greek writer, made it the stage for the conclusion of his popular romance novel *Aethiopica*. As much as Meroë provided a physical network for regional travelers, it also provided an intellectual link between Eurasia and Africa; the people of Meroë facilitated this important cultural link through their adaptation.

The Kingdom of Aksum

Meroitic trade with the Red Sea had to cross through the Ethiopian highlands. Exposed to this trade, highlanders gradually acculturated to urbanized Meroë as well as Yemen. Sometime in the early first century CE, a king replaced the chiefdoms of the highlands and established the kingdom of Aksum (300–600 CE). Based on a relatively abundant, plow-driven agriculture, this kingdom assumed control of the trade from Meroë, which declined subsequently. Aksum became the major supplier of African goods to the Roman Empire, from where it accepted Coptic Christianity in the early 300s.

Meroë's Decline and Aksum's Rise   Three factors contributed to Meroë's decline in the third century CE. First, the iron industry devoured immense amounts of charcoal, which is made by burning wood in earth-covered mounds. Once the forests in the east were gone, the iron industry in the capital city was doomed, depriving the kings of a major source of their income. Second, beginning in the late 200s BCE, camel nomads from the deserts east of the Nile raided northern Meroë. Third, the eastern neighbor, Ethiopia, acculturated to Meroë, thanks to the trade that crossed its land. Ethiopian guides and owners of transportation animals became participants in the trade, and then chiefs in the agriculturally rich high plain of Aksum took it over. Aksum was located close to the coast, where the port of Adulis (today Zula) was one of the main transshipment ports in the Red Sea. Thus, a combination of agricultural and commercial wealth enabled the chiefs of Aksum to assume the succession of Meroë.

The agricultural bounty of the Ethiopian highlands southeast of Meroë was due to its plains at 5,000–6,000 feet elevation and surrounding mountains 15,000 feet high. Deep valleys, notably of the Blue Nile and of the Rift Valley, cut into these highlands, which were therefore accessible only over steep ascents. The summer monsoon from the south Atlantic brought sufficient and, in places, abundant rain to the plains and mountains and supported large forests and a productive subtropical agriculture in the lower elevations.

As in the Nile valley, agriculture in the Ethiopian highlands was of considerable age, with evidence—from a rock painting and archaeological finds—of the existence of plow, oxen, barley, and wheat going back several thousand years. In higher elevations where barley and wheat did not prosper, farmers grew teff, a high-yielding grain. Plenty of grasslands supported cattle breeding. The Red Sea coast was dry and hot, with today's Djibouti sporting the highest average temperatures in the world. The coast supported little more than a few ports dependent on their hinterland. Ethiopia was a largely self-contained region in Africa, remaining outside the large population movements and cultural assimilation characteristic of West and East Africa.

Aksum's Splendor   Aksum, founded around 100 CE, came into its own around 300 CE. Its king, Ezana (ca. 303–350 CE), adopted Christianity as the state religion in 333 CE, thereby making Aksum the third Christian kingdom, after Armenia (301 CE) and Georgia (319 CE). Like his Armenian and Georgian counterparts and, somewhat later, the Roman emperor, Ezana replaced tolerance for a multiplicity of polytheistic religions with the requirement of conversion to a single faith (see Chapter 7). When the Roman emperors, however, embraced what would become the Roman Catholic interpretation of Christianity at the Church Council of Chalcedon (451 CE), Aksum opted for Coptic Christianity, which was dominant in Egypt. The emperors clearly considered the religious unity of the western and eastern halves of the empire as more important than the religious unity with their Middle Eastern provinces. Aksum, on the other hand, embraced union with the Coptic church. Although it did not break with the Roman Empire and even sided with it in the second half of the 500s CE (against the Sasanid Persians), Aksum kept its distance.

Another centralizing policy characteristic for Aksum was the use of a gold-based currency with which the taxation of the market for the import and export of luxury goods was facilitated. The kings of Aksum acquired their gold by sending merchants, protected by accompanying troops, to the southern highlands outside the kingdom, where the gold was mined. The merchants paid with salt, iron, and cattle. Finally, a small central administration of tax collectors, tax farmers, and provincial tribute collectors assured delivery of agricultural surplus to granaries in the towns and the capital. The provinces outside the capital, however, were in reality small kingdoms, federated with Aksum through some kind of tribute system, the details of which are unknown. Even though more centralized than Meroë, Aksum was well below the level of administrative coherence of a typical Middle Eastern or Mediterranean kingdom or empire, such as Ptolemaic Egypt (305–30 BCE) or Antigonid Greece (301–168 BCE).

Imperialism and Crisis   In the 500s CE, Aksum briefly engaged in imperialism—the only imperialism coming out of sub-Saharan Africa in its entire history. This century was a time of profound crisis in both the Roman and Sasanid Persian Empires, which were under threat by nomadic invaders from the central Asian and Russian steppes (see Chapter 7). Naval trade in the Red Sea declined and the kingdom of Yemen increasingly relied on camel caravan trade along the west coast of Arabia. Perhaps under the influence of Jewish communities at the northern end of the caravan route, a Yemeni usurper who had converted to Judaism seized the throne and persecuted the Christians in his land. In response, and with the encouragement of Rome, the Aksumite king invaded Yemen and defeated the usurper. After a period of political instability, Aksum was able to make Yemen a regular province (543–570 CE).

But Aksum eventually lost this province when the Sasanid Persians invaded by land and sea in 570 CE, to establish their own proxy regime at the commercially important entrance to the Red Sea. The Sasanids had re-covered earlier than the Romans from nomadic invasions and were determined to turn the long competition be-tween the two empires (discussed in Chapter 7) to their favor. Seizing control over the entire India and East Af-rica trade was part of the Sasanid strategy to defeat Rome in the Middle East.

As a kingdom dependent to a considerable degree on transcontinental luxury trade, Aksum eventually became a collateral victim of this new Persian ascendancy. After 570 CE, Aksumite trade in the Red Sea declined precipi-tously. The capital city shrank to a shadow of itself, and in the following centuries provincial rulers in the highlands farther south rose to prominence. In addition, there were signs of internal problems: Timber resources for Ak-sum's iron industry in the vicinity of the capital became scarce. Although Ethiopia did not disintegrate, as Meroë had done, after 600 CE it played a much more modest regional role.

Aksumite Stela, pre-400s CE. This is the largest of hundreds of stone monoliths, some with tombs and altars, attesting to the architectural sophistication of the kingdom. Workmen transported them from quarries 3 miles away where they had cut the stelae with iron tools. Some of the stelae, like the one to the right, have false windows and doors, looking like modern art deco buildings.

The Spread of Villages in Sub-Saharan Africa

By about 600 BCE, agriculture and pastoralism were common not only in East Af-rica but also in West Africa. Both emerged when a majority of people retreated from the increasingly dry Sahara southward into West Africa. They followed the gradual southward shift of West Africa's three ecological zones, stretching from west to east in the form of more or less broad bands. The first and northernmost zone was the steppe, or **Sahel** (Arabic *sahil*, or "coast" of the "sea" of the Sahara Desert). The sec-ond zone was the *savanna*, an expanse of grassland with stands of trees. The third zone was a relatively narrow, up to 150-mile-wide belt of rain forest along the coast from Guinea to Cameroon. Farming villages were dispersed by 600 BCE over all three zones, although they were most numerous in the savanna, where farming was most productive.

Sahel: An area of steppe or semidesert bordering the Sahara.

West African Savanna and Rain-Forest Agriculture

During the period 600 BCE–600 CE the densest village networks were located in the savannas of the inland delta of the Niger and middle Senegal Rivers. The village of Jenné-jeno [Jen-NAY-JEN-no] in the delta developed into a major urban center during 300–900 CE. Indications are that it was a chiefdom with a developing re-gional trade for raw materials and luxury goods. In the rain forest, the evolution of slash-and-burn agriculture is still largely undocumented by archaeology, although its end result, the so-called Bantu dispersal with its combination of yam and oil palm village agriculture, is well established.

Inland Delta Urbanism   The river Niger originates in the far west of the West African rain forest and flows northeast from the savanna to the Sahel, before turning at a right angle southeastward in the direction of the Atlantic Ocean. Midway along its northeastern leg, it slows and divides into several branches, the 250-mile-long and 50-mile-wide inland delta. In the first millennium BCE, when the climate was still relatively humid, the delta was located entirely in the savanna, forming a huge area of canals, islands, and swamps. Villagers in the delta grew millet and African rice, the latter domesticated around 1500 BCE.

Over time, a dense network of villages developed. After 300 BCE a village division process began, by which some villages, increasing to town size, became the center of satellite villages. This is how Jenné-jeno at the southern end of the delta originated. By 900 CE, so it is estimated, Jenné-jeno was a *city*—that is, a dwelling place for a nonagricultural crafts-based population—of between 5,000 and 13,000 inhabitants. It was surrounded within a circle of half a mile diameter by 25 villages. Other towns with satellite villages developed farther downstream as well and made the delta the most populated area in West Africa.

Unfortunately, the archaeology of the period under discussion (chiefly by Susan Keech McIntosh and Roderick J. McIntosh) has not revealed much yet about the social stratification and power structures of Jenné-jeno. It is clear that this urban–rural center had a line of chiefs, some basic administrative offices, and craftspeople. The strongest evidence is a gold ring and many objects made of copper and bronze dated to 850–900 CE. Copper and iron ore had to be carried in by donkey or camel from a distance of 30 miles or more from the desert and savanna to be smelted and manufactured in town into weapons and implements. Two chemically analyzed glass beads, dated to the pre-600 CE period, seem to have come from overseas, one from India, southeast Asia, or east Asia and the other from Roman Italy or Egypt. Thus, trans-Saharan trade seems to have been in existence, supporting an incipient urban demand for luxuries.

Rain-Forest Settlements   The earliest evidence for rain-forest agriculture comes from the Kintampo complex of 2250–750 BCE, located in today's Ghana. Here, archaeologists have found traces of wood and mud huts on stone foundations, domesticated cattle and dwarf goats, rats, pottery, terra-cotta figurines, and polished stone implements. The assumption is that the villagers practiced slash-and-burn farming to grow yams and oil palms. Unfortunately, no archaeological evidence of the cultivation of yams has been found, and the earliest evidence for oil palm cultivation dates to an 800–BCE site in the Atlantic Niger delta. Rain-forest archaeology, burdened by the tendency of the environment to break down the organic matter of artifacts, is lagging behind; and archaeologists have begun producing good data only from the 1990s onwards.

Slash-and-burn farming consisted of clearing small areas of rain forest for the establishment of villages of up to 500 inhabitants, as well as for yam and oil palm plantations. Virgin rain forest was relatively easy to cut, even with stone tools, prior to the arrival of iron axes in the 800s BCE. Trees between 80 and 125 feet high formed a thick canopy, allowing relatively little light to penetrate and, therefore, not much undergrowth to develop and obstruct the clearing process. Each clearing was large enough for a village of a few hundred farmers, family fields, communal fallow land, and small numbers of cattle and goats.

If a village grew beyond its population capacity, a group had to depart and select a new site in the rain forest for clearing. Yam fields could be cultivated for up to 3 years and had to lay fallow for 10–15 years. During the fallow years, the rain forest grew back, although it now no longer returned to its virgin state. A secondary rain forest developed, with few tall trees and a proliferation of vegetation up to 30 feet high. Given several millennia of slash-and-burn cultivation, over time nearly all virgin African rain forests were replaced by secondary forest. As in so many other places in the world, what many might perceive as pristine "jungle" was in fact the creation of human hands, as emphasized by Jan Vansina in his classic on African rain-forest settlement. The transformation of the environment by humans, for better or for worse, is a process that began early on in world history.

The Spread of Village Life to East and South Africa

Groups of yam and oil palm farmers of southeast Nigeria, at the eastern end of the West African rain-forest belt, calling themselves "Bantu" or "the people," exhausted their area for clearings around 2000 BCE. In contrast to their westerly neighbors, they were favored in their search for new spaces to clear because they had the equatorial rain forest of the Congo to the southeast at their disposal. Once there, a northerly group, the Mashariki Bantus, began to disperse around 1500 BCE, this time, however, eastward into the savanna of the Great Lakes in East Africa. On their way, they adapted to the cereal agriculture and iron crafting of the savanna villagers. The Bantu villages of the Great Lakes became the center for one of the great transformation events of history. Under Bantu impact, during 600 BCE–600 CE, nearly all foragers in the southern cone of Africa became either villagers or cattle nomads and adopted Bantu dialects and culture (see Map 6.2).

Inland Villagers and Nomads   At the time of the Mashariki Bantu arrival around 600 BCE, much of the land around the Great Lakes was still heavily forested savanna. As the villagers cleared the forest, the threat of the tsetse fly diminished and nomads from the north were able to expand southward. Many nomads gave up their minimal farming, which they traditionally tended from campsites. As in the Middle East, these nomads entered into a symbiotic relationship with the villagers, from whom they acquired their necessary grain supplements. In the meantime, the descendants of the original Bantu dispersal of 2000 BCE had settled the Congo equatorial rain forest and, under the impact of their eastern cousins, had complemented their yam and oil palm agriculture with millet and sorghum, as well as iron working. Only small pockets of the original Paleolithic foragers of the virgin rain forest, the pygmies, continued their traditional lifestyle, although they eventually adopted Bantu languages.

The conversion of the foragers on the savanna south of the Congo rain forest to farming, from the Great Lakes westward to Angola and southward to the tip of South Africa, was the work of both eastern Great Lakes and western Congo branches of Bantus. The foragers either retreated before the farmers with their iron implements and weapons or adapted voluntarily to farming and speaking a Bantu language. Small numbers of savanna foragers, speaking Khoisan-derived languages, retreated into the Kalahari Desert and steppe in western and central South Africa, hanging on to a precarious hunting-and-gathering survival. As could be expected, the process from Mashariki Bantu origins and Bantu interaction with the nomads and foragers of East and South Africa to the eventual mutual adaptations took time and was still incomplete in 600 CE.

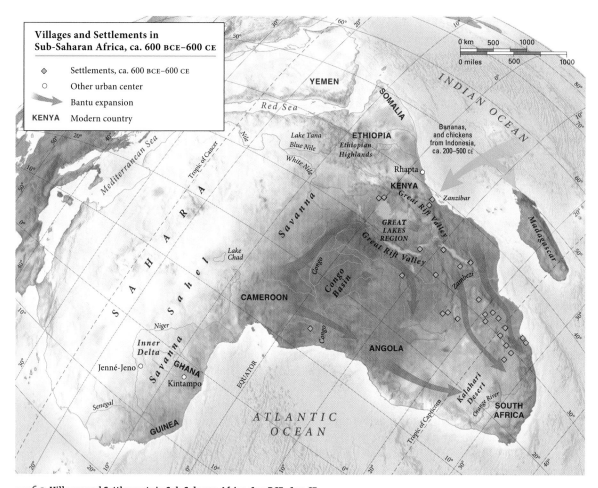

MAP **6.2** Villages and Settlements in Sub-Saharan Africa, 600 BCE–600 CE.

African Traditional Rituals   The results of an analysis of Bantu linguistic roots and of early Iron Age (350–900 CE) sites in South Africa provide a glimpse into African **animism**, summarized by Jan Vansina, a pioneer of Bantu studies. In this animist perception of reality, Bantus distinguished between the daily world of more or less regular cycles of renewal and disintegration in the village (birth, puberty, adulthood, marriage, old age), the fields (rain, plantation, harvest, and dry season), and the calendar movements of heaven (described in the beginning of this chapter). Elaborate rituals, including a scrupulous observance of taboos and omens, had to be followed to keep the village and field cycles in their regular paths. For example, South African sites contain stone cairns marking the space of male circumcision lodges, stone-walled pits for rain-making ceremonies, broken pots symbolizing deflowering in female puberty rites, and ceramic masks used for the representation of ancestors in village feasts. Rituals were the guarantee that the human and field cycles would remain in sync.

Ancestor and nature spirits pervaded the village and fields, and they had to receive their respect through regular sacrifices, lest they disrupt the cycles of renewal

Animism: Perception of reality based on the concept of a life force pervading humans, other animals, and, by extension, plants and inanimate objects.

and disintegration. Charms, mixed from herbs, protected against unintended insults of the spirits. The worst disruption, however, threatened to come from male or female witches in the villages who, acting out of envy, revenge, or malice, could severely harm or even kill their victims. The only way to avoid death from bewitchment was to seek a diviner or healer (shaman) in the village who, through trances, dreams, oracles, or charms, was able to enter the spirit world, recognize bewitchment, and stop it through **witchcraft**. It appears that in the early African Iron Age the adoption of elaborate rituals involving the human and field cycles—and, in some places, the calendar cycle, as evidenced by the Borana calendar discussed in the vignette at the beginning of this chapter—represented the main changes in the patterns of shamanic conceptualizations dating back to the African origins of humanity.

Witchcraft: An animistic belief in which an evil person (male or female) can harm an innocent victim at a distance and cause the victim to become possessed, with attendant illnesses.

Indonesian Contacts   Village agriculture received a big boost in 200–500 CE when Indonesian sailors brought the banana and chicken to East Africa. These sailors were descendants from Austronesian farmers, who had dispersed to the islands of the Pacific, Philippines, and Indonesia, beginning around 2000 BCE. They sailed on large outriggers. These watercraft were rigged with canted square sails, which made it possible to sail a course at an angle from the aft wind. Prevailing wind patterns in the southern Indian Ocean would otherwise have made sailing westward from Indonesia to Africa difficult. Where on the African coast the Indonesians landed is unknown, although they definitely settled the still-uninhabited tropical island of Madagascar, the fourth largest island in the world.

The banana tree yields 10 times more fruit per acre than the yam plant and the fruit is just as nutritious. It was highly adaptable not only to the rain forest, from where it came, but also to the savanna as well as irrigated orchards in dry climates. In the rain forest it did not require the full clearing that was necessary for the yam and, above all, it demanded far less labor. Chickens, domesticated perhaps in Thailand or India about 5000 BCE, were well represented in the Middle East and Mediterranean from 3000 BCE onward. Curiously, however, the keeping of chickens apparently did not begin in sub-Saharan Africa until the arrival of Indonesian sailors. The practices of cultivating bananas and keeping chickens soon spread all across sub-Saharan Africa, with the rearing of chickens spreading faster than the cultivation of bananas. These two food sources were crucial for the improvement of the meager food supplies in sub-Saharan Africa to a level where dense village networks, towns, and chiefdoms could develop in the period after 600 CE.

Incipient Urbanism on the East Coast   Apart from being the first to improve their agriculture by cultivating bananas and raising chickens, East Africans also benefited from trade with the Middle East. Archaeological evidence points to the inclusion of the northern East African coast into the Yemeni commercial network in the last centuries BCE, which connected Meroë, Ptolemaic and Roman Egypt, Parthian and Sasanid Persia, the Indian west coast, Sri Lanka, and (indirectly) Indonesia and China. Remnants of two camps on the northern coast of Somalia, dating to 150 BCE–500 CE, contain shards of ceramics from all these places. But as impermanent fixtures, these camps do not indicate regular commercial journeys.

The mid-first century CE seems to have been the transition point in the construction of permanent ports. The *Periplus of the Erythraean Sea*, a Greek-Hellenistic

Stone Relief of a Large Outrigger Merchant Ship, Buddhist Temple of Borobudur, on the Indonesian Island of Java, ca. 800 CE. This type of ship traveled regularly from Java to East Africa on the cinnamon trade route, with its merchants exchanging spices for ivory, wild animal skins, and slaves during the early centuries of the first millennium.

source describing for the Romans the monsoon winds for journeys to and from India, mentions Yemenis intermarrying with locals in the town of Rhapta along the Kenyan coast.

The archaeological remnants of this place have not yet been located, but Roman glass beads and shards found in digs on the island of Zanzibar and the nearby coast suggest regular journeys beginning around 200 CE. The beads and ceramics were presumably intended to be exchanged for ivory, rock crystal, ostrich feathers, and hardwood. If true, the roots of the later Swahili cities antedated the spread of Islam by several centuries—just as they did in the case of Jenné-jero in West Africa before the rise of Islamic Saharan kingdoms.

Patterns of African History, 600 BCE–600 CE

Based on a modestly productive agriculture, sub-Saharan Africa evolved along two basic patterns in the period 600 BCE–600 CE. First, in the northeast Meroë and Aksum adapted themselves to Middle Eastern agriculture, including the plow and irrigation techniques. In addition, both domesticated sorghum and millet—teff as well in Aksum—indigenously. With the help of irrigated farming and long-distance trade, chiefs built kingdoms, which lasted as long as the urban infrastructure could be supported. The exhaustion of timber in the vicinity of the capitals ended the royal pattern of social and political evolution in the sub-Saharan northeast.

Second, in the northwest of sub-Saharan Africa inhabitants pioneered the agricultures of the steppe, savanna, and rain forest on the basis of millet, rice, yam, and the fruit of the oil palm. Millet was productive enough to support the rise of villages. In one steppe region, the inland delta of the Niger, the irrigated farming of millet and rice allowed for the rise of a dense village network, village nucleation, and eventually a city, Jenné-jeno. With its incipient long-distance trade, this city foreshadowed the post-600 rise of Saharan kingdoms. Farther south, in the rain forest, the farming of yam and oil palm supported the emergence of small and widely dispersed villages. The arrival of the banana and the chicken from southeast Asia enriched all African agricultures and the expansion of the Bantus and their culture brought village life as well as iron smelting to all parts of sub-Saharan Africa.

Africa and the Americas   The Americas displayed striking similarities to the internal sub-Saharan interactions and adaptations. The latter, as we have seen, were responsible for patterns of village, city, and kingdom formation. In Mesoamerica as well as the Peruvian Andes mountains, internal processes of interaction and adaptation based on increasingly productive agricultures also supported a pattern of village, city-state, and kingdom development from 600 BCE to 600 CE.

The principal difference, however, was that in sub-Saharan Africa this evolution gradually expanded also to the central and southern regions, whereas in the Americas no such expansion took place until after 600 CE. Social and political formation patterns spread to North America only after 600 CE, as represented by the Pueblo and Cahokia cultures in what are today the US states of Arizona, Utah, New Mexico, and Missouri.

Early States in Mesoamerica: Maya Kingdoms and Teotihuacán

In Chapter 5 we saw that the chiefdoms of Caral-Supé (2600–2000 BCE) and Chavín de Huántar (1000–200 BCE) in the Andes as well as of the Olmecs (1200–600 BCE) in Mesoamerica represent early examples of social processes from agriculture and villages to urbanization, chiefdoms, and kingdoms. In the period 600 BCE–600 CE, in the Yucatán Peninsula of modern southeastern Mexico and the Mexican basin in south-central Mexico, chiefdoms evolved into full-fledged kingdoms. In the Andes, urban centers continued to form under chiefly rule, although in Teotihuacán and Moche the urban culture was nearly as diversified as in the Mesoamerican kingdoms.

The Maya Kingdoms in Southern Mesoamerica

Closeness to the equator and a long rainy season supported a dense rain forest in the central Yucatán Peninsula. By creating clear cuts and heaping up the soil on elevated fields or terraces on hill slopes, Maya villagers built a rich agriculture based on squash, beans, and corn. Around 600 BCE towns evolved into cities, where chieftains transformed themselves into kings. By organizing the labor of the farmers during slack agricultural times in the winter, they created city-states with imposing temple pyramids and palaces, surrounded by outlying villages. Among these city-states, the most powerful during the period 600 BCE–600 CE were Tikal and Kalakmul (see Map 6.3).

Mayaland on the Yucatán Peninsula   The climate of the Yucatán Peninsula is subtropical, with a rainy season extending from May to September. The base of the Yucatán Peninsula consisted of rain-forest lowlands and swamps, traversed by rivers. To the south were rain-forest highlands, sloping from a chain of mountains about 80–110 miles wide, which descended gradually toward the lowlands in the north and abruptly to the Pacific coast in the south. The northern region comprised the tip of the Yucatán and consisted of dry and riverless lowlands. Maya culture began in the center and far south and later radiated into the southern mountains and northern lowlands. Underlying the northern lowland areas was a limestone shelf that provided stone for construction. Here, local *chert* (a fine-grained sedimentary silica rock) and flint deposits provided for the fashioning of tools with which to quarry the limestone. The volcanic south was quarried for its lava stone and was also rich in obsidian and jade. Quetzal birds, whose feathers were used for prestigious ornamentation, inhabited this region as well (see Map 6.3).

The people in the Yucatán, the highlands and lowlands, spoke a variety of Mayan dialects. Even though they were early on exposed to Olmec cultural influence, it does not appear that there was much Olmec immigration as Maya culture formed. As the early Mayas became sedentary in the center of the peninsula and along the Pacific, they cut down the rain forest in order to clear fields, dry out swamps, and build villages on low stone platforms near water sources. Drainage ditches in fields indicate a beginning intensification of agriculture. By around 1000 BCE, some villages evolved into towns, dominating village clusters around them. Elite lineages under chieftains resided in the towns and controlled the best lands, while more humble lineages in

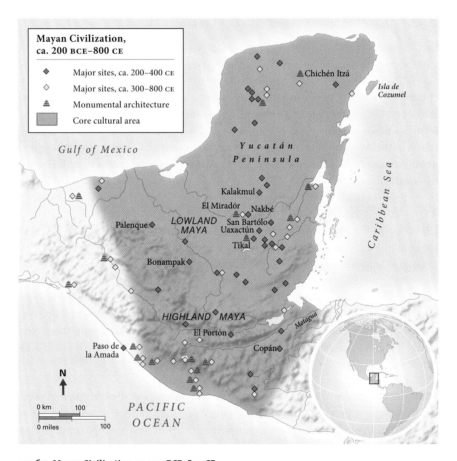

MAP **6.3** **Mayan Civilization, ca. 200 BCE–800 CE.**

the surrounding villages were on less productive soils. Although society continued to be organized by familial descent, social stratification by wealth began to differentiate the lineages. This stratification is archaeologically recognizable from rich tomb gifts as well as corrective dentistry: Then as now, the wealthy had enhanced means to beautify themselves.

Early Kingdoms   As in the agrarian centers of Eurasia, debt dependence was probably the earliest lever of power in the hands of the Mayan chieftains. Poor farmers, it can be assumed, borrowed seeds from rich farmers and during droughts were often unable to return what they had borrowed. Rich farmers had larger families, built bigger homes, and had more domestic workers producing pottery and textiles. They traded manufactured goods for goods not locally available, such as obsidian and jade. Thus, in the period 1000–600 BCE, these wealthy farmers transformed themselves into chieftains, exerting family rule for more or less extended periods over a central town surrounded by satellite villages.

Beginning in the seventh century BCE, chieftains in some agriculturally rich areas increased their wealth so that they could claim to be kings (sing., *ajaw*). Wealthy chieftains were able to surround themselves with military forces through which they made themselves the ultimate arbiters in all town disputes. They began to collect taxes, enlarge their towns into *cities*—that is, centers in which craftspeople and merchants who did not practice agriculture lived—and conquer other villages. During slack times in the agricultural cycle, these kings commanded farmers to construct the first ceremonial monuments—rectangular platforms up to 50 feet in elevation with temples and royal residences on top. Olmec-inspired stone stelae with images of human figures, dressed in Maya-style clothing, were placed around the platforms. Nakbé (700 BCE–150 CE), a city in the north of the central lowlands, was the site of the first temple pyramids on ceremonial platforms. These pyramids were stepped stone structures, as high as 200 feet, with staircases to the temples on top. In those elevated temples, kings conducted their sacrifices in tribute to the gods of the emerging divine pantheon.

A nearby town, El Miradór (600 BCE–150 CE), became a city with surrounding villages about a century after Nakbé. Perhaps favored by better trade connections than Nakbé, El Miradór gradually surpassed its neighbor in size and monumental ambitions. With about 100,000 inhabitants, hundreds of ceremonial and palatial structures on its platforms, and a 216-foot pyramid built around 300 BCE, this Mayan city was the largest early center of what ultimately were more than 4,400 Mayan urban and rural sites. Only the later Tikal (200–600 CE) reached a similar size. El Miradór was explored systematically by archaeologists for the first time only in 1978–1983 and then again beginning in 2003. To their surprise, this site turned out to be as fully Mayan, with its temple pyramids, elite structures, stelae, ball courts, sweat houses, and commoner quarters, as the later and better-known centers of the so-called Early Classic Period (250–600 CE). Maya culture at its peak has to be considered—as is being done in this chapter—under the much longer time horizon that began around 600 BCE.

El Miradór, La Danta Temple, 600 BCE–150 CE. By height (230 ft), volume and ground plan, this pyramid was the largest of all Maya sacred structures and one of the largest buildings of the premodern world. At present, the site is only partially excavated and archaeological work is still ongoing. The temple visible atop the pyramid is surmounted by a roosterlike roof comb, once covered by stucco figurines of Maya deities.

Progress made since the 1990s in deciphering the Maya glyphic script has allowed the conclusion that "Mayaland" consisted of some 15–17 fully evolved, dominant kingdoms in the central lowlands during the Early Classic Period, each with a capital and one or more secondary cities, plus countless towns and villages nearby. Marriage alliances among the royal lineages of the capitals and secondary cities served to maintain the cohesion of the kingdom. Rebellions by secondary cities, however, often called the power of the kings into question. Many scholars think that the frequent wars in Mayaland were either intra-kingdom rebellions or wars among secondary cities in different kingdoms. The only exception was the direct military competition between the kingdoms of Tikal and Kalakmul, which endured for many centuries.

Animism and Polytheism   The kings and their royal households lived in palaces adjacent to the temple pyramids. When they ascended the throne, in the tradition of animism, kings often assumed the names of animals or combined them with the names of human-made objects, for example, "Spearthrower Owl," "Shield Jaguar," and "Smoke Squirrel." Heirs to the throne, usually the eldest son, used the same name but with the suffix II, III, etc. On wall paintings, earthenware vessels, and stelae, kings were recognizable through their elaborate headdresses decorated with quetzal feathers, animal masks, and richly embroidered clothing. When sons were still minors, their mothers assumed the roles of regents. Occasionally, women ruled as queens. After death, kings were buried in pyramids or in separate tombs. Dead kings were assumed to have taken their place among the gods, residing in abodes both above and beneath the earth.

Polytheism: Personification of the forces of nature and performance of rituals and sacrifices to assure the benevolence of the gods and goddesses.

Polytheism had begun to develop on top of animism after the emergence of the first villages around 2500 BCE. Gods were the embodiments of forces of nature whose favor had to be curried if rich harvests were to result. The Mayan kings considered themselves servants of the many animal, nature, star, and war gods which had come to populate the divine pantheon by the time of the Olmecs in the eleventh century BCE and continued to grow during the Maya period. They fulfilled the demands of these gods for sacrifices during daily rituals in the temples atop the pyramids. The main sacrifice was the gift of blood—a heritage from animism—which Mayan kings drew from their ear lobes, tongues, and penises. During times of war, captured enemies, from kings to commoners, were also sacrificed. Through their blood, the kings nourished nature and supported the human and divine worlds.

The Ruling Classes   Apart from their temple service, kings and leading officials also assembled for the administration of justice, the collection of rents and tributes, commercial exchanges, and diplomatic relations. Many of these functions required expert knowledge of the annual calendar as labor on palaces or pyramids could be required from farmers only during specific times in the agricultural cycle. Other functions, such as military action, required divination so as to discover the most favorable star constellations under which to proceed. The tracking of these units of times required a specialized group of calendar specialists, mathematicians, and astronomers.

The Mayan calendar was an outgrowth of developments that began sometime after 1000 BCE in Olmec-influenced Paso de la Amada. One calendar was the

260-day, or 9-month, divinatory calendar, which scholars interpret as being related to the human gestation period. A second calendar, based on the solar year of 365 days and important for determining the beginnings of the agricultural seasons, was nearly as old. A third calendar was the Mayan Calendar Round, calculated as occurring every 52 years when the divinatory and solar calendars began on the same day. The Mayas believed that this calendar inaugurated cycles of calamitous as well as fortuitous times. The fourth calendar in use among the Mayas was the Long Count Calendar, which counted the days elapsed since the mythical origin of the universe (corresponding to August 11, 3114 BCE, in the Gregorian calendar). A sophisticated mathematics, based on a *vigesimal* system of numbers (twenty-based, in place of our modern decimal system), undergirded the calculations necessary for the coordination of these four calendars.

Other occupations of the royal family and leading courtiers consisted of daily processions and feasts during which copious amounts of cacao, spiced with chili, vanilla, and honey, were consumed. Alternatively, the elite consumed chocolate wafers, forerunners of our modern chocolate bars, which were also used as easily transportable nourishment on journeys. Finally, the court attended ball games in stadiums, which formed part of the temple-palace grounds. As in the kingdoms of Eurasia, but without evidence of any influence, in Maya kingdoms the occupations and functions of the ruling class were ritualized, refined pastimes far beyond the reach of common farmers and craftspeople. A stratified social hierarchy typified the Maya kingdoms (see "Patterns Up Close" on pp. 160–161).

The Commoners   The commoners, whose taxes supported the royal courts, lived in housing compounds of a few thatched huts or clusters of huts erected around courtyards on stone platforms, which allowed them to be above the floodwaters during the rainy season. In these houses, women were in charge of cooking, weaving, pottery making, the growing of garden vegetables and fruits, and the rearing of domestic animals (including dogs, turkeys, and pigeons). Garden fruits included avocado, guava, papaya, vanilla, and pineapple. Within the household, women and men shared the crafts of tool making, fabricating tools from chert, bone, and wood. In larger Maya kingdoms some households seem to have specialized more than others in tool manufacturing and weaving, with both women and men participating.

Men were in charge of growing corn in fields which were cut into the rain forest through slash-and-burn techniques. Fields near rivers and in swamps were "raised fields" (Spanish *chinampas*), rectangle-shaped islands on which the mud from adjacent canals had been heaped. The main agricultural implement was the digging stick (Mayan *kool* [kohl]) with which farmers loosened the soil and dropped corn kernels into a hole. Slopes along river valleys were terraced in order to retain rain or irrigation water. Cotton, cacao, and tobacco fields formed special plantations because of either special soil preparation or intensive labor needs. Hunting and fishing with bow and arrow, blowguns, and harpoons, skills inherited from forager times, remained important occupations among both royals and commoners.

The hard agricultural labor of the commoners produced an agricultural surplus, which supported ruling dynastic families as well as craftspeople in the cities. Craftspeople worked for the construction and maintenance of royal palaces, creating monuments, wall paintings, pottery, and inscriptions on stone pillars or stelae.

Glyphic script: The
Maya developed a script
of some 800 images.
Some are pictograms
standing for words,
others are syllables to
be combined with other
syllables to form words.

Mayan Writing   Excavations in El Portón and San Bartoló in the early 2000s
suggest that Mayan writing might have begun as early as 400–300 BCE. These early
texts—although similar in appearance to the fully evolved script of the later centuries—still await decipherment. Their age raised the important question among
Maya specialists, whether the notion of the late Olmecs having developed writing
first can still be maintained. The Mayas might very likely have been the originators.

Mayan writing is a **glyphic** as well as a syllabic script, numbering some 800 signs.
It is structurally similar to Sumerian cuneiform and Egyptian hieroglyphic. The
glyphic part consists of *pictograms*, one-word images of the most essential features
of what is to be depicted (for example, the glyph for a human being would be a stick
figure with body, legs, arms, and a head). Glyphs as syllables consist of one, two, or
three signs, which stand for the combination of a consonant and a vowel. Combina-
tions of syllabic glyphs, or *syllabaries*, are pronounced as a series of syllables. Given
the mixture of pictograms and syllabaries, which is potentially immense, the complexity of Mayan writing appeared for a long time to be an insuperable obstacle to
any effort at deciphering.

A breakthrough came only in the 1960s and 1970s when scholars successfully interpreted a number of stelae monuments to kings recording the dates of their birth,
accession to the throne, and death. First, scholars realized that Mayan writing had
an important syllabic component; then, the Russian-born American architect and
Maya specialist Tatiana Proskouriakoff discovered that the inscriptions on many
royal stelae contained information on dynastic dates and events. The final breakthrough came during a conference at the Maya site of Palenque in 1973 when participants recognized the syllables *k'inchi* as referring to the Mayan sun god as well
as individual kings. As first in Mesopotamia and then in many other places, kings
invoked patron gods that symbolized forces in nature and thereby became founders of polytheism, as mentioned above. In one inspirational afternoon, a working group consisting of the art historian and epigrapher Linda Schele, the linguist
Floyd Lounsbury, and the undergraduate Peter Mathews, deciphered the king list of
Palenque, containing eight rulers. Since then, scholars have assembled a dictionary
of as many as 1,000 words and it has become possible to embark on a systematic
chronicling of the dynasties of Maya kingdoms.

The Crisis of the Kingdoms   Spectacular building activities characterized
Mayaland during the Late Classic Period (ca. 400–600 CE). Ruling classes must
have grown to considerable sizes, and it is possible that farmers in some kingdoms
were no longer willing to produce food staples as well as provide labor for the
pyramid temples and palaces. Destruction identified in some archaeological sites
could be interpreted as the result of revolts. In other places, overexploitation of
the soil, loss of topsoil on terraces, or salinization of lowland fields as the result of
neglected drainage might have increased the imbalance between the peasants and
ruling classes. Frequent wars among the kings might have reduced the size of the
ruling class, but their wars clearly also had negative consequences for the farmers.

The interplay between the ruling class, farmers, and the environment produced a
crisis beginning in the late 500s CE and extending through the mid-600s CE, leading
to the collapse of many older Mayan kingdoms and endangering the survival of the
strongest newer ones in the southern lowlands. When the crisis ended, the political
weight of Maya power shifted to the northern lowlands of the Yucatán Peninsula.

The Kingdom of Teotihuacán in the Mexican Basin

The subtropical climate of Yucatán extended northward into the highlands, in which the Mexican basin was the largest agricultural region. Although the high elevation did not allow for the full breadth of Maya agriculture, the alluvial soil and water from the surrounding mountains supported a productive agriculture of beans, squash, and corn. The northern part of the basin developed a rich village life later than the south, but its closeness to obsidian quarries gave these villages commercial advantages. Militarily and economically, the town of Teotihuacán in the north caught up to the south around the early 100s CE and developed into a city-state that became politically and culturally dominant across all of Mesoamerica.

The Mexican Basin   The Mexican basin is a large, 7,400-foot-high bowl without river outlets in southern Mexico. In the center of the bowl was Lake Texcoco [Tes-CO-co], nourished by rivers flowing down from 15,000-foot-high mountain chains on the eastern and western sides. As in Mayaland, the basin enjoyed a rainy season from May to September. River water, channeled through irrigation canals to terraces and the flatlands around the central lake, as well as numerous bays, supported a moderately productive agriculture.

During the period of village expansion (1200–600 BCE), many of the slopes surrounding this bowl were forested. There was plenty of firewood and timber for construction, as well as abundant wildlife for the hunt. Fish in the freshwater bays of the lake was another important food source. Clay deposits in the flatlands and obsidian quarries on the slopes of the still active volcanoes in the northeastern mountains provided resources for the manufacture of ceramics, tools, and weapons. However, the high elevation and temperature differences between winter and summer did not allow for cultivation of the cotton, cacao, vanilla, and tropical fruits which enriched lowland Maya agriculture. These latter products had to be acquired by trade.

The principal plant fiber for the weaving of clothes came from the *maguey* [Ma-GAY] plant, a large, deep-rooted, agave-like cactus that could grow in poor soil and did not need much water. The fiber was gained from scraping the sweet-tasting flesh off the interior of the long, stalk-like leaves. The flesh contained a juice which, in its fermented state, was consumed as an alcoholic drink called *pulque* [Spanish, PULL-kay; Nahuatl, *octli*]. If people wished to manufacture clothes from cotton or acquire cacao, vanilla, jade, or quetzal feathers, they had to trade their obsidian. Commercial exchange was a firm ingredient of the period of village expansion and played a major part in the subsequent pattern of kingdom formation.

Teotihuacán   In a wide valley to the northeast of Lake Texcoco, traversed by the San Juan River and endowed with rich alluvial soil, villagers in the early centuries CE dug a large canal system with raised fields similar to those of the Maya. Around 100 BCE, villages around this canal network began to cluster, eventually forming the city of Teotihuacán. When the transition from chieftains to kings and chiefly

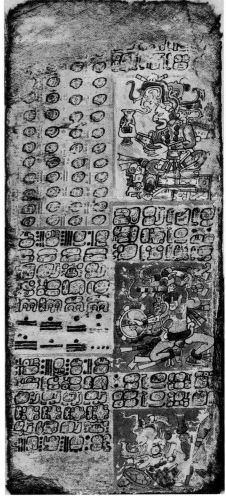

Mayan Glyphs. Beginning in the fourth century BCE, scribes in the Maya kingdoms developed a written language composed of morphemes (word elements) and syllables, eventually numbering about 800 signs. This language allowed communication among educated people in the different Maya kingdoms who spoke often mutually unintelligible local languages. Because of the double meaning of each glyph as morpheme and syllable, it took most of the twentieth century for scholars to decipher the Mayan language. The example shown here is from the Dresden Codex.

The Mayan Ball Game

One of the most remarkable features in Mesoamerica was the team ball game. Although it shares its ancient age with similar games in China, the Persian Middle East, and the Greek and Roman Mediterranean, only in Mesoamerica was it a game with formal rules, played in stadiums constructed specifically for this purpose. In Mesoamerica, archaeologists in 1985 discovered the oldest stadium to date, 1400 BCE, in the ruins of Paso de la Amada, a chiefdom town with surrounding villages in the far southeast of today's Mexico. Adjacent to the palace of the chief, this ball court measures 260 by 23 feet, with two 7-foot-high spectator platforms on both long sides. Later on, during the Maya period, these platforms usually rose theater-style on both sides, for better viewing from farther away. Given the proximity of the ball court to the chief's residence, it is possible that other chiefdoms in the area engaged in what we would call today "league tournaments."

The Mayan Ball Game. Note the strong body protection around the mid-section of the players as well as the elaborate headdresses, symbolizing animals.

The ball was made of solid rubber, from a gum- or latex-producing tree growing in the area of Paso. Balls were around 2 feet or more in diameter and weighed 8 pounds. Given these dimensions, players often wore protective gear around their hips and helmets on their heads, as shown in murals and on ceramics.

dynasties occurred is impossible to determine on the basis of the present archaeological record. The iconic writing system, less developed than that of the Mayas and lacking syllabic elements, does not allow for identification of any rulers or lineages. Teotihuacán was a city-state with an anonymous dynasty, centered in a city and surrounded by villages. In its physical appearance it was even more imposing than most of the Maya kingdoms (see Map 6.4).

In the first century CE, the rulers of Teotihuacán began spectacular building projects. They laid out an urban grid along a north–south axis, dubbed the "Avenue of the Dead" by archaeologists, which included two densely constructed city quarters of some 2,200 housing units. Each unit housed a patrilineal clan of 60–100 members. Near the central avenue, closely packed and plastered adobe houses were divided by alleyways. Some 600 houses have the appearance of workshops, primarily for the making of tools from the gray and green obsidian mined near Teotihuacán. The workshops indicate a degree of nonagricultural crafts specialization, which one would expect from a city. Farther away, houses and fields were interspersed. Canals, reservoirs, and an extensive drainage system facilitated the transportation of food, the provision of drinking water, and the elimination of waste. By around 300 CE, Teotihuacán had grown to as many as 100,000 inhabitants. It was a metropolis easily comparable to Rome, Ctesiphon, and Alexandria in the Roman Mediterranean and Persian Middle East; Patliputra in Gupta India; and Chang'an in Han China.

An aerial view of Teotihuacán's ruins conveys an idea of the vast scale on which the temple pyramids, palaces, markets, and city quarters were built. The Temples of

Under the Maya, who called the game *pitz* and built about 1,500 courts, the rules became more formalized. A basic rule was that the ball had to be hit with the hip only and had to remain aloft. But variations are also known, in which players struck the ball with their forearms, bats, or hand stones. The size of a team extended from one to seven players. The team that lost was the one that dropped the ball most often.

The significance of the Mayan ball game fits into the larger picture of agrarian–urban society and its chiefdom and kingdom patterns when polytheism with its innumerable rituals and sacrificial practices assumed elaborate proportions. Although the archaeological record is debatable, it appears that ball games took place during chiefly or royal festivities and fertility rituals, perhaps also human sacrifices. The apparent but also disputed role of some players as human sacrifices on a number of murals was a late Mayan phenomenon. Today, in scientific–industrial society, these roots of "games" in past rituals, processions, and reenactments of divine events are largely forgotten. Instead, sports have their own modern rituals, such as flag waving, parading, tailgating, and hooliganism. Whether religious or secular, rituals are a permanent fixture that follow their own patterns, parallel to those of society at large.

Questions

- How did the ball game serve as a microcosm for larger patterns in Mayan society?
- What function could the ball game have played in relations among the various Mayan chiefdoms?

the Moon and the Sun, built at the northern end of the city, represent the earliest structures. They were ceremonial centers which attracted pilgrims from everywhere in the Mexican basin and beyond. Archaeologists interpret the Temple of the Sun as a construction on top of a cave symbolizing the entrance to the nether world. In the third century CE, the temple of the god of the feathered serpent (Nahuatl *Quetzalcoatl* [Ket-sal-COA]) followed, probably built in honor of the then reigning dynasty. The founding king sacrificed some 260 humans, probably war captives, to garner the good will of the god. After what appears to have been an internal uprising and change in leadership in the 400s CE, the new rulers destroyed the temple's facade and erected an attachment (Spanish *adosada*) in front of it. Colorful wall paintings and pottery, depicting rulers, priests, gods, and mythical figures in processions, rituals, and dances, still survive, attesting to a highly developed aesthetic culture. Today, after a century of intermittent excavations, much has been learned about the city's architecture, but little is yet known about its rulers and inhabitants.

The Decline of the City   As in the case of the Maya kingdoms, the balance among the peasantry, urban inhabitants, dynasties, and construction programs was not always easy to maintain. Hints at an internal upheaval in the 400s CE point to the balance being lost at least once during Teotihuacán's existence. Another such upheaval occurred in the early 500s CE, to judge from fires and destructions along the Avenue of the Dead, possibly in the course of a popular uprising against the rulers. Thereafter, the population of the central city quarters declined rapidly, although

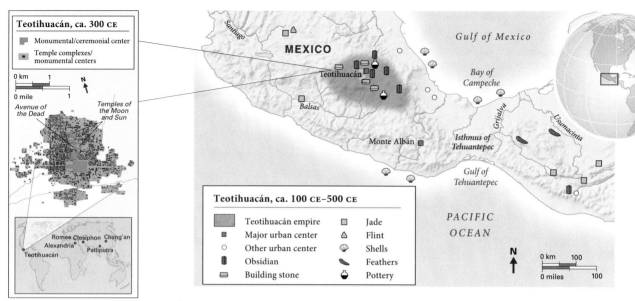

MAP **6.4** Teotihuacán, ca. 100 CE–500 CE.

the outlying quarters continued to exist, reverting back to the village level as farming communities for centuries to come. The mid-500s CE saw prolonged periods of cooler weather and droughts and were generally a more difficult time for farming in the Americas. As we shall see in Chapter 15, in contrast to the agriculturally richer Maya kingdoms, the less endowed Mexican basin found a return to urbanism and dynastic states more difficult.

At its height, Teotihuacán exerted a commercial, cultural, and perhaps even political influence considerably greater than the Maya kingdoms. Its trade reached deep into Mayaland and beyond, to the Isthmus of Panama. Teotihuacán exchanged its obsidian for cotton, rubber, cacao, jade, and quetzal feathers from the subtropics. Its gods, especially the deity of the feathered serpent, were sacrificed to everywhere in Mesoamerica. Similarly, Teotihuacán was instrumental in spreading the so-called *talud-tablero* architectural style (sets of inward-sloping platforms, surmounted by temples) from the basin of Mexico to the Yucatán Peninsula. In the later 300s CE and throughout the 400s CE, Maya rulers of Tikal, Uaxactún [Wa-sha-TOON], and other kingdoms claimed descent from rulers of Teotihuacán, evidently seeking to benefit from the city's prestige as a ceremonial center.

The Andes: Moche and Nazca

In Andean South America, a pattern of chiefdom formation, wherein chieftains controlled urban ceremonial centers and surrounding villages, evolved between 3000 and 2000 BCE, a millennium earlier than in Mesoamerica. Given the absence of large plains and the enormous differences in elevation within short distances, however, relatively small chiefdoms remained the dominant social formation in the Andes. Still, around 1000–200 BCE, a major ceremonial center like Chavín de Huántar (north of present-day Lima) was a town with fewer than 5,000 inhabitants, even though it was a pilgrimage site for most of the Andes. Chavín's successors, the chiefdoms of Moche and Nazca, although somewhat larger, remained within the chiefdom pattern during the period 600 BCE–600 CE.

The Moche in Northern Peru

The Moche Valley was the place of the two largest ceremonial centers in the Andes, the Temple Pyramids of the Sun and the Moon. The power of its main chiefdom must have been impressive since large numbers of farmers had to be mobilized for the construction of these pyramids. But it remained a federation of village chiefdoms clustered around an urbanized temple center with a dominant chiefly lineage.

Teotihuacán, Temple of the Feathered Serpent God, Quetzacóatl. This sculpture of a serpent's head with its exposed, menacing fangs and the collar made of feathers is one of many along the front wall of this temple. The hybrid deity (green quetzal bird and cóatl snake) bridged the fertile earth and the planet Venus, bringer of rain in the summer.

Moche Origins The Moche Valley was at the center of nine coastal valleys in what is today northern Peru. It had a subtropical climate south of the equator with moderately wet winters from April to November and dry summers from December to March. It was based on an irrigated agriculture of corn, pulses, cotton, and peanuts; llamas and alpacas from the highlands were domesticated for wool and light transportation. Here, the earliest evidence of the emergence of the Moche chiefdoms (100–750 CE) is the tomb of the "Lord of Sipán," dated to 50 CE. The tomb contained the chief's mummy, clad in warrior clothing and richly decorated with gold and silver necklaces, nose rings, ear rings, helmets, and bracelets. Eight people were buried with him, including his wife, two other women (perhaps concubines), a military officer, a watchman, a banner holder, a child, and a dog. This chieftain was wealthy and powerful indeed.

A Federated Chiefdom Half a century later, Moche chieftains began the construction of the two Temple Pyramids of the Sun and the Moon, huge stepped temple pyramids made of adobe bricks. Markers on the bricks indicate the participation of about 100 village teams in the construction, which lasted intermittently for centuries. The platforms contain the burial places of Moche chieftains and priests and the remains of human sacrifices brought during ceremonies and rituals. At the feet of the two temples was a city that included administrative offices and workshops. Lesser chieftain lineages ruled in the more remote valleys. Altogether the chiefdoms formed a loose federation around a main ceremonial center and pilgrimage place.

None of the participating villages appears to have grown beyond the moderately large spaces at the mouth of valleys, and it seems that they coexisted peacefully for the most part. When the generally cooler and drier climate of the sixth century CE arrived, it had a greater negative impact on the agriculture of the central chiefdom in Moche, closer to the coast and more remote from the river waters, than on the chiefdoms upstream in the adjacent smaller valleys. In the Moche Valley with its two huge temples the balance between chiefly elites and farmers was more difficult to maintain than in the farther valleys with smaller elites and comparatively larger peasantries. Eventually, in the early 600s CE, the Moche elite dissolved, while smaller elites in other valleys carried on and eventually disappeared also, sometime around 750 CE (see Map 6.5).

Paracas and the Nazca in Southern Peru

Southern Peru was much drier, and its agrarian population density lagged behind that of the north. The chiefdoms were correspondingly more modest. Nevertheless, Paracas [Pa-RA-cas] represents one of the earliest burial places for mummies in the world, and Nazca offers the most elaborate petroglyphs of the Americas. The two possess, therefore, considerable cultural significance.

Paracas Chiefs   Desert conditions on the southern Peruvian coast and full dependence on runoff water from Andean snowmelt between January and March after the Andes winter required more elaborate irrigation works than on the northern coast. The patterns of social formation from foraging to villages and chiefdoms with ceremonial centers were correspondingly slower and more modest. Shamans and chiefs on the Paracas peninsula and the Ica valley set the pattern in motion when they unified a number of hamlets. Subsequently, other Paracas chiefdoms appeared in neighboring valleys, forming a loose confederation (750 BCE–1 CE). A necropolis on the peninsula contained hundreds of mummies of chieftains, wrapped in the colorful, high-quality wool and cotton mantles still today characteristic of southern Peru. It was primarily through the icons woven into the mantles and painted on pottery that modern scholars identified the Paracas chiefs. These icons included figures—shamanic ancestors or early agricultural, polytheistic deities—holding weapons, plants, or skulls. Other icons were felines, birds, or whales, often with human-like features reminiscent of Paleolithic cave paintings in other parts of the world. Although contemporary with the Maya kingdoms in Mesoamerica, the Paracas chiefdoms in the Andes were culturally still compact.

Moche Terracotta Portrait Vessel with Handle, ca. 100–800 CE. Archaeologists assume that the vessel shows a chief. Other types of Moche vessels show deities, animals, ritual objects, sexual acts (for education?), domestic objects, and crafts activities. Potters often used stone molds for making their wares. Among the Andes people, the Moche potters were among the most imaginative and versatile.

The Nazca Ceremonial Center

The transition from pottery painted after firing to predecorated or slipware ceramics defines the shift from the Paracas to the Nazca chiefdoms (1–650 CE). Nazca chiefs built ceremonial centers, not the monumental freestanding ones as on the northern Peruvian coast but more modest adobe structures, which actually covered preexisting mounds. Cahuachi [Ca-wooh-WAH-tshee], the main pilgrimage center, contained 40 such structures, assumed to represent the contributing chiefdoms.

During the extended cold weather and drought periods of the sixth century CE, when a number of rivers dried out, Nazca chiefs mobilized the villagers in the valleys for the construction of an extensive tunnel network for irrigation. Workers tapped underground water in the mountains and guided it onto the slopes of the valleys and into reservoirs. These highly sophisticated constructions, with intermittent shafts and manholes for cleaning and repair, were built so sturdily that many of them are still in operation today. Called *puquios* [Quechua, POO-kyos], they are reminiscent of the much later *qanat* [Arabic, Ka-NAHT] structures of Islamic Iran and Morocco. In the agrarian age, chiefdoms could be technologically just as innovative as kingdoms and empires.

Geoglyphs: Long geometric lines and figures as well as outlines of animals formed in the desert by picking up darker stones and exposing the lighter sand underneath.

The Nazca Geoglyphs

Another Nazca innovation were the so-called Nazca **geoglyphs**, large geometrical and animal figures laid out in the dry highlands and on the valley slopes of the chiefdoms. Villagers constructed straight and zigzag lines,

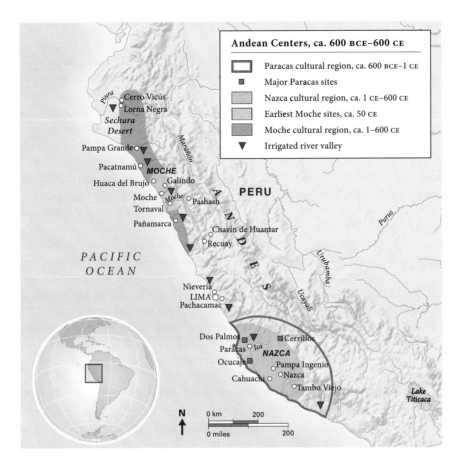

MAP **6.5** Andean Centers, 600 BCE–600 CE.

triangles and trapezoids, as well as images of a monkey, spider, whale, and several birds with astounding precision, by removing dark-colored rocks and exposing the lighter sand underneath. These geoglyphs are unique in the Andes, and the closest parallel did not occur until nearly a millennium later when the Incas arranged sacred objects (Quechua, *huacas*) outside their capital, Cuzco, in straight lines.

There are, however, vague parallels with a considerable number of undated later geoglyphs in the Great Basin and other western regions of North America. Native Americans under the leadership of shamans used these geoglyphs during rituals in which they evoked honored figures, animals, and events of the mythical past. Processual archaeologists (archaeologists applying concepts of cultural evolutionism), relate the Nazca symbols to the abstract Paleolithic geometrical cave symbols found in Africa, Europe, and Australia (see Chapter 1). Eventually, the Nazca came under the influence of the highland state of Wari, a later city-state in the Andes (see Chapter 15). This state expanded its political and cultural influence toward the southern Peruvian coast in the first half of the 700s CE and gradually gave the Nazca chiefdoms a new identity.

Nazca Lines. Spider. These lines can only be seen from the air—perhaps by a sky god?

Putting It All Together

In the period 600 BCE–600 CE, agriculture and life in villages became near universal in the world. Only Australia remained outside this development from foraging to agrarian settlement. Of course, remnants of foraging societies survived, notably in sub-Saharan Africa and even more so in the Americas. But it is nevertheless striking that humans on the latter two continents developed in the same direction as those in Eurasia toward cities, kingdoms, and long-distance luxury trade.

Agrarian-based urban culture, however, was a fragile achievement in Eurasia and even more so in sub-Saharan Africa, Mesoamerica, and the Andes. Irregularities of the weather and, in the latter regions, the slow improvement of food plant productivity (as revealed by plant archaeologists) meant that agriculture was a tenuous enterprise. Corn, especially, evolved only slowly toward a greater cob length and was still quite short during the Maya period. Only by the time of the Aztecs, selective breeding had produced corn of modern proportions. As a rule, dynastic cities regularly outstripped the natural resources of their local environments, as was the case in Meroë, Aksum, the Maya cities, and Teotihuacán. But once the option of urbanization had arrived, it was usually not lost again and sooner or later new city-based states arose.

As we have seen in this chapter, the primary dynastic urban achievements were monumental architecture, sophisticated metal and textile craftsmanship, and, in some cases, forms of intellectual expression. Typical examples covered in this chapter were the remarkably similar monumental temple pyramids and stelae of the kings in northeastern sub-Saharan Africa, Mesoamerica, and the Andes. Metal and textile craftsmanship, of course, had deep village roots on both sides of the Atlantic. Gold, silver, copper, and bronze jewelry was often exquisite; and the iron manufacture in African villages was remarkably developed. In cities these crafts became the refined products of specialized workers who did not participate in farming.

Similarly, precocious intellectual achievements appeared both in nomadic contexts (complementary to agriculture), as witnessed by the Borana calendar of the Kushite nomads in Kenya, and in small-town agricultural chiefdoms, as seen in the giant geometrical lines and animal outlines created in the desert landscape by the Nazca of Peru. By comparison, the intellectual pursuits in royal cities were on a much larger scale. Here, the Mayas took the prize with their complex calendar and script, as well as their elaborate divine pantheon and cosmogony.

Altogether, evolving largely on their own, both sub-Saharan Africa and the Americas made long strides in the period 600 BCE–600 CE toward expressing the same depth of humanity which was already on display in Eurasia. They did not yet have empires or possess the literary breadth that favored the rise of the visionaries of transcendence, hallmarks of the Middle East, India, and China during 600 BCE–600 CE. But their more compact cultures were not lacking in any of the overall patterns that characterized Eurasia.

▶ For additional resources, including maps, primary sources, visuals, and quizzes, please go to www.oup.com/us/vonsivers. Please see the Further Resources section at the back of the book for additional readings and suggested websites.

Thinking Through Patterns

▶ **How does comparing and contrasting sub-Saharan Africa with the Americas during 600 BCE–600 CE help in understanding the agrarian–urban patterns of social and political development across the world?**

Innovations in world history usually originated in one specific place and then radiated outward into new populations through interactions among different peoples. Through adaptation, the new populations incorporated innovations into their own cultures. Adaptation was never slavish imitation; it was always a creative process of shaping something from a different culture to the new culture's needs and circumstances. Sub-Saharan Africa and the Americas were partially or entirely limited to their own internal innovation patterns, given their relative or absolute isolation from Eurasia. Encountering the same experiences and challenges as humans in Eurasia, albeit somewhat later, their responses were remarkably comparable. Thus, the history of the world was not merely the history of peoples coming into more and more intensive contact with each other. It was also the history of peoples experiencing similar challenges without transcontinental interaction.

Agrarian sub-Saharan Africa during 600 BCE–600 CE is an example where interaction with the Middle East—as well as, in some periods, its absence—formed the background for comparable processes of economic, social, and political developments. The middle Nile valley and the highlands of Ethiopia gave rise to the plow-based agrarian kingdoms of Meroë and Aksum, both receiving their original plows and grain from the Middle East and maintaining a lively trade for luxury goods with that region. By contrast, the West African inland Niger delta grew into the urbanized chiefdom of Jenné-jero without recognizable external interactions. Through interaction and adaptation, forms of farming as well as iron smelting (the latter perhaps received from the Middle East) migrated south in sub-Saharan Africa, together with called Bantu expansion.

▶ **Where did chiefdoms, cities, and kingdoms arise in sub-Saharan Africa and why? On which forms of agriculture, urbanization, and trade were they based?**

▶ **Which areas in the Americas saw the development of a corn- and potato-based agriculture that did not depend on the plow, the wheel, and iron making?**

Three regions in the Americas were favorable for the development of densely settled villages, some of which subsequently evolved into cities and kingdoms: Yucatán with its Maya kingdoms, the Mexican basin with the city-state of Teotihuacán, and Peru with the Moche and Nazca chiefdoms. The Maya kingdoms were economically and culturally the most differentiated polities—and the only ones to record the histories of their kings in writing on stelae and other monuments. Highly productive farming took place on riverbanks or hill terraces, with a surplus that supported the construction of elaborate temple pyramids and structures containing painted ceramics and wall paintings.

Chapter 7 550 BCE-600 CE

Persia, Greece, and Rome

PERSIA, GREECE, AND ROME

Mediterranean Sea

At one of his banquets after vanquishing the Achaemenid [A-KEE-ma-need] Persian Empire in 330 BCE, the world conqueror Alexander the Great (r. 336–323 BCE) had a violent confrontation with one of his leading commanders, Cleitus. Flatterers at the banquet compared Alexander to the gods, and Alexander himself boasted that his conquests were far superior to those of his father, Philip. Cleitus, older than Alexander and an officer in Philip's army who had been engaged in the preparations for the Greek conquest of Persia, angrily interjected. It was the army that was the true victor, he objected, noting that he himself had saved Alexander's life in at least one of the battles against the Persians.

The exchange became heated, fueled by copious amounts of wine. At one point, Cleitus loudly complained about Alexander demanding everyone, Greek and Persian, to fall on their knees when entering his presence. As the shouting match continued, Alexander first threw an apple at Cleitus, then reached for his sword—which guards had prudently removed—and finally grabbed a javelin, killing Cleitus with a lightning-like thrust. Almost before the blow had been struck, Alexander regained his senses. Deeply remorseful, he grieved over the death of his companion; according to one source, he abstained from food and drink for several days, bewailing the loss of his veteran commander.

Although the sources that report the incident vary considerably in detail, they agree that the quarrel was about the question of Alexander remaining

ABOVE: Detail of the Ludovisi sarcophagus (c. 175 CE), depicting battle between Romans and "barbarians."

true to his Macedonian/Greek heritage or becoming a Persian "king of kings." Was he still a first among equals? Was he still bringing liberty to the Greeks of Asia? Or was he becoming a divinely mandated monarch who could command Persians and Greeks alike to obey him on bended knee? Not surprisingly, these questions arose right at the time that Alexander had completed the liberation of the Greeks from Persian rule, destroyed the Persian Empire, and was about to begin his conquest of India. He was on his way to becoming the exalted single ruler of the then known world, encompassing all nations, languages, and religions on earth, a world similar to that heaven where Zeus ruled all gods and goddesses (or the Libyan god Ammon, from whom Alexander believed he was descended).

Seeing Patterns

▶ Why should the Middle East and Mediterranean Europe during the period 600 BCE–600 CE be studied as a single unit?

▶ What is transcendence, and why is it important to understand its importance in world history?

▶ Which elements characterize the institutions growing out of the Middle Eastern monotheisms of Judaism and Christianity and the monism of Greek philosophy and science?

The Middle East and Mediterranean during 600 BCE–600 CE was a region that was culturally diverse, as illustrated by Cleitus' contrast between Greek liberties and Achaemenid Persian royal power. It was also an area of intense military rivalry, as we see in Alexander's avenging the Persian dominance of Greece in 386 by his own conquest of Persia in 334. Later on, as we shall learn in this chapter, the successor states of Parthian and Sasanid Persia and Rome continued the rivalry. However, already in the sixth century BCE, Greek, Jewish, and Iranian visionaries introduced very similar *monotheistic* (single personal god) and *monist* (single impersonal principle) forms of thought into the region. Centuries later, in the rivalry between Persia and Rome, the opposing state religions of Christianity and Zoroastrianism also faced off against each other. In short, this chapter focuses on one single region that had evolved from its Mesopotamian and Egyptian agrarian–urban origins and shared such basic patterns as imperialism, monotheism, and monism but was also torn apart by concrete and unbridgeable political and cultural differences. Intense internal interaction and adaptation characterized the Middle East and Mediterranean in the period 600 BCE–600 CE.

Interactions Between Persia and Greece

The Achaemenid Persian conquest of the Middle East, from Anatolia and Egypt in the west to northwestern India in the east, was a relatively easy affair compared to the conquest of Greece, where inhabitants resisted fiercely. Although Persia was able to subjugate the Greek city-states of the Anatolian coast, it proved unable to conquer the Greek mainland. A century and a half later, Alexander the Great unified Greece and led it to victory over Persia, establishing a short-lived Macedonian–Greek Empire. Alexander's generals divided the empire into three successor kingdoms under which politics stabilized until the Persians, under the Parthians and Sasanids, renewed the Persian imperial tradition.

The Origins of the Achaemenid Persian Empire

The Persians originated as agrarian villagers and nomadic horse and sheep breeders during the Bronze Age in central Asia south of the Ural Mountains. Toward the end of the third millennium BCE, groups of nomads migrated from the Urals southward and, by the middle of the second millennium BCE, reached the Aral Sea region. From here, some migrants pushed farther, establishing themselves in Upper Mesopotamia and India around 1200 BCE. The Persians were a branch that migrated sometime before the 800s BCE from the Aral Sea region to the southwestern Iranian province of Fars, from which the name "Persia" is derived.

Persian Conquests   The first Persians to appear in the historical record were the Medes, who presided over a loosely organized kingdom with provincial vassals adjacent to the Assyrian Empire in Fars. The head of one vassal family, Cyrus II the Great (r. ca. 550–530 BCE) of the Achaemenids, assumed the crown of the Persians in 550 BCE and, in contrast to the Medes, embarked on an ambitious imperial program. Cyrus first expanded into Anatolia, where he conquered the kingdom of Lydia [LEE-dee-ya]. The Lydians are notable for having created in 615 BCE the first minted money in world history, coins made of silver and gold and used in trade. Next, Cyrus turned to the neighboring Greek city-states of Ionia on the southwestern Anatolian coast. His generals besieged these cities one by one, until their inhabitants either surrendered or returned to the Greek mainland.

Cyrus himself was busy with the conquest of the Iranian interior and north, as far as Afghanistan. In 540 BCE he began his campaign against Neo-Babylonia in Mesopotamia, capturing the capital of Babylon a year later. The Phoenician city-states in Syria submitted voluntarily in the following years. Within a little more than a decade, Cyrus had defeated the most important powers of the period and had unified all of the Middle East except Egypt, which Persia conquered a little later, in 525 BCE (see Map 7.1).

Persian Arms   The Achaemenids achieved their conquests with the help of lightly armed, highly mobile mounted archers as well as heavily armored, slow-moving **cataphracts**—horsemen with protective armor consisting of iron scales sewn on leather shirts. The archers fought with composite bows and the cataphracts, with 5-foot-long, iron-tipped lances for thrusting. Saddles and stirrups had not yet been invented, and hence, the lance—requiring the mounted user to have a firm footing with which to brace himself—was still a relatively short, modest weapon.

Cataphracts: Heavily armed and protected cavalry soldiers.

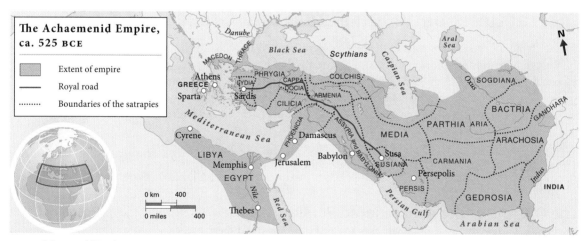

MAP **7.1 Achaemenid Persian Empire.**

Infantry soldiers armed with bows, arrows, shields, and javelins provided support for the cavalry, complementing its tank-like thrust.

Early on, Persian kings supplemented their armies with heavily armored infantry recruited from among the Anatolian Greeks. These foot soldiers, called **hoplites**, fought shoulder to shoulder in ranks, called "phalanxes." They were equipped with 8-foot-long, iron-tipped thrusting spears, short iron swords, large shields held on the left forearm, helmets, and iron-scale protective armor. In close quarters, hoplite phalanxes were nearly invincible. Even in the open, however, phalanxes were difficult to crack, unless attacked by mounted archers on their right, unshielded flank.

Hoplites: Greek foot soldiers fighting in closed ranks, called "phalanxes."

The Persian navy comprised as many as 1,200 galleys during its peak in the fifth century BCE. The Ionian and Phoenician provinces of the Persian Empire constructed and staffed these galleys, which were long, narrow ships, approximately 100 feet long and 15 feet wide. Apart from fighting naval battles against the Greeks, the navy also explored the western Mediterranean and even unsuccessfully attempted the circumnavigation of Africa. Altogether, the Persian military was a formidable fighting machine stationed in garrisons and ports in the various provinces of the Middle East and eastern Mediterranean.

Persian Administration   The Achaemenid Persian Empire, encompassing not only the Middle Eastern agrarian centers of Mesopotamia and Egypt but also those of the Indus valley, is estimated to have had some 15 million inhabitants. The kings prided themselves on having at their palace in southwestern Iran containers of water from both the Nile and the Danube, which they served at their banquets to demonstrate their vast power. (King Darius I, the Great [r. 522–486 BCE], campaigned in 514 or 513 BCE against the Scythians in Russia, across the Danube.) The enormous size of the Persian territories demanded creative assimilation of the institutions they inherited. The empire consisted of some 70 ethnic groups, hundreds of temple cults, a small Persian aristocracy, and a limited central bureaucracy. Most kings prayed to the god Ahuramazda of the Zoroastrians, but others selected other deities from the Persian pantheon. Since the Achaemenids granted considerable autonomy to their 30 provinces, many of which retained their native ruling dynasties, temples, and legal systems, a bewildering number of languages, ethnic groups, and religious pantheons coexisted in the empire.

Around 500 BCE, the empire had become integrated enough that the kings could replace indigenous rulers with their own governors from the Persian aristocracy. These provincial governors, or *satraps*, supported by Persian troops in fortresses, were powerful rulers. They administered the Persian law, to which all imperial subjects could appeal from their own legal systems. The satraps also collected tributes and taxes, with which they maintained themselves and their troops, forwarding the

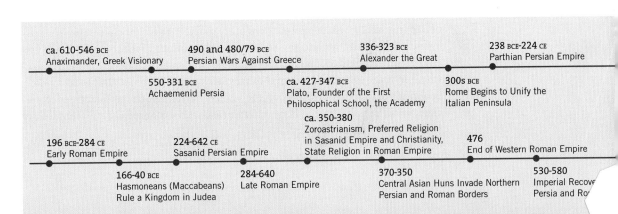

ca. 610-546 BCE
Anaximander, Greek Visionary

490 and 480/79 BCE
Persian Wars Against Greece

336-323 BCE
Alexander the Great

238 BCE-224 CE
Parthian Persian Empire

550-331 BCE
Achaemenid Persia

ca. 427-347 BCE
Plato, Founder of the First
Philosophical School, the Academy

300s BCE
Rome Begins to Unify the
Italian Peninsula

ca. 350-380
Zoroastrianism, Preferred Religion
in Sasanid Empire and Christianity,
State Religion in Roman Empire

476
End of Western Roman Empire

196 BCE-284 CE
Early Roman Empire

224-642 CE
Sasanid Persian Empire

166-40 BCE
Hasmoneans (Maccabeans)
Rule a Kingdom in Judea

284-640
Late Roman Empire

370-350
Central Asian Huns Invade Northern
Persian and Roman Borders

530-580
Imperial Recove
Persia and Ro

Persepolis. This relief from the stairs that approach the royal audience hall shows ambassadors from the various lands under the power of the "king of kings" humbly offering tribute.

Shahinshah: "King of kings," the title of Persian rulers.

remainder to the kings. When called upon by the kings, the governors contributed their provincial troops to the royal army. Officially, the Achaemenid king called himself "king of kings" (**shahinshah** [SHAW-in-shaw]), that is, emperor, in order to make his elevated status clear to all princes and governors of regional and Persian aristocratic origin, as well as the populace.

The venerable, 2,500-year-old Mesopotamian administrative institution, the assembly (*pukhru* [POO-kroo]) of urban citizens (see Chapter 1), remained in place. As in Greece, the members of this assembly were landowners with estates in the villages around the cities, but their formerly unlimited powers were now restricted to judicial matters. Transplanted ethnic groups also administered themselves within their own autonomous communities. This was the case among the Jews and Egyptians in the cities of Babylon, Sippar, and Nippur. Councils of elders in these communities were responsible for distributing water and land, prescribing internal tax assessments, and settling property disputes.

The *shahinshahs* had a number of palaces in Iran and Mesopotamia, among which Persepolis [Per-SAY-pow-lis] is the best known. Here, they maintained the central administration with its treasury and archive. The language used for administrative purposes was imperial Aramaic, a special bureaucratic version of the spoken and alphabetically written Aramaic that had become the predominant language of Mesopotamia and Syria in the previous centuries. Clay tablets continued to be used as writing material, particularly in Mesopotamia; but scribes preferred parchment or papyrus scrolls, which offered them more space. A basic principle of the empire's financial administration was the hoarding of all incoming silver and gold. Trade was not yet fully monetized, and the kings minted only small amounts of coins. As elsewhere in Asia, villagers continued to pay taxes or rents in kind and local markets continued to function primarily on the basis of barter. Enormous quantities of precious metal piled up in the Persian treasuries, with no purpose yet except luxury trade and the giving of presents.

The vast size of the empire dictated that the imperial administration pay close attention to its communication networks. Thus, the Persians created their famous "royal roads," perhaps the first such highways in the world. They consisted mostly of regularly maintained paths connecting Persia with Anatolia and Mesopotamia as directly as possible. Governors provided the roads with distance markers, constructed inns and depots at regular intervals, and protected them through a chain of police and army posts. The roads were intended primarily for quick troop movements, although traders with carts and pack animals used them as well.

Greek City-States in the Persian Shadow

In the sixth century BCE, while Persia evolved into an empire, hundreds of city-states— cities (singular *polis*; plural *poleis*) with surrounding villages—dotted the landscape in Anatolia, Greece, and Italy. The most populous of these *poleis* were Athens and Sparta. The two competed for dominance; but neither could overcome the other, and their rivalry eventually benefited Persia in its attempt to assume power over Greece.

Athens and Sparta   Most of the hundreds of city-states of which Greece was composed ruled themselves independently. The only common bonds, besides language, history, and culture, were a number of so-called **oracles** and the Olympic Games. Greeks went to the oracles to settle disputes or to divine their future. The Olympic Games, in the *polis* of Olympia, brought together the Greek youth for athletic competitions. Athens, with 200,000 inhabitants, and Sparta, with 140,000 inhabitants, were the largest city-states and exerted a certain dominance but ultimately accomplished little in terms of unification (see Map 7.2).

Oracles: Temples situated on the no-man's land between city-states and guided by priests or priestesses.

MAP **7.2 Greece in the Sixth Century BCE.**

Athens is located on the small peninsula of Attica in southeastern Greece. Its limited agricultural resources forced inhabitants to specialize in the growing of cash crops, such as wine, olive oil, nuts, and dried fruits. They traded these crops, together with woolen textiles and metal goods, for grain and metals from Italy and the Black Sea region. The growing focus on trade helped in the emergence of mercantile interests among the landowning citizenry. Disputes about representation in the ruling council and chronic debt among farmers forced the first among several reforms in 594 BCE under Solon. In 508 BCE, Cleisthenes, a prominent landowner, forged an alliance between merchant landowners and smallholders to bring about further constitutional reforms, broadening the citizenry to more modest property owners and ending the arbitrary rule of self-appointed strongmen. He expanded the rights among citizens to sit on juries and participate in the legislative assembly, which was enlarged to 500 members. Proposals adopted by the assembly were to be ratified by the citizenry, and executive power was vested in boards of elected magistrates. The reforms of Solon and Cleisthenes are often cited by scholars as the first steps toward the creation of Athenian democracy in the middle of the next century.

Sparta was another major city-state of Greece and Athens' principal rival. It was located on a plain in the Peloponnesus [Pay-lop-pon-NEE-soos] Peninsula southwest of Athens. Unlike the land-poor Athens, Sparta had room to enlarge its agricultural base before eventually turning to maritime trade. Its constitutional organization preceded that of Athens by a century and, therefore, embodies more traditional traits. Citizenship was based on landownership, and Spartan citizens were entitled to stand for participation in the 30-member Council of Elders and the five-member Board of Overseers, the decisions of which were ratified by the assembly of owners of medium-sized properties. Executive power was in the hands of two hereditary kings.

Army service was of crucial importance in Sparta. At age 7, boys left home and entered military camps to train as hoplites. Until the age of 30, married soldiers were not allowed to live with their wives but received extended military leaves in order to create large families. A thoroughgoing code of male citizen discipline dominated Sparta. Women also received rigorous physical training and were fully imbued with the Spartan military ethic: Wives or mothers seeing their men off to battle customarily handed them their shields with the parting words, "with it or on it."

The village farmers who tilled the land in Athens, Sparta, and the other Greek city-states were noncitizens of unfree status, in contrast to the free farmers in the Middle East. In Athens, they possessed basic rights and, as we have noted, were at the center of early reform efforts. In Sparta, however, the farmers, called *helots*, were the descendants of surrounding peoples conquered by Sparta during its years of expansion and tied to the land in perpetuity.

Since, in addition to villagers, women were excluded from political participation, constitutional rule benefited only small minorities in the Greek city-states. This was true even in the mid-fifth century BCE, when the final round of Athenian reforms under Pericles extended voting and office rights to all male citizens. While Athens' "golden age" of democracy was arguably the most open of the ancient world, it was still restricted to no more than one-third of the population at its height. Thus, what has been idealized by people in the modern era as a forerunner of our own institutions was in fact not very different from the urban assemblies in Mesopotamian cities or those of some of the early Indian city-states in the Ganges valley (see Chapter 3). In retrospect, Greece was thus not the only pioneer of constitutional rule:

It shared this role with other societies, although each adopted rule by assemblies independently and not as a result of interaction.

Greece and Persia   Their maritime commercial wealth made the Greek city-states irresistible targets of Persian imperialism. When Athens supported a revolt of the southwest Anatolian city-states in 499–494 BCE, the Persian monarchy found its justification to wage war against the Greeks. They suppressed the revolt and organized two large-scale invasions of the Greek mainland in the following years (492–490 and 480–479 BCE). Both invasions were well planned and included vastly superior land and sea forces. Storms took their toll on these forces, however, and long supply lines further compromised Persian military efficiency. To meet the invasion, the Greek city-states on the mainland united under the joint leadership of Athens and Sparta. In two battles, on land at Marathon (490 BCE) and on the sea at Salamis (480 BCE), the united Greeks took advantage of their better knowledge of local conditions and the utility of the phalanx against larger massed forces in narrow areas and repelled both Persian invasions. Greece managed to preserve its liberty and escape Persian imperial dominance. Soon, however, the Greek world was plunged into a long and devastating internal conflict.

After the repulsion of the Persian invasions, Athenian–Spartan unity fell apart. As a substitute, Athens formed a league with as many as 200 *poleis* around the Aegean and Black Seas and for about two decades harassed the Persians in the eastern Mediterranean. When Athens diverted a portion of the league's membership contributions to the reconstruction of its Persian War–damaged citadel, the Acropolis, however, anger against this perceived self-service erupted into the Peloponnesian War (431–404 BCE). During this war, Sparta made itself the champion of liberation from what many Greek cities viewed as an Athenian empire. After depleting Athens' land forces, Sparta—with Persian financial support—built a navy, which won a brilliant victory over Athens, forcing the latter to sue for peace in 404 BCE.

Once involved again in Greek politics, the Achaemenids played their cards carefully, this time stoking fears of Spartan dominance. During yet another round of hostilities, a coalition of city-states led by Athens and backed by Persia defeated Sparta. In the King's Peace of 386 BCE, the Persians granted the Greeks autonomy, or self-rule, according to their city-state constitutions, provided they recognized Persia's overall dominance. Persia held the purse strings, employing some 50,000 Greek hoplite mercenaries who became jobless in Greece after the King's Peace. Persian imperial lordship over Greece had finally become a reality, to last for about half a century.

Alexander's Empire and Its Successor Kingdoms

The one Greek area that remained outside Persian control was Macedonia, on the northern periphery of the Greek city-states. Although the Macedonians spoke a Greek dialect, the city-state Greeks considered them barbarians, that is, people mired in tribal customs and without an urban culture. In the middle of the 300s BCE, however, a king, Philip II (359–336 BCE), unified the country and provided it with a disciplined infantry army. He conquered the Greek city-states to the south, and his son, Alexander, continued the expansion with the conquest of Persia.

Alexander and His Successors   In 337 BCE, Philip employed his greatly enhanced military strength to declare war on the Persian Empire, in revenge for

East Meets West. A turbaned man stands next to a Corinthian capital in the Hellenistic city of Ai-Khanoum founded in what is today northern Afghanistan—ancient Bactria—in the fourth century BCE after Alexander's conquests. Ai-Khanoum was one of the focal points of Hellenism in the East. Archaeological excavations in the 1970s revealed a flourishing city, with a Greek-style theater, a huge palace, a citadel, a gymnasium, and various temples.

the Persian invasion of Macedonia and Greece a century earlier. He made himself the champion of Greek liberty in Asia, the "liberator" of the city-states in Anatolia. Just as Philip was getting ready to invade Anatolia, he was assassinated in a court intrigue. Philip's 20-year-old son, Alexander, took over both throne and campaign, setting off for Persia in 334 BCE. In three fiercely fought battles (334–330 BCE), Alexander outmaneuvered the Persian defenders with his highly motivated soldiers. The Persian king was the lesser strategist and tactician, but he and the Persian aristocracy resisted tenaciously. The Persian forces retreated slowly into what is today Afghanistan. Alexander occupied the Persian royal towns and confiscated the Persian treasury, including some 7,000 tons of precious metals. During a drunken revelry in the palace town of Persepolis, Alexander had the imperial palace burned down, as a final act of vengeance for the destruction of the Acropolis by the Persians.

After finishing off the Achaemenid forces in Afghanistan and occupying Bactria (modern Uzbekistan) to the northeast, Alexander invaded India. When he reached the Ganges basin, however, persistent monsoon rains and exhausted troops forced him to retreat. As he left, he appointed governors over northwest India. Under these governors, Greek culture entered the subcontinent and exerted a palpable influence even beyond 305 BCE when the expanding Maurya Empire conquered India (see Chapter 8). Alexander returned to the Middle East and made plans to trump the Persians by executing their unfulfilled plan to circumnavigate Africa. Before he could depart, however, a fever seized him; and within 10 days, at the age of 33, Alexander was dead (323 BCE). In the stupendously short time of just 11 years, he had turned the mighty Persian Empire into a Macedonian–Greek one (see Map 7.3).

Not surprisingly, this empire did not hold together. Alexander's one legitimate son was born after his father's death and had no chance to assume the throne. Alexander's generals divided the empire among themselves, founding kingdoms, among which Antigonid Greece (276–167 BCE), Ptolemaic Egypt (305–30 BCE), and Seleucid southwest Asia (305–64 BCE) were the most important.

Hellenistic: Period of Greek history from 323 BCE to 31 BCE.

Altogether, about 1 million Greeks emigrated during the 200s BCE to the Middle East, assimilating gradually into the local population of some 20 million and imprinting their **Hellenistic** (Greek-influenced) culture on urban life. Thus, even though the Macedonian–Greek Empire failed politically almost immediately, its cultural legacy lasted for centuries, even in far-away central Asia and India.

Interactions Between the Persian and Roman Empires

A century after Alexander's conquests, a resurgent Persia—in the shape of Parthia—appeared on the northeastern border of the Seleucid kingdom. This resurgence coincided with Rome's imperial expansion after the unification of Italy. On the periphery of the successor kingdoms of Alexander's Macedonian–Greek Empire, both Parthia

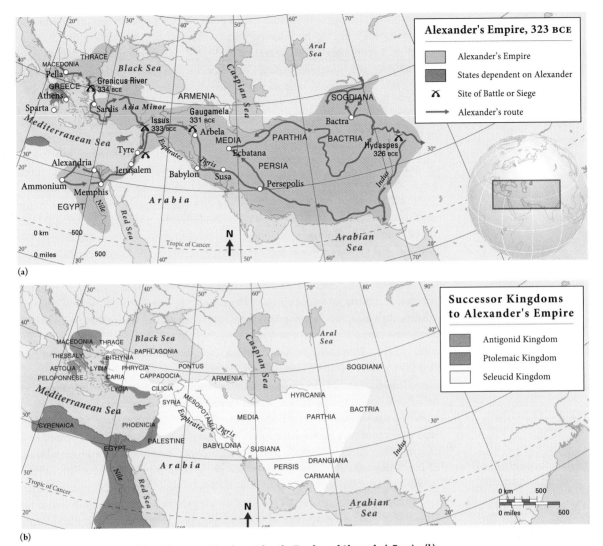

MAP **7.3** Alexander's Empire (*a*) and Successor Kingdoms After the Breakup of Alexander's Empire (*b*).

and Rome pressed against the Antigonids, Seleucids, and Ptolemies. After conquering these kingdoms, Rome and Parthia eventually came face to face in Anatolia and Syria in the early second century BCE. Neither, however, succeeded in eliminating the other, as strenuously as they tried in a long series of wars. As a result, the Middle East and the Mediterranean remained politically as divided as they had been in the previous centuries under the successor states of Alexander the Great.

Parthian Persia and Rome

Parthia was originally the name of the northeasternmost province of the Seleucid kingdom. In the 240s BCE, the tribal federation of the Parni, distant relatives of the Achaemenid Persians, migrated from the region east of the Aral Sea in central Asia to Parthia, where they defeated the Seleucid governor. The Seleucids, distracted by conflicts on their western front with Ptolemaic Egypt, were unable to prevent the Parthians from seizing provincial power. Initially, the Parthians recognized Seleucid overlordship, but they also expanded their power and in 141 BCE conquered Iran and Mesopotamia, reducing the Seleucids to a small rump kingdom in northern Syria. In 109 BCE, Mithridates II, the Great (r. ca. 123–88 BCE), formally renewed the Persian Empire in his newly founded capital Ctesiphon, today a suburb of Baghdad, by assuming the title "king of kings" and taking over the traditional Iranian pantheon of gods.

Parthian Diplomacy   Parthian Persia was a major power, in large part because of its diplomacy. In 115, Wudi [Woo-DEE] (r. ca. 140–87 BCE), the emperor of Han China, sent a diplomatic mission to Mithridates II, to explore the possibilities of an alliance as well as trade. The mission was part of Wudi's efforts, lasting nearly a quarter of a century, to secure his northern border against Turkic nomadic invaders and find allies among the nomads in Bactria across the Pamir mountains in the northwest of China. Bactria, consisting of the fertile Ferghana [Fer-GAH-nah] valley plain and surrounding mountain chains, had been governed previously by the Achaemenid Persians, Alexander, and Greek generals but had become independent after the end of the Seleucids.

When the first Chinese missions arrived in the valley, many nomads were in the process of settling into agricultural villages and displayed less desire for a military alliance than for trade. The missions then moved westward, where they encountered a militarily strong power in Parthian Persia. No alliance between Persia and China came to pass, however. Instead, this first diplomatic contact opened up the Silk Road, which, for many centuries to come, was the main central Asian trade route.

At the other end of this empire, on the upper Euphrates River, the Persians established first contacts with Rome, which in 103 BCE had occupied Cilicia, in southeastern Anatolia, and thereby had become Parthian Persia's western neighbor. In a diplomatic meeting, in which the envoy of the small, Persian-descended principality of Pontus in northern Anatolia participated as well, the three sides exchanged vows of friendship. The meeting, however, did not end on a positive note. The Roman governor seated himself in the middle and thereby sought to pull rank on the other two envoys, causing an infuriated Mithridates II to have his ambassador executed for allowing the Roman envoy to claim superiority. Not surprisingly, Rome and Persia soon came to blows.

Paestum, Southern Italy. By the sixth century BCE, Greek city-states were flourishing across southern Italy and Sicily, including Paestum, which has some of the best preserved temples outside of Greece, including the Temple of Hera shown here.

Roman Republican Origins   The western Mediterranean, adapting to agriculture around 3000 BCE and to the Iron Age after 1000 BCE, became part of the Middle Eastern and eastern Mediterranean agrarian centers in the course of the first millennium BCE. Phoenicians from the eastern Mediterranean established ports along the northern shores of Africa, in Spain, and on the islands of Sicily and Sardinia, attracted by the prospects of rich mineral resources. Their principal port at the entrance to the western Mediterranean, in today's Tunisia, was Carthage. Later on, Greeks established city-states in southern Italy and Sicily. In north-central Italy was the kingdom of the Etruscans, a local people assumed in recent scholarship to be linguistically related to the Hungarians and settled in Italy since ca. 2000 BCE. The kingdom included Rome, founded around 1000 BCE.

Subsequently, around 500 BCE, the Romans made themselves independent and overthrew their kings. They created a **republic** (from Latin *res publica*, "public matter"), that is, a state without a king, electing leaders and forming a constitutional government. Around 450 BCE, the Romans adopted the Twelve Tablets, a set of laws covering a variety of legal matters, such as procedure, property, inheritance, constitution, due process, family, and crime. A chief priest was responsible for administering the cult of the patron god, Jupiter, and fixing the calendar. Later on, the Romans sacrificed to hundreds of gods and their polytheistic religious practices acquired a close resemblance to those of the Greeks and Persians. Indeed, the chief gods in the Roman pantheon were taken directly from the Greeks.

Republic: State without a royal dynasty and with an elected executive.

Expansion of the Republic   In the 300s BCE, when Rome began to unify the peninsula, it organized its citizen army more formally into legions. The heavily armed infantry of **legionaries**, forming the center of each legion, consisted of landed citizens able to pay for their swords, javelins, helmets, shields, and scale armor. Wealthy Romans also manned the light and heavy cavalry, including cataphracts, while small landholders made up the light infantry of skirmishers. With the help of these legionaries, Rome unified Italy and in three wars (246–164 BCE) conquered its strongest rival, Carthage, across the Mediterranean in what is today Tunisia.

Legionaries: Roman foot soldiers fighting in closed ranks.

Around 200 BCE, during the second war when Carthage was still relatively strong, it sought to protect itself against Rome through an alliance with the kingdom of Antigonid Greece. In a first expansion east, the Romans defeated the Antigonids and, in 196 BCE, issued the Isthmus Declaration, according to which the Greeks of Greece, Anatolia, and farther east were to be "free" of Antigonid overlordship and governed by their own laws. In Roman eyes, the Greek cities were now clients. When the Greeks resented this restriction of their laws and rebelled, in the middle of the second century BCE, they were ruthlessly repressed by the Romans, who eventually reduced Greece to provincial status. The Isthmus Declaration was Rome's decisive step toward becoming an empire. It continued its republican institutions for another two centuries and never formally abolished them. Historians usually date the beginning of the Roman Empire to 27 BCE, when the Senate bestowed the title "Augustus" on Octavian; but by that time Rome had been an empire for 200 years in all but name.

In the wake of the imperial expansion of Rome to North Africa, Greece, and Anatolia during the second and first centuries BCE, a new ruling class of wealthy landowners emerged. These consisted of Italian aristocrats who had appropriated the land of smallholders absent for extended periods during their military service as legionaries, turning these lands into large estates called **latifundia**. Ruling-class members also acquired leases of conquered lands overseas, where they established latifundia with enslaved war captives who grew cash crops. Discharged legionaries and dispossessed farmers crowded Rome, while rebellious slaves on latifundia in southern Italy and Sicily rose in massive revolts. The most dangerous revolt was that of Spartacus in 73–71 BCE. Spartacus was an army deserter from Thrace who had been recaptured, enslaved, and trained as a gladiator. The sources describe Spartacus as a skillful tactician who devastated latifundia throughout Italy and held the Roman army in check for 3 years before it succeeded in defeating him.

Latifundia: Large, ruling class–owned estates with tenant farmers or slaves.

Efforts by a few social reformers at improving the lot of the poor through food subsidies, land reforms, and public work projects failed against the fierce resistance of the landowners. About the only reform that succeeded was that of Marius, who was senator from 107 to 85 BCE and a successful general in North Africa. He opened the army ranks to the landless, equipped them with arms, and enlisted them for up to 20 years of service. Upon retirement, soldiers received plots of land in conquered provinces. This reform greatly benefited imperial expansion as well as Romanized conquered provinces through settled veterans. But it also encouraged generals to use the now fully professionalized army for their own ambitions.

In the middle of the first century BCE, three ambitious generals were vying for control of the empire. One of them was Julius Caesar (r. 60–44 BCE), from a prominent family of administrators and a successful conqueror of northwestern Europe. Recently returned from triumphant conquests in Gaul (modern France), he defeated his two rivals. When he then assumed several offices traditionally held by separate magistrates, including the title "dictator for life," he provoked much opposition. An assassin, Marcus Junius Brutus, eventually struck Caesar down and a new "triumvirate" of generals assumed power.

The triumvirate did not last. Civil war broke out, and the ultimate victor was Octavian (r. 31 BCE–14 CE), a distant younger relative of Caesar whose career the latter had furthered. More subtle than Caesar, Octavian gradually created a new constitutional order with himself as leader, always maintaining the pretense of being merely the executive officer of the state. In practice he possessed unlimited powers under the title of Augustus ("the Revered One"), bestowed on him in 27 BCE.

The Augustan Age   To consolidate his power, Augustus limited imperial expansion in the north to France and Germany, west of the rivers Rhine and Danube. He ordered the construction of a wall, called *limes*, linking the two rivers, to keep the Germanic tribes on the other side at bay. In the east, a series of wars with the Persian Parthian Empire (56 BCE–1 CE) over the control of Armenia, Upper Mesopotamia, and Syria ended inconclusively. Egypt, Syria, and Judea came under direct Roman rule, Armenia became a Roman client state, Upper Mesopotamia east of the Euphrates remained Parthian, and peace reigned between Rome and Parthia for two generations. At this time, the Roman Empire had about 55 million inhabitants (see Map 7.4). It was considerably more populous than its Middle Eastern competitor, Parthia, with 10 million, but less so than its territorially smaller contemporary, Han China (202 BCE–220 CE), with 58 million. In addition, the Roman and Parthian Empires were geographically far less compact and had more vulnerable borders than China, disadvantages which hampered political cohesion.

All 44 Roman provinces outside Italy had to pay heavy poll and agricultural taxes in kind and silver coins, primarily to support a standing army, which Augustus reduced by half compared to the earlier civil war armies. Legionaries came from not only Italy but also Gaul and Hispania (modern France and the Iberian Peninsula). In addition, tax money went into the building and upkeep of roads and ports, as well as wheat subsidies and circuses for the inhabitants of Rome and other large cities. In contrast to the huge military, the number of civilian Roman administrators in the provinces was small. The Roman Peace (*pax romana*) clearly rested more on the projection of military might than on a civilian administration, as in Han China.

The Roman Peace on the borders was rarely disrupted during the first two centuries following Augustus. Not surprisingly, the disruptions that did occur were on the border with Parthian Persia. Here, the flashpoint was the kingdom of Armenia,

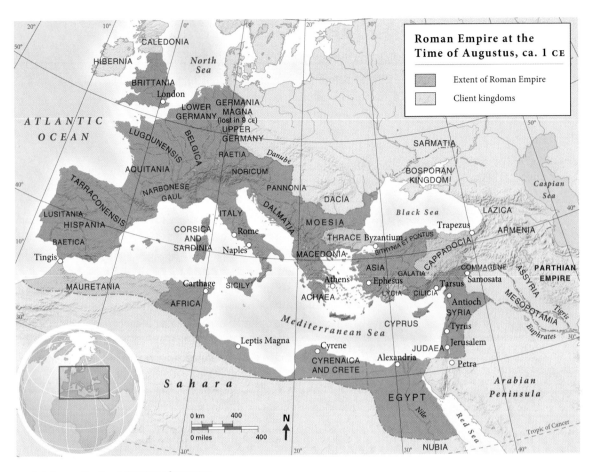

MAP **7.4** Roman Empire at the Time of Augustus.

which both Parthia and Rome coveted as a client state. Compromise solutions collapsed twice (54–63 CE and 112–117 CE). On the second occasion, Rome came close to destroying Parthia when it succeeded in occupying Mesopotamia for a short time. The subsequent puppet kingdom, however, was unable to maintain itself, and the Parthians returned to independence.

The Sasanid Persian and Late Roman Empires

After renewing its independence, Parthia challenged Rome twice (161–166 CE and 193–198 CE). It lost both times and had to give up the province of Upper Mesopotamia and much of its economic wealth to pay tributes. Divisions in the ruling class of the Parthians began to appear. In the early 200s, the priestly family of a temple to Anahita, the goddess of water and fertility in the Iranian pantheon in Fars, assumed provincial leadership functions in opposition to the dynasty. Ardashir, a descendant of this priestly family, finally ended Parthian rule in 224 CE and declared himself king of kings of the Sasanid Persian Empire (224–642 CE).

Roman Crisis   Just as Persian imperial power was rejuvenated through a new dynasty, the Roman Empire fell into a political and economic crisis, which lasted half a century (234–285 CE) and profoundly changed its organization. As in all empires,

The Plague of Justinian

At the end of the 500s, neither the Roman nor the Sasanid Empire was as populous and wealthy as before the nomadic invasions from the north. For the first time, in 541 CE, a mass epidemic, the bubonic plague, hit the world, breaking out first in the Roman Empire and traveling thereafter to Persia and, in cycles of 15 years, by the 600s CE as far as China and England. This plague, recorded as the "Plague of Justinian"—it sickened the emperor himself for several weeks—dramatically reduced population levels everywhere. The Plague of Justinian originated either in East Africa or in Burma. It reached the Mediterranean through black rats traveling in ships on the Indian Ocean and Red Sea.

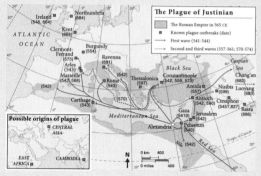

MAP **7.5** The Plague of Justinian.

Historians know now that for the plague to spread from fleas and rats in one of its endemic regions and become a pandemic the region's average temperatures must have declined. Fleas are most likely to jump from rats to humans, at 59–68 degrees Fahrenheit. Such a temperature decline might have occurred a few years prior to 541 CE, with the eruption of the volcano Krakatau in Indonesia in 535 CE, the ashes of which obscured the sun for a number of years. Although the climate returned to normal a few years later, recurrent cycles of the plague every decade or two until well into the 700s CE prevented population levels from recovering.

Observers in various cities of the Roman Empire, some afflicted by the plague themselves, have left us vivid accounts. People infected by the plague bacillus

the balance between war booty, tax revenue, and military expenditures was always precarious. Booty acquired in the Parthian wars kept the empire afloat until the 220s, but thereafter emperors had to dilute the silver money paid to the legionaries with cheaper metals. The ensuing inflation angered the soldiers, who supported any claimant to the imperial throne promising higher wages. Some two dozen emperors followed each other in rapid succession on the throne, and for a while the empire even fragmented into three pieces.

In addition to the internal conflicts, Germanic tribes broke through the northern defenses and during 260–276 CE pillaged as far as northern Italy. At the same time, both Rome and Persia were afflicted by what historians of science assume was an outbreak of mass disease along the trade routes in 251–266 CE, foreshadowing the plague of 541 (see "Patterns Up Close"). The number of deaths was estimated in the hundreds of thousands. At the end of the 200s it appeared as if Rome was at its end.

Emperor Diocletian (r. 285–305 CE), however, salvaged the empire. He divided it into an eastern and a western half, doubled the number of provinces and civil administrators, and created a separate set of military districts. In addition, he ended Italy's tax exemption, regularized tax collection, increased the number of legions by one-third, and created a mobile field army under his command. Civil peace returned to the empire, albeit at the price of an increased militarization.

Adoption of Monotheism Since the early Sasanids had to consolidate their rule in a large territory, stretching from Upper Mesopotamia to Uzbekistan and northwestern India, they could not exploit the Roman crisis to the fullest. Although typically developed a high fever, followed by swelling of the lymph nodes in the groin, the armpits, and the neck. In great pain and delirious from fever, most people died quickly after a few days. Although the concept of quarantine was familiar, there was no known medicine. Survivors tried folk remedies, to no avail. Many clerical observers at the time were convinced that sinfulness was what had attracted God's wrath. For us modern observers, the most important lesson of the Plague of Justinian is the evidence it provides of how interconnected the various parts of Eurasia and Africa were toward the middle of the 500s CE (see Map 7.5).

The Plague of Justinian shows us how climate and disease followed their own natural patterns in world history, patterns different from those of the polytheistic and monotheistic city-states, kingdoms, and empires. By killing up to one-third of the population and keeping population levels low for at least a century, the Plague of Justinian severely impacted city-state, kingdom, and empire patterns. The reduced population levels led to increased labor costs and food shortages; it also made survivors wealthier. On the other hand, since the plagues were equal-opportunity killers, they hit states and societies with the same ferocity. Justinian's plague favored neither Rome nor Persia and, thus, had more quantitative than lasting qualitative effects on the process of world history.

Questions

- What does Justinian's plague tell us about the interconnectedness of Afro-Eurasia at this time?
- How does understanding the impact of disease and climate on human societies add a new dimension to the patterns of world history?

they led lightning invasions into Roman territories in Syria and Anatolia, acquired immense booty, received large indemnity payments, and even captured the Roman emperor Valerian in battle in 260 CE, the Romans always in the end regained control over Armenia and Upper Mesopotamia. Diocletian, after his reforms, was even able to push the border eastward to the Tigris River.

In the first half of the 300s, while the inconclusive wars between the two imperial rivals of Rome and Persia continued, both empires took first, halting steps toward a profound internal transformation, that is, a shift away from polytheism and toward the elevation of monotheism to the status of state religion. During the previous polytheist millennia in the Middle East and the Mediterranean, kings and emperors had supported imperial temple priesthoods in their capitals for the justification of their rule. Temples devoted to many other deities existed in their realms, and rulers did not seek their elimination. But when the Romans and Persians suffered their severe internal crises—the former nearly falling apart and the latter changing dynasties—rulers became aware of the need for a unifying single religious bond.

At the beginning of the reign of Emperor Constantine I, the Great (r. 306–337 CE), Christianity's adherents numbered about 10 percent of the Roman population. Christianity had begun three centuries earlier with the preaching of Jesus of Nazareth and Paul of Tarsus. Its growth, despite periodic persecutions, was impressive enough for Constantine to take a first step toward making Christianity the state religion by sponsoring the Nicene Creed in 325 CE as the common doctrinal platform among Christians, as well as granting tax privileges and jurisdictional powers to the Christian

Church. Baptized shortly before his death, Constantine can be considered the first Christian Roman emperor.

In Persia, under the sponsorship of Shapur II (r. ca. 307–379), Zoroastrian priests began to write down the Gathas, the oldest holy scripture of Zoroastrianism. In Rome, several pagan emperors succeeded Constantine, and it was only in 380 that Christianity became the sole state religion. Persia, with its large Jewish and Christian minorities in Mesopotamia, went the different route of making Zoroastrianism the preferential religion in ca. 350, with Christianity and Judaism being accorded a protected status. Thus, both empires sought to strengthen internal unity through the adoption of a single monotheistic faith.

Nomadic Invasions   The adoption of Christianity and Zoroastrianism to strengthen the cohesion of the Roman and Sasanid Empires came just in time, before the great migration of peoples across Eurasia caused severe disruptions. The migration began in the mid-300s CE when the western branch of the Huns—horse- and sheep-breeding nomads in the steppes between Mongolia north of China and central Asia east of the Ural Mountains—moved westward and southward on the Silk Road. As in the case of the previous migrations out of central Asia in the second millennium BCE, the reasons that the western Huns packed up and journeyed westward remain unclear. One possible factor was the success of the Chinese in driving away nomadic invaders from their Great Wall in the north, resulting in a chain reaction of migrations among neighboring tribes, including the Huns. During their journey westward, the Huns grew into a large federation of nomads, farmers, and town dwellers of mixed ethnic and linguistic composition (Huns, Turks, Mongols, and Iranians).

As the Huns entered the Russian plains, they encountered local Germanic farming populations, whom they defeated. Other Germanic peoples, such as the Visigoths, fled from the Huns and negotiated their entry into the Roman Empire. In the early 400s CE, both Hunnish and Germanic peoples overcame the defenses of the Romans, poured into the western half of the Roman Empire, and eventually ended the western line of emperors, an event remembered as the fall of Rome in 476 CE (see Map 7.6).

The emperors in the eastern half of the empire withstood the migrants' threat, in part because of Constantinople's strategic location. This city, made the capital by Constantine in 330 CE, was relatively close to the endangered northern and eastern borders, allowing for a more rapid deployment of troops than was possible from faraway Rome. The Sasanids initially repelled an attack by another branch of the Huns on their central Asian border in the early 400s CE but succumbed to renewed invasions in 483–485 and were forced to pay tribute for a number of years. A third branch of Huns invaded the Gupta Empire of India toward the end of the 400s CE. In the mid-500s the Sasanids eventually recovered from the invasions, but the Guptas were reduced to small remnants. Further compounding matters, plague struck the Middle East and Europe in 541 BCE (see "Patterns Up Close" on pp. 182–183).

Roman and Persian Recovery   The architect of reconstruction of the Roman Empire was Justinian I, the Great (r. 527–565 CE). Although not a military campaigner himself, Justinian employed talented generals who reconquered most shores of the western Mediterranean from the Germanic invaders, including all of

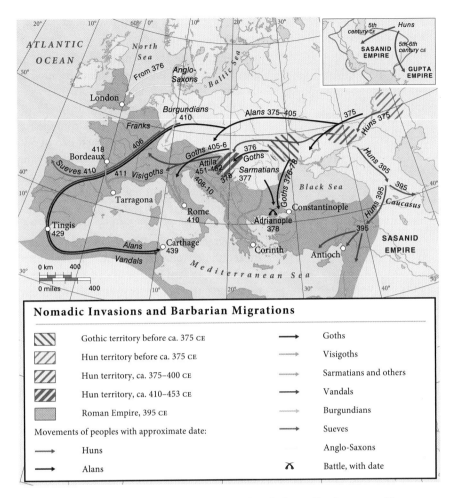

MAP **7.6** **Nomadic Invasions and Barbarian Migrations into the Roman Empire, 375–450 CE.**

Italy. As the empire stabilized, prosperity returned. With improved tax revenues, Justinian was able to finance reform measures. The best known of these reforms was the reorganization of the legal system, based on the codification of the huge body of Roman law that had grown from the initial Twelve Tablets in republican Rome. In addition to the *Codex Justinianus* and *Digests,* he issued an instructional textbook, the *Institutions,* used by law students for centuries after Justinian's death. Originally written in Latin, Justinian's *Codex* was translated later into Greek and became the legal foundation for the Roman Empire's successor, the Byzantine Empire (640–1453 CE), as well as the Islamic empire of the Abbasids (750–1258 CE).

In Persia, it was Khosrow I (r. 531–579) who rebuilt the Sasanid Empire (see Map 7.7). He began his rule in the aftermath of a civil war that pitted Mazdak, a renegade Zoroastrian priest and social reformer, and the dynasty against the Zoroastrian priesthood and the ruling class. In this war, the dynasty confiscated landed estates from the ruling class, opened the latter's granaries to the poor, and distributed its lands to small military landowners (*dihqans*). Khosrow, scion of the dynasty but siding with the ruling class, seized power and had Mazdak executed, ending the social reforms. But he maintained the military reforms in favor of the *dihqans,* thereby

MAP **7.7** **The Sasanid Empire.**

distancing himself from the traditional ruling class. After a census of the population, which allowed him to raise taxes and hire bureaucrats, he greatly expanded the central administration at the expense of the ruling class.

Like Justinian, Khosrow also pursued military expansion. Acceding to pleas from the Armenians after a revolt against Justinian in 530 CE, Khosrow reopened hostilities against the Romans. Initially, his armies broke through to the Mediterranean and returned with rich loot, but the campaign stalled and the war once more ended in 577 CE with a draw. The Romans agreed to pay a tribute, and Khosrow returned the conquered territories. In the north, Khosrow defeated European and Turkic tribes, expanding the border eastward to Turkistan. A plea from the king of Yemen in southwestern Arabia to aid him in his efforts to repel a Roman-backed Ethiopian invasion brought Khosrow's fleet to southern Arabia in 575–577 CE. On land, Arab vassal kings established Persian control over much of the rest of Arabia. In contrast to Rome, the reach of Persia was much expanded at the end of the sixth century.

Adaptations to Monotheism and Monism in the Middle East

Although demographically weakened by plague, Rome and Sasanid Persia were comparatively strong unitary empires at the end of the 500s CE. Both had regained territories lost to the Asian tribal migrations two centuries earlier and were religiously unified through the adoption of the monotheisms of Christianity and Zoroastrianism as obligatory or preferential state religions. The adoption of these religions, however, had been of relatively recent vintage, as we have seen. It came at the end of a lengthy process that originated at the beginning of the Achaemenid Persian Empire (550–330 BCE). At that time, visionaries arose to whom a single god revealed himself or who discovered fundamental truths. At first, these visionaries of religious monotheism and philosophical monism had only small numbers of followers. It took many centuries before followers of each faith became more numerous and organized themselves in local communities dispersed over the empires' territories until the creeds achieved imperial sanction as the preferred or obligatory state religion.

Challenge to Polytheism: The Origins of Judaism, Zoroastrianism, and Greek Philosophy

Religious visionaries of the sixth century BCE arose in a polytheistic environment, a culture of many gods who embodied overpowering as well as benign natural forces and phenomena. In Egypt these gods numbered in the thousands; in Mesopotamia, Greece, and Rome their numbers were smaller; and among the Persians and ancient Israelites they numbered fewer than a dozen. Regardless of specific numbers, all polytheisms had one basic characteristics in common: The gods all descended from something unnameable that existed prior to creation (Nothing, the Abyss, Darkness, Waste, or Chaos). Unity preceded multiplicity and even though perceived reality consisted of both, in thought they could be separated from each other. Unity **transcended** multiplicity.

Transcendence: Realm of reality above and beyond the limits of material experience.

Judaism   Remarkably, the discovery of transcendence occurred more or less simultaneously during the 600s BCE in Mesopotamia, Iran, and Anatolia. The historically most influential case was that of an anonymous Jewish visionary, whom scholars dubbed "Deutero-Isaiah" or "Second Isaiah" (fl. ca. 560 BCE) in Mesopotamia. After their deportation by the Neo-Babylonians from Palestine (597–582 BCE), as we saw in Chapter 2, a majority of Israelites lived in Babylonian exile, scattered over areas of Upper and Lower Mesopotamia as well as western Iran and earning their livelihood as scribes, craftspeople, and soldiers. After the establishment of the Achaemenid Persian Empire, these scribes began to compile their Israelite religious traditions from Palestine into larger collections of writings. They became the founders of what is called today "Judaism" and one of them, Deutero-Isaiah, was the first to declare Yahweh [YA-ha-way], or God, to be the only god of the Jews.

In Deutero-Isaiah's words, there are no gods but Yahweh: "Thus says the Lord the king of Israel, and his redeemer the Lord of hosts; I am the first, and I am the last; and beside me there is no other god" (Is. 44:6–8). Yahweh is completely distinct from the traditional gods of polytheism. Yahweh is invisible and cannot be represented by visible images: "Verily you are a God who hides himself, O God of Israel, the Savior" (Is. 45:15). God in Deutero-Isaiah is the single, invisible creator and sustainer of the world. He is transcendent—a conceptual reality beyond the empirical reality of this world.

Some of Deutero-Isaiah's followers inserted revisions in the corpus of early scriptures that the Jews had brought with them into Babylonian exile to emphasize Yahweh's transcendence, particularly in the book of Genesis dealing with creation. (A new element they also introduced in Genesis was the 7-day calendar, an innovation which is today recognized everywhere.) Other followers petitioned the Persian king to allow them to leave for Jerusalem and restore the temple destroyed by the Neo-Babylonians. The Persian king issued the permit in 538 BCE, and a small but determined group of monotheists returned to Jerusalem to construct the Second Temple (completed in 515 BCE). A new priesthood took up residence in the Temple and, on the basis of new rituals and laws, administered the emerging monotheistic faith of Judaism.

Zoroastrianism   Zoroastrians attribute their origin to Zoroaster (also called Zarathushtra), who, like Moses of the Israelites, is supposed to have lived around 1200 BCE, long before the rise of monotheism. The earliest recorded references to Zoroaster's teachings, however, date only to the rise of the Achaemenid Persian Empire in 550 BCE. These teachings were handed down orally by a priestly class, the magi. The main oral text is the Avesta, a body of liturgical texts which the magi used in their religious ceremonies.

Zoroastrian Fire Temple. Consisting of a cube with a superimposed dome, this Zoroastrian temple, one of the best preserved, is located outside Baku, in present-day Azerbaijan. Zoroastrianism was prevalent in the Caucasus region until the arrival of Christianity and Islam.

The earliest text forms the section called "Yasht" in the Avesta. Zamyad Yasht 19, or "Hymn to the Earth," speaks of the glories of Ahuramazda (God), to whom the priests are bringing sacrifices. The last of his glories, bestowed on humankind at the end of history, is that of the savior (Avestan *saoshyant*):

> He will restore the world "which will [thenceforth] never grow old and never die, never decaying and never rotting, ever living and ever increasing." The end will be a time "when the dead will rise, when life and immortality will come" and "when the creation will grow deathless." Yasht 15:89–90

Other sections of the Avesta describe in considerable detail an additional period of time just prior to the arrival of the savior, a time of trial and tribulation with horrible calamities and devastations, later called the "apocalypse" (Greek *apocalypsis*, revelation). Both themes—Savior or Messiah and apocalypse—are trademarks of Zoroastrian monotheism. In later centuries they became central in Judaism, Christianity, and Islam. They replaced the polytheistic notion of a shadowy afterlife in the underworld with salvation in the righteous in God's transcendent kingdom.

Unfortunately, the extant sources do not present a clear picture of the evolution of Zoroastrian monotheism after the 500s BCE. It appears, however, that under the Parthians the magi introduced traditional Iranian and Anatolian cults of fire, maintained in fire temples, into Zoroastrianism. Similarly, they adopted customs of exposing the dead on rooftops to vultures before burying the bones cleansed of mortal flesh in graves. How far the fire temples evolved into congregational places for priests and laity, however, similar to Jewish synagogues, Christian churches, or Greek philosophical schools, is not known from the available sources.

Greek Philosophy   While the author of Deutero-Isaiah and the Zoroastrian reformers of the 500s BCE are unknown to us today, the first Greek philosophers are known by name: Thales, Heraclitus, and, especially, Thales' pupil, Anaximander, who lived during the first half of the 500s in the city of Miletus on the Anatolian coast. In contrast to Judaism and Zoroastrianism, Anaximander formulated the impersonal, or *monist*, "principle of the infinite" (*apeiron*) as the invisible cause underlying the world (*kosmos*). A lively debate over principles ensued after Anaximander and his successors, also mostly from Anatolia, proposed several other cosmic principles. This debate became the basis for the rise of the mathematical and physical sciences in the subsequent centuries.

The Athenian Plato (ca. 427–347 BCE) was the first systematic thinker who extended the debate from principles in nature to a principle common to all areas of reality, such as politics, ethics, and the arts, calling it Being (*on*, originally coined by his predecessor Parmenides, fl. fifth century BCE). In his thinking, called "philosophy," meaning love of wisdom, Being is embodied in the three transcendent forms (*eidai*) of Truth, Justice, and Beauty. These forms, so Plato argued, represent objective standards against which all earthly assertions about truth, justice, and beauty in daily life are to be measured. Anaximander's monism thus formed the stem from which two major branches, science and philosophy, sprouted.

The Break from Polytheism to Monotheism   The common thread linking the three visions of transcendence is that they all involve transcendent symbols, such as God or Being, which can only be thought but not experienced. For the Greek, Zoroastrian, and Jewish visionaries, reality consisted of two separate halves, the one that can be comprehended only through abstract thought and the other that can be comprehended concretely by being sensed. Polytheist reality is undivided, with gods and corresponding natural phenomena conjoined. Given this contrast, it is not surprising that monotheism was incompatible with polytheism. Deutero-Isaiah expressed this incompatibility explicitly; in Greek philosophy and Zoroastrianism it was more implicit. Nevertheless, in the long run, polytheism disappeared from the Middle East and Mediterranean, ceding its long reign to monotheism and subsequent religious civilizations.

Toward Religious Communities and Philosophical Schools

The visionaries were founders of small religious communities and philosophical schools amid an initially continuing polytheism in the Greek city-states and the Persian Empire, both in the Iranian–Mesopotamian imperial center and the Jewish province of Palestine. The small Jewish community that built the Second Temple in Jerusalem grew more rapidly than the Zoroastrian fire temple communities and Greek philosophical schools and led the way to monotheism. It furthermore spawned a Jewish reform movement, Christianity, which in turn changed the Roman Empire from polytheism to monotheism (see Map 7.8).

Judaism in Palestine   The Achaemenid Persian kings allowed the Jews, who had moved from Mesopotamia to Palestine and had founded the Second Temple in Jerusalem, a large degree of autonomy. Under their successors, the Ptolemaic and Seleucid kings in Alexander the Great's successor states, this autonomy declined substantially. These kings introduced Greek-Hellenistic institutions and culture into Palestine, forcing the Jews to allow the *gymnasium* (the basic school which included Olympic sports exercises in the nude) as well as polytheism and philosophy in their midst. A majority resisted the introduction of the gymnasium and Zeus into the temple with fierce and eventually successful rebellions. As a result, the Jews established

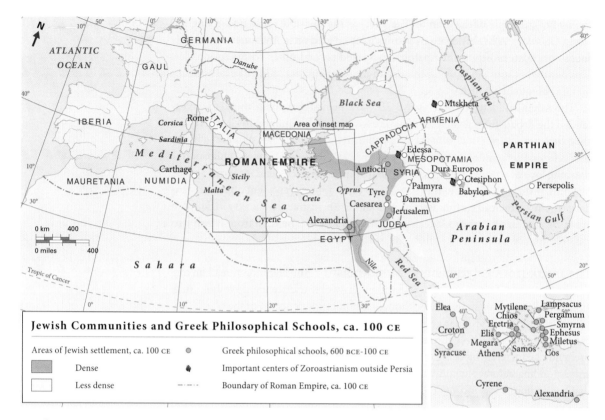

MAP 7.8 **Jewish Communities and Greek Philosophical Schools, ca. 100 CE**

the autonomous Hasmonean (also called "Maccabean") kingdom (140–37 BCE), which sought to limit the Hellenization of society.

In spite of all Hasmonean attempts to keep Judaism pure, educated Jews learned Greek and read the writings of the Greek philosophers, especially the so-called Cynics who advocated the virtues of natural simplicity far removed from power, wealth, and fame. Scribes translated Jewish scriptures into Greek, and in the second half of the 200s BCE prayer houses, called "**synagogues**," emerged in cities and towns for the study of the scriptures and of the new Jewish law that had evolved since the foundation of the Second Temple. The monotheism of Yahweh continued to be exclusively administered by priests. But preachers in the synagogues, called "pharisees," made this monotheism an increasingly popular faith among ordinary Jews.

Synagogues: Jewish meeting places for prayer and legal consultation.

In the first century BCE, the Romans and Persian Parthians replaced the Seleucids and the Herodians replaced the Hasmoneans in Palestine. The Jews interacted not only with the culture of Hellenism but also with the culture of the Romans, their new overlords, and the Parthian Persians, their new neighbors to the east. Many Jews adapted to the Roman philosophical school of the Stoics (who, like the Cynics, advocated an ethics in harmony with the laws of nature) and to the Persian Zoroastrian-inspired apocalypse, which predicted God's final war against evil (that is, foreign domination by Rome), the resurrection of the dead, the day of judgment, and salvation in the heavenly kingdom. Elements of philosophy and the apocalypse, coming together in the teachings of the pharisees in the synagogues, found widespread followers in the Jewish population. Palestine was a cauldron of cultural influences—some monotheistic, others monist, many clashing with polytheism.

The Origins of Christianity   It was from this cauldron that the Jewish reform movement of Christianity arose in the first century CE. The earliest scriptures of the Christians, contained in the New Testament, describe the founding figure, Jesus of Nazareth, as a preacher in Galilee or northern Palestine, far from Jerusalem. After he was baptized by John, an ascetic preacher on the Jordan River, Jesus is reported to have left the Mosaic as well as the Pharisaic law aside, including the stringent purity laws, and to have preached instead the spirit of the law, which he expressed as the "law of love" (Greek *agape*, Latin *caritas*; Mark 12:29–30). Only if one loved God and one's neighbor as one loved oneself would one acquire the proper understanding of law and be prepared for the apocalypse and salvation in the heavenly kingdom soon to come.

When Jesus is reported to have gone to Jerusalem during Passover, one of three times a year when Jews were enjoined to visit the Temple for sacrifices, he provoked the Temple priests with his ultimate challenge to Jewish law: He overturned the tables of the money changers and sellers of sacrificial birds to Jews who performed the required animal sacrifices. For Jesus, obedience to all these detailed laws and regulations was quite unnecessary in the anticipation of the heavenly

kingdom. According to the New Testament, his actions in the Temple initiated the chain of events which ended with the priests turning Jesus over to the Roman governor for death on the cross.

Again according to the New Testament, shortly after Jesus' death, the Pharisee, Roman citizen, and philosophically trained Paul of Tarsus in Anatolia converted to Jesus' law of love. Paul dispensed with another Jewish law, circumcision, and thereby liberated Jesus' message from its last tie to Judaism: Henceforth, anyone could become a follower of Jesus. Paul retained the concept of the apocalypse with its tribulations but also argued that salvation had already begun with Jesus' resurrection from death, ascension to heaven, and imminent return—the Second Coming as the Messiah or Christus, hence Jesus' divine name, "Christ"—and ruler of the heavenly kingdom. According to the letters attributed to his name, Paul traveled widely and preached to numerous small Christian communities, called "churches" (Greek, sing. *ekklesia*), which formed in the Roman Empire during the middle of the first century CE.

Mural from Dura Europos on the Euphrates. The city, founded in 303 BCE, was home to a sizeable Jewish community whose synagogue was adorned with murals in the Parthian-Hellenistic style. Shown here is a depiction of the infant Moses being rescued from the Nile.

The Christian Church   Paul trained the first missionaries, and after him proselytizing became a regular feature of the emerging Christian community. The missionaries preached Christianity in the Roman Empire from scriptures which evolved in the first three centuries CE. At this time, the first basic canon of accepted writings, the New Testament, was assembled. A hierarchy of bishops and priests preached from these scriptures to laypeople who congregated in local churches for regular communal services. From an early period, however, Christians were divided on how to understand the New Testament. The philosophically educated tended to interpret it figuratively, that is, by reading their philosophical concepts into scripture. Others, opposed to Greek philosophy, preferred a literal interpretation, even though Paul's Christianity was already philosophically tinged. A long struggle over the integration of scripture and philosophy into a single Christian civilization ensued in the church.

Principal figures in the struggle were bishops, called "church fathers." The earliest among them was Origen of Alexandria (ca. 185–254 CE), who focused not only on the allegorical but also on the ethical interpretation of scripture. The intellectually most versatile church father was Augustine (354–430 CE), from what is today Algeria. His two main works are the *Confessions*, in which he describes his conversion to Christianity and reflections on spirituality, and *The City of God*, in which he defends Christianity against the accusation by many Romans that its adoption as the state religion in 380 contributed to the decline of the empire. Although his philosophical training was limited, he was a strong proponent of the allegorical interpretation, which became a principal pillar of church doctrine. Thanks to the church fathers, the church was set on a path of merging monotheism and philosophy, as the basis for the rise of a Christian civilization.

The Beginnings of Science and the Cultures of Kings and Citizens

Monotheism and philosophy entered society early in the Jewish Second Temple kingdom in Palestine. In the Persian and Roman Empires this incorporation, in the form of preferred or state religions, took longer. Greek science became important in Ptolemaic Egypt (305–30 BCE). The Ptolemies provided state support for the development of mathematics, physics, astronomy, and the applied science of mechanics as new and independent fields of culture. The other, inherited forms of cultural expression—painting, sculpture, architecture, and literature—remained within traditional polytheistic confines. Nevertheless, in Greece and Rome these cultural forms underwent substantial innovation and differentiation, influenced by Hellenism as well as Parthian and Sasanid Persia.

The Sciences at the Museum of Alexandria

In Athens and other city-states, citizens supported philosophical schools, such as the Academy of Plato or the Lyceum of Aristotle (384–322 BCE), one of Plato's students and tutor of Alexander. These institutions were small if compared with the enormous resources the Ptolemies and their Roman successors poured into a new type of institution of Greek learning, the institute for advanced study, as we would say today. This institute was the Museum of Alexandria (280 BCE–ca. 400 CE), which was devoted primarily to research in the mathematical and natural sciences. At times, some 100 resident fellows did research in its library holdings of half a million scrolls, dissected corpses in laboratories, gazed at the stars in the astronomical observatory, strolled through the botanical gardens, and shared meals.

The most developed branch of the sciences at the museum was geometry. Euclid (fl. ca. 300 BCE), one of the founders of the museum, provided geometry with its basic definitions and proofs in his *Elements*, still important today. In addition to geometry, mathematicians laid the foundations for algebra. The pioneer was Diophantus (ca. 214–284 CE), with his exploration of the properties of equations. Hypatia (ca. 360–415 CE), the first known female scientist in world history, is said to have contributed further to the development of algebra; but her work is unfortunately no longer extant. In the absence of a Greek number system, however, algebra remained ultimately stunted in its growth in Alexandria and had to await the Muslims and the Arabic numeral system—originally devised in India—to evolve fully.

Alexandrian geographers and astronomers, trained in geometry, made important calculations of the earth's circumference and tilt and formulated the first heliocentric astronomical theory, according to which the earth spins around the sun. Unfortunately, this theory remained mathematically unsupported, so the opposite theory of the earth at the center of the planetary system became dominant. Claudius Ptolemy (ca. 87–170 CE) devised such a detailed and precise geometric system of the planets' movements that his geocentrism reigned for the next millennium and a half in the astronomies of the Islamic Middle East and western European Christianity, dethroned eventually only by Copernicus in the sixteenth century.

Apart from astronomy, physics also flourished at the museum. The outstanding physicist was Archimedes (287–212 BCE), who investigated the behavior of floating bodies in the new science of hydrostatics—bold investigations, which had to wait a millennium and a half before being fully appreciated in the works of Galileo Galilei, one of the pioneers of modern physics.

The museum came to its end under unknown circumstances at the beginning of the 400s CE. Its legacy, however, was such that later Islamic rulers resumed the tradition of sponsoring institutes for advanced study.

Royal Persian Culture and Arts

The Achaemenid Persians arrived in Mesopotamia with their rich Indo-European traditions of divine and heroic myths, which were also characteristic of Aryan migrants to India. These myths told of deities and heroes mingling in a verdant landscape of mountains, rivers, and pastures. Major themes included the protracted, sometimes noble, and occasionally treacherous struggles between the Persians and their tribal rivals in central Asia, whom they called "Turanians." After 600 BCE, monotheistic Zoroastrians reworked the pagan myths in the Avesta so that under the one, invisible God (Ahuramazda) the other deities became lesser beings, such as angels and demons. The myths and epics were handed down orally until the 400s CE, well after the disappearance of the Achaemenids, before they were finally written down.

As heirs of both Achaemenid Persian and Greek traditions, the Parthians forged a new synthesis between inherited styles and adopted Greek-Hellenistic elements, while maintaining an overall palace-focused culture of their own. For example, courtiers listened to bards who recited the exploits of Hercules and other Greek heroes, thereby laying the foundations for the Rustam story cycle written down several centuries later. Other bards and minstrels traveled among aristocratic families, composing stories of their masters' courtly loves and intrigues or their exploits in battles against nomadic invaders from central Asia. After the Parthians, these stories were handed down orally and grew in both length and complexity. They exist today in a modern Persian version, called the *Book of Kings* (*Shahname* [Sha-ha-na-MAY]), compiled by the poet Firdosi [Feer-dow-SEE] in the eleventh century CE.

The Sasanids were major transmitters of Indian texts to the Middle East and Mediterranean. The most popular text was a translation of animal fables, known in

Barrel Vault of the Sasanid
Royal Reception Hall,
Ctesiphon.

India as *Five Treatises* (*Panchatantra* [Pan-sha-TAN-trah]) and in Arabic as *Kalila wa dimna* [Ka-LEE-lah wa DIM-nah].

In these fables, animals appear in witty, cleverly constructed stories intended to teach lessons to palace courtiers and retainers. Other texts were instruction manuals on chess, a game which made its way to the West during Sasanid times. Also from India came medical texts complete with discussions of anatomy, diseases, and herbs. All these texts, which were both useful and entertaining, played important roles at the Sasanid court.

In architecture, the characteristic feature of Sasanid palaces was the monumental dome and barrel vault. Arches, domes, and barrel vaulting had been pioneered in Mesopotamia in the second millennium BCE but only for small structures. These earlier curved constructions consisted of bricks laid and mortared at an angle in the so-called pitched brick style. It is possible that during the Parthian period, when fire temples began to appear among the Zoroastrians, domes topped the cube-shaped chambers of those temples, although the earliest extant domes date to the Sasanids.

Sasanid vaults and domes were massive structures. The central audience hall of the palace in the capital, Ctesiphon, built ca. 250 CE, had a barrel vault 118 feet high. Other palaces had "squinched" domes of up to 45 feet across, covering square audience and banquet halls. *Squinches* were curved triangular transition spaces between the dome and the corners of the halls. In order to contain the outward thrust of the dome's weight, buttresses supported the walls on the outside. The techniques of both barrel vaulting and the dome were transmitted from Sasanid Persia to Christian Armenia, Rome, and ultimately western Europe, where they appeared in church architecture.

Greek and Roman Civic Culture and Arts

The disappearance of kings and aristocracies in the Greek city-states during the sixth century BCE had momentous consequences for Greek culture. Instead of merely a handful of kings and aristocrats sponsoring the arts, thousands of wealthy citizens began to patronize artists or even create themselves works of literature, sculpture, painting, and architecture. A broad civic artistic creativity arose. Although polytheism, myths, and other ancient traditions remained central for the majority of the citizens and only a minority adapted to the new philosophical and scientific monism, the heritage lost its symbolical, stylized, and generic royal orientation. Instead, Greeks began to experiment with a variety of individual shapes, types, and models, seeking realistic representation in their art.

Greek Literature and Art

The Greek theater emerged around 500–480 BCE out of the stylized traditions and rituals of the Dionysiac cult. Every year in March, during the Dionysiac processions, competitions took place among groups of citizens (later wealthy noncitizens also competed) for the presentation of the best tragedy or comedy. These competing groups, or *choruses*, dressed in sumptuous robes and elaborate masks to perform the chosen dramatic or comic piece through declamation and dance. In the course of time, individual actors emerged from among the chorus members and presented dialogues on which the chorus commented as the plot evolved. Tragedy developed out of Dionysiac myths and comedy from the Dionysiac processions.

Among the most important writers who composed for the early Greek stage were the tragedians Aeschylus, Sophocles, and Euripides, as well as the comedian Aristophanes. All four authors, and many of their successors, continue to exercise a profound influence on the evolution of Western literature today.

Just as democracy encouraged the exploration of individual character in tragedy and comedy, so it supported the search for character representation in Greek painting and sculpture. Unfortunately, no murals or panels exist today, although a few Roman reproductions survive. Vase painting gives us a good impression of scenes of daily life, even though the medium imposed severe limits of color and composition on artists. Surviving examples of sculptures are plentiful, even if primarily in the form of later Roman copies, which often lack the original Greek refinement.

In the fifth century BCE, sculptors abandoned the last traces of the traditional Middle Eastern symbolic royal style that required figures to be in tranquil repose, projecting dignity and sternness. Instead, sculptors began to explore physical movement and individual emotional states. In terms of themes, poses, and individuality, Greek vase paintings and sculptures achieved a remarkably wide range, from figures exerting themselves in their chosen sports to serene models of human beauty. Greek sculptors and painters abandoned symbolism and, instead, embraced realism as their style of representation (what we would call today "photographic representation").

Roman Literature and Art

Greece influenced Roman culture early on. As early as the middle of the third century BCE, Romans had translated Greek plays and poetry into Latin. After the adaptation of Greek poetic metrical patterns to the Latin language, a long line of poets emerged. Prose writings on political and historical themes, also modeled on Greek precursors, appeared in large numbers. Emperor Augustus and his wealthy friend Maecenas, renowned for his sponsorship of the arts, stimulated an outburst of early imperial pride. For example, in his epic poem the *Aeneid*, Virgil (70–19 BCE) played down the influence of Greece by positing the origins of Rome in Troy, the rival of Greece. In his *Odes*, Horace (65–8 BCE) glorified courage, patriotism, piety, justice, and a respect for tradition, which he regarded as uniquely Roman virtues. These writers viewed Rome as the culmination of civilization.

Roman sculpture followed the Greek civic style closely by emphasizing proportion, perspective, foreshortening, and light and shadow. Among the earliest

Greek Realism. The Greeks used decorated stelae to mark the burial places of the dead in much the same way tombstones function today. This intimate relief, from about 450 BCE, memorializes a young girl. The treatment of the child's body is realistic—note the chubby arms—and the way the girl tenderly holds her pet doves transforms the little scene into a touching story.

Scene from the *Aeneid*. According to Virgil's *Aeneid*, on his journey from Troy, Aeneas landed in North Africa and fell madly in love with Dido, the queen of Carthage. One day, as they were hunting, a storm forced the two to seek shelter in a cave. Destiny, however, demanded that Aeneas travel on to Italy and found Rome. In her disconsolate grief of being without Aeneas, Dido committed suicide. The cave episode is illustrated here in a manuscript of the fifth century CE.

Pompeii, Mural Executed with Careful Attention to Perspective, Light and Shadow, and Foreshortening. An eruption of the Vesuvius volcano buried the city in 79 CE in ash and, thereby, preserved the murals of the city. They provide some of the best evidence we have of life in ancient Rome.

sculptures were marble busts which aristocratic Romans had made of their patri-archs, cast from wax masks and plaster models. These busts, kept in family shrines, were a central part of aristocratic life in the republic. During the imperial period prior to Christianity as the state religion (31 BCE–380 CE), life-size imitations of Greek and Egyptian statues were commonly found in the households of the wealthy. On columns and triumphal arches, reliefs similar to those of the Persians celebrated military victories. In contrast to the Parthians and Sasanids, civic Romans adorned their cities with numerous monumental structures and, hence, provided their empire with much greater visibility.

Roman pictorial art existed mostly in the form of wood panels, wall paintings, and floor mosaics. In the fifth century CE, the first illustrated book appeared, depicting scenes from Virgil's *Aeneid*. Nearly all panel paintings have perished, but wall paintings have survived in larger numbers, ironically due to their preservation in Pompeii and other cities buried by the eruption of Mt. Vesuvius in 79 CE. The paintings demonstrate Roman art at a remarkably skilled level, with perspective emphasized and executed just as precisely as in Greek art.

Rome's architecture was initially closely modeled on the Greek and Etruscan heritage in Italy. In the imperial age, when the desire for monumental architecture developed, the Romans—shortly after the Parthians—adopted the elements of arch and dome for large buildings. An example is the Pantheon in Rome, built in 118–126 CE. This building, a temple dedicated to all the Roman gods, consists of a dome placed on top of a drum and lit by a round open skylight at its apex (diameter and height both 142 feet). The circular foundation wall made squinches unnecessary. The courtyard of Emperor Diocletian's palace in Split, Croatia (ca. 300 CE), contains the first example of arches set on pillars, which later acquired crucial importance in Islamic and medieval Christian architectures.

Beginning with the first Christian emperor, Constantine, in the early fourth century CE, there was a return from realistic to symbolical representation in the arts. The rich variety of literature shrank to the one category of religious poetry and hymns. Pagan Greek and Roman realistic artists had emphasized emotional variety in their art, playing with surface detail, perspective, foreshortening, light and shadow, and full and empty space. In contrast, Christian artists began to emphasize what they considered essential. Instead of seeking emotionally diverse forms and expressions, they drew from Middle Eastern models, which retained connections to symbolism. Accordingly, characters and objects became generic and lost their detailed psychological and physical characteristics. Space became two-dimensional and figures were large or small according to their religious importance, not their closeness to or distance from the viewer. What mattered was the paradigmatic saintly comportment of figures, whom the believers were supposed to imitate. Religious uniformity came to dominate culture in the Roman and Sasanid Persian Empires, as it dominated their politics in the form of state religion.

Putting It All Together

In 590/591 the Sasanid Empire suffered a war of succession during which one of the rivals, King Khosrow II (r. 590–628), fled to the Romans. Before he arrived in Constantinople, he sent an embassy that pleaded for military support: "it is impossible for a single monarchy to embrace the innumerable cares of the organization of the universe . . . it is never possible for the earth to resemble the unity of the divine and primary rule." As Khosrow had hoped, his ambassadors' arguments were persuasive, and he received Roman military support, with which he defeated his rival and regained the Persian throne.

Khosrow's argument is a fitting conclusion to this chapter on world empires, which began with Alexander's bold quest to unite the Mediterranean, Middle East, and India. For Alexander it was still possible to think in terms of one supreme god in heaven and one empire on earth. But after the introduction of monotheism, the situation changed. For the Persian ambassadors it was impossible for a human empire not only to ever resemble the kingdom of God but also to reign alone on earth. For the Persians and Romans—Theophylactus cites the Persian ambassadors approvingly—the one single God anywhere and nowhere disapproves of all imperial projects on earth and prefers a commonwealth of multiple kingdoms. It is this reevaluation of politics and history which the visionaries can be seen as having contributed to world history. Obviously, many kings and emperors later in history did not accept the idea of the futility of empires. But after monotheism, they had to reckon with forceful critics who would cut their ambitions down to size and remind people of the fundamental difference between the imperfect earthly states and the heavenly kingdom.

▶ For additional resources, including maps, primary sources, visuals, and quizzes, please go to www.oup.com/us/vonsivers. Please see the Further Resources section at the back of the book for additional readings and suggested websites.

Thinking Through Patterns

▶ **Why should the Middle East and Mediterranean Europe during the period 600 BCE–600 CE be studied as a single unit?**

The sharp division between Europe and the Middle East that exists today is a recent phenomenon. During the period of late multireligious and early monotheistic empires, from 600 BCE to 600 CE, the two regions were tightly intertwined. Initially, the sequence of the multireligious Persian and Macedonian Empires dominated the Middle East and eastern Mediterranean. Later, the competition between the subsequent two empires, Rome and Persia, inaugurated a pattern of urbanization, a deepening gulf between the wealthy and poor, and the immigration of tribal people from central Asia.

The experience of transcendence happens constantly, even if it remains for the most part unexpressed and little thought about. In its most common form, it is encountered as the unknown future: You dream of getting a college degree as the entry ticket to your future academic career. After years of toil, sacrifices, and financial cost, the day of graduation arrives. In one moment, as your name is called, the transcendent expectation becomes a reality: As you clutch the diploma, a thrill goes down your spine. Apart from the future, the past as well as space can be thought of as transcendent. The great visionaries of 700–500 BCE abstracted a separate, transcendent God or first principle from the world where there had been, in polytheism, a single cosmos in which heaven with its high god, plus all the other gods and goddesses, intermingled with the world. The visionaries did not merely reflect on gods and humans mixing *in* the world, as in the polytheism of the past. They rather directed their focus on God or the first principle *separate from* the world, thereby creating religious monotheism and philosophical monism. Following the visionaries, thinkers explored new, abstract dimensions of thought in the new intellectual disciplines of science, philosophy, and theology.

▶ **What is transcendence, and why is it important to understand its importance in world history?**

▶ **Which elements characterize the institutions growing out of the Middle Eastern monotheisms of Judaism–Christianity and monism of Greek philosophy-science?**

In the Middle East and eastern Mediterranean, visionaries were the creators of bodies of transcendent thought that evolved into the Zoroastrian and Jewish religions as well as Greek philosophy and science. The visionaries and their early followers created scriptures which expounded in great detail the nature of God or the first principle. Anyone could read or listen to the scriptures and, accordingly, the visionaries and their successors attracted communities of like-minded followers. Zoroastrianism, Judaism, and Christianity were religions of salvation: Firm believers in the power of God's forgiveness would be saved in a transcendent kingdom of heaven. For Zoroastrians, Jews, and Christians—cogs in the giant, brutal, and meaningless multireligious machines of the Persian and Roman Empires—this religious promise of salvation was the only way of making sense out of life. Eventually the emperors themselves converted, making monotheism the state religion.

Chapter 8 600 BCE-600 CE

Empires and Visionaries in India

It was one of the most intriguing meetings of the ancient world, though no one could have foreseen its ultimate significance at the time. One of the participants, Alexander the Great, as we have seen, had already become by the age of 30 the most successful military leader the world had ever seen. His present interest, however—the conquest of northern India—had so far proved difficult in the face of the huge armies and terrifying ranks of war elephants massed by his opponents. Now, as he prepared to invade the most powerful Indian state, Magadha, Alexander's men were growing anxious about the seemingly insatiable ambition of their commander. Given the opposition within his own ranks and on the battlefield, Alexander had retreated to the northern city of Taxila, near the modern capital of Islamabad in Pakistan, to replenish his forces and rethink his situation.

While in Taxila, Alexander met with a man identified by his biographers simply as "Sandrokoptros," who had recently fled the Magadhan court after a failed attempt to overthrow its government. Though we can only speculate about the substance of the talks between the two men, Alexander's use of local politics in his past military campaigns suggests that he sought to take advantage of Sandrokoptros' knowledge of Magadha and its leadership in planning his attack. The intelligence Alexander obtained must have been discouraging, for he soon abandoned his plans to invade India and, facing the possibility of mutiny among his men, withdrew to the safer confines of Persia, where he died in 323 BCE. Following Alexander's death, one of his

INDIA,
800 BCE–800 CE

ABOVE: "Sutra of the 1000 Buddhas," from a seventeenth-century Tibetan manuscript.

commanders, Seleucus Nikator [See-LOO-kus Nee-KAY-tor], gained control of the eastern reaches of his empire. By 321 BCE, however, Seleucus Nikator found his territory around the Indus River threatened by a powerful new Indian state created by none other than Alexander's former ally, Sandrokoptros. But it was not until the end of the eighteenth century CE that the shadowy "Sandrokoptros" was identified by English Sanskrit scholars as Chandragupta Maurya [Chahn-drah-GUP-tah MOORY-ah], the founder of India's first and largest empire.

The meeting between Alexander and Chandragupta was significant for many reasons. For one thing, it took place between two men with similar desires for world empire, whose models of leadership inspired a host of imitators. More significant for our purposes, however, was what this meeting symbolized for the future of India: intensifying exchanges of ideas and goods between peoples of vastly different cultures and beliefs.

Indian visionaries and innovators made contributions that would have a profound effect on patterns of world history as they made their way throughout Eurasia and North Africa. In turn, India's place as a crossroads of trade and invasion continually replenished the subcontinent with innovation from outside. Many centuries later, the lore of India's wealth and culture would fire the imaginations of Europeans and drive them to seek out the connection first established by Alexander and Chandragupta so many centuries before.

Patterns of State Formation in India: Republics, Kingdoms, and Empires

When Alexander arrived, the pattern of state formation in India had shifted permanently to the plains and hills of the Punjab and Ganges valley. The shift had begun when tectonic movements in the Himalayas around 1900 BCE caused the drying up of the Sarasvati River in northwest India. People abandoned the agrarian–urban center of the Indus valley and migrated eastward. Much of the land to which they migrated in the Punjab and Ganges valley consisted of rain forest and marshes that required laborious land-clearing. But the settlers drew on their past experience as they built the new agrarian–urban centers of northern India. In contrast to Africa and Mesoamerica where the patterns of state formation from villages and chiefdoms to kingdoms developed slowly, state formation proceeded rapidly. The earliest traces of villages date to about 1200 BCE. Thereafter, polities emerged quickly, in the form of warrior republics and kingdoms. Both flourished in the early first millennium BCE.

A gradual consolidation process set in from about 800 BCE onward, with a few kingdoms emerging as the strongest states while warrior republics disappeared from the scene. At the height of the wars for predominance, around 700–400 BCE, visionaries similar to those appearing at the same time in the Middle East and China offered reforms of the Vedic traditions: the Upanishads, Jainism, and Buddhism. The process of state formation reached a first peak with the Mauryan Empire, which

▶ Think about the reasons for the spread of Buddhism inside and outside of India. How have historians seen the decline of Buddhism in India?

▶ What do you consider to be the most influential patterns in Indian history to this point? Why?

▶ Do you think some of Ashoka's ideas could be implemented by governments today? Why or why not?

united northern and central India and experimented with Buddhism as a privileged religion. A firm marriage between state and religion, however, occurred with the Hindu Gupta Empire (320–550 CE), which, along with its contemporary, Christian Rome, became the first state in world history to lay the foundation for a religious civilization.

The Road to Empire: The Mauryas

In the early first millennium BCE, the emerging states along the Ganges River valley developed political systems ranging from *gana-sanghas* [GAH-nah SAHN-gahs]— often termed "republics" by scholars—to centralized monarchies whose rulers were accorded god-like status. The agricultural advances made in these formerly forested areas, particularly through the use of iron tools—and the dikes, ponds, flooded fields, and drainage systems necessary for growing rice—resulted in the emergence of wealthy, centralized states led by Magadha and Kosala, along with the lesser kingdoms of Vatsya and Avanti farther west (see Map 8.1).

During the half-century before Alexander attempted to expand his empire into northern India, Mahapadama Nanda [Mah-hah-PAH-dah-mah NAHN-dah], a member of the *shudra varna*, seized power in Magadha and embarked on a series of military campaigns against Vatsya and Avanti, both of which he conquered. By the 330s BCE, the Magadhan state stretched across the entire breadth of northern India and the taxes imposed by the Nandas brought unprecedented wealth to their capital

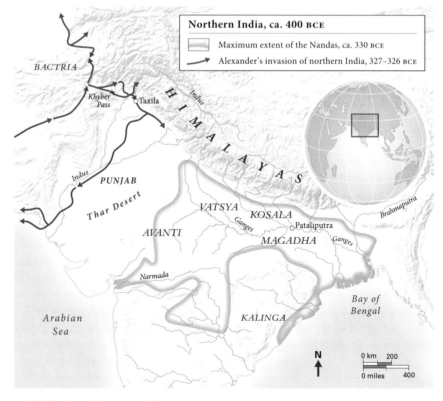

MAP 8.1 Northern India, ca. 400 BCE.

of Pataliputra [Pah-tah-lee-POO-trah], the modern city of Patna, on the Ganges. The Nandas, however, were not alone in their aspirations for universal empire.

Chandragupta Maurya   Little is known of Chandragupta's early life. It is believed that at a young age he was put under the care of the philosopher Kautilya, whose *Arthashastra* became the most influential political treatise in Indian history (see Chapter 3). Contemporary accounts of Chandragupta's court and the structure of his government suggest a strong connection to the political practices of the idealized ruler outlined in the *Arthashastra*. At this stage, however, Kautilya was instrumental in the young Chandragupta's first attempt to seize power from the ruling Nandas. Playing on discontent over Nanda taxation and the threat to religious order posed by rulers from the lowest shudra varna, he used his considerable influence to back a palace revolt by the young Chandragupta. When the revolt was unsuccessful, the two fled to Taxila, a dominant trade crossroads strategically located near the Khyber Pass, where they encountered Alexander.

Kautilya and Alexander played important roles in building Chandragupta's empire, though Alexander's role is less obvious. The dislocations in the northwest caused by Alexander's attempted invasions allowed Chandragupta to pursue a patient strategy of securing the most vulnerable and least contented of the Nandas' client states while methodically surrounding and, ultimately, conquering Magadha. By 321 BCE Chandragupta had secured the capital and embarked on a campaign to enlarge his empire. Following a series of battles with Alexander's successor, Seleucus Nikator, the Greeks surrendered their north Indian and Indus territories to Chandragupta. Though forced from his Indian holdings, Seleucus and his successors maintained cordial relations with the Mauryas and posted the ambassador Megasthenes to the Mauryan capital of Pataliputra. Though little survives of his reports, Megasthenes' accounts of the enormous wealth and population of the capital and the efficiency of Mauryan government formed the basis of much of the classical and medieval European understanding of India.

Although his motivations for doing so are unclear, Chandragupta stepped down from his throne around 297 BCE and joined an ascetic religious order, the Jains, formed on the basis of the teachings of the visionary Mahavira. Legend has it that he ended his life in the Jain monastery at Karnataka, where, in imitation of the order's founder, he refused all food and starved himself to death rather than consume any living thing. Chandragupta's son continued to expand the Mauryan domains to the west and south, but it was his grandson, Ashoka (Ah-SHOW-kah) (r. ca. 273–231 BCE), who emerged as perhaps India's most dominant ruler until the nineteenth century CE.

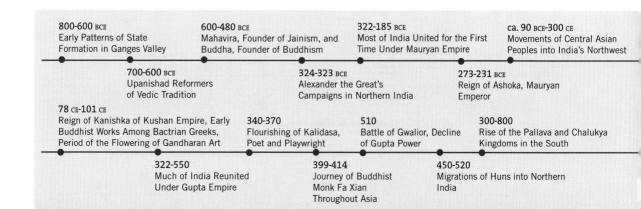

| 800-600 BCE Early Patterns of State Formation in Ganges Valley | 600-480 BCE Mahavira, Founder of Jainism, and Buddha, Founder of Buddhism | 322-185 BCE Most of India United for the First Time Under Mauryan Empire | ca. 90 BCE-300 CE Movements of Central Asian Peoples into India's Northwest |

700-600 BCE Upanishad Reformers of Vedic Tradition — 324-323 BCE Alexander the Great's Campaigns in Northern India — 273-231 BCE Reign of Ashoka, Mauryan Emperor

78 CE-101 CE Reign of Kanishka of Kushan Empire, Early Buddhist Works Among Bactrian Greeks, Period of the Flowering of Gandharan Art — 340-370 Flourishing of Kalidasa, Poet and Playwright — 510 Battle of Gwalior, Decline of Gupta Power — 300-800 Rise of the Pallava and Chalukya Kingdoms in the South

322-550 Much of India Reunited Under Gupta Empire — 399-414 Journey of Buddhist Monk Fa Xian Throughout Asia — 450-520 Migrations of Huns into Northern India

Ashoka   Born around 304 BCE, Ashoka may have actually seized the throne from his father. Like his predecessors, he soon began a series of military ventures to drive the Mauryan Empire deeper into the south (see Map 8.2). The climax of his efforts was a fierce war he fought with the kingdom of Kalinga, the last adjacent region outside of Mauryan control, on the eastern coast. Though figures given in ancient sources must always be treated with suspicion, by Ashoka's own admission, 100,000 people were killed in the conflict. Yet, it was also here, at the height of his power, that, deeply moved by the carnage in Kalinga, in around 260 BCE he abruptly abandoned the path of conquest, converted to Buddhism, and vowed to rule his kingdom by "right conduct" alone.

Scholars know perhaps more about Ashoka's reign than that of any other ancient Indian monarch. He told much of his own story and outlined his Buddhist-inspired ideas for proper behavior on inscriptions in caves and on rocks and pillars set up in strategic places throughout his empire. Written mostly in Prakrit, the parent tongue of many of the modern north Indian dialects, these inscriptions present a fascinating and human glimpse of the ruler and his personal vision of the idea of dharma (see Chapter 3).

Departing somewhat from the Bhagavad Gita's concept of dharma as duty (see Chapter 3), dharma for Ashoka was simply "that which is good." Among other

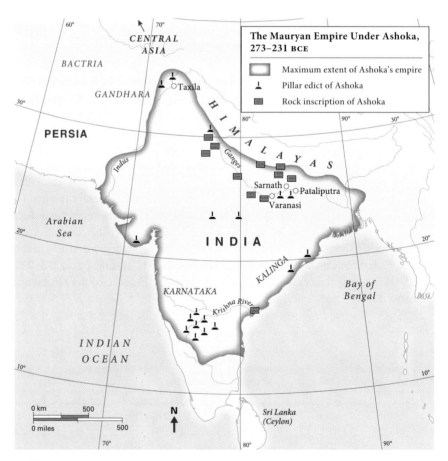

MAP 8.2 The Mauryan Empire Under Ashoka, 273–231 BCE.

things, this involved living a life of "kindness, liberality, truthfulness, and purity." Moreover, he believed that following the path of dharma represented the only way one could achieve happiness. One distinctive innovation growing out of Ashoka's support of dharma was his taking up of the Buddhist concept of *ahimsa*, or nonviolence: People should be kind to the weak and disadvantaged and do no harm to any living creature. By way of setting an example, Ashoka declared dozens of animal species to be under his protection, forbade the wholesale burning of forests, and even warned his people not to burn grain husks in order to avoid injuring any creatures living within them. Ashoka's devotion to dharma even extended to sending his sons as Buddhist missionaries to Sri Lanka, where it has remained the principal faith to this day.

Although Ashoka advocated the peaceful principles of dharma, the records of his reign also indicate that his empire was, in many respects, an early kind of police state. He followed many of the political practices suggested in Kautilya's *Arthashastra*, which emphasizes that a monarch must be alert to the moods of his people, on the lookout for enemies, and ready to capitalize on opportunities to exercise power. While allowing the practice of many religions in addition to Buddhism, Ashoka kept a tight rein on his officials and people through a vast network of spies and informers, a practice begun by his grandfather, Chandragupta. The empire itself was divided into four large regional districts, each with a governor. They and all the officials under them were subject to periodic review by roving special commissioners appointed by the throne, whose chief task was to check on everyone's adherence to dharma. Thus, the entire governmental apparatus was now geared toward uplifting the people's morality and supervising their happiness.

Ashoka also encouraged a unified system of commercial law, standardization of weights and measures, and uniform coinage throughout his realm, innovations that greatly facilitated trade and commerce. A majority of state revenues came from taxes on harvests of wheat, rice, barley, and millet plus those on internal and external trade. Under the Mauryans, India was the major crossroads in the exchange of gold and silver sought by the Hellenistic kingdoms and for the expanding maritime trade accompanying the advance of Buddhism into southeast Asia. In the north, Taxila and the cities and towns along the caravan routes from China to the west grew wealthy from the increasing exchange of silk and other luxury goods.

Within India, the circulation of tropical fruits, medicinal barks, and innumerable other forest products augmented trade still further. Thus, the immense wealth and power flowing into Ashoka's court in Pataliputra made that city of half a million perhaps the richest in the ancient world. The wealth at Ashoka's command and his devotion to dharma allowed the government to spend lavishly in sponsoring public works—palaces, roads, rest stops and hostels for travelers, and parks—as well as temples and shrines for various religious groups.

In all, Ashoka's regime represents a pioneering attempt to construct a workable moral order, a pattern of world history that emerged repeatedly as states seeking to become world empires increasingly turned to religious and philosophical systems that proclaimed universal truths. In India, as in southwest Asia and the Mediterranean, and as we will see in China, these universal truths were proclaimed by visionaries who sensed problems developing in the old order of their respective societies.

Capital of Ashoka Pillar of Sarnath. The triple lion motif atop the *chakravartin* wheel, symbolizing universal kingship, topped one of Ashoka's famous pillars. The one from which this capital was taken had been set up to commemorate the Buddha's first sermon in Sarnath's Deer Park.

**MOVEMENT OF
NOMADIC PEOPLES,
300 BCE–100 CE**

The ultimate end of this process, which we will explore in detail in Part 3, was the development of religious civilizations.

The Nomadic Kingdoms of the North   With the end of the Mauryan Empire, northern India was transformed into a series of regional kingdoms run by local rulers. Greek-speaking peoples from Bactria—descendants of troops and colonists who had come to the area under Alexander the Great—controlled some of these territories. Their most famous ruler, Menander, achieved immortality in Buddhist literature as "King Milinda" by engaging in a debate at court with the philosopher Nagasena. Their talks, as later set down, became an important exposition of Buddhist ideas and purportedly led to Menander's conversion.

By the first years of the Common Era, the Bactrian Greek rulers of northern India confronted new nomadic groups from central Asia, who eventually put an end to Greek rule in the region. These groups had been put into motion by repeated Chinese campaigns against the Xiongnu [SHIUNG-noo] (the Huns) and the Yuezhi [YOO-eh-jih]. As they moved into northern India sometime around 25 CE, the Yuezhi became known as the "Kushans." Under its most famous ruler, Kanishka (r. ca. 78–101 CE), the Kushan Empire expanded into not only northern India but also much of modern Pakistan and Afghanistan. Kanishka, like Menander, adopted Buddhism and actively propagated the faith within his growing kingdom and beyond. Through his efforts, the new religion expanded along the caravan routes of central Asia and shortly afterward appears for the first time in Chinese records.

Although the continual arrival of new groups expanded the cultural resources of northern India and greatly aided the spread of Buddhism, it also worked against the development of stable states in the region. With the intensity of the migrations abating by the end of the third century, however, a new and aggressive line of rulers, the Guptas, established power in the Ganges valley and stood poised to reunite the old Mauryan heartland. Under their rule would come India's great classical age.

The Classical Age: The Gupta Empire

The origin of the Gupta line is somewhat obscure, though scholars agree that, like the Mauryans, it originated somewhere near Magadha. The first major ruler of the dynasty was Chandragupta I (ca. 320–335 CE, no relation to the Chandragupta of the Mauryan Empire), whose new state occupied much of the old heartland of Magadha and Kosala. With recognition of the rising power of the Guptas extending from Nepal in the north to the Shaka territories in the west, the way lay open for his successor, Samudragupta [Sahm-OO-drah-ghup-tah] (r. ca. 335–380 CE), to expand the borders of the empire even further.

Under Samudragupta, the Gupta sway extended both north and south, securing a swath of territory extending far up the Ganges River to the borders of the Kushans south of Taxila and down the coast deep into the territory of the Pallavas in the south. Like Chandragupta I, he forged ties to regions outside of Gupta control, the people of which in turn pledged their loyalty to him. As was the case of the states of Zhou China, this arrangement has often been characterized as "feudal" in that it resembles the relationships among the states of medieval Europe, though scholars are careful not to push the parallels too far. Samudragupta's son, Chandragupta II (r. ca.

Coins of the Northwest, Second Century BCE and Late First Century CE. The complex history of the area encompassed by modern Afghanistan and Pakistan has been understood principally through the coins minted by the many rulers of frequently shifting territories. The silver coin on the left was minted by a Bactrian Greek king, probably in the second century BCE. The gold coin beside it with the Greek inscription was the product of the reign of the famous Buddhist King Kanishka (78–101 CE) of the Kushans and depicts the king himself.

380–413 CE), seized the throne from his elder brother and continued to expand the empire, adding the southern and western Gujarati territories of the Shakas. The cumulative effect of this string of conquests over barely a century was that, once again, the Indian subcontinent stood on the threshold of unity (see Map 8.3).

Court and Culture   The Gupta era is considered to be the classical age of Indian culture and religion. During the reign of the Guptas, the collection of religious traditions called "**Hinduism**" flourished, becoming the dominant faith of the time. Indeed, the Guptas actively used the gods and practices of Hinduism, particularly in their devotion to Vishnu and Shiva, to extend their legitimacy not just as kings but as universal rulers.

Hinduism: A convenient, shorthand term for the vast multiplicity of religious practices derived from the Vedic, Brahmanic, Upanishadic, and later traditions in India and those places influenced by Indian culture.

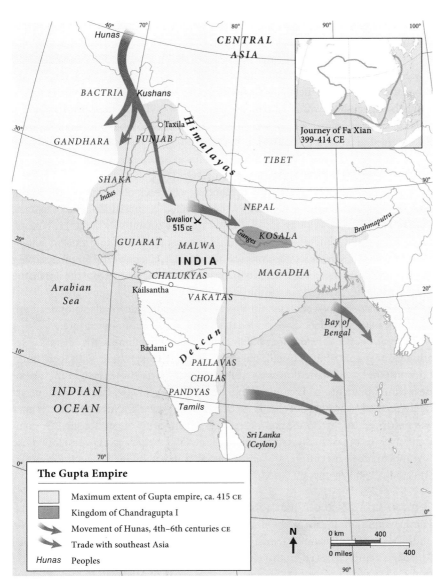

MAP **8.3 The Gupta Empire.**

Although the Guptas preferred the king-centered, hierarchical Brahmanic tradition of Hinduism, which they made the privileged religion in the state, they permitted the practice of other faiths, including both Jainism and Buddhism. Under their influence and with their financial support, the first distinctly "Hindu" art is recognizable in the temples and shrines to a variety of deities that were built in staggering profusion. In addition, the era marked a peak of popularity for classical treatises on political and social behavior such as the *Arthashastra* and the *Kama Sutra*, the famous manual of sexual practices and personal deportment, as well as, it is often supposed, the works of the playwright and poet Kalidasa (fl. fifth century CE), sometimes called the "Indian Shakespeare."

The Waning of Gupta Power   Gupta power began to fade under the reigns of Chandragupta II's son and grandson, whose weakened authority was challenged by groups seeking greater autonomy in the vicinity of Malwa, in central India. By this time, however, a new wave of central Asian nomads, the Hunas, sometimes called the "White Huns," had appeared. By 510 CE, having defeated the Guptas at Gwalior, some 200 miles south of the modern city of New Delhi, the Hunas established themselves as the dominant force in northwest India, and once again the areas along the Ganges were thrust into political disunity. By 515 CE, the eastern tributary states of the Guptas had broken away, while in the west the kingdom of the Rajputanas emerged in Gujarat by mid-century.

The Southern Kingdoms, ca. 300–600 CE

Though their states were constantly contending with each other for wealth, power, and territory, the southern regimes of the so-called "imperial Pallavas," Pandyas, Cholas and Chalukyas of peninsular India were comparatively stable in cultural terms from the decline of the Guptas until the installation of the Muslim sultanates of the north. One reason for this was the absence of a powerful empire pushing south. Freed from the need to defend themselves from incursion from the north, the southern kingdoms could pursue the pacification of their own realms. Their political and religious systems were also still largely dominated by descendants of northern colonists, so their ruling classes shared to some degree a common culture.

In addition, the development of Hinduism among the Tamils, the region's chief ethnic group, contributed to cultural stability, while its synthesis with local traditions inspired a dramatic flowering of literature and art. These include the rise of **devotional** branches of Hinduism and an outpouring of spectacular religious art rarely equaled in any area of the world. Finally, the power and wealth of the region was enhanced by the promotion of trade, especially with the established "Indianized" enclaves of southeast Asia and the Indonesian archipelago. As a result of these ties, Indian religions, culture, and economics dominated Indian Ocean trade until it was gradually taken over by the Muslims after the fourteenth century CE.

Devotional: In the context of this chapter, dedicating oneself to practices that venerate, honor, or adore a particular god or divinity.

Temple Complexes   The southern kingdoms' most tangible remains are the Hindu temple complexes left behind at a number of sites. The Pallavas, for example, under Mahendra Vikruma Varman I (r. ca. 590–630 CE), constructed the famous Mandapa Temple, carved from solid rock. His descendant, Narasimha Varman II (r. 695–728 CE), sponsored the seven rock pagodas of Mahabali Purana. Perhaps most spectacular of all was the eighth-century CE Rashtakutra complex of Krishna I

The Kailasantha Temple. Hewn from a single, solid rock, the Kailasantha Temple, part of an elaborate complex in east-central India, is considered the world's most monumental sculpture. Strongly influenced by south Indian architectural traditions, the temple complex dazzles the visitor with carvings of innumerable deities, mythic figures, and erotic imagery.

at Kailasantha again carved from solid rock. The work was so complex, detailed, and painstakingly done that it was said to have moved its master builder to cry, "Oh, how did I do this?"

Regional Struggles The long process of interaction and adaptation in India had already created a recognizably different society as one moved south from the Ganges. For one thing, the systems of *varna* and *jati* (see Chapter 3) tended to revolve more around where one lived than they did in the north. For example, there were major differentiations between those living in the cities and flatland farming communities and the "hill peoples" and "forest peoples," still considered largely uncivilized. A major division also existed between the local leaders, whose families had in many cases emigrated from the north and were members of the upper varnas, and their subjects. Within these divisions, rulers tended to be more predatory in their efforts to enrich themselves and their kingdoms.

The rise of the Chalukya state on the western side of the peninsula in the midsixth century CE, along with that of the Vakatakas of the Deccan Plateau and the Rashtakutras in the early eighth century CE, resumed the struggle for wealth and territory among the older southern kingdoms. As we will see in Chapter 13, by the middle of the eighth century CE, the Chalukya state spawned a potent rival when the areas to the north and west broke away from its grasp. The leaders there became known as the "Rashtakutras" and shortly thereafter captured the capital at Badami.

The Vedic Tradition and Its Visionary Reformers

Beginning around 700 BCE, visionaries appeared, seeking to reform a Vedic tradition that they believed had grown overly formalistic and unresponsive to the needs of the people. As we noted in Chapter 3, the first of these men were the thinkers who created the Upanishads, a set of spiritual writings that lay the foundations of *monism*—the belief in a single transcendent first principle—in Hindu thought. In the next two centuries, Mahavira and the Buddha followed, becoming the founding figures, respectively, of Jainism, a small community in today's India, and of Buddhism, today a major religion in southeast Asia, China, and Japan.

Reforming the Vedic Tradition

The Vedas consisted of 10 books of hymns to the gods and goddesses of the Hindu pantheon and described in detail the rituals and sacrifices required to keep the world in harmony with these deities. They thus framed the culture of the period 1200–600 BCE, when the inhabitants of the Indian subcontinent initiated the pattern of Punjab and Ganges valley state formation. As we saw at the beginning of this chapter, several dozen warrior republics and kingdoms competed against each other for wealth and power, similar to the warring states of China that we will explore in Chapter 9. It was against the backdrop of this competition that visionaries critical of the polytheistic Vedic heritage arose and sought to reform it through the formulation of a single first principle. The main figures of these reform efforts were the authors of the Upanishads (ca. 700–300 BCE), Mahavira (trad. 599–527 BCE), and Gautama, the Buddha or Enlightened One (trad. 563–483 BCE).

The Upanishad Visionaries   Many authors of the more than 100 Upanishads are known to us by name. They were Brahmanic priests—and also the daughter of one—whose principal concern was to penetrate beyond the complexities of the tens of thousands of gods (as one of the Upanishads mockingly asserts) to a vision of cosmic unity. This Upanishadic vision, with its opposition to polytheism and the proclamation of monism, was remarkably similar to those propounded in the Middle East and China during the same time: They proclaimed a transcendent first principle as universal truth, addressed to anyone anywhere.

The Indian visionaries were hermit teachers living in the forests of the Gangetic states to "draw near" to themselves (the meaning of the Sanskrit "Upanishad") disciples who did not want merely to understand the transcendent unity of the universe outside of the individual but also to attain this unity by merging their personal selves (*atman*) into the universal self (*brahman*) and thereby achieve salvation. These visionaries did not develop this theme of the unity of atman–brahman systematically in the form of treatises. Instead, they concentrated on leading their disciples through brief aphorisms, paradoxes, and negations ("not this, nor that") step by step into deep meditation, which they considered as the activity through which salvation could be achieved. As time went on, however, contemplation of the Upanishadic scriptures and their hidden meanings concerning the mysteries of atman–brahman also became a vital part of a new evolving tradition. In the highest state of understanding of atman–brahman, one could attain release from the bounds of the cycles of death and rebirth and thus enter into transcendence, or *moksha*.

Criticism of the Vedic Rituals and Sacrifices   Although they were advocates of monism, or first principle, the authors of the Upanishads remained faithful to the Vedic rituals, sacrifices, and doctrines. Their reforms were limited to creating a meditative supplement to the Vedic religion. However, as strong kingdoms emerged in the 500s BCE and conquered smaller kingdoms and warrior republics, criticism of religious ritual grew. Urbanization and trade created new classes of inhabitants, such as merchants and craftspeople, to whom rituals and sacrifices meant far less than they did to the kings and the priestly class. The merchants and craftspeople viewed the rituals as formalistic and the sacrifices, consisting of burning large quantities of food and killing many animals, as wasteful. For the kings and priests, these religious practices were essential to legitimize their power. The Vedic doctrine that eventually caused the break between the priests and their strongest critics, however, was that of the cycle of karma–samsara (see Chapter 3), death and rebirth.

The Ascetic Break: Jainism   The founder of the Jains, Nigantha Nataputta [Nee-GAN-tah Nah-tah-POO-tah], whose title of Vardhamana Mahavira means "the great hero," was born the son of a warrior chief perhaps around 540 BCE. At the age of 30 he left home and gave up all his worldly possessions to become an ascetic, and after 12 years he found meditative enlightenment. From this point on he was given the title of *jina*, or "conqueror," and from this his followers became known as "Jains." For the next 40 years, he wandered throughout India without clothes or possessions, spreading the new sect's principles and practices. Finally, as the ultimate exemplar of the movement's ideal of not taking the life of any being whatsoever, Mahavira refused all food and performed a ritual fast that led to his death in Pava, near Pataliputra.

Statue of the Jain Saint Gomateshwara at Karnataka. The world's largest statue cut from a single stone, this statue was built at the site of the famous Jain monastery, where, it was said, Chandragupta Maurya entered the order and fasted to death, following the example of the sect's founder, Mahavira.

While much of the earliest Jain doctrine was lost during its first two centuries of oral transmission, it begins with a universe in which all things possess *jiva*, a kind of "soul" that yearns to be free from the prison of the material world. Jains believe that even inanimate objects, such as stones—as well as plants, human beings, and other animals—possess *jiva*, though at different levels or "senses." These "souls" are governed in turn by the degree to which a thing's past karma stands between it and its release from material bondage. For human beings, karma builds up according to the injuries one does to other beings and objects, intentionally or not. The way to enlightenment is to act in such a way that one acquires as little karma as possible, while performing actions of suffering and self-sacrifice to atone for and reduce the karma one already has. In this sense, karma might be thought of as a kind of weight on the "soul": As karma dissipates, the soul becomes lighter until, finally free, it rises to the very heights of the cosmos and lives for eternity.

Ahimsa   Jain monks take extraordinary pains to prevent injury to any object, especially living things. For example, from the first centuries of the movement there has been a **schism** between those who insist on complete nakedness—to avoid injuring creatures that might be trapped in one's clothing—and those who wear a simple white robe. Other measures include wearing gauze masks to filter out invisible organisms that might be breathed in and carrying brooms to sweep small creatures out of one's path. Monks live by begging food from others—so that they themselves do not have to kill it and add to their karma. Because suffering reduces karma, they frequently undergo extraordinary ordeals, such as allowing themselves to be covered with biting insects or lying on beds of nails. The most dedicated perform the

Schism: A division; when used in a religious context it usually refers to the splitting of members of a certain religion into two or more camps over matters of doctrine, ritual, etc.

supreme sacrifice and ritually starve themselves to death, which, because of the intense suffering involved and the resolute refusal to harm living things, is seen as the ultimate act of ahimsa, or nonviolence.

Not surprisingly, the strict practices of the Jains did not appeal to most people. As a result, an extensive laity, especially among the lower castes who identified more with the sacrifices of the monks, grew to support them. The patronage of kings, most famously Chandragupta Maurya, helped ensure the sect's vitality. As a matter of course, Jains would not take up farming, so monastic and lay followers were often involved in business, study, and writing—occupations they still favor today. The religion's most distinctive element is that it is rigorously **atheistic**, choosing not to worship any god but insisting instead on meditatively merging into an eternal, uncreated, indifferent unity that is both universal and transcendent.

Atheistic: Not believing in a god or supreme being.

The Middle Way: Buddhism   The other major movement, Buddhism, began in part as a reaction against such extreme ascetic practices. Siddhartha Gautama, whose title of "Buddha" means "the Enlightened One," is believed to have been born a prince in the Sakya republic in the Himalayan foothills. His traditional birth date is given as 563 BCE, though recent accounts have moved it to at least the mid-400s BCE. Because of his royal pedigree, he is frequently referred to as "Sakyamuni," or prince of the Sakyas. Seeking to shelter him from the evils of the world, Gautama's father secluded him in the palace. At the age of 29, however, Gautama left his world of privilege and followed the paths of various Vedic schools. At one point, following a discipline of extreme asceticism, his path of self-deprivation led him to nearly fast to death.

During his travels, Gautama was exposed to the entire range of human suffering and death from which his father had tried so hard to shelter him. His shock and compassion for the world around him drove him to find a way to understand the endless round of death and rebirth to which all creatures were apparently subject. According to Buddhist accounts, the insight gained from his experiences and a long period of deep meditation sparked his enlightenment one day under a pipal tree in the town of Gaya. Shortly afterward, Gautama went to a deer park in Sarnath, close by the great city of Varanasi (Benares) where he found five former disciples and preached a sermon to them outlining what became known as the Middle Way—the path of moderation.

The Four Noble Truths, the Eightfold Path, and Nirvana   Gautama believed that the fundamental nature of the perceived universe is change. In a constantly changing world, suffering is the common lot of all because they attach themselves to what will ultimately be taken from them. Although they crave permanence, they rely only on their senses, which provide the illusion of stability but actually give a false picture of what is the true, ever-changing nature of things. Pushed into evil deeds in pursuit of whatever they desire, they accumulate karma. Over many lifetimes, the karma they acquire stays with them even after the separation of the material "soul" from the immaterial at death. It builds up with each life and keeps them from breaking free of the cycle of death and rebirth. In that first sermon in Sarnath, Gautama distilled these insights into what he called the Four Noble Truths:

1. that all life is suffering
2. that suffering arises from craving

3. that to stop suffering, one must stop craving
4. that one stops craving by following the Eightfold Path of right views, right resolve, right speech, right conduct, right livelihood, right effort, right mindfulness, and right concentration

Later sermons and vast numbers of commentaries outlined the specifics of the Eightfold Path. Essentially, the path represents a course of life in which one avoids extreme behaviors of any kind, adheres to a code of conduct that favors **altruism** and respects the life of all living beings, and through meditation and "right mindfulness" reaches a state of calm nonattachment with an uncluttered mind able to grasp the universal truth. On reaching this stage during this same lifetime, the karmic traces of past lives are "blown out" like a lamp flame, the literal meaning of the Sanskrit word associated with this final state of enlightenment: *nirvana*, or nothingness. In Buddhism, this nothingness is a more explicit version of the logic of *moksha*—transcendence—first explored in the Upanishads.

Altruism: The practice of acting in an unselfish manner for the good of others.

Even during the Buddha's lifetime his followers had organized into a brotherhood, despite his dying injunction that the true path to enlightenment resided in them as individuals. As in other movements, the void left by the Buddha's death resulted in disputes about the authenticity of certain teachings and questions about how the group should now conduct itself. Over the following two centuries, several Buddhist councils were held and, during one of these meetings, a division developed, resulting in one group separating from the main body of adherents. The now separate group became known as Theravada [Ter-rah-VAH-dah], "the teachings of the elders." Under Ashoka's influence, Theravada Buddhism became the approved sect, with the first complete surviving texts dating from this time.

Buddhist Texts   The *Pali Canon*, written in Pali, the sacred language of Buddhism, is a collection of texts that forms the foundation of Theravada Buddhism and serves as the fundamental body of scriptures for nearly all Buddhist schools. The collection consists of the *Tripitaka* [Tree-pee-TAH-kuh], or "Three Baskets"; the *Vinaya* [Vee-NAI-yah], treatises on conduct and rules of discipline for monks; the *Sutras* [SOO-truhs], or "discourses," of which there are five groups, with most of them believed to have originated with the Buddha; and the *Abhidhamma* [Ah-bee-DAH-mah], doctrines of philosophy and metaphysics.

As Theravada Buddhism developed and spread in northern India and beyond, a number of developments changed its character, making it more accessible to a larger group of followers. The rich cultural interaction of the many peoples encountering it resulted in a great number of religious ideas and traditions circulating around the region. Questions and problems among Buddhist adherents from these different areas required broader solutions than in earlier times. For example, stories of the Buddha's last days implied that he would save everyone who followed his path, opening the way for the potential enlightenment of all. Coupled with this was a developing tradition of the Buddha as one in a long line of past and future Buddhas, suggesting the potential for a devotional component to the religion. In addition, there was the concept of the *bodhisattva* [boh-dee-SAHT-vuh]—one who, having achieved enlightenment, does not proceed to nirvana but is dedicated instead to helping the suffering achieve their own enlightenment.

Great Buddhist Stupa at Sanchi. The need for commemorative burial mounds and reliquaries for the Buddha's relics spawned a characteristic structure called a *stupa*, meaning "gathered." Brimming with symbolic motifs representing the stages of enlightenment, the structures changed considerably from this example—built in the first century BCE over an earlier one from the Mauryan period—as they spread through east Asia, where they assumed the shape of the pagoda.

Theravada and Mahayana   All of these ideas took shape around the first century CE in what became the largest branch of Buddhism, Mahayana [Mah-hah-YAH-nah], the "greater vehicle." Dismissing Theravada Buddhism as Hinay-ana [Heen-ah-YAH-nah], or "the lesser vehicle," Mahayana spread along the trade routes into central Asia, into the borderlands of the Parthians, and ultimately to China, Korea, Japan, and Tibet (see Map 8.4). As it spread, its different interpretive schools were, broadly speaking, divided into *esoteric* branches—those seeking enlightenment through scriptural or other kinds of deep knowledge—and devotional branches. Of the devotional schools, that of Amitabha [Ah-mee-TAH-bah], the Heavenly Buddha of the Western Paradise, is today the most popular Buddhist sect in both China and Japan (see Chapters 9 and 13).

As Buddhism was spreading across the greater part of Asia, however, its decline had, in a sense, already begun in the land of its birth. With the revitalization of the older Vedic and Brahmanic traditions into Hinduism, all the schools of Buddhism were to face strong competition for converts and noble patronage.

The Maturity of Hinduism: From the Abstract to the Devotional

The period from the Mauryans to the rise of the Guptas brought about a number of changes within the orthodox traditions of Indian religion. On the one hand, the continuing push of state formation to the south carried with it the older Vedic and Upanishadic traditions. Along the way, these traditions had incorporated many local

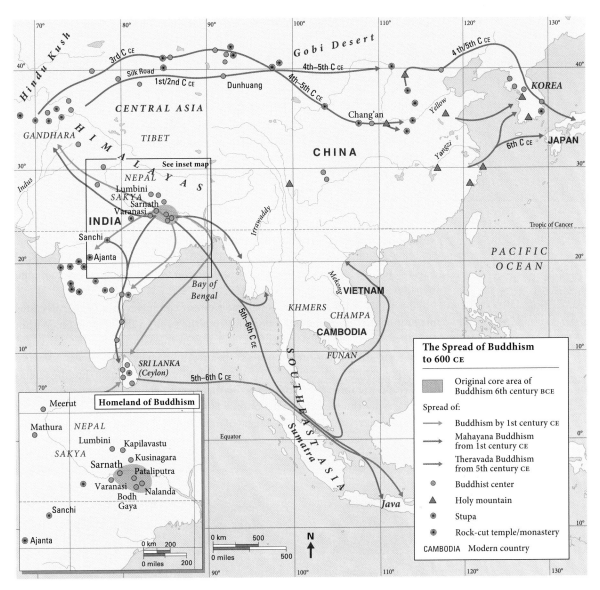

MAP 8.4 **The Spread of Buddhism to 600 CE.**

deities into their pantheon of gods. Over the next several centuries these southern areas would lead in the rise of devotional cults, especially those of Vishnu and Shiva, culminating in the *bhakti* movements beginning in the seventh century CE.

On the other hand, the growth of new religions like Buddhism and Jainism challenged such cultural mainstays as the caste system, the inevitability of the karmic cycle, and the domination of society and salvation by the traditional ruling classes. As a result of these challenges and through the popularity of the grand epics of the Mahabharata and Ramayana, the spreading of the classical texts of the first and second centuries, and Gupta patronage, a rejuvenated brand of religious experience, Hinduism, is distinctly recognizable by the fourth century CE.

Avatars and Alvars Among the most consistent Hindu beliefs was the idea that the subcontinent was a land united by faith—*Bharata*—a name used to describe India ever since. Another is the development of a full continuum of religious experience, ranging from the highly abstract to the emotional and mystical, springing from devotion to a particular god. Perhaps due to the egalitarian influence of Buddhism and Jainism, salvation was increasingly seen as accessible to all, according to one's abilities and the restrictions of caste and one's social position.

Of the many gods singled out for special attention, the most important were the so-called Indian trinity: Brahma, Vishnu, and Shiva. Of these, the main divisions of devotion emerged between Vishnu, the beneficent preserver, and Shiva, the powerful, fertile giver and destroyer of life, the "Lord of the Dance" of the universe. Both Vishnu and Shiva can manifest themselves through avatars or incarnations, the most popular of which is Krishna, an incarnation of Vishnu, who plays such a central role in the Bhagavad Gita. In addition to guiding that epic's hero, Arjuna, to an understanding of fulfilling his dharma—regardless of the immediate consequences—Krishna reveals to him the true power of devotion to himself as transcending the transitory nature of the material world.

The ability of the new devotional traditions of Hinduism to appeal to all castes made the religion increasingly popular from the time of the Guptas on. Within the all-encompassing character of Hinduism grew the assumption that one could achieve salvation according to one's caste and ability, whether one was a *shudra*, worshiping Shiva with a pure heart, or a highly educated brahman, finding liberation within the most profound texts. By the seventh century CE, religious poets were carrying the message of devotional Hinduism to all believers in vernacular languages. *Alvars* and *nayanars*, singers of praise for Vishnu and Shiva respectively, created some of the most passionate and beautiful religious poetry in any language

Representations of Brahma, Vishnu, and Shiva. From the time of the Guptas, a growing movement within Hinduism was that of devotional practices directed at the trinity of Brahma, the Creator; Vishnu, the Preserver; and Shiva, the Destroyer. The gods are frequently represented with multiple limbs to symbolize their different roles and superhuman functions.

over the next five centuries and helped bond the people to the orthodox religion as a whole.

Shakti and Tantra   A related development was that of Shakti, literally "power," sometimes called "tantra." Shakti practitioners often probed the darker edges of the multiple natures of the gods—especially Shiva and his consort Kali, or Durga—associated with death and destruction. Toward this end they purposely violated social norms—by eating meat, having illicit sex (even committing incest), eating human excrement, and, on rare occasions, committing ritual murder. The idea behind such perverse behavior was both to prove one's mastery over attachment to the acts them-selves and to push beyond the ordinary dualities of good and evil. Such extreme activities were comparatively rare, though the idea of transcending ordinary norms also passed into Buddhism at about the same time, in the fourth and fifth centuries CE. Here, it was also referred to as "tantra" and often as "the vehicle of the thunderbolt." In this modified form it passed into Nepal and Tibet, where its mysticism and interest in magical practices formed important elements of Tibetan Buddhism.

Stability Amid Disorder: Economics, Family, and Society

Despite India's tumultuous political history, the agrarian-based economy of the sub-continent remained for 2,000 years the richest (along with China) in the world. Its agriculture was enormously productive in its most fertile areas, and the topography and climate allowed an astonishing variety of products, from fragrant woods to pep-per and other tropical spices, to be produced for domestic consumption and export. As the economy flourished, society as a whole remained relatively stable. The hier-archical nature of the caste system maintained continuity through times of political turmoil, prescribing set duties and standards of behavior according to social position. Although the newly emerged religions of Buddhism and Jainism did not recognize the caste system, their appearance and spread did not fundamentally alter that system.

The relationships between men and women and among family members out-lined in Chapter 3 grew increasingly complex, particularly from the classical age of the Guptas onward. Despite the trend in Buddhism—and, as we shall see in Chap-ters 10 and 12 in Islam—toward greater equality between men and women, beliefs such as the strictly delineated spheres of husband and wife, the idea of the female as a fundamental force of the universe, and a male vision of women as simultaneously desirable and threatening were considerably enlarged during this time.

Tax and Spend: Economics and Society

By 600 BCE, the inhabitants of the emerging Gangetic states had long since made the transition to being settled agriculturalists. With the vast majority of inhabitants of the new states being peasants from the lowest *shudra varna*, the chief form of rev-enue was harvest taxes. The average tax levied on the people of these early states appears to have been around one-sixth of their annual harvest.

Accelerating Taxes   With the expansion of Magadha in the fifth and fourth centuries BCE, the agricultural tax increased to one-quarter of the harvest and even higher on royal lands—as much as half the cultivable land in the kingdom. By this time, the accelerating pace of urban life, the explosion of trade, and the increasingly differentiated castes expanded the economy even more, allowing whole new classes of items to be taxed. Thus, the immense wealth wielded by the Mauryans was accumulated through harvest taxes as high as one-half of all the produce raised in the empire, as well as taxes on livestock, internal trade, imports and exports, and such commodities as gold, textiles, salt, horses, and a variety of forest products and spices. Moreover, the increase in trade had led to a growing commercial class expanding beyond the traditional *vaisya* (merchant) *varna*, while the growing need for capital and credit was met by guilds of bankers and traders in precious metals.

Tariffs: Taxes levied on imports.

Agricultural taxes of about one-quarter to one-third of the harvest continued under the Guptas. The various working guilds, or *sreni* in the major cities were highly organized. As under the Mauryans, bankers and merchants were frequently tapped by rulers for ready cash to fund armies, buy off intruders, or finance other emergency measures. Despite low **tariffs**, the Guptas enjoyed a highly favorable balance of trade. Indeed, the empire's self-sufficiency in nearly all commercial items meant that foreign traders had to pay for their goods in gold or silver. Because of this, the Romans were eventually forced to stop much of their Indian trade because of its drain on their supply of precious metals.

Trade and Expansion   By the time of Persia's invasion in the late sixth century BCE, the reputation of the wealth of northern India was already well established among the Greeks. The historian Herodotus (ca. 484–425 BCE), for example, noted that the yearly tribute of gold from the region was several times that of Persian Egypt. Interactions with the expanding Hellenistic world extended the reach of Indian markets and trade through the eastern Mediterranean and, shortly, into the expanding Roman domains.

Nexus: A means of connection, a bond or link; also, a series of connections.

With the decline of the Mauryans and the adoption of Buddhism by peoples of the northwest, the region around Taxila became the **nexus** of a caravan trade that from the third century BCE to the third century CE, linked nearly all of Eurasia from Roman Britain to Han China and beyond along the famous Silk Road (see Chapter 9). In addition, Buddhist, Jain, and Brahmanic religious elements all spread westward over time to enrich in varying degrees the intellectual climate of the Parthians, Greeks, and Romans.

Indians also dominated the region's maritime trade until they were gradually displaced by the Arabs from the ninth to the fifteenth centuries CE and by the Europeans shortly thereafter. The reputations of "Chryse" and "Cheronese," the lands of gold of southeast Asia, were well established among the Romans through Indian trade by the first centuries CE, while Roman and Greek jars and coins could be found as far away as Vietnam, Cambodia, and Java. Colonies of Greek, Roman, Persian, and Arab traders clustered in the western port cities of Broach and Kalliena, trading tin, copper, hides, and **antimony** for the teak, ebony, ivory, spices, and silks available there. A testament to the importance of the trade in the Greco-Roman world was the first-century guide to the Indian Ocean, the *Periplus* (marine atlas) *of the Erythrean Sea* (see "Patterns Up Close: The Global Trade of Indian Pepper").

Antimony: A metal widely used in alloys.

Indian Influence Beyond India   By the first century CE, this expanding trade region had established a network of outposts in southeast Asia and the Indonesian archipelago. Buddhist influence in the area may have come soon after. Though it is unclear whether merchants or missionaries made the first contacts, a series of small settlements of Indians on the Malay Peninsula launched the founding of the first of the Indianized kingdoms in the area, that of Funan in the Mekong delta of southeast Asia by the Brahmin Kaudinya in the second century CE. The spread of both Buddhism and the Indian system of "god-kings" soon reached the nearby Khmers [Khe-MARES] and the state of Champa [KHAM-puh] in modern Cambodia (Kampuchea) and Vietnam. By the seventh and eighth centuries CE, these areas became important trade centers in their own right, connecting the Indian states with Tang China and Heian Japan.

In addition, these countries formed important way stations in the expanding traffic of Buddhist pilgrims. The widespread appeal of Buddhism enhanced the Indian economy by both increasing the volume of trade on the subcontinent and providing a uniform structure for its expansion abroad. The mobility of pilgrims and monks, their role as missionaries, and their aversion to a number of lower-caste occupations made them natural candidates to assist in the increasingly far-flung circulation of goods and ideas. Monasteries served as hostels and way stations along well-traveled routes; larger complexes along branches of the Silk Road often had commercial centers grow up around them, particularly if they were destinations for pilgrims as well. The international character of Buddhism also facilitated contacts among long-distance traders. Perhaps most important, it linked India to an emerging cultural sphere that soon spanned Eurasia from the borderlands of the Persian empires to Japan. By the fourth century CE, firm trade ties had been established with the Romans, the Sasanids, the remnant states of Han China, and the Buddhist and Indianizing territories of southeast Asia (see Map 8.5).

Caste, Family Life, and Gender

As with the economy, the basic patterns of Indian society were already being forged by the seventh century BCE. The integration of Aryan migrants, the peoples of northwestern India, and the early inhabitants of the Ganges valley had been largely completed. Thereafter, the fusion of Vedic traditions into a distinct form of Hindu culture, drawn heavily from the Brahmanic religious and social practices, proceeded apace. In the Gupta Empire, when Hinduism became the privileged religion of the state and the subcontinent was largely decentralized as regional kingdoms competed with each other, Hinduism evolved into a religious civilization, the form of social organization dominant during the period 600–1450 in world history (see Part 3).

Maturation of the Caste System   Perhaps the most distinctive marker of Hinduism as a religious civilization is the caste (Sanskrit *jati*) system. Scholars are still uncertain as to whether this system originated with the four varnas in the Punjab–Ganges states or whether it evolved later. In any case, varna and caste seem to have merged over time to create a markedly stable, adaptable, yet also repressive system that continues even today, despite being technically unlawful under the Indian constitution. One of the caste system's chief functions was to provide a mechanism for absorbing and acculturating peoples of widely divergent languages, ethnicities, and religious practices into an integrated social whole. Within the framework of caste, all people lived within an interlocking system of reciprocal rights and

The Global Trade of Indian Pepper

Pepper was perhaps the world's most sought-after commodity for thousands of years. Indeed, its primacy among such other rare spices as nutmeg, ginger, cinnamon, and cloves ultimately drove European adventurers and traders to the Americas as they sought a direct all-water route to its source in India.

The pepper plant (*Piper nigrum*) is a vine native to the Malabar Coast of India in the modern state of Kerala. The two main varieties of pepper, white and black, are derived from the same berries: white pepper is the product of crushing the dried seeds (peppercorns), while black pepper comes from soaking and drying the seeds with their fruit coating still attached. As far back as the thirteenth century BCE, Egyptian records show black pepper being used in mummifications, a testament to its early place as a valued import.

By the third century BCE, pepper had become a mainstay of south India's burgeoning Indian Ocean trade, with growing annual cargoes going to China, southeast Asia, and Egypt. The Hellenistic cultural exchange conducted through Ptolemaic Egypt spread the use of pepper throughout the Mediterranean world. By the first century BCE, traders from Egypt, coastal Arabia, and northeast Africa were regularly availing themselves of the monsoon winds to make annual voyages to the Malabar ports for pepper. But it was after the Roman acquisition of Egypt that pepper became a kind of mania throughout their empire. Contemporary Romans like Pliny the Elder regularly complained of the huge drain of gold required to keep the empire adequately spiced, and the export of gold to India was ultimately curtailed.

How does one account for the huge popularity of a food product that has no nutritive value and burns the tongue? Initially, part of pepper's attraction may have been its exotic quality as a mysterious spice from a faraway land. But it had also long been used for medicinal purposes in India, and from Roman times through the European Middle Ages it was hailed in European and Arab treatises as healthful in a number of ways. Most useful of all, perhaps, was its capabilities as a preservative. Long used to preserve fish, meat, and vegetables in tropical south India, pepper was

Pepper Pot. The earliest records of pepper being imported into Britain are from the first century. Discovered in 1992, this exquisite pepper pot—a special container intended to keep this expensive spice—is designed in the shape of an "empress" and dates to the fifth century CE. Made of gold and silver, it testifies to the high value placed on such a precious commodity, especially in a remote place like Britain.

responsibilities in which even those at the bottom levels had a necessary, if disagreeable, societal function.

During the Mauryan era, Ashoka's advocacy of dharma also reinforced older notions of duty according to social position, while such treatises on proper behavior as the *Code of Manu* (written down by 200 CE) helped solidify concepts of model conduct among the various classes of society. By the Gupta period, renewed interest in societal stability after nearly five centuries of disorder prompted increased attention to stricter boundaries for acceptable behaviors within the different jati. Along with this, the idea of **ritual pollution** resulting from unsanctioned contact with lower castes—requiring ever more elaborate purification rites to cleanse oneself after such contact—becomes increasingly common. This

Ritual pollution: The act of making something or someone "unclean" in terms of their religious taboos or prohibitions.

avidly sought throughout Eurasia to treat perishables—particularly during the winter months when fresh food was difficult to obtain.

The Arab occupation of the prime transshipment areas of the eastern Mediterranean, the termini of the Silk Road, and, by the fourteenth century, domination of Indian Ocean trade caused the price of Indian commodities to soar in Europe. The urge to break the Islamic monopoly of the spice trade ultimately drove the Portuguese, and Columbus, to set off for India by sailing into the Atlantic, hoping to go directly to the Malabar Coast. The commercial network built on pepper and other spices was now positioned to drive what would grow into the world's first global trading system.

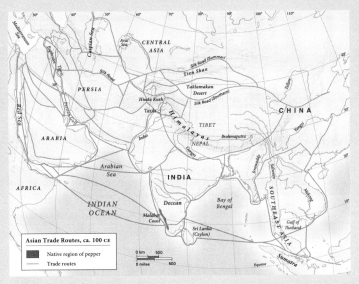

MAP 8.5 **Asian Trade Routes, ca. 100 CE.**

Questions

- How does the global trade in Indian pepper show the connectedness of Eurasia in this period in world history?

- What are the origins of the pepper trade? How did it change over time through interactions? What adaptations, if any, resulted from these interactions?

increasing trend in social segregation led to such things as small closets, nooks, and other places of concealment built into the houses of the upper castes so that their lower-caste servants could instantly hide themselves if their masters suddenly happened upon them.

Yet, such repressive extremes also mask some of the strengths that gave the caste system its vitality and longevity. Like religious organizations and guilds in medieval Europe, jati membership provided a kind of extended family, giving each person a recognized and valued place in society, despised as they might be by their "betters." In some areas, especially in the south, entire villages or clans were incorporated into their own jatis; in others, ethnicity or occupation might be the determining criteria. Although the upper castes dominated the political structure of rural society, social power was in fact more diffuse than is usually appreciated. For example, the members of various caste and guild councils were customarily represented at state functions. In addition, different castes became associated with special feasts and their sponsoring gods or goddesses, giving them a degree of informal power within the larger social structure.

Jainism, Buddhism, and Caste

Jainism and Buddhism had a considerable influence on the caste system as well. Although both religions accepted the theory of karma–samsara, their followers saw their own distinct practices as ways to break out of the cycle of death and rebirth. They thus represented powerful alternative traditions to the acceptance of varna and jati. Moreover, the potential for anyone, regardless of social position, to practice these methods undermined the hierarchical order of the caste system and made Jain and Buddhist practitioners equals in a society of believers. Their alternative institutions such as monasteries for men and women as well as their self-sufficiency, good works, and commercial expertise also gave them considerable material power in the larger community, particularly when patronized by nobles or monarchs.

Family Life and Hindu Culture: Men

Despite the attractiveness for some of monastic or ascetic life, the family remained the primary social unit of Indian society. Norms of proper moral behavior for family life were explicitly outlined in the *Code of Manu* and other legal and religious treatises. Married couples were expected to be monogamous, though in some cases, when they could not have children, it was permissible for a man to take a second wife while remaining married to the first.

A number of texts were devoted to outlining the correct conduct of the "four stages of life" for men: student, householder, hermit, and wanderer. In the first stage, that of the student, boys of the "twice-born" upper castes were to be taken into the household of a *guru*, or teacher, for a minimum of 12 years. During this time, they were expected to study the works of the Vedic–Brahmanic–Upanishadic tradition. Upon entering into the second stage (householder), more mature men with sufficient savings should marry young women of good character and appropriate caste membership. In addition to providing for his household, servants, and relatives, a man should get up before dawn, offer the appropriate sacrifices throughout the day and busy himself studying the Vedas, Puranas [Poor-AHN-ahs] (genealogies and histories), and Itihasas [Ee-tee-HAH-sahs] (legendary histories). As old age approaches, he enters the third stage (hermit) and should retreat to the forest, live on the roots and berries he can gather, and work to master the self in preparation for the end. In the final (wanderer) stage, he moves beyond desire for life or death, wandering without home or possessions. Caring not for anything of this world, he returns good for any evil done him and, ideally, attains moksha or release from the cycle of death and rebirth at his journey's end.

Family Life and Hindu Culture: Women

As we saw in Chapter 3, the role of women both in the family and in Indian society was perhaps more complex than in any other agrarian-based culture. On the one hand, the idea of female "dependence" was central to the Hindu conception of the family. That is, a woman without the support and protection of a web of family relations was cast adrift in society, a kind of "nonperson." Thus, to protect women was to safeguard the family and the social order. It followed from this that obedience and loyalty to senior female and male authority within the hierarchy of the family was the keystone of a woman's dharma, her duty according to her position. This fundamental duty was consistent regardless of her position in the caste system. In some regions, such loyalty found extreme expression in the act of *sati*. This controversial practice of a widow committing suicide by throwing herself on her husband's funeral pyre, however, remained largely confined to northern India and is legally prohibited today.

As in the strict division between men's and women's spheres in Confucian China we will see in Chapter 9, women's education and legal responsibilities in India were considerably narrower than those for men and tended to revolve around maintaining the home. Although in the Tamil areas of the south families remained matrilineal, property rights were limited. Yet, wives customarily exercised the important responsibility of controlling the household accounts and supervising servants and hired help. For the more well-to-do, an appropriate knowledge of poetry, literature, and conversational skills was required, along with other attainments necessary for well-rounded, gracious living. And while men were somewhat less restricted in terms of marrying for love, the vast majority of men and women were united through marriages arranged by their families after careful negotiation and often betrothed before adolescence.

Balancing Male and Female Roles   Although women were, for the most part, treated as subservient members of a patriarchal society, they were also seen by men as complementary opposites, as symbols of harmony and balance, though also as real and imaginary temptations and impediments to their ultimate release (moksha). On the one hand, women in epic and popular literature were often depicted as heroic and resourceful—Draupadi in the Mahabharata, for example, married five brothers in the Pandava family and aided all of them in their battles. Moreover, from the Gupta period on, a bewildering number of goddesses were increasingly appealed to by devotees for a variety of reasons. Fertility, sexuality, and growth, largely associated with femaleness, were all celebrated in Hindu literature, statuary, and religious symbolism. The lush depictions of frank sexuality in Hindu temples are among the most erotically charged artworks produced anywhere in the world. In contrast with this celebration of sexuality, on the other hand, was the perception of women as temptresses who anchored men to the sensual world. This in turn diverted them from the fundamental truth of the material world as transitory, thus potentially delaying their release from the karmic cycle through moksha.

The tensions growing from this duality and the difficulties of controlled enjoyment of the senses for both men and women as part of approved religious practice are graphically illustrated in Vatsyayana's [Vaht-see-ai-AH-nah] famous *Kama Sutra*, or *Aphorisms of Love*, written perhaps sometime in the first or second century CE. Its frank handling of a multiplicity of sexual practices has created an aura of pornography about it for readers outside of India. Within a wider context, however, it should be seen more as a manual on the everyday worship of living. While the more sensational aspects of the arts of sexual love are certainly present, the majority of the text deals with how to become a well-rounded person of taste and culture. For women,

Gandharan Buddhas. One of the most stunning syntheses of artistic and religious traditions occurred in the wake of the decline of the Seleucid states and the invasion of the Kushans. In the area centered around Gandhara (modern Kandahar in Afghanistan) Hellenistic artistic techniques of realistic human representation fused with the developing practices of Mahayana Buddhism to create sculptures like the head pictured here, from the second or third century CE, believed to be that of a bodhisattva, or perhaps of Siddhartha Gautama.

no less than 64 separate skills are detailed, including singing, dancing, cooking, chemistry, first aid, metallurgy, architecture, and even driving horses and elephants. Here, at least, the "proper" sphere for women's activities was greatly expanded.

Strength in Numbers: Art, Literature, and Science

The vast number of artistic, literary, cultural, and scientific contributions arising from India makes it impossible to do more than hint at their richness here. One area worth noting in terms of its cross-cultural fertilization, however, is that of Gandharan art. During the time of the Kushan Empire, the powerful influences of the old empire of Alexander the Great were meeting the new religious movements arising within Buddhism to create a new "Gandharan" style of art.

Previous representations of the Buddha had not been human but were instead symbols associated with his life and lore: the "wheel of dharma," an empty throne, or a footprint. Around the beginning of the Common Era, perhaps coinciding with the development of Mahayana Buddhism, the distinctly realistic forms of Greek sculpture and the tradition of depicting the Greek gods as human merged with the new Buddhist sensibilities to create the first images of the Buddha, which looked remarkably like the Greek god Apollo. This synthetic Gandharan approach spread across northern India, and soon images of the Buddha were being turned out in great profusion. Over time, however, the more familiar, stylized, less realistic, and heavily symbolic representations became standard throughout the Mahayana religious sphere.

The Classical Age While relatively little art from the Mauryan era has survived, the Gupta period brought an explosion of art and literature from a multitude of artists patronized by the court and the upper classes. The "perfection" of Sanskrit as the medium of the sacred texts of Hinduism under the scholar and grammarian Panini and its systematic study under the **philologist** Patanjali several centuries later solidified the sacred language and caused it to be viewed and preserved as unchanging. As a classical language, Sanskrit was used in a staggering variety of works of poetry, prose, and drama, as well as in the *Puranas*—religious and secular historical genealogies. Other noteworthy works may include the poems and plays of "India's Shakespeare," Kalidasa (though some scholars place his life in the first century CE), such as the poignant romance *Shakuntala* and the poetic yearnings of *The Cloud Messenger*.

Philologist: A specialist in language study, particularly in the history and provenance of important terms.

In addition to Sanskrit literature, scholarship of all types, including Buddhist works and scientific treatises, was undertaken at the great Buddhist monastery and university of Nalanda in northeastern India, founded in the fourth century CE.

Science and Mathematics In addition to Buddhism, the most profound intellectual influences from India on the surrounding regions were in science, especially mathematics. Despite the highly sophisticated speculative philosophy of the Upanishads, during the period from the second century BCE until the second century CE India was an importer of scientific and mathematical concepts from the Greco-Roman and Persian spheres. Greek geometry, for example, made its way into northern India during this time. In exchange, however, concepts of Indian health regimens—some involving yoga discipline—along with the vast body of Indian medicine, with its extensive knowledge of herbal remedies, also seem to have moved west. The second century CE medical text *Charaka Samhita* for example, like its counterparts in the Mediterranean and later European world, taught a health regimen based on the balance of humors.

In the area of mathematics and astronomy an important synthesis of ideas took place from the time of the Mauryans through the twelfth and thirteenth centuries CE. Like the early Chinese methods of reckoning time, the first Indian calendars were based on the lunar months, though a year consisted of six seasons and an intercalary period was inserted every 30 months to make up the difference with the solar year. During the Hellenistic period, Indians adopted the calendar of the eastern Mediterranean and southwest Asia, which had a 7-day week, a 24-hour day, and a 365-day solar year—along with the 12 zodiacal signs of the Greco-Roman world.

Indian thinkers refined these imported concepts to levels unsurpassed in the ancient world. The subtleties of some of the philosophical schools had already required intervals of time and numbers that still stagger the imagination today. For example, cycles of time marking eternity in some philosophical schools were measured in intervals larger than current estimates of the age of the universe; the shorter *kalpa*, reckoned at about 4 billion years, is only slightly less than current estimates of the age of the earth. Philosophical discussion on the nature of matter in infinitesimal space among some schools anticipated key arguments of modern physicists regarding the principle of indeterminacy.

The ability to conceive of mathematics on at once such a grand and such a tiny scale seems to have also helped Indian mathematicians and astronomers during the Gupta period to calculate a precise length for the solar year. Like the Chinese, they had already developed a decimal system; however, they now employed the first use of the zero, initially marked by a dot, as a placeholder, and developed a system of positive and negative numbers. Their work with the geometry of the Greeks enabled them to calculate pi to four decimal places as well as develop methods for the solving of certain kinds of algebraic equations. By the eleventh and twelfth centuries CE, the acquisition of these techniques by the Arabs and their transmittal of them to the new universities of Christian Europe gave us the system we still use today, known by the somewhat erroneous name of "Arabic numerals."

Putting It All Together

In roughly a millennium, a number of important patterns of world history emerged in India. The political, cultural, social, religious, and economic systems of the states along the Ganges River were diffused to all parts of the Indian subcontinent, where they were substantially—though by no means completely—received by the surrounding peoples. With the maturing of these patterns came the tendency to see the subcontinent as a unified entity in nearly every way except in politics. Here, despite the accomplishments of the Mauryans and Guptas, unity would prove elusive—in some respects even to the present day. This would prove particularly true, as we will see in later chapters, with the coming of Islam.

In terms of its regional influence and beyond, India's impact was disproportionately large. By at least the time of Ashoka, the population of the subcontinent was second only to that of China. Within it was contained the world's most active source of religious traditions, next to southwest Asia and the Mediterranean. The influence of one of these religions, Hinduism, spread to Indonesia and southeast Asia; that of the other, Buddhism, could lay claim through this period to be the world's largest religious system as well as the first "universal" one.

Paradoxically, many of the factors that allowed for this tremendous richness of religious, cultural, and intellectual traditions also tended to abet the subcontinent's chronic political instability, particularly in the north. Here, continual migrations of outside peoples cross-fertilized the cultural resources of the region but also impeded political unification.

▶ For additional resources, including maps, primary sources, visuals, and quizzes, please go to www.oup.com/us/vonsivers. Please see the Further Resources section at the back of the book for additional readings and suggested websites.

Thinking Through Patterns

▶ **Think about the reasons for the spread of Buddhism inside and outside of India. How have historians seen the decline of Buddhism in India?**

An important historical pattern we examine in this Part is that of individuals we call "visionaries"—people who, as the saying goes, "think outside the box" in their own societies. In this chapter, we place the Buddha in this category as a man who sought—and satisfied himself and his followers that he succeeded—to go beyond the Hindu bounds of death and rebirth. Like the other visionaries we examine, however, the Buddha's fundamental message of transcendence and enlightenment can be adapted to any belief system. As his message moves along the trade routes in India, central Asia, and, as we will see in later chapters, China, Korea, Japan, and southeast Asia, it adapts to local customs by borrowing bits of indigenous religious mythology and belief to make it attractive to converts while keeping the fundamental message intact. Local people in turn adapt it to their own beliefs and make it their own. In the case of east Asia, this will receive a large boost by the translation of Buddhist scriptures into literary Chinese and the circulation of Buddhist practitioners, monks, merchants, and pilgrims throughout the Buddhist cultural sphere. Its decline in the place of its birth appears to be due in part to the shift of its cultural center to China and Japan and the official support of the Guptas for Hinduism.

How do historians establish criteria of "importance"? One measure of this is to assess the influence of certain patterns and practices on a culture or society over time. Change over time or the lack of it is an important indicator of the prevalence and kind of innovation taking place in a society. So some influential patterns in Indian history might include the permeation of religion in all aspects of Indian life, the search for transcendence of the material world, the caste system as the social fabric of the subcontinent, and the prominence of India as a trade crossroads astride the trade routes of the Indian Ocean and the great land routes across Eurasia.

▶ **What do you consider to be the most influential patterns in Indian history to this point? Why?**

▶ **Do you think some of Ashoka's concepts could be implemented by governments today? Why or why not?**

Ashoka's ideas seem quite modern in many ways, and his decrees regarding the protection of animals and ecological matters might certainly have some current application. His ideas of not taking life except in extreme circumstances and of giving prisoners time to repent also parallel modern concepts. Yet, it must also be remembered that he is still far removed in time and culture from the modern world. His ideas of dharma as duty might not carry exactly the same import as today. Historians are routinely conscious of the pitfalls of identifying too closely with peoples in very different cultures in the remote past. "The past is a foreign country," it is often said. "They do things differently there."

Chapter 9 722 BCE-618 CE

China

IMPERIAL UNIFICATION AND PERFECTING THE MORAL ORDER

"Venerable sir, since you have not considered a thousand *li* too far to come, may I presume that you bring something that may profit my kingdom?" Even today one can sense the air of challenge, however polite, as the two men begin to take each other's measure. The speaker, King Hui of Liang, had seen his kingdom steadily eroded by the powerful surrounding states of Chu, Jin, and Qin, vying for supremacy at the height of China's Warring States period (403–221 BCE). Given the increasing desperation of his situation, perhaps he can be forgiven his somewhat sharp tone.

The "venerable sir" to whom he addressed his question, however, was in no mood to banter: "Why must Your Majesty use that word 'profit'? I bring only humanity and righteousness," he thundered. Warming to his topic, the Confucian sage Mencius now laid out his rebuttal:

> If Your Majesty says, "How may I profit my kingdom" the great officers will say, "How may we profit our families"; and the lesser officers and common people will say, "how may we profit ourselves." Superiors and inferiors will try to snatch this profit from each other and the kingdom will be endangered. . . . [but] There never has been a humane man who neglected his parents. There never has been a righteous man who made his ruler an afterthought.

> James Legge, trans. *The Works of Mencius.*
> New York: Dover Reprint, 1970, pp. 125–126

THE FIRST CHINESE EMPIRES

ABOVE: "The Admonitions Scroll: The Instructress Writing the Admonitions," a handscroll painting from the Tang dynasty.

Chastened by this confrontation, but also intrigued, King Hui now sought Mencius out for advice on a number of fronts. Through it all the sage refused to mince words with him about the extent of his misgovernment. Finally, both Hui and his son and successor, Xiang, said, "I wish quietly to receive your instructions."

This story from the opening pages of the fourth-century BCE *Mengzi*, the *Book of Mencius*, illustrates several important points not only about late Zhou China but also about the role of intellectual innovation, the ultimate direction of Chinese political thought, the way Chinese ideas would influence nearby peoples, and, more generally, the larger pattern of empires and states adopting the ideas of visionary thinkers. As we noted in Chapter 4, the Spring and Autumn and the Warring States periods in China during the final centuries of the Zhou era were socially and politically tumultuous. In spite of, or perhaps because of, this, the period was also the most fertile one in China's long intellectual history. As we shall see, starting with Confucius—from whom Mencius drew his ideas—Chinese thinkers suggested ways of looking at the world, how to behave in it, and how to govern it that ranged from radically abstract to firmly practical, from collective to individualistic, and from an absence of active government to near totalitarianism.

Seeing Patterns

▶ Was the First Emperor's ruthlessness justified by his accomplishments in his empire?

▶ How would you compare the values expressed by Confucius and Mencius to those of contemporary society?

▶ How have historians viewed the role of women in early imperial China?

From the time of the Han dynasty (202 BCE–220 CE) until the twentieth century, Confucianism, as interpreted by Mencius and adopted as a means of bureaucratic control, would be the governmental system of China. Moreover, as Chinese is adopted as the first written language by Koreans, Japanese, and Vietnamese, Confucian concepts will be firmly planted in these lands as well. So, in China, as in India, Persia, Rome, and eventually the Islamic world, the legacy of innovators we have identified as "visionaries" will be picked up and adopted by rulers as officially approved thought. As we will emphasize in this and the following chapters, an important pattern of world history emerges by the beginning of the Common Era. Large "world" empires utilize religions and systems of thought that have universal application and appeal.

Visionaries and Empire

The period from the eighth century BCE until the first unification of China under the Qin in 221 BCE is universally regarded as China's most fertile period of intellectual exploration. The foundations of nearly every important school of Chinese philosophy were laid during this era. By the time of the Confucian ethicist and political thinker Mencius in the fourth century BCE, so many competing thought systems had emerged that Chinese chroniclers refer to them as the "hundred schools." Of these various systems, those that are best known and that had the greatest impact were Confucianism, Legalism, and Daoism.

Confucianism, Legalism, and Daoism

Like so many important figures in the world of ideas, the historical Confucius is an elusive figure. Contemporary researchers have widely differing views on his identity and his works. According to traditional accounts, he was born in 551 BCE to a family named Kong. Even today, the Kong family, some of whose members still live in the original family compound at Qufu [CHOO-foo] in modern Shandong Province, maintains what is claimed to be a continuous genealogy of the sage's descendants that are now said to number in the millions.

In Confucian texts he is referred to as "the Master" (*zi* or *fuzi*) or "the Master Kong" (*Kong fuzi*) [Koong-FOO-zuh]. European Roman Catholic missionaries in China during the seventeenth century rendered *Kong fuzi* into Latin, where it became "Confucius." As a member of the growing *shi* class of well-to-do, educated commoners and lower aristocracy (see Chapter 4), Confucius spent much of his early career seeking a position as political adviser to the courts of several of the Zhou states in northern China. Though tradition has him holding a minor position in his native state of Lu, his search for employment was largely unsuccessful. As did the visionaries we saw in the previous chapter in India, he ended up spending most of his life as an itinerant teacher, spreading his ideas about ethics and politics to a growing group of followers. Like the Buddha, however, it would be centuries before his ideas were applied on a large scale by a state.

Confucian Doctrine   Confucius has been called "China's first great moralist." His teachings—as presented in the *Lunyu* or *Analects*, the central Confucian text—have at their core a view of human beings as inclined toward ethical behavior and of human society as a perfectible moral order. According to Confucius, there are certain fundamental patterns that are manifestations of the *Dao* ("the Way") of the universal order.

One of these fundamental patterns is the relationship between parent and off-spring. A child owes its life and body to its parents. Because of this, a child—even a grownup, who was, after all, once a child—dares not injure him- or herself or others. People develop their moral character to reflect well upon their parents and serve those in higher social or political stations as they serve their own parents. This example of human society as a kind of extended family applies at every level, from the peasant to the ruler—and even beyond: Drawing on the idea of the Mandate of Heaven (see Chapter 4), Confucius makes the ruler himself responsible to heaven for the state of his country. Indeed, emperors in later regimes would habitually refer to themselves as "son of heaven," to emphasize this filial duty.

Though this view is avowedly hierarchical rather than egalitarian, the mutual obligations present at every level serve as checks for Confucius on the arbitrary exercise of power. Hence, when asked to sum up his thinking in one word, Confucius answered "**reciprocity**": Do not do unto others what you would not have them do unto you. Confucius believed that individuals should strive for the qualities of *ren* (kindness or humaneness toward others) by faithfully following the practices of *li* (the observance of rules of decorum as guides to appropriate behavior toward others). People who did so would not only perfect their own character but also set an example for the rest of society.

Reciprocity: Mutual exchange of things, ideas, etc.

Confucian Government   Confucius lived during a time of great social and political disorder, and as a result, many of his teachings center on ways to restore order and make government and society more humane. But because Confucian doctrine places great emphasis on personal responsibility, the structure of government is far less important than the ethical fitness of the ruler and the people. Good government, according to Confucius, begins with educated leaders and officials of strong moral character, like the Zhou kings Wen and Wu and the Duke of Zhou (see Chapter 4), who are often cited in the *Analects* as examples. To describe this ideal of behavior, Confucius introduced the concept of the **junzi** ("the superior man" or "gentleman").

> **Junzi:** According to Confucius, the "superior man" or "gentleman" who behaves according to an ethical and moral ideal. A society run by *junzi* would foster social institutions that encourage proper behavior.

Those able to attain these ideals would comprise for Confucius a kind of aristocracy of merit, while rulers who possessed these qualities would set a sound example for their subjects to follow.

Just as the *junzi* cultivated his personal ethics and morals, a society run by *junzi* would spread these values to society by fostering social institutions that encouraged proper behavior among the people. In the same way that a musician's consistent practice of scales eventually makes playing them correctly second nature, the consistent observance of *li* would help make appropriate behavior routine among ordinary people. Not everyone would necessarily develop the high moral standards of the *junzi*, but at the very least, the majority of people would almost involuntarily develop a sense of right and wrong and thus acquire a stake in the social order.

By the time Confucius died in 479 BCE, he had attracted a loyal following of adherents to his teachings. Two later students of Confucian doctrine, Mencius and Xunzi [SHWUN-zuh], continued to spread the teachings of the master, though with their own distinctive contributions. Despite challenges from a number of competing philosophical schools, Confucian ideals ultimately became the standard for Chinese politics and scholarship.

Mencius   By Mencius' time, in the fourth century BCE, the intensity of the competition and continual warfare among the Zhou states had spawned most of the so-called hundred schools of thought as thinkers questioned fundamental assumptions about private and social good. Not surprisingly, given the chaotic times, their answers varied from radical individualism to universal love and altruism, with some, like Sun Zi [Sun Tzu] in *The Art of War* examining the nature and practice of armed struggle.

Mencius (*Mengzi*, or Master Meng; ca. 385–312 BCE), like Confucius, believed that people were fundamentally good and that individuals must continually work to understand and refine this goodness in order to avoid being led astray by negative influences. Mencius used water, the nature of which is to flow downhill, as a familiar metaphor for human nature. It is possible, of course, to force water out of

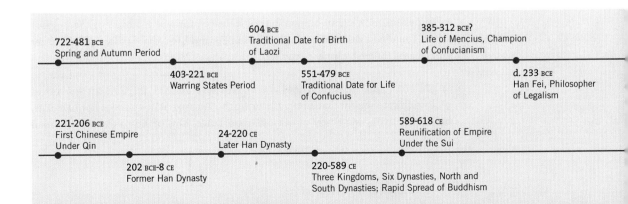

The Kong Family Mansion in Qufu. Though scholars have debated many aspects of the life and activities of the historical Confucius, his descendents have maintained the family line and compound over the centuries at Qufu in modern Shandong province. Since 1055 CE, Chinese emperors have bestowed on the eldest male family member in the direct line from the Sage the title of "Duke Yansheng." The most recent holder of the title, Kung Te-cheng (Kong Dezheng), died in October 2008 on Taiwan at the age of 89. He was the 77th main-line descendent of Confucius.

this natural tendency, said Mencius; but once such artificial means are removed, it reverts to its original course. Hence, he concluded, the way to proper behavior is to cultivate the Confucian virtues as a bulwark against forces pushing toward "unnatural" behavior.

Mencius traveled throughout China spreading Confucian ideals, especially as a basis for government practice. The *Mengzi* or *Book of Mencius*, is written in more of a narrative form than the *Analects* and supplemented by stories, parables, and debates with advocates of other schools of thought. Its most powerful sections deal with the obligations of rulers to their subjects. As the center of power and moral authority, in Mencius' view a ruler's primary duty is to maintain the "people's livelihood" and uphold the "righteousness," *yi* (appropriate behavior by and toward all according to social rank), of the state. As an appropriately ideal way to maintain the people's livelihood, for example, Mencius advocated the "well-field" system (see Chapter 4) as a means of ensuring crop surpluses and equality among peasant cultivators.

As for the state, as we saw with King Hui of Liang in the chapter-opening vignette, "I bring only humanity [*ren*] and righteousness [*yi*]; why must Your Majesty use that word 'profit'?" Mencius argued that rulers who sought to profit from their states sowed the seeds of their own destruction by encouraging their subjects to profit only themselves. A state ruled by righteousness and humanity, on the other hand, ensured that the people would be prosperous and orderly, which automatically contributed to the "profit" of the ruler. A ruler who abused or neglected his subjects upset the social order and the natural tendency of people toward good. In such a case, the people had not only the right but also the obligation to invoke the Mandate of Heaven and depose him. In the end, said Mencius, anticipating a host of later Chinese thinkers, the people, not the ruler, are the foundation of the state.

Xunzi   As states grew increasingly powerful, their armies larger, and warfare more deadly, Mencius' optimistic view of human nature seemed less and less practical to many thinkers. Like Mencius, Xunzi (trad. ca. 310–219? BCE) was also a student of Confucian philosophy but had a much darker view of human nature. Living during the apogee of the Warring States period, Xunzi came to believe that individuals were self-involved creatures with little interest in society as a whole and capable of regulating themselves only through immense effort. Only by enforcing the restraints of civilization, such as ritual, law, and the example of past model rulers, could individuals approach the Confucian ideals of virtue and humanity. Thus, by the end of the third century BCE, Confucian thinkers had come to radically opposed conclusions about their most fundamental premise: the authentic nature of human beings. In the long run, the more moderate views of Confucius and Mencius won out. Xunzi's more pessimistic view of human nature, however, formed the basis of the Legalist school founded by two of his students, Han Fei and Li Si, that finally restored order and created the first Chinese empire.

Legalism   The Legalist school is the most severe of the three major schools of philosophical thought that emerged during the Warring States period. For Legalists, building a strong state was of utmost importance. Out of Xunzi's view of human beings as inclined toward evil and drawing on the earlier practices of the Qin minister Lord Shang (d. 338 BCE), Han Fei (d. 233 BCE), and Li Si (d. 208 BCE) developed a system of uniform laws and practices based on the absolute will of the ruler. Order in a state, they claimed, could be implemented only through the institution of strict, detailed, and explicit laws diligently enforced on all subjects without regard to rank or class. Since Legalists believed that compliance on small matters led to compliance on larger ones, they imposed harsh punishments—forced labor, mutilation, in some cases death—for even the tiniest infractions.

The Legalists argued that the state was all-important; therefore, all subjects must serve the state through productive activities. Among these activities, agriculture and military service were the highest priorities. Individuals were encouraged to take up farming or military service as their livelihoods; any other occupation was discouraged. Idlers were put to work by force. Since dissent led to disorder, only government-approved history and literature were tolerated.

Although Legalism had many critics, it was its strict practices, not the more moderate ideals of Confucianism or Daoism, that imposed order on China. The price it exacted for doing so, however, was considered by succeeding generations to have been intolerably high.

Daoism   While most Chinese philosophical schools accepted the concept of the Dao as the ordering principle of the universe, they varied considerably as to the best means of achieving harmony with it. For Confucians, as we have seen, study and self-cultivation to the point of intuitive understanding put the individual in tune with the Dao. For followers of the Daoist tradition, attributed to Laozi (Lao Tzu), however, the Confucian path prevented genuine understanding of and harmony with the Dao.

The historical Laozi is an even more obscure figure than Confucius. In fact, many scholars believe Laozi to be a mythical figure. Chinese tradition cites his birth date as 604 BCE and his name as Li Er. The honorific title "Laozi" is translated as either "the Old Master" or "the Old Child." The translation "Old Child" captures something of the Daoist belief that only a return to child-like simplicity would lead to union with the *Dao*.

For Daoists, in contrast to the Confucians, the Dao was not the ordering force *within* the universe but the transcendent first principle *beyond* the universe. The Confucian Dao, dealing with the particulars of this world, can be named; the Daoist Dao, like the relationship between atman and brahman we saw in Chapter 8, transcends all particulars and therefore cannot be named. The Dao is thus beyond all dualities and unifies them in a great oscillating whole.

In fact, the vocabulary Laozi used for this new measure of all phenomena is remarkably similar to that of other Eurasian visionaries during the 600s BCE discussed previously: Deutero-Isaiah, the Zoroastrian reformers, Anaximander, and the Buddha, as well as the Upanishad writers. All were striving in their volatile kingdoms and empires, many of which worshipped large pantheons of gods, for one, single, unchangeable, and all-encompassing standard for morality and understanding.

Since the Dao transcended the world—including all such opposites as "good" and "evil"—no single path of action would lead an individual to union with it. To choose the good, as the Confucians do, is therefore to follow only a limited part of the universal Dao. Instead, the Daoists taught that only through a life of quiet self-reflection and contemplation of opposites and paradoxes might an individual come to know the Dao. A classic tale that expresses this aspect of Daoist thought is the story of the philosopher Zhuang Zhou [JWONG-Joe], who lived in the fourth century BCE and awoke from a dream unsure of whether he had dreamed he was a butterfly or whether he was a butterfly dreaming he was Zhuang Zhou.

Daoism and Government Daoist political theory held that the best government was that which governed least. Here, the key idea is one from the most famous Daoist work, the *Daode Jing* (*The Classic of the Way and Virtue*, often spelled as the *Tao Te Ching*): "By non-action there is nothing that is not done." This is not to say that the ruler literally does nothing; rather, his role is to create the conditions that naturally lead to a society in which everyone spontaneously acts in accordance with the Dao. The ruler should not push specific policies but rather let all things take their natural courses, for even as they run to extremes they will always reverse. The ruler's understanding of the flow of these universal cycles leads to union with the Dao and keeps the world in equilibrium.

These three schools of thought were all to play a role in the development of China's political and cultural life. Confucianism would provide the basis for the bureaucracy of China's empires and ideals of a perfectible moral order; Daoism would provide the mystical dimension of Chinese culture and a profound love and idealization of nature; finally, Legalism would provide the brute muscle of unifying the last of the warring states into a single structure under the Qin [CHIN].

The Qin Dynasty

As the period of the Warring States continued, the Qin state ultimately claimed victory over its opponents and established centralized rule throughout China. At first glance, Qin might seem unpromising as a candidate for empire. It was the smallest and poorest of the Zhou dependencies, located far to the west of most of the other Zhou states. However, Qin had several powerful advantages over its competitors. Its position on the fringe of the Zhou world meant that it was free to expand its economic base by promising land to peasant cultivators as the state seized territory on its western frontier.

Qin and Zhou The agricultural surplus that resulted from these land grants led to increased prosperity for the small but growing state. Qin's location was also a benefit when it came to military preparedness. Many of the warring states were in close proximity to each other, and the constant battles among them depleted their economic and military resources. Qin, on the other hand, did not have to fight off other states at its borders. Consequently, the Qin participated in limited military campaigns, mostly against nomadic groups, which strengthened their fighting skills but did not upset their economy or weaken their army. By 350 BCE, Qin rulers, particularly the famous Shang Yang, reorganized the state by eliminating the last of the old Zhou institutions and replacing them with a uniform, centralized system that anticipated a number of later Legalist principles. In 256 BCE, the Qin conquered Zhou itself and began the drive for empire in earnest (see Map 9.1).

With its strong economy, expert military, and the Legalist theorists Han Fei and Li Si advising the court, Qin took advantage of the collective exhaustion of the other

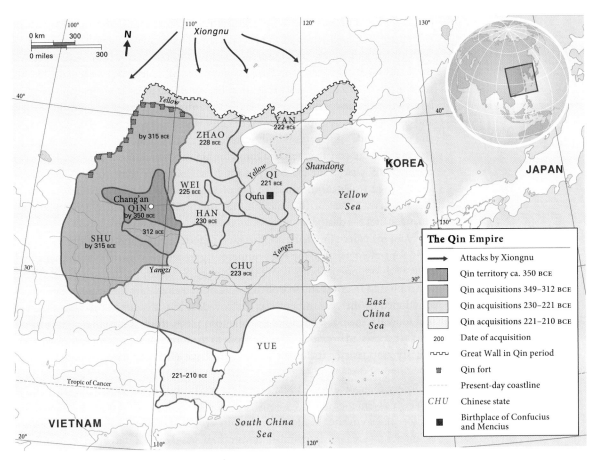

MAP **9.1 The Qin Empire.**

northern Chinese states and conquered them at a pace reminiscent of Alexander the Great's campaigns of the previous century. With stunning swiftness, Qin armies, now swelling to hundreds of thousands of men, drove south and eliminated the opposition of the many tribal peoples below the state of Yue.

The Qin then continued into the northern part of modern Vietnam—thus beginning a long, and often bitterly contested, relationship with southeast Asia. The Chinese would attempt to rule the area with limited success for over 1,000 years and claim it as a protectorate for nearly another thousand until they were ousted by the French in 1885. In the north and west, Qin armies fought a series of campaigns to drive nomadic peoples, especially the *Xiongnu*, or Huns, from newly established borders and secure the trade routes into central Asia. By the end of the 220s BCE, the Qin had subdued all of the states that would constitute what was about to become the first Chinese empire.

The First Emperor   In 221 BCE, the Qin ruler Cheng (r. 246–221 as Qin ruler; 221–209 BCE as first emperor) proclaimed himself Qin Shi Huangdi, the first emperor of the Qin, and with Li Si as his chief minister instituted the Legalist system throughout the new empire. As a safeguard against attacks by nomadic peoples in the north, the First Emperor deployed tens of thousands of forced laborers to join together the numerous defensive walls of the old Zhou states. This massive project stretching over 1,400 miles would become the Great Wall of China.

With virtually unlimited resources and the ruthless drive of the Legalists to expand and fortify the state, the First Emperor began a series of projects during his reign of less than a dozen years that are still astonishing today in their scope and ambition. The Chinese writing system was standardized, as were all weights, measures, and coinage. Hundreds of thousands of conscript laborers worked on roads, canals, and a multitude of irrigation and water conservancy projects. The First Emperor also ordered the construction of a tomb for himself, a mammoth complex meant to celebrate his legacy. The discovery of the First Emperor's tomb in 1974 by a peasant digging a well near the modern city of Xi'an unearthed an army of thousands of life-sized terra-cotta warriors marching in orderly ranks, intended to protect Qin Shi Huangdi after his death.

From his palace in Chang'an, the site of modern Xi'an and the ultimate capital of 13 separate dynasties, the First Emperor tightened his control over the state and dealt with opponents with ruthless efficiency. Scholars, particularly Confucians, who objected to government policies were buried alive. Any literature not officially sanctioned by the government was destroyed. While it is difficult to assess the extent to which the book burnings actually took place, it is believed that a great many works that existed before the Qin were put to the torch. Writers of the following Han dynasty, emphasizing the horrors of the Qin, have left a number of accounts of mass executions of dissenting scholars.

After a reign of about 12 years as emperor, Qin Shi Huangdi died. His strict laws, severe punishments, and huge construction projects had angered and exhausted the people; and soon after his death the empire erupted in rebellion. Ironically, the government's severe laws and punishments now worked against it as officials attempted to conceal the revolt's severity for fear of torture and execution. At the same time, Minister Li Si provoked additional discontent by conspiring to keep the First Emperor's death a secret in order to rule as regent for the monarch's son. He was captured attempting to flee the rebellion and executed in 208 BCE. In an attempt to make the punishment fit the crime, his captors lashed him to a board and slowly sawed him in half, lengthwise, in accordance with Qin law. After a brief civil war, a

Terra-cotta Warriors at the First Emperor's Tomb. One of the most important archaeological finds of the twentieth century, the Qin burial complex was discovered in 1974 by local farmers digging a well. Over 5,000 figures have been unearthed so far, all with individualized features. The dig has been enclosed and a museum built on site. Along with the Great Wall, it is one of China's most popular tourist destinations.

general named Liu Bang put an end to the fighting and restored order to the region. He proclaimed himself emperor in 202 BCE and called his new dynasty the Han.

The Han Dynasty

If the Qin constructed the Chinese empire, the Han perfected it. The Han developed over time a centralized political system of rule that blended the administrative structures of the Qin with more moderate Confucian ideals of government as a moral agent. This model of rule endured—with some interruptions and modifications—for over 2,000 years, by having its power tempered by a bureaucracy that saw its role as both carrying out the will of the court and acting as advocates for the people.

Unlike earlier rulers who came from aristocratic families, Liu Bang, who had taken the reign name Gaozu (r. 202–195 BCE), had been a peasant. Perhaps because of this background, he had little interest in restoring the decentralized system of the Zhou, which favored the aristocratic classes. Instead, he left intact the Qin structure of centralized ministries and regional **commanderies**. This structure seemed the only sensible way to keep such a large empire under control. To mollify advocates of returning to the old Zhou system, Han rulers offered them token distributions of land. They also reduced taxes and labor obligations and rescinded the most severe punishments imposed under the Qin. Han rulers altered the Qin system of leveling social classes by instituting uniform rules for different segments of society—aristocrats as well as commoners. Under the Han, the upper ranks of society were taxed at lighter rates and exempted from most forms of corporal punishment.

As the Han Empire expanded—reaching a population recorded in 2 CE of just under 60 million—so did its bureaucracy. Within a century of Liu Bang's reign, the number of government officials had swollen to 130,000. Officials were divided into graded ranks ranging from the heads of imperial ministries to district magistrates. Below these officials were clan leaders and village **headmen**. Landowners were to collect and remit the taxes for themselves and their tenants, while the lower officials recorded the rates and amounts, kept track of the labor obligations of the district, and mobilized the people during emergencies.

Wudi, the Martial Emperor   A high point of the Han dynasty came during the rule of the emperor Wudi, whose reign name means the "Martial Emperor" (r. ca. 140–87 BCE). Like both his predecessors and successors, Wudi faced the complex problem of defending the empire's northern and western boundaries from diverse groups of nomadic peoples, especially the Xiongnu. He therefore extended the Great Wall begun by the Qin to provide greater protection. Hoping that a strong Chinese presence would discourage potential invasions, Wudi encouraged people to move to areas along the northern and western borders of the empire (see Map 9.2).

In addition to securing the empire, Wudi had to suppress Xiongnu raids on central Asian trade routes, especially the Silk Road. He made diplomatic efforts, offering the Xiongu food and other necessary supplies; but when those efforts failed, he mounted military campaigns against them. Over the long term, the Han also adopted the practice of "**sinicizing**" the nomadic peoples, a process similar to that pursued by their contemporaries, the Romans, toward the peoples surrounding their empire. The practice

Han Dynasty Gilt Bronze Lamp. The sophistication and craftsmanship of Han art can be seen clearly in this bronze oil lamp overlaid with gold— much of which is now missing, revealing the oxidation of the bronze underneath. The three-legged style of the vessel itself goes back at least to the Black Pottery period, while the dragon motif, superficially whimsical in its design, is meant to symbolize strength and is a favorite device of the imperial courts of successive dynasties down to the Qing (1644–1912), who incorporated it into the the first modern Chinese national flag.

Commanderies: Districts under the control of a military commander.

Headmen: Local leaders; these are usually chosen by the people of the village, clan, district, etc., rather than appointed by the government.

Sinicize/sinicizing: The pattern by which newcomers to areas dominated by Chinese culture were encouraged to interact and adopt that culture for themselves.

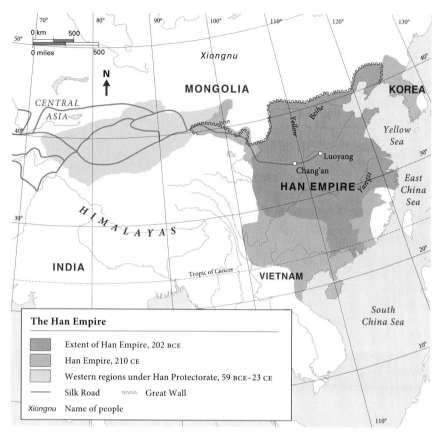

MAP **9.2 The Han Empire.**

of sinicizing involved encouraging nomadic peoples to assimilate themselves to Chinese culture and identity. Once they had been assimilated, the threat of nomadic invasion would be lessened. Wudi drove his armies into central Asia, where he established a lucrative trade with the peoples there, and again into northern Vietnam and Korea, extending Han rule into those areas. Along with the imposition of Han rule came the Chinese writing system and the infusion of Confucian ideology and practices.

Wang Mang and the Red Eyebrow Revolt   Lasting more than 400 years, the Han era has traditionally been divided into the Former or Western Han (202 BCE–8 CE) and the Latter or Eastern Han (24–220 CE). During the brief interval between 8 and 24 CE, Han rule was temporarily interrupted when a relative of the royal family, Wang Mang (45 BCE–23 CE), seized power. Wang Mang attempted to introduce a number of reforms in land distribution in an effort to reduce the huge disparity between rich landowners and peasants, which had been inherited from the Warring States period. Wang Mang's proposed reforms provoked a revolt led by a Daoist secret society called the Red Eyebrows. The rebels killed Wang Mang and sacked the capital of Chang'an. An imperial relative restored the Han dynasty in 24 CE but moved the capital to Luoyang, where the empire continued in somewhat reduced size.

Wang Mang's attempts at land reform and the Red Eyebrow revolt hastened the collapse of the last of the old aristocratic landholdings. Together with the sense of renewal accompanying the restoration of the Han dynasty, these events helped to temporarily mask the empire's growing weakness.

Han Decline   By the late second century CE the Han dynasty was showing signs of strain. Ambitious internal improvements ordered by Han emperors were carried out by *corvée* labor—labor required by the government as a form of taxation. These labor obligations made it increasingly difficult for peasants to tend their lands, and as a result, agricultural productivity declined. Furthermore, the loss of some borderland territory reduced the tax base just when the empire required more taxes to maintain the Great Wall and far-flung military outposts also meant to protect the empire from nomadic invasions. Economic crises, however, were not the only threats to the empire. A series of internal battles within the royal family, aggravated by increasing regional power falling into the hands of Han generals and the rise of the Daoist Yellow Turban revolt after 184 CE, finally brought the Han dynasty to an end in 220 CE.

Between Empires   Like the Romans of the late fourth century CE, who saw Germanic migrations as temporary disruptions rather than fatal blows to their empire, the Chinese expected that a new dynasty would shortly emerge after the collapse of the Han. Instead, China experienced its most chaotic postimperial political period. This interlude of turmoil is traditionally divided into the era of the Three Kingdoms (220–280 CE), the overlapping Six Dynasties period (222–589 CE), and the also overlapping period of the North and South Dynasties (317–589 CE).

From the initial Three Kingdoms period through the numerous small, weak, and short-lived "dynasties" that followed, the aim of reconstituting the empire was always present. Many of the factors that had undermined the Han, however—the growing power of landed elites, the increasing weakness of the bureaucracy, the chronic defense problems of the north and west—continued and even multiplied. In the absence of effective centralized administration, the infrastructure fell into disrepair, the enormous internal economy grew more regionalized, external trade declined, and warfare, famine, and banditry haunted the land.

Not until the fifth century CE did the rebuilding process begin, when an eastern Mongolian people known as the Toba established the state of Northern Wei in northern China. Taking advantage of the possibilities of the new military tactics growing from the development of the stirrup, Northern Wei established itself as a dominant power in the region. By the beginning of the sixth century, the Toba had enacted a formal policy of assimilating into Chinese culture—taking Chinese names, marrying into leading families, reviving old imperial rites, and taking on the perennial problem of land reform. In organizing a program of land redistribution to the peasants, they helped pave the way for the return of centralized administration, military service, and tax collection. A Toba general named Yang Jian succeeded in uniting most of the old Han lands in 589 and called the reunified dynasty the "Sui" (see Map 9.3).

MAP **9.3 China in 589 CE.**

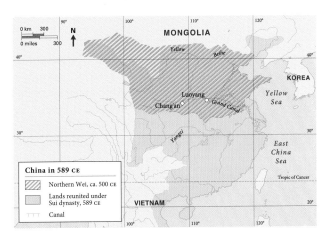

China in 589 CE
- Northern Wei, ca. 500 CE
- Lands reunited under Sui dynasty, 589 CE
- Canal

Patterns Up Close | The Stirrup

Given the long list of familiar Chinese pathbreaking technologies such as paper, the compass, the sternpost rudder, printing, the horse collar, and, of course, gunpowder, it may seem strange that we would feature something as simple as the stirrup. Yet, the stirrup's understated presence has long been recognized by historians as being of major importance. The reason is that it not only completely changed the way humans used horses but ushered in a new type of warfare that altered the structure of societies and dominated military strategy for 1,000 years.

Despite the fact that the horse had occupied a prominent place in Eurasian warfare for over 2,000 years, its utility had been limited to pulling chariots and supporting mounted archers and riders with light spears. The central problem of using horses in pitched battles was that the back of a horse was a precarious perch: It was difficult to mount a horse when one was weighed down with armor and weapons but easy to be knocked from one, especially when one was engaged in close combat and swift maneuvering.

Around the beginning of the Common Era the first attempts at saddles with straps for supporting a rider's feet began to appear in northern India. But these employed only a simple toe loop, and the saddle concentrated the rider's weight on a small area of the horse's back, tiring and hurting the animal. This basic idea for the stirrup, however, appears to have spread via the Silk Road, and by the early 300s CE a recognizably modern iron stirrup with a flat bottom and semicircular top began to be used in north and central China; the earliest remains discovered so far date to 302 CE. At about the same time, saddles with a rigid frame to distribute the rider's weight more evenly and better padding to cushion its effects on the horse began to be employed.

The effects of these changes were swiftly apparent in a China now dominated by feuding states and marauding nomads in the post-Han era. With his legs secured to his mount and a high saddle back to cushion him in combat, a mounted warrior

Jin Dynasty Iron Stirrups. Widespread use of the stirrup not only brought the use of cavalry back to the forefront of warfare, but led to a resurgence in power of Eurasian mounted nomadic peoples. The ornate stirrups pictured here helped the nomadic Jurchen people displace the Northern Song Dynasty (see Chapter 12) and set up their own Jin Dynasty that lasted from 1127 to 1234. Their downfall was brought about by another mounted nomadic people—the Mongols—who not only displaced the Jurchens but went on to conquer the Southern Song in 1279 and incorporate their new Yuan Dynasty into the short-lived Mongol super-empire spanning Eurasia in the late thirteenth and early fourteenth centuries.

The Empire Reclaimed: The Sui Like the Qin before them, the forcefulness with which the Sui pursued empire building—particularly in an ill-conceived invasion of the Korean peninsula after their ascension in 589 CE—prompted unrest among the people. The Sui used forced labor for several elaborate construction projects, including palatial palaces, roads, and, perhaps the most ambitious project of all, the Grand Canal. Linking the Yangzi River with the Yellow River, the Grand Canal facilitated shipment of large quantities of rice and other food crops from the south directly to the refurbished capital at Chang'an. This was to prove a vitally important highway over the coming centuries as northern capitals increasingly depended on food supplies shipped from the south. The Grand Canal, still in operation today, would eventually be extended all the way to the Beihe River, which leads to Beijing.

could use a long lance to charge directly into enemy formations without fear of being immediately unhorsed. Furthermore, he could wear a full complement of armor and armor his horse. The stirrup proved so effective that by the fifth century CE the armies of all the states in China had adopted and refined the technology. In China, it helped pave the way for the Sui reunification in 589.

It was in western Eurasia, however, that the new technology saw its greatest impact after its arrival in the seventh century CE. It has even been argued that the feudal society of Europe was ultimately derived from the stirrup. The ability of a heavy cavalry of armored warriors to break infantry formations and fight effectively at close quarters from horseback placed a premium on refining armor and weapons, training warriors, and breeding bigger, faster, and stronger horses. The politically fractured eras of post-Roman and post-Carolingian Europe meant that local elites and regional strongmen had to mount their own defenses. The stirrup and the military innovations it spawned allowed them to do this without heavily equipped armies, while the expenses necessary to adopt the new technology ensured that it would remain a monopoly of the rich and powerful. Thus the relationships comprising feudalism matured as peasants placed themselves in the service of their mounted protectors. The rough parity and independence of this widely dispersed warrior elite proved a powerful obstacle to the patterns of centralized state formation and empire building. Ironically, it would be another Chinese invention that would ultimately end this way of warfare many centuries later: gunpowder.

Questions

- How does the stirrup show how a technological innovation can lead to cultural and societal adaptations across many regions and across time?

- Which environmental and geographical conditions facilitated the impact of the stirrup across Eurasia in a way that would not have been possible in the Americas?

The outbreak of rebellion following the death of the second Sui emperor, Yangdi, brought the precocious 16-year-old commander Li Shimin to power. Li had the Sui emperor killed, placed his own father on the throne, and announced the founding of the Tang [Tahng] Dynasty in 618 CE. In less than a decade, he forced his father to abdicate and took power in his own right in 627 CE.

As we will see in the next part, the reconstitution of the Chinese empire under the Sui and its expansion and consolidation under the Tang not only marked a dramatic turning point in Chinese political history but also placed China among the world's regions marked by the ascendancy of religious civilizations. Like Christianity in the late Roman Empire, Buddhism made remarkable inroads in China during the period of fragmentation following the collapse of the Han. Indeed, through the work of Chinese monks it had also become firmly established in the Korean kingdoms and the Yamato state in Japan. The Tang would see the completion and high point of this process.

Buddhism and its institutions permeated Tang China to an extent never surpassed or even equaled in later dynasties. For a period in the late seventh and early eight centuries CE it even became the established Chinese state religion, under the remarkable Empress Wu Zetian. In this regard, China became not only part of a giant regional religious and cultural sphere during the Tang but an important part of a new world pattern that would encompass the sway of Islamic civilization, orthodox Christianity in the eastern Roman (Byzantine) Empire and much of eastern Europe, and the Christian civilizations of Roman Catholicism and Protestantism.

The Domestic Economy: Society, Family, and Gender

Throughout Chinese history, various dynasties actively encouraged and supported agriculture as the basis of the domestic economy. Yet, from the Han dynasty on, China exported far more in luxury goods and technology than it imported. Unlike the various regimes in India, which actively sought to foster trade, the Confucian view of the pursuit of profit as corrupting meant that Chinese governments seldom encouraged merchants and generally preferred to adopt a passive, but controlling, role in trade. Although merchants were held in low esteem, the state recognized that trade was indispensable to the financial health of the empire and saw it as an expandable source of tax revenue.

Industry and Commerce

Goods made in and distributed throughout the empire by the time of the Han included some of the best-known items of Chinese production. By the first century CE, Chinese manufacturers were making paper using a suspension of mashed plant fibers filtered through a fine-mesh screen and set aside to dry, a method still considered to produce the highest-quality product for painting or literary work.

Coal Mining. While the miners shore up a tunnel and gather coal into a basket lowered from above, a large bamboo pipe is thrust into the mine to draw off poisonous gases.

Perhaps even more impressive, by this time, too, artisans were producing a kind of "proto-porcelain" that, with increasing refinement, would be known in the succeeding centuries to the outside world as "china." The earthenware produced during the Tang dynasty is among the most coveted in the world today. In other arts, the use of lacquer as a finish, as well as in artwork created by sculpting built-up layers of it, was also well established. By the second century CE, the Chinese had perfected silk production and had become world leaders in textile weaving. Both treadle and water-powered looms were in widespread use, and bolts of silk with standardized designs were produced for export. The Chinese supply of silks could barely keep pace with demand, especially from Persia and Rome. But much of the most important domestic production centered on bulk strategic goods that sparked some of the world's first debates on the government's role in economics.

Iron and Salt   By the Han period, the Chinese were producing cast iron in huge foundries. According to one estimate, by 2 CE, there were no fewer than 48 major ironworks in north China, while the mining industry as a whole may have employed as many as 100,000 people. The foundries, which produced ingots of standardized sizes and weights, used sophisticated systems of forced-air control, including water-powered bellows. Salt mines employed complex gearing for lifting brine from deep wells, systems of bamboo piping for transferring it, and evaporators fired by natural gas for extracting the salt. Because of the enormous productivity of the iron-making and salt-mining industries, the government continually sought ways to regulate and control them.

Despite the increasing importance of industry and commerce to the imperial economy, the Han and succeeding dynasties continued to view merchants as a parasitic class, with no ties to the idealized relationships of agrarian life, trade as a necessary evil. Nevertheless, government programs aimed at improving the empire's infrastructure facilitated commerce. The unpredictable flow of China's rivers required dikes, dredging, reservoirs, and especially canals to ease transportation. Along with roads, canals grew in importance as the empire relied more and more on the produce of the rich lands of the south to supply the capitals of the north. The Han emperor Wudi, as we have seen, began work on the Grand Canal that linked the Yangzi and the Yellow Rivers (see Map 9.4).

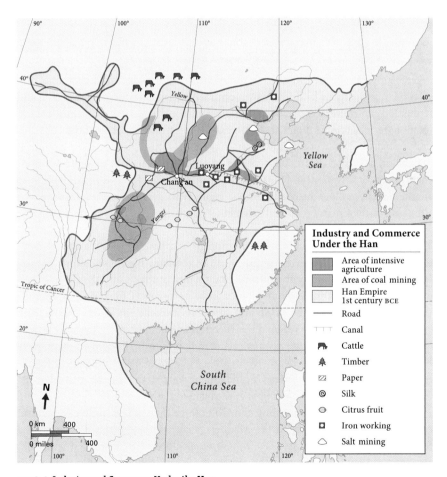

MAP **9.4** Industry and Commerce Under the Han.

Land Reform   By the time of the late Han, China's old aristocracy had largely died out, its place at the top of the social hierarchy assumed by the so-called *scholar-gentry*—the educated large landholders who constituted the Confucian bureaucracy. Despite the elimination of the old aristocracy, landlord holdings continued to expand. Since the upper ranks of the landowners and bureaucrats either were exempt from taxes or paid reduced amounts, the tax burden fell increasingly on tenants and owners of small parcels of land. Poor harvests or bad weather, particularly in the arid north and west, made the situation even worse for those already heavily taxed. Because the north, despite its elaborate irrigation works, was far less productive and more prone to crop failure than the south, it was also proportionally more heavily taxed.

Such problems made land reform and redistribution an ongoing concern. The Tang, for example, continued the policy of land redistribution begun during the brief Sui dynasty by allotting each peasant family a tract of 100 *mou*, one-fifth of which was inheritable, while the remainder reverted to the state for redistribution. Although the Tang land redistribution policy resulted in a relatively high level of prosperity, absentee landlordism, tenancy, and usury also rose again, particularly during times of economic stress. The continual problem of land tenure and attempts at reform and redistribution marked every dynasty and modern government down to the People's Republic—where it is even today a major concern.

Agricultural Productivity   A number of technical and systemic innovations steadily increased agricultural productivity. In addition to such staples as wheat, millet, and barley in the north and rice in the south, a wide variety of semitropical fruits and vegetables were cultivated within the empire. New strains of rice resulted in larger harvests on more marginal land. Trade with central Asia had introduced wine grapes, and fermented grain beverages had become a substantial industry. New techniques of crop rotation, fertilization, and plowing were gradually introduced, as were the collar for draft animals and the wheelbarrow; oxen-drawn, iron-tipped plows; treadle hammers; undershot, overshot, and other types of waterwheels; the foot-powered "dragon" chain pump for irrigation; and the *fengche*—a hand-cranked winnowing machine with an internal fan to blow the chaff from the grain. With this basic, reliable technology, China led the world in agricultural productivity until the eighteenth century CE.

The Silk Road   The dramatic expansion of maritime and caravan trade from the seventh century CE on, particularly within the huge Buddhist cultural sphere, spread Chinese technology abroad and brought new products into the Chinese empire. During the first millennium and a half of its history, China made numerous connections throughout the world and spread its influence in all directions. Early examples of silk may have reached the Mediterranean and North Africa through a long train of middlemen as early as the first millennium BCE. By the first century BCE, a variety of artifacts clearly identifiable as Chinese had turned up in Egypt; by the fourth and fifth centuries CE, Indian and Persian middlemen extended the Chinese trade to the African empires of Kush and Aksum.

Silk Road: Overland trade routes that connected eastern and western Eurasia, beginning at the end of the fourth century BCE.

The principal route connecting the Chinese to the various trading centers of central Asia, and ultimately to the Mediterranean and Rome, was known as the **Silk Road**. Along this route, the Chinese would forever be identified with silk; and though they tried to guard the secrets of its production, the demand was so high that many peoples along the caravan routes were soon engaged in making silk

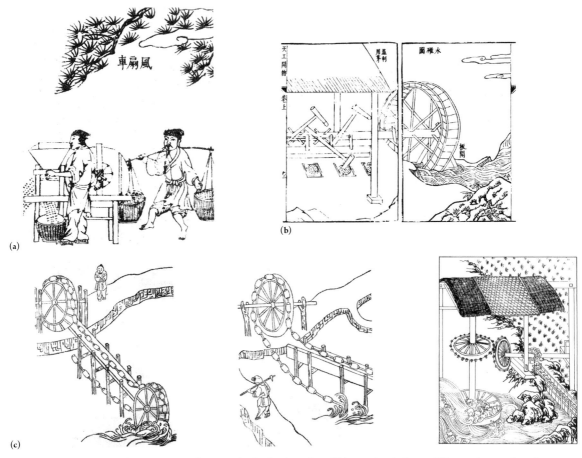

Han Era Technology. By the first century CE, Chinese sophistication in crafts and labor-saving devices could be seen in a number of areas. While the illustrations here are from the famous seventeenth-century compendium of technology *Tiangong kaiwu* (*The Works of Nature and Man*), all of them illustrate techniques in use during the Han period. (*a*) *Fengche* winnowing machine. (*b*) Undershot waterwheel driving hammers in a pounding mill. (*c*) Horizontal waterwheel driving a chain-bucket "dragon pump" for irrigation.

themselves. The techniques of raising silkworms and weaving silk reached the eastern Mediterranean between the third and fifth centuries CE. Competition among silk producers in western Eurasia became so keen that the Roman emperor Justinian allied with the African kingdom of Aksum in the sixth century CE to try to break the Persian near-monopoly on fine silks. In the process, the Romans created their own monopoly to service the western trade.

Gender Roles

Women in imperial China, as in agrarian-based societies in general, were subordinate to men. Early Confucian works, while emphasizing reciprocal responsibilities within the family, were relatively flexible about the position of women. However, with the rise of the imperial bureaucracy during the Han and the increasing emphasis on filial piety within its new Confucian curriculum, a more rigidly hierarchical, patriarchal model of proper women's behavior gradually developed. At the same time, the emphasis on sons within the extended family as carriers of the ancestral line and their potential to win admission to official state service led to a gradual devaluing of daughters. In times of severe economic stress, when families had difficulty supporting several children, young

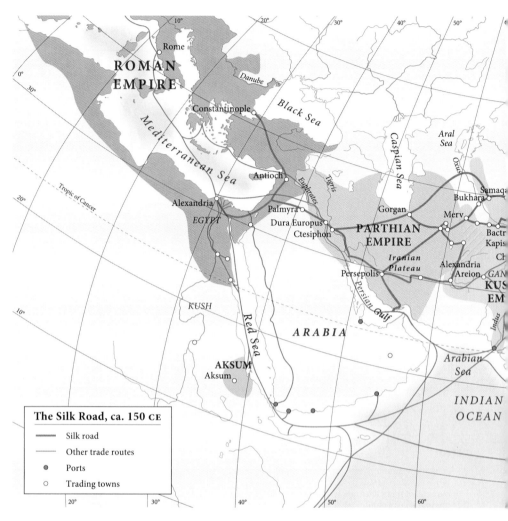

MAP **9.5** The Silk Road, ca. 150 CE.

girls were the first to suffer. Families, especially in rural areas, would sometimes sell their daughters into prostitution or kill female infants. By the Song era (960–1279 CE) problems relating to the treatment of young girls had become so acute that China's first foundling hospitals were opened in 1138 CE.

Although some elite women achieved prominence in intellectual pursuits, like the historian Ban Zhao (48–116 CE), women's education centered primarily on cultivating the domestic virtues of devotion and obedience, as well as mastering crafts such as spinning and weaving. Daughters were "expendable" in the sense that they would marry or be placed with another family through adoption or servitude. Since these last options often brought advantages to the girl's family, daughters were frequently educated in singing, playing instruments, chanting poetry, etc., in order to make them desirable candidates for placement.

From the fifth century CE on, the popularity of monastic Buddhism created attractive alternatives for those fleeing family pressures, especially women. Those women enrolled in Buddhist schools that required extensive scriptural study became highly educated, and the communities themselves, like Christian monasteries in

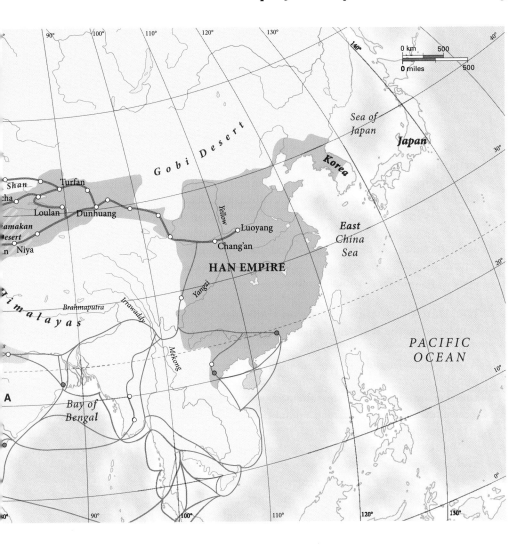

Europe, often owned large tracts of land and wielded considerable local influence. At the same time, the relative strictness of the practices regulating sexual and family life varied, particularly among high officials and the growing urban commercial classes. Foreign influences and fashions also affected behavior, particularly in Chang'an and places engaged in international trade. Tantric Buddhist (see Chapter 8) and Daoist sexual practices, which were used by their followers as a means of spiritual liberation, undoubtedly contributed to a more relaxed approach to relations between men and women during the Tang as well.

Intellectual Trends, Aesthetics, Science, and Technology

As we saw in the opening of this chapter, the period from the sixth century BCE until the first unification of China under the Qin in 221 BCE was marked by a dynamic collision of economic and social forces and is universally regarded as China's most fertile period of intellectual exploration. Long-term contacts with the east Asian Buddhist sphere from the end of the Han through the Tang era resulted in a number of new Buddhist schools being founded and spread throughout east Asia.

Confucianism, Education, and History During the Han

While the first Han rulers tended to favor a philosophical system that combined a more lenient Legalism with aspects of other surviving schools, over time a form of Confucianism became the preferred governmental doctrine. Confucian emphasis on the ethical correctness of officials, caring for the people, filial piety, and the study of history tended to make it a good fit for Han administrators. By the second century CE, the steadily growing popularity of Confucian academies led to their subsidization by the state, in effect placing all official education in the hands of these academies. Since the purpose of such education was state service, it also made knowledge of Confucianism the principal test for entrance into the bureaucracy. This situation, expanded and elaborated over nearly two millennia, would remain in force until the opening years of the twentieth century.

The Han Confucian Synthesis   Although Confucianism served as the foundation for the Han educational curriculum, Confucian doctrine had changed somewhat from the early teachings of Confucius and his disciples. During the Warring States period and the era of Qin rule, much Confucian thought—along with that of other philosophical schools—had been altered to suit the times, while a great many texts had been lost along the way. Thus, the Confucianism that finally received state approval included a number of elements reflecting the new realities of the Han dynasty.

This so-called Han synthesis of Confucian philosophy is evident in the era's chief treatise on government, the *Huainan zi*. In this document, a number of Confucian ideals, all calling for humane, righteous, and filial behavior by the powerful, are linked with Daoist ideas of the ruler as divorced from day-to-day administration and Legalist notions on the role of officials. As the intermediary between heaven, humankind, and earth, the emperor occupied a position of cosmological significance by nourishing the people and holding all in balance. For continuity's sake, a dynasty had to be hereditary—in contradiction to Confucius' ideas. But the idea of dynastic cycles and the Mandate of Heaven became even stronger during this period as they were elaborated by the great Han historians.

Han Historians   As we saw in Chapter 4, while there had been no shortage of history writing in the late Zhou period, much of it was seen even by contemporaries as overly partisan, fanciful, or tied to teaching moral lessons at the expense of accuracy. Mencius, for example, doubted the truthfulness of most of the *Book of History*. By the Han period, with the ideal of empire now encouraging a new sense of cultural unity, a series of court historians attempted to collate historical materials that had survived the Qin purges and to unify and systematize the writing of history.

For these men and women, the purpose of history writing, much as it was for the great Greek historians Herodotus (ca. 484–425 BCE) and Thucydides (ca. 460–ca. 395 BCE), was the accurate transmission of information—often with verbatim copies of important documents—and analysis of the events portrayed in terms of a larger vision of the direction and purpose of human history. For the Han historians, as for Chinese historians throughout the imperial era, history was cyclical: Human events, as manifestations of the great universal cycles of being, are a constant succession of birth, growth, decay, death, and rebirth, in which older ideas of the Mandate of Heaven, dynastic cycles, and yin and yang theory are imbedded. The moral lessons learned are therefore tied to actions taken at various stages of these cycles.

The basic format of long-term history was laid out by the father-and-son team of Sima Tan (d. 110 BCE) and Sima Qian (145–86 BCE). Their *Shiji* (*The Records of the Grand Historian*) attempts the first complete history of the Chinese people from the mythical Yellow Emperor to their own time. One particularly valuable section that became a staple of later histories was a survey of non-Chinese peoples encountered along with their habits, customs, religions, geography, and other significant traits. Hence, the Han records give us our first written accounts of Japan and other places on the Chinese periphery.

Like other Chinese officials, the historians took their role of "conscience" of the government seriously, sometimes at severe peril to themselves. As historian to the powerful Emperor Wudi, for example, Sima Qian offended the ruler by exonerating a general in his writings whom the emperor and court had accused of cowardice. Given the choice between execution and castration, Sima chose the latter; if he were dead, he explained, he could not finish his history, which he believed was his highest duty.

Several generations later, the Ban family comprised another dynasty of Han court historians. Writing after the Wang Mang interval, Ban Biao (3–54 CE) and his son Ban Gu (32–92 CE) pioneered the writing of dynastic history with their *Hanshu* (*The History of the Former Han*), which laid out the format followed by all subsequent dynastic histories. Ban Gu's daughters were also scholars and writers, and his sister Ban Zhao (48–116 CE) carried on the family tradition of history writing as well as a treatise on proper women's behavior, *Admonitions for Women*.

Interestingly, accounts of the historians' activities themselves may be found in the *Hou Hanshu* (*The History of the Latter Han*), written after the fall of the dynasty by Fan Ye (398–446 CE).

Buddhism in China

The growth of Buddhism as a universal missionary religion came, at least in part, from the adaptability of its doctrines to widely diverse peoples and belief systems. As we saw in Chapter 8, by the mid-first century CE, when it is first mentioned in Chinese accounts, Buddhism had already split into the major divisions of Theravada (Hinayana), which had established itself in southern India and Sri Lanka and was moving into southeast Asia, and Mahayana, which would be established in China, Korea, Vietnam, and Japan.

The introduction of Mahayana Buddhism into China presents a number of interesting parallels with that of Christianity into Rome, though there are important differences as well. Rather than focusing on the problems of practical government, both religions emphasized instead personal enlightenment or salvation. Both, to some extent, were initially seen as "foreign" systems and subjected to periodic persecution before emerging triumphant. Finally, while both challenged existing political and social hierarchies, the institutions of both were also adopted by rulers who wanted to strengthen or expand their power.

**Bodhisattva
Guanyin, Sixth Century CE.**
Originally incorporating aspects of both genders, Guanyin (also Kuan-yin) came to be depicted as female as Buddhism became firmly established in China. For Pure Land adherents, she was the bodhisattva invoked in times of extreme peril, and "the miracles of Guanyin" (*Kannon* in Japan) was a favorite theme of both Chinese and Japanese artists.

Aesthetics (Esthetics):
The study of the beautiful; the branches of learning dealing with categorizing and analyzing beauty.

Language and Scripture   The incompatibility of the Chinese written language with Sanskrit and Pali scriptures complicated the introduction of Buddhism to China. The earliest Buddhist missionaries had to rely heavily on transliterations, borrow extensively from Daoist terminology, and invent a new and diverse vocabulary of Chinese terms. Over the next several centuries, this eclecticism resulted in a proliferation of sects and a growing need on the part of Chinese and, later, Korean, Japanese, and Vietnamese converts to travel to India for study and guidance. The travel account of the Chinese monk and early pilgrim Fa Xian (see Chapter 8), who journeyed throughout central Asia and India from 399 to 414 CE in search of Pali copies of Buddhist works, contributed greatly to Chinese understanding of the growing Buddhist world. The most famous pilgrim, Xuan Zang (596–664 CE), went to India in 623 CE and brought back the extensive collection of scriptures still housed in the monastery he founded just outside Xi'an. His travels were later immortalized in the popular collection of fabulous tales called *A Journey to the West*.

Buddhist Schools   The period between the dissolution of the Han and the ascendancy of the Tang was also marked by the founding of several of the most important schools of east Asian Buddhism. By the fifth century, the school of popular devotion to Amida, the Buddha of the Pure Land, was spreading rapidly in China. Like the *bhakti* sects in India, no immersion in the texts is necessary for enlightenment for Pure Land followers; merely invoking Amida's name is sufficient for salvation. Even today, it remains the most popular Buddhist sect in both China and Japan. Amida is often pictured with the bodhisattva Guanyin [GWAHN-yin]—*Kannon* in Japan—the Goddess of Mercy who, like the Virgin Mary in Catholicism, is frequently invoked during times of peril.

Another influential Buddhist school was Tiantai, centered on the scripture of the *Lotus Sutra*. Tiantai emphasized contemplation of the sutras as the vehicle to enlightenment and later inspired several schools of esoteric (see Chapter 8) paths to enlightenment. These schools exercised considerable influence over both the Tang and the Japanese court at Heian during the eighth and ninth centuries CE.

Finally, one school that later achieved fame, if not widespread popularity, was Chan Buddhism, better known by the name given it in Japan: Zen. As outlined in its central text, *The Platform of the Sixth Patriarch*, by Hui Neng (638–713 CE), enlightenment is transmitted not through scriptural study or personal devotion to a particular figure but rather through the discipline of meditation and the active example of a master. The intense give and take between master and pupil, the discipline involved in performing humble tasks, and the contemplation of paradoxical questions are all meant ultimately to generate an intuitive flash of enlightenment. While limited in its influence in China, the emphasis on discipline and obedience made Zen the preferred Buddhist school of Japan's warrior aristocracy after the twelfth century CE.

Intellectual Life

To a considerable degree, Chinese concepts of **aesthetics** developed during the first millennium CE became the founding principles for the arts throughout east Asia. The most important developments during this period were the maturation of three disciplines: poetry, painting, and calligraphy. An important part of a well-rounded

Calligraphy. Detail of calligraphy from Wang Xizhi (303–361). The styles of Chinese characters were standardized for use in formal documents during the Qin and Han eras but have since been endlessly refined as art by master calligraphers. Along with painting and poetry, calligraphy was esteemed as one of the "three excellences" (*sanjue*) of the scholar. Wang Xizhi is, even today, revered as the master of the *xingshu*, or "running script," a cursive form used for private correspondence. This sample is from an early Tang tracing copy of Wang's hand.

education even today, these three disciplines are considered to be closely interrelated and governed by the same overriding principles. Central to each discipline is the idea of spontaneous creation as a reflection of the inner state of the artist. The artist in each of these media seeks to connect with the Dao by indirectly suggesting some aspect of it in the work itself. For example, Chinese landscape paintings often feature misty mountains, lone pines, and tiny human figures, with the action and occasion implied rather than detailed, because too much detail would place limits on the illimitable.

The Sciences   Because the imperial establishment relied on the prediction of comets, eclipses, and other omens to monitor the will of heaven, astronomy and mathematics were especially important disciplines. Chinese mathematicians had long used a decimal system and had worked out formulas and proofs to figure the areas of most standard geometrical forms. They had also calculated pi to four places and were able to solve simultaneous algebraic equations. The astronomers Zhang Heng (78–139 CE) and Wang Chong (27–100) had each championed theories of a universe governed by comprehendible natural forces. Zhang built a water-powered *armillary sphere*—a hollow globe surrounded by bronze bands, representing the paths of the sun, stars, and planets—and, in 134 CE, devised what was perhaps the world's first practical earthquake detector: Small balls were delicately balanced on tracks inside a sculpture faced with frogs, representing the directions of the compass. Even a slight tremor would send one of the balls down the appropriate track and out of the frog's mouth, indicating the direction from which the quake came.

Earthquake Detector. One of the more ingenious pieces of high technology to come out of the Han period was the creation of a working earthquake detector by Zhang Heng (78–139 CE) in 134 CE. In the model illustrated here, carefully balanced balls were placed inside the large, hollow egg-shaped vessel. A tremor coming from a particular direction would jar the ball closest to the direction of the quake loose and send it down a track where it would fly from the mouth of one of the dragons on the outside of the "egg" and fall into the yawning mouth of the frog underneath. Thus, anyone checking the device could tell at a glance that a quake had occurred and from what directions by seeing which frog held a ball.

Printing and Proto-Porcelain   One of the signal innovations of Eurasia was printing. Believed to have its origins in the ancient practice of taking rubbings on paper or silk of gravestone inscriptions, by the eighth century CE woodblock prints of popular Buddhist works had become available in major Chinese cities. By the end of the Tang and the beginning of the Song dynasties, presses employing both carved block and movable copper type were in regular use in China, Korea, and Japan. As it would later in Europe, the innovation of printing dramatically raised the literacy rates in all the areas it touched. By the beginning of the Song era, China had some of the highest preindustrial literacy rates achieved in human history—despite the difficulties of the written language.

The techniques involved in generating the extremely high temperatures required for cast iron were also transferable to porcelain production. Though there is debate about when the breakthroughs resulting in true porcelain first occurred, by the Tang period, distinctive brown and green glazed figures, often depicting the vibrant parade of peoples and animals of the caravan trade, were widely exchanged. By the Song, delicate white, cracked glaze and sea-green celadon ware were produced and sought by connoisseurs as the height of aesthetic refinement. Today, such pieces are considered to be among the world's great art treasures.

Putting It All Together

The political and social turmoil of the late Zhou era also marked an enormously innovative period in Chinese intellectual and cultural history. During this era the most important schools of Chinese thought and philosophy developed: Confucianism, Daoism, and Legalism. While Confucianism ultimately triumphed as the ideology of imperial China, it was the Legalist state of Qin that created the empire itself.

When the Qin dynasty fell in 206 BCE, much of the infrastructure of the early empire—including the Great Wall—was in place. The Han dynasty, from 202 BCE to 220 CE, retained the administrative structure of the Qin but softened the harsh laws and punishments of the Legalists. Eventually, the form of Confucianism practiced by the empire's administrators was taught in the imperial schools, becoming in effect the imperial ideology. By the end of the Han, China had created a solid alliance between the state and this all-encompassing ethical and legal system.

Perhaps more important than even the structures themselves, however, was that, like the Egyptians and Romans, the Chinese had become accustomed to what has been called the "habit of empire." As suggested in this chapter, 400 years of unity under the Qin and the Han had conditioned the Chinese to believe that empire was the natural goal of the patterns of political formation in China and that any interruptions in these patterns would be but brief interludes in the dynastic cycle. Thus, Chinese history has been marked by rhythms of inwardness and outwardness, inner renewal and usurpation of rule from the outside. Along with these rhythms came an inherited belief, reinforced by the theories of dynastic historians, that human society and the cosmos were knit together in a moral order, made perfectible by the power of the empire and the dedication of a bureaucracy selected for its understanding of ethics in human affairs. Throughout the imperial era—and even in our own time—the students and scholars of China have tried to keep faith with this heritage by guiding and remonstrating with those in power.

▶ For additional resources, including maps, primary sources, visuals, and quizzes, please go to www.oup.com/us/vonsivers. Please see the Further Resources section at the back of the book for additional readings and suggested websites.

Thinking Through Patterns

▶ **Was the First Emperor's ruthlessness justified by his accomplishments in his empire?**

Addressing this question raises a very basic problem: Why do we study history? In ancient times, most people studied history for the moral lessons it offered and to avoid making the same mistakes their ancestors did. As we have also seen, some cultures, like the Chinese, studied it in hopes of grasping its basic patterns so as to understand the present and anticipate the future. Modern historians have generally taken their cue from Leopold von Ranke (1795–1886), who felt that scholars should rise above preconceived ideas and simply seek the past "as it really was." For most of the twentieth century, historians have sought to avoid making moral judgments about the past, to see their job as being "detectives" rather than "judges." By that standard, the historian should empathetically enter the past and seek to understand it; to judge it by the standards of the present is to be "presentist." But how does one deal with such things as genocide, extreme cruelty, or slavery? Thus, one way out of this dilemma might be to weigh the actions of the First Emperor against the standards of morality current in *his* day. Yet here, too, we encounter a problem: There were so many new schools of thought emerging in China then that no single one dominated; moreover, the First Emperor himself created his own system of morality based on Legalism. Perhaps, then, the best that we can do at this point, aside from judging him privately by our personal standards, is to note that he set the fundamental pattern for Chinese imperial government for the next 2,000 years—but at considerable cost.

Perhaps the biggest difference between Confucian society and modern American society is in the way both see the ideal forms of societal relations. Americans see the individual, the rule of law, democracy, and equality as fundamental to a good society. The purpose of government is to allow people to do as they wish but to provide the bounds within which they can do so. Confucian concepts of government and society put a premium on holism, hierarchy, and harmony. People are not seen as mere individuals but as part of larger patterns: family, clan, village, society, state.

▶ **How would you compare the values expressed by Confucius and Mencius to those of contemporary society?**

These are seen as part of a hierarchy that stretches from the poorest peasant to the emperor himself. Reciprocal rights and responsibilities are present at every level for protection of the weak, but equality is not seen as important. The role of government itself is seen in large part as being able to provide a moral example to the people. It if teaches them well through regulations, customs, and ritual, then the people aspire to be good and will police themselves to a great extent.

▶ **How have historians viewed the role of women in early imperial China?**

One of the most unattractive things about imperial China to the majority of us today is that it often appears that women were held in low regard, abused, denied basic human rights, and even tortured for fashion's sake, as with foot binding. The Confucian emphasis on hierarchy within society and the family tends to reinforce this impression. But scholars have in recent years begun to study the role of women at different times and in different regions of China, and the picture now appears much more complex than before. While scholars agree that in some respects, particularly foot binding from the Song period on, women's roles deteriorated, there were also times when the evidence suggests they exercised considerable freedom and influence, such as during the Tang and early Song periods. The pattern of "inner" and "outer" as it governed the traditional Chinese family is still discernable in many Chinese households today: While husbands go off to work, women definitely hold sway within the "inner" realm of the house.

PART THREE

The Formation of Religious Civilizations

600–1450 CE

A vitally important pattern of world history during the period 600–1450 was the emergence and development of what may be called "religious civilizations." By this we mean the formation of religions and cultures in entire world regions, shared by the states and empires in these regions. In all cases, religious, philosophical, and/or ethical traditions based on monotheism or monism helped give legitimacy to the polities that adopted them. They helped link individual states by providing them with a common set of cultural norms and bonds. Six religious civilizations emerged in a relatively short space of time in Eurasia and, to some extent, in Africa during the second half of the first millennium. They were, from west to east, western Christianity (from 476), eastern Christianity (640), Islam (750), Hinduism (550), Buddhism (Korea 550, Japan 594, Vietnam 971), and Neo-Confucianism (China 960, Vietnam 1010). Each occupied a world region.

Uniqueness and Comparability

Uniqueness. The rise of religious civilizations on the continents of Asia, Europe, and Africa is a striking phenomenon that unifies the period 600–1450. In this respect, it may be considered as a continuation of the intellectual and institutional transformations that began with the emphasis on transcendence by the visionaries of the mid-first millennium BCE as a key aspect in understanding the world in which they lived.

Comparability. The religious civilizations were not monolithic and displayed many regional variations. Internal diversity notwithstanding, they shared a number of common characteristics:

- Religious civilizations formed in regions which were larger than any single state within them: They superseded empires as the largest units of human organization. They often consisted of commonwealths of competing states sharing common characteristics and even a common culture.

- The civilizations were *scriptural*, that is, based on bodies of texts inherited in most cases from earlier periods. In each religious civilization, followers were

628–651
Arab Kingdom in Syria; Conquest of Iraq, Egypt, and Iran

1204
Sack of Constantinople by Crusaders

1268
St. Thomas Aquinas' *Summa Theologica*

1453
Constantinople Falls to Ottoman Empire

1336–1564
Dominance of Hindu State of Vijayanagar in Southern India

1238–1492
Muslim Kingdom of Granada

1206–1310
Mongol Conquests of Asia, Eastern Europe, and the Eastern Middle East

1348–1352
Black Death in Middle East and Europe

1206–1526
Muslim Delhi Sultanate at Height of Power

618–960
Tang Dynasty in China

preoccupied with harmonizing the often conflicting texts into one coherent *canon:* a single, official interpretation adhered to by all.

- The guardians of the canon (clergy, scholars, sages) were members of educated elites who taught and interpreted it to laypeople.

- Despite hostilities among religious civilizations, merchants, missionaries, pilgrims, and travelers visited each other's areas in large numbers. They fostered a lively exchange of innovations from one end of Eurasia and Africa to the other.

Origins, Interactions, and Adaptations

The era of religious civilizations provides some striking examples of the processes of origins, interactions, and adaptations that we have emphasized in this book.

Internal Forces. The elements with which people built their religious civilizations came from the intellectual and institutional traditions of empires and kingdoms from the pre-600 period. These elements were for the most part found inside the territories of the evolving religious civilizations. Some exceptions include Korea, Japan, and Vietnam, which adopted Chinese Buddhist civilization more or less ready-made from the outside.

In the majority of religious civilizations, the scriptural canons were completed within two or three centuries. Thereafter, refinement within the confines set by the canons continued for many more centuries, in some cases even beyond 1450. Without outside challenges, however, these refinements slowed. Over time, scholars, thinkers, and artists tended to exhaust the possibilities which their civilizations offered them.

External Challenges. External intellectual challenges contributed to the reshaping of two religious civilizations during the period 600–1450: Neo-Confucian China and western Christianity. China's intellectual foundation from the Han dynasty on was based on Daoism and Confucianism, harmonized with some difficulty during the early centuries of the millennium. Buddhism, coming from India, became a full-blown intellectual and institutional challenge by the 800s. In response, the Chinese reconfigured their canon from the mid-tenth century with the creation of Neo-Confucianism.

In western Christianity, Latin Christians enlarged their canon twice, as a result of adapting to intellectual challenges coming from the outside: first around 1100–1250, after the arrival of Arabic and Greek texts, and second around 1400, after the arrival of another set of Greek and Hellenistic texts.

Thinking Like a World Historian

▶ How were the religious civilizations of the period 600–1450 unique? How were they comparable?

▶ What impact did internal forces and external challenges have on the patterns of development in the religious civilizations of the period 600–1450?

▶ Why do the civilizations of the Americas fall outside the patterns that characterize Eurasian and African civilizations during this period?

960–1127
Neo-Confucian Synthesis in China

794–1185
Heian Period, Japan

1257–1287
Vietnamese Repel Three Attempted Mongol Invasions

1250–1505
Kingdom of Great Zimbabwe in Southern Africa

850–1000
Kingdom of Chichén Itzá in Northern Yucatán Peninsula

1438–1533
Inca Empire in Andes

918–1392
Koryo Kingdom, from which the Name "Korea" Is Derived

ca. 1000
Tale of Genji, perhaps World's First Novel, Japan

ca. 1000–1400
Kingdom of Ife in West African Rain Forest

1240–1645
Empire of Mali in West Africa (Rain Forest, Sahel, and Savanna)

1427–1521
Aztec Empire in Mesoamerica

Chapter 10 600-1300 CE

Islamic Civilization and Byzantium

One cannot help but feel sympathy for Safra, a jilted wife whose husband left her for a more attractive woman in twelfth-century Cairo. Two letters by Safra to her estranged husband Khidr tell of her deep hurt and bitter anguish. She is offended that Khidr denigrates her as unattractive and reveals marriage secrets to his new lover, who is also married. In her words, his "repulsive, shameless talk" causes her deep suffering. Were she not a good Muslim, she says, she would curse him roundly and loudly, both privately and in public.

The letters also reveal that she was independently wealthy, while her husband was not. She freely admits that when they were married 3 years earlier, she did not realize that he was unreliable. Since he could not pay the obligatory portion of the "bride wealth" payable to her at the time of the wedding, she let it stand as a loan. Not only did he not make payments, but he did not even feed and clothe her or pay the rent. When he began his affair 2 years earlier, she went to the countryside to find distance and rest. But he tortured her with insistent demands to return, promising her to leave his mistress. The moment she gave in and returned to Cairo, he went back to his lover. Like a ghost, he slipped into Safra's house at night for a few

Byzantium

Islamic Civilization

BYZANTIUM AND THE ISLAMIC WORLD, ca. 1000 CE

ABOVE: The constellation Aries, from *Book of the Fixed Stars* by Abd al-Rahman al-Sufi (903–986).

hours of sleep in his room, only to disappear the next morning. During his nightly visits he stole most of the household furnishings so that in the end she found herself in an empty house.

Safra's reflections and actions provide an important glimpse into the legal side of Islamic civilization. Contrary to the widely held opinion in the contemporary West, Islamic law afforded women considerable protections. Safra was a woman of property, holding personal title to possessions as well as to debts payable to her. She could go to court where she had standing as a complainant. She could initiate divorce proceedings, even if a wife's proceedings were more complicated than those of a husband. In short, even though Islamic civilization was as patriarchal as the other religious civilizations of the time, women exercised considerably more rights than in the Persian and Roman Empires.

The central patterns of Islamic civilization flowed from an empire that conquering Arabs from northern Arabia built during 628–750. These patterns would then develop across a 5,000-mile swath ranging from Spain to Turkestan. The empire, ultimately ungovernable as a single unit, evolved into a **commonwealth** of smaller states. From 750 to 950 it underwent a formative period during which its inhabitants adapted to inherited Greco-Roman and Persian cultures. By the mid-tenth century, historians consider the empire "fully developed," meaning that it was subjected to few outside influences that changed it in substantive ways. After this time, Islamic civilization continued to be shaped by its patterns of characteristic religious, political, and cultural traditions and institutions. These patterns remained largely unchanged and unchallenged by new stimuli coming from the outside until well into the modern period. In this respect, Islamic civilization was similar to Byzantine eastern Christian, Hindu Indian, neo-Confucian Chinese, and Confucian–Buddhist Japanese civilizations. All of these, after their formation by the end of the first millennium, developed stimulation more along their established internal patterns than as a result of innovation, interaction, and adaptation coming from the outside.

The Rise of Arab Dominance in the Middle East and Mediterranean

Arab conquests and the rise of the religion of Islam were foundational events during the period 600–900. In the 600s, the Arabs carved out a kingdom for themselves by exploiting the preoccupation of the eastern Roman and Sasanid Persian Empires with their destructive wars of conquest in 610–628. Two Arab dynasties, the Umayyads succeeded by the Abbasids, built a vast empire stretching thousands of miles from east to west. Given the enormous distances, the Abbasids were forced to grant autonomy to many outlying provinces. Their empire thus changed into a commonwealth of many states sharing a single Islamic religion.

Seeing Patterns

▶ Why can the period 600–1450 be described as the age of religious civilizations? How do eastern Christian and Islamic civilizations fit this description?

▶ Which cultural traditions combined to form Islamic religious civilization during its formative period? What were the most characteristic patterns?

▶ How did eastern Christian or Byzantine civilization evolve over time? On which institutions was this civilization based, and how did it evolve, wedged between Islamic and western Christian civilizations?

Commonwealth: An association of self-governing states sharing similar institutional and cultural traits.

From Rome and Persia to the Arab Empire

At the beginning of the 600s, the Sasanid Persian and Roman Empires battled each other in a lengthy and destructive war, which left the Arabs in Syria and Mesopotamia (which the Arabs subsequently called "Iraq") to their own devices. The Arabs had been nomadic inhabitants of the Syrian-Arabian desert since the domestication of the camel and were founders of sedentary kingdoms and city-states around the rim of the desert on the Arabian Peninsula in the early centuries CE. In the mid-600s a group of Arabs declared a kingdom in Mesopotamia and Syria, captured Egypt from the eastern Roman Empire, and destroyed the Sasanid Persian Empire. Through further conquests, the Arab kingdom became an empire, stretching by the mid-eighth century from Iberia (Spain and Portugal) in the west to the Indus in the east.

Final Showdown Between Persia and Rome

As we saw at the end of Chapter 7, Khosrow II (r. 590–628) regained the Sasanid Persian throne thanks to Roman help. In gratitude for this help, Khosrow made territorial concessions, ended Roman tribute payments, and terminated the Persian–Roman war inherited from his predecessors. When a mutiny in 602 overthrew his Roman benefactor, however, Khosrow reacted by invading the Roman Empire. By avenging the emperor, Khosrow hoped that he could overcome the stigma of having owed his throne to the Romans. During the first phase of what was to become a new, 26-year-long war, Khosrow succeeded in reconquering Armenia and Upper Mesopotamia.

As the Roman defenses crumbled, a new emperor, Heraclius (r. 610–641) took the throne. To deny the Romans any chance of recovery, Khosrow II initiated the second phase of the war with the conquest of Syria, Palestine, and Egypt (614), as well as the abduction of what was believed to be the "true Cross" (on which Jesus was supposed to have died) from Jerusalem. In 626, one of Khosrow's generals even fought his way to the Bosporus opposite Constantinople, stopped only by Heraclius' fleet in the Bosporus.

The Persian failure to cross the Bosporus was the turning point in the war. Within just 2 years, Heraclius was able to push the retreating Persians to the outskirts of their own capital, Ctesiphon, about 20 miles south of modern-day Baghdad. Khosrow fled from his palace and courtiers murdered him in the ensuing anarchy. After reoccupying the provinces lost in the war and restoring the purported "true Cross" to Jerusalem in 628, Heraclius returned to Constantinople in triumph. He left governance of the coastal and interior cities of Palestine and Syria in the hands of bishops supported by a few garrisons and governance of the interior countryside to the Arabs.

Theology and the Origins of Islam

Like scholars seeking the founding histories of many religions or philosophical traditions, modern students of Islam find themselves confronted by a dilemma. On the one hand, they possess a large number of often richly detailed Arabic narratives on the origins of Islam. But the earliest of these narratives date to the early 800s—two centuries *after* 628—and scholars have found it impossible to separate history from theology. In the early 800s, Islamic religious civilization was forming and it was only natural for Muslims at that time to project the tenets of the then evolving Islamic theology and law back into the 600s. On the other hand, narratives by Christians and Jews purportedly from the 600s are brief, lacking in detail, and often confused. Their reliability is frequently questionable, even if they provide seemingly useful information: Later copyists often changed the texts or added details not contained in the original texts. As a result, historians have to be extremely cautious with the available sources.

The theological account of Islamic origins, elaborated during the period 800–950, became the primary narrative of Islamic civilization. Usually referred to as "Islamic tradition," this account includes a number of theological doctrines:

- the revelation of the Quran as the Arab holy scripture
- the role of Muhammad as the Prophet, as told in his biography
- the establishment of a model community in Medina with Muhammad as the lawgiver
- the holy war (**jihad**, also "struggle") of the followers of Muhammad against the paganism (ignorance, or *jahiliyya*) of the Arabs
- the providential Islamic conquest of Sasanid Persia and much of the eastern Roman Empire
- the handing down of reports recording pronouncements and decisions of Muhammad and his companions in the early community, collectively called "tradition"

Jihad: According to Islamic tradition, war against unbelievers or pagans.

In short, Islamic tradition is the theology of Islam as the completion of the previous revelations of Christianity and Judaism and its mission to bring the world under God's rule.

More specifically, Islamic tradition begins with Muhammad's birth during the "year of the elephant." It was in this year, assumed to be 570 or 571, that Aksum's vice-regent in Yemen led an unsuccessful expedition (with elephants in his war train) against the western Arabian trading and pilgrimage city of Mecca. He laid siege to Mecca either in the name of the king of Aksum (in today's Ethiopia) or as a rebel seeking to consolidate his own rule but was beaten back by a flock of birds that supposedly dropped deadly rocks on the besiegers. Muhammad is described as a descendant of a prominent Meccan family of guardians of the sanctuary but also as an early childhood orphan who had to struggle for recognition. As a mature man, Muhammad received Allah's (God's) calling as a prophet of the Last Judgment, soon to arrive. The Meccans not only rejected his message but forced Muhammad and his small band of followers into an emigration (*hijra*) northward in 622, which became the first year of the Islamic calendar.

Muhammad resettled with his small band of followers in Yathrib, an oasis city farther north where he had ancestors on his mother's side. Local notables hired him as an arbiter among warring factions, including pagan Arab and Jewish tribes. In this city, renamed "Medina" (city [of the Prophet]), he molded a nascent community (*umma*) of Muslims by eliminating polytheism and expelling the Jewish tribes.

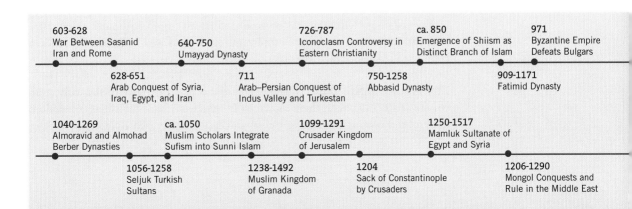

603-628 War Between Sasanid Iran and Rome		726-787 Iconoclasm Controversy in Eastern Christianity	ca. 850 Emergence of Shiism as Distinct Branch of Islam	971 Byzantine Empire Defeats Bulgars
640-750 Umayyad Dynasty				
628-651 Arab Conquest of Syria, Iraq, Egypt, and Iran	711 Arab–Persian Conquest of Indus Valley and Turkestan	750-1258 Abbasid Dynasty	909-1171 Fatimid Dynasty	
1040-1269 Almoravid and Almohad Berber Dynasties	ca. 1050 Muslim Scholars Integrate Sufism into Sunni Islam	1099-1291 Crusader Kingdom of Jerusalem	1250-1517 Mamluk Sultanate of Egypt and Syria	
1056-1258 Seljuk Turkish Sultans	1238-1492 Muslim Kingdom of Granada	1204 Sack of Constantinople by Crusaders	1206-1290 Mongol Conquests and Rule in the Middle East	

**Circling the Ka`ba.** Muslims on pilgrimage perform a number of rituals, among which is the sevenfold counterclockwise circumambulation of the Ka`ba, the sanctuary at the heart of Mecca. A large black cloth, called the kiswa, covers the sanctuary and is renewed annually. According to tradition, Abraham was the founder of the Ka`ba.

Sharia: The entirety of Islamic morality and law, revealed in the Quran and the tradition.

Muhammad continued to receive divine revelations, and he undertook military campaigns against the Meccans, who persisted in their hostility. After 8 years of warfare and damage to their trade, the Meccans capitulated, agreeing to give up their paganism and convert to Islam.

According to the traditional account, the Prophet briefly returned to Mecca to rededicate the pilgrimage sanctuary of the city to monotheism. Called the Ka`ba [KAH-bah], this sanctuary was said to date back to Abraham, the father of both Israelites and Arabs in the Hebrew Bible. Two years later, in 632, Muhammad died in Medina, survived by several wives and daughters but no son. The first four successors in the leadership of the community—early converts and companions of the Prophet—kept the Muslims from dividing into warring factions and guided the early conquests of Syria, Iran, and Egypt. Paganism in Arabia ended, and Muslims established their own imperial rule over the Zoroastrians, Christians, and Jews of the Middle East.

As is clear from this summary of the tradition, Islam is not only a monotheistic religion opposed to paganism but also a faith that united a community of converts from paganism, which Muhammad governed through God's commands and laws of revelation. The Quran, the holy scripture that contains God's commandments and laws, speaks about a chain of preachers of monotheism, including biblical figures such as Joseph, Moses, and Jesus as well as Arab figures. Islamic tradition depicts Muhammad as the final prophet who laid the base for the moral and legal code, the **sharia**, which functioned as the blueprint for the perfect community that was Medina. In sum, this theology, created during 800–950 and projected back into western Arabia in the early 600s, is that of a communally organized Islam, destined to rule the world as the final revealed religion.

From the Arab Empire to Islamic Civilization

While the theology of a fully evolved Islamic community in Medina in the early 600s is a vital topic for religious scholars to discuss, historians working with verified documents can say only that from 628 to 651, in the wake of the Roman–Sasanid war, Arabs from the north of the Arabian Peninsula conquered Sasanid Persia and assumed power in Roman Syria. In the course of the following century, Arabs established an empire extending to the Iberian Peninsula in the west and central Asia and northwestern India in the east. In this empire, they interacted with conquered Romans, Persians, North African Berbers, Iberian Visigoths, and central Asian Turks, incorporating them into their administration and adopting the cultural heritage of both Rome and Iran. Toward the end of the 700s the Arabs began to shape an emerging Islamic religious civilization patterned by influences from Christian theology, Roman and Jewish law, Greek philosophy and science, as well as Persian and Indian literature and science (see Map 10.1).

The Arab Empire   The Umayyads were the ruling dynasty of the early Arab empire (640–750), with their capital in Damascus. After establishing a kingdom in Syria and conquering Iran as well as the agriculturally rich Roman province of

Egypt, the Umayyads led several campaigns by land and sea as far as Constantinople. The conquering Arab armies were increasingly composed of cavalry forces which had adopted the Chinese innovation of saddle frames and stirrups (see Chapter 9). This innovation was first recorded toward the end of the sixth century in an eastern Roman war manual. In both Roman and Persian armies, saddle frames and stirrups allowed for the riding of horses over long distances without injury to the horses' backs. They

Gold Coin of Abd al-Malik, ca. 696. The coin displays the characteristics of what were to become Islamic coins; that is, the avoidance of images and the use of religious phrases.

anchored riders firmly on their steeds, enabling them to fight not only with bow and arrow in quick maneuvers but also in frontal attacks with heavy armor and long lances. With their new form of cavalry, the Arabs inaugurated the cavalry age, which lasted in Eurasia until the 1400s when firearms became sufficiently effective to swing the advantage back toward infantries.

Under the reign of Abd al-Malik (685–705), the first signs of a religious orientation in the Arab Empire became visible. Earlier coins minted in the empire made no religious pronouncements, although the rulers were depicted with Christian crosses. By contrast, on a coin of 687, Abd al-Malik inscribed the formula "in the name of God, *muhammad* the servant of God." The meaning of the Arabic word is ambiguous, for it can be read either as the name of the prophet called "Muhammad" or as the epithet "the Praiseworthy." Accordingly, the inscription would read either as "Muhammad is the servant of God" or as "the Praiseworthy Servant of God." In the context of the inscription, this servant is Jesus.

The discussion among historians on how to read the word has barely begun and is still marred by polemics. However this discussion will be settled, one conclusion can definitely be drawn: Abd al-Malik had a strong interest in shaping religious doctrine for the empire. Since Arab coins from the 690s show Christ with either a flaming halo or a sword, indicative of his second coming, we can furthermore conclude that Abd al-Malik saw himself as the last **caliph** (from Arabic *khalifa*, or representative of God) before the end of time who would turn over his Islamic or Christian caliphate to God or Christ at the Last Judgment.

Caliph: Representative of God, later of Muhammad, on earth.

Abd al-Malik's view of the end of time led him to renew Arab efforts to take over Byzantium. (According to convention in recent scholarship, the Roman Empire after 640 is called "Byzantium.") Umayyad armies composed of Arabs and Berbers conquered Byzantine North Africa in 686–698, reducing Byzantium to Anatolia, the Balkans, and parts of Italy. Once North Africa was conquered, Abd al-Malik's successors became entangled in western Christian politics. In 711, dissident Visigothic nobles called Berber and Arab troops into the Iberian Peninsula to help them in their bid to oust the dominant Visigothic king. After destroying the Visigothic kingdom, the Berbers, Arabs, and Visigothic allies divided Iberia among themselves.

Two decades later, the Iberian Berbers and Arabs pushed into France. One of these raids is commemorated in western Christianity as the Battle of Tours in central France (732 or 733). Here, the founder of the western Christian Carolingian Empire, Charles Martel (r. 714–741), beat back the invading raiders. Similarly, Arab campaigns in the Caucasus to take the Russian steppes failed around 740. By contrast, in the east of the Arab Empire, Persian and Arab troops advanced to the lower

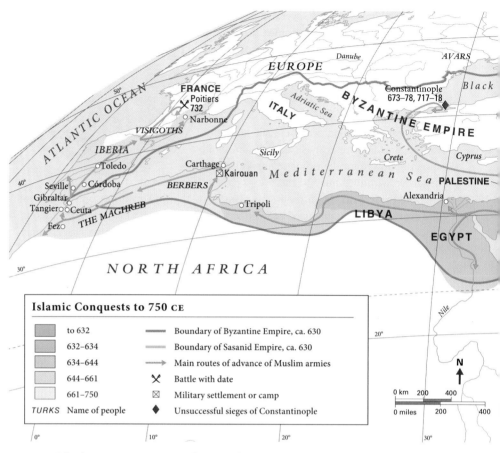

MAP **10.1** **Islamic Conquests to 750s, According to Tradition.**

Indus valley, as well as Turkestan in central Asia, at the western end of the Silk Road from China. In 751, a Persian-Arab army defeated Chinese and Uighur forces and turned the Silk Road into an Arab caravan route.

Arabs disappointed in the setbacks of the Umayyad conquests, however, turned to a radical movement that renewed Abd al-Malik's preaching of the end of time. In 750 they succeeded in overthrowing the Umayyad dynasty. The movement began in the distant province of Khurasan with local Persian military lords and Arab settlers, stirring them to arise under the banner of a "rightly guided" leader (*Mahdi*, or Messiah) and establish a realm of justice on earth at the end of time. The beneficiary of the overthrow was the new dynasty of the Abbasids, who derived legitimacy from their claim to belong to the "family of Muhammad" from which the Mahdi would rise. In order to distinguish themselves from the Umayyads, the Abbasid caliphs moved the capital from Damascus to the newly founded city of Baghdad in the center of Iraq, an agriculturally highly productive province since Sasanid times (see Map 10.2).

The Mahdi, however, did not arrive and the Abbasids quickly squashed all end-of-time expectations. They also realized that the far-flung Arab Empire could be governed only if they bestowed autonomy to the provinces of Iberia, North Africa, Egypt, Iran, and central Asia. Emirates (from Arabic *amir*, or "leader")

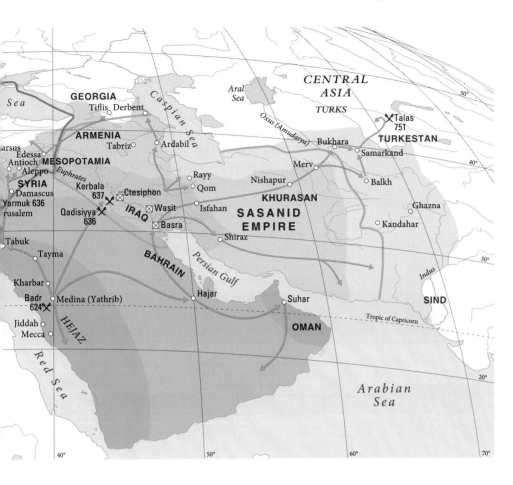

under provincial leaders developed their own administrative and fiscal offices and pursued conquests of their own. The Abbasids themselves maintained an active military front against the Byzantines in Anatolia. In the early 800s, the Abbasids' emphasis shifted from territorial expansion to consolidation, focusing on the development of the new civilization of Islam. A world region emerged that was no longer ruled by a single emperor but was instead a commonwealth of states in which Islamic religious civilization formed.

The Beginnings of Islamic Civilization   At the center of the emerging new Islamic civilization, Baghdad became a magnet for the bright and ambitious in the Middle East and Mediterranean. Christians, Jews, and Zoroastrians settled with their intellectual, literary, and artistic heritages in this metropolis of several hundred thousand inhabitants. The Abbasid caliphs established an institute for advanced study (*dar al-hikma,* "house of wisdom," 813–833), to which they invited scholars from across the Islamic world as well as Byzantium. At this institute and elsewhere during the 800s and early 900s, teams of scholars translated large numbers of legal, philosophical, scientific, and literary works from Syro-Aramaic, Greek, Pahlavi, and Sanskrit into Arabic. By interacting with the cultural heritages of the conquered provinces, Muslims engaged in a selective adaptation to these heritages

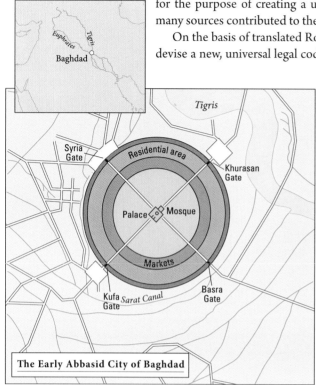

The Early Abbasid City of Baghdad

MAP 10.2 **The Early Abbasid City of Baghdad.**

Sunna: The way of life prescribed as normative for Muslims on the basis of the traditions about the teachings and practices of Muhammad.

for the purpose of creating a unified religious civilization. Thus, influences from many sources contributed to the shaping of Islamic civilization.

On the basis of translated Roman law handbooks, the caliphs had legal scholars devise a new, universal legal codex to replace the diverse legal systems inherited in the provinces from pre-Islamic times. The court jurist Muhammad al-Shaybani (d. 805) used Roman law to arrange caliphal case law in the same way as Roman jurists did but in addition provided it with a religious grounding. He declared the individual laws to be based on pronouncements of Muhammad, called *hadiths*. These pronouncements, taken together, became subsequently known as the **Sunna**, that is, the "path" of Muhammad to be emulated by each Muslim.

The Separation of State and Religion

The caliph's claim for divinely based legislative authority did not go unopposed in the first half of the 800s. At this time, a debate developed between the government lawyers and theologians, on one hand, and critics in the population at large, on the other. The latter claimed that all doctrines and laws of Islam had been revealed to the Prophet Muhammad and that the caliphs had no right to add any new ones. The critics busily collected traditions far more numerous than those employed by Shaybani, provoking the government to denounce them as forgers who invented hadiths for their own political purposes. Other traditionalists gained popular support with their literalist doctrine of the Quran as the eternal word of God, while the government theologians rejected this doctrine as incompatible with the notion of God's transcendence. In a more general sense, the debate between the caliphal government and the traditionalist opposition pitted the proponents of a figurative interpretation of scripture (Quran and Sunna) against the proponents of a literal interpretation.

In order to break the opposition of the traditionalists, the caliph decreed in 833 that all religious scholars and jurists occupying government positions had to swear a loyalty oath (*mihna*) in support of caliphal legislation. Supported by a reported groundswell of popular support in Baghdad, however, a minority of traditionalists refused to give the oath, even going to jail for their conviction. Unnerved, in 849 the government ended the enforcement of its decree.

Although the caliphs continued to rely on religious advisors to their liking, they gradually gave up their legislative powers. Around 950, the two sides reached a compromise, in which the caliphs gave up any further legislation in return for the religious scholars recognizing the caliphs' executive power. Caliphs and opposition agreed to share in the administration of scripture: The religious scholars were to be the interpreters of the Quran and Sunna, while the caliphs were the only authorities to apply law and theology. The compromise resulted in an early instance of separation between state and religion. This separation became the basic characteristic of

Sunni Islam, the branch to which the vast majority of Muslims subsequently adhered and still adhere today.

Sunni and Shia Islam

At its core, **Sunnism** consists of five basic ritual obligations, the so-called Five Pillars: the profession of faith, prayer, fasting, alms giving, and pilgrimage to Mecca. The profession of faith is summed up in the formula "There is no God but God and Muhammad is his messenger." The five-times daily prayer requires the washing of hands and feet for ritual cleanliness and the performance of a sequence of bodily motions and prayers. On Fridays the noon prayer is to be performed in the congregational mosque. Fasting means a month-long abstinence from food, drink, and sex during the daylight hours. Alms giving is a small (2.5 percent) donation or tax to the poor, and the pilgrimage is a journey made at least once in one's life to Mecca. The adherents of minority **Shiism** observe the Five Pillars with the key addition of an additional prayer formula in praise of Ali, Muhammad's relative, who is considered by the followers of this minority branch of Islam, the Shiites, to have been the true successor of the Prophet. According to Muslim doctrine, fulfillment of these basic religious obligations defines a "good" Muslim in the eyes of God.

Abbasid Glory. Little is left of the Abbasid splendor during the 800s since Iraq suffered several invasions in later history, in which palaces, mosques, and other structures were destroyed. This is the eighth-century Abbasid palace of Ukhaydir, south of Baghdad. The palace included gardens, baths, residential suites, courtyards, and audience halls.

The Abbasid Crisis

During the second half of the 800s—around the same time that religion and state were beginning to separate—there was a fiscal crisis in the caliphal administration in Iraq. The Sasanid Persian expansion of agriculture between the Euphrates and Tigris Rivers, continued by the Abbasids, reached the limits of its potential in the mid-800s. The soil became too salty due to poor drainage in the fields in the flat terrain of lower Iraq. Crop yields declined and agricultural tax revenue shrank. As a result, the administration found it increasingly difficult to pay the military, causing its officers to take over still fertile tax districts directly as personal assignments.

Shiism: Minority faith in Islamic civilization, based on the figure of the Hidden Imam, who is expected at the end of time to establish a realm of justice in which state and religion are one.

At the same time, there was a generational shift in ethnic composition in the ruling class from Arabs and Persians to Turks from central Asia. Muslim slave raiding parties had captured non-Muslim boys and girls during campaigns into Turkish central Asia. Merchants sold these youths to the caliphs in Baghdad, where they were trained in the palace and converted to Islam. From 861 to 945, Turks seized power over the Abbasid caliphs in Baghdad while retaining the caliphs as titular heads of the government. The main function of the Turkish generals was the control of political affairs in Iraq. But they also provided important military services. Like their Umayyad predecessors, the Abbasids devoted themselves to the completion of the jihad against the eastern Christian empire of Byzantium in order to fulfill the original dream of uniting the Sasanid and Byzantine Empires into one single Islamic Empire—the last one before the end of time, to be handed over to God at the Last Judgment.

Byzantium: Survival and Recovery

Under siege by the Umayyads and Abbasids, the old eastern Roman Empire, now "Byzantium," had retreated to Anatolia and parts of the Balkans. It survived because its emperors reconstituted the state on a new military and religious basis: locally organized border defense and redefinition of Christian doctrine. Fortunately, its capital, Constantinople, was situated at a significant distance from the Muslims and was protected by thick walls on a nearly impregnable peninsula on the European side of the Bosporus, astride the entrance to the Black Sea. Under difficult circumstances, Byzantine emperors overcame outside attacks by Muslims and Norsemen and the loss of the Balkans to the Slavs and Bulgars, as well as internal religious conflicts. When the principality of Kiev in modern-day Ukraine adopted Christianity, Byzantium eventually changed into a commonwealth of eastern Christianity similar to the Islamic one of the Abbasids.

Survival Strategies   Under constant Arab pressure in eastern Anatolia and northern Africa (636–863), the Byzantine Empire shrank to a small Anatolian–Balkan realm. Both the Umayyad and Abbasid caliphs either led or sent invasion forces a total of seven times between 653 and 838 by land and sea to attack Constantinople. The empire survived the onslaught only by completely reorganizing its armed forces. Emperors after Heraclius restructured the mobile field armies into four stationary cavalry and auxiliary infantry regiments settled in Anatolia along the border with the Arab Empire. To reinforce these regiments, the emperors withdrew troops from the Balkans, which they abandoned to recently arrived Slavic tribes.

A nucleus of Slavs probably originated in the large lowland area extending from Poland eastward across modern Belarus and northern Ukraine into northwestern Russia. They, together with people of other ethnic backgrounds, migrated in the 500s from there southward into the Balkans, the Ukraine, and eastern Russia. Although linguistically related, in the Balkans the Slavs became a composite ethnic population, incorporating speakers of other languages, such as Turkish-speaking groups of Bulgars from eastern Russia. These Bulgars migrated in the 500s to the Byzantine lower Danube, where they were influenced by Slavic culture and asserted their independence from the empire in 681. As the Byzantines were fighting for survival against the Arabs in Anatolia, the Bulgars became a major power in the Balkans.

External and Internal Threats   The Anatolian regiments of Byzantium were known as "themes" (Greek *themata*). New research has demonstrated that the central administration in Constantinople recruited the themes from among volunteers in the interior Byzantine provinces. It paid them in cash and food provisions, which were collected as taxes from estates and free farmers. Since the 25,000 cavalry troops making up the Anatolian themes were only half the number of their Muslim opponents, cunning had to substitute initially for brute force. The themes' main task was to shadow and harass their mightier Arab rivals, waiting for a lucky moment to strike back. One effect of these tactics was an impoverishment of the Anatolian interior, which suffered deeply from constant Muslim raids. Provincial life in Anatolia became increasingly hard for its Christian inhabitants, and even Constantinople declined in wealth.

Iconoclasm: Removal of all religious images from churches and monasteries during a period in the Byzantine Empire, under orders of the emperors and patriarchs of Constantinople.

Throughout this difficult period the Byzantine emperors continued to be active in the shaping of religious doctrine and law. One of the most important religious disputes to wrack the empire was the **iconoclasm** controversy (726–787 and 814–842). Christians of all theological directions had been embroiled for centuries in controversies over the visual depiction of Jesus and Mary. By the eighth century proponents argued for a total ban on holy pictures and statues, based on the biblical injunction against "graven images." In 726 the emperor Leo III (r. 717–741) decided to reform Christian theology by imposing a ban on all such art (*ikons*). He ordered the destruction of religious art, hence the term *iconoclasm*—smashing the icons. The reform pitted the emperor and his clerical advisors against the imperial church hierarchy, including the papacy in Rome, which defended what it considered the legitimate tradition of Christian imagery. As in the case of the Islamic traditionalists insisting on the literal reading of the Quran, eastern Christian traditionalists sided with church practices which were widely shared by ordinary believers.

Even though belief in God *and* divine images violated strict interpretations of monotheism—as with the doctrine of God's transcendence in Islam—for ordinary believers such imagery was seen as a tangible link to the divine. Pressured by popular demand, in 842 the Byzantine emperor, like the Abbasid caliph a few years later, ended his control over religion and law. Although the emperors did not become figureheads like the caliphs, their authority nevertheless was considerably diminished vis-à -vis an invigorated church hierarchy. As we will see shortly, similar disengagement between politics and religion occurred in western Christianity during the investiture conflict two centuries later. In this respect, the religious civilizations of Islam, Byzantium, and western Christianity followed similar patterns of development.

Transformation into a Commonwealth   As the internal doctrinal quarrel over iconoclasm was being settled in the mid-800s, the strategy of using themes to harass and carry out counterstrikes against the Muslims in Anatolia finally paid off. By exploiting the fiscal crisis of the Abbasids, theme commanders were able to go on the offensive and raid Arab settlements in eastern Anatolia and northern Iraq. A century later, in 965, Byzantium regained all of Anatolia and the emperors were able to turn their attention to the Balkans. Here, the Bulgars had converted to eastern Christianity in 864 and, under their own emperors, had forced Byzantium to pay tributes in the early 900s. But in 971, the Byzantines crushed the Bulgars and reintegrated their realm into the empire. Toward the middle of the eleventh century, Byzantium encompassed again a respectably large territory, extending from Belgrade across the Balkans some 1,100 miles southeast to Antioch in northern Syria (see Map 10.3).

The settlement of the iconoclasm controversy and recovery of imperial power formed the background for the transformation of Byzantium into a commonwealth of Christianity in eastern Europe. In the late 700s, Kiev in the Ukraine had emerged as a western outpost of the large, ethnically Turkish, and religiously mixed Jewish, Christian, and Muslim Khazar realm in southern Russia. The traders in Kiev were "Rus" (from which the name "Russia" is derived), of Scandinavian Norsemen (Viking or Varengian) origin. By the 800s, most had intermarried with Slavs and become culturally Slavic. The Rus traded furs from Scandinavia and the Urals and wine from western Europe for Indian spices and Chinese silk, traveling on the Dnieper and Volga Rivers and the Baltic Sea between the Abbasid and Carolingian Empires. In addition to trading, the Rus repeatedly raided Byzantium, thereby adding to the difficulties of the empire during the 800s and early 900s. By the mid-900s, Rus trading and raiding had made Kiev a regional power.

In 988, Grand Prince Vladimir I of Kiev (r. 980–1015) decreed the conversion of his subjects to Christianity. The conversion was part of a deal whereby Vladimir would convert and receive a Byzantine princess for marriage if he would assist the emperor Constantine VII with Kievan troops against internal rebels. With

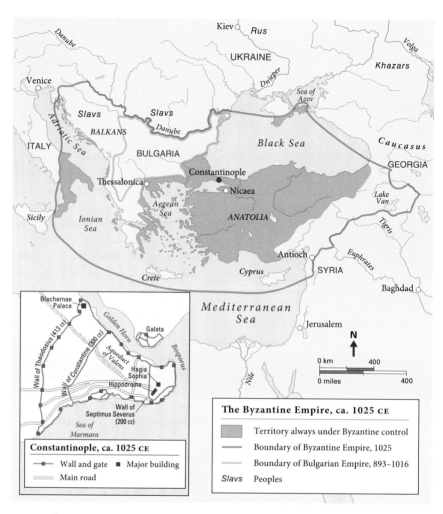

MAP **10.3** The Byzantine Empire, ca. 1025 CE

this conversion of the Ukraine, eastern Christianity expanded beyond the Byzantine Empire into the much larger region of Russia. Thus, a commonwealth of states emerged in this region similar to that of Islam.

Islamic Civilization in the Commonwealth of Dynastic States, 900–1300

In the Islamic commonwealth in the early 900s, the Fatimid caliphate challenged the rule of the Abbasids as well as the Umayyads of Iberia. (In 756, an Umayyad refugee prince had declared an independent emirate in Iberia.) In a parallel development, Islamic civilization took root among non-Arabs on the margins of the commonwealth, among such peoples as the Berbers in North Africa and the Turks in central Asia. These newly converted people migrated into the Islamic heartland, establishing new states which assumed leadership in the commonwealth. But this leadership was short-lived since western Christians (such as the Spanish kings and the European crusaders) as well as central Asian Mongols similarly established themselves

through conquest. For about two centuries, from 1100 to 1300, political instability reigned until the Egyptian Mamluks defeated the crusaders and Mongols. When the Mongols converted to Islam, Islamic civilization returned to its previous condition of competitive politics in a commonwealth of states.

The Fatimid Challenge   The Abbasid fiscal difficulties and declining power encouraged the formation of a new group of oppositional Muslims, the party (*shi`a*) of Ali. Islamic tradition projects the origins of the Shi`a to an early period of the Arab Empire (656–685), but the Shiites, as the followers of this minority branch of Islam are called, emerged as identifiable believers only in the second half of the 800s. At that time, their leaders claimed to be descendants of Muhammad via a different line from that of the Abbasids: Instead of an uncle of the Prophet, they claimed the Prophet's daughter Fatima and her husband Ali (in Islamic tradition also the cousin of Muhammad) as their ancestors. The eldest male in each generation since the 600s was held to have been infallible, possessing knowledge of the "inner" or figurative meaning of the Quran. He, therefore, was empowered to issue new doctrines and laws, in contrast to the Sunni caliph. He was also entitled to be the leader (imam) of the Islamic community. However, since the Abbasids were the reigning titular rulers in the commonwealth, Shiite leadership remained purely theoretical. In contrast to the Sunni religious scholars who had wrested the power to control doctrine and law away from the Abbasids, the Shiites acknowledged leaders who claimed full powers over doctrine and law, even though in practice these leaders were private persons keeping a low profile to protect themselves from the Abbasid police.

According to Shiite tradition, the line of firstborn males descended from Fatima and Ali died out in 874. This event was at the root of the belief that the last childless imam went into hiding and would return at the end of time as the Mahdi, or "rightly guided one." As the Savior or Messiah, he would establish a realm of justice. Since the last imam was the twelfth in descent, beginning with Ali, the followers became known as Imami or "Twelver" Shiites. There was, however, a minority of so-called Sevener Shiites forming at the end of the 800s, who claimed that the line of descendants had actually ended well before 874, with the seventh imam, who was the one to return as the Mahdi. Followers of this doctrine of the seventh descendant revived the belief in the apocalypse, suppressed earlier by the Abbasids, and expected the

The Byzantine Commonwealth. Characteristic of eastern Christianity are the many churches dedicated to Hagia Sophia, "holy wisdom," which can be found throughout the Byzantine commonwealth, from the Balkans to the Caucasus. Though each region developed its own architectural style, they all organized sacred space in similar ways. A masterpiece of design and engineering based in part on the theories of the third-century BCE mathematician Archimedes, the Church of Hagia Sophia in Constantinople was dedicated in 537 by the emperor Justinian on the foundations of an earlier structure (a). Its massive dome was often compared to the great dome of heaven itself, and the church would become the prototype for many others throughout the commonwealth in subsequent centuries, including the Cathedral of Saint Sophia in Kiev, whose foundations were laid early in the eleventh century (b). While it exhibits a distinctly Kievan style of church architecture, including over a dozen cupolas, the cathedral nonetheless embodies an unmistakable Byzantine tradition whose roots extend deep into the past.

Mahdi's return and the establishment of the realm of justice to occur prior to the year 300 AH (after hijra, i.e., 912 CE). They engaged in underground preaching and agitation against the Abbasid regime. Followers of the idea of the twelfth descendant were quietists, waiting for his arrival without calculating the date and willing to endure Abbasid rule.

Propagandists among the Sevener Shiites or Fatimids chose the faraway province of eastern Algeria in the early 900s to preach their revolutionary cause to remote mountain Berbers, who probably were not yet Muslims. After coming to power, the first Fatimid imam claimed to be the Mahdi at the end of time, who would conquer the Abbasids and bring justice to the world. At the head of Berber armies, the imam's successors created a powerful empire in North Africa, Egypt, Syria, and western Arabia (909–1171). But the revolutionary zeal gradually died down, and by the eleventh century it was clear that the Fatimid countercaliphate was unable to expand from Syria to Iraq and replace the Abbasids.

A similar initial effort of the Fatimids to conquer Iberia fizzled early. Here, the governing Umayyad caliphs, descendants from a refugee of the defeat in 750 at the hands of the Abbasids, arrested a Fatimid advance party sent to probe the weak spots in the Iberian emirate. In response, the Umayyads elevated the peninsula in 929 into a caliphate in its own right, in competition with both the Fatimids and Abbasids. Meanwhile, in 945 there was a change of leadership in Baghdad. In the place of the military regime of Turkish generals, the new military regime of Persian Buwayhids from the Caspian Sea confined the Abbasids to their palace. The Buwayhid generals were Twelver Shiites opposed to revolutionary beliefs and with no interest in making common cause with the Fatimid Seveners. Like their Turkish predecessors, the Buwayhids retained the Abbasids as figureheads, even though they disagreed with the latter's Sunnism. By the mid-900s, a commonwealth of three competing caliphates and numerous provincial dynasties in Arabia, Iran, and Turkmenistan had emerged within Islamic civilization (see Map 10.4).

The Great Mosque of Córdoba. This congregational mosque, called *Mezquita* in Spanish, was built in the years following 784 and was enlarged twice until it reached its final dimensons in 987. To heighten the ceiling, the architects topped the short marble pillars taken from Roman ruins with brick pillars and double arches, covered in white and red plaster. Light entered through three domes above the wall facing Mecca.

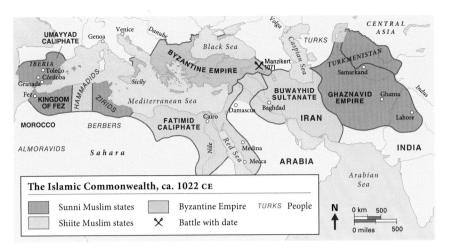

MAP 10.4 **The Islamic Commonwealth, ca. 1022 CE.**

The Umayyads in Iberia

The westernmost competing state, the caliphate of the Iberian Umayyads, covered three-quarters of the peninsula at its height. Visigothic refugees, who in the late 700s had survived precariously in their small mountain refuge in the northwest of the Iberian Peninsula, improved their livelihood in the 800s through raids against the Umayyads and founded a number of small Christian kingdoms. The kings took the apostle James, said to have converted Iberia to Christianity, as their patron saint for the proclamation of the reconquest (Spanish *reconquista*) of Iberia and parts of North Africa, once ruled by the Visigoths, from the Muslims.

In the 900s, however, the Umayyads checked the Christian military advances. The caliphate prospered, thanks to an expanding long-distance trade through the Moroccan Sahara for West African gold. The caliphs and their administrators spent lavish sums on monuments, libraries, court physicians, poets, musicians, and scholars. Umayyad Córdoba became the political and cultural center of the Islamic west, or Maghreb. Perhaps 90,000 inhabitants called the city their home, more than in any other European city except Constantinople. The Córdobans were a cosmopolitan mix of Arab- and Berber-descended Muslims, Islamized Iberians, Arabic-speaking Christian Iberians, and Sephardic Jews, that is, Jews who had migrated from Palestine to Spain during Roman times. By about 1000, Muslims were a majority in the Umayyad caliphate.

The military of the caliphate became increasingly diverse in the early 1000s, with regiments composed of Arabs, Berbers, Christian mercenaries from the north, and military slaves called *saqaliba* [sa-KAH-lee-bah] from the Balkans. The caliphs bought the *saqaliba* from Christian merchants in Venice and Prague, who acquired them from raiding parties roaming in the then not yet fully Christianized parts of eastern Europe. In spite of their wealth, the caliphs lost control over the army, just like their Abbasid colleagues had a century earlier. In 1031, the caliphate disintegrated altogether, leaving a collection of provincial emirates in its wake.

Emboldened, the Christian kings demanded tributes in gold from the Islamic emirates. The emirs had no choice but to pay, given the same problem of heterogeneous troops as in the preceding caliphate. In 1085, the kings grew even bolder and conquered the emirate of Toledo in the center of the peninsula. This conquest was a pivotal event in western Christianity: Thanks to Toledo's collections of Arabic manuscripts containing the Greek heritage, Europe experienced its first outside cultural stimulus (after inheriting Roman culture in 476). The far-reaching consequences of this stimulus for the growth pattern of western Christianity as a religious civilization are discussed in Chapter 11.

To block Christian advances in central Iberia, the remaining Muslim emirates in 1086 turned to the newly Islamized Berber dynasty of the Almoravids (1086–1147) for military support. Astride the Saharan trade route for gold from West Africa, the Almoravids had converted to Islam in the mid-1000s. They and their successors, the Almohads (1147–1269) from the southern Moroccan mountains, held power among the Iberian Muslims and stopped the Christian *reconquista* for nearly two centuries. Under the Almohads, who sponsored theology, law, philosophy, medicine, and architecture, Islamic civilization in the west experienced its most active period.

Almohad dominance, however, did not last long. Both Almoravids and Almohads were handicapped by the economic weakness of their North African base. The central Moroccan plains were too small to support numerous villages and large cities. The two dynasties did not dispose of sufficient manpower and tax resources to stabilize their initial conquests and recruit new troops in North Africa. The Christian kings succeeded in 1212 at inflicting a crushing defeat on the Almohads, forcing them to retreat back to North Africa. Only the well-protected Muslim mountain kingdom of Granada in southern Iberia, with its rich silk, cotton, and sugar cane production and flourishing Mediterranean trade, remained under Muslim rule for several more centuries (1238–1492).

The Seljuk Turks and Byzantium   Similar to the conversion of the pagan Berbers to Islam under the Almoravids and Almohads in Morocco, there was a contemporaneous Islamization process among the Turks in the steppes of eastern Russia and western central Asia around the Ural Mountains. Turkish rulers astride the Volga trade route to the Baltic Sea had initiated this process in the early 900s and a century later Turks east of the Ural Mountains converted to Islam. Among the converts was a Turkish confederation led by the Seljuks [Sel-JOOKS], a dynasty of rulers that conquered the steppes from Turkmenistan to Iran and Iraq. In 1055–1059, these rulers ended the Buwayhid regime in Baghdad and assumed power under the title "sultan" (from the Arabic for "power"). As newcomers to Islam, the Seljuk sultans made themselves champions of campaigns against Christians and heretical Muslims, among whom they counted the Fatimids. In eastern Anatolia they defeated the Byzantines at Manzikert in 1071, and in Syria they conquered Damascus from the Fatimids in 1079. By the early 1080s, the Seljuks had become rulers of a large sultanate comprising nearly all of the Middle East, except Egypt (see Map 10.5).

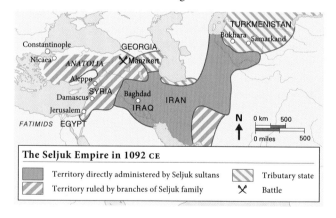

The Seljuk Empire in 1092 CE

| Territory directly administered by Seljuk sultans | Tributary state |
| Territory ruled by branches of Seljuk family | Battle |

MAP 10.5 **The Seljuk Empire in 1092 CE.**

The Seljuk defeat of the Byzantines was possible because of a change of policies that had taken place in Constantinople during the 900s and early 1000s. After the theme commanders had regained eastern Anatolia and northern Syria from the Muslims, the emperors—concerned about the rising power of these commanders—had systematically expanded their palace regiments stationed in Constantinople, avoiding recourse to the themes. Included among the palace regiments were contingents of Norman mercenaries from France. Altogether, these regiments, however, were not large enough without theme reinforcements to halt the Seljuks. After a resounding victory at the battle of Manzikert in Armenia 1071, the Seljuks advanced across Anatolia to Nicaea, which they took in 1087, bringing them within 100 miles of Constantinople.

By this time, Emperor Alexios I (r. 1081–1118) was thoroughly alarmed. He was wary of his Norman mercenaries in the palace guards who had developed ambitions of their own, conquering Sicily from the Muslims as well as invading Byzantine Greece. In spring 1095, the emperor requested military aid from Pope Urban II (r. 1088–1099), in the hope that he would receive western European soldiers more reliable than the Normans to reinforce his palace troops and beat back the Seljuks.

The Crusader Kingdom of Jerusalem

As we will see in Chapter 11, Urban II granted Alexios' request, taking into consideration a number of his own religious and political ambitions vis-à-vis the European kings. The pope and his clergy preached what was later called the Christian "Crusade" to an enthusiastic nobility chafing under efforts by the French and English kings at political centralization. On their way during 1096–1099 from western Europe to the Middle East, the crusaders returned Nicaea to Byzantium and captured Jerusalem. They overcame extremes of hot and cold weather, disease, and the determined resistance of the Seljuks as well as the Fatimids (who had reconquered Jerusalem from the Seljuks in 1098); but in all likelihood the Crusade probably would have failed had it not been for the timely disintegration of the unified Seljuk realm after the death of its sultan in 1092.

By the mid-1100s, the crusader kingdom centered on Jerusalem had evolved into a strategically placed, well-organized, 300-mile-long state along the Syrian and Palestinian coast (see Map 10.6). It possessed fortified seaports and a string of defensive castles on the edge of the desert east of the Jordan River. Two further Crusades and newly founded military orders which recruited unmarried knights in Europe provided a minimum of cavalry

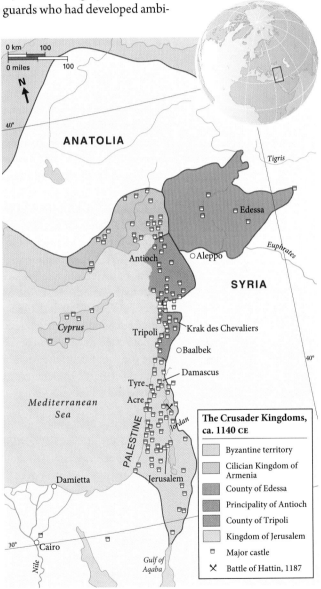

MAP 10.6 The Crusader Kingdoms, ca. 1140 CE.

The Crusader Kingdoms, ca. 1140 CE

- Byzantine territory
- Cilician Kingdom of Armenia
- County of Edessa
- Principality of Antioch
- County of Tripoli
- Kingdom of Jerusalem
- ☐ Major castle
- ✕ Battle of Hattin, 1187

forces to defend the kingdom. Traumatized at first by the unanticipated appearance of the crusaders, who they considered to be barbarian cousins of the Byzantines, the Seljukids (successors of the Seljuks) recovered gradually and, in the middle of the twelfth century, regained the initiative.

Saladin [Arabic Salah al-Din] (r. 1174–1193), the Kurdish successor of the Fatimids in Egypt and Seljukids in Syria, nearly ended the crusader kingdom in 1187. He trapped and destroyed almost the entire military forces of the kingdom in the Battle of Hattin near the Sea of Galilee and reconquered Jerusalem. But a remnant of these forces was able to reconstitute a small kingdom limited to the coast, with Acre as its capital. This state survived for another century, until 1291, because Venice and Genoa made it a commercially viable transit zone for Indian spices and Chinese silk via the Gulf of Aqaba. Since the Muslims profited from this trade as well, they tolerated the small crusader state.

Beginning in the mid-1200s, however, it was only a question of time before the crusader kingdom would become the victim of new and powerful political forces arising in the Middle East. In 1250 the Mamluks—Turkish military slaves from the Russian steppes and dominant in the armies of Saladin's successors—established their own regime in Egypt (1250–1517). Barely in power, in 1260 the Mamluks had to face the Mongols, who had emerged in the previous half-century under Genghis Khan (r. 1206–1227) and his descendants as a major power (see Chapter 13). The Mongols were conquerors of a giant but loosely organized cavalry-borne empire in central Asia, China, eastern Europe, and the eastern Middle East—so they were tough competition for the Mamluks.

The Mongols stormed into the Middle East in 1255, conquering Iran and Iraq, ending what had remained of the Abbasid caliphate in Baghdad in 1258 and advancing into Syria. After conquering Baghdad, they tolerated the weak crusader kingdom since their main target was the Mamluk sultanate as the last remaining Islamic power in the Middle East. The Mamluks, however, defeated the Mongols in several battles between 1260 and 1281, thanks to their much heavier cavalry, and pushed them from Syria back into Iraq and Iran. Under the name of "Ilkhanids," the Mongols converted to Islam and became linguistically and ethnically Persian. Finally free of the Mongol threat, the Mamluks terminated the crusader state in 1291 with the conquest of Acre. The commonwealth of Islamic dynastic states thus returned to self-determination.

A Shrinking Byzantium
The Crusades had initially helped the Byzantines to halt the losses of imperial territory. Energetic emperors extended eastern Christian sovereignty across western Anatolia and into northern Syria in the middle of the 1100s, where they gained control over the crusader principality of Antioch. But the Fourth Crusade of 1204 reversed these gains. The knights and foot soldiers of the Fourth Crusade were the compliant instruments of a conquest scheme hatched by Venice, the German Hohenstaufen emperor, and a refugee claimant of the Byzantine throne at the Hohenstaufen court, with the compliance of the pope. As a result, western Christians conquered Constantinople from the Byzantines and established a Latin empire.

After the crusaders stormed Constantinople, Venice plundered the city of its riches and the pope appointed a Catholic archbishop. But the supply of manpower from western Europe did not flow any better to Byzantium than to the kingdom of Jerusalem. By 1261 the emperor of the Byzantine successor state of Nicaea had been able to drive the western Christians from Constantinople. Subsequently, Byzantium regained a semblance of power but within a much smaller territory, limited to western Anatolia and the eastern end of the Balkans.

Islamic and Eastern Christian Civilizations at Their Height

While the western Christians lost the crusader kingdom and Byzantium in the Middle East, they gained the Muslim emirates of Iberia (except for Granada) in western Europe. By 1300, the borders between western and eastern Christianity and Islam were again clearly drawn. At this time, the Mamluk sultanate, victorious against the crusaders and the Mongols, was the richest and most powerful state in the region, enduring for nearly three centuries (1250–1517). It represented Middle Eastern Islamic civilization at its peak, eventually succeeded only by the Ottoman Empire, which then shifted the center of Islamic civilization from Egypt northward to Anatolia and the Balkans.

State and Society in Mamluk Egypt

Few in the Mamluk ruling class spoke Arabic or intermarried with the indigenous population of their realm in Egypt and Syria. The indigenous population in turn possessed its own autonomous institutions, which provided for most of its needs. Although the Mamluks provided military protection, the indigenous population had to pay for it dearly with high taxes and often arbitrary rule.

THE MAMLUK EMPIRE, ca. 1300

The Mamluk State   At the top of the ruling class was the sultan, who controlled the annual purchases of slaves and commanded the largest cavalry regiment. Raiding parties in the Mongol state of the Golden Horde (1241–1502) on the Russian steppes (later on the Caucasus) captured boys and girls from nomadic tribes and sold them to Genoese merchants, who shipped the slaves to Alexandria. The popes protested against the slave trade but to no avail.

Mamluk Cavalry. Mamluk horsemen engaged in military exercises, wielding swords and protected by chainmail armor. Stationed in barracks on Nile islands near Cairo, the pagan, Asian-born but Muslim-educated Mamluks formed a standing army of a dozen regiments that trained daily and could be mobilized within a short time. Their children were not slaves but freeborn Muslims, who were admitted only to auxiliary military units.

Divorce Court. Husband and wife arguing about a divorce before a judge; scene from al-Hariri, *Maqamat* (ms. dated 1222). Hariri's stories, among the most popular during the classical period, involve a poor but eloquent storyteller traveling from town to town in changing disguises but being recognized each time by the fictional author. The stories include occurrences of everyday life, like this divorce.

The Mamluk sultan governed in consultation with a group of a dozen or so emirs, stationed in the provincial cities of Egypt and Syria and each commanding a cavalry regiment of his own. Additional auxiliary troops, both infantry and light cavalry, consisted of sons of Mamluks, tribal nomadic contingents, and freeborn Turks. The sultans maintained a lavish court, which included a splendid kitchen and some of the finest cooks of their time. A large civilian bureaucracy in Cairo, composed of Muslim, Coptic Christian, and Jewish scribes and accountants, staffed the three main ministries—correspondence and archives, tax collection, and army administration. Other officials oversaw the construction and/ or administration of granaries, oil presses, the mint, hospitals, the postal service (including pigeon courier), water supplies, sanitation, stud farms, horse stables, and the hippodrome (for polo games).

Mamluk power was based on a large, state-centered economy. The Mamluks owned buildings and collected rents from residences, mills, ovens, workshops, inns, public baths, and bazaars. They hired large labor forces for the construction or repair of mosques, city walls, fortresses, and water-works. Sultans and emirs even built entire city quarters. They usually paid regular wages to their workers but occasionally also used forced labor. The sultans had their own permanent labor force, which included prisoners and slaves; and they occasionally rented laborers to emirs for large construction projects. From time to time, the sultans sent craftspeople and laborers to Medina and Mecca to keep the pilgrimage sanctuaries in good repair. The importation of timber and metals was a state monopoly, providing the raw material for the shipyards. As consumers of all manner of crafts products, for both military needs and extravagant luxuries, the Mamluks by far outpaced the wealthy urban merchant class. Their military campaigns were occasions for large numbers of craftspeople, traders, storytellers, entertainers, prostitutes, and other hangers-on to find additional employment.

The Religious System   On the intermediate level of authority were the Muslim religious scholars. They were of indigenous Arab origin and often came from a merchant or craftspeople background. If they could afford it, they pursued their scholarship independently. But many depended on appointments by the sultan's administration to positions at courts, mosques, colleges, lodges, orphanages, and hospitals. Although dependent for their personnel on state appointments, these institutions were financially autonomous since they were supported by fees as well as endowments, that is, revenue accruing from urban property or rural farmland originally deeded by pious individuals.

At the head of the juridical system were the chief judges of the four legal traditions in Islamic civilization. These traditions, distinguished by their broader or narrower interpretations of law, were Hanafism (today central Asia, Turkey, Syria, and Iraq), Shafiism (Yemen, East Africa, and Indonesia), Malikism (northern and West Africa), and Hanbalism (Saudi Arabia). In larger cities all four traditions were usually represented. Lower-level judges staffed the courts in towns and large villages. They could decide cases only if an aggrieved party sought relief, as exemplified by the story of Safra at the beginning of this chapter. In preparation for their decisions, judges employed one or two investigators to establish the facts of the legal cases brought before them. In addition to their juridical functions, judges were responsible for the appointment and supervision of the mosque officials (preachers, scripture reciters, and prayer callers). They were also responsible for the office of the market inspector and his deputies. The market inspector was a religious official who prosecuted and punished violations of the public order on markets and thoroughfares, thus cooperating with the Mamluk ruling class for police functions.

Similar to the juridical system, the educational system was based on a combination of state appointments and endowment finances. Primary schools, attached to mosques, taught children to read and write using the Quran and quranic recitation. Colleges (*madrasas*) provided basic instruction in logic, mathematics, and astronomy but focused on a mostly religious curriculum of prophetic traditions, law, and theology. The professors taught courses from specific books assigned to each class, reading and commenting as they went along. Colleges often had substantial libraries, dormitories, and kitchens and provided scholarships to their students. For graduation, a college required a certain number of books to be read and the contents thereof to be mastered. Wealthy urban families sent both boys and girls to primary schools and colleges, and a small number of professors were women. Since education was not compulsory, however, literacy was largely limited to the religious, mercantile, and crafts elites of the urban centers.

Gender Relations   Islamic civilization followed the traditional Middle Eastern patriarchal family system. Within this system, as we saw at the beginning of the chapter, married women had definite rights and were no longer the chattel they were in the Assyrian Empire. But the Muslim Usama Ibn Munqidh (1095–1188) was shocked when he saw the behavior of the men and women in the crusader kingdom: Husbands allowed their wives in public to walk around alone and shake hands and converse with men to whom they were not married. The patriarchal order in Islamic civilization was clearly stricter than that in western Christianity, and Ibn Munqidh had only contempt for crusaders who had such a low sense of honor that they even went home alone when their wives wished to continue their chats (perhaps even flirtations) with other men. Evidently, a significant cultural difference existed between western Christianity and Islamic civilization.

The Urban Working Population   Below the Mamluk ruling class and the intermediate urban elite were craftspeople, laborers, domestics, and farmers. Urban laborers lived in city quarters, which were organized according to religious (Christian, Jewish), ethnic (Arab, Kurdish, Iranian), and, in the case of the Sunni majority, clan ties. The city quarters were not closed communities, however, and always contained minorities.

City quarters, crafts clusters, and neighborhood mosques and lodges were autonomous structures in urban life. Although overseen by appointees of the market inspectors, the residents often engaged in acts of resistance and rebellion against the

Mamluks in times of famine, overtaxation, or arbitrary rule. In addition, Syrian cities, such as Damascus and Aleppo, had a long tradition of rebellious youth gangs fomenting unrest in suburbs and adjacent villages outside the city walls. The gang members wore distinctive hairstyles and cloaks and found their recruits mostly from among ditch diggers, canal dredgers, and brick layers as well as from among the occasional discontented cooks, traders, spinners, and carpenters. During times of peace these gangs collected protection money from owners of workshops and market stalls, inevitably coming into conflict with the market inspectors and their deputies whose turf they invaded. At times of economic or political distress they linked forces across city quarters and transformed themselves into formidable militias, holding down entire Mamluk regiments for days or weeks. Given the relatively slight state–society relations, the gangs provided a degree of protection for society from the state.

Commercial Relations from the Atlantic to the South China Sea

The Persians and Romans had pioneered the trade of gold and silver for subtropical and tropical luxuries during the period 600 BCE–600 CE, as we discussed in Chapter 7. An enormous leap forward in this trade occurred during the rise and flourishing of Islamic civilization in Mamluk Egypt. The Islamic imperial unification of most of the Middle East and the Mediterranean, the urbanization process exploding in its wake, and the western Christian recovery after ca. 1050 all contributed to this leap. In short, an Afro-Eurasian world commercial system, extending from West Africa to China and regularly connected by seasonal travel, emerged where there had been none before. The accounts that the Moroccan-born scholar Ibn Battuta (1304–1369) left of his 30 years of journeying along the trade routes from West Africa to China provide an invaluable source of information about the cultures and peoples that were connected by this vast network (see Map 10.7).

Trade Routes and Commerce   To understand the West Africa–China world trade, we begin with West Africa. Villagers mined gold in the rain forest on the upper Niger and Senegal Rivers and traded with African merchants from Islamic kingdoms located along the middle Niger. The kings sent raiding parties to other regions in the rain forest to capture slaves. Merchants and kings then sold the gold and surplus of slaves not employed in the kingdoms to visiting Muslims from North Africa and Iberia.

The visitors from the north paid with North African and Iberian manufactures and with salt from mines in the Sahara. In the Mediterranean basin, Muslims, Jews, and western and eastern Christians shared the trade of West African gold (minted into coins) and European timber for Indian and Indonesian spices, dye stuffs, ointments, and cottons as well as Chinese silks, porcelain, and lacquerware. The Mamluks did not allow Christians to travel beyond the Mediterranean, and thus, Muslims, Jews, and Indians were the only ethnic groups who participated in the Indian Ocean and Chinese Sea trade of gold for luxuries.

In addition to these main routes, there were three secondary trade routes. First, there was the overland Silk Road with its gold-for-luxuries trade that connected Iran with China via central Asia. Second, there was the maritime East African trade route, where merchants exchanged manufactures for ivory, gold, and slaves. The

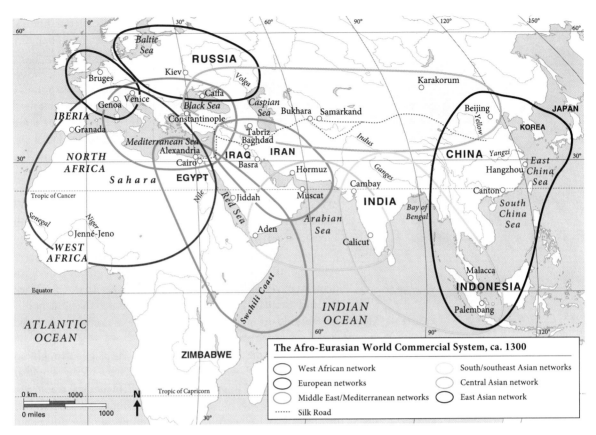

MAP 10.7 **The Afro-Eurasian World Commercial System, ca. 1300.**

latter route connected Egypt and Iraq with the Swahili coastal Muslim city-states along the African coast and the gold mines of Zimbabwe (see Chapter 14). And third, there was the Volga route, where Norman merchants traded gold, silver, spices, ivory, silk, wine, and fur, connecting the Middle East with western Europe. The Mamluk military was a major consumer of the goods that flowed down from the Volga trade route, using Russian and Scandinavian furs for the designation of its ranks. Both primary and secondary trade routes yielded immense supplementary tax revenues, which added to the basic and highly dependable agricultural tax income of the Mamluks.

Islamic and Jewish merchants in the Egyptian center of this network were for the most part wholesalers for whom the import and distribution of eastern luxuries formed only a part of their overall commercial activities. They also organized the regional production and distribution of raw materials, such as textile fibers (wool, flax, cotton, and silk), chemicals for dyeing and tanning, metal ingots for making utensils and jewelry, and pitch for caulking ships' planks. They contracted with craftspeople for the production of soap, glassware, candles, and perfume. Tailors, cobblers, and sugar mill owners delivered robes, slippers, and bags of refined sugar to the merchants. To provide their accountants, scribes, porters, and guards with daily food, these merchants had caterers deliver lunches and dinners to their residences and warehouses. Merchants who were also **tax farmers** maintained grain stores, with employees responsible for collecting, shipping, brokering, and marketing the grain.

Tax farming: A system for collecting taxes and rents from the population, where the state grants the right of collection to private individuals.

Maritime Trade. This image, an illustration in Hariri's *Maqamat* (ms. dated 1236), depicts an oceangoing sailboat used between Arabia and India.

Others "farmed" the taxes from ports or public auction houses. Diversification was the preferred path to consistent profitability in the merchant class.

The Black Death   Extensive travel, however, yielded not only profits but also unforeseen horrors. The more densely people lived together in cities and the more frequently they traveled, the more often they incurred the risk of spreading terrifying and lethal diseases hitherto confined to small, isolated regions of the world. The Black Death of 1346 was the second time that an outbreak of this ghastly plague occurred in world history (the first was the Plague of Justinian in 541, see Chapter 7). Scholars, such as William McNeill and Stuart J. Borsch, agree that the Mongol invasion of Vietnam set off the spread of this horrific mid-fourteenth-century pandemic. The Mongols acquired the bubonic plague bacillus in southeast Asia, one of its permanent breeding grounds, from rodent fleas and dispersed it via China and the Silk Road to the Black Sea area. From here, Genoese merchants carried the virulent disease to the Mediterranean and northwest Europe (see Chapter 11 for a more detailed discussion of ravages of the bubonic plague).

Egyptian sources vividly recount the devastation which the plague wrought on the population. The plague was both sinister and incomprehensible to people at the time who had never experienced it, possessed no effective medical resources, and thus, found themselves powerless to fight it. Similarly difficult to fathom was the recurrence of the plague every generation or so for another century and a half, hitting rulers and subjects; rich and poor; men, women, and children with equally appalling force. Not until the 1500s did Middle Eastern population levels recover to pre-1346 levels.

Religion, Sciences, and the Arts in Two Religious Civilizations

Despite the impact of the Black Death, Mamluk Egypt and reconstituted Byzantium during the 1300s and 1400s were highly active cultural centers. Although they received little further cultural stimuli from outside their civilizations, scholars and artists developed their respective cultures further within traditional boundaries. In Islamic civilization, the most important new cultural phenomenon was mystical Islam, and in eastern Christianity it was a revival of Platonism.

Sufism: Meditative devotion to faith, expressed in the form of prayer, ecstasy, chanting, or dancing.

Islamic Culture: Intellectual and Scientific Expressions

Like a number of other religions we have examined, Islam developed a devotional mystical tradition of its own. Mystical Islam, or **Sufism**, was an outgrowth of meditative thought and practices developed from the Christian, Zoroastrian, and Greek philosophical heritages interacting within the Muslim world. Around 1050 Muslim scholars integrated Sufism into the Sunni-dominated Islamic civilization, and around 1200 Sunni mystics adapted Sufism to Islamic civilization in the form of popular brotherhoods. Educated Muslims, in addition, were conversant in philosophy or the sciences, both of which experienced an important flowering in the period 1050–1300.

Sunni–Sufi Islam The pioneer of Sufism was the Persian Mansur al-Hallaj (858–922), who was a popular preacher in Iraq when Sunnism was not yet fully formed. The proponents of Sunnism accused Hallaj of heresy for claiming identity with God in his moment of ecstasy. They persuaded the political authorities to execute him but were unable to halt the growth of Sufism's popularity. A century and a half later, Sunnis and Sufis agreed to a compromise. The major mystics representing this compromise were the Persian Abd al-Hamid al-Ghazali (1058–1111) and the Iberian Muhyi al-Din Ibn Arabi (1165–1240). Ghazali acquired fame as a figure who succeeded in expanding Islam from the highly technical Sunnism focusing on law to the personal commitment to God. Ibn Arabi provided Muslims with perhaps the most sophisticated conceptualization of God, both in transcendence and in the world. Ghazali and Ibn Arabi struggled with the problem that absolute transcendence can be thought but not experienced unambiguously (see the discussion in Chapter 7). Ghazali introduced a persuasive metaphor to overcome this problem with his wine glass example: Believers, looking at a glass of red wine from a distance, are unable to decide whether they are not instead seeing an empty red glass. God, being both beyond and in the world, can only be "seen" like one sees the one or the other aspect of the glass but never both simultaneously.

Execution of Mansur al-Hallaj. This miniature shows the gruesome last moments of the mystic. Hallaj's sermons included the bold proclamation "I am the Truth," which alluded to one of God's 99 names in Islam. Sunni scholars interpreted this proclamation as blasphemy, hence the trial, condemnation, and execution. Sufis, of course, wrestle with the difficult problem of having to express the simultaneity of God as in the world (present in one's consciousness) and transcendent (utterly other)—this is how "I am the Truth" has to be understood. But it is also easily misunderstood, as the Sunni scholars did.

Through meditative practice, however, so Ghazali and Ibn Arabi taught, Muslims can reduce the ambiguity in thinking/experiencing God. The more Muslims removed themselves, step by step, from the distractions of daily life and focused only on their inner self through meditation, the more they would be able to approach God. In the 1200s, mystics—often revered as saints—founded lodges in which they provided instruction and training in meditative practice for Muslims. With time, these lodges branched out, with hundreds of sublodges organized along the specific practices of its founder saints. The lodges represented widely dispersed brotherhoods in Islam, located in urban centers as well as in rural areas, and even difficult-to-organize nomadic areas. Sunni Muslims of all walks of life joined, from legal scholars and judges to craftspeople, farmers, and nomads. By around 1450, Islamic civilization was a commonwealth not only of competing states but also of competing Sufi brotherhoods. The Sunni–Sufi compromise dominated in Islamic civilization until 1900.

Philosophy and Sciences As in the case of Sufism, philosophers also encountered opposition from among the proponents of early Sunnism and did so for the same reason of violating the transcendence doctrine. Greek philosophical writings were accessible in translation since the 800s and had attracted Muslim thinkers well before the emergence of Sunnism. As in philosophy, scientific texts were also available in translation from around 800 onward. Islamic scientists made major contributions early on, pushing beyond the discoveries of the Greeks. The Greeks had excelled in developing geometry into a mathematical science, but in the absence of a numbering system—they used letters as numbers—they had left algebra undeveloped until the Alexandrian period of Hellenism. The Persian Muhammad Ibn Musa al-Khwarizmi (ca. 780–850) laid the foundations for the conversion of algebra into a science. In his textbooks, computation is based on a decimal system of "Arabic" numerals, from 0 to 9. He borrowed this system from India (where it had been developed 150 years earlier) and introduced algebraic equations for the determination of unknown quantities, expressed through letters, as is still done today.

The proponents of Sunnism in the tenth century left the scientists largely alone, in contrast to Sufis and philosophers. The sciences were useful for the determination of the month of fasting, the direction of prayer toward Mecca, and astrological predictions. After 950, mathematicians developed decimal fractions, raised numbers to high powers, extracted roots from large numbers, and investigated the properties of complex equations with roots and higher-degree powers. Other scientists used applied mathematics in engineering, such as the Arab, al-Jazari (see "Patterns Up Close"). Persian and Arab astronomers simplified the work of the Hellenistic astronomer Ptolemy (d. ca. 168), whose trigonometry was based on an awkward geometric plurality of world centers. Physicists elaborated on Archimedes' investigations into the physics of balances and weights and developed the impetus theory of motion (force applied to thrown objects) adopted in western Christian physics and dominant there until the time of Galileo in the 1500s.

Medicine was based on comprehensive handbooks, with chapters on anatomy, bodily fluids or "humors," diseases, diagnosis, surgery, therapy, and drugs. Specialized medical fields included ophthalmology (the treatment of eye diseases); obstetrics and pediatrics (which also dealt with sexual hygiene, birth, breast-feeding, childhood, and related diseases); and pharmacology, with descriptions of medicinal plants. The discovery in the 1200s of the pulmonary circulation system of the body anticipated similar European medical discoveries by several centuries, underlining the high degree of specialization which the sciences had reached in Islamic civilization.

Artistic Expressions in Islamic Civilization

During the formative period of Islamic civilization (800–950), secular poetry and prose flourished. As Sunni–Sufi Islam fully evolved (1050–1200), religion was interwoven with the telling of stories, the painting of miniatures, and the building of mosques and palaces. Persian artistic traditions reemerged from pre-Islamic times, and Turkish central Asian steppe traditions entered Islamic culture. In the eastern Christian civilization of Byzantium, the arts suffered greatly during the defensive period against the Arabs, Slavs, Bulgars, and Rus of Kiev. They rebounded after 950, and the painting of icons experienced a veritable explosion, making icons the distinctive feature of eastern Christian art.

Islamic Literature   The first extant poems in Arabic were odes celebrating the tribal ethos of courage, trust, generosity, and hospitality in Arabia (800s). They follow the quest theme common to many folktales and myths, with its three distinct stages of loss, marginality, and reintegration that the hero has to experience to find peace. New forms of literature evolved in the cosmopolitan culture of Baghdad, which brought together highly literate secretaries and officials from a variety of non-Arab ethnic backgrounds. They cultivated poetry with urban themes, such as the pleasures of sensual abandonment, seduction, and homosexual love.

Cosmopolitan Córdoba in Iberia was famous for its sensual *muwashshah* [moo-WASH-ah] poetry, which was composed in Arabic but also contained Romance language verses and was influential in the development of medieval troubadour lyrics in western Europe.

Essays expressing refined taste, elegance, and wit also circulated widely in the Baghdad of the 800s, on topics such as "The Art of Keeping One's Mouth Shut," "Against Civil Servants," "Arab Food," "In Praise of Merchants," and "Levity and Seriousness." The most popular collection of short stories was the *Maqamat* about an impersonator telling tall stories to gullible listeners, collecting money for his tales, and traveling from city to city in ever-new disguises. Another collection of stories, the *Arabian Nights*, was first written down in Mamluk Damascus during the 1300s. Even today, one admires the refined taste, elegance, and wit that people of cosmopolitan Islamic urbanity possessed.

Persian and Turkish Muslims preserved their pre-Islamic pasts in epics celebrating the heroic deeds of their ancestral leaders in central Asia. In the case of the Iranians, the poet Firdosi (940–1020) spent a lifetime collecting the traditions of the Persians and rendering them into the 60,000 verses of the *Book of Kings* (*Shahnameh*). The anonymous epic *Dede Korkut* originated among the central Asian Turks at the time of the Arab conquests and was written down in the 1300s. Both ethnic groups also produced outstanding poets, especially mystical poets, among whom the Afghanistan-born Jala al-Din Rumi (1207–1273) acquired worldwide popularity.

Painting and Architecture in Islam

In the visual arts, Arabs and early Muslims embraced the eastern Roman-Sasanid symbolic style which Christians, Jews, and Zoroastrians preferred over the realistic style of the Greeks and Romans. In this style, artists sought to capture the inner essence of their subjects, rather than draw them according to their surface. The distinction was not always rigid however, and Islamic artists sometimes applied subtle techniques of shading and modeling, with which they approached realism.

Moreover, since Islamic law contains prohibitions against painting and sculpting, similar to Byzantine iconoclasm, the visual arts disappeared entirely from public spaces and retreated to the domestic sphere of the households of rulers. The Umayyad and early Abbasid caliphs loved frescoes with hunting, drinking, and dancing scenes but confined them to the chambers of their palaces. The rulers of Granada in the 1400s enjoyed scenes of courtly love in their royal chambers. The Seljuk and Ilkhanid rulers were lavish sponsors of miniature painters, as we have seen in the case of Jazari and his book on mechanical devices. They delighted in richly illustrated biographies and histories, which played the role in their libraries of what we would consider today coffee-table books.

By contrast, the architecture of mosques and palaces was intended for public use, often in commemoration of their state sponsors. Mosques followed the architectural style of the Arab open courtyard and covered prayer hall or Persian open courtyard with surrounding half domes and galleries, both with roots in the pre-Islamic past of the Middle East. Among the surviving palaces, the best preserved is the Alhambra of Granada (ca. 1350–1450), with its exquisite honeycomb-style decorations. Religious and palace architectures were perhaps the most direct forms in which the identity of Islamic culture was expressed. They are still admired today for their variation and richness.

Patterns Up Close | Play Toys for Princes—al-Jazari's Ingenious Mechanical Devices

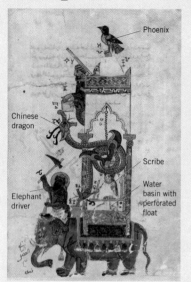

Elephant Clock.

Many Islamic courts employed engineers for entertainment as well as military tasks. One of these engineers was Abu al-Izz al-Jazari (1136–1206) at the court of the Artukid beys (1092–1409) in what is today Diyarbakir, southeastern Turkey. Jazari was a gifted engineer in the Greek and Hellenistic tradition as well as a fine painter of miniatures in the Syrian–Iraqi style. He left us a work entitled *The Book of Knowledge of Ingenious Mechanical Devices* (1206), with descriptions of the devices he built, together with rich illustrations of their functions. It contains chapters on water clocks, drinking machines, music boxes, fountains, water lifting devices, and locks. Many of the devices were driven by water or air and their power was transmitted by pipes, valves, gears, pistons, and crankshafts (the latter a first in history). Precision was achieved through laminating the wooden pieces and sand-grinding the gears and pistons. Unfortunately, we know nothing about Jazari's life, except that his patron commissioned the book.

Mechanical devices also enjoyed wide distribution in the other religious civilizations of the age. Elaborate Chinese water clocks, employing floats, wheels, gears, and chains, were used during the same time period for the determination not only of daily time but also of the imperial Chinese astronomical and astrological calendars. In Europe, monks used simpler water clocks during the

Intellect and the Arts in Byzantium

In contrast to Islamic civilization, the eastern Christianity of Byzantium was a fully formed religious civilization from its beginning in 640, even if it underwent major doctrinal changes thereafter. During its difficult struggle for survival against the Arabs, Slavs, Bulgars, and Rus, Constantinople declined in both wealth and sponsorship of knowledge and the arts. The teaching of the liberal arts inherited from the earlier Roman period barely survived.

The Veroli Casket. We tend to associate Byzantium with religious art, but secular works, such as this tenth century trinket box decorated with scenes from antiquity, provide a different glimpse into Byzantine daily life. The casket's panels depict scenes from Classical mythology. On the left is the hero Bellerophon with the winged horse Pegasus, and on the right is Iphigenia who, according to Euripides, was willing to sacrifice herself so that the Greeks could sail to Troy. The Byzantines consciously cultivated their Greek roots.

The liberal arts included the preparatory *trivium* (grammar, rhetoric, and dialectics), advanced *quadrivium* (arithmetic, geometry, music, and astronomy), and philosophy as the capstone. The Hagia Sophia, for centuries the largest church in the Christian world and seat of the patriarch, the highest eastern Christian official, was about medieval period in monasteries for their prayer hours. The privilege of inventing the first mechanical, weight-driven clock goes to Norwich, England, where the citizens could watch the lapse of time beginning in 1325 on their cathedral tower.

Perhaps the most elaborate device was Jazari's 6-foot-high elephant clock, which contained a water basin with a perforated float inside the elephant. Included in the actions were a phoenix, chirping on top; a scribe in the middle, marking the hours on a dial; and a driver, exhorting the elephant. The hourly mechanism functioned—verified through a modern reconstruction—by a perforated float in the interior of the elephant, slowly filling with water. When full, the float activated a lever connected to a trap, which released a ball on top of the clock. When this ball fell into the mouth of a Chinese dragon (causing the dragon to pivot), it rolled into a container connected to a cymbal and struck the hour. A chain attached to the pivoting dragon's tail lifted the float inside the elephant out of the water. After being drained of the water, the float repeated the mechanical action and did so as long as there were balls in a container on top to drop. What a conversation piece this clock must have been, in the middle of the table around which the bey and his visitors were feasting!

Questions

- How do Jazari's mechanical devices show the many ways classical learning was expressed and adapted in the postclassical era?
- Which specific features of Jazari's clock show the wide diffusion of varied cultural influences across Eurasia during this time?

the only place where eastern Christians could pursue the study of the liberal arts, theology, philosophy, and science.

In the arts, Byzantine iconoclasm during the 700s and 800s caused the destruction of innumerable and irreplaceable icons and mosaics. It also disrupted the transmission of artistic techniques from masters to subsequent generations of artists. When the public display and veneration of images became the officially sanctioned doctrine again in the mid-800s, it took a while for the arts to recover. As artists were relearning their craft, they engaged in much initial experimentation. The subsequent mature period of ca. 950–1200 saw a veritable explosion in the production of icons, mosaics, and frescoes as well as the building of new churches and monasteries. Byzantine mosaic craftspeople and painters were also much sought after by the caliphs in Córdoba, who avoided hiring artists from their Abbasid and Fatimid rivals. Byzantine craftspeople were also popular with the princes of Kiev, who, after their conversion, carried the Byzantine arts into the commonwealth of eastern Christian states.

The Latin disruption of 1204–1261 saw again a tremendous loss of Byzantine art as well as manuscripts, this time to Venetian pillage after the Fourth Crusade. When Byzantium recovered, Plato scholars initiated a strong philosophical recovery, which resulted in a return of western Christians, this time peacefully, to that city in search of Platonic writings. The Academy of Florence invited Byzantine Plato scholars, and further scholars emigrated to Italy after the fall of Constantinople to the Ottomans in 1453. Thus, western Christianity renewed its adaptation to stimuli from a neighboring civilization, in contrast to eastern Christianity and Islamic civilization, which continued within their existing traditions.

Putting It All Together

Both Islamic civilization and eastern Christian civilization were based on a synthesis of religious revelation and Greek philosophy and science. This synthesis had begun in the Roman and Sasanid Persian Empires. Muslims accomplished their cultural synthesis after the period of Arab conquest, roughly during 800–950. Eastern Christians completed their synthesis in the period 950–1050, after their recovery from the Arab, Slav, Bulgar, and Rus onslaughts. Both refined their internal civilizational achievements to a high degree well into the 1400s. Thereafter, they did not absorb substantial new cultural stimuli from the outside until about 1700 when the Muslim Ottoman sultans and the Russian czar Peter the Great invited western Europeans to reform their respective empires.

Islamic civilization was an outgrowth of the Arab conquests in the Middle East, central Asia, northern Africa, and Europe in the 600s and early 700s. It emerged as an adaptation of the Arabs to the heritages of the Jews, Christians, Greeks, Romans, and Persians. Its core was the monotheism of Allah, and its cultural adaptations were to Greek philosophy and science, Roman law, Persian statecraft, as well as a variety of artistic and architectural traditions of the Middle East and Mediterranean. At its height, during 950–1450, a commonwealth of competing Islamic states represented Islamic civilization. This ethnically diverse commonwealth with Arab, Turkish, Persian, and Berber rulers and states shared a number of common characteristics, among which were the same canon of scriptures (the Quran and the Sunna), laws and moral norms (sharia), and religious institutions (separate state and religious authorities as well as Sunni–Sufi brotherhoods). These characteristics endured to 1450.

The Byzantine Empire succeeded the Roman Empire around 640 when the emperors, under attack by the Arabs, reorganized their military forces and redefined the inherited Christian theology. This Christianity acquired its specific eastern identity by becoming clearly separate from the other Christianities outside the Byzantine Empire, such as Catholic western European, Syrian and Egyptian Monophysitic, and Asian Nestorian Christianities. Byzantium recovered politically and culturally in the mid-900s, and the empire changed into a commonwealth when Russian Kiev converted to eastern Christianity. Unfortunately, the recovery lasted only a century. The Seljuk Muslim Turks conquered most Anatolian provinces of Byzantium (1071–1176), and the Venetians conquered Constantinople in the Fourth Crusade (1204–1261). Byzantium recovered thereafter for another two and a half centuries and even flourished culturally, but after 1453 the center of eastern Christian civilization would shift northward to Russia.

▶ For additional resources, including maps, primary sources, visuals, and quizzes, please go to www.oup.com/us/vonsivers. Please see the Further Resources section at the back of the book for additional readings and suggested websites.

Thinking Through Patterns

▶ **Why can the period 600–1450 be described as the age of religious civilizations? How do eastern Christian and Islamic civilizations fit this description?**

The adoption of Christianity and Zoroastrianism as state or privileged monotheistic religions in the Roman and Sasanid Empires was late and ultimately did not prevent these empires from eventual collapse. But both empires helped launch the period of religious civilizations. New empires arose in this period, beginning around 600. Byzantium was Christian from its inception. The Arab Empire adopted Islam early on, initially under the Umayyads and fully in the Abbasid-led commonwealth of states. Eastern Christian and Islamic civilizations were characteristic of religious civilizations because both embraced basic religious scriptures, upheld a form of separation of state and religion, and adapted to inherited cultural traditions.

Specifically, the pattern of Islamic included revealed scriptures, a religiously interpreted history, the separation of state and religion, the fusion of revealed religion and Greek philosophy, and the adaptation to the scientific and artistic heritage from Rome and Persia. The pattern was completed early, by about 950 with the emergence of Sunni Islam, but continued to evolve internally, without further outside stimuli, through Sufi Islam and a myriad of Sufi brotherhood lodges. The result was an Islamic civilization around 1450 which was composed of many states and even more autonomous religious congregations existing alongside the mosques.

▶ **Which cultural traditions combined to form Islamic religious civilization? What were the most characteristic patterns?**

▶ **How did eastern Christian or Byzantine civilization evolve over time? On which institutions was this civilization based, and how did it evolve, wedged between Islamic and western Christian civilizations?**

The late Roman Empire achieved a close integration of Christianity, Greek-Hellenistic philosophy and science, as well as Roman law; but it was hard-pressed for survival by the conquering Arabs. When the eastern Roman, or Byzantine, Empire recovered, it elevated eastern Greek Orthodox Christianity to a supreme position. A powerful recentralization effort strengthened the empire, especially in the Balkans. But in the wake of the Seljuk invasions and Western Christian Crusades, the empire weakened again, surviving in a much diminished form until it was conquered by the Ottoman Muslims in 1453. Eastern Christianity survived in Russia.

Chapter 11 600-1450 CE

Innovation and Adaptation in the Western Christian World

Latin
Christendom,
ca. 700

Canterbury
Paris•

Area converted to
Latin Christianity
ca.1000

Rome•

**LATIN
CHRISTENDOM,
ca. 700–1000**

A round 575 a casual encounter took place in Rome that had enormous implications for the future of western Europe. While strolling through the Forum, a young monk from the monastery of St. Andrew came upon several boys for sale in the slave market. Struck by their fair skin and light hair, he asked about their ethnic origin. He was informed that the youths were from the far-off island of Britain and were called "Angles." The monk replied that because of their angelic appearance they should instead be called "angels." He then asked whether the inhabitants of this far-off land were Christians. When told that they still clung to pagan beliefs, he remarked that it was a pity that such beautiful young persons were not blessed with Christian worship.

In the year 1096 the young monk, now elevated to the papacy as Pope Gregory I (r. 590–604), dispatched a group of monks to Britain, led by Augustine (later named the first archbishop of Canterbury), on a missionary campaign of conversion among the Anglo-Saxons of southern England. Throughout the seventh century Roman Christianity slowly spread northward into Anglo-Saxon England, eventually eclipsing the already established Celtic form of the faith brought over from Ireland in the fifth century.

ABOVE: Detail from *The Effects of Good Government on Town and Country*, a fresco by Ambrogio Lorenzetti (ca. 1290–1348).

During the first half of the eighth century English missionary monks, most notably St. Boniface (680–754), carried Christianity to the continent.

T he papal reign of Gregory I represents the dawn of a new era in the history of western Europe. By encouraging the conversion of Germanic kings to Christianity in return for the sanction of the Church, Gregory studiously advanced the role of the papacy in both ecclesiastical and secular affairs throughout Europe. Thus, Gregory was responsible for making the Roman papacy a significant power in the West. In the process, Gregory inaugurated new links between Rome and northwest Europe that went a long way toward the emergence of a new civilization distant from the Mediterranean. In addition, Gregory's efforts led to the assertion of the independence of **Latin Christendom** from the Eastern Greek Church at Constantinople. Moreover, Gregory established an effective institutional structure and organized a hierarchy that provided the framework for a unified and well-regulated Christian civilization in emerging Europe that would endure until around 1450, when the Renaissance ushered in a new phase in European history.

The Formation of Christian Europe, 600–1000

During the fifth century, Roman provincial rule in the West collapsed and a new post-Roman period of cross-cultural interactions began, which included not only Greco-Roman traditions but also Germanic contributions, as well as Christian spiritual and educational values. Gradually, these various ways of living coalesced to form the foundation of a distinctively Christian European civilization. An important feature of this new civilization was the overarching importance of the Church, whose alliance with Frankish kings—particularly Charlemagne during the eighth century—initiated a new church–state relationship in the West. This civilization nearly dissolved during the internal civil wars among Charlemagne's successors and the ninth-century invasions by non-Christians (Norsemen, Muslims, and Magyars). During the tenth century, however, the slow process of restoring order was under way in post-Carolingian Europe. Despite the turbulence of the ninth and tenth centuries, a new cultural and religious cohesiveness—realized in the age of Charlemagne—provided a new sense of forward-looking optimism; Latin Christendom had survived.

Frankish Gaul and Latin Christianity

Amid the chaos and confusion caused by Germanic invasions and the breakdown of Roman rule during the fifth century, the first attempt to restore a semblance of political order appeared in Frankish Gaul. Merovingian kings relied on brute force to begin the slow process of assembling a unified kingdom. Significantly, however, they also recognized the importance of the Church and its leaders as a unifying force. After an interim period of political confusion a new line of Frankish kings, the Carolingians, emerged during the eighth century. At the same time, the Christian Church played an integral role in the shaping of Frankish Gaul and, in a larger sense, early

Seeing Patterns

▶ How did the Merovingians and Carolingians construct a new Christian European civilization during the seventh and eighth centuries?

▶ What were key factors in the political, economic, and social recovery of Europe during the eleventh and twelfth centuries?

▶ What were some of the cultural and intellectual developments during the "twelfth-century renaissance," and how did they contribute to medieval civilization?

▶ How did the Church influence political developments in Europe during the twelfth and thirteenth centuries?

▶ What events made fourteenth-century Europe so dismal? How did these combine to spell the gradual demise of medieval institutions and perspectives?

Latin Christendom: Those countries professing Christian beliefs under the primacy of the pope.

medieval European civilization. It was during this period that the concept of *Christendom* as a common identity through the practice of western Christianity began to crystallize.

The Merovingians

Unlike other Germanic tribes, the Franks did not invade the western Roman Empire but, rather, expanded from within the confines of its borders. Again, unlike most other Germans, the Franks became western Christians, rather than Aryan Christians. As a result, they were not rejected as heretics by native Gallo-Romans. For these reasons, Frankish Gaul was ideally suited to lay the foundation for the emergence of a Christian state in post-Roman Europe.

The first Frankish dynasty, the Merovingians [Mer-oh-VIN-gee-anz], was firmly established by the Frankish king Clovis (r. 481–511), who succeeded in unifying a number of northern Frankish tribes and defeating neighboring Germanic states. At some point in his reign, perhaps in 498, Clovis adopted Christianity, which gave him the backing of Christian bishops in Gaul. As a result, Clovis had powerful allies in his attempt to solidify his control over a unified Christian kingdom. However, because of the Merovingian practice of dividing inheritances among surviving heirs, soon after his death Clovis' kingdom was split up into Austrasia in the east, Neustria in the west, and Burgundy in the southeast.

The Carolingians

During the eighth century one aristocratic family, the Carolingians, gradually rose to power in Austrasia and eventually took control of all of the Frankish lands. The power of the Carolingians was greatly enhanced during the eighth century by two outstanding leaders. Charles Martel, "The Hammer"—so called because of his military prowess (ca. 714–741)—increased the authority of the Carolingians by encouraging the expansion of Christianity by supporting Christian missionaries and by establishing administrative centers and monasteries. Martel also actively promoted his ties with the Church, as attested by his affiliation with the abbey church of St. Denis near Paris. Then, as a result of his defeat of advancing Muslim armies at the Battle of Tours in 732, he emerged as not only the most powerful man in Frankland but also the leader of the most powerful force in Latin Christendom.

Martel's son, Pepin III ("The Short") (751–768), succeeded his father as mayor of the palace in 741, and enhanced ties with the Church in two ways. First, in 751 he was crowned by the reigning pope as the king of the Franks, thereby replacing the former Merovingian line of kings with a new Carolingian dynasty. Second, the coronation established a new Franco-papal alliance. One consequence of this was the establishment of a closer affinity between Rome and Frankish Gaul, an important factor in allowing Europe to develop independently of the Byzantine Empire in the East. In addition, in the **coronation** of Pepin, the pope included the ceremony of **unction** (used earlier by the Visigoths), in which the newly crowned person was anointed with holy oil. Historians have seen in this practice the introduction into western European history of the concept of sacred kingship, whereby kings now began to call themselves "kings by the grace of God."

Coronation: The act or ceremony of crowning a sovereign.

Unction: The act of anointing with oil as a rite of consecration.

The Early Medieval Church

The Church contributed greatly to the development of a new era in Western history during the early medieval period. The *secular clergy* (from the Latin *saeculum* [CY-cu-lum] or "world") included bishops—among them bishops of Rome, who later became popes—and priests in the cities. The *regular clergy* (from the Latin *regula*, or "rule") were monks who adopted a particular monastic rule and who lived in rural monasteries. Each of these monasteries made distinctive contributions to early medieval culture.

The model for monastic living and organization was established by St. Benedict (ca. 480–543), who provided a set of guidelines, known as Benedict's *Holy Rule*, governing such matters as the times for rising, praying, eating, and retiring, all supervised by an *abbot*, or head of the monastery. The daily lives of Benedictine monks were devoted to prayer and work and were regulated by a series of "offices," or times of the day given over to communal prayer and to manual labor around the monastery.

In economic terms, Benedictine monasteries helped to revitalize rural agricultural production because of their emphases upon economic self-sufficiency and manual labor as a form of prayer. Most monasteries had a watermill and a forge (for wrought iron implements), and the large landholdings of monasteries produced significant quantities of grain, along with wine from vineyards. In addition, Benedictine monks expanded arable lands within their regions by draining swamps and clearing forests. Benedictine monasteries also stood as havens of security and civility amid the social and economic turbulence of the post-Roman, Germanic West.

Above all else, monasteries preserved classical and early Christian culture in the midst of a mostly illiterate Germanic population. The limited education available during the early medieval period took place mostly in monasteries and emphasized not only studying the Bible and church doctrine but also the "seven liberal arts"—consisting of the *trivium* (grammar, rhetoric, logic) and the *quadrivium* (arithmetic, geometry, music, astronomy). Monks copied and studied the works of the Church fathers (Augustine, Jerome, and Ambrose), along with texts from the Bible and scattered papal decrees, thus laying the foundation for a new, Christian civilization for medieval Europe.

The Papacy   While monks lived and worked in isolated monasteries in rural areas, bishops of the Church resided in urban centers. Although major cities throughout the Roman Empire had bishops, the bishop of Rome emerged as spiritual head of the Christian Church in western Europe. The most important of the early medieval popes, and indeed the pope usually credited with the foundation of the medieval papacy, was Gregory I.

In a wider sense, however, Gregory was responsible for making the Roman papacy a power in the West and for establishing the independence of Latin Christendom from the Eastern Greek Church at Constantinople. Gregory clearly understood that by 600 the Latin west was emerging as a distinct civilization, and he recognized

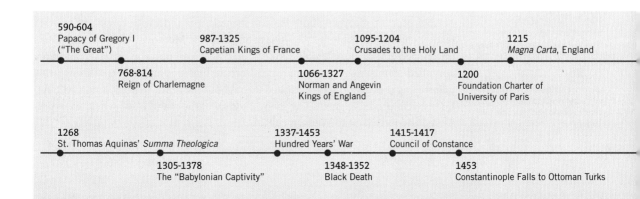

590-604
Papacy of Gregory I
("The Great")

768-814
Reign of Charlemagne

987-1325
Capetian Kings of France

1066-1327
Norman and Angevin
Kings of England

1095-1204
Crusades to the Holy Land

1200
Foundation Charter of
University of Paris

1215
Magna Carta, England

1268
St. Thomas Aquinas' *Summa Theologica*

1305-1378
The "Babylonian Captivity"

1337-1453
Hundred Years' War

1348-1352
Black Death

1415-1417
Council of Constance

1453
Constantinople Falls to Ottoman Turks

that an alliance with the Frankish kings would benefit both parties. Gregory's letters to Childebert II (r. 575–595), king of the Franks, laid the foundation for the Franco-papal alliance that came to fruition in the eighth century. Gregory also enhanced the prestige of the Roman papacy in Italy, which laid the foundation for the Papal States, separating the Roman from the Byzantine Church.

The Age of Charlemagne

Following the death of Pepin III in 768, his son Charlemagne ("Charles the Great") (r. 768–814) inherited the Frankish crown. In his personal preferences and in his official policies, Charlemagne represents the first full synthesis of Roman, Germanic, and Christian elements to forge a unified Christian empire. Charlemagne also established what many consider the "first Europe." By creating a distinctive Western cultural identity and by raising the status of western Europe to rival the civilizations of Byzantium and Islam, the Mediterranean was no longer the center of civilization in the West.

Charlemagne was a born leader. At above 6 feet, 4 inches tall he towered over other men, whose average height was around 5 feet, 5 inches. Recent analysis of his remains indicates he weighed a lean 180 pounds. He was known for boundless energy and athletic prowess. Even more remarkable were his intellectual interests.

Through a combination of extensive military campaigns and attention to effective rule, Charlemagne constructed and administered the largest empire in Europe since the collapse of Roman rule in 476 (see Map 11.1). An important step was the creation of a magnificent palace complex at Aachen [AH-ken] (Aix-la-Chapelle in French). Although most of its buildings have long since been destroyed, its Palatine chapel housed Charlemagne's throne—and both have survived to this day. From here Charlemagne ruled over a highly centralized empire, that is, a polity comprised of many different ethnic and linguistic groups. Charlemagne also reformed legal practices by instituting the Frankish inquest, a forerunner of the jury system, which was carried to England at the time of the Norman Conquest.

Charlemagne's reign also resulted in significant intellectual contributions to medieval Europe. Scholars have debated whether or not the new intellectual climate at his court was indeed solely owing to Charlemagne's personal influence. Nevertheless, in an attempt to both revive and reform learning, especially among the aristocracy and the clergy, Charlemagne orchestrated and oversaw a program of educational reform throughout his vast empire. Key to this effort was the appointment of Alcuin of York (ca. 735–804), the leading intellect of his age, as master of the palace school. Monks in several monastic schools were instructed to engage in the laborious process of copying both Roman manuscripts and a wide range of Christian texts, including the Bible and the *Rule* of St. Benedict. Moreover, Carolingian monks introduced a new, more legible script known as "Carolingian minuscule," and they compiled manuscripts in expensive and ornate bindings and covers. Through this painstaking process, which continued throughout the ninth century, around 50,000 books were produced, including many classical authors and texts, which were preserved and passed on to Western culture.

Charlemagne's Throne. Charlemagne frequently traveled throughout his realm, and one place where he stopped several times was Ravenna on the Adriatic coast of Italy, where he would admire the magnificent sixth-century church of San Vitale. Inspired by its harmonious proportions and stunning mosaics, Charlemagne determined to build a replica at Aachen. The Palatine Chapel, the only surviving component of his palace, combines Byzantine and Carolingian architectural styles.

MAP 11.1 **The Empire of Charlemagne.**

Like his forebears, Charlemagne also took an active interest in affairs of the Church. Not only did he promote the interests of Christianity throughout his kingdom, but he also intervened in papal affairs in Rome. In 774 Charlemagne journeyed to Rome to offer protection against the Lombards, and in 800 he gave assistance to Pope Leo III (r. 795–816), who was attacked by rivals. While attending mass at St. Peter's on Christmas day, Charlemagne was suddenly crowned "emperor of the Romans" by a grateful Leo III.

The creation of a new Roman emperor in the West announced the new independence of western Europe from the Byzantine East, and it signaled a shift in the center of power away from the Mediterranean and toward Europe north of the Alps. Charlemagne's new imperial status was recognized (reluctantly) not only by the Byzantine court but also by the Abbasid caliph in Baghdad, Harun al-Rashid (r. 786–809).

Post-Carolingian Europe   Charlemagne's empire did not long survive his death in 814. Soon after his passing it was torn apart by a series of internal wars and divisions. Charlemagne's eldest son, Louis the Pious (r. 814–840), followed the old Frankish custom of dividing the empire among his three sons, who then proceeded to squabble over their respective shares. By the terms of the Treaty of Verdun in 843 the empire was divided into eastern, western, and central portions. At the same time, a series of devastating raids from outside Europe further disturbed the situation. From the north came the Norsemen, or Vikings, motivated by the quest for land and treasure. They sailed from Scandinavia into West Frankland and England in shallow-draft "long ships," causing terror and destruction wherever they landed along Europe's rivers. From the south, marauding bands of Muslim pirates created fear and destruction along the French coast of the Mediterranean and even penetrated inland as far as the Alps and into Rome itself in 846. Magyar horsemen from the plains of Hungary terrorized East Frankland in the same period, although they were more inclined to settle onto farmlands than to merely plunder (see Map 11.1).

Feudalism: An arrangement in which vassals were protected and maintained by their lords, usually through the granting of fiefs, and required to serve under them in war.

The Feudal Age   The name traditionally given to the form of governance that arose in West Frankland during the ninth through the eleventh centuries is **feudalism**. But what, precisely, was feudalism? Historians have never fully agreed on a precise definition of the term, and some have suggested abandoning it altogether as essentially meaningless. Complicating the picture further for world historians, the term is often used to describe similar arrangements that arose, in different periods, in Zhou China and Tokugawa Japan. It is true that feudalism was not a system *per se*; it was based on no theory, and it was nowhere uniform or consistent. Yet, amid the growing chaos and confusion of the ninth and tenth centuries, feudalism provided security at the local level in the absence of central government.

Essentially, feudalism represented a new form of governance at the regional and local levels instead of from a centralized royal court. Feudalism consisted of powerful landed aristocrats (lords) who gathered together small private armies consisting of dependents (vassals) in order to meet the military emergencies posed by the Norsemen, Muslims, and Magyars. Since wealth and power were now measured in terms of landholdings, vassals were rewarded for their services with grants of land, known as *fiefs* [feefs].

Lord–vassal relationships and institutions marked a turning point in European history in that they laid the foundation for the later formation of centralized kingdoms. Most important was the concept of honor and loyalty to someone higher in the feudal hierarchy. Even though in *practice* the local aristocratic lords were sometimes stronger than royal figures, in *theory* all land and power were possessed by kings, who stood at the apex of the feudal hierarchy. By using these and other elements of feudal relationships to his advantage, a royal figure could convert the feudal relationships to royal control in his realm.

Manorialism: The medieval European system of self-sustaining agricultural estates.

Whereas feudalism refers to the political and governmental aspects of life in the ninth and tenth centuries, **manorialism** refers to social and economic affairs of the time. Large manorial estates were established in rural areas and constituted self-sustaining agricultural communities. In appearance, the manorial estate consisted

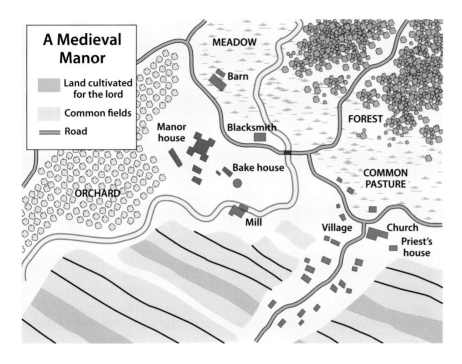

Figure 11.1 A Medieval Manor. This illustration shows the layout of a typical manor, with the manor and its satellite buildings next to a village surrounded by fields for planting and common (waste) land.

of several prominent buildings: the castle or manor house, the church, the barn, and the mill (see Figure 11.1).

Peasants lived in small cottages or huts in a confined area of the estate. The typical cottage was constructed of mud and straw, with an earthen floor and without windows. A small stone hearth was used for cooking, with a hole in the roof to allow smoke to escape the interior. Interiors were without light of any kind, and privacy was nonexistent. Surrounding all this were fields for agricultural production, a large wooded area for timber and fuel, and a fish pond. The fields were arranged into long, narrow strips, some farmed by peasant families and others owned by the lord of the manor, on which the peasants had to provide free labor, called "boon work." The physical pattern of such manors may still be seen in many areas of France even today.

Recovery, Reform, and Innovation, 1000–1300

From about 1000 to 1300 medieval Europe experienced a period of revitalization, expansion, and cultural creativity and innovation. The period began with the appearance of several competing, politically centralizing kingdoms and with advancements in agriculture, commerce, and trade. Reforms in the Church provided an overarching framework that defined a unified western European Christian religious civilization, culminating in papal supremacy over Europe around the beginning of the thirteenth century. During the so-called twelfth-century renaissance, extending from ca. 1050 to 1250, a cultural revolution in universities produced new philosophical and scientific perspectives that, along with interaction with the Islamic world, came to distinguish western Europe from other world civilizations.

The Political Recovery of Europe

If we survey Europe in the middle of the ninth century, we find chaos and confusion everywhere, caused by internal civil wars and external invasions from nearly all directions. As we have seen, all signs of central government had disappeared as a result of the collapse of the Carolingian empire. In this turbulent setting most people were ruled by local lords—dukes, counts, barons, or other regional officials. By around 1300, however, each of these areas was governed by well-run centralized administrations headed by kings, who restored both political and fiscal health to their realms.

France and England   The French nobility elected Hugh Capet (r. 987–996) as their king in 987 CE, beginning a long process of restoring centralized monarchy. This event marked the beginning of a new royal dynasty, the Capetians, in place of the former Carolingians. Although relatively weak in relation to powerful lords, the Capetians could claim several theoretical advantages. For one thing, the king's court served as the place where all disputes among his vassals were resolved, and the location of Hugh's royal **demesne** [deh-MAIN] in the lands around Paris meant that he was at the strategic and commercial center of events in France. The Capetians also enjoyed the support of the Church. Not only did they have control over dozens of bishoprics and monasteries but they alone were anointed with holy oil as a part of the coronation ceremony, making their persons sacrosanct and safe from bodily injury.

Demesne: All territories within France controlled directly by the king.

Over the next 300 years, Capetian kings extended royal control in France. Success in petty wars against the nobles and arranged marriages between Capetian heirs and members of the nobility helped extend the domain and enhance Capetian power. Determined to make France the most powerful country in Europe, Philip IV (r. 1285–1314) established a representative assembly in France, the **Estates-General**, in order to raise needed revenues. Comprised of the three social "estates" in France—the clergy, the nobility, and the townspeople—this body played an important role in later events leading up to the French Revolution.

Estates-General: The French representative assembly, comprised of the three social "estates" in France, first convened by Philip IV.

Compared to the long and slow process of building a centralized monarchy in Capetian France, the establishment of centralized rule in England took place over a much shorter period of time. After the Norman duke William the Conqueror defeated an Anglo-Saxon army at the Battle of Hastings in 1066, he was proclaimed king of England as King William I (r. 1066–1087). William then proceeded to seize control of all lands in the realm, to distribute them to his followers, and to secure his claim to the throne by building castles throughout the country.

William's successors continued his practice of centralizing authority. Henry II (r. 1154–1189), the first of the Plantagenet kings of England, reformed the judicial system by making royal courts the final courts of appeal, particularly in disputes over land, thereby overriding the authority of baronial courts. Moreover, Henry established a uniform code of justice (known as English common law) throughout the realm, which replaced the complex and frequently contradictory jurisdictions of baronial and local courts. Even more effective was Henry's reliance upon roving royal justices and the use of royal **writs** and the jury system, which provided justice for all disputants.

Writ: A written order issued by a court, commanding the party to whom it is addressed to perform or cease performing a specified act.

Henry's son John (r. 1199–1216), however, alienated the baronage of England, who forced the king to sign Magna Carta ("The Great Charter") in 1215. Magna

Carta established several important principles: the king must rule in accordance with established feudal practices; he must consult with the barons before levying taxes; and all free men have the right to trial by jury if charged with a crime. Many of these concepts also contributed to the appearance of a new institution known as **Parliament**.

Across the thirteenth century the English Parliament increased its power and scope. It also established certain principles that would be contested periodically by English monarchs over the next five centuries. In order to raise money for an anticipated French attack against England, Edward I (r. 1272–1307) found it expedient to convene in 1295 the so-called Model Parliament, comprised of an upper house of nobles and a lower house of "knights of the shires and burgesses of the towns." This precedent established the origin of Parliament's House of Lords and House of Commons, which continues today.

Parliament: A representative assembly in England that, by the fourteenth century, was composed of great lords (both lay and ecclesiastical) and representatives from two other groups: shire knights and town burgesses.

Germany   Events in East Frankland, or Germany, took a different turn. One setback to centralized rule was the division of the eastern portion of Charlemagne's realm into five regional groupings, or *duchies*, each under the control of a powerful duke. The result was that successive kings were chosen by the five regional princes, making it difficult for kings to centralize royal authority.

Furthermore, imperial involvement in papal affairs in Italy provided another impediment to centralization. When Otto I of Saxony (r. 936–973) took power as king of the Germans, he extended Germanic influence in Italy in order to reestablish Charlemagne's protection of the papacy. In 962, Otto put down political disturbances and protests against the Church. In gratitude, Pope John XII (r. 955–964) proclaimed Otto "emperor of the Romans," forming the basis of what has been termed the "Holy Roman Empire." Otto's successors continued the policy of interfering in papal affairs, with momentous results for both church and state.

The Economic and Social Recovery of Europe

Yet another area of recovery for Europe around the year 1000 was in economics. In the year of the millennium there was little manufacturing and commerce in Europe, agriculture was still the mainstay of its economy, there were few cities (and even these were underpopulated), and society was broken up into only three classes: those who work, those who fight, and those who pray. By 1300, however, the map of Europe was crisscrossed by scores of trade routes, trade and commerce were important features, urban life was humming, and a new social class of businesspeople had emerged in cities. How are we to explain this remarkable economic resurgence?

The Agricultural Revolution   We can begin to account for Europe's economic revival by studying developments in agriculture. The first step in this direction was land reclamation. During the tenth and eleventh centuries the cessation of internal wars and outside invasions provided the freedom to undertake the arduous work of reclaiming land for increased cultivation—primarily clearing forests and draining swamps. In addition, many areas of northern Europe, particularly France, enjoyed deep deposits of topsoil rich in nutrients, which, combined with a climatic warming trend, provided a perfect environment to grow new crops.

An important factor in the agricultural revolution was the heavy-wheeled plow, fitted with an iron blade and a *moldboard* (a curved iron blade to cut through the heavy sod of the region and lift and turn the newly dug soil). The use of new fertilizers and the transition from a two-field to a three-field system also provided a 33 percent increase in crop production. In the three-field system, one field was planted in the spring for a fall harvest, another was planted in the winter for a spring harvest, and the third remained fallow to enable its soil to regenerate nutrients. The three-field system resulted from the introduction of pulses (beans, peas, lentils, etc.), which added nitrogen as the new fertilizer.

Apart from European contributions, however, it is important to note that the agricultural revolution was in large part the result of innovations that originated elsewhere in Eurasia (perhaps in China), which were transmitted to Europe through cross-cultural interactions, mostly via trade across the Silk Road network. Among these innovations were the the use of horses with collar harness (instead of slower-moving oxen), which provided a fivefold increase in traction, not to mention less injury to the animal; the use of iron horseshoes; the use of the tandem harness, allowing horses to work in pairs and further increasing production; the vertical water-wheel; and the single-wheeled barrow.

Moreover, new forms of mechanical energy—also of Asian origin—were introduced to Europe through interactions and contacts with the Islamic world. As early as 1050 watermills were in wide use; and although some historians attribute the water-mill to Roman origin, its design—particularly the incorporation of the trip-hammer—indicates an Asian origin. Windmills were subsequently borrowed from Islamic Iran during the twelfth century. The circular motion of the wheel, driven by either water or wind, was then converted by a series of cranks, gears, and camshafts into pounding and grinding motions, thereby greatly increasing the production of cloth goods, beer, and especially grain products, which in turn led to an increase in food production. Even the first deep-drilled water well, introduced in the twelfth century, was of Chinese origin. Finally, through Muslim Spain the Europeans benefited from several Islamic advances in agriculture, such as the new crops of rice, sugarcane, watermelons, bananas, and improvements in techniques of irrigation and drainage.

These new techniques meant an increase not only in the quantity of agricultural production but also, more importantly, in the quality of new foods. Before the agricultural revolution, European diets were based mainly on grains and, thus, were rich in carbohydrates but low in protein. Peas and beans provided much needed proteins, which when combined with chicken, fish, and eggs resulted in a more balanced and nutritious diet. Improvements to the European diet resulted in an increase in Europe's population: in 1000, the population stood at about 36 million; by 1100 it had jumped to 44 million and by 1200, to 58 million. By 1300 the European population reached about 80 million.

Commerce and Trade

Commerce and Trade   The revolution in agricultural production sparked in turn a rejuvenation of commerce and trade that spread throughout and beyond medieval Europe. As Europe's population grew, so did the demand for all manner of consumer goods, ranging from agricultural implements to household utensils, clothing and shoes, and numerous other commodities. The expansion of mercantile elites in thriving urban centers also provoked a brisk demand for luxury goods from beyond Europe, including silks, spices, and sugar.

One focal point of the revival of trade and commerce developed in northern Europe. Cloth goods, especially woolen products, had been a staple item in Flanders (modern-day Belgium) along the coast of the North Sea in northeastern France, even before the Carolingian era. After the cessation of Viking raids, Flemish weavers began a flourishing exchange with wool-producing centers in England, particularly with monasteries in the north of the island, in the twelfth century. Another very productive source of the commercial trade revival in northern Europe was the importation of French wines into England beginning in the later eleventh century, occasioned by the Norman Conquest in 1066. German merchants established trade routes to London in the west and to Russian cities like Riga and Novgorod in the east.

Far more vital, however, was the remarkable revival of European commerce and trade across the Mediterranean. When Umayyad rulers were displaced by the Abbasids, who ruled from 750 to 1258, maritime contacts between Islamic and Christian merchants resumed. At around the same time, the Byzantine Empire turned its attention to extending its power into the Balkans and northeastward toward Russia. As a consequence, its military interests lay more in developing landed, rather than naval, forces, thereby ceding involvement in the Mediterranean to European traders. In addition, the Norman conquest of southern Italy and Sicily (1046–1091) afforded the northern Italian maritime cities of Pisa, Genoa, and Venice the opportunity to collaborate with Islamic merchants in Alexandria and the Levant. By the end of the eleventh century, Italian traders had established commercial ties with Constantinople, Syria, and Cairo and had begun the exchange of all manner of goods between Europe and Asia.

The most momentous change in European trade and commerce took place near the close of the thirteenth century. Around 1275, first Genoese and then Venetian maritime traders sailed westward across the Mediterranean, through the Strait of Gibraltar, and then out into the Atlantic. Then, Fernando IV (r. 1295–1312) claimed control of Gibraltar from the Muslims in 1309, ensuring full access to the waters of the Atlantic. Before these developments, trading patterns were primarily of a one-way nature: European merchants imported modest quantities of goods like *alum* (a mineral essential for dyeing cloth), spices, and silks from China and India. Thanks to economic advances in the West, however, European merchants now had products to export to the East: wool and tin from England, finished French and Flemish cloth goods, and manufactured items like iron agricultural and household implements (see Map 11.2).

Cross-Mediterranean trade and commerce were facilitated by several innovations, some of which were assimilated as a result of interactions with Islamic and Byzantine merchants, while others were of independent origin.

Navigation was tremendously improved by advances in European ship design. Among the most important was the incorporation of the sternpost rudder. This concept was familiar to Chinese and Muslim sailors, but the European version—in use on ships of the Hanseatic League as early as 1180—was unique in its design and function in that it used hinged iron plates firmly mounted to the ship's stern. The principal advantage of the stern-mounted rudder was that it allowed for the construction of larger ships, which in turn greatly increased the volume of transported goods. Another improvement was provided by the adoption from Muslim sailors of the *lateen sail*, a front-mounted triangular sail that allowed for tacking into the wind. It was largely owing to this navigational device that Italian ships were able to sail into the westerly winds that had previously prevented their sailing through the Strait of Gibraltar into the Atlantic. Most important was the introduction of the magnetic compass. Whether of independent invention or derived from China, where it was

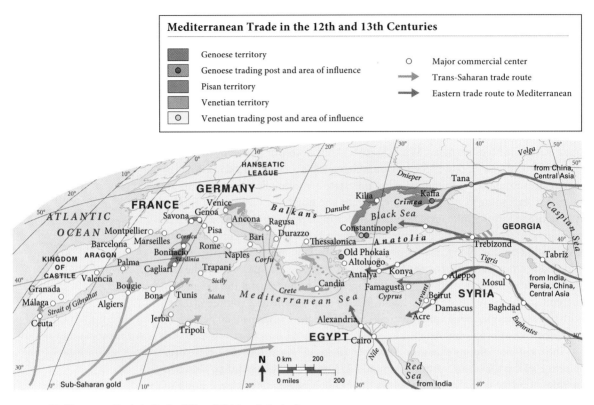

MAP 11.2 **Mediterranean Trade in the Twelfth and Thirteenth Centuries.**

used on Chinese ships as early as around 1090, the magnetic (or mariner's) compass first appeared in Europe in 1190. Use of the compass greatly facilitated maritime travel beyond the sight of land, particularly across the Mediterranean.

Early Capitalism and a Cash Economy   This renewed trans-Mediterranean commercial activity resulted in several innovations in commerce and monetary exchange that laid the foundation for the development of European **capitalism**. Increasing commercial transactions prompted a need for coined money—mostly in the form of silver coins—in order to arrange easy payment for exchanged goods and products. Meanwhile, medieval fairs gradually created new business procedures like record keeping and accounting practices, along with bills of exchange (the forerunner of the modern bank check) to replace transport of large amounts of coins. These transactions were facilitated by the use of paper, invented in China during the Han dynasty (see Chapter 9), then adopted by Islamic merchants, and subsequently transmitted to Europe in the eleventh century through Muslim Spain.

Several innovative financial and legal instruments were also devised to facilitate long-distance trade. Among these was the *commenda*, first in use by Venetian traders in the eleventh century and borrowed from interactions with their Byzantine and Islamic counterparts. Essentially, the *commenda* was a legally binding partnership in which one partner provided the funds to initiate a seagoing venture, and the other carried out the voyage; upon a successful conclusion, both partners shared an agreed-upon portion of the profits.

Capitalism: An economic system characterized by private or corporate ownership of capital goods, by investments that are determined by private decision, and by prices, production, and the distribution of goods that are determined mainly by competition in a free market.

Marco Polo's Departure from Venice. From at least the ninth century, Venice's political and economic fortunes were linked inextricably to the East; and by the fifteenth century it had gained undisputed supremacy over its rivals, Genoa and Pisa, in the trade with the Levant. Overseas commercial ventures, such as the famous journey of Marco Polo to Asia in the late thirteenth century, involved a great degree of risk; but the prospect of lucrative profits was irresistible.

Urban Growth   The revitalization of trade and commerce contributed to the rejuvenation of urban life in eleventh-century Europe. Many Roman towns survived the tribulations of the early medieval period, although most resembled underpopulated ghost towns. The repopulation of these existing urban sites plus the creation of new cities attests to the influence of the economic revival of the eleventh century. Artisans and merchants were drawn to these vibrant urban centers, along with craftspeople and laborers, many of whom fled rural manors in order to begin new lives in cities. These cities were small in comparison with today's standards. Most numbered around 5,000 people, although cities like London and Bruges held about 40,000 inhabitants, while cities like Venice and Genoa in northern Italy boasted populations of around 100,000. Churches and castles were the most prominent physical sites in cities, and most urban areas were enclosed within stone walls outside of which were surrounding agricultural fields.

Social Patterns   Social patterns within the revitalized urban centers of the eleventh and twelfth centuries underwent change for several reasons. Of primary importance was the return of a money economy, which not only spelled the demise of feudalism—in that kings and nobles could now pay for armies with cash rather than with grants of land—but also resulted in the appearance of a new social class: the military. The effects of a new cash economy were noticeable especially in cities, which benefited from the cash contributions of wealthy businessmen in order to build cathedrals and large town halls. Finally, cities produced a new class of people, the **bourgeoisie**. Comprised of merchants and artisans who lived in "burghs" (or cities) the bourgeoisie made their livings from producing and selling goods for commercial exchange. This new, "middle class" of people was destined to exert an enormous influence on the development of medieval representative

Bourgeoisie: The urban-based middle class between the wealthy aristocracy and the working class.

The Virgin Mary Knitting. This fourteenth-century drawing of the Virgin Mary knitting a garment for her unborn child is the earliest known representation of knitting, a medieval innovation. Knitwear was unknown in the ancient Mediterranean but was essential in the cold, damp climate of northern Europe.

governments, primarily because their access to liquid cash made them attractive to European rulers.

Urban women worked in a variety of occupations, especially craft industries. Among these crafts we find women employed as butchers, candlemakers, metal crafters, silk weavers, and bookbinders. Nevertheless, women were rarely admitted as full members to craft guilds, and even in the silk industry—the one area where women did predominate—there is no evidence of a guild. For the great majority of working women, better opportunities were available in what were known as "bye industries," or home-based enterprises, like spinning cloth and brewing ale. In some cases widows took over their late husband's trade and worked as single women.

Jews occupied a distinct position in medieval towns and cities during the early years of the urban revival in the eleventh century. Comprising a small but distinct minority of the European population, communities of Jews were spread around the Mediterranean world. Through their travels and interactions with a wide variety of peoples, Jews developed both wide geographical knowledge and the command of multiple languages. For these reasons they sometimes served as diplomats, and they engaged in money lending and banking.

As the eleventh century unfolded, however, tolerance toward Jews began to wane. Jews were increasingly vilified as murderers of Christ, a sentiment sparked by the First Crusade in 1096. In 1144 a full-scale assault against Jews was unleashed in the English town of Norwich. In many cases Jews were forced to live together in walled-off, gated ghettos in towns, which frequently held charters of liberty separate from those of the towns. Ghettos appeared as early as the thirteenth century in Spain, Portugal, Germany, and elsewhere. Several countries expelled Jews—England in 1290, France in 1306, and a number of continental cities in the early 1400s—resulting in their dispersal throughout eastern Europe.

Religious Reform and Expansion

During the period from 1000 to 1300 the clerical establishment of medieval Europe underwent dramatic reform as the Church struggled to recover from nearly two centuries of decentralization and decline of learning. The reform movement in the Church began in monasteries, then spread to the ecclesiastical hierarchy in cities, and eventually resulted in a new age of religious enthusiasm throughout Europe.

Monastic Reform   The effort at monastic reform began in France in a monastery founded at Cluny in 910 by Duke William I (875–918) of Aquitaine. Cluny was established as a monastery totally free of obligations to either feudal lord or local ecclesiastical control, being subordinated only to papal control. Another objective of the Cluniac reform movement was strict adherence to the Benedictine rule, which laid down strict guidelines for the monastic life. The number of reformed monasteries increased across the eleventh and twelfth centuries. The most successful of new monastic orders was the Cistercians, founded in 1098 in a remote area of France at Citeaux. At its inception the order numbered only a handful of monastic houses, but by 1200 nearly 500 Cistercian monasteries were active throughout France. The appeal of the Cistercian order lay in its simple and austere way of life; Cistercian monasteries were founded in remote areas of wasteland, and their interiors were bare and stripped of expensive adornments. They were enjoined to work and live in poverty and to devote their total beings to "God's work" (*opus Dei*).

Papal Reform and the Investiture Controversy

As the monastic reform movement progressed, a similar reform effort took place in the papacy. One of the major concerns of the Church was to establish its independence from secular influence, particularly the practice by which lay rulers appointed clergy, including the pope, to their offices. Popes, however, believed it was the exclusive right of the clergy to make such appointments. After Pope Leo IX (r. 1049–1054) created the College of Cardinals Pope Nicholas II (r. 1059–1061) proclaimed the Papal Election Decree in 1059, which began the practice whereby only the College of Cardinals is empowered to elect the pontiff of the Holy Catholic Church. The result was the elimination of the role of the Holy Roman (German) emperor in the appointment of popes.

This conflict came to a head in what is known as the "investiture controversy." Pope Gregory VII (r. 1073–1085), a staunch advocate of papal reform, insisted that appointment of the clergy was in future to be controlled solely by the Church. When the German emperor Henry IV (1056–1106) openly challenged Gregory's proclamation, the pope excommunicated him. The struggle between popes and emperors dragged on for more than 40 years, until 1122 when an agreement known as the Concordat of Worms (named for the German city where the agreement was made) was reached. This agreement stipulated that German bishops must be elected by Church officials.

The investiture controversy produced mixed results. On one hand, Gregory's actions represented the enhanced power of the Church and proved that popes could force emperors to acknowledge papal authority. Henry had famously traveled to the papal residence at Canossa and waited barefoot in the snow for Gregory to lift the ban of excommunication on him. On the other hand, Henry IV's struggle with the Church proved disastrous for his successors. Later German emperors never fully recovered from this policy of attempting to control matters in both Germany and Italy. Even such otherwise strong figures as Frederick I (r. 1152–1190) and Frederick II (r. 1215–1250) were unable to establish centralized rule in Germany. Moreover, efforts by German emperors to exert political influence over northern Italy also kept that region divided between partisans of the emperor and those of the pope for centuries to come. After Frederick's death, the five Germanic principalities reasserted their independence from royal control, and Germany remained disunited until the later nineteenth century.

Popular Piety and a Religious Society

As early as the eleventh century Europe experienced a dramatic increase in popular piety, when ordinary people took a more active interest in religion and religious issues. This movement was caused by

(a)

(b)

Changing Views of Christ. The Crucifixion scene from the door of the basilica of Santa Sabina, Rome, ca. 430, is formal and stylized: Christ is remote. *(a)* In contrast, the Crucifixion commissioned by the archbishop of Cologne, Germany, just before 1000 shows a suffering Christ—a human being in agony and sorrow, hanging from a cross *(b)*.

several factors. One was the reform movement in the Church, which resulted in both higher standards of conduct among regular and secular clergy and the increased visibility and temporal authority of the pope following the investiture controversy. Another factor was the construction of numerous shrines dedicated to Christian saints, whose *relics* (venerated items connected with their lives) were considered powerful aids in the quest for personal salvation.

Additional factors responsible for generating a wave of renewed enthusiasm for religion concerned new depictions of Jesus and Mary, the mother of Jesus. Whereas in the earliest years of the Church in the fifth century CE the Crucifixion of Jesus was rarely shown—and, if at all, in a stylized and unemotional manner—by the tenth century Christ was depicted as a compassionate figure, whose tragic death on the Cross was portrayed as a reminder of his sacrifice for the redemption of humanity's sins.

Another important contribution of the popularization of Christian piety is evident in the introduction of new concepts of time. One concept derives from the book of Genesis in the Bible, where the creation of the earth took 6 days, leaving the seventh day as a day of rest, set aside for Sunday. Moreover, the numbering of years in accordance with the Christian era was introduced in 532 by Dionysius Exiguus (ca. 470–544), a Roman monk. For Dionysius historical time really began with the birth of Christ, hence his designation of *Anno Domini* ("in the year of the Lord") to denote a new dating system. The new system was used by the eighth-century Anglo-Saxon scholar Bede (ca. 673–735) in his *Ecclesiastical History of the English People* and then popularized in Europe by Alcuin of York during the reign of Charlemagne.

Easter: Christian celebration of the Resurrection of Christ; celebrated on the Sunday following the first full moon after the vernal equinox.

These and other associations with Christianity carried with them several implications that altered the lives of Europeans. For one thing, two crucial Christian feast days now became standard: the birth of Christ was celebrated on December 25 (Christmas) and his resurrection on a movable date called **Easter**. For another, saints' days, set aside for reflection and celebration, constituted major events around which Europeans' lives centered. Finally, the ringing of church and monastery bells announced the hours of the day, which provided for regulation of daily routines. Mechanical clocks, introduced into Europe in the early fourteenth century—and most likely derived from earlier Chinese models—provided for more precise measurement of the daily hours.

A less benign aspect of popular piety was an alarming trend toward the appearance of heretical movements within the Church. Criticisms of Church practice and doctrines, especially over the Church's growing worldliness and political maneuvering, began to arise, particularly in the cities and towns of southern France. In an effort to channel the devotion of the faithful, particularly in cities, Pope Innocent III (r. 1198–1216) licensed two new religious orders of friars ("brothers"), the Franciscans and the Dominicans.

Founded by St. Francis of Assisi (1181/82–1226), the Francisan order inspired a new dedication to Christianity by living simply among the people, preaching repentance for sins and aiding the poor and the sick. The Dominicans, founded by St. Dominic (1170–1221) in 1216, also lived among the people; but they were more interested in preaching and teaching, believing that the best way to combat heresy was to teach the doctrines of the Church. The Dominican order included many famous medieval theologians in its ranks, such as St. Thomas Aquinas (ca. 1225–1274).

The Crusades   A movement that reflects both the growing appeal and power of the Church as well as the renewed energy of a revitalized Europe centers on the Crusades. Like the reform movement of the Church, the Crusades were in part inspired by the new wave of religious enthusiasm sweeping Europe during the period of recovery from the horrors of the ninth and tenth centuries. But there were other causal factors as well. One of the most fundamental causes was the so-called *Reconquista*, or reconquest, of formerly Christian lands that had been taken over by Muslims.

Until the year 1000 Spanish Christians were forced to retreat into the far northwestern section of the peninsula, while the Muslims controlled most of the lands from their capital in Córdoba. In 1031, however, internal squabbling among Muslim factions led to a loosening of Muslim control over all of Spain, which in turn prompted two kings of Christian territories to launch an offensive in order to reclaim land from the Muslims. The real breakthrough occurred in 1085 when Toledo was liberated from Muslim control, resulting in almost half of Spain returning to Christian control.

A similar effort to retake Christian territory from Muslim control took place in southern Italy and Sicily. Beginning in 1061, a group of Norman knights began wresting Sicily from Muslim control. Across the twelfth century their successors established a strongly centralized Norman kingdom in Sicily. The Norman kings of Sicily allied themselves with the papacy, and in return for their protection of the papacy, they were given the status of permanent papal legates, which in turn gave them total control over all the higher clergy in their realm.

These spectacular successes against the Muslims in the western Mediterranean occurred simultaneously with alarming developments in the eastern Mediterranean. At the same time, a new menace appeared from the east, the fearsome Seljuk Turks. After their conversion to Islam, the Seljuks launched a series of raids against the Byzantines; and at the Battle of Manzikert in 1071 they routed their Christian opponents, resulting in the loss of all Christian lands in Asia. In 1076 the Turks overran Jerusalem itself. Fearing for the survival of the Byzantine state, the Byzantine emperor Michael VII (r. 1071–1078) sent an appeal for aid to the Roman pope, Gregory VII. As we have seen, Gregory was preoccupied with the investiture controversy, so he declined to intervene in the east.

But when the next emperor, Alexius Comnenus (r. 1081–1118) followed up with another request to Gregory's successor Urban II, the latter felt it was time to intervene against a total Muslim takeover in the eastern Mediterranean. Inspired by recent victories over Muslims in the western Mediterranean, Urban II wanted to liberate the Holy Land in order to guarantee the safety of Christian pilgrims anxious to view the holiest Christian sites in Syria and Palestine, and he was anxious to enhance papal prestige in the contest with the German emperor.

Accordingly, on November 27, 1095, Pope Urban II called for the launching of a crusade to the Holy Land during the Council of Clermont in France. Urban called particularly on the great barons of Europe to gather together their feudal armies and march to the east to liberate Jerusalem from Muslim control. For their part, although they may have been partially driven by religious enthusiasm, Europe's feudal nobility most likely saw in this expedition the promise of new lands and a chance to use their military training in a good cause. In the summer of the following year the main force, consisting of approximately 7,000 mounted knights along with around 35,000 infantry and augmented by thousands of attendants, suppliers, and prostitutes, gathered for the journey eastward. When the eastern emperor realized the size and potential unruliness of the approaching crusader army, he is supposed to have said, "I asked for rain and have been given a flood." Eventually, the entire army crossed over into Asia Minor and in 1097 took Nicaea from the Turks; and two years later, in the summer of 1099, Jerusalem was finally freed from Islamic control at a terrific cost in human life. As a result of the crusaders' victory, new "crusader states" were established along the eastern Mediterranean and papal authority gained new respect among western secular rulers (see Map 11.3).

Other crusades followed throughout the twelfth century. In 1144 the fall of the crusader state of Edessa (in present-day Syria) to a resurgence of Islamic militancy caused renewed interest in a second crusade. Called for in a sermon by Bernard of Clairveaux, the crusade was led by King Louis VII of France and Conrad III, Holy Roman emperor. The two leaders failed to coordinate their movements once they reached the east, and the result was the failure of the expedition to reach Jerusalem. A surge of renewed interest in the crusading movement occurred in 1187, when Jerusalem was overrun by the renowned Muslim leader Saladin. Known as the "Crusade of the Three Kings," the army was led by Frederick I of Germany, Philip II of France, and Richard I of England. The accidental drowning death of Frederick I removed the German contingent from the force, but the combined English and French forces managed to capture Acre from the Muslims in 1191. At that point, however, dissension between Philip I and Richard I resulted in Philip's hasty return to France, where he engaged in stirring up trouble against the English monarch.

Yet another crusading effort, the Fourth Crusade, instigated by the leader of Venice, was launched in 1201. Consisting mainly of French knights, the crusading army desired to travel to the Holy Land by sea instead of taking the usual landed route. When they reached Venice, the Crusade's leaders contracted with the Venetians for passage by ship to the east. The crafty Venetians were quick to realize the advantage of transporting a crusading army and, after leaving port attacked the Adriatic port city of

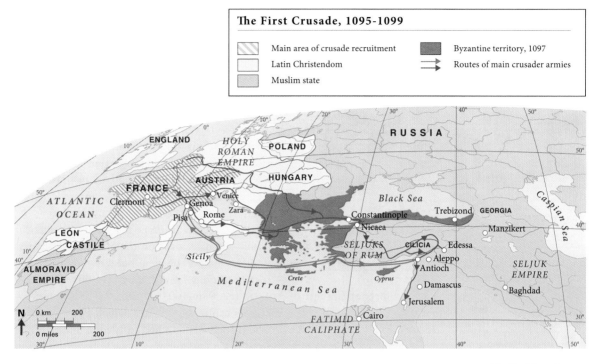

MAP 11.3 **The First Crusade, 1095–1099.**

Zara, their commercial rival. Outraged by an attack on a Christian city, Innocent III excommunicated the crusaders, who blithely ignored the papal ban. From Zara the Venetians transported the army to Constantinople in 1204, where they plundered the city. Nicetas Choniates (ca. 1155–1215), a Byzantine historian, provides a gruesome eyewitness account of the crusaders' rampage.

Although the crusading movement ultimately failed to liberate Jerusalem from Muslim hands and although the cumulative casualty estimates run into the millions, the Crusades produced some positive achievements for Europeans. The ability of Western popes to organize European knights into armies and to send them far afield in service of the Church enhanced their prestige in both the west and the east. The Crusades also helped to establish western Christian dominance of sea traffic in the Mediterranean. Finally, the retaking of Christian territories in southern Italy, Sicily, and Spain—an effort that began in local areas before the First Crusade—provided European scholars access to new sources of Greco-Arabic scientific advances, known collectively as the "New Logic."

Intellectual and Cultural Developments

Closely associated with the religious recovery of Europe during the High Middle Ages (ca. 1000–1300) was a series of important new directions and institutions reflective of the intellectual and cultural expressions of western Christian religious civilization. Perhaps the two most visible symbols of this civilization—the Gothic cathedral and the university—were produced during the "twelfth-century renaissance" (see "Patterns Up Close"). It was in the university that the study of Aristotle provoked a renewed interest in science and the natural world.

A Medieval Italian Classroom.
As the master recites passages from a text, some students copy verbatim what is read aloud, while others either listen attentively or even sleep.

Scholasticism: A medieval method of determining theological and philosophical truth by using Aristotelian logic.

Universities   As a result of the urban revolution of the eleventh century, monastic schools in rural areas began to lose ground to cathedral schools in urban centers, which offered more relevant instruction in reading and writing, mathematical reckoning, and logical reasoning—skills needed for success in the commercial world of the twelfth century. The most creative thinkers were now attracted to cathedral schools in the larger cities of Europe, where they in turn began to attract eager young students. In time, larger groups of students and teachers formed the first universities at Salerno, Bologna, and Paris.

Particularly in Paris, the university curriculum began to focus on the philosophy of Aristotle, who had been all but ignored during the early Middle Ages. In large part this was owing to the efforts of Gerbert of Aurillac (ca. 946–1003), known by his contemporaries as "the most learned man of his century" and later named Pope Sylvester II (r. 999–1003). As a young man Gerbert had studied in Islamic Spain, where he acquired an interest in mathematics and astronomy, along with a fascination with Aristotelian logic. Later, as deacon of the cathedral school at Reims, Gerbert introduced both the sciences and Aristotelian logic to his students, many of whom in turn helped spread the new learning throughout cathedral schools in Europe.

During the eleventh and twelfth centuries, two important developments in universities resulted from the growing popularity of Aristotelian logic. One of these was the emergence of a new method of pursuing philosophical and theological truth by use of Aristotelian logic, known as **scholasticism**. Adherents of this new methodology began to subject long-held doctrines of the Church to rigorous scrutiny. The problem was that Aristotle posed a serious threat to Church authority since a better understanding of his ideas revealed just how incompatible his thinking was with religious doctrine. For example, Aristotle denied the creation of the world in favor of the world's eternity, and he denied the immortality of the soul.

What emerged was a fundamental disagreement between those who placed the truths of *faith* before the truths of *reason* in attempting to gain knowledge of God's existence and those who held the opposite view.

The most famous advocates of these opposing schools of thought were St. Anselm (ca. 1034–1109) and Peter Abelard (1079–1142). Anselm argued that faith must precede reason ("I believe in order that I might understand"). He further argued that proof of God's existence could be deduced by first accepting Church doctrine on the basis of faith and then proceeding to support these notions by reasoned argument. Abelard, the most popular teacher at the cathedral school of Notre Dame in Paris during these years, disagreed, arguing that "I understand in order that I might believe." Abelard's apparent favoring of reason over faith tipped the balance in favor of those who were inclined to question traditional Christian doctrine.

So alarmingly popular was Aristotle by the middle of the thirteenth century that in addition to the earlier division between those who advocated either the truths of faith or reason, a third perspective was offered by those who took a middle path. It was from the latter camp that St. Thomas Aquinas (ca. 1224–1274) originated. In his famous *Summa Theologica*, Aquinas argued that, instead of considering the truths of reason as being totally irreconcilable from the truths of faith, it was possible to consider a compromise, or a synthesis of the two, that would in the end lead to a knowledge of God's existence and, thus, to personal salvation. According to this construct, one could begin an upward journey to an understanding of God by first relying upon the truths of reason; but at a certain point one would have to abandon pure reason for the more enlightened approach afforded by faith, which would then allow an understanding of the mysteries of Christian doctrine and, thus, of God. Aquinas put it this way: "Grace (faith) does not destroy nature (reason)—it perfects her."

Law and Medicine   Consistent with the necessity of providing the requisite skills for advancement in the new urban and cosmopolitan ambience of twelfth-century urban life, universities began to offer training in law and medicine. By the early years of the twelfth century scholars at Bologna discovered the Roman legal tradition preserved in Justinian's celebrated *Corpus Iuris Civilis*. It was at Bologna around 1140 that the *Corpus* inspired a monk named Gratian to compile a comprehensive compendium of ecclesiastical law known as the *Decretum*. Gratian's student Peter Lombard's *Book of Sentences*, produced in 1150, served along with the *Decretum* as the foundation for the development of **canon law**, utilized by the papacy in its struggles to contest secular power.

> **Canon law:** The law of the Church.

Medical studies were taught at Salerno in the late eleventh century. Thanks to its location in Sicily, Salerno was able to assimilate Islamic and Byzantine medical advances. Serving as the nucleus of medical studies at Salerno were the works of the Roman physician Galen and the *Canon of Medicine* compiled by the Islamic scholar Ibn Sina (or Avicenna, 980–1037). These works formed the foundation of medical studies throughout medieval European universities.

Medieval Science   Another consequence of the appeal of Aristotle was a corresponding fascination with scientific texts of the ancient Greeks. The initial impulse in this direction was provided not only by Gerbert of Aurillac but also by Christian advances into Spain and southern Italy during the waning years of the eleventh century. The Christian conquest of Toledo in 1085, followed by the retaking of Sicily in 1091, provided opportunities for so-called wandering scholars from all over Europe to gain access to Islamic treasure troves of scientific learning. Adelard of Bath (ca. 1080–1152) was one of the forerunners of twelfth-century Western scholars who translated Greek scientific texts from Arabic into Latin. As such, Adelard served as an important bridge, or conduit, between the Islamic and western Christian worlds; and it was largely owing to his efforts that a new awareness and sense of curiosity about the mysteries of natural science began to circulate in Western intellectual circles.

Adelard contributed to what is often referred to as the age of Latin translators. The most prolific of these translators was Gerard of Cremona (ca. 1114–1187), who provided Latin translations of over 70 Greek scientific texts, including Ptolemy's *Almagest* and most of Aristotle's works on physics, along with numerous mathematical treatises such as Euclid's *Elements* and al-Khwarizmi's *Algebra*, and several medical treatises such as Galen's text and Avicenna's *Canon of Medicine*.

Perhaps the most important of Adelard's successors in England was Robert Grosseteste (ca. 1175–1253). Grosseteste represented a rare combination of ecclesiastical

The Gothic Cathedral

Of all the contributions of medieval Europe, the best-known and most readily recognizable is the Gothic cathedral. But the origins and evolution of this iconic symbol of medieval European Christianity are less familiar.

The origin of the cathedral can be traced back to late imperial Rome. Following Constantine's Edict of Milan in 313, Christians were no longer forced to worship in secret locations, and Church leaders began the quest to identify a type of public building that could accommodate larger congregations. Disused Roman temples were deemed unsuitable because of their pagan associations.

Many features of the Roman *basilica*, a civic hall traditionally used for public functions, rendered it ideally suited to the needs of early Christian worship. Its design was therefore assimilated by the early Church and transformed from pagan to Christian usage. The basilica style featured a long central aisle (or nave), roofed over with timber, ending with an intersecting transept and an arched passage into a semicircular *apse* (or sanctuary) with a raised platform where the presiding magistrate sat in judgment. The first adaptation of the pagan basilica plan to Christian usage appeared in several churches constructed during Constantine's reign.

St. Denis Cathedral—Nave.

Several factors combined during the post-Roman, early medieval period to produce the assimilation of some earlier Roman and Christian architectural styles with evolving European circumstances. The result was the Romanesque style of church architecture, which appeared in different guises across the period ca. 800–1000. Most important, however, was the incorporation of several features associated with Romanesque architecture: the replacement of the basilica's low timber roofs with heavy stone barrel vaults, which spanned the space over the nave and in turn required massive stone piers and exterior walls to support the weight, and the resulting gloomy interiors. In addition, the apse was expanded beyond the transept by the addition of a circular walkway (the ambulatory) to allow crowds of pilgrims to view Christian relics; and the focal point of the exterior was now the western façade, flanked by two towers, with a tympanum featuring scenes like the Last Judgment. The spread of Benedictine monasteries as well as the emergence of powerful German emperors during the tenth and eleventh centuries provoked additional changes in Romanesque churches. Among these were the enlargement of interiors, the increased height of the nave—utilizing vaulting and groin arches—and the addition of a clerestory with rounded arches above the nave to admit more light into the interior, as in Speyer Cathedral.

and secular interests; he was for a time bishop of Lincoln but also a dabbler in the new scientific studies of natural phenomena. Grosseteste made a distinctively important contribution to the advancement of science in that he recognized the value of mathematics, and he was among the earliest scholastics to question the scientific

The revitalization of urban life in the eleventh and twelfth centuries, along with a marked increase in lay piety, prompted architects to assimilate some features of the Romanesque into a new design more in keeping with changing tastes and practices. The first attempt to open up gloomy Romanesque interiors—and to lay the foundations for what emerged as the new Gothic style—was made at the abbey church of St. Denis in Paris under the direction of its abbot, the famous Suger (1085–1151). In his rebuilding of the abbey church of St. Denis near Paris in 1144, Suger's intention was to enlarge the interior spaces of Romanesque churches, to provide more light, and at the same time to increase the upward reach of their exteriors. Among the innovations at St. Denis was the incorporation of stained glass panels in the outer walls, which provided dazzling arrays of color in the interior and presented stories from the Bible. Thus, Suger writes, "the whole [church] would shine with the wonderful and uninterrupted light of most sacred windows, pervading the interior beauty."

Three subsequent architectural inventions of the twelfth century enabled architects to expand on Suger's original contributions: the ribbed vault, the pointed arch, and the flying buttress. The ribbed vault allowed for thinner outer walls, with the result that they could be opened up to contain large glass windows that allowed more light. Pointed arches, copied from earlier Islamic architecture through cultural interactions in Sicily and Spain, allowed for higher vertical thrusts in weight distribution, resulting in soaring naves, many well over 100 feet in height. Flying buttresses—perhaps the most innovative feature of the Gothic style—were then used to support the thinner outer walls, distributing the thrust of the ribbed vaults and pointed arches away from the outer wall and down toward the ground.

From 1170 to 1270, 80 Gothic cathedrals (including Chartres and Notre Dame in Paris) and nearly 500 churches were built throughout France. From France the Gothic style spread throughout Europe; in 1175 the cathedral at Canterbury, England, was rebuilt in the Gothic style. That these monuments of Christian devotion and medieval architectural ingenuity continue to inspire awe is a testament to the cultural contributions of medieval European civilization.

Speyer Cathedral—Interior.

Flying Buttress.

Questions

- How does the Gothic cathedral demonstrate the origins-interactions-adaptations process in action?

- What types of cultural adaptations are evident in houses of worship built today?

authority of Aristotle, particularly Aristotle's theory of the formation of rainbows. Grosseteste's arguments were absorbed and carried forward by his student Roger Bacon (ca. 1214–1294), whose principal contribution to the development of Western science was to emphasize the role of induction and experimentation.

The advances made by Grosseteste at Oxford were carried across the Channel to Paris, where scholars like Jean Buridan (ca. 1300–1370) and Nicole Oresme (1323–1382) continued the assault on Aristotle's credibility. Through a series of experiments, Buridan disproved Aristotle's theory of motion, which erroneously argued that objects remain in motion only through the continuous application of an external force. Rather, Buridan demonstrated that some sort of inner force, imparted to an object at the moment it was set in motion, was the agent. Like Buridan, Oresme also took issue with many of Aristotle's scientific propositions, particularly the idea that the earth is immobile at the center of the cosmos.

Crisis and Creativity, 1300–1415

The fourteenth century marks the final phase of European Christian civilization and is often considered an age of transition to the European Renaissance. The early part of the century witnessed a series of economic reversals. Near mid-century a devastating plague originating in southeast Asia ravaged Europe, killing as much as one-third of its population and generating further social upheaval. Centralized kingdoms developed a sense of national identity and consolidation; one result was a long, drawn-out period of war between England and France that began in 1337 and ended in 1453. In addition, the authority of the papacy was challenged from without by powerful European secular rulers and weakened from within by a series of internal problems and philosophical disputes. As bleak as things were, however, the fourteenth century can be considered a time of transition from medieval institutions and perspectives to early Renaissance ideals. Signs of new creative forces arising from the ashes of the fourteenth century appeared as early as the middle of the century.

The Calamitous Fourteenth Century

Fourteenth-century Europe experienced all manner of dearth, disease, death, and dissolution. The early part of the century witnessed a series of reversals in the economic and social realms, brought on initially by a dramatic climatic change in the year 1315 that resulted in a prolonged period of poor harvests followed by famine. Near mid-century a disastrous plague added to the misery of daily life.

Famine   During the early years of the fourteenth century Europe was hit by a disastrous combination of factors that produced a prolonged period of famine. One factor was a sudden disparity between an expanding population and its available food supply. From ca. 1000 to 1300 Europe's population had nearly doubled to a total of around 80 million, thanks to advances in agricultural technology. By 1300, however, no new advances were forthcoming. In addition, after centuries of expansion and clearing of lands, Europe suddenly ran out of new frontiers, resulting in a shortage of land available for increased agricultural production. To make matters worse, the average annual temperature dropped during this period, which shortened the summer growing season. At the same time, an unusually prolonged series of rainy seasons in the spring and summer planting seasons, followed by a succession of harsh winters, resulted in a famine that extended from 1315 to 1322.

Plague   Near mid-century, Europe's already weakened populations suffered a horrific outbreak of bubonic plague. The disease originated in Cambodia, Burma, and Vietnam; it was then transmitted across Asia in goods and wares transported by Mongol traders in the 1330s. From there it spread westward along trade routes to the Black Sea. The plague was introduced to the West when grain-carrying Genoese merchant ships, infested with diseased rats, sailed from the Crimea to ports in Sicily and northern Italy in 1346–1347. Within a year, the plague had spread into northern Europe via trade routes, carried by infected rats and fleas, fanning out across Europe north of the Alps.

The disease took its name "Black Death" from the appearance of blackened body sores, called

Burial of Plague Victims. With up to 50 percent of the people in some places in Europe dying of the plague, burial scenes, such as this one depicted in a Flemish manuscript, were common throughout the middle and late fourteenth century.

"*buboes*" (hence the name "bubonic plague"), especially in the lymph nodes, that announced the arrival of the disease. Once the dreaded black sores appeared, infected people suffered horribly with high fevers, swollen lymph nodes, and painfully aching joints and usually had only 3 days to live. The plague ran unchecked throughout Europe from 1348 to 1352 and returned sporadically in the 1360s, 1370s, and 1390s. The highly contagious disease was next to impossible to contain for a variety of reasons. For one thing Europe's population was weakened and ravaged as a consequence of the great famine. For another, overcrowded European cities, with their lack of sanitation, created ideal breeding conditions for the rapid spread of the disease. Mortality figures are difficult to establish with certainty. Nevertheless, it has been estimated that England alone may have lost nearly 1 million from a total population of around 4 million. Urban areas were the hardest hit; Florence suffered losses amounting to around 50,000 out of a total population of 85,000. A reasonable estimate of the number of people who died throughout Europe as a result of the first wave of the plague puts the total loss at about one-third of the entire population (see Map 11.4).

A series of economic and social consequences of the Black Death resounded throughout Europe. The falling off of Europe's population resulted, in urban areas, in less demand for goods and manufactured items, causing a downturn in commerce and trade, and, in rural areas, in a similar decline in demand for grain products. Another result of the overall decline in Europe's population was the reduction in the number of agricultural workers, whose labor was suddenly more sought after than before the plague. The result of these increasing tensions between the well off and those less well off was a series of social uprisings throughout Europe. In Paris a disturbance known as the "Jacquerie" broke out in 1358, and in Florence the Ciompi rebellion flared up in 1378. The most serious social revolt occurred in London in 1381. Known as "The Peasants' Revolt," the uprising was more broadly based and included wealthy country residents as well as participants from the ranks of the urban working classes.

The Hundred Years' War   From the mid-fourteenth to the mid-fifteenth century, Europe was embroiled in a disastrous conflict, coined the "Hundred Years' War" by nineteenth-century historians. At issue was a long-simmering dispute over English landholdings in France, the result of the Norman Conquest. More immediately, when the English king Edward III (r. 1327–1377) laid claim to the vacant French throne

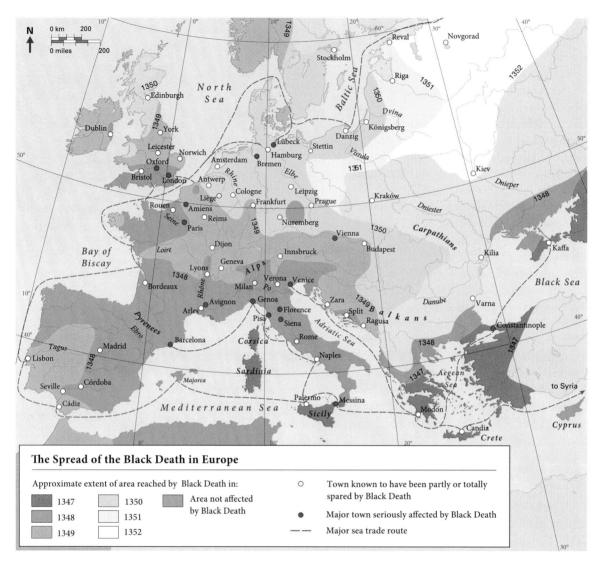

The Spread of the Black Death in Europe

Approximate extent of area reached by Black Death in:

1347	1350	Area not affected by Black Death
1348	1351	
1349	1352	

○ Town known to have been partly or totally spared by Black Death

● Major town seriously affected by Black Death

– – – Major sea trade route

MAP **11.4 The Spread of the Black Death in Europe.**

in 1328, his claim was rejected in favor of Charles IV (r. 1322–1328), the first of the Valois rulers. These issues came to a head in 1337 when Philip VI (r. 1328–1350) seized control of Gascony and fighting erupted in earnest between the two countries.

The conflict was fought in three phases. Early on, English forces racked up significant victories at the Battle of Crécy in 1346 and then again at the Battle of Poitiers in 1356, where English longbowmen handed smashing defeats to the mounted French knights. The same thing occurred later at the Battle of Agincourt in 1415, where Henry V (r. 1413–1422) led vastly outnumbered English forces (only 6,000 as opposed to 20,000) to score a surprising victory while suffering relatively few casualties. Suddenly, however, when it seemed that English forces were on the verge of declaring victory, a 17-year-old peasant girl named Joan of Arc (ca. 1412–1431) encouraged the uncrowned Charles VII (r. 1422–1461) to relieve the siege of Orleans in 1429, where English forces were routed. The victory at Orleans inspired the French to one success after another. The conflict finally came to an end in 1453, when the English conceded a French victory in terms agreed to in the Treaty of Paris, leaving the English in possession of only the port of Calais (see Map 11.5).

The Hundred Years' War affected almost every aspect of European life. Like the plague, the war was a constant reminder of the omnipresence of death. The economic consequences of the war were equally serious. The war—fought entirely on French soil—destroyed both crops and small farms. In both England and France, financing the war meant new and increased taxes—and further woes for the peasantry, who bore the brunt of these increased financial obligations. The war even affected the religious realm. It prevented the resolution of the **Great Schism** as rival popes sought the support of contending French and English kings and their subjects.

Over 100 years of war brought about a number of innovations in weaponry, military tactics, and strategy. The English use of foot soldiers armed with longbows resulted in the dominance of the infantry over the cavalry of armored, mounted knights. Important advances in warfare resulted from the first extensive European use of various sorts of firearms, invented in China and transmitted to the West by Muslims.

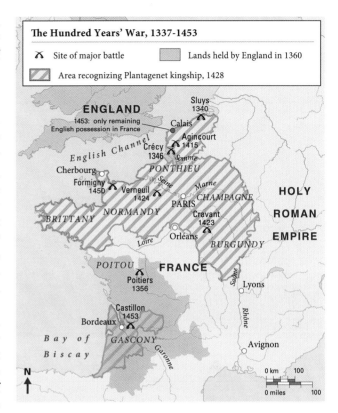

MAP **11.5** The Hundred Years' War, 1337–1453.

Crises in the Church

Troubles began during the papacy of Pope Boniface VIII (r. 1294–1303), whose stubborn personality clashed with the ambitious national interests of Philip IV (r. 1285–1314) of France. Philip, desperate for money in order to consolidate royal power, levied a tax on the French clergy. In response, Boniface excommunicated Philip; he retaliated by ordering the imprisonment of the pope in 1303, who subsequently died from the shock of this rude treatment. Boniface's successor, Clement V (r. 1305–1314), left Rome and took up residence in a splendid palace at Avignon, on the French border. Clement appointed a number of French clergymen to the College of Cardinals. From 1305 to 1378 successive French popes continued to reside at Avignon, a period known as the *Avignon Papacy*.

In 1378 Pope Gregory XI (r. 1370–1378) returned to Rome, but he died shortly after his arrival there. Acting, as they later said, under pressure of a Roman mob to elect "a Roman, or at least an Italian" as the next pope, the predominantly French College of Cardinals elected an Italian archbishop, Urban VI (r. 1378–1389). Urban badly mistreated the cardinals and insisted on a series of outlandish reforms. The cardinals, regretting their selection of Urban, returned to Avignon and promptly elected a Frenchman as the new pope, Clement VII (r. 1378–1394). An attempt of the Council of Pisa in 1409 to resolve the conflict merely intensified the embarrassment. The council deposed both reigning popes and named a new one, Alexander V (r. 1409–1410). However, the two reigning popes refused to step down, with the result that the Church had not one or two but *three* popes.

Great Schism: The period 1378–1417 marked by divided papal allegiances in Latin Christendom.

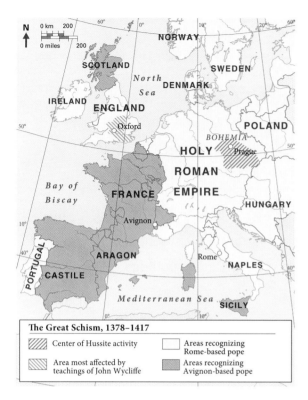

MAP **11.6 The Great Schism,**
1378–1417.

Adding to the Church's problems were several outspoken critics of its doctrine. One of the earliest of these critics was John Wycliffe (ca. 1330–1384), an Oxford theologian. Wycliffe railed against the wealth and abuses of the higher clergy, denied the power of priests to act as intermediaries between believers and God, and disputed the validity of many **sacraments**, including the most central of Christian dogmas, the sacrament of the Eucharist (sometimes referred to as Communion or the Lord's Supper), which holds that Christ's presence is revealed in consecrated bread and wine. Wycliffe also oversaw the translation of the Bible into Middle English. Wycliffe's teachings reached Bohemia in eastern Europe when the English king Richard II (r. 1377–1399) married the princess Anne of Bohemia. John Huss (1370–1415), a radical religious reformer and preacher at Prague, enthusiastically supported Wycliffe's ideas, especially the English theologian's argument for the primacy of scripture as the basis for all Christian doctrine (see Map 11.6).

Signs of a New Era in the Fifteenth Century

All of the instances of doom and gloom we have mentioned signaled the waning of earlier medieval values, perspectives, and institutions. Yet, at the same time, dire situations in the fourteenth century prompted adaptations and subsequent transformations in the succeeding century that prefigured the transition to the Renaissance. We can observe these adjustments in political, economic, and cultural aspects of fifteenth-century Europe.

Political Reorganization in France and England   Out of the ashes of the Hundred Years' War arose new conceptions of royal authority in both England and France that in many ways set the stage for the appearance of the "new monarchies" in the second half of the fifteenth century. In France, for example, fifteenth-century rulers utilized the demands and pressures of warfare as rationales to centralize their authority. One expedient was to overhaul the royal bureaucracy in order to enhance its efficiency and power. Another, more profitable tack was the raising of new taxes without consulting the Estates-General.

The state of politics in England was similarly affected by the course of the Hundred Years' War. Across the course of the war English monarchs were repeatedly forced to convene Parliament in order to gain quick access to much needed funds to prosecute the war effort. Before granting monies to the crown, however, the House of Commons, consisting of merchants and lesser nobility, insisted on "redress of grievances before consent to taxation." As a result, the House of Commons eventually gained the right to introduce all important tax legislation in Parliament, it was granted its first speaker in 1376, and it was given the right to impeach irresponsible members of the king's government.

Sacrament: An outward and physical sign of an inward and spiritual grace.

European Commerce and Trade   Europe's fifteenth-century economic recovery was even more pronounced in commerce. When France regained control of Flanders during the course of the Hundred Years' War, England—currently at war with the French—was forced to abandon its profitable wool trade with Flemish merchants. As a result, England developed a far more lucrative trade in manufactured cloth products, of which by 1500 it had become a leading exporter. Flemish towns changed practices as well, switching from the sale of expensive finished garments to trade in cheaper cloths that were sold to wider markets.

When the Hundred Years' War disrupted trade in France, new lanes of commerce opened up across Europe. Germanic towns in northern Europe had formed a trading alliance, known as the **Hanseatic League** (from *hansa*, meaning "company") as early as the thirteenth century. The league reached the peak of its influence during the later fourteenth and fifteenth centuries, with trading links from London in the west to Novgorod in eastern Europe. A new commercial axis extended from the cities of the Hanseatic League in the north southward to the northern Italian cities of Venice and Genoa. Crossing the Alps, this new trade route stretched through the German states to the northern reaches of Europe.

Hanseatic League: A trade network of allied ports along the North Sea and Baltic coasts, founded in 1256.

Of crucial importance for the future of European trade was the collapse of the so-called Pax Mongolica in 1368. Following the expansion of the Mongol Empire during the thirteenth and fourteenth centuries, travel and trade networks flourished between China and the West across the Silk Road. Thus, the Mongols facilitated the transfer of significant technological innovations from China to Europe, including gunpowder and mechanical clocks. When, however, Mongol rule in China dissolved and was replaced by the Ming dynasty, less interested in ties with the West, travel on the Silk Road was no longer safe or profitable. Faced with the necessity of reaching the riches of the East by alternate means, European merchants were forced to resort to southern maritime routes, in use from the 750s onward.

Innovations in Business Techniques   A combination of innovative economic practices contributed to a revitalization of Europe's economy during the fifteenth century. Smaller markets, caused by the economic crises of the fourteenth century, brought on increased competition among merchants, who sought ever more creative business methods in order to remain solvent. New accounting procedures, such as double-entry bookkeeping, increased the efficiency of record keeping. In addition, the introduction of maritime insurance, which protected investments in risky seaborne trade, fueled an increase in trans-Mediterranean trade and commerce, while at the same time increasing profits for individual investors.

New banking procedures also facilitated the expansion of Europe's economy by providing loans to merchants and manufacturers. Florence emerged across the fifteenth century as the center of huge banking partnerships, like the Bardi, Peruzzi, and Medici; and although the Bardi and Peruzzi eventually collapsed, the Medici family went on to dominate Florentine civic affairs by 1500.

Developments in the Church   As a consequence of the disintegration of papal leadership during the fourteenth century, the Church was controlled by councils of bishops in the early fifteenth century. The movement that emerged from the decisions made by the Council of Constance was known as *conciliarism*. In order to resolve the crises of the fourteenth century, the Council of Constance

(1414–1417) was convened by the Holy Roman emperor. Its first order of business was to depose the three reigning popes and to restore papal authority to a single pontiff, who took the name Martin V (r. 1417–1431). Second, to put an end to heretical movements, principally the followers of John Wycliffe, the council convicted John Huss of heresy and burned him at the stake. The execution of Huss had momentous implications for the future of the Church, especially in Germany. Huss's region of Bohemia emerged as a hotbed of heresy, and these anticlerical sentiments helped fuel Martin Luther's Protestant Reformation, which began in neighboring Saxony in the next century. Finally, to improve the management of the Church, the council declared that henceforth councils of bishops would meet frequently in order to place popes under their strict control.

The conciliar movement was an attempt by the bishops to wrest control of the Church from popes. The popes resisted the conciliar movement but had to make concessions to secular rulers to gain their support. In 1438, for example, the Pragmatic Sanction of Bourges granted the French king control over Church affairs in France. The Pragmatic Sanction of Mainz, issued the following year, conceded control over Church matters to the Holy Roman emperor. The result of these concessions was the further weakening of the Roman Church and the creation of national churches, independent of control from Rome.

Literature   Equally as dramatic as new directions in religion were significant and widespread changes in literary expression. Most basic was the growing popularity of cultural expression in the vernacular instead of Latin. Although the vernacular first made its appearance in France in the later 1100s, education in the vernacular was especially popular in the city-states of northern Italy, where the emphasis was on educating students for productive careers in the secular world, rather than training them to become priests.

Consistent with the increase in vernacular literacy, particularly in Florence, a number of Italian authors chose to write in the vernacular rather than in Latin. A particularly noteworthy example is the poet Dante Alighieri (1265–1321), author of *The Divine Comedy*, a long epic poem written in Italian and completed in 1321. The theme of Dante's *Divine Comedy* is the author's journey from the pit of hell, through the torments of purgatory, and into the blessings of paradise.

Two Italian authors of the next generation continued Dante's legacy. Francesco Petrarch (1304–1374), known as "the father of Renaissance humanism," turned to Roman authors and classical texts, whose values more closely resembled the secular, materialistic world of everyday life in Florence. Petrarch also wrote a series of love sonnets to his beloved Laura, in Tuscan Italian. In Giovanni Boccaccio (1313–1375) also we move even further from the medieval toward the Renaissance. Boccaccio's *Decameron*, written between 1352 and 1353, represents a further drift away from medieval literary conventions—and toward the Roman classical past—in that it draws its inspiration from the first-century Roman author Petronius and his scandalous *Satyricon*.

English and French writers of the fourteenth century also began to produce works in their native languages. *Piers Plowman*, composed in Middle English by William Langland (ca. 1332–1400), presents a series of complaints and laments about current abuses in late fourteenth-century England, especially among the aristocracy and the clergy. Geoffrey Chaucer (ca. 1340–1400), a friend and contemporary of

Langland's, also wrote in Middle English. Like Langland, Chaucer satirized abuses in contemporary society. His *Canterbury Tales* are a series of stories told by travelers making their annual pilgrimage from London to the shrine of St. Thomas Becket in Canterbury. Christine de Pizan (ca. 1364–1430) of France composed both poetry and prose; she was primarily concerned with advancing the status of women and for her criticisms of male behaviors is often considered the first feminist writer. In her *Epistle to the God of Love*, for example, she criticizes the Roman poet Ovid for attributing to women "… nasty ways."

Philosophy   Running parallel with new dimensions in literature were bold departures in philosophy that challenged basic medieval theological beliefs. In place of St. Thomas Aquinas' attempt to reconcile differences between the truths of faith and reason, the intellectual world of fourteenth-century Europe turned decidedly toward the latter, especially toward Aristotle. The earliest philosopher to take this approach was the Oxford Franciscan John Duns Scotus (ca. 1266–1308). Critical of Aquinas, Scotus argued for the strict separation of reason from theology. William of Ockham (ca. 1285–1349), another Oxford Franciscan, carried the assault on the Aquinas synthesis even further. He argued for extreme nominalism, arguing that only the truths of reason, vested in individual things, could be known for certain. Therefore, no metaphysical knowledge is possible; and from this, it is impossible to have any sure knowledge of the existence of God. That being the case, only a personal, mystical association with God was available to the believer.

Putting It All Together

Following the collapse of the united Mediterranean Roman Empire, a new postclassical, Christian religious civilization gradually developed in western Europe during the period ca. 600–1400. The Germanic invasions that brought down Roman rule in the western provinces destroyed imperial unity in the West and created in Europe a series of smaller political entities. After a brief period of centralized imperial rule during the reign of Charlemagne in the later eighth century, medieval Europe fell back in the ninth and tenth centuries into a pattern of decentralized political entities that provided for law and order at the local, instead of an empire-wide, level. Feudalism, as this arrangement is known, prevented the reassertion of a centralized European empire and prepared Europe for the appearance of several highly centralized, competing kingdoms. One advantage of this "political pluralism" was the appearance of competition among the states of Europe, which in turn created a sense of vitality and progress in the West.

In terms of cultural developments, the Germanic invasions and subsequent destruction of Roman rule in the West were far more disruptive than anywhere else on the globe and forced the formation of a new, distinctly European, postclassical culture. Whereas other civilizations experienced similar periods of chaos, these were often mere interruptions, to be followed by the reappearance of slightly altered preexisting cultural patterns. In Europe, however, a brand new culture began to emerge from the rubble of the disintegration of the Greco-Roman classical civilization, formed from a blending of three elements that had formerly been antagonistic to each other: Roman legacies, Germanic customs, and Christian institutions (see Concept Map). Of these, the role of the Christian Church would prove the most important in the long run in shaping a new European religious civilization. In much the same way that Buddhism, Hinduism, Confucianism, and Islam undergirded civilizations in Asia and Africa, Christianity served as the basic unifying force that held together the new European civilization.

During the fourteenth century Europe experienced several transforming events. The horrors of famine and plague, accompanied by over a century of warfare between England and France, cast a pall of gloom over European society, which in turn called into question traditional medieval values and perspectives. In addition, a series of internal problems in the Church resulted in a lessening of its authority and prestige. At the same time, however, several developments—particularly in the cultural arts— prepared Europe for the transition to Renaissance secularism and humanism.

▶ For additional resources, including maps, primary sources, visuals, and quizzes, please go to www.oup.com/us/vonsivers. Please see the Further Resources section at the back of the book for additional readings and suggested websites.

Thinking Through Patterns

▶ **How did the Merovingians and Carolingians construct a new Christian European civilization during the seventh and eighth centuries CE?**

The Merovingians and Carolingians constructed a new Christian European civilization during the seventh and eighth centuries by utilizing the support of the Christian Church. Through their conversion to Christianity, as well as their support and encouragement of monastic expansion, they earned the support of bishops, priests, and monks in all regions of their kingdom. In addition, the creation of the Franco-papal alliance during the eighth century, followed by Charlemagne's personal involvement in Church affairs, ensured the emergence of a new Christian foundation for Europe.

Some key factors in the political, economic, and social recovery of Europe during the eleventh and twelfth centuries included the emergence of centralized kingdoms in France and England, which replaced the decentralized cells of political authority during the ninth and tenth centuries. The expansion of agricultural advances and the development of commerce and trade produced a population surge, which in turn resulted in urbanization and the emergence of a new bourgeois middle class of merchants and traders.

▶ **What were key factors in the political, economic, and social recovery of Europe during the eleventh and twelfth centuries?**

▶ **What were some cultural and intellectual developments during the "twelfth-century renaissance," and how did they contribute to medieval civilization?**

During the "twelfth-century renaissance" urban-centered cathedral schools developed into universities in Europe. In order to serve the needs of an expanding urban and commercial economy, more practical disciplines like law and medicine were developed in revised curricula. The influx of Aristotelian logic and science, assimilated from contacts in Spain and Sicily between Latin scholars—known as the Latin translators—and their Islamic counterparts, resulted in a prolonged debate between the truths of reason and the truths of faith. Although temporarily resolved by Aquinas in the later thirteenth century, Aristotelian nominalism dominated philosophy and theology in the fourteenth century. Another result of the fascination with Aristotle was the development of natural science at Oxford and Paris, which during the later thirteenth and early fourteenth centuries began to uncover flaws in Aristotelian celestial and terrestrial scientific conceptions.

As a result of a series of ecclesiastical reforms in both the monastic and episcopal arms of the Church, a series of increasingly powerful popes began to assert papal primacy over secular rulers and, indeed, over all European institutions. Pope Gregory VII humbled the German emperor Henry IV in the eleventh century, and Pope Innocent III did the same with King John of England in the beginning of the thirteenth century.

▶ **How did the Church influence political developments in Europe during the twelfth and thirteenth centuries?**

▶ **What events made fourteenth-century Europe so dismal? How did these combine to spell the gradual demise of medieval institutions and perspectives?**

The "calamitous fourteenth century" witnessed several unprecedented setbacks that, taken together, signaled the end of the medieval era and the early stages of the Renaissance era. Among these events were the Black Death, the Hundred Years' War, and the Avignon papacy followed by the Great Schism, which produced not one, not two, but eventually three popes. At the same time men of letters, philosophers, as well as theologians began to challenge earlier assertions of papal authority, resulting in the Council of Constance in (1414–1417), which ultimately replaced papal control of the Church with councils of bishops during the fifteenth century.

Chapter 12 600-1600 CE

Contrasting Patterns in India and China

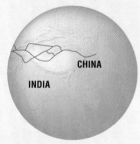

While Arab armies had worked their way through Sasanid Persia by the middle of the seventh century CE, their first reports on northwest India were not terribly encouraging. The land was described as desert waste, with few resources and a hostile populace. They made at least 10 attempts to invade the northwest Indian region of Sind, and all 10 times they were defeated by local rulers. According to the *Chachnama* (the history of the campaign written hundreds of years later, in the thirteenth century), following these failed attempts a more ambitious invasion was mounted by Muhammad Ibn Qasim, a cousin of the governor of Iraq who was responsible for the conquest of eastern lands.

Ibn Qasim's army pursued the move into India with brutal efficiency. Wearing coats of chain mail armor and equipped with siege machinery for hurling projectiles and battering down walls, they decimated the major cities, executed most of the defenders, and extracted plunder and slaves before moving in to completely occupy the area in 711. Though Ibn Qasim's rule in the wake of his violent conquest was considered relatively moderate, the *Chachnama* claims that he met his death through a spectacular episode of duplicity concocted by his new subjects.

ABOVE: Mongol archers depicted in the Djamil el Tawarika, *a fourteenth-century history of the world written by the Persian scholar Rashid al-Din Tabib (1247–1318).*

When the daughters of Dihar, the ruler of the conquered city of Dehal (Karachi in modern Pakistan), were taken back to the governor of Iraq as tribute, they accused Ibn Qasim of making sexual advances toward them. The governor immediately ordered his cousin Ibn Qasim to be sewn up in a stifling raw leather sheath and transported home. This torturous mode of transport was meant to inflict maximal suffering, and indeed, the heat and lack of room for breathing soon did their work. Ibn Qasim died 2 days into the journey, and when his putrefied body was shown to the women who had accused him, they proudly confessed their deception and revenge on their conqueror.

Though the reliability of the *Chachnama's* account is questionable, it has come to symbolize the dramatic clash of cultural and religious outlooks that have marked the history of the Indian subcontinent ever since. In this contested area between radically different religious civilizations, the Hindu vision of Islam has remained one of ruthless conquest and purposeful disregard for long-established religious traditions. Muslims, on the other hand, have tended to view Hindus as despised infidels for whom no act of treachery is out of bounds. Such competing visions, despite periodic efforts to find common ground, have created over the centuries the pattern of *syncretic* social and political formation (a pattern in which two different traditions evolve with little or no common ground). In this case, the two cultures actually coexist with considerable hostility toward one another. Despite extensive interaction, neither side has adopted much from the other; in fact, the dominant pattern has been that each has used the differences of the other to define its own religious civilization more consciously and distinctly.

The case of China provides a useful contrast. Here, despite a pervasive belief among officials and scholars of the Song dynasty (960–1279) that the fall of the previous dynasty, the Tang, had come about in large part because of the influence of the "foreign" religion of Buddhism, there were no mass persecutions or forced conversions. While Song Confucian scholars tended to lecture their audiences about "unseemly" Buddhist "superstitions," they also borrowed from Buddhist cosmological perspectives and Daoist beliefs to create a pattern of *synthetic* social and political formation (a pattern in which the most durable opposing elements merge together into a compatible whole). The result was a coherent Chinese religious civilization for the next 1,000 years, based on Neo-Confucianism, the fused body of Daoist and Buddhist religious traditions, and Confucian ethics.

India: The Clash of Cultures

As we saw in Chapter 8, the early centuries of the Common Era marked the maturing of two large divisions among the multiple varieties of religious and cultural experience of India. The first was the rise and spread of Buddhism out of northern India into central Asia via the Silk Road and on to China and ultimately to Korea, Japan, and Vietnam. Along the way, the main branches of the various Buddhist schools were created—Theravada and Mahayana—and their scriptural foundations solidified.

Seeing Patterns

▶ How did interactions between Muslims and Hindus in India lead to religious syncretism?

▶ What steps were taken by Hindus and Muslims to lessen the conflicts between the two rival religious traditions?

▶ How was the Tang dynasty in China different from its predecessors and successors?

▶ How effectively did the religious and philosophical traditions of Buddhism, Confucianism, and Daoism blend together in creating Neo-Confucianism? Where did they clash?

More important for the long term of Indian history, however, was that the efforts of the Guptas during India's "golden age" from the fourth to the sixth centuries CE helped in the maturation of the vast variety of religious practices that we know as "Hinduism." For it was Hinduism, rather than Buddhism, that would dominate Indian cultural and religious life until Islam ultimately established itself in the north. In the south and some areas of the north, however, Hinduism remained the dominant religious tradition down to the present day. Hence, India was transformed from a Hindu religious civilization into a frontier between the competing religious civilizations of Islam and Hinduism.

India After the Guptas

By the 500s CE, the last Gupta monarchs were under increasing pressure from a branch of the central Asian Huns pressing on their borders. Following the old invasion routes through the Khyber Pass into northern India, the Huns established themselves in the Punjab and adjacent regions and soon settled in to create new states as the Gupta lands shrank and finally dissolved.

Harsha Vardhana   One relatively stable regime that achieved a certain degree of power in the north following the Guptas was that of Thanesar [TAHN-uh-sar] under its ruler Harsha Vardhana (r. 606–647). Like Ashoka of the Mauryans, Harsha is one of the few Indian monarchs about whom we know a good deal. The *Harshacarita* or *Life of Harsha*, by the poet Bana and the account of the famous Chinese Buddhist pilgrim Xuan Zang (see Chapter 9), who traveled throughout India from 630 to 644, offer a number of insights into Harsha's reign.

When Xuan Zang met Harsha in his capital at Kanauj on the Ganges River, he discovered that the ruler was a devout Buddhist. Xuan Zang's account notes the degree to which Buddhism had once permeated the land, despite the favoritism shown by the Guptas earlier toward Hinduism. It was also clear, however, that many Buddhist monasteries were now abandoned or in disrepair. Bolstered by the new devotional strains of Hinduism, the decline of Buddhism on the subcontinent as a whole was well advanced.

MAP 12.1 Harsha's Empire, ca. 645 CE.

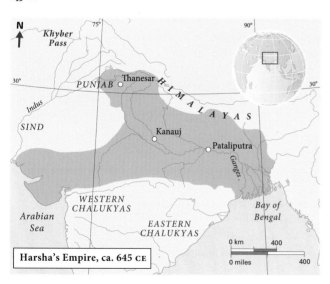

Harsha's Empire, ca. 645 CE

Still, Xuan Zang found Harsha's kingdom well run, wealthy, justly administered, and in many ways a model state. The state, however, barely outlived its ruler. The middle years of Harsha's reign saw the new power of the Arabs probing the borders of Sind, the arid plain to the east of the Indus River, in advance of their full conquest in 711. Meanwhile, following Harsha's reign, northern India was once again divided into regional kingdoms (see Map 12.1).

In the interim, the political center of the subcontinent had shifted south. By the latter part of the ninth century, a Chola [KO-luh] state based in Tanjore [Tan-JO-ray] had concluded its long and bitter contest with the Pallavis. In 897 they captured Kanchipuram [Kan-chih-POOR-um], advanced into the Pandya kingdom in the southern tip of the peninsula, and captured their capital at Madurai. In the next century, the Cholas conquered Kerala, invaded Sri Lanka, and launched campaigns aimed at expanding their control of the trade with southeast Asia. The Cholas then advanced northward, allying themselves with the eastern Chalukyas in 1030. In the west, however, the revived western Chalukyas absorbed the Rashtakutras in 970 and repeatedly fought the Cholas to a standstill.

In the meantime, the development of the clove trade of the Moluccas (in what is now Indonesia) vastly increased the strategic value of the area, which the Indian-influenced Sumatran state of Srivijaya attempted to exploit in the tenth and eleventh centuries. In response to the exorbitant rates and threats of piracy Srivijaya posed, the Cholas sent a maritime expedition in 1025 that smashed its major ports and reduced its power for a time. In this context, the coming of the

Rajarajeshwara Temple, Tanjore India. This early eleventh-century Hindu temple is the largest in all of India and one of the most beautiful. It was richly endowed with spoils taken from Chola conquests.

Arabs to India resulted in a broadening of the subcontinent's position in world trade. Along the western ports of India, Arab merchants continued to ply their trade much as before. Despite the newfound religious antagonisms, caravan traffic also continued much as before and India became the bottom leg of a triangle of trade that spanned Eurasia (see Map 12.2).

Vijayanagar   After several centuries of expansion southward by Muslim sultanates in north and central India, a new Hindu state emerged in 1336 with the founding of the city of Vijayanagar ("City of Victory"). The last in the two-millennium pattern of rule by god-kings, the new state was deemed fabulously wealthy by visitors to its capital, including the first Portuguese traders in the sixteenth century. From the City of Victory, the rulers presided over an arrangement that, like the Gupta Empire, some scholars have described as feudal as it absorbed the remnants of the older southern kingdoms. For example, local leaders called *nayaks* collected taxes and provided men and provisions for the army, while retaining considerable autonomy within their own realms.

For more than 200 years the state of Vijayanagar withstood penetration by the various Islamic sultanates of the north. In fact, following the destruction of the Tugh-Lug line of Muslim rulers in Delhi in 1398, Vijayanagar and its associated Hindu *nayaks* expanded their control to nearly the entire southern third of India. In 1564, however, their huge armies were decimated by a regional coalition of northern sultanates whose forces were equipped with the newest technologies—cannon

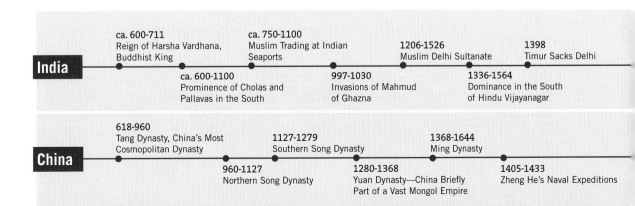

India

ca. 600-711 Reign of Harsha Vardhana, Buddhist King	ca. 750-1100 Muslim Trading at Indian Seaports	1206-1526 Muslim Delhi Sultanate	1398 Timur Sacks Delhi

ca. 600-1100
Prominence of Cholas and
Pallavas in the South

997-1030
Invasions of Mahmud
of Ghazna

1336-1564
Dominance in the South
of Hindu Vijayanagar

China

618-960
Tang Dynasty, China's Most
Cosmopolitan Dynasty

1127-1279
Southern Song Dynasty

1368-1644
Ming Dynasty

960-1127
Northern Song Dynasty

1280-1368
Yuan Dynasty—China Briefly
Part of a Vast Mongol Empire

1405-1433
Zheng He's Naval Expeditions

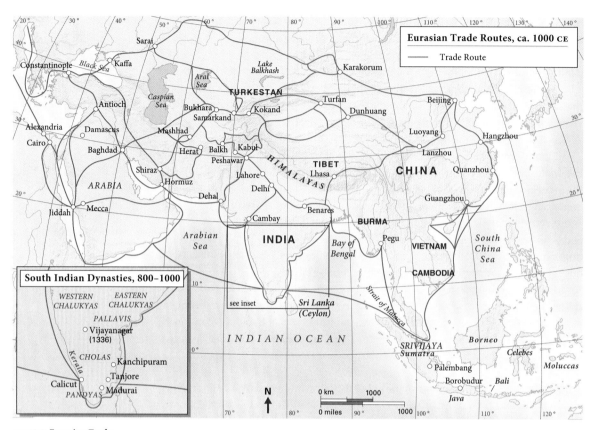

MAP **12.2 Eurasian Trade
Routes, ca. 1000 CE.**

and small arms. The city of Vijayanagar was abandoned, and for the next several
centuries various *nayaks* ruled independently in different areas of the peninsula. By
this time, however, Hindu India was already centuries into an ideological, political,
and military struggle that continues in many respects to this day. For despite their
cultural domination, the power of the Hindu southern states was being eclipsed by
the most potent outside force the region had yet faced: Islamic religious civilization.

Islam in India, 711–1398

As we have seen, conquering Arabs incorporated much of modern Afghanistan,
Pakistan, and some parts of northwest India into their empire during the early 700s.
But for several centuries the rest of India experienced the religion of Islam, which
arose in the wake of the Arab conquests, more peacefully through maritime trade
conducted by Muslim merchants. In central Asia, Arab armies moving eastward
along the caravan routes advanced through conquest, settling in the cities of Turkestan and raiding into the territories of Turkic nomadic tribes. During 700–1000,
first Arab governors and later Persian autonomous rulers supported a profitable
slave trade.

The Career of Mahmud of Ghazna   The Persian rulers in Iran and central Asia
enrolled these slaves in their palace guards and converted them to Islam. The son of
one of these slave officers was Sultan Mahmud of Ghazna, who declared himself independent of his Persian overlord and conquered the city of Ghazna in Afghanistan. In

997 Mahmud embarked on a career of expansion lasting three decades, until his death in 1030. His tactical brilliance and utter ruthlessness have left his name both revered and reviled in Muslim and Hindu circles ever since.

Early in his career, Mahmud conquered an immense territory comprising part of Iran as well as Afghanistan and Turkestan. The wealth he extracted from this empire turned Ghazna into an opulent city and left the door open for the next round of expeditions into the old Ganges River states.

A New Style of Warfare

For those encountering Mahmud and his successors for the first time, the scope and ferocity of these raids were especially unsettling. Warfare among the Hindu states had been the exclusive domain of the military castes. With casualties largely limited to the combatants and the various opponents sharing the same religious and cultural traditions, society as a whole generally suffered a minimum of disruption. The Muslims, however, tended to practice warfare on a much wider scale and saw their role of spreading the rule of Islam as central. Consequently, in addition to the destruction involved in the conquest and looting of an area, they frequently attempted widespread changes involving the destruction of temples; the establishment of sharia, or quranic law, in occupied areas; and the imposition of the head tax (*jizya*) on non-Muslims—though practical rulers learned over time to go about this judiciously.

The Northern Sultanates

Mahmud and his successors, the Ghaznavids, ruled for nearly two centuries. The provinces of their empire, however, were too disparate—ranging from the central Asian desert to the rain forests of northern India—to cohere. A Persian ruler subject to the Ghaznavids, Muhammad of Ghur, declared his independence and conquered most Ghaznavid lands. In 1192, he defeated the Rajputs, considered Hindu India's most ferocious warriors, allegedly killing 100,000 soldiers. Striking deep into northern India, Muhammad set up a Muslim state at Delhi. He subsequently lost his territories in the north, but the Indian state he had set up endured (1181–1526) under the name of the "Sultanate of Delhi." The founders of this state were, like many state builders we have seen in Islamic history, Turkic generals of slave origin who seized power after the death of Muhammad. Their successors were Turkic and Afghan dynasties who ruled until the invasion of Babur, the Mongol-descended founder of the Mughal Empire of India in 1526 (see Map 12.3).

The Delhi Sultanate successfully weathered an attempted invasion by Genghis Khan in 1222, whose military campaigns had so devastated the lands of southwest Asia and central Europe. Among the more colorful rulers of the Delhi Sultanate was the female sultan Raziya, who ruled from 1236 to 1240. Raziya seized the throne from her dissolute brother and, in an even more provocative move, dispensed with the veil required of Muslim women and wore male attire on the battlefield. During her short reign, she pressed south and east to Bengal and settled Muslim refugees from Mongol-controlled lands within her own domains. A scandal involving her liaison with an Ethiopian adviser soon sparked a conspiracy against

Qutb Minaret, Delhi. The sense of the northern Indian sultanates being a sanctuary for Muslims from other locales translated into efforts on the part of rulers to outperform their counterparts. The wealth of the area allowed them the resources with which to build a number of spectacular structures. The Qutb Minar, built next to Delhi's first mosque, is said to still be the world's largest minaret, requiring the efforts of two rulers before being finished by the Tugh-Lug sultan Feroz Shah (d. 1388).

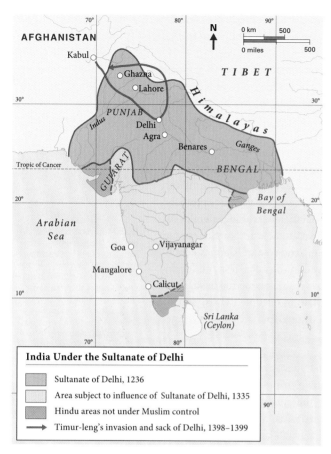

India Under the Sultanate of Delhi

- Sultanate of Delhi, 1236
- Area subject to influence of Sultanate of Delhi, 1335
- Hindu areas not under Muslim control
- → Timur-leng's invasion and sack of Delhi, 1398–1399

MAP **12.3 India Under the Sultanate of Delhi.**

her. Captured while suppressing one of the accompanying revolts, she won over and actually married one of the conspirators. Defeated in an attempt to retake Delhi, Raziya and her new husband were ultimately killed as they tried to escape.

The renewed Mongol expansion which led to the sack of Baghdad and the destruction of the Abbasid caliphate in 1258 was accompanied by raids along the Delhi Sultanate's borders. Out of this unsettled period came the long reign of Balban, who exercised power informally in Delhi for 20 years before ruling in his own right from 1266 through 1287. Balban's iron hand in suppressing potential rivals resulted in a succession struggle at his death, and a new set of sultans, the Khalijis, came to power in 1290. Like nearly all of their predecessors, the Khalijis soon expanded into southern India, where they acquired loot and established a short-lived overlordship. The court politics of the sultanates were always ripe with intrigue because of the vulnerability of the relatives of the heir apparent. On accession to the throne, a sultan's family members were routinely executed to prevent succession battles. Frequently, they secured the loyalty of ambitious allies on the outside in order to forestall their own deaths. Slaves were largely insulated from these intrigues and, thus, constituted a favorite group of potential supporters; indeed, it was possible for an ambitious slave to seize power in his own right.

A product of this situation was Ala-ud-din, who gained the sultanate by assassinating his predecessor. On his death in 1316, a short period of uncertainty prevailed until the 1320 accession of the Tugh-Lug rulers, who held power until 1413. Perhaps the most controversial ruler of the line was Muhammad Ibn Tugh-Lug (d. 1351), named by his detractors "Muhammad the Bloody." Discontent over high taxes, debased coinage, famine, and ruthless atrocities against his enemies was prevalent during his reign. Such acts, however, seemed to contradict his considerably more peaceful personal attainments. By all accounts he was highly educated, a renowned poet and calligrapher, and humble and chaste in his behavior at court. Regardless of the ultimate effects of his rule, by the time of his death at mid-century, powerful forces were once again gathering to the north. Within a few decades they would bring about the end of Tugh-Lug rule and alter the region's politics for generations to come.

Toward the Mughal Era, 1398–1450

In 1398, one of the last great invasions of central Asian nomads, that of Timur—also Timur-leng or Tamerlane, "Timur the Lame" (r. 1370-1405) on account of a riding accident—descended on northern India and southwest Asia. Though himself a Muslim, Timur did not spare the Muslim capital of Delhi. He went on in 1402 to defeat the Ottoman Empire in the Middle East, but his giant empire did not survive his death in 1405. Nevertheless, though the wave of violence accompanying his conquests quickly subsided, his invasion had broken the power of the ruling Tugh-Lugs. Two smaller sultanates, those of the Sayyids (1414–1451) and the Lodis (1451–1526), held the area around Delhi. Once again, northern India had moved into a period of political disorder.

Economics in Islamic India

India's rich economy generated repeated political problems. It continually attracted invasions by outsiders eager to take advantage of its wealth. While scholars have long debated whether the first Arab and Turkic incursions into India were motivated primarily by religious or economic reasons or a combination of the two, the vast wealth accumulated as a result provided ample justification for continuing them. Like the constantly feuding southern states of the subcontinent, the turnover of goods acquired through raids and warfare helped finance the economies of the emerging northern Muslim sultanates. Even after these states became financially stable, the attraction of the wealth of the southern states resulted in frequent expeditions against them for financial gain.

The northern sultanates also supported their economies through heavy taxation. In addition to the *jizya* tax on nonbelievers, Ala-ud-din of the Tugh-Lugs, for example, instituted a 50 percent land tax, taxes on the ownership of milk cows, and a household tax. Beyond this, he embarked on an ambitious campaign to institute wage and price controls on a dizzying array of occupations and commodities in order to keep food prices low and urban granaries full. In this, Ala-ud-din was surpassed in zeal by the notorious Muhammad "The Bloody" Tugh-Lug, who had one tax offender flayed alive, his skin stuffed and mounted, and his remains served as a meal to his unfortunate relatives.

Muhammad also instituted price controls and attempted to stabilize the currency by minting new gold coins, debasing silver ones, and manufacturing bronze tokens for use as temporary currency, measures ultimately abandoned as disruptive to the economy. Despite the sultans' constant need for money, however, Muslim prohibitions against **usury** kept banking and capital firmly in the hands of Hindus, Buddhists, and *Parsees* (descendants of Zoroastrian emigrants from Persia).

Muslims and Caste

The role of Islam in calling the faithful together as equals tended to appeal to those most discontented with the caste system. Islam's minority status in India, however, meant that it was never possible to carve out an Islamic state within the sultanates in the same fashion as had been the case in other parts of the Muslim sphere.

Over time, a certain amount of cross-cultural compromise was reluctantly granted on both sides. Nearly all Hindu and Muslim sects were eventually allowed to practice to some degree, with the dress and markings distinguishing different castes allowed to continue. Muslim repugnance toward Hindu nakedness—as in the case of devotees of certain gods and the working attire of some of the lower castes—as well as discomfort with Hindu concepts of religious sexuality, gradually became less overt. At the same time, Hindus in some areas adopted the Muslim practice of veiling women.

Usury: For Christians, the sin of lending money at high rates of interest; for Muslims, charging any interest at all on money loaned.

The Sikhs   Despite their profoundly different worldviews, traditions, and practices, by the fifteenth century the unique position of the Muslim sultanates of northern India as havens for refugees from the ravages of the Mongols, as well as for Sufis (practitioners of Islamic mysticism) and Muslim dissidents, provided a rare opportunity for interchange between Muslim and Hindu sects. Starting with the poet Kabir (1440–1518), the commonalities of the ecstatic, mystical experience of communion with the absolute shared alike by Hindu and Muslim devotional sects was the subject of repeated attempts to find common ground between their two faiths.

Sikhism: Indian religion founded by Guru Nanak that combines elements of Hindu and Muslim traditions.

The climax of this movement came with the guru ("teacher") Nanak (1469–1539), who founded the faith of **Sikhism**, *sikh* meaning "disciple," which also emphasized a direct emotional experience with the divine. Combining elements of Hinduism and Islam, the Sikhs, due to religious persecution in the seventeenth century, eventually became more of a fighting faith, a stance that, even to the present, has served to continually place them at odds with various Indian governments.

While Sikhism at first appeared to be a step toward reconciliation between Islam and Hinduism, it in fact became the exception that proved the rule of their competition. Indeed, both Hindus and Muslims opposed the Sikhs and they were persecuted a number of times under the Mughals. India thus remained a syncretic religious and cultural society among the world's religious civilizations. The experience of China, on the other hand, would be far less traumatic.

Interactions and Adaptations: From Buddhism to Neo-Confucian Synthesis in China

The Tang dynasty (618–907) marked the completion of the reconstitution of the Chinese empire begun under the Sui. At its height, the influence of Buddhism at the imperial court, especially with the famous Empress Wu, made China a Buddhist empire. Since the Han, China's ideology had been based on the ethics of Confucianism combined with the imperial structure inherited from the Qin (see Chapter 9). By the mid-600s this ideology of statehood had fused with Mahayana Buddhism to give China for the first time an overtly religious civilization. China thus dramatically joined the ranks of Hindu India (soon to be split by Islam), the growing spread of the Islamic caliphates, the Christian eastern Roman Empire, and the developing states of western Christian Europe as states dominated by a universal religion. Such states would dominate world history until the European Enlightenment and Industrial Revolution created an entirely new type of society.

Nestorian Christianity: Christian sect that was condemned as heretical by Orthodox Christians and Catholics but which spread across central Asia along the Silk Road.

But the Tang, with their connections to the larger Buddhist cultural sphere, ultimately fell. The dynasty of their successors, the Song (960–1279), has often been seen as the beginning of China's early modern period, supported by the world's largest and most productive agrarian state. The political system that marked China from this period until the twentieth century, however, was in part derived from a departure from Buddhism, which was blamed for the downfall of the Tang. Instead, the new synthesis of official beliefs blended the ideas of three ethical-religious schools—Confucianism, Daoism, and Buddhism—to create a system called "Neo-Confucianism." Unlike India's competing religions, Neo-Confucianism in China had no real religious competitors inside or outside the empire and its debates centered instead on interpretations and approaches to understanding its core teachings—not on the teachings themselves.

Creating a Religious Civilization Under the Tang

As we saw at the end of Chapter 9, the installation by Li Shimin of his father on the throne in 618 saw the founding of the Tang. His dismissal of his father in 627 saw it begin in earnest. For the next 150 years, the dynasty expanded its reach deep into central Asia and made incursions into Korea and Vietnam until its shape resembled a dumbbell, bulging at both ends connected with the narrow territory adjacent to the Silk Road.

Expansion and Consolidation   Determined to complete the consolidation begun under the Sui and expand the empire, the Tang led military expeditions into central Asia. By the end of the seventh century, they had expelled the major nomadic groups from the empire's western borderlands, pushing them west to Anatolia, eastern Europe, and the Mediterranean. The Tang reestablished rule in Korea and opened diplomatic relations with Japan, which in 645 announced the *Taika* (Great Reform)—a wholesale adoption of Tang imperial institutions, Buddhism, Confucian bureaucracy, record keeping, and even architecture.

The Tang Empire's position as the eastern terminus of the Silk Road; its enhanced maritime trade with India, Japan, southeast Asia, the Middle East, and even Africa; and its integration of Buddhist culture led to China's first extensive encounter with the major agrarian–urban societies to the west. During the seventh century, the Umayyad–Abbasid conquests in southwest Asia brought China into contact with the rapidly expanding Arab Empire. In 674, members of the Sasanian Persian royal house fled the advancing Arabs to the Tang capital at Chang'an, bringing in their wake communities of merchants who established a taste among the Tang elites for Arab, Persian, and central Asian musical forms (China's first real orchestral music), dance, silver artwork, and a host of other items.

China's major cities now had quarters set aside for foreign traders, which by the end of the Tang era included Jews, **Nestorian Christians**, Zoroastrians, members of the major Indian traditions, and the beginnings of what would one day be a substantial Muslim minority. Indeed, the modern Chinese city of Xi'an (old Chang'an) even today has a large historic Muslim market area. Arab and Indian intermediaries extended trade from China all the way to the East African coast.

With the Tang Empire expanding, trade booming, and the bureaucracy well staffed and run, the Tang capital of Chang'an grew into perhaps the largest city in the world, with its core comparable in size to Baghdad or Constantinople in the same era and as many as 2 million people living in its metropolitan area. Its streets, official

Camel with Musicians. Music played an important role in Tang China and was enjoyed privately as well as on public occasions. This brightly colored glazed earthenware sculpture, dated to 723 CE, shows three musicians riding a Bactrian (two-humped) camel. Their long coats, facial hair, and hats indicate that they are from central Asia; indeed, the lute held by one of the figures is an instrument that was introduced to China from central Asia in the second century CE.

buildings and residences, and south-facing imperial palace dominating the center became the model for urban planning throughout eastern Asia (see Map 12.4).

The Examination System   The Tang refined the bureaucratic structure pioneered by the Han into a form that, with only minor alterations, survived into the twentieth century. The most noteworthy aspect of the Tang bureaucratic structure was the introduction of an examination system for entry into government service. The initial entry-level tests, based on knowledge of the Confucian classics and, for most of the Tang era, Buddhist and Daoist texts, were open to men of all classes except merchants, artisans, and convicted criminals. The few who passed the initial, district-level tests could sit for provincial exams and, if successful, would be eligible for minor posts. Individuals who passed the metropolitan tests, usually held every 3 years in the capital, were eligible for national service. Other reforms undertaken by the Tang included the creation of a board of censors to check arbitrary behavior among officials, the obligation of lower officials to report the infractions of those above them, and the practice of rotating official posts to prevent individuals from developing local power bases.

The Confucian educational system had a huge impact on Chinese history. Until the twentieth century, it was the only sure route to both wealth and power. Because the exams were open to a relatively large portion of the male population, the goal of state service ensured a degree of social mobility based on merit rather than birth. Schools and academies educated and socialized large groups of people in the Confucian canon, not only in China but also in areas subject to Chinese influence.

Prosperity and Its Discontents   As the prosperity of the Tang dynasty expanded, many of the problems of uneven growth that had plagued the Han dynasty began to reassert themselves. For example, as the center of population continued to move south, the northern regions languished in relative poverty, while the capital grew economically isolated. The agriculturally productive subtropical areas south of the Yangzi now yielded about 90 percent of the empire's taxed grain and contained as much as 70 percent of the population. Moreover, as maritime trade grew and ports increased in size and number, the connecting infrastructure of roads, courier stations, and especially canals required ever more investment and attention. This was a particularly acute problem in the case of communication with the capital. As an administrative center and trade crossroads, the capital city of Chang'an had ballooned to a size that was now unsustainable without constant grain shipments from the south, while its isolation made it particularly vulnerable to attack. Thus, even before the Tang, work on the Grand Canal, connecting the Yangzi and Yellow Rivers, had been pushed forward to enhance water-based transport in the north. Since the capitals of succeeding dynasties tended to be in the old northern heartland as well, this problem of maintaining communication with and provisioning them remained a chronic one throughout the imperial era.

Tang efforts to control military outposts along the Silk Road, with its lucrative trade and Buddhist shrines, brought the empire into conflict with Arab expansion by the early eighth century. Despite some early successes, Tang armies suffered a decisive defeat by the Arabs at the Battle of Talas in 751. This loss followed a series of setbacks at the hands of the Tibetans from 745 to 750 and simultaneous uprisings in the border areas of Manchuria, Korea, and the southern province of Yunnan. From 755 to 762 a general revolt initiated by the Tang commander An Lushan (703–757)

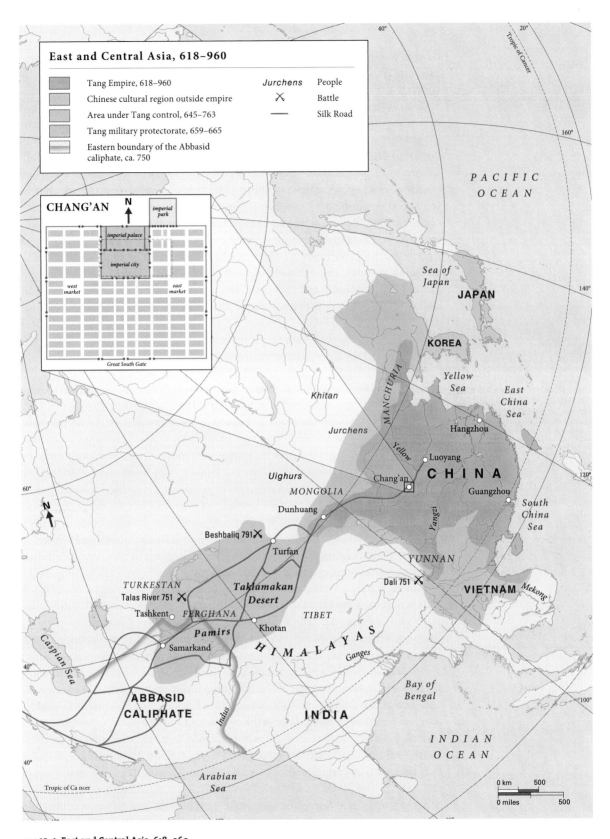

MAP **12.4** East and Central Asia, 618–960.

East and Central Asia, 618–960

Tang Empire, 618–960
Chinese cultural region outside empire
Area under Tang control, 645–763
Tang military protectorate, 659–665
Eastern boundary of the Abbasid caliphate, ca. 750

Jurchens   People
✗   Battle
——   Silk Road

CHANG'AN   N

imperial park
imperial palace
imperial city
west market
east market
Great South Gate

PACIFIC OCEAN

Sea of Japan   **JAPAN**

KOREA

MANCHURIA

Khitan

Jurchens

Yellow Sea

East China Sea

Hangzhou

Yellow

Luoyang

Chang'an   **CHINA**

Uighurs

MONGOLIA   Guangzhou

South China Sea

Dunhuang

Beshbaliq 791✗

Turfan

Yangzi

YUNNAN

Dali 751✗

VIETNAM   Mekong

TURKESTAN

Talas River 751✗

Taklamakan Desert

Tashkent   *FERGHANA*   *TIBET*

Pamirs   Khotan

Samarkand   H I M A L A Y A S   Ganges

Caspian Sea

ABBASID CALIPHATE

Indus

INDIA

Bay of Bengal

I N D I A N   O C E A N

Arabian Sea

Tropic of Cancer

0 km   500
0 miles   500

devastated large sections of the empire and resulted in heavy land taxes after its suppression. As with the later Han, the dynasty was now in a downward spiral, from which recovery would prove increasingly difficult.

For the next century and a half some economic and political recovery did in fact occur, but the problems of rebuilding and revenue loss persisted, accompanied by a questioning of a number of the premises of the regime, particularly by the Confucians. For example, Confucians criticized Buddhism for being patronized and subsidized by the Tang court. They were particularly critical of its "foreign" ideas and practices, such as monasticism, celibacy, and personal enlightenment, which contradicted the Confucian standards of filial piety, family life, and public service. At the same time, Buddhist monasteries, which paid no taxes, were tempting targets for an increasingly cash-strapped government. In 845, despite Tang sponsorship of Buddhism, the government forcibly seized all Buddhist holdings, although followers were allowed to continue their religious practices. Even with renewed campaigns against border peoples and other attempts at reinvigorating the empire, sporadic civil war continued for the remainder of the century, leading to the collapse of the Tang dynasty in 906. Following this collapse, China again entered a period of disunity as regional states battled for ultimate control. None of these states would be victorious until the emergence of the Song in 960.

Cosmopolitan Commerce   From the capital in Chang'an, merchants, monks, pilgrims, diplomats, and travelers made their way along the Silk Road, while Chinese, Indian, and Arab ships plied the seas as far away as Africa. The compass, invented by Chinese fortunetellers and adapted for use in keeping to a constant direction at sea, now guided ships throughout the Indian Ocean and southeast Asia. In the Chinese versions of this instrument, however, the needle was considered to point due south—the preferred direction of good fortune and architectural orientation. Spurred by lucrative opportunities, colonies of Chinese merchants could be found throughout the Indian Ocean and southeast Asia; colonies of foreign merchants, including East Africans, Arabs, Persians, Indians, Jews, and Nestorian Christians, all had their own quarters in China's larger port cities, at trade crossroads, and most prominently in the capital.

Among the export items most coveted by foreign merchants were tea and silk. Initially brought to China from southeast Asia, tea quickly established itself as the beverage of choice during the Tang and vied with silk for supremacy as a cash crop during the Song. Tea had a profound effect on the overall health of the population in China, Vietnam, Korea, Japan, and central Asia. Middle Easterners, however, did not adopt it until early modern times. The simple act of boiling water renders tea potable, while the tea itself contains a number of healthful, even medicinal, properties. In addition, its caffeine makes it desirable for those who need to keep alert, such as monks in meditation. Tea production, particularly in the region near the city of Hangzhou, became a major industry and for hundreds of years remained China's most lucrative export item.

The influence of foreigners in art and artifact, fashion, taste, music, and dance marks a radical departure in many respects from the more demure Chinese styles that came before and after. For example, the Persian-influenced costumes of Tang dancers—with their daring and distinctive bare midriffs and transparent tops and trousers—were celebrated at the court in Chang'an but scandalized the more modest sensibilities of later centuries. Indeed, the period saw a number of controversial trends regarding the role and deportment of women.

Empress Wu   The most noted exemplar of these contradictory trends toward both greater restrictiveness and wider latitude in personal behavior was the Tang ruler Wu Zetian, or Empress Wu (r. 690–705). The daughter of a public works official, she spent a brief period at court as a servant to the empress. Disillusioned at life in the capital and drawn to the austerities of Buddhism, she joined a women's monastery, only to return to the palace when her beauty piqued the interest of an imperial prince. Seeing the opportunities this opening presented, she exploited them ably and ruthlessly.

Like Cleopatra in Egypt, hostile chroniclers in subsequent dynasties attributed much of her success to her sexual exploits, though the records also note that she was well educated, shrewd in her dealings with ministers, and a polished hand at employing imperial spectacle. In 684, after the death of her husband, who had become the emperor, she ruled as **empress dowager** and as regent for her son. In reality, however, she held all the real power. A devout Buddhist, she declared Buddhism the state religion. She intrigued and maneuvered to rule in her own right, and in 690, she inaugurated a new Zhou Dynasty. The final step came in 693, when she took the Buddhist title "Divine Empress Who Rules the Universe." Though an able ruler according to the Tang official histories, the act of creating her own dynasty and new titles for herself was considered usurpation by many of her subjects and a resistance soon followed. Unlike many other Chinese rulers, she was able to put the revolt down and preserve the continuity of the dynasty, only succumbing to natural causes in 705. Following the Confucian backlash of the Song era, no woman in imperial China would wield this kind of power again until the reign of the Empress Dowager Cixi in the late nineteenth and early twentieth centuries. Even today, however, she is widely celebrated in China as an early feminist role model.

Empress dowager: In monarchical or imperial systems in which succession is normally through the male line, the widow of the ruler.

Tang Poetry   Tang poetry, especially the compressed "regulated verse" of eight five-character lines and the terse four-line "cut-off line" poems, attempts to do the same thing: suggest powerful emotions or themes in minimalist fashion. For example, the deep Confucian sensibilities of the Tang poet Du Fu (ca. 721–770) are often detectable in his emotionally charged poems such as "Mourning Chen Tao." Li Bai (or Li Bo, 701–762), his friend, was in many ways his opposite in both the way he lived his life and the emotions he sought to stir. Carefree, witty, a lover of wine and women—according to legend, Li Bai drowned after a drunken challenge to "embrace the moon" reflected in the water—his poetry evokes happier moments but frequently conveys them as fleeting and bittersweet. Wang Wei (ca. 699–759) was a third renowned Tang poet. Of him, it was later said that "in every one of his poems is a painting, and in every painting a poem."

For all the accomplishments of the Tang, however, the role of Buddhism as a privileged religion left the dynasty open to severe criticism. With the coming of the Song, China would become a religious civilization in which its people reemphasized the indigenous traditions of Confucianism and Daoism, with elements of Buddhism on a more reduced level.

The Song and Yuan Dynasties, 960–1368

During the Song dynasty, China achieved in many ways its greatest degree of sophistication in terms of material culture, technology, ideas, economics, and the amenities of urban living. Its short-lived incorporation into the huge empire of the Mongols opened the country to renewed influence from neighboring peoples and helped to spread Chinese influence westward, most famously through the accounts of the travelers Marco Polo and Ibn Battuta. Finally, the new synthesis of Neo-Confucianism would carry China as a religious civilization into the twentieth century.

Reforms of Wang Anshi   Like the Tang, the Song instituted a strong central government based on merit rather than heredity. The Song, however, broadened the eligibility of those seeking to take the civil service exams; and with increased opportunities to join the government service, a huge bureaucratic system emerged. This unwieldy system placed an enormous financial burden on the state, which, to secure revenue, placed heavy taxes on individuals outside the bureaucracy. The constant demand for revenue by the state would ultimately lead to rebellion.

The need for administrative reform spurred the official Wang Anshi (1021–1086) to propose a series of initiatives designed to increase state control over the economy and reduce the power of local interests. Wang proposed state licensing of both agricultural and commercial enterprises, the abolition of forced labor, and the creation of a system of government pawnshops to loan money at reduced rates, in order to break the power of usurers and middlemen. He also urged greatly reducing the number of bureaucratic positions in order to lessen the power of local officials and clan heads.

Opposition to his proposed reforms forced Wang from office in 1076. The question of government involvement in commerce and the economy has been the subject of vigorous debate throughout the history of imperial China, particularly during times of internal crisis.

In addition to internal problems, such as the financial strain of maintaining a huge bureaucracy, the Song faced external problems. Because the Tang had lost much of northern China, including the Silk Road, to nomadic groups, Song lands from the start were substantially smaller than those of the Tang. Although the Song spent a great deal of treasure and energy to maintain a professional army of more than 1.5 million as well as a formidable navy, this massive but ponderous force ultimately proved ineffective against the expert militaries of invading nomadic groups using swiftness to their advantage. The Song also tried careful diplomacy and bribery to maintain China's dominance. Such efforts, however, were unable to keep the northern part of the empire from falling to the nomadic Jurchens in 1127. Forced to abandon their capital at Kaifeng on the Grand Canal just south of the Yellow River, the Song created a new capital at Linan, the modern city of Hangzhou (see Map 12.5).

The decreased size of the Song Empire resulted in a more southern-oriented and urbanized economy. The new capital at Hangzhou, described by Marco Polo as the most beautiful city in the world, may also have been the largest, with a population estimated at 1.5 million. Despite the bureaucracy's disdain for the merchant and artisan classes, the state had always recognized the potential of commerce to generate revenue through import, export, tariffs, and taxes. Thus, while attempting to bring the largest enterprises under state

MAP 12.5 **East Asia in 1150.**

control, the government pursued measures to facilitate trade, such as printing the world's first paper notes, minting coins, and restraining usury. These practices, combined with an excellent system of roads and canals, fostered the development of an internal Chinese market. The Song conducted a lively overseas trade, and Chinese merchants established colonies in major ports throughout southeast Asia and the Indian Ocean.

The Mongol Conquest   Commercial success, however, could not save the Song from invasion by neighboring nomadic peoples. For centuries, disparate groups of nomadic Mongols had lived in tribes and clans in eastern central Asia. There was no real push to unite these groups until the rise to power of the Mongol leader Temujin (ca. 1162–1227). Combining military prowess with diplomatic strategy, Temujin united the various Mongol groups into one confederation in 1206. Temujin gave himself the title "Genghis Khan" ("Universal Ruler") of the united Mongol confederation.

Following confederation, the Mongols launched a half-century of steady encroachment on northern China. The Mongols had several enormous advantages over the infantry-based armies of their opponents:

- their skill at horsemanship and archery
- their unsurpassed ability to fire arrows at pursuers while galloping away from them at full speed
- their repeatedly successful tactics of feigned retreat

Genghis Khan's grandson Khubilai Khan (1215–1294) resumed the Mongol offensive in southern China after the Song unwisely attempted to enlist Mongol aid against the Jurchens. In 1267 he moved his capital from Karakorum to Khanbaligh, called by the Chinese "Dadu"—the future city of Beijing—and steadily ground down the Song remnant. Hangzhou fell to the Mongols in 1276; the death of the young Song emperor in 1279 as he attempted to flee by sea brought the dynasty to an end.

The Yuan Dynasty   In 1280 Khubilai Khan proclaimed the Yuan dynasty. This short-lived dynasty pulled China into an empire spanning all of Eurasia from Korea to the interior of Poland and probing as far as Hungary, Java, and Japan. Like their

Khubilai Khan as the First Yuan Emperor, Shizu (Shih-tzu).

predecessors in the Northern Wei and Sui dynasties, however, the Mongols found themselves adapting to Chinese culture in order to administer the densely populated and complex society they had wrested from the Song. Thus, while some senior Song bureaucrats resigned in protest from the new Mongol government, most carried on with their posts, and the examination system begun under the Han dynasty was finally reinstated in 1315.

Now that China was part of a much larger empire, its culture was widely diffused throughout Eurasia. In addition, China was open to a variety of foreign goods, ideas, and travelers. Paper money, gunpowder, coal, the compass, and dozens of other important Chinese innovations circulated more widely than ever, while emissaries and missionaries from the developing states of Europe traveled east to the Chinese capital city of Khanbaligh. Rabban Sauma, a Turkish Nestorian Christian who had been born in China, traveled from Khanbaligh to Paris and Rome, even

Patterns Up Close | Gunpowder

Korean Rocket Launcher. Adapting Mongol and Chinese military technology, the Koreans repelled a Japanese invasion in 1592 with *hwacha*, mobile rocket launchers that were used with great effect against both enemy land forces and ships.

If fine porcelain, lacquerware, landscape painting, poetry, and calligraphy marked the refined side of Song life, the most momentous invention to emerge from the era was gunpowder. The substance was originally used as a medicine for skin irritations until its propensity to burn rapidly was established. The early Chinese term for gunpowder, *huoyao* (火药) "fire medicine," preserves this sense of its use.

Though long packed into bamboo tubes to create fireworks ignited during religious festivals, it is unclear when the first weapons employing gunpowder were used. By the Southern Song, however, the Chinese army and navy had a wide array of weapons that utilized gunpowder either as a propellant or as an explosive. The use of "fire arrows"—rockets mounted to arrow shafts—was recorded during a battle with the Mongols in 1232. The Song navy launched missiles and even employed ships with detachable sections filled with explosives with which to ram other ships. By the end of the century, primitive cannon were also employed as well as gunpowder satchels to blow open city gates and fortifications.

The widespread use of gunpowder weapons by the Song against the Mongols was a powerful inducement to the invaders to adopt them for themselves. Indeed, toward the end of the war, the Mongols increasingly employed explosives in their siege operations against Chinese walled cities. They also used them in the 1270s and 1290s during their failed invasions of Japan. The need for these weapons pushed their dispersion throughout the Mongol holdings and beyond.

Huang Gongwang's (Huang Kung-wang's) Dwelling in the Fu-ch'un Mountains (1350). Like the era immediately after the Han, the turbulent political situation of the Yuan dynasty forced many of the educated elite to withdraw from the bureaucracy and cultivate aesthetic pursuits. The period thus saw some of the most expressive examples of Chinese monochrome ink landscape painting. In this section from Huang's scroll, the artist has encoded subtle messages to the knowledgeable viewer. Among these is that the site itself was famous as the retreat of a first-century Daoist hermit who chose to live in seclusion rather than serve the government.

celebrating a mass with the pope in 1278. The two most famous travel accounts of the era, those of the Venetian Marco Polo (1254–1324) and Ibn Battuta of Tangier (1304–1369), who lived and traveled throughout the Mongol Empire, are testament to the powerful impact of Mongol rule on facilitating travel over such a vast area. Indeed, it was during the brief rule of the Mongols that the European image of China as a fairyland of exotica, fabulous wealth, and wondrous inventions was firmly set (see Map 12.6).

For Chinese historians, however, the Yuan period is almost universally regarded as one of imperial China's darkest times. Although the Mongols quickly restored order, administered the empire effectively, and allowed a relative tolerance of religious practice and expression, the Yuan period was seen as an oppressive time of large standing armies, withdrawal from service of many Chinese officials, forced labor, and heavy taxes. Compounding the

It is difficult to overestimate the importance of gunpowder in human affairs. The next round of empires, the Ottomans, Safavids, and Mughals, made its use in warfare so central to their efforts that historians often refer to them as "the gunpowder empires." Its use in sixteenth-century Japan was so important in battle that the Tokugawa Shogunate banned it for two centuries once peace had been established. But it was among the states of Europe that these weapons achieved their highest levels of development over the following centuries. Incessant warfare among the European states and against the Ottomans fueled the development of bigger and deadlier cannon and lighter and more accurate small arms. The use of these weapons helped speed the decline of the heavily armed and armored mounted knight and brought on the age of the infantry armed with muskets as "the queen of battles." By the end of the eighteenth century, even though muskets and artillery were technologically more or less the same world over, a high degree of drill among bayonet-equipped grenadiers gave European armies an edge against the Ottomans, Mughals, and Africans.

Questions

- How do gunpowder's origins as a medicine complicate the way we typically view technological and cultural adaptations?

- What would have been the consequence for world history if the military uses of gunpowder had never been discovered?

intensity of these conditions was perhaps the single worst disaster of the fourteenth century, the bubonic plague, as we saw in Chapter 11. While scholars have only recently begun to examine Chinese mortality rates resulting from the plague, Chinese accounts suggest that they were in all likelihood similar to those of Europe in some areas, with perhaps one-third of the population of about 100 million dying from the 1340s until the end of the century.

By mid-century, all of these factors contributed to outbreaks of rebellion in China. Moreover, the Mongol Empire spanning Eurasia had now begun to dissolve into a series of increasingly squabbling regional states. By 1368, a coalition led by the soldier-Buddhist monk Zhu Yuanzhang (1328–1398) had driven the Mongols from the capital at Khanbaligh and proclaimed a new dynastic line, the Ming. A final measure of revenge came when the last Mongol pretender to the throne was driven into the sea—just as the last Song emperor had been by the Mongols.

The Ming to 1450: The Quest for Stability

The "Pig Emperor," as Zhu was sometimes derisively called because of his ungainly features, took the reign name of "Hongwu" and spent much of his rule driving the remaining Mongols out of his empire. Under Hongwu's leadership, Chinese politics and customs were restored and a powerful centralized government was put into place. This new imperial state that Hongwu and his successors created would, with minor modifications, see China into the twentieth century.

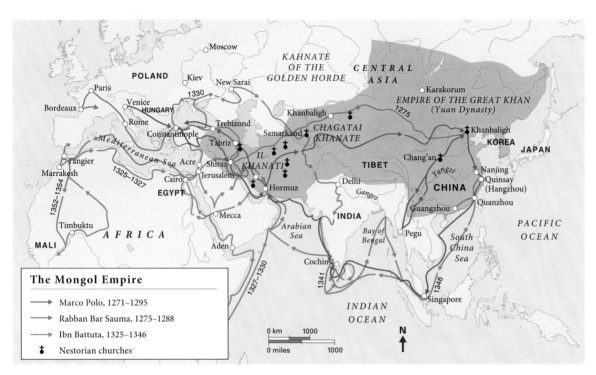

MAP **12.6** **The Mongol Empire.**

The Grand Secretariat

Hongwu sought to streamline this newly reconstituted bureaucracy by concentrating power and governmental functions around the emperor, a practice that had been common during the Qin, Han, and Tang dynasties. Thus, one of his first steps in reshaping the government was to create the Grand Secretariat in 1382. This was a select group of senior officials who served as an advisory board to the emperor on all imperial matters. The Grand Secretariat became the highest level of the bureaucracy and the most powerful level of government after the emperor. Although military needs eventually moved much of its power to the Grand Council set up by the Qing in the mid-1700s, the secretariat remained at the apex of imperial Chinese power into the twentieth century. With a powerful, centralized government in place, Ming emperors now had a base from which to take measures to protect the empire from incursions by Mongols and other nomadic groups in the north. One step to protect against invasion was taken in 1421, when the capital of the empire was moved from Nanjing in the south to the old site of Kambaligh, now renamed "Beijing" (northern capital) so that a strong Chinese presence in the region would discourage invasion. Further safeguards against invasion included the upgrading of the fortifications along the Great Wall.

Population Recovery

While the country fortified its borders and reinstated political systems that had been dismantled by the Mongols, it also had to contend with a sharp drop in population due to warfare and the lingering effects of the bubonic plague that ravaged the country in the 1340s. The population rebound, however, did not assume significant proportions until it was aided by the introduction of a number of new food crops in the sixteenth and seventeenth centuries, which boosted agricultural productivity.

With the coming of new food and cash crops from the Americas by way of Spanish and Portuguese merchants, including potatoes, sweet potatoes, maize (corn), peanuts, and tobacco, the country's population grew from a low of perhaps 60 million at the end of the Yuan period to an estimated 150 million in 1600. The efficiency of Chinese agriculture and the consequent growth of the empire's immense internal trade contributed to another doubling of the population to perhaps 300 million by 1800.

The Interlude of Naval Power   Thanks to the foundation laid by Hongwu, the dynasty's third emperor, Yongle, inherited a state in 1403 that was already on its way to recovering its economic dynamism. Taking advantage of this increasing prosperity and fearful of potential usurpers, he ordered China's first and last great naval expeditions. These voyages, sent out from 1405 to 1433 under the command of his childhood friend and imperial eunuch, Zheng He (1371–1435), were perhaps the most remarkable feats of their day.

The story of Zheng He himself is equally remarkable. Born to a Muslim family in the southern province of Yunnan in 1371, Zheng was taken captive when Ming armies conquered Yunnan in the bloody war to recover the last Mongol strongholds in the region. Ten-year-old Zheng's quick wit impressed a Ming general, who spared the boy's life and placed him as a servant in the household of the future Yongle emperor.

The vast fleets that Zheng commanded were the largest amphibious forces the world would see until the twentieth century. With a length of over 400 feet, the largest of Zheng's "treasure ships," as they were called, were more than four times the length of Columbus' *Santa Maria* and many times its bulk and were accompanied by a diverse array of smaller vessels that carried cargo, supplies, and troops. There were even tankers that carried fresh water for the fleet, while the larger ships grew fresh fruits and vegetables on their aft decks. Zheng's ships also carried a formidable arsenal of cannon, bombs, rockets, and other weaponry and a force of nearly 30,000 men. In addition, they featured such technological innovations as watertight compartments, sternpost rudders, magnetic compasses, and paper maps.

The first voyages were expeditionary forces aimed largely at overawing any nearby foreign powers that might be harboring pretenders to Yongle's throne. As the realization set in that these foreign threats were nonexistent, the voyages became focused on trade and exploration and ranged farther and farther afield, ultimately covering the Indian Ocean, the Persian Gulf, and the East African coast. Along the way they planted or reestablished contact with Chinese merchants in south and southeast Asia. Of particular interest were the first direct Chinese contacts with the Swahili-speaking states of East Africa. In one famous exchange of gifts, the king of Malindi (modern Kenya) sent Yongle a giraffe, which found the emperor among the awestruck admirers of the creature at the imperial court. Even today one can still see the stone markers left by the Chinese along the East African coast where their ships landed (see Map 12.7).

Although Zheng He's explorations firmly established Chinese predominance in naval technology and power, Yongle's successors put an end to the expeditions. The reasons for this abrupt turnabout were both political and strategic. By the 1430s the Mongols, having regrouped from their defeats, were again threatening the northern frontiers. The huge expense of the voyages and the realization that there were no significant naval rivals were convincing arguments to discontinue them in the face of the Mongol threat. In addition, the Confucian officials, always suspicious of the

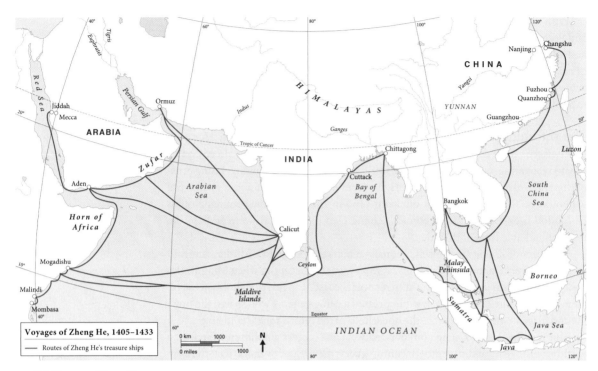

MAP 12.7 **Voyages of Zheng He, 1405–1433.**

profit motive, argued that maritime trade was not useful to the overall welfare of the empire.

Toward the Ming Decline   The activist style of Hongwu and Yongle proved to be the exception rather than the rule during the nearly three centuries of Ming rule. As had so often been the case in Chinese history, a degree of weakness at the center of power encouraged probes of the frontier by nomadic peoples on the empire's periphery, a condition neatly summarized by the Chinese proverb "disorder within, disaster without." A disconcerting foretaste of this occurred in 1449, when the emperor was taken prisoner by the Mongols following the defeat of his expeditionary force. Through most of the sixteenth century, a succession of weak emperors would erode the stability of the reformed Ming imperial system, which had been based on enhancing the emperor's power. To compensate for the chronic weakness at the center, power was increasingly diffused throughout the system. Over time, much of it was acquired by the grand secretaries and provincial governors, while at the village level magistrates and village headmen assumed the bulk of power and responsibility.

Society, Family, and Gender

With the refinement of the examination system and the elaboration of the bureaucracy during the Song, which was renewed during the Ming, the key point of intersection between the people and the government was the district magistrate. While magistrates occupied the lowest official rung of the bureaucracy, they wielded considerable power at the local level and constituted the entry-level position for the majority of those called to service. Some experience at the magistrate's level was considered essential for ambitious officials, and the wide-ranging skills developed during one's district tenure often proved indispensable for advancement to the higher levels of the bureaucracy.

"Father and Mother to the People"   The position of magistrate brought with it enormous responsibility. Even in rural areas, the magistrate might have charge of 100,000 people—and in urban areas perhaps 250,000. Assisted by a small group of clerks and secretaries, messengers, and constables, he supervised all aspects of local government: collecting taxes, policing and security, investigating and prosecuting crimes, settling legal disputes, sentencing and overseeing punishments—including executions—presiding over all official ceremonies, conducting the local Confucian examinations, and setting an exemplary moral example for his constituents. He was constantly on the move, traveling around his district and discharging his duties. When disaster struck, it was the magistrate who had charge of organizing local relief efforts; if floods, disturbances, or famines were the result of negligence, it was he who would be punished—in especially serious cases, by death or banishment. The magistrate's responsibilities and powers were so all-encompassing that he was referred to as "father and mother to the people."

Despite the hectic schedule of the magistrate, he remained a remote figure for the vast majority of the people in his district. "Heaven is high and the emperor is far away" was a Chinese proverb that seems to have been equally applicable to the local officials. For most people, the main figures of authority remained the leading families of the village, their own clan leaders, and the headmen in the *lijia* and *baojia* systems of village organization.

The Scholar-Gentry and Rural Society   While China boasted some of the world's largest cities, more than 85 percent of the country remained rural during the period from the Song to the Ming. At the top of the local structures of power and influence were the *scholar-gentry*. As a class, they were by definition the educated and included all ranks of degree holders, whether in or out of office, and their families.

Scholar-gentry membership was in theory open to most males and their families, though in practice it seldom exceeded 1–2 percent of the population in most areas of the empire. The chief qualification was attainment of at least the lowest official degree, *shengyuan*, which enabled the bearer to attend a government-sponsored academy for further study and draw a small stipend. The demands of memorizing the classical canon and learning to write in the rigid essay format required for the exams, however, were such that the wealthy had a distinct advantage in their leisure time, access to tutors, and the connections required to pass the exams. Still, there were enough poor boys who succeeded by hard work and the sacrifices of their families and neighbors to provide a surprising degree of mobility within the system.

Since prestige within the scholar-gentry derived from education even more than wealth, it was not uncommon for individuals to purchase degrees, though technically they were barred from doing so in the upper three categories. Thus, there was considerable snobbery among the upper gentry of advanced degree holders and officials toward the lower gentry. This was reinforced by an array of **sumptuary laws** and a court-directed protocol of buttons worn on the hats of officials signifying to which of the nine official grades—each with an upper and a lower rank—they belonged. Individuals could also attain honorary ranks, awarded by the emperor, for meritorious service in the military, outstanding ability during times of emergency,

Sumptuary laws: Regulations mandating or restricting the wearing of certain clothes or insignia among different classes of people.

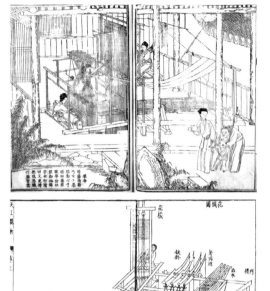

Song Women Weaving Silk on a Draw Loom. Increased commercialization and the demand for silk in the national and international markets made sericulture and weaving two of Song China's largest industries. Women played a predominant role in the industry as well as in the production of cotton and hemp textiles. The illustration on the top is taken from a thirteenth-century copy of a Song text on silk manufacture; the diagram on the botom of the workings of the draw loom—a device dating from the Former Han used for weaving intricate designs—is from the *Tiangong Kaiwu*.

decades of diligent study unaccompanied by success in the exams, and even living to a ripe old age. Commoners reaching the ages of 80, 90, and 100 were awarded official ranks of the ninth, eighth, and seventh grades, respectively, and given the honorary title of "Elder."

In keeping with their role as the informal administrative apparatus of the magistrate, the scholar-gentry enjoyed a number of privileges as well as responsibilities. At the same time, their position as community leaders and their grounding in Confucian ethics frequently placed them in tension with the official bureaucracy, especially when local interests appeared at odds with regional or imperial ones. Along with the district magistrate, they presided over all ceremonies at temples, and those holding the highest ranks led all clan ceremonies. In addition, the scholar-gentry mingled with the official authorities more or less as social equals; in the case of those in between appointments to high office, they frequently outranked the local magistrate.

Local government relied to an extraordinary degree on the cooperation of the gentry and people with the magistrates, subprefects, and prefects in order to function. Because the presiding officials were moved so frequently, the gentry represented a consistent network of people to carry out the day-to-day work of government. They took very seriously the Confucian injunction to remonstrate with officials, especially when their complaints coincided with local interests. Thus, they could—and did—rally the people to subvert the policies of unpopular magistrates. Moreover, as influential men themselves—and often officials with national connections—they could force the resignation of officials and sometimes even bring about changes in regional or imperial policy.

Village and Family Life   The tendency toward greater centralization under the Ming also reverberated within the structures of Chinese village life. While much of local custom and social relations among the peasants still revolved around family, clan, and lineage—with the scholar-gentry setting the pace—new institutions perfected under the Ming had a lasting impact into the twentieth century.

Originally conceived during the Song dynasty, the *baojia* system of village organization called for families to register all members and be grouped into clusters of 10. One family in each cluster was then assigned responsibility for the others. Each group of responsible families would then be grouped into 10, and a member would be selected from them to be responsible for the group of 100 households, and so on up to the 1,000-household level. The *baojia* headmen at each level were to be chosen by the families in the group, though they received their office from the magistrate. They were to report to the magistrate on the doings of their respective groups and were held accountable for the group's behavior. The system was especially important in that it allowed the authorities to bypass potential gentry resistance to government directives and guaranteed a network of informers at all levels of rural life.

Peasant Women's Lives   Despite China's technological prowess and the introduction of new rice strains during the Song period that propelled a surge in population, the patterns of work and the overall rhythms of peasant life changed little from the Song through the Ming. The tools available to the vast majority of cultivators, as later depicted in the seventeenth-century technology manual *Tiangong Kaiwu* (*The Works of Nature and Man*), had remained fundamentally unchanged from their prototypes of the preceding centuries. The very simplicity and efficiency of such tools in such a labor-rich environment encouraged their continued use.

Tensions in the older patterns of village life tended to be magnified during times of stress in the lives of women and girls. On the one hand, the education of upperclass women tended increasingly toward those areas aimed at making them more marriageable. Study of proper Confucian etiquette (as outlined in Ban Zhao's *Admonitions for Women*, discussed in Chapter 9), light verse, and a heavy dose of filial piety occupied a large portion of their curriculum. The custom of painful **foot binding** originated during the Song, gained ground during the Ming, and continued until it was banned by the People's Republic of China after 1949. **Female infanticide** also rose markedly in rural areas during times of famine or other social stress. As in previous periods, rural girls were frequently sold into servitude or prostitution by financially pressed families.

Foot binding: The practice of tightly wrapping the feet of young girls in order to break the bones and reset them in such a way that the feet are compressed to about one-third of their normal size; this was generally done by mothers to their daughters to make them more marriageable since tiny feet were considered the epitome of female beauty.

Female infanticide: The killing of girl babies.

Perceptions of Perfection: Intellectual, Scientific, and Cultural Life

The period from the Tang to the Ming was marked by unsurpassed technological prowess. Indeed, according to the leading scholar of China's record of innovation, Joseph Needham, China remained the world's leading producer of new inventions until roughly 1500. So striking is this record, and so suddenly does it subside after this time, that historians sometimes refer to the problem of why it took place as "the Needham question." One possible answer may be simply that the Chinese considered that they had achieved a degree of perfection in so many areas that, like their great naval expeditions, there was simply no pressing need to advance them further. Within a few hundred years, however, the momentum of technological innovation had shifted decisively to the small, feuding states of Europe.

The Neo-Confucian Synthesis   The long period of the intermingling of Confucianism with Buddhist, Daoist, and other traditions of thought forced an extensive reformulation of its core concepts by the Song period. During the twelfth century, this reformulation matured into Neo-Confucianism, which combined the moral core of Confucian ethics with a new emphasis on speculative philosophy borrowed from Buddhist and Daoist thinkers.

Neo-Confucianism holds that one cannot sit passively and wait for enlightenment, as the Buddhists do, but must actively "seek truth through facts" in order to understand correctly the relationships of form (*li*) and substance (*qi*) as they govern the constitution of the totality of the universe, or "supreme ultimate" (*taiji*). As self-cultivation of the Confucian virtues is the means of discovering one's true *li*, so investigation of the

Bound Foot. One of the Song practices that would have long-term repercussions for Chinese women was the fashion of foot binding. These so-called lily buds represented the height of male eroticism well into the twentieth century and were the result of years of careful, painful wrapping of the feet of young girls until they assumed the misshapen form depicted here.

physical world is a means of discovering one's place in the larger *li* of the supreme ultimate. Hence, knowledge is a cumulative, unified whole, with the moral dimension of knowledge taking precedence over mere observation.

One experiences the ethical and epistemological strands of this exploration holistically in a manner beyond mere analytical reason and more akin to a Buddhist flash of enlightenment. Exploration of the physical universe undertaken in this spirit is thus the ultimate act of Confucian self-cultivation in that one apprehends the Way (*Dao*) on every level. This vision of Neo-Confucianism was propounded by the Cheng brothers, Hao (1032–1085) and Yi (1033–1107), and perfected by Zhu Xi (ca. 1129–1200), generally recognized as the leading Neo-Confucian thinker. Not surprisingly, these ideas came to prominence during the Song period, riding a wave of anti-Buddhist reaction in the wake of the fall of the Tang. The incorporation of Buddhist approaches to cosmology made the philosophy attractive to those who were intrigued by inquiries into the nature of the universe while retaining the Chinese ethical precepts of family relationships and behavior.

Zhu Xi's speculative Neo-Confucianism lost favor somewhat during a Buddhist revival of sorts during the Ming, in favor of the more direct ethical action favored by Wang Yangming (1472–1529). For Wang, as for Zhu Xi, truth, whether in terms of epistemology or ethics, was unitary. He believed that all people carry within them an "original mind" in which rests an intuitive sense of the fundamental order of the universe. It is out of this instinct toward the right that one investigates the physical and moral universe in order to refine one's conclusions.

Wang, however, departed from Zhu Xi's emphasis on a rigorous "investigation of things" as the necessary route to understanding the nature of the world. Instead, he insisted that such investigation merely hones one's existing instincts in these areas to a higher degree. For example, the innate feelings one has toward one's parents naturally lead one to see filial piety as a fundamental condition of the universe; further investigation allows one to grasp its subtleties.

Wang's other area of emphasis, nurtured by a long study of Buddhism—especially *Chan* (*Zen*)—and Daoism, was the unity of knowledge and action. While everyone has the spark of intuition, he argued, true understanding is inseparable from active pursuit and cultivation of that spark. Moreover, the sage must act in the world as his knowledge becomes increasingly refined, both to be a moral example to others and to complete his own self-cultivation.

Technological Peaks   In many respects, the notion of perfectibility woven through Song and Ming philosophy presented itself in the scientific and technical realms as well. A number of previous innovations were refined and, in some cases, brought to highly developed states. In a great many other cases, however, high points were achieved early on and continued substantially unchanged. For example, Zheng He's ships, with their dazzling array of innovative features in the fifteenth century, remained unsurpassed triumphs of Chinese naval architecture until the mid-nineteenth century, when the empire's first steamships were launched from Western-style dockyards. While new firearms were introduced in the seventeenth and eighteenth centuries, they came in part by way of Jesuit missionaries from Europe and remained essentially unchanged until the 1840s—yet another revealing pattern of core innovation (gunpowder weapons) reintroduced in improved form from the periphery.

From the Tang through the Southern Song, China was the site of an unprecedented number of technological innovations that would have a profound effect inside and outside the empire. The horse collar, moldboard plow, wheelbarrow, advanced iron casting, compass, gunpowder, porcelain, and paper diffused widely throughout Eurasia and the Indian Ocean basin. By the height of the Song period, tea, sugar, silk, porcelain, paper, and cotton cloth had all become major industries and China dominated—in some cases, monopolized—production and distribution of all of them. An increasingly sophisticated infrastructure of commercial credit, printed paper money, and insurance for merchant houses and their agents supported and secured China's vast network of industry and trade.

Song Porcelain. Porcelain reached its full maturity during the Song Dynasty and objects from that period are even today highly coveted. This white-glazed ding jar is from the Northern Song (960–1127).

Porcelain and Literature   As we can see, many of the technical advances that took place revolved around luxury items. Most notable in this regard was the development of true porcelain. Following centuries of experimentation with kaolin clays, glazing mixes, and extremely high firing temperatures, Song craftspeople hit upon the formula for creating the world's most celebrated ceramics. Elegant white and celadon (a shade of green) porcelain vessels were manufactured in great numbers, and the surviving examples of Song wares today are among the world's most precious art treasures. Techniques for using distinctive blue cobalt oxide pigments were originally introduced from Iraq in the ninth century and were being utilized by Song and Ming potters to brighten their porcelain ware. Government-sponsored and -run kilns, notably at the Jingdezhen works in Jiangxi Province, allowed for unprecedented volume and quality control.

The growing wealth, leisure, and literacy of the scholar-gentry and urban classes also created an increased demand for popular literature. The novel as a literary genre first made its appearance in China during the Yuan period but emerged as a form of mass entertainment only in the sixteenth century. Written in a rapidly evolving combination of classical and colloquial language, the swashbuckling adventures of the multiauthored *Water Margin* (or *All Men Are Brothers*) and the tale of family intrigue and woe of Cao Xueqin's *The Dream of the Red Chamber* captured the imaginations of seventeenth- and eighteenth-century readers.

Putting It All Together

The experiences of India and China during the period from the seventh through the fifteenth centuries provide us with several important areas of comparison. The first is in the realm of political continuity. India was subject to a succession of governments set up by invaders from the north and west, while the kingdoms to the south jockeyed for power among themselves and for power over the Indian-influenced states of southeast Asia. While there was considerable cultural and religious continuity in the south, the north was alternately dominated by the Hinduism of the late Gupta period, the revived Buddhism of the seventh century, and ultimately by Islam. In the end, none of these claimed full dominance, though Islam remained the religion of the rulers after the twelfth century.

In the case of China, despite the Mongol invasion and political domination of China during the fourteenth century, the basic political structure changed relatively little and reemerged with greater centralization than ever during the Ming dynasty. Culturally, the Mongols' influence on China was negligible; moreover, the Mongols increasingly were compelled to make themselves culturally "Chinese" in order to rule, despite their concerted efforts to maintain their ethnic autonomy. Through it all, not only did Chinese leadership in technical innovation in so many fields keep up its former pace but the brief incorporation into the Mongol Empire helped to greatly facilitate other cultures' interaction with and adaptation to Chinese advances.

The most dramatic difference, however, came in the realm of interaction with and adaptation to religion. India, from the time of Mahmud of Ghazna, never completely adapted itself to Islam—a situation that continues to the present day. Thus, northern India became a *syncretic* area—an area in which the worldviews of rival religious civilizations confronted each other but were not significantly adopted or adapted by the other. Instead, Hindus and Muslims attempted to coexist with each other. Even notable attempts to bridge the gulf between Hindus and Muslims, such as the Sikhs, were not successful in attaining widespread acceptance.

In China, however, the dominant political structures of empire and the cultural assumptions of Confucianism not only resisted Mongol attempts to circumvent them but in the end were largely adopted by the conquerors. Unlike the Muslim conquerors in India, the Mongols did not adhere to a powerfully articulated universal religion. In fact, they proved receptive to several of the religious traditions they encountered in their conquests: Islam, Buddhism, and Nestorian Christianity all gained Mongol adherents. Even before this, however, in marked contrast to India's encounter with Islam, the very real tensions between Buddhism and Confucianism in China resulted not in persecution of the Buddhists but in Confucian thinkers borrowing their approaches to speculative philosophy and creating an expanded synthetic ideology, Neo-Confucianism.

Thus, until the nineteenth century, these religious and cultural trends would continue: India, dominated by the Muslim Mughals in the north and increasingly by the British from the eighteenth century on, would struggle to reconcile and balance the tensions of syncretism. The British, quick to sense these tensions, increasingly exploited them in their strategy of "divide and rule." The Chinese, firm in the belief that all outsiders could ultimately "become Chinese" continued to pursue this policy through the same period. Ultimately, both empires would be reduced by the British and their fellow European powers, whose centuries-long rise was shortly to begin.

▶ For additional resources, including maps, primary sources, visuals, and quizzes, please go to www.oup.com/us/vonsivers. Please see the Further Resources section at the back of the book for additional readings and suggested websites.

Thinking Through Patterns

▶ **How did interactions between Muslims and Hindus in India lead to religious syncretism?**

In contemplating this question, we must consider what the fundamental beliefs of these two religious traditions were and what kinds of changes take place as religions move from one place to another and interact with other long-established beliefs. For Hindus, this is somewhat difficult because Hinduism encompasses many different religious assumptions. Moreover, it has a long tradition of trying to fit newly arrived belief systems into its own traditions. This is where the clash with Islam is most evident. Islam teaches that there is no God but God (Allah); Hinduism would place Allah next to its other gods, which Muslims find intolerable. This fundamental clash of views makes any compromise difficult. But Muslim leaders find that they simply cannot coerce their Hindu subjects, who vastly outnumber them, to accept the new religion by force. They must therefore find ways to lessen its impact while holding true to the strictures of Islam. Thus, some leniency must be given, or rule becomes impossible; but each side keeps its distance from the other for fear of giving up core values. Thus, they coexist, albeit very uneasily.

Some compromises were made along the way to lessen conflict between the major traditions. Muslim rulers routinely had to suspend their insistence on governing by strict Islamic law and let the Hindu majority govern itself according to their own traditions. In some cases, Hindu women even adopted the veil, like their Muslim counterparts. The most spectacular steps were the founding of new religious traditions incorporating both Hindu and Muslim elements—the Sikhs, for example, and, as we will see in Chapter 19, the Mughal ruler Akbar's attempt at a synthetic religion.

▶ **What steps were taken by Hindus and Muslims to lessen the conflicts between the two rival religious traditions?**

▶ **How was the Tang dynasty in China different from its predecessors and successors?**

As we saw, the Tang was China's most cosmopolitan dynasty, and this alone made it quite different from its predecessors. But why was it so cosmopolitan? Here, a large part of the answer must be seen in the widespread practice of Buddhism. China was now integrated in a Buddhist cultural sphere that allowed a greatly enhanced circulation of ideas and goods. Thus, China's rulers knew a good deal more about their neighbors than ever before and through Buddhism shared a community of religious interest with them. The reaction to Buddhism as a "foreign" faith in the Song period made China turn more inward; consequently, its larger ties with the Buddhist world deteriorated, never to reach Tang-level connections again.

The longevity and diversity of Neo-Confucianism over time suggest that the blending was quite effective. It represented a synthesis in which ethics and epistemology—Confucian, humanist-based morality coupled with the speculative ventures of Daoists and Buddhists—created a complete, self-sustaining system. In this, it parallels attempts by contemporary Christian and Muslim thinkers to marry faith and reason into an all-encompassing system designed to provide a means to answer both concrete and speculative questions.

▶ **How effectively did the religious and philosophical traditions of Buddhism, Confucianism, and Daoism blend together in creating Neo-Confucianism? Where did they clash?**

Chapter 13 550-1500 CE
Religious Civilizations Interacting
KOREA, JAPAN, AND VIETNAM

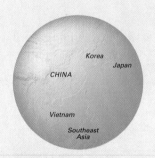

The brushstrokes flowed across the fine rice paper, as they had thousands of times since she began carefully practicing them as a young girl. For Murasaki Shikibu (ca. 973–1025), the daughter of a minor noble in the court at Heian-Kyo in central Japan, the words that now came so effortlessly had become her refuge from the rigid routine of palace life, where a woman's every move was carefully prescribed. The court women of Heian Japan (794–1185 CE), in their thick, stiff winter kimonos, their teeth blackened and faces powdered white to enhance their beauty, were carefully monitored by palace chamberlains and commented on by court gossips. Some of the women, like Murasaki's older contemporary, Sei Shonagon, responded to this restricted life with savage wit and scathing commentary, skewering its pretentions in her scandalous *Pillow Book*.

Murasaki's literary interests, however, took a somewhat different turn. Though trained in *kanji*, the literary Chinese that functioned as Japan's first written language, her private writings, as were those of the handful of other literate Japanese women, were written in the simpler *kana* script based on a **syllabary** of sounds in the Japanese spoken language. Like Sei's, her work also centered on court life. But her subject was the adventures, loves, trials, and triumphs of a fictional prince named Genji. When it was finished, she had created in her *Genji Monagatori*, the *Tale of Genji* (ca. 1000), what

ABOVE: Detail from twelfth-century Japanese scroll depicting *The Tale of Genji*.

scholars have since recognized as the world's first novel. It remains even today Japan's most popular work of fiction and one of the world's great literary masterpieces.

The story of Murasaki, the court women of Heian-Kyo—the city we know today as Kyoto—and eleventh-century Japan more generally all help to illustrate the patterns of world history featured in this book.

Seeing Patterns

▶ How was the history of Korea affected by its relations with China? With Japan?

▶ Which important elements of Chinese culture were adapted by the Japanese for their own purposes? What advantages did Japan have over Korea and Vietnam in this regard?

▶ Which Japanese adaptations of Chinese institutions did not work well in Japan? Why?

▶ In what ways was the experience of Vietnam similar to that of Japan and Korea? How was it different?

In the sixth century CE, Chinese writing, culture, thought, and Buddhism arrived simultaneously in Japan and were swiftly adopted by the ambitious Japanese state of Yamato. Sensing that power and prestige would grow from adapting China's centralized imperial institutions to Japanese conditions, Yamato leaders thoroughly remade their state along these lines over the next two centuries. But in many ways, as we shall see, the suitability of these institutions to Japan's clan-based society was at best uneven.

The tensions in state formation, both large and small, created by this situation were noticeable as well in Korea and Vietnam, also in the process of interaction and adaptation to Chinese institutions. Like the Japanese, the Koreans and Vietnamese would go on to create their own writing systems while retaining Chinese as a literary language. They would also struggle, like the Japanese and Chinese, to balance the differing traditions of Buddhism with the practical elements of Confucian government. The dynamism within these tensions would allow each to ultimately make Chinese imported culture their own as they followed their own distinct courses of state formation: Korea and Vietnam, often struggling under China's political shadow, and Japan, clinging fiercely to its independence and protected by the intervening Sea of Japan.

Korea to 1450: Innovation from Above

Like the influence of the Greek-Hellenistic and Roman worlds, that of imperial China became widespread throughout east, northeast, and southeast Asia. Chinese writing, literature, law, government, and thought, as well as imported religions such as Buddhism, came to overlay local social, cultural, and religious customs and practices. But as these imports were often imposed from the top down, they met frequent resistance at the village and clan levels. Thus, tensions between elites and locals continually played out in the assorted Korean kingdoms against a backdrop of invasion and collaboration. From the beginning these societies asserted their political independence from the Chinese. However, their position on or near the Chinese border, the role of the Korean kingdoms as havens for refugees, and the continual pressures of possible invasion provided a conduit for the spread of Chinese innovations—even to the islands of Japan. For the Koreans themselves, shifting relations with China provided both unity and disarray in the struggles of different kingdoms for dominance.

People and Place: The Korean Environment

The terrain of the Korean peninsula resembles in many ways that of the adjacent region of Manchuria. The north is mountainous, marked by the Nangnim and Hamyong ranges running northeast to southwest, with the Taebaek chain running

Syllabary: A system of written characters representing the sounds of syllables, rather than individual sounds.

north and south along the coast facing the Sea of Japan. The Amnokkang, better known as the Yalu River, and Kangnam Mountains form the present dividing line with Manchuria; but Korean kingdoms have at times extended far beyond them into modern China's northeast. The areas south of the modern city of Seoul are somewhat flatter; but the entire peninsula is generally hilly, and agriculture has historically been concentrated in the river floodplains and coastal alluvial flats.

Climate and Agriculture   The climate of Korea is continental in the north but influenced by the monsoon system in the south. As in northern China, summer and winter temperatures tend to be extreme, with distinct rainy (summer) and dry (winter) seasons. Because of the configuration of the mountains and the peninsula's position along the northern perimeter of the monsoon, annual rainfall amounts differ widely: from average lows of 30 inches in the northeast to 60–70 inches in the southwest. Like the western side of the Japanese islands, however, Korea is largely blocked by Japanese mountain ranges from the moderating effects of the Japan Current.

The difficulties of the terrain and the ever-present possibility of drought have rendered the challenges of the region similar to those facing agriculturalists in northern China, with crops such as millet and wheat dominating and rice farming catching on only much later in the south, where rainfall and the terracing of hillsides made it feasible. Scholars have noted similarities to archaic Greece, where geography fostered the development of isolated, independent communities and worked against political unification, though early on a degree of cultural unity appears to have prevailed (see Map 13.1).

Ethnic Origins   The ethnic origins of the Koreans are still obscure, though the slim archaeological and linguistic evidence seems to point to a central Asian homeland and links to the **Altaic**-speaking peoples. In this sense, the modern Korean language may be distantly related to such languages as Mongolian, Manchu, and possibly Japanese. East and northeast Asia, as we have seen, was home to some of the world's first pottery, though the potter's wheel did not arrive in the area for millennia. In the case of the Korean peninsula, potsherds dating from 4000 BCE have been uncovered in **striated** styles not unlike the Jomon wares of Japan, which some scholars have suggested points to an early period of interaction or perhaps even a common ancestry.

Altaic: In language studies, referring to the family of languages descended from that spoken by inhabitants of the region of the Altai Mountains in central Asia. Examples include the Turkish languages, Mongolian, and Manchu.

Striated: Having thin lines or bands.

Conquest and Competition: History and Politics to 1598

Though developments in northern China have long had a bearing on events on the Korean peninsula, the first Korean state predated any such influence. Zhou Chinese annals contain apparent references to the kingdom of Choson—"The Land of the Morning Calm." Choson seems to have extended deep into southern Manchuria, with its capital located on the site of the modern city of Pyongyang. It is believed to have been founded sometime after 1000 BCE. In the absence of a Korean written language, however, no indigenous records exist of its early years.

The "Three Kingdoms"   Such Chinese cultural influences as the use of written language appear to have been present in the region even before the first attempt at invasion under the Qin (221–206 BCE). By 108 BCE, their successors, the Han, briefly succeeded in bringing much of the peninsula under their sway. It is from this period that the first written records of exchanges with such outlying peoples as the Koreans, Japanese, and Vietnamese find their way into Han histories. Long before this, however, Chinese agricultural techniques and implements, methods of bronze and iron smelting, and a wide variety of other technologies found their way to Choson and beyond. Early contacts between Choson and the Zhou Chinese states from the ninth century BCE on saw the arrival of bronze tools, coins, and weapons. By the fifth century BCE, the technology of iron smelting was also firmly established on the Korean peninsula.

Following the Han conquests, a more systematic Chinese transformation was attempted. The Han incorporated approximately two-thirds of the peninsula into their empire and took over Pyongyang as their regional capital. They also encouraged Chinese settlement in the newly acquired territories in order to help ensure loyalty. One of the indirect effects of the conquest was a steady stream of refugees into the unoccupied regions of the south and to the small tribal societies of Japan. This constant traffic back and forth across the narrow, 100-mile strait separating the Japanese islands from the mainland created a transient population of colonists in both places and greatly facilitated cultural exchanges. Koreans became established as important factors in early Japanese history, and with the founding of the small Japanese holding of *Kaya* [Gaya] in 42 CE, Japanese territorial claims were established on the peninsula.

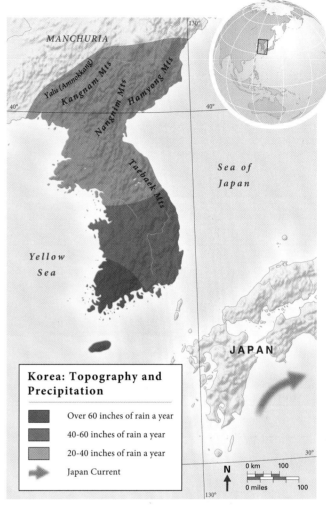

MAP **13.1** **Korea: Topography and Precipitation.**

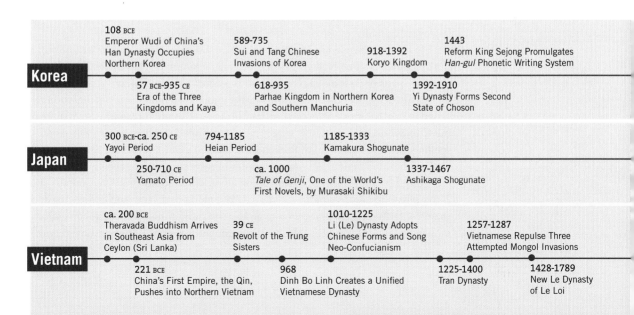

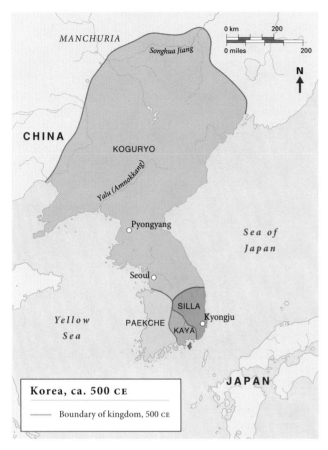

MAP **13.2** **Korea, ca. 500 CE.**

At the same time, the foundations had been laid for the so-called Three Kingdoms of Korea: *Koguryo* [Go-GUR-yo] (37 BCE–668 CE), *Paekche* [BAAK-chih] (18 BCE–660 CE), and *Silla* [SEE-lah] (57 BCE–935 CE). By the fourth century CE, the dissolution of the Han Empire encouraged the Koreans to push the Chinese out of the peninsula. In the wake of their retreat, the three rival kingdoms began a process of intrigue and intermittent war among themselves for dominance. Koguryo, in the extreme north, formed the largest state as the Chinese evacuated, moving into southern Manchuria in the absence of any strong rivals. In the south, the areas that had never been under Chinese control had a history of close ties to the developing Japanese clan powers and, consequently, tended to be more outward-looking (see Map 13.2).

In 372 the Chinese state of Jin began sending Buddhist missionaries to Koguryo. With them came Chinese writing and literature—and, significantly, ethics and political thought. Within a few decades, as the elites of Koguryo sensed the power of these tools to enhance their statecraft, a Confucian academy was established in the kingdom. In 427, Koguryo remade itself along Chinese lines. From Pyongyang a central Confucian bureaucracy was set up, examinations were instituted, and a reconstituted land tax and conscription system were installed.

Meanwhile, the two southern kingdoms fought continually to stave off domination by their northern rival. Paekche's maritime contacts with south China aided the spread of Buddhism there, as did, to some degree, its wars with Koguryo from 364 to 371. Buddhism had also come to Silla, but Chinese political institutions did not take the same form there as elsewhere. A clan-based, autocratic monarchy, Silla adopted a Chinese-style bureaucracy but retained its system of hereditary ranks, leaving power largely in the hands of warrior aristocrats.

The power struggle among the peninsular states was long and bitter and from time to time also involved China. In 550, Silla allied with Paekche against the renewed expansionist aims of Koguryo, in the course of which Kaya was eliminated in 562. The reunification of China under the short-lived Sui dynasty in 589 soon resulted in another invasion of the north. After several Tang campaigns were repulsed, the Chinese decided on a new strategy and concluded an alliance with Silla in 660, spelling the immediate end of Paekche. Threatened along two fronts, Koguryo itself finally submitted in 668. Following decades of resistance against the Tang, Silla was recognized by the Chinese as controlling all of Korea south of Pyongyang in 735. Although politically free of the Chinese, Silla remained a client state of the Tang and shared with them incorporation into an east Asian Buddhist cultural sphere, which now included Japan as well. Meanwhile, remnant forces of Koguryo moved north

Pulguksa Temple. Buddhism put down strong roots in Silla after its introduction in the fourth century. The Pulguksa temple was first built in Kyongjiu, the Silla capital, in 535 as part of the state Buddhist school. The stone pagodas were built in the ninth century under the auspices of the new Son school, better known by its Japanese name, Zen.

and set up a state called Parhae [BAHR-hay] in northern Korea and Manchuria that lasted until 926, when it was overrun by the Qitans [Khitans] (see Chapter 12).

Korea to the Mid-Fifteenth Century By the middle of the eighth century, Silla was in decline. In 780 the king was assassinated, and revolts led by various pretenders threatened to leave the country unstable for some time to come. Among the most restive members of Silla society were the merchants who, like their counterparts in China, were aware of their growing economic power, though sensitive to the fear and contempt in which they were held by the Confucian-influenced aristocracy and bureaucrats.

One such merchant, Wong Kon (d. 943), subdued the crumbling kingdom and reconstituted it as Koryo—from which comes the name "Korea." The Chinese imperial model of state formation proved attractive to Wong, who, after the practice of Chinese emperors, was accorded a posthumous reign name, Taejo. He moved the capital to Kaesong, where he laid out a city in the grid pattern of the Tang capital of Chang'an and adopted Chinese-style bureaucratic and tax systems, with military and labor conscription. Koryo even built its own version of the Great Wall near the Yalu River as a barrier to the nomadic peoples of the north (see Map 13.3).

By the middle of the thirteenth century, Koryo, like much of the rest of Asia, had begun

MAP **13.3 Korea Under the Koryo, 936–1392.**

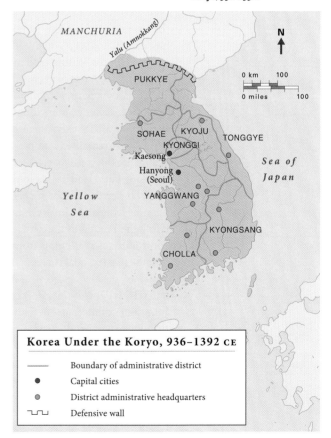

Korea Under the Koryo, 936–1392 CE

——	Boundary of administrative district
●	Capital cities
●	District administrative headquarters
⌐⌐	Defensive wall

to feel the power of Mongol expansion. In 1231, with rockets, bombs, and assorted other new military items acquired from their victories over the Chinese, Mongol forces laid siege to Kaesong. The fall of the city inaugurated four decades of irregular warfare against the occupiers and forced the withdrawal of the government to the south. The Mongols' imperial ambitions prompted the deportation of perhaps 250,000 Koreans as slave laborers to other parts of the Mongol Empire, beginning in 1254. The Koryo court finally capitulated in 1259, following which, as they had in other areas, the Mongols intermarried and assimilated to Korean culture. As in most of the occupied areas of Eurasia, the advantages wrought by Mongol unity in terms of easier travel and transport and increased public works were eclipsed in Korea by the cruelty of the conquest itself, the widespread perception of misrule, and oppressive taxation.

In 1368, the Mongol Yuan dynasty in China was overthrown by the forces of the soldier monk Zhu Yuanzhi, who inaugurated the Ming dynasty (1368–1644). As had nearly every previous dynasty, the Ming laid plans to invade Korea. In 1388 the Korean leader Yi Song-gye made the strategic decision not to resist the Ming but moved against the Korean court instead, founding the Yi dynasty in 1392 and resurrecting the name of Choson for the new state. The Yi proved to be Korea's final imperial dynasty, ruling until the peninsula was annexed by Japan in 1910. The Yi concluded an agreement with China that formed the heart of what is often, though somewhat erroneously, referred to as the Ming "tribute system" (see Chapter 12).

Meanwhile, the Yi polity once again adapted to Chinese-style institutions. The highly centralized governmental structure of the Ming was echoed in Choson, and the adoption of Neo-Confucianism slowly began to drive out older local customs. A new capital was set up on the site of present-day Seoul, and the state was divided into eight provinces. Within each of these, the Chinese model of prefectures and districts was followed. A uniform law code was later promulgated in 1485, calling for, among other things, a permanent hereditary class structure. The Confucian exam structure was also broadened to include a two-tiered official class, the *yongban* and *chongin*.

Yet, for all the advantages created by the new class structure, old cleavages in many cases remained and new unanticipated ones soon developed. As a means of stabilizing the *yongban* class (and, so it was assumed, society as a whole), the Yi rulers made large land grants to the great officials of the kingdom. These landholders, however, tended to use such grants to amass more and more local power. Unlike Chinese officials, who were moved from place to place for just this reason, they tended to remain in their own territories, where they could use a host of informal controls to resist attempts from the throne to rein in their excesses. Over time, many became like regional rulers.

Economy, Society, and Family

Like their counterparts in China, rulers and government officials in the various Korean kingdoms tended to be preoccupied with recurrent problems of landlordism and tenancy, land reform, and maintenance of local infrastructures—especially in wet rice-producing areas—and alleviating want during times of shortage.

Land Reform   At various times, therefore, those under Chinese influence proposed schemes of land redistribution based on the Chinese "well-field" model (see Chapter 4). More ambitious was the *chongjon* system of Silla, begun in 722. Following a combination of Buddhist and Confucian precepts and with an eye to local custom, the *chongjon* system mandated a government-sponsored distribution of land, with taxes paid in kind. Additionally, peasants were instructed to develop specialized cash crops or engage in small-craft manufacture. A prime example was the planting of mulberry trees as food for silkworms and the development of **sericulture**.

Under the Yi dynasty of Choson, the implanting of Neo-Confucian values in the countryside as well as among elites became a prime consideration. Edicts were handed down about proper deportment of family members, inheritance practices, and relations between men and women, as well as land policy. Here, a new system of land tenure was made part of a more general stabilizing of all classes. Peasant rents were fixed at half the crop and a hierarchy of village headmen, bureaucrats, and magistrates similar to the Chinese system was set up to collect taxes, settle disputes, and dispense justice.

As noted previously, the institution of Chinese systems in Korea tended to attract the elites more than the peasant and artisan classes. Their spotty success in taking root tended in many ways to aggravate societal tensions, despite the governmental efficiencies they created. One factor in this was a repeated attempt on the part of the bureaucracy to enhance its power at the expense of the merchant and artisan classes. In the countryside, power remained in the hands of the landholder aristocracy, which tended to ensure that the peasants would be bound to them in a fashion not unlike the serfdom of their European contemporaries.

Neo-Confucian Influence   Particularly in the cities, the high level of Song Chinese-influenced material culture was increasingly evident. Interregional trade was brisk, and luxury items like silk, porcelain, and lacquerware were widely available. Korea's position at the center of the east Asian Buddhist world tended to make it a trade and pilgrimage crossroads, and its artisans became highly proficient in the new technologies of porcelain making and book printing. Many of the oldest Chinese, Korean, and Japanese works extant were printed by Korean publishers.

Under the Yi, the Confucian exams became more open, though the new arrangement called for two official classes, the *yongban*, or scholar-gentry, drawn from high civil and military officials, and the *chungin*, or minor officials. Below these were the *yangmin*, commoners of different professions as well as peasants and serfs, while the lowest group, the *chonmin*, consisted of bond slaves, laborers, and prostitutes.

Though approximating the class structure in China, the new system was more like the composite one created in Heian Japan. As in Japan, it proved a troublesome fit, particularly in remote rural areas. Though the Confucian exams theoretically allowed for some degree of social mobility, they tended to be monopolized by the *yongban*. The institution of hereditary classes, intended to create a stable and harmonious social structure, instead concentrated wealth in the hands of the rural gentry, who often lacked a proper Confucian sense of the official responsibilities of their positions. In many places, the older patterns of aristocratic local power simply continued with only cosmetic changes. Thus, by the sixteenth century, the divide between the wealthy, educated, sophisticated capital and large provincial cities and the tradition-bound countryside was steadily increasing.

Women and Society   Until the arrival of Confucian institutions in the Korean countryside, local village life, as in Vietnam and Japan, tended toward more

Sericulture: Raising silkworms in order to obtain raw silk.

egalitarian structures, especially between men and women, than would later be the case. In Korea, this egalitarianism retained a remarkable vitality in the face of Neo-Confucian precepts. Even today, there is far less of the traditional emphasis on filial piety and patriarchal custom than in China. Until the sixteenth and seventeenth centuries, for example, bilateral and **matrilocal** marriage patterns tended to be the norm. As in Japan and Vietnam, the communal nature of rice agriculture, and its emphasis on meticulous, intensive cultivation, tended to lessen the division between "male" and "female" work roles and made women and girls more equal partners in local rural society. Women's property and inheritance rights, far more expansive than in Confucian China, also reflected this.

Matrilocal: Living with the family of the bride.

Under the Neo-Confucian reforms of the Yi, however, some of these practices began to change. The idea of strictly delineated gender roles, of men dominating in the "outer" world and women being preeminent in the "inner" world of the home—long a staple among the urban elites and official classes—now became a cornerstone of moral training in rural academies and in the home.

Religion, Culture, and Intellectual Life

As with many peoples of north and central Asia, early Korean religion appears to have been animistic. One could appeal to the spirits through shamans or animals believed to have certain powers. Like Shinto in Japan, these beliefs continued at the local level for many hundreds of years after the introduction of more formalized systems. The invasion of the Han brought the Chinese concepts of heaven, earth, and humankind along with the imperial rituals associated with them. Of more long-term importance, however, was the introduction of Buddhism to the Three Kingdoms during the fourth century CE.

Impact of Buddhism All the Korean kings seized to varying degrees on the combination of Buddhism, Han Confucian political and moral philosophy, and their supporting institutions as ways to enhance their own state formation. In Silla, for example, the court pursued a course of striving for Buddhist "perfection." It patronized a popular Buddhist-Confucian society, Hwarang—the "Flower of Youth Corps"—that helped to build the 210-foot Hwang Nyonsu temple in 645. Others sponsored mammoth publication projects of Buddhist works: Koryo produced a version of the *Tripitaka* printed on 80,000 hand-carved wood blocks as an act of piety and supplication during the war with the Mongols. Indeed, the relatively high level of functional literacy in written Chinese among Korean elites was greatly aided by the immense popularity of the many schools of Buddhism—Tiantai, Amida (Pure Land), and, by the 1100s, Zen. As a result, twelfth-century Korea developed into one of the world's handful of centers of printing and publishing due in large part to the demand for Buddhist works. By the 1100s as well, publishers were employing what may have been the world's first movable, cast metallic type (see "Patterns Up Close: Printing").

Korea's leading role in world literacy in the preindustrial era received a further boost during the reign of King Sejong (r. 1418–1450). Here, the development of the Korean phonetic script **han-gul**, like the use of *kana* in Japan, made the introduction of writing much simpler and closer to the vernacular than literary Chinese. Like the *kana* system in Japan, *han-gul* helped the spread of literacy in a far more efficient manner than had been the case with literary Chinese. Yet, like *kana* in Japan, it also tended to create a two-tiered system of literacy: Chinese tended to remain

Han-gul: Korean phonetic script, first introduced in the middle of the fifteenth century.

the written medium of choice among the highly educated and largely male elites, while *han-gul* became the language of the commoners and, increasingly, women. One of the best examples of this is the anonymous, autobiographical *Memoirs of Lady Hyegong*, written in the eighteenth century. Such divisions notwithstanding, however, the explosion of vernacular literature—satires on *yongban* manners, social criticism, fiction, advice manuals for a variety of tasks—all contributed to Korea attaining, with Japan, some of the highest levels of functional literacy in the preindustrial world.

Vowels Consonants	ㅏ [a]	ㅑ [ya]	ㅓ [ŏ]	ㅕ [yŏ]	ㅗ [o]	ㅛ [yo]	ㅜ [u]	ㅠ [yu]	ㅡ [ŭ]	ㅣ [i]
ㄱ [k,g]	가	갸	거	겨	고	교	구	규	그	기
ㄴ [n]	나	냐	너	녀	노	뇨	누	뉴	느	니
ㄷ [t,d]	다	댜	더	뎌	도	됴	두	듀	드	디
ㄹ [r,l]	라	랴	러	려	로	료	루	류	르	리
ㅁ [m]	마	먀	머	며	모	묘	무	뮤	므	미
ㅂ [p,b]	바	뱌	버	벼	보	뵤	부	뷰	브	비
ㅅ [s,sh]	사	샤	서	셔	소	쇼	수	슈	스	시
ㅇ²	아	야	어	여	오	요	우	유	으	이
ㅈ [ch,j]	자	쟈	저	져	조	죠	주	쥬	즈	지
ㅊ [ch']	차	챠	처	쳐	초	쵸	추	츄	츠	치
ㅋ [k']	카	캬	커	켜	코	쿄	쿠	큐	크	키
ㅌ [t']	타	탸	터	텨	토	툐	투	튜	트	티
ㅍ [p']	파	퍄	퍼	펴	포	표	푸	퓨	프	피
ㅎ [h]	하	햐	허	혀	호	효	후	휴	흐	히

The Conventions and Alphabet of Han-gul. As originally given by King Sejong in his 1446 *Hunmin chong-um* ("Proper Sounds to Instruct the People"), *han-gul* contained 28 syllables. These have now been reduced to 24, with five double consonants and the additional vowels shown. The ease of learning the system is such that Korea has one of the highest levels of literacy in the world.

Japan to 1450: Selective Interaction and Adaptation

Of all the places we have examined in east and south Asia thus far, Japan raises the most exciting questions about the effects of relative isolation. Like Britain in its "splendid isolation," Japan's geographical position allowed it to selectively interact with and adapt to continental innovations, experimenting, refining, and occasionally abandoning them as needed. Indeed, having never experienced a successful invasion, Japan's acculturation was almost completely voluntary, a position unique among the societies of Eurasia.

The Island Refuge

Japan's four main islands, Honshu, Hokkaido, Kyushu, and Shikoku, contain a varied set of climatic conditions. The northernmost island of Hokkaido has cold, snowy winters and relatively cool summers; the central island of Honshu, bisected roughly north to south by substantial mountain ranges, has a temperate to subtropical climate on the eastern side—where it is moderated by the Japan Current—and a colder, more continental climate to the west of the mountains on the side facing Korea and northeastern China. The small southern island of Shikoku and the southernmost island of Kyushu have an abundance of warm, moist weather and are largely governed by the Pacific monsoon system (see Map 13.4).

The Limitations of the Land   The formation of Japan's islands from volcanic activity means that only about one-fifth of the territory has historically been arable. In the narrow plains and valleys, however, the majority of which are on the temperate Pacific side of the mountains, the soil is mineral-rich and the rainfall abundant. But the islanders from early on have also had to face the limitations of the land in supporting a steadily growing population. Like the Korean peninsula, the ruggedness of the land tended to force its people to live in politically isolated, culturally united communities. Thus, communication by water was often the most convenient method, both among the Japanese home islands and across the hundred-mile strait to southern Korea.

Adaptation at Arm's Length: History and Politics

Like the first peoples to inhabit the Korean peninsula, the origins of the Japanese are obscure. Two distinct groups appear to have migrated to the islands from the

Printing

While the invention of the printing press and movable type is widely recognized as having revolutionized the intellectual life of early modern Europe, it is equally true that these developments seven centuries before in east Asia had a similar effect. Yet, in many respects, the consequences of these innovations were different because of the requirements of the languages used and the technical media with which printers in China, Korea, Japan, and Vietnam worked. As in other places, the cultural patterns of handwriting and calligraphy as artistic skills necessary for elites to cultivate in order to complete their moral development also hampered the spread of printing to some degree. Yet, for all these differences, by the fourteenth century, the societies of east Asia still achieved the highest preindustrial literacy rates in the world. These would be unmatched in Europe until centuries after the use of printing had become widespread there.

By the fall of the Han dynasty in 220 CE, we have the earliest remnant examples of woodblock printing. Printers carved single- or double-page blocks of text on book-sized boards, inked them, and pressed the cloth or paper pages on them to get their copies. The boards could then be shaved down and carved again as needed. By the eighth century the Chinese had also begun to experiment with copper movable type inserted vertically into standardized rows in a system very much like the one Gutenberg devised centuries later. But, ironically, these presses remained more curiosities than practical devices for printing a variety of documents. Here, the chief problem was the nature of the Chinese written language—and at this time, the written languages of Korea,

The Korean Printing Industry.
Because of its position as the northern crossroads of the Buddhist and Chinese literary world, Korea was a major center of printing. Printing with carved wooden blocks had been developed during the eighth century, and large publishers and academies kept great numbers of them on hand. The most famous was this storehouse, which still preserves the 80,000 blocks of the *Tripitaka*, carved between 1237–1257.

Asian mainland via Ice Age land bridges, perhaps 10,000–20,000 years ago. Their descendants, the Utari are today regarded as Japan's aboriginal peoples and referred to by the Japanese as *Ainu* the "hairy ones," or in early imperial times as *Emishi*. Their physical features, tribal hunting society, and language mark them as distinct from the later arrivals. Details of their religious practices have led some anthropologists to link them to the peoples of central Asia, Siberia, and the Americas.

The later inhabitants may have originally come from the peoples who migrated into southeast Asia, Indonesia, and eventually the central Pacific. They may also have been descended from later Polynesian travelers and later migrants from the Asian mainland. Linguistic evidence suggests a very tenuous connection to Korean and even to the Altaic language family. Japan's long linguistic isolation, however, renders its ultimate origins obscure at the present time.

Jomon and Yayoi   Japan's prehistory, which lasted from ca. 10,000 BCE down to 300 BCE, has been designated by archaeologists as the Jomon period. The most distinctive artifacts from the era are lightly fired clay vessels marked with a unique horizontal herringbone pattern and often fanciful decorations, clay female figurines called *dogu*, and **phallic** symbols called *bo*. Others include a wide assortment of **microlith** items: arrowheads, spear points, tools made of bone and antler, and nets and fishhooks. **Matriarchal** and **matrilineal** clans appear to have dominated society,

Phallic: Of, relating to, or resembling a penis.

Microlith: A very small blade made of flaked stone and used as a tool, especially in the Mesolithic era.

Matriarchal: A social system in which the mother is head of the family.

Matrilineal: Relating to, based on, or tracing ancestral descent through the maternal line.

Japan, and Vietnam as well. Unlike the English alphabet with its 26 letters, literary Chinese has thousands of different characters. It was simply impractical for type-setters to cast adequate supplies of even the most common characters, organize them, and sort through them to compose the text to be copied. It was far less work to just carve the text blocks from scratch, especially of popular works that would be widely copied and circulated.

In this case, one of the chief catalysts for printing was the growing popularity of Buddhism throughout east Asia. As would be the case centuries later with the spread of religious tracts during the Protestant Reformation, the desire of Buddhists to read scriptures and the openness of the various schools to all classes proved a stimulus to literacy, though in practical terms only those with considerable leisure could master the literary Chinese of the scriptures. Still, by the fourteenth century, the pattern of woodblock printing as a major industry in east Asia, with printing centers in the major cities of China, Japan, and Korea, has been seen by a variety of scholars as one of the hallmarks of early modernity centuries before that term is applied to Europe.

Questions

- How did the innovation of woodblock printing facilitate the spread of Buddhism throughout east Asia?

- What does the use of *han-gul* script in Korea say about the relationship between literacy and state formation?

clustered mostly near the sea or slightly inland. Because game was increasingly limited on the islands, fishing and harvesting seaweed were the major forms of subsistence. As among the American peoples of the Pacific Northwest, the bounty of the sea and forests enabled substantial settled village life to develop in the absence of an early agricultural revolution.

During the final half-millennium before the Common Era, increased intercommunication among Japanese, Koreans, and some members of the Late Zhou Chinese coastal states laid the groundwork not only for the introduction of agriculture to the Japanese islands but for an almost simultaneous Bronze Age as well. During the last centuries of the Jomon period, it appears that some of the grain crops of northern Asia (such as millet) found their way to the islands. During a 600-year period designated Yayoi (300 BCE–300 CE), imported and domestically manufactured bronze and iron articles made their appearance. The fertile plains of southern Honshu and Kyushu also saw the cultivation of northern Eurasian veg-etables and fruits and, most significantly, rice. The swiftness of these changes came in part because of the dislocations resulting from the creation of China's first empire in 221 BCE and the influx of Korean refugees in the wake of the initial Chinese inva-sion of Korea.

Jomon Jar and Yamato Sharinseki Disk. The distinctive herringbone pattern and flared top mark this pottery as Middle Jomon, perhaps 5,000–6,000 years old. The disk made of finely worked steatite was taken from a third-century CE *kofun* burial mound in central Japan. It may be related as a religious object to similar kinds of ornaments found in China.

MAP 13.4 Japan: Topography and Climate.

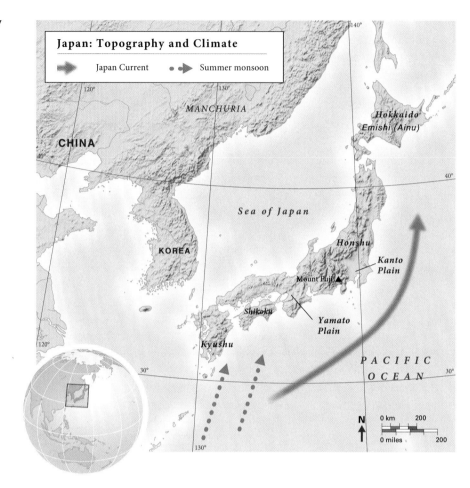

Japan: Topography and Climate

Japan Current ● ▶ Summer monsoon

As it had in other areas of Asia, the rice revolution not only allowed the development of larger populations in Japan but also demanded them for efficient cultivation. The movement away from fishing and gathering combined with the efficiency of metal tools and weapons also fostered state formation among the larger and more powerful clans, or *uji*. The role of the new technologies is witnessed by the items included even now in the imperial regalia at the Shrine of Ise in southern Honshu: a jewel, a bronze mirror, and an iron sword, all of which date from about 260 CE. Thus, sometime after 250 CE, Japan's first fully evolved state, Yamato, centered on the Kanto Plain near modern Tokyo, emerged and quickly expanded, absorbing its weaker rivals on Honshu. Japan's first monumental architecture, enormous burial mounds called *kofun* date from this period.

Toward the Imperial Order While the nature of rulership in Yamato is still clouded by myth, the earliest written records describing the state, composed by Chinese chroniclers in 297 CE, attest to the increased notice it had achieved—though, characteristically, the writers considered their subjects scarcely civilized.

Although there had been steady diplomatic and cultural contact back and forth across the Sea of Japan from the first century CE, a particularly high level was reached during the later sixth century CE. In 552, tradition has it that Buddhism was introduced to the islands from Paekche. With it came the Chinese writing system and written works of every description. A decade later, in 562, the Korean kingdom of Silla eliminated the Japanese colony of Kaya on the peninsula, precipitating a new flow of refugees to Japan. As we have seen, the years from 589 into the early seventh century saw the rise of the Sui and Tang dynasties in China, resulting in yet more Chinese attempts to dominate the Korean kingdoms, and pushing the level of emigration to new levels.

The impact of these events on Yamato cannot be overstated. The growing power of China and Silla helped prompt the Soga *uji*'s Empress Suiko (r. 592–628) and her nephew, Prince Shotoku (ca. 573–621), to connect Yamato more firmly to the mainland and its conceptions of politics, culture, literature, and, ultimately, the imperial system itself. A few signposts along the way include the adoption of Buddhism as a state religion (594), the adoption of the Chinese lunar calendar for state record keeping (604), and the adoption of the prince's 17-article constitution modeled on Confucian and Buddhist precepts (604). But perhaps the most far-reaching changes came later in the century, with the *Taika*, or Great Reform, of 645.

The systematic remaking of the Yamato regime along Chinese lines in the wake of the *Taika* marks the beginning of the imperial Japanese state, that is, of a kingdom bent on expansion over multiple political groups and clans. Among other things, Soga clan control of the court was overturned and Fujiwara No-Kamatari, who emerged as adviser to the new emperor, Tenchi, ushered in a connection between his family and the imperial court that continued into the twentieth century. In less than a century the first Chinese-style imperial histories, the *Kojiki* (712) and *Nihongi* (720), were composed; the concept of the "Mandate of Heaven" was adopted to justify the overthrow of the Sogas; the emperor as the center of a hierarchical system of government run through a rigorously selected bureaucracy was institutionalized; and a census, uniform taxation on land and produce, and systems of conscription and labor service were enacted. The edicts mandating these changes were promulgated as the Taiho Code of 702, which remained the basis of Japanese law until the late nineteenth century.

Yamato's spiritual roots in Shinto, with its connection to the rhythms of nature and renewal, had dictated that the seat of the state be frequently moved. Even today, the sacred shrine at Ise is disassembled and rebuilt every 20 years. Because of the requirements of a far larger and more sophisticated system of government, however, it was decided that a permanent capital be built. The first site selected, at Nara, saw the creation in 710 of a close replica of the Tang capital at Chang'an, down to the axial boulevards, grids of streets, and propitious placement of temples and government buildings. In 794, a larger capital was completed nearby along the same lines called Heian-kyo, the future city of Kyoto. The era of imperial rule from this capital, which lasted until 1185, is thus often referred to as the "Heian" period (see Map 13.5).

Heian Japan   As the imperial order penetrated all the Japanese home islands except Hokkaido and the widespread adoption of Buddhist culture plugged Japan into an enormous, interconnected economic and cultural Asian sphere, Heian Japan increasingly became a land of contrasts, with local rumblings of discontent never far below the surface. For the elites of the capital and provincial administrative centers, life was not unlike that of their counterparts in Korea, Vietnam, or even China itself. The spread of literacy at the top and the common currency of Confucianism,

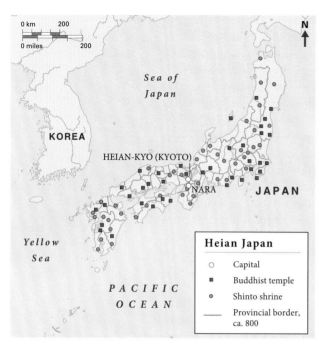

MAP **13.5** Heian Japan.

Chinese literature, and the various Buddhist schools helped these elites see themselves as part of a cosmopolitan world, as did frequent travel for trade and pilgrimage. The latest fashions in poetry, literature, fine arts, calligraphy, music, and (to a lesser extent) clothing all found their way to court and beyond.

For the members of the new classes into which the vast majority of Japan's people had now been placed (peasants, artisans, and merchants—with Buddhist monks occupying an increasingly significant position in the hierarchy), many of the changes had been disruptive at best. Perhaps most tellingly, power, and soon military strength, was diffusing from the court and capital out into the countryside. This was particularly true in more remote regions where the most aggressive *uji* had assembled forces in support of their battles with the *Emeshi*. The bureaucracy, a tenuous institution at best during the Heian period, became weaker as the local *uji* began to reassert power. This was given a considerable push in the wake of a virulent smallpox epidemic (735–737), during which the population may have been reduced by as much as one-third.

Despite court attempts to create a Chinese-style "well-field system," tenancy became a chronic problem. In many cases, the *shoen*, or clan estates, were given tax-exempt status because of their military contributions. The estates of Buddhist monasteries were similarly exempt and provided social services and refuge for outcasts, in effect becoming shadow societies of their own. By the late eleventh century, perhaps half of the land in the empire had become exempt from taxes. As the countryside became more self-sufficient, the capital became more isolated—and more reliant on local military cooperation.

In addition, the court itself was often divided by factional disputes, spurred by the practice of emperors abdicating but staying on as regents or advisers. Three decades of civil war between factions supporting the claims of the Taira clan and those pledged to the Minamoto, or Genji, finally ended in 1185 with the defeat of the Taira. Shortly thereafter, Minamoto Yoritomo was given the title Sei-i-tai **Shogun** (the "Great Barbarian-Suppressing General") and the period of the **Shogunates** was inaugurated, lasting until 1867.

Shogun: The chief military official of Japan. The office later becomes hereditary under the Tokugawa family from 1603 till 1867.

Shogunate: The government, rule, or office of a shogun.

Japan Under the Shoguns
Though the emperor at Kyoto theoretically remained in charge with the shogun as his deputy, the arrangement in fact hastened the drain of power from the capital. Because of its parallels to the political and social order in Europe at the time, the term "feudal" has sometimes been applied to this period. As we saw in Zhou China, however, such similarities should not be pushed too far. In order to restore order in the hotbed of Taira opposition, Yoritomo set up his headquarters at Kamakura, several hundred miles from Kyoto, beginning an interval known as the "Kamakura Shogunate," 1185–1333. The court itself remained the center of religious and ceremonial life as well as a forum for intrigue, but the real

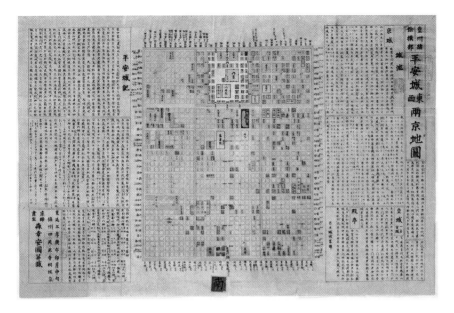

Plan of the Capital at Heian-kyo (Kyoto). The desire to copy the grandeur of Tang institutions extended even to city planning for the eighth-century Japanese court. The capital city at Heian was a faithful copy of the plan of the Tang capital of Chang'an, at the time one of the world's largest cities. The city grid was strictly laid out on a north–south axis, with the most important structures like the imperial palace placed in the northern section and their courtyards and main gates all facing south, the most propitious direction, indicated by the Chinese character highlighted in red at the bottom of the page, meaning "south." The placement of gardens and outlying structures was also carefully calculated according to Chinese notions of *feng shui* geomancy regarding trees, hills, and water.

center of power now resided at the shogun's headquarters. Meanwhile, in 1274, the Mongols launched the first of two major attempts to invade Japan. Their first armada was defeated handily, while in 1281 a much larger second fleet was smashed by a typhoon, known ever after by the Japanese as *kamikaze*, "the divine wind." Though the country was briefly roused to common action in the face of this threat, the dissipation of imperial power for the most part continued unabated.

Court life became even more stilted and formalized, while emperors very occasionally led unsuccessful attempts to reassert power for themselves. The most ambitious of these, though ultimately unsuccessful, was the revolt by Emperor Go-Daigo in 1333. Securing the support of the powerful leader Ashikaga Takauji [Ah-shee-KAH-gah Tah-kah-OO-jee], Go-Daigo's faction was crippled when the opportunistic Ashikaga switched sides twice during the conflict. Ashikaga finally placed his own candidate on the throne, drove the old emperor into exile, and moved his headquarters to the Muromachi [Moo-roe-MA-chee] district in northern Kyoto. For the first time in nearly 200 years, the seats of political and cultural influence were reunited in the same city (see Map 13.6). Even more important for the future of Japanese aesthetics and cultural institutions, the refinements of court life were now available to the warrior classes. There thus was born the union of *bu* and *bun*, the "dual way" of the sword and writing brush. The patronage of the *daimyo*, or regional lords, and their retainers, the **samurai**, ensured steady development of the Chinese-inspired arts of painting, poetry, and calligraphy, while the introduction of Zen and tea in the twelfth century forged an armature of discipline in both the martial and courtly arts that helped to foster the preservation of both for centuries to come.

While the aesthetic refinement of the warrior classes proceeded, the size and scope of warfare itself grew larger and ever more deadly. Like the codes of chivalry current in Europe at this time, *daimyo* and samurai prided themselves on acting according to a strict system of loyalty and honor, *bushido*, "the Way of the Warrior." A samurai was expected to be not just expert with sword and writing brush but unswervingly loyal to his *daimyo* to the point of death. Indeed, the tradition of *seppuku*,

Samurai: A Japanese warrior who was a member of the feudal military aristocracy.

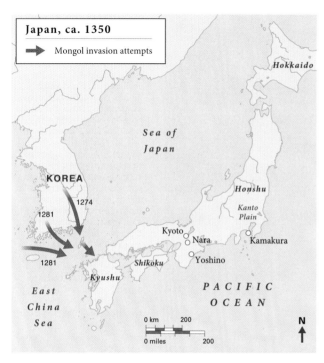

MAP 13.6 **Japan, ca. 1350.**

or *hara kiri*—ritual suicide—developed originally as a way to show one's "sincerity" and disdain for death and capture on the battlefield. One was also expected to show honor and respect to one's opponents, and tales abound from the period of warriors perfuming their helmets and decorating themselves so that whoever killed them would have a tolerable aesthetic experience amidst the gore of the battlefield.

By the fifteenth century, however, these personal touches were giving way to armies increasingly dominated by massed ranks of infantry, in some cases ballooning into the hundreds of thousands of men. By the middle of the following century, the adoption of firearms and accompanying advances in fortification made Japan perhaps the most heavily armed country on earth. The fluidity of the military situation had major social consequences as well, and by the middle of the sixteenth century it was increasingly possible for commoners to rise through the ranks and become commanders and even *daimyo*.

One important reason for these conditions was the chronic instability of the Ashikaga Shogunate. The position was never intended to be hereditary and was always the subject of *daimyo* intrigue both in Kyoto, where manipulation of the emperor was vital in order to achieve favor, and in the countryside, where power had become increasingly concentrated. In 1467, factional struggles would finally erupt into all-out war for 10 years, the effects of which would last more than a century.

Economy, Society, and Family

The real beginning of the diversification of Japan's economy came with the Yayoi period, beginning around 300 BCE. As the early Japanese communities adopted wet rice and vegetable agriculture they gained the ability to sustain a sedentary population, which would prove crucial for assimilating new technologies and allowing the concentration of power for state formation. The limited amount of arable land also meant that the populations of the few large open areas like the Kanto Plain were in an advantageous position to subdue their less numerous neighbors. In addition, they were better able to adopt technologies like bronze and iron making, silk weaving, and so forth that required an increasingly complex infrastructure. By the high point of the Yamato period, therefore, one finds Chinese accounts describing an economy that seems to resemble that of the Chinese or Korean countryside, with the majority of inhabitants engaged in agriculture and identifiable merchant and artisan classes coming into view.

The New Economy   The introduction of Chinese writing, concepts of law, and Buddhism during the sixth century allows historians to view in far greater detail the workings of Japanese economics. By this point, nearly every appropriate domesticated plant and animal from the mainland had been introduced to Japan; and the efficiency of the island's agriculture would soon approach levels comparable to those in China and Korea. Like its counterparts on the mainland, the Yamato court and its successors at Nara and Heian-kyo attempted to regulate economic activity in the form of land and produce taxes, taxes on trade, monopolies on strategic commodities, and requisitions of labor for infrastructural projects.

Yet almost from the beginning, as we noted earlier, these efforts at centralization were only partially effective. The larger *uji*, whose power had theoretically been cut by the creation of a state bureaucracy, got around the problem by supplying many of the officials for the new body. They took advantage of government incentives to reclaim land from the wilderness and the Ainu. By such means the large *shoen* and monastery estates with their tax exemptions tended to acquire regional political and military power.

Such multiple centers also produced an increase in and decentralization of trade. The period from 1250 to 1450 saw cycles of expansion in overseas commerce, with colonies of Japanese merchants—and often, Japanese pirates—operating in the Philippines, Java, and Malacca as well as Korea and China. Through their wares, the *daimyo* and samurai became increasingly sophisticated connoisseurs of luxury goods such as silks, jade, porcelain, lacquerware, rare woods, and books and paper. As the early ports, market towns, regional capitals, and, by the sixteenth century, castle towns, grew, Japanese craftspeople became adept at imitating and refining Chinese crafts, in some cases surpassing the quality of the originals. Moreover, a growing and increasingly diverse middle class of merchants, artisans, actors, dancers, **sake** brewers, ship builders, and others organized into trade guilds (*za*) all partook of such luxury items. The increased demand for capital among them spurred a monetization of the economy and the beginnings of banking and credit systems.

Advances in Agriculture

Most of this would not have been possible without dramatic increases in food production. The period from 1250 to 1600 saw a vast increase in both intensive cultivation of Japan's limited arable land and the introduction of a host of new crops to multiply its productivity. As it had throughout east Asia, the widespread use of fast-ripening Champa rice strains from southeast Asia in southern Honshu, Kyushu, and Shikoku vastly enhanced stocks of this staple. In Kyushu it allowed three crops a year; in other areas, the wet paddy fields it required allowed dry raised beds for vegetables to be made from the soil taken out of the paddies. At the same time the introduction of the Chinese "dragon wheel pump" (see Chapter 9) allowed for easy, small-scale irrigation. Finally, a triple-cropping system consisting of buckwheat in winter, wheat in spring, and rice during the monsoon, with vegetables grown on the raised beds in between fields, allowed an average family to sustain itself on only a few acres of land.

If one factors in the use of terracing and dry rice cultivation in more marginal areas, and the introduction of oranges, grapes, and tea, the leaps in population seem almost inevitable. From an estimated population of about 5 million in 1100 a doubling occurred, perhaps as early as 1300; by 1450 it was on its way to doubling again.

Family Structure

As in Korea, the earliest social structures of Japan appear to have been matrilocal and, most likely, matriarchal. *Uji* before the sixth century were organized around female lineages, and the first Chinese accounts mention semi-mythical figures such as "Queen Pimiko." With the coming of Chinese institutions,

Japanese *Daimyo* Armor. This extraordinarily well-preserved torso armor and helmet is believed to date from the fourteenth century and may have belonged to the Shogun Ashikaga Takauji (r. 1338–1358). The helmet is bronzed iron, while the cuirass is made of thousands of overlapping iron and lacquered leather scales held together in horizontal rows by means of rivets. The combination made for effective protection against swords and arrows while allowing considerable freedom of movement.

Sake: Traditional alcoholic drink brewed from rice.

however, this changed radically at the uppermost levels and more gradually below. As we have seen, during the early importation of Chinese influences in the sixth and seventh centuries, women at the top could still wield considerable political power, as witnessed by Empress Suiko of the Soga clan. By the height of the power of the Heian court, Confucian patriarchal institutions had made a great deal of headway in Japan but were moderated somewhat by the pervasive influence of Buddhism and Shinto. Thus, aristocratic women controlled property, though they increasingly tended to wield political power through men. They were sequestered at court and forced into a highly refined and regulated ritual life, yet they created their own highly influential cultural world. Women like Murasaki Shikibu and Sei Shonagon (ca. 965–1025) defined the guidelines for literary and aesthetic appreciation for generations to come in the *Tale of Genji* and *The Pillow Book*, respectively.

Outside the court, the moderating institution for commoners, and particularly women, was the Buddhist monastery. As in China and Korea, the monasteries provided havens for women and men who did not marry or had fled bad marriages. They provided enough education to read the **sutras**, thus helping to increase literacy. They also provided important avenues of political power as large landholders, innkeepers, peacekeepers, and advisers. A famous example was the monastery at Mt. Hiei above Kyoto, whose monks provided guidance to the court for centuries.

Sutras: In Buddhism, a collection of aphorisms relating to some aspect of the conduct of life.

As in China and Korea, however, the family life of commoners was mostly governed by a mix of Confucian filial piety, local clan relations, and the desire to improve the family's position through marriage. As in China, girls came to be considered "expendable" because they would move in with their husband's family. Arranged marriages were the norm, and by way of forcing such issues, rape, kidnapping, and family vendettas were all too common. A woman who would not consent to such a marriage, for example, could evade it only if she fled to a monastery before the groom's relatives caught up with her. Failure to escape could result in a beating or even murder. Such informal sanctions eventually gave way under the Tokugawa Shogunate to strictly regulated Neo-Confucian family codes enforced by the shogun's local officials.

Religion, Culture, and Intellectual Life

The foundations of Japan's original religion, Shinto, go far back into remote antiquity. Some scholars have used the word "vitalism"—akin to animism in Africa and shamanism in Siberia and the Americas—to describe its common features: a deep-seated belief in the power of *kami*—spirits of divinities, beings living and departed, nature as a whole, and even inanimate objects like mountains and streams. Reverence for these forces extended early on to fertility and earthly vitality. Even today Shinto priests commonly wear a stiff black hat that has a phallic figure rising prominently from it.

The importance of ritual vitality was reinforced by a tremendous emphasis on ritual purity—as Chinese observers recorded nearly 2,000 years ago, the Japanese seemed to bathe constantly—and waterfalls were enormously popular as places of ritual ablution and even miracle working. On the other hand, death and corruption were things to be separated from as much as possible—hence the practice of distancing shrines from burial mounds.

The Way of the Gods   Shinto means "the way of the gods," and Japanese mythology recognized a staggering array of deities. Chief among these were Izanagi and

Izanami, whose initial sexual act created the Japanese home islands, as well as Amaterasu, the sun goddess, considered the ancestor of Japan's emperors, purportedly starting with Jimmu in 660 BCE. Until the emperor Hirohito officially renounced his divinity at the end of World War II, every Japanese emperor has been considered a god in the Shinto pantheon by believers.

Although it had undoubtedly arrived some time before, the customary dating of the introduction of Buddhism to Japan is 552 CE, when the king of Paekche sent a collection of Buddhist scriptures as a present to Yamato. Under the missionary Kwalluk, the new religion soon became well established among Japanese elites. As we have seen, after four decades of struggle with the Shinto establishment at court, Buddhism had become the state religion of Yamato in 594. Both religious traditions, however, were ultimately able to coexist and, to some extent, fuse. The ability of Buddhism to adapt the cosmologies of other traditions to its core beliefs, its reverence for nature, emphasis on the transcendental, and lack of a priestly hierarchy made it an easy fit for Shinto. For their part, Shinto believers could add the bodhisattvas and other Buddhist entities to the list of *kami*. Coupled with an already great admiration for things Chinese in Japan, such accommodations made the spread of the religion relatively easy.

Most of the schools of Buddhism established in Japan had first become popular in China. With the exception of the earliest variants, all of them were Mahayana schools. The first to establish itself at Nara was the Hosso school, based on the newly recovered texts brought back by the Chinese monk Xuan Zang from India. This was shortly displaced by the highly influential Tendai (from the Chinese Tiantai) school of Saicho (767–822) and the Shingon sect of Kukai (774–835), which dominated the imperial court for most of the Heian period.

As noted in Chapter 12, for Tendai followers, the most important scripture was the Lotus Sutra. This sutra includes the key revelation that all beings possess a "Buddha nature" and, hence, the potential for salvation. Esoteric Buddhism, on the other hand, placed more emphasis on scriptural study and aesthetics. For both, the degree to which one can grasp the central truth varies according to the capacity of the individual to study and contemplate it but that central truth is in theory open to all at some level. The popular devotional schools of Buddhism also came to Japan during the eighth and ninth centuries. Their simplicity and optimism—simply bowing repeatedly and calling on Amida Buddha with a sincere heart in order to be saved (*nembutsu*)—and the hope for a place in the Pure Land, or Western Paradise, ensured widespread adherence. Even today, it remains the most popular of the Japanese Buddhist schools.

Though neither achieved widespread popularity, two other Buddhist schools deserve mention because of their influence. The first is a wholly Japanese development. Nichiren (1222–1282) advocated a Japan-centered, patriotic form of Buddhism. Japan, he believed, because of its unique history and centrality in the Buddhist world, had become the repository of "true" Buddhism in the present decadent age and must be defended at all cost, a view that he believed was confirmed by the miraculous Japanese deliverance from the Mongols.

Perhaps more influential was the practice of **Zen**. Again, the Chinese origins of this movement, known as *chan*, were introduced in Chapter 12. Arriving in Japan in the twelfth century, its popularity spread among the *daimyo* and samurai, who had the discipline to pursue its rigors. Zen seeks to achieve *satori*, a flash of

Zen: A form of Buddhism that exhorts each person to attain enlightenment by his or her own efforts, under the guidance of a master.

The Miracles of Kannon.
Amida Buddhism was the most popular school throughout east Asia, and the most popular figure of the many bodhisattvas was Kannon (Guanyin in China). On this long hand scroll dated to 1257, Kannon saves her followers from assorted tribulations: Here, she appears to two men set upon by soldiers or brigands.

enlightenment signaling the recovery of one's Buddha nature. Everyone's path to this is different, so one must follow the instructions of an experienced master rather than engage in prolonged scriptural study. Zen practitioners seek to open themselves to enlightenment by humble, repetitive tasks, contemplating paradoxes (*koans*) and, in some schools, sitting in meditation (*zazen*).

All of these practices can be useful to a warrior. Endless drilling with bow and arrow or sword to the point that the use of each weapon becomes instinctive certainly refines one's martial talents. Such an approach is equally useful in painting, poetry, and calligraphy, where a distinct Zen style of spontaneous, minimalist art suggesting the true inner nature of subject and artist is still a vital area of Japanese aesthetics today.

One final area in which Zen permeated the life of the warrior classes was in the use of tea. Introduced from China by the Zen monk Eisai (1141–1215), tea drinking in Japan became widely adopted as an aid to discipline and meditation among monks in the twelfth century. Soon, however, it became quite popular among the upper classes, and its presentation was ultimately refined into the ritual of the tea ceremony. Here, inside the teahouse where all were equal, under the movements prescribed by the sixteenth-century tea master Sen-no Rikyu (1522–1591), host and guest were to approach their encounter as if they were sharing their last moments together on earth. Since the ceremony was a popular preparation for battle among *daimyo* and samurai, this was often the case.

Forging a Japanese Culture   With the importation of Chinese political theory to Japan came an understanding of the importance of histories and record keeping. Thus, the first Chinese-influenced Japanese histories, the *Nihongi* (*Chronicles of Japan*) and *Kojiki* (*Records of Ancient Matters*), made their appearance during the early eighth century. At about the same time, the first collection of Japanese poetry published in Chinese, the *Man'yoshu* (*The Ten Thousand Leaves' Collection*) appeared in 760. This work, however, also illustrated the problems inherent in using Chinese as a method of rendering Japanese sounds.

The *Man'yoshu* uses one-syllable Chinese characters picked for their similarity to Japanese sounds and strings them together into Japanese words. If one can follow the *sounds* of the words, one can grasp the meaning of the poems; if, however, one attempts to read them based on the *meaning* of the characters, they become gibberish. This fundamental problem was solved by devising the *kana syllabary*, a system of 50 sounds that form the building blocks of Japanese words. By the late ninth century, a kind of social divide had arisen—as it did later with *han-gul* in Korea—between predominantly male, Buddhist, elite users of literary Chinese and literate women and members of the lower elites who favored the convenience of the *kana* system. As in China and Korea, the technology of printing greatly spurred the circulation of these works and over the centuries helped push functional literacy to some of the highest premodern levels in the world.

In addition to the development of the 31-syllable *tanka* poetry form, perhaps the most important literary developments to come from the use of *kana* were the novel and the prose diary. The former, as we have seen, is credited to Murasaki Shikibu, whose *Tale of Genji* is often considered the world's first novel. A skilled diarist as well, Murasaki was a tutor to the powerful courtier Fujiwara Michinaga, and she put all of her acute observations of the subtleties of court life into *Genji*. Seclusion for court women fostered a considerable amount of self-analysis, and one sees in Murasaki's writing a tension between Buddhist ideas and the requirements of place, name, reputation, and hierarchy at court. Enduring aesthetic guidelines that emerge in the work include the concept of *aware* (a-WAHR-ei), an intensity of feeling with elements of sadness, melancholy, fragility, and the fleetingness of life, often symbolized by cherry blossoms; *okashi*, an ability to make light of the tragic; *en*, an appreciation for visible beauty; and *miyabi*, courtliness and refinement. Similarly, her older contemporary, Sei Shonagon, in her *Pillow Book*, sets an almost modern tone in her astute, funny, and sometimes spiteful categories of likes and dislikes at court.

Vietnam: Human Agency and State Building

For much of the twentieth century, the history of southeast Asia was written according to the cultural divisions separating the areas influenced by China from those influenced by India. In the 1960s, however, this concept of a derivative "Indo-Chinese" history was challenged by scholars, who emphasized the similarities of the lived experience of the common people on both sides of the cultural divide. Of equal importance in this new approach was the *agency* of the people in question: their taking of the initiative in deciding matters of acculturation, political systems, and so forth. Our focus on the interactions and adaptations here is to explore the agency of people in their acceptance and rejection of certain influences and innovations.

The Setting and Neolithic Cultures

The topography of southeast Asia as a whole is similar from the borders of Assam in India to the Mekong delta in the south of what is now Vietnam. Divided by several major river systems—the Irawaddy, Salween, and Mekong—running roughly north to south, and by the Red River, running northwest to southeast through Hanoi and meeting the Gulf of Tonkin at Haiphong, their watersheds are separated by low to medium mountain ranges running generally parallel to them. Even today much of the region is heavily forested, with abundant rainfall supplied by the summer monsoon, which acts as the region's principal climatic regulator. The river valleys and coastal plains are believed to have supplied the wild ancestors of the first rice plants, as well as some of the world's first domesticated fowl sometime after 8000 BCE (see Map 13.7).

The Neolithic revolution appears to have taken place in southeast Asia at about the same time as it did in southwest Asia. This Hoabinhian culture was characterized by the cultivation of root crops, millet, and rice and by about 6000 BCE saw the domestication of pigs and chickens. By 4500 BCE, the famous Dongsan cultures had come on to the scene, marked shortly after by some of humankind's earliest bronze artifacts. The origins of these peoples are still obscure, with contemporary speculation centering on a homeland perhaps in southern China, like the Thai, Laotians,

MAP **13.7 Southeast Asia: The Physical Setting.**

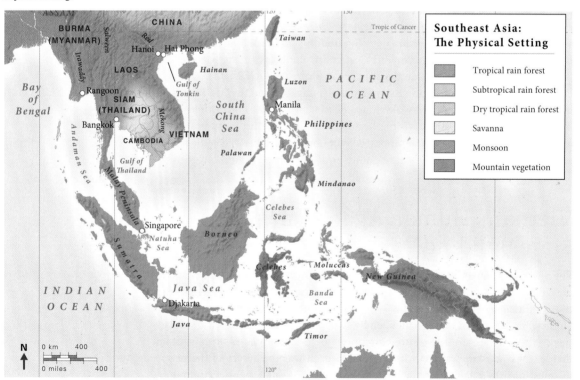

Burmese, and Cambodians. Out of the fertile, subtropical and tropical regions in which they settled, it is believed that the basics of wet rice agriculture and the domestication of chickens and pigs may well have diffused north into China and perhaps west to northern India.

Village Society and Buddhism

The earliest records of the peoples and states in the region are likewise fragmentary. Late Zhou Chinese references frequently mention the state of Yue, but its southern borders appear to have been fluid and probably included parts of the modern provinces of Guangdong and Guangxi and perhaps the northern part of Vietnam. Once more, the social structure suggests a village-based agricultural system in which women enjoyed far more equality than would later be the case. Villages and clans were often bilateral or matrilineal and matrilocal. Men paid a **bride price** to the families of their wives, and divorce for either spouse appears to have been relatively easy. As in other places in east Asia during the first millennium BCE, women occupied roles as officials, diplomats, merchants, and small-business operators. The area also became one of the first outposts of Theravada Buddhism outside India through the efforts of missionaries from Ceylon (Sri Lanka) in the second century BCE. It would come to be the majority religion in the region for the next 2,000 years.

Bride price: Amount negotiated between the family of the groom and the family of the bride to be paid by the former to the latter in some marriage traditions, as compensation for the loss of her labor.

The "Far South": History and Politics to 1450

With the unification of China under the Qin in 221 BCE, Yue was incorporated into the First Emperor's new state. Thus began a prolonged period of Chinese occupation and local resistance in the area, ultimately lasting over 1,000 years. As in Korea, the occupation brought with it a cultural invasion, including the full spectrum of Chinese writing, political ideas, and cultural preferences. Like their counterparts in Korea and Japan as well, the new Vietnamese literate elites were incorporated into the increasingly far-flung world of Chinese civilization and the Buddhist cultural and religious sphere. Southeast Asia's geographical position in the center of the maritime portion of this economic and cultural sphere encouraged a considerable openness to outside influences.

Sinification and Resistance

On the other hand, the repeated invasions from the north also went far to cement a Vietnamese ethnic identity. The collapse of the Qin in the period 206–202 BCE encouraged a rebellion against the local Chinese officials of "Nam Viet"—the Vietnamese name for the Chinese *Nanyue* ("Far South"), as the Qin had called their new southern province. The Han emperor Wudi reoccupied northern Vietnam in 111 BCE, however, and swiftly reimposed Chinese institutions on the region.

Han attempts at sinification raised tensions between the new Chinese-influenced elites and those who thus far had managed to retain their cultural independence. The situation was sufficiently volatile that in 39 BCE another rebellion began that to this day is commemorated as helping to form the modern Vietnamese national identity. Trung Trac, the widow of a local leader executed by the Chinese, and her sister Trung Nhi (both ca. 12–43), led their local militia and defeated the Han garrison, sparking a general revolt. The Chinese shortly regrouped, however, and overpowered the forces of the Trung sisters, who drowned themselves rather than be taken alive. For the next millennium, northern Vietnam would be firmly within the imperial Chinese orbit.

In the three and a half centuries following the breakup of the Han Empire in 220 CE, the region was able to gain a degree of political autonomy, but the power of Vietnam's sinified elites continued to ensure their cultural loyalty to China. The growing regional power of the north allowed it to expand into the more Indian-influenced Buddhist kingdoms to the south. With the reunification of China under the Sui and Tang, the drive for Chinese political control of the region was taken up again and the north was soon fully reincorporated into imperial China. During the political chaos following the fall of the Tang, however, the long-awaited opportunity for independence arrived again.

Independence   Dinh Bo Linh, the first emperor of Vietnam, solidified his control of the region in 968. Though politically independent of China, Vietnam's new Li dynasty (1010–1225), long immersed in Chinese notions of Confucianism and statecraft, swiftly instituted Song-style institutions and created its own bureaucracy. Continuing what by now was a long-established pattern of expansion, the Li systematically pushed south during their two centuries of control.

With the fall of the Li dynasty, the Tran dynasty (1225–1400) soon faced the potent threat of the Mongols, who in 1280 would subdue the southern Song in China and form the Yuan dynasty. The first Mongol attempt at invasion, in 1257, was mounted as the Mongols were busily reducing the last strongholds of the southern Song. Once this was accomplished, the attempt was renewed in 1285 and again in 1287. The unsuitability of Mongol strategy and tactics and the stubborn resistance of the Vietnamese ultimately prevented further Mongol expansion and allowed the Tran to keep the dynasty intact.

MAP 13.8 Vietnam, ca. 1428.

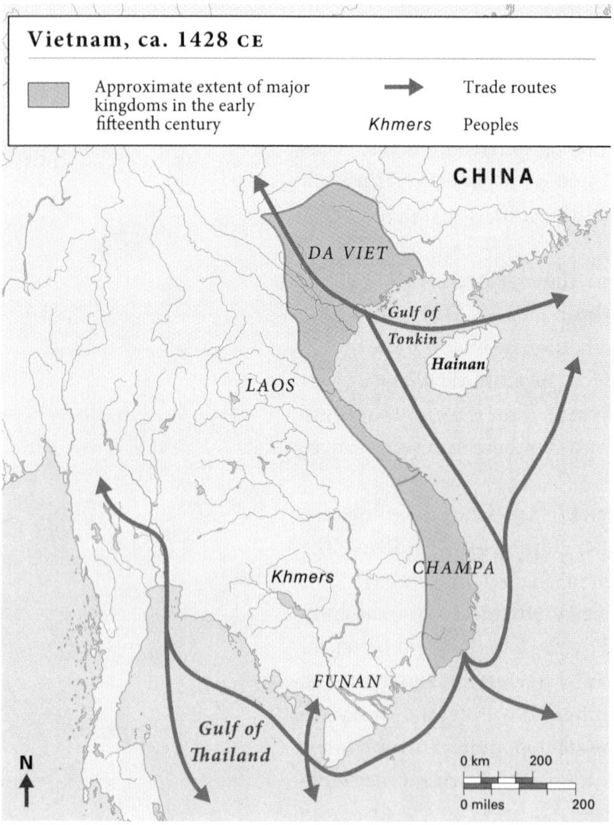

Cultural and Political Conflict   Even during the height of the Mongol threat, the Tran continued to push southward. Much of this drive was aimed at the state of Champa—the site of the fast-growing rice strains that would do so much to increase east Asian populations. Champa itself had ambitions to achieve regional dominance. Centuries before, in the complex interplay of political and cultural rivalries marking the region, the Vietnamese had expanded at the expense of Champa. Champa and the Khmers, heavily influenced by India, had briefly united to subdue another Indian-influenced state, the trading kingdom of Funan, in the 600s. Now a reconstituted Champa represented not just a strong political threat but, as a Sanskrit, Hindu, and Theravada Buddhist state, a cultural rival as well. In the resulting war, the new Le dynasty of Dai Viet ("Great Viet"), founded in 1428 by Le Loi, decisively broke the power of the Chams in 1471. The remnants of their state were incorporated into Vietnam in 1720 (see Map 13.8).

Economy, Society, and Family

Since the Neolithic domestication of rice, Vietnam has been one of the world centers of wet rice cultivation. Perhaps 300 strains of rice were cultivated in northern Vietnam by the mid-fifteenth century, with yields running as high as 25 bushels per acre (seed-to-harvest ratio of 1:25, compared to the much smaller ratio of 1:5 in wheat-growing Europe at the same time). Roughly 90 percent of the people were engaged in agriculture, a figure consistent with other east Asian agrarian-based societies. Like them, too, the rhythms of the agricultural year were governed by the monsoon cycle. During the long rainy season of the summer, rice, vegetables, and commercial crops such as hemp would be cultivated.

As in southern China and Japan, families could be sustained on relatively small amounts of land and required few complex tools beyond the treadle-powered "dragon pump" or a hand-cranked winnowing machine (see Chapter 9). Along with draft animals like water buffalo, these would often be held communally by clans within the *xa*, or village. Villages commonly consisted of raised, thatch-roofed dwellings, surrounded by a bamboo fence and centered on the shrine to the ancestral spirits.

Politics, Labor, and Trade

Two key political institutions kept order and acted as checks upon each other. The village headman, the *xa troung*, was elected but had to be approved by the imperial court, which, like its Chinese counterpart, ruled through a Confucian bureaucracy of provincial governors, prefects, and magistrates. The magistrate and his staff were the last official layer above the *xa troung*, so the headman had considerable power and responsibility at the local level. He collected the taxes and dues and sat with a council of notables. His powers, however, were checked by the council itself, which consisted of members of a scholar-gentry class much like that in China and who had to share in all major decisions, especially those regarding the use of communal land, about 20 percent of the total by the end of the sixteenth century. Thus, there was a balanced tension between the power of the central government and local interests. As in both China and Korea, however, the power of the local council often resulted in periods of increased landlordism and tenancy.

One legacy of the long period of Chinese occupation was the use of conscription and **corvée** labor by Vietnamese dynasties. Peasants were required to serve in the army 4 months per year—indefinitely during national emergencies. They could also be sentenced to slave labor for various offenses. In many cases, they would be sent to open up virgin land for agriculture, which was theirs to keep upon the expiration of their sentences.

Corvée: Labor exacted by a local authority for little or no pay or instead of taxes.

Changing Position of Women

One pattern of history the Vietnamese shared with the other societies we have examined in this chapter is that of changes in the status of women over time. The nature of the agricultural work undertaken was communal, and men and women tended to work in the fields together. As in Korea and Japan, kinship lines were bilateral—traced through either spouse—or matrilineal. Here again, the long period of Chinese influence and Neo-Confucian emphasis on filial piety, hierarchy, and sharply separate roles for men and women eroded this equality somewhat, though much less markedly than in Korea or Japan. In the villages, or in the ports and market cities, women commonly exercised prominent roles as merchants, entrepreneurs, and craftspeople. This was reinforced by the prominence of the different Mahayana schools of Buddhism. Once more, as in China, Korea, and Japan, the role of the monastery for both men and women allowed a place for and gave an education to those who for whatever reason were on society's fringes. Buddhist nuns and abbesses thus wielded considerable power, though their positions were often at odds with the Confucian precepts of the elites. Still, women's rights to divorce and property ownership were upheld in the Neo-Confucian law code of 1460.

Religion, Culture, and Intellectual Life

Just as the Vietnamese struggled to maintain their political independence, they continually labored to develop their own cultural distinctiveness. While the porous border region with southern China and geographical and ethnic ties to other southeast Asian peoples assured a constant flow of influences, not all were readily absorbed and some were played against each other.

Mahayana Buddhism   Among the most important of these influences was that of religion. Whether the practice of ancestor veneration arrived with the Chinese or whether it was present before is as yet unsettled. Nearly all villages even into the twentieth century, however, had a shrine for a founding ancestor or famous headman where periodic ceremonies honoring him would take place. As in Korea, the coming of the Han emperor Wudi's armies in the second century BCE brought the imperial system of the Son of Heaven as intermediary between heaven and earth. At about the same time, however, Theravada was being established in the Indianized ports of southeast Asia and became the first branch of Buddhism to be established there. Thus, as the Han retreat from the north allowed some political breathing space, the barest beginnings of Mahayana began to come into the area as well. For several hundred years, though, Indian-influenced Theravada dominated

Temple of Literature, Hanoi. The independent Vietnamese states, beginning with Dai Viet in 939, instituted Chinese-style examinations for their civil service. The Temple of Literature was the first national academy for Confucian training, founded in 1076. This building was the examination hall for those testing for the equivalent of the Chinese *jinshi*, or metropolitan degrees. The large Chinese characters, read right to left, carry the motto "A Pattern for Emulation Through the Ages."

the religious and cultural life of Vietnam. Buddhist stupas were erected and the austere, mendicant, saffron-robed monks held sway in northern Vietnam, as they still do in much of southeast Asia.

The Tang occupation brought a large infusion of Mahayana influence with its vibrant art motifs, temples, and monasteries as well as the entire spectrum of Confucian and Daoist ideas. While Mahayana became the dominant division from this time on, the Vietnamese at the local level tended to pursue a synthesis of all of these systems in their beliefs. As in China, this collection was often referred to as *tam giao*, after the Chinese *san jiao*—"the three religions."

Similarly, the Vietnamese court sought to reconcile the differences among the systems by promulgating edicts on their compatibility. Indeed, some emperors sought to take a leading role in developing a unique strain of Vietnamese Buddhism. The later emperor Minh Mang (r. 1820–1841), for example, advocated combining the opposites of "abstention" from the world and "participation" in it.

Chu Nom   During the fifteenth-century consolidation of Dai Viet, the Le dynasty undertook a thoroughgoing sinification of the country, in much the same way as under the Yi in Korea. Chinese law codes and even dress was adopted. As in Korea and Japan, Chinese-style histories were also compiled and court-sponsored literary projects of various sorts commissioned. Yet here again, the literary language favored by the court for such projects continued to be the Chinese of the elites who had the time and means to undertake its study. As in Korea and Japan, an attempt was made to develop a vernacular writing system, in this case sometime during the tenth century. Called *chu nom* ("southern characters"), the new script combined existing Chinese characters picked for the similarity of their sounds to Vietnamese words with newly invented Chinese-style characters for meaning. It was similar in this respect to the formation of many complex Chinese characters but would in theory be easier to use as a tool for literacy. Poets like Nguyen Thuyen and his contemporary Ho Quy Ly in the fourteenth century used this system, translating Chinese works into the script. However, it never had the widespread circulation of *han-gul* or *kana* in Korea or Japan.

Putting It All Together

While there are a great many commonalities among the patterns of state formation and religious interaction among the states along the outer ring of Chinese influence, each responded to that influence in its own way. From the beginning, each state sought to maintain its political independence, though all acculturated to some degree to Chinese models. Yet, here it should be stressed that the relative attractiveness of those models was largely related to their usefulness in state building. That is, while the Koreans and Vietnamese struggled to throw off the Chinese political yoke, the systems and values of the invaders also gave powerful tools to the invaded, allowing them to organize their new regimes after they had won independence. In a sense, the invaders had provided a ready-made package of laws, moral codes, and social organization for the new states but also came with moderating institutions like Mahayana Buddhism. They were therefore equipped with a wide range of options to adopt or discard as the situation demanded. In that sense, the cultural intrusion was far more successful than the political one.

In the case of Japan, since the early Yamato state did not have Chinese traditions imposed on it from the outside, its leaders could afford to be more selective in what to adopt. However, the wholesale adoption of Chinese institutions proceeded even more quickly in Japan than on the mainland. Part of this may be attributed to the growing sense of the power that such institutions could provide to a government; part of it may also have been a growing sense on the part of the Japanese that states on the mainland based on these institutions were a potential threat. In essence, they felt they had to "join them" before they were beaten by them.

By the end of the fifteenth century, all three of these states were in the process of consolidating civilizations based to varying degrees on Chinese models and prominently included Neo-Confucianism and Buddhism among their governing traditions. They may therefore be considered part of the dominant trend toward the formation of religious civilizations, a pattern we have emphasized in Part 3 of this volume. However, given the specific adaptations to local conditions, the three states were quite different from each other and from China. Even at the most signified level of governmental organization, the Japanese role of *daimyo* as feudal lords and samurai as retainers, to cite just one example, would have been unthinkable in China, Vietnam, or Korea. Yet all four of these countries, faced with varying degrees of dislocation, foreign intrusion, or rebellion, would seek similar solutions to solve these problems.

▶ For additional resources, including maps, primary sources, visuals, and quizzes, please go to www.oup.com/us/vonsivers. Please see the Further Resources section at the back of the book for additional readings and suggested websites.

Thinking Through Patterns

▶ **How was the history of Korea affected by its relations with China? With Japan?**

The most obvious and dramatic way the various Korean kingdoms were affected by China was through conquest. Chinese culture and institutions were firmly planted in Korea during the Qin, Han, Sui, and Tang eras. In many respects this also prompted the Korean kingdoms to assert their political independence and to be discriminating about which Chinese institutions to adopt. Thus, Neo-Confucianism was adopted because of its use as a state-supporting ideology. Chinese writing, though quite useful as the means of acquiring the literature of China, ultimately yielded to the *han-gul* system as more convenient and user-friendly.

In the case of Japan, Korea's situation was as a cultural intermediary and as a mainland target for conquest. Thus, during certain periods, Korea's status as a buffer between the two regional powers made its position precarious.

In addition to the Bronze Age elements of wet rice cultivation and bronze implements—which moved Japan ultimately toward agrarian–urban society—the cultural elements, beginning with the Chinese writing system, were the most influential. With the writing system came ideas of government, ethics, philosophy, literature, and, of course, Buddhism. Unlike Korea and Vietnam, Japan acquired all of these more or less voluntarily and had the leisure to adopt them according to its own needs, rather than have them imposed by conquest.

▶ **Which important elements of Chinese culture were adapted by the Japanese for their own purposes? What advantages did Vietnam have over Korea and Japan in this regard?**

▶ **Which Japanese adaptations of Chinese institutions did not work well in Japan? Why?**

While the Chinese writing system gave Japan a ready-made literature, the language itself was not well suited to the Japanese vernacular. Thus, by the 800–900s it had to be supplemented with the *kana* systems. But more serious was the less than perfect fit of the Chinese government structures on Japan's still clan-based society. Here, the cleavages developing during the Heian period would cause the social breakdown that resulted in the era of the shoguns, lasting until 1867.

Like Japan and Korea, much of Vietnam was influenced by the importation of Chinese culture, including Buddhism, the imperial system, and Confucianism. Like Korea, and unlike Japan, Vietnam suffered centuries of Chinese invasion and occupation. But Vietnam, positioned on the border with the Indianized states of southeast Asia, also was influenced by Indian culture in its southern and western areas, causing interactions and adaptations that did not take place in the other states inside the Chinese sphere of cultural and political influence.

▶ **In what ways was the experience of Vietnam similar to that of Japan and Korea? How was it different?**

Chapter 14 600-1450 CE
Patterns of State Formation in Africa

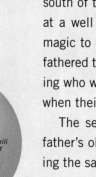

According to local tradition, the founder of the gold-trading kingdom of ancient Ghana (ca. 400–1200) in West Africa was Dinga. He was a descendant of Bilal, the Ethiopian who was chosen by the Prophet Muhammad as the first *muezzin*, or crier who calls the Muslim faithful to prayer. When Dinga arrived from Arabia in the Sahel, the east–west belt of steppe south of the Sahara Desert in West Africa, he asked a many-headed snake at a well for water. The snake refused, and Dinga subdued her through magic to receive his drink. After marrying the snake's three daughters, he fathered three sons, the eldest of whom was a half-human, half-serpent being who went to live underground. The two younger sons were still growing when their father left to return to Arabia.

The second son grew into an inconsiderate man who mistreated his father's old servant. The third son turned into a much kinder person, giving the same servant his leftovers. Years later, Dinga, nearly blind, felt his end coming and summoned his two sons, to give them their respective heritages. The elderly servant, who had never forgotten the kindness of the younger son, persuaded the youngest son to go first, disguised as his older brother, to receive the lion's share of Dinga's estate. Indeed, the father

ABOVE: Detail from the *Catalan Atlas* (1375), showing Mansa Musa, the king of Mali, on his throne.

bestowed his power of magic as well as the kingdom on the youngest son, while the older son received the more modest power of rain making.

The two sons struck a deal whereby Ghana would receive enough rain and gold as long as its people would sacrifice every year a virgin and a colt. After many years of human and animal sacrifices, a Wagadu man and admirer of a virgin about to be sacrificed slew the snake brother. As he was dying, the snake brother cursed the people of Wagadu, which lost its abundance of rain and gold. A parched and impoverished Ghana fell to its enemies.

This story gives us a glimpse of the main pattern underlying the history of sub-Saharan Africa between 600 and 1450. In this period, rulers converted to Islam and incorporated its beliefs and practices into their traditional African spirituality of animism.

While the Eurasian and North African pattern during 600–1450 was that of the formation of religious civilizations that contained commonwealths of states, the pattern of sub-Saharan Africa in the same period was that of religious kingdom and empire formation. In the northeast of sub-Saharan Africa, kingdoms had already adapted to Christianity prior to 600, and the new kingdoms of Nubia and Ethiopia continued the Christian heritage. In West Africa, Mali, the successor of ancient Ghana, adapted to Islamic imperial traditions and became the only multilinguistic, multiethnic, and multireligious empire of sub-Saharan Africa during 600–1450. On Africa's east coast, a set of small Islamic merchant states emerged, the Swahili port cities, under either kings or councils of notables. Finally, in the interior of central and southern Africa, indigenous kingdoms rose on the basis of the African tradition of magic-empowered authority, descended from the **animist** heritage.

Christians and Muslims in the Northeast

During 600–1250, Nubia was a Christian kingdom along the middle Nile in the Sahara and sub-Saharan steppe, built on agriculture and trade between tropical Africa and the Middle East. Ethiopia, Nubia's neighbor in the highlands to the southeast, was similarly Christian but, unlike Nubia, was initially a collection of decentralized chiefdoms. When one of the chiefs eventually centralized rule in 1137, the new kingdom of Ethiopia unified the highlands, sent missionaries to the southern provinces to convert non-Christian Africans, and battled the Muslims in the lowlands on the Red Sea coast in the name of a Christian Crusade. Both Nubia and Ethiopia were fascinating cases of sub-Saharan polities adopting patterns of state formation from the Middle East into their African heritage: They adapted to Middle Eastern plow agriculture and Christianity, while long retaining African traditions of decentralization.

Seeing Patterns

▶ What patterns of adaptation did the Christian kingdoms of northeast Africa demonstrate in their interactions with the civilizations of the Middle East and eastern Mediterranean?

▶ What were the responses of Africans to Muslim merchants who connected them with the trading zone of the Indian Ocean and Mediterranean? As these Africans adapted to Islam, which forms of political organization did they adopt?

▶ In what ways did the economic and political transformations on the east African coast and West Africa affect developments in the interior?

Animism: The experience of and/or belief in the presence of a life substance or spirit shared by all living beings and things in nature.

Nubia in the Middle Nile Valley

About a century after the end of the kingdom of Meroë, sometime around 350 (see Chapter 6), small Nubian successor states dominated the middle Nile valley from north to south. In the course of the mid-500s, these states converted to Coptic Christianity and subsequently united into a single kingdom. Open to trade with the then rising empire of the Arab Umayyads, Nubia experienced a gradual ascendancy of Arab merchants to dominance in Nubian commerce. Eventually, the enhanced position of these merchants led to Muslim political control: In 1276, the Egyptian Mamluks defeated the Christian king of Nubia and installed a puppet regime. By around 1450 Christianity in Nubia had largely given way to Islam.

The Rise of Christian Kingdoms in Nubia   Meroë's power ended as a result of deforestation near the capital and nomadic attacks against its northern provinces. The nomads had adapted to the use of the camel in the early centuries of the Common Era, which allowed them to carry out swift long-distance raids over vast tracts of inhospitable territory. Indeed, the use of the camel created a transportation revolution in the Sahara in general and opened up new routes for commerce and invasion. One immediate result of this was that a new ruling class of Nubians arose in the middle Nile valley during the 400s. Nubian chiefs and their followers established three small kingdoms along the middle Nile that prospered in large part as the result of the rapid spread of the animal-driven waterwheel (*saqiya* [SAH-qee-ya]) invented in Egypt in the first century CE. Water could now be lifted into channels all year round, even at some distance from the river, for the purpose of planting two annual grain crops. Archaeological evidence points to a substantial increase in the number of villages in the region as a result of this innovation.

In the 500s, Egyptian missionaries converted the Nubians to Christianity. Pagan temples became churches, and new churches and monasteries were built, ultimately in nearly every village. Kings and members of the ruling class sponsored these Christian institutions. As did their contemporaries in the Mediterranean and Middle East, the Nubian rulers appreciated the unifying effect of a single state religion over the multiplicity of local temple cults.

Barely Christianized, Nubia now had to withstand an invasion of Arabs from Egypt. After the establishment of the Arab caliphate of Syria, Iraq, and Egypt (see Chapter 10), the new governors in Egypt organized military campaigns into neighboring countries. In 652, one of these campaigns penetrated deep into Nubia. The Arab military used siege engines and caused considerable damage to one of the Nubian capitals. But an army of Nubian archers, long famous for their skill with bow and arrow, defeated the Arabs, forcing them to retreat. In a subsequent agreement, the two sides formally recognized each other, made a pact, and drew up a schedule of future friendly exchanges among their respective rulers. Later Muslim historians reinterpreted this pact, ignoring the defeat and presenting it as a treaty of submission to Islamic hegemony. Such differing interpretations notwithstanding, the pact endured and blocked the advance of Islam into East Africa for 600 years.

Royal Power and Governance   At of the turn of the 700s, a "great king" emerged who unified the three Nubian kingdoms. Power remained largely decentralized, however, with a dozen vassal rulers and an appointed—later hereditary—official called an "eparch." This official governed the northern subkingdom and was responsible for its defense against Egypt. The Coptic patriarch of Alexandria appointed the bishops, who, therefore, were independent from the kings, in marked contrast to Ethiopia as well as Catholic Europe in the early Middle Ages, where the kings appointed church officials (see Chapter 11).

In terms of financial administration, archaeologists have so far discovered no evidence of a kingdomwide taxation system. The dozen vassal rulers were probably powerful landlords who might have sent presents to the great king as tokens of their position. As in Europe, abbots of monasteries were also landlords, endowed with royal grants of villages, where peasant-farmers paid rent. Monasteries, however, were not numerous, given the scarcity of fertile land on the Nile banks, in contrast to Ethiopia, western Europe, and Byzantium. Most likely, in the vicinity of the great king's residence some basic fiscal mechanisms existed whereby village headmen delivered taxes in kind. Another, perhaps even the principal, source of income for the kings and eparchs was long-distance trade, which they controlled. In this respect, the Christian great kings of Nubia were similar to their Islamic counterparts in eastern and western Africa.

Agriculture   The farmland of the Nubian villages consisted of small strips of arable land on the up to 2-mile-wide fertile banks of the Nile. The annual summer floods between June and September inundated these strips, leaving them covered with rich sediment. In a few places, a wider valley or low-level islands in the river allowed for the farming of additional fields. Palm orchards helped to anchor the silt, and stone walls and jetties built into the Nile captured additional amounts of alluvial soil. As the floods receded in fall, villagers grew sorghum, millet, barley, wheat, and cotton with the help of plows pulled by oxen.

Higher fields away from the banks, which required waterwheels for irrigation, were planted during the winter with pulses, okra, melons, and other garden crops for spring harvesting. In the spring, farmers planted second crops on both the banks and higher elevations. Vineyards became more important as the kingdoms evolved, and wine was consumed by villagers in taverns as well as by priests and monks in daily religious services. Farmers also planted limited amounts of alfalfa for the feeding of cattle and donkeys. Sheep and goats fed on the stubble of grain fields and on scrubland, while pigs ate household remnants. Arabic written sources report the necessity of occasional food transports during local famines on the Nile, but generally the Nubian villages were self-supporting.

Long-Distance Trade   The pact of 652 between the Arabs and Nubia included clauses concerning the trade of Egyptian cloth, pottery, iron utensils, leather goods, and wine for ivory and slaves. The latter two items came from the tropical territories on the White Nile, though nothing is known about how Nubian merchants and

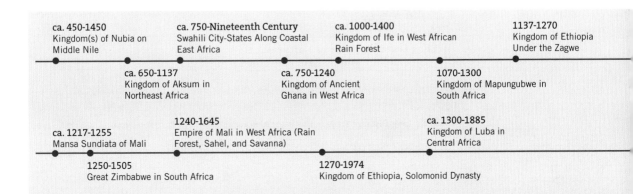

ca. 450-1450
Kingdom(s) of Nubia on
Middle Nile

ca. 750-Nineteenth Century
Swahili City-States Along Coastal
East Africa

ca. 1000-1400
Kingdom of Ife in West African
Rain Forest

1137-1270
Kingdom of Ethiopia
Under the Zagwe

ca. 650-1137
Kingdom of Aksum in
Northeast Africa

ca. 750-1240
Kingdom of Ancient
Ghana in West Africa

1070-1300
Kingdom of Mapungubwe in
South Africa

ca. 1217-1255
Mansa Sundiata of Mali

1240-1645
Empire of Mali in West Africa (Rain
Forest, Sahel, and Savanna)

ca. 1300-1885
Kingdom of Luba in
Central Africa

1250-1505
Great Zimbabwe in South Africa

1270-1974
Kingdom of Ethiopia, Solomonid Dynasty

slave raiding troops operated in these territories. Whatever the specifics of the Nubian activities along the White Nile, the kings taxed the merchant caravans at various resting places along the way.

In the period between 800 and 1200, the long-distance trade attracted Muslim merchants and craftspeople from beyond Aswan to the northern province of the Nubian kingdom, where they settled in a number of villages and possibly built mosques. A ruling in the mid-800s by an Egyptian Muslim judge recognized by Nubia allowed the Muslims in Nubia to acquire private property. A money economy then emerged, based on Islamic gold dinars. Muslim merchants also settled along the Red Sea coast, especially once the North African Fatimid caliphs had conquered Egypt in 969. To compete with the Iraqi Abbasid caliphs on the Persian Gulf, the Fatimids developed maritime trade with India through the Red Sea. Both of these trade avenues would bolster the commerce of the entire Mediterranean region and even reach to far-off western Europe (see Map 14.1).

From Christian to Islamic Nubia   In the mid-1000s, to secure their hold on the Red Sea, Egyptian rulers resettled nomadic tribes from Arabia to Upper Egypt. Unfortunately for Nubia, these tribes and their neighbors began raiding the kingdom in the 1100s. The local rulers in northern Nubia, principal defenders against the raids, gained in power vis-à-vis the Nubian kings. Perhaps as a consequence, dynastic rivalries broke out; and in the 1200s both usurpers and pretenders to the throne appealed to Egypt for support. The Mamluks, who governed Egypt at this

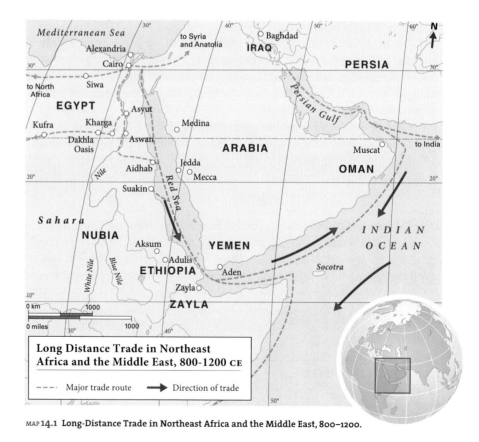

MAP 14.1 **Long-Distance Trade in Northeast Africa and the Middle East, 800–1200.**

time (1250–1517), responded to the appeals with enthusiasm, adding Nubia to their anti-Christian holy war effort. They propagated the reinterpretation of the pact of 652 as a treaty requiring regular tributes, particularly the delivery of slaves, from Nubia. In 1276, they conquered Nubia, installed a Christian vassal king, and levied the head tax, which non-Muslims in Islamic lands had to pay. In due time, the Christian dynasty gave way to Muslim rulers; and in 1365, after a new wave of Arab nomadic incursions, the Nubian kingdom ceased to exist altogether.

Viewed in retrospect, through interaction with the Roman Empire Nubia adapted itself to the Christian institutions of sacred kingship. A specifically Nubian pattern of political formation emerged that resembled the feudal practices (see Chapter 11) of many other places around the world, in which kings acted as representatives of God on earth but lacked the resources to govern with the help of centralized institutions. Instead, they relied on the support of federated chiefs, who functioned much like vassals. The kings were also not strong enough to incorporate the clerical hierarchy into their states, so the patriarch of Alexandria never lost control over the appointment of Nubian bishops—unlike the pope in his struggles with the Holy Roman emperors over lay investiture. Nubian churches were outposts of the Egyptian **Coptic** Church rather than indigenous institutions with their own hierarchy intertwined with the Nubian royal dynasty. Had the Nubian Church been a "national church" like those we will examine in Europe (see Chapter 17), it might have been in a better position to resist Islamization once Muslim rulers took over.

Coptic Christianity: A branch of Christianity centered in Egypt that emphasizes the sole divine nature of Jesus, in contrast to Catholic western and Orthodox eastern Christianities, in which the combined divine and human nature of Jesus is proclaimed.

Ethiopia in the Eastern Highlands

After the Christian kingdom of Aksum had lost Yemen to the Sasanid Persians in 570 and had exhausted the timber resources around its capital in the 600s, it shriveled to a chiefdom. However, in cooperation with the Coptic Church, Aksum continued to represent the church's mission to convert the southern highland Africans. Eventually, new dynasties arose and renewed the mission, among which the Solomonids and their Christian Crusades were the most successful. In Ethiopia, the adaptation to Christianity was more thorough than in Nubia. The Ethiopians embarked on a pattern of forming an African Christian civilization, including the Judeo-Christian symbolism of Zion and Christian law.

Christianity in the Highlands   The kings of Aksum and the patriarch of the Coptic Church abandoned the capital perhaps as early as the mid-600s and reestablished themselves in a modest chiefdom with better agrarian resources farther south. They continued to trade ivory, ostrich feathers, musk, and myrrh for linen and cotton textiles as well as spices on the Red Sea but no longer issued coins. When Muslim rulers in Egypt in the late 800s occupied ports on the west coast of the Red Sea and expanded trade with India and East Africa, Aksum became a partner in this trade. In addition to these goods, it sold slaves captured in raids in the lowlands to the south. The main effort of the small Aksum kings was directed toward campaigning southward, taking priests and settlers with them to convert, and pacify the defeated highland Africans. A monastery, founded in the late 800s some 200 miles southwest of Aksum, became the main center for sending out missionaries to the south. Reduced as it was, Aksum continued to be a factor in highland politics.

Quite dramatically, however, in the 970s the Africans subjected to conversion struck back. A mysterious queen, Gudit or Judith, led several destructive campaigns in which churches and monasteries were burned, towns destroyed, and thousands of people killed or enslaved. The situation was so chaotic that the patriarch of Alexandria refused to appoint the customary metropolitan bishop from Egypt to the country. Scholars, scouring the scant evidence to identify the area of this queen's origin, have determined that she might have been from the recently Christianized parts of the highlands. After her regime of terror of allegedly 40 years, a remnant of the Aksumite kingdom recovered and survived modestly for another century; but little is known about its kings and nothing about the extent of their rule.

State and Church Under the Zagwe Kings

Political stability eventually returned to the highlands with the foundation of the Zagwe dynasty (1137–1270), centered on a Christianized province some 300 miles south of Aksum. To its neighbors, the Zagwe kingdom was "Ethiopia" or "Abyssinia," names rooted in the Hebrew and Christian Bibles. The Zagwe kings laid the foundation for a return to dominant royal power and continued the Aksumite tradition of church sponsorship and missionary work in the south.

A first step toward reunification was the request of an early king in the mid-twelfth century to his metropolitan bishop to appoint seven additional bishops. The idea was that this nucleus of an Ethiopian episcopate would later grow to the 10 members required for a vote of independence from the patriarch of Alexandria. The king, however, did not get far with his attempt to create an independent Ethiopian Church. After lengthy negotiations with the patriarchs of Egypt and Syria and the Muslim ruler of Egypt, the latter refused the split. The Muslims were not about to relinquish the indirect leverage they possessed in Ethiopia through their political control over the patriarchs in Egypt. Had Ethiopia succeeded, the interesting development of a "national church" would have occurred: just the opposite of the situation in Europe at that time, where the pope wrested control of the church from the kings during the investiture controversy.

Church of St. George, Lalibela, Ethiopia. Stone masons cut this church and its interior from the surrounding rock formation. This and 10 other churches, built in the early 1200s, are part of a pilgrimage center created in the image of the Holy Land in Palestine.

Church sponsorship expressed itself in the construction of 11 remarkably innovative structures carved out from subterranean rock during the early 1200s, called the Lalibela churches. The kings arranged the churches in two groups, separated by a stream named Yordanos, named after the biblical Jordan River. The policy of the Zagwe dynasty was the recreation of Zion, perhaps in succession of Jerusalem, which the Muslims reconquered in 1187 from the western European crusaders. Accordingly, the dynasty used these churches for elaborate annual masses and processions during Passion Week. The Lalibela monoliths are unique in the history of Christian church construction and have no parallels elsewhere.

Under the Zagwe kings, the conversion of the peoples in the central and southern highlands to Christianity resumed. In addition, the kings encouraged the colonization of the land with Christian settlers from the north. These settlers introduced the plow and cereal agriculture, replacing the previous hoe and tuber crops (ensete, taro, and yam). The central and southern highlands were geographically much larger than the north and offered ample opportunities for the establishment of new villages, fields, and pastures. With its fertile volcanic soil, southern Ethiopia became one of the most productive agricultural regions of sub-Saharan Africa.

The political system that emerged in the center and south was an extension of what Aksum had pioneered in the north. Under a king ruling by divine right, Ethiopia was a confederation of provincial lords, some of whom also used royal titles. These lords lived in villages among their farmers and collected rents, consisting of grain, pulses, and cattle. Legally, ownership of the land was vested in families and had the status of inalienable property, even if the lords had the right to collect rents.

The Solomonid Dynasty   Once Christians from the north had settled as farmers in the central highlands and had converted the locals to Christianity, they shifted the focus of their missionary efforts southward. In 1270, a new dynasty of kings, the Solomonids, emerged some 300 miles south of Aksum, in the region of today's capital of Ethiopia, Addis Ababa. These new kings claimed descent from the Aksumite kings and sponsored the composition of an elaborate foundation narrative, the *Kebra Negast*, which legitimized the Solomonid dynasty until its fall in 1974. According to this narrative, the kings of Aksum were not only the descendants of a union between the queen of Sheba and the Israelite king Solomon but also the heirs to the Israelite Ark of the Covenant after the destruction of the First Temple by the Neo-Babylonians. The Ethiopians thus appropriated the biblical heritage more thoroughly than any eastern or western European Christian peoples did. The religious heritage of the Solomonids still lives on in Ethiopia. Outside Africa, this heritage has been embraced by the *Rastafarians*—Afrocentric Christians who form a small minority in Jamaica and have found many admirers, some perhaps more because of the popular reggae music of Bob Marley (1945–1981) than its doctrines.

Ethiopian Christians and Coastal Muslims   During the 1300s and most of the 1400s, Ethiopia was a powerful kingdom. The kings continued to depend on the collaboration of their provincial lords, but they also commanded a sizeable mercenary army of their own. With this army, they extended their authority over small principalities of Christians, animists, and Muslims in the southern highlands and Rift Valley, as well as Muslim sultanates along the Red Sea coast. This extension

The Ethiopian Highlands, ca. 1450 CE

☐ Maximum extent of Ethiopian kingdom under the Solomonids, ca. 1450 CE

☐ Muslim sultanates, ca. 1450 CE

MAP 14.2 **The Ethiopian Highlands, ca. 1450.**

began with the conquests of King Amda Seyon (r. 1314–1344), who in effect doubled the kingdom's territory. An unknown priest accompanied the king on his campaigns, which he related to posterity in vivid prose and with great detail in *The Glorious Victories of Amda Seyon*, one of the earliest written histories in sub-Saharan Africa. A century after the Mamluks had eradicated the crusader kingdom of Jerusalem in the Middle East (1291), Solomonid Ethiopia was carrying on the Christian holy war in sub-Saharan Africa (see Map 14.2).

Foremost among the Muslim sultanates along the Red Sea coast, which came under Ethiopian authority, were Ifat (1285–1415) and its successor state Adal (1415–1555) on the west coast of the Red Sea, at the entrance from the Indian Ocean. Both relied principally on trade, linking East Africa via the Rift Valley with the India–Mediterranean sea lane. Only the sultanate of Zayla, near modern Djibouti, and a few other places along the coast had sufficient water from wells to allow for a modest garden agriculture. The steppe lowlands farther away from the coast were too dry to support more than widely dispersed populations of camel nomads, who supplied animals and guides to the trade caravans and soldiers to the wars of the sultans against Ethiopia. Urban dwellers, nomads, and pastoralists astride the trade route through the Rift Valley had converted to Islam gradually in the centuries after 800 when autonomous Muslim rulers in Egypt began the expansion of trade via the Red Sea with India and East Africa.

The Ethiopian kings were ruthless in their efforts to subdue the sultans. But the kings' crusading image notwithstanding, they were also pragmatic enough to exempt Muslim merchants and pastoralists from the church's missionary efforts in the south of the kingdoms. Similarly, the kings had little choice but to tolerate the sultans of Ifat and Adal as Muslim vassals. Ethiopia became de facto a multiethnic, multilinguistic, and multireligious state in which the kings limited the church's conversion efforts.

Legally, however, the kings continued to emphasize their Christian identity, adopting in the mid-1400s a Christianized version of Roman law, *The Law of the Kings* (*Fetha Nagast*), from the Egyptian Copts. The law trailed behind it an intriguing history. According to Islamic law, Christians in Islamic civilization were entitled to self-rule; and for this purpose, the Coptic Church in Egypt adopted portions of Justinian's code and resolutions of church councils for its governance. In the mid-1300s, an Egyptian Copt compiled these law books and resolutions into a single codex governing church affairs, civil law, and criminal law, translated from Greek into Arabic. The Ethiopian translator added a section on kingship, and as such, *The Law of the Kings* remained the law of the land until 1930, when the Ethiopian emperor Haile Selassie issued the first modern constitution.

The reinvigorated Ethiopian kingdom of the Solomonids was keenly interested in establishing contacts with western Christianity, wishing especially for the dispatch of craftspeople (and receiving a few). A first embassy of 30 members traveled in 1297–1312 to visit the popes. A churchman in Genoa reported on these visitors, identifying their king for the first time with the mythical Prester John, a great Christian ruler in the "east" expected to come to the aid of the crusaders in recovering Jerusalem and the Holy Land. Previously, Prester John had been considered to be an Indian priest-king, commander of a huge army; but now after the loss of the Holy Land in 1291, Ethiopia appeared as a better hope for an ally than the more distant India.

Adaptation to Islam: City-States and Kingdoms in East and South Africa

During the period 600–1450, the Swahili people emerged as an indigenous African population of Muslims. They formed a society with common features but were divided into dozens of city-states along a 2,000-mile stretch of the African east coast, from today's Somalia in the north to Mozambique in the south. The Swahilis' most common feature was their function as merchant middlemen between the interior of East Africa and the Middle East as well as India. In the interior, increasing agricultural resources and trade with the Swahilis encouraged the expansion of chiefdoms but not yet the rise of kingdoms, except in the far south, in the middle Limpopo valley and on the Zimbabwean plateau where local people mined gold. Here, beginning around 1075, towns, cities, and kingdoms arose, the best known of which was Great Zimbabwe (ca. 1250–1505).

The Swahili City-States on the East African Coast

Dissenting Arabs, driven by the centralizing caliphs to the margins of the Arab Empire in the Middle East, were the first to establish trade contacts in the 700s with Bantu-speaking villagers in coastal East Africa. In the following centuries, these villagers adapted themselves to long-distance trade and Islamic civilization. They evolved into an urban society of kings, **patricians**, religious scholars, sailors, fishermen, and farmers based in small port cities. The kings and patricians were consumers of luxury goods brought to them by Middle Eastern and Indian merchants. As sellers of goods manufactured in their cities to the populations of the interior, the patricians acquired goods from the interior, which the Muslim merchants from overseas took back home. Thus, the Swahilis were brokers in a complex system of exchanges among the people around the Indian Ocean.

Swahili Beginnings   The East African coast follows a fairly straight line from the northeast to the southwest, with few bays and natural harbors. For the most part, the coast is low, in most places rising only gradually. Many small rivers open into the Indian Ocean, and their estuaries provide some room for anchorage. Only the Zambezi River in the south was large enough to allow longer-range water traffic and the building of inland towns. Islands, reefs, and mangrove swamps were numerous and limited the construction and use of large vessels among the Swahilis. Under the influence of the monsoons blowing from the northeast from April to September, the northern half of the East African coast—from today's northern Tanzania to southern Somalia—receives most of its annual rain during the summer. These monsoon winds supported sailing with the wind to the Middle East and India. The opposite direction

Patrician: Term used in this chapter to denote Muslims in Swahili society claiming Middle Eastern descent and, by virtue of profiting from long-distance trade with the countries around the Indian Ocean, either ascended to the throne of their cities as kings or governed their cities in councils, together with other patricians.

of the winter monsoons facilitated the return voyages. The southern half of the coast, from northern Tanzania to Mozambique, has rainy winters and no reliable seasonal winds, making sailing conditions less predictable. Accordingly, the southern half was less settled than the northern part.

The main ethnic group in the interior of sub-Saharan Africa was the Bantu, who had migrated to central, eastern, and southern Africa from roughly 600 BCE to 600 CE (see Chapter 6). The Bantus possessed a diversified agriculture and a wide variety of iron implements. In the mid-700s CE, a cultural differentiation between the Bantu of the interior and the east coast began to emerge. Archaeological remnants from Shanga, near today's Somali–Kenyan border, indicate the existence of a small wooden Islamic congregation hall, holding perhaps 25 people, and Muslim burials with an orientation toward Mecca. Small silver coins with Islamic inscriptions similar to Yemeni coins of the same period but minted in Shanga have also been found. The coastal population thus adapted to Islam, while the hinterland remained wedded to traditional animist spirituality.

The earliest Muslim merchants in East Africa were Khariji dissidents from the Middle East. These Muslims were sectarians who opposed the emergence of a centralized empire, the caliphs of which were actively shaping the emergent Islamic state religion. The caliphs pursued them relentlessly, pushing them into political insignificance in far-away provinces, such as Oman at the mouth of the Persian Gulf and oases in the North African Sahara. Given the agricultural limits in these regions, the Kharijis took to trade, in both East and West Africa.

Early on, the Kharijis were mostly interested in slaves, who were in great demand in the Islamic empire. Merchants in Basra, the main port for the Indian Ocean trade, invested their profits in the purchase of marshland around the mouth of the Tigris River and in the acquisition of slaves from East Africa to clear this land for the planting of rice and sugarcane. From 868 to 883, a revolt among these slaves disrupted the Abbasid Empire's entire trade through the Persian Gulf with India, East Africa, and China. When the caliphs finally succeeded in suppressing the revolt, large-scale agricultural slavery in the region ended. Black slave imports from East as well as West Africa continued on a smaller scale, however, primarily for domestic purposes.

Adapting to Islam   After the Kharijis lost their edge in the trade, mainstream Muslim merchants from the heartland of the Islamic empire traveled with textiles, glazed pottery, and glassware to East Africa to purchase luxury goods, such as ivory, hardwoods, and skins. One of the heartland cities was Shiraz, the capital of the Shiite dynasty of the Buyids (945–1055) in Iran. Their prestige appears to have surpassed that of the Kharijis since wealthy Swahili merchant families associated themselves with them, claiming Shirazi descent. Members of these families migrated from the northern Swahili city of Shanga southward and founded new trading centers as far away as the Comoros Islands. After 1050, mainstream Islam, with its mixture of Sunnism and mysticism, rose in prestige. *Sharifian* descent, that is, the possession of a genealogy going back to the Prophet Muhammad, began to rival Shirazi descent among the coastal elites. Leading Islamic families claiming Shirazi or Sharifian descent thus assumed a dominant position in the Swahili cities, from Mogadishu in the north to Chibuene (in Mozambique) in the south.

Urbanism   Swahili urbanism along the East African coast encompassed several hundred towns and about two dozen city-states of up to 10,000 inhabitants, either on the mainland or on islands off the coast (see Map 14.3). The mark of many cities was the central open space containing the Friday mosque for the congregational noon prayer, the main city well, and tombs of Islamic saints. Around the mosque and usually facing the sea were the densely built inner cities of the patricians. In the

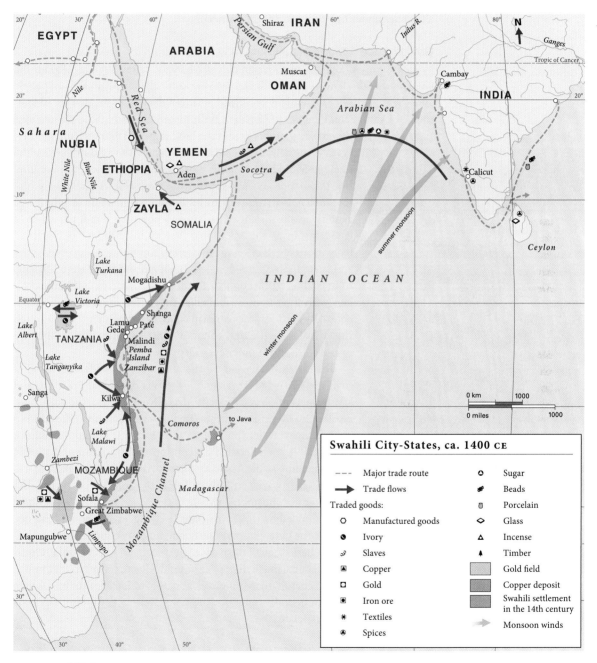

Swahili City-States, ca. 1400 CE

- - - Major trade route	○	Sugar
→ Trade flows	🐚	Beads
Traded goods:	🗻	Porcelain
○ Manufactured goods	◇	Glass
◑ Ivory	△	Incense
✏ Slaves	▲	Timber
▣ Copper		Gold field
▢ Gold		Copper deposit
◉ Iron ore		Swahili settlement in the 14th century
✳ Textiles	→	Monsoon winds
◓ Spices		

MAP **14.3 Swahili City-States, ca. 1400.**

less densely settled outskirts, nonpatricians from overseas or the interior and manumitted slaves earned their living as craftspeople. On the perimeter were cemeteries, pastures, brushland, and mangrove swamps. Separate commoner towns housed fishermen, boat builders, and sailors. Their families grew vegetables and fruits in their gardens and sold the surplus in the nearby patrician cities. Further inland lived various non-Muslim client populations who traded meat and food staples, primarily sorghum, to the cities. Cities, towns, and inland people thus formed loosely organized city-states under the leadership of the patricians.

Governance In the period 600–1450, the Swahili city-states were governed by kings and/or councils of patrician elders. Mainland cities, such as Mogadishu, Gede, and Malindi, were more vulnerable to occasionally hostile hinterland people and, therefore, more dependent on inland alliances than cities located on islands, such as Lamu, Paté, Pemba, or Zanzibar. Both hinterland and inland populations

Musician, in Traditional Garb, Blowing the Siwa Horn. Magnificent horns such as this were part of the royal music repertoire of the mainland city-state kingdoms of the Swahili coast. This musician is from Lamu, in today's Kenya.

were trade partners whom the Swahili patrician merchants or their agents—usually slaves—visited but where they did not settle. The merchants did not establish mosques in the interior, and the interior population did not convert to Islam. Nor did holy men venture into non-Islamic territories to establish retreats or pilgrimage centers. In the absence of Islam as a common bond, the office of chieftainship as the traditional African institution binding tribal federations together served to express the communality of the cities and surrounding rural peoples. The mainland kings were Muslims from leading Shirazi or Sharifian patrician families, but in the dealings with their non-Muslim allies they acted more like traditional chiefs. By contrast, the patrician councils in the island cities—often clusters of several cities, commoner towns, and villages—had no inland allies and at times even dispensed with kings.

The Swahili city- or port-states were considerably smaller than the Christian or Islamic kingdoms of Nubia, Ethiopia, and southern, central, and western Africa. Nevertheless, the patricians' regalia clearly expressed the same royal aspirations. The Moroccan Muslim traveler Ibn Battuta (1304–1369) visited Mogadishu in 1331 and left a detailed description of the animist and Islamic royal customs as displayed by Sheikh Abu Bakr, who claimed Yemeni Sharifian descent. Every Friday, so Ibn Battuta writes, the king attended the noon prayer in his enclosed space in the mosque. Afterward, in a procession led by royal musicians (playing large drums, trumpets, and wind instruments), the king, judge, officials, and military commanders walked through town to the audience hall of the palace. The most important royal prerogative was the minting of coins, made of copper or gold. Given, however, that power on the Swahili coast was based on commercial, and not landed, wealth from which to collect taxes, in administrative practice the kings were never more than firsts among equals in the patriciate.

Traditional Kingdoms in Southern and Central Africa

The first region in the interior where a pattern of increasing wealth and population density became visible during the period 600–1505 was southern Africa, on and around the Zimbabwean plateau. Here, the original foragers of the vast grasslands were in the process of adapting to the Bantu culture arriving from the north, which included the influx of herders and farmers discussed in Chapter 6. Chiefs became powerful on the basis of large herds of cattle. Later, by trading first ivory and then also gold to coastal Swahili merchants, the chiefs initiated a pattern of political formation, building cities and kingdoms, such as Mapungubwe and Great Zimbabwe. Adapting their new economic power to indigenous traditions, these kings assumed the same exalted status which we encountered in the cases of Christian Nubia and Ethiopia.

The Kingdom of Mapungubwe In the course of the 700s, hunters increasingly went after elephants for their ivory. Khariji Swahili merchants from the north had founded the coastal town of Chibuene for the purpose of buying ivory, in return for textiles, glass beads, glazed pottery, and glass bottles. These items, being storable goods, added to the wealth accumulated by chiefs. Thus, the ivory trade marked the beginning of the south African hinterland being incorporated into Swahili long-distance trade.

When chiefs acquired cattle and imported goods from the coast, the first towns arose in the interior. Larger towns with around 1,500 inhabitants followed during the next few centuries, culminating with Mapungubwe [Mah-poon-GOOB-way], the capital of the first full-fledged kingdom (1070–1300), with some 5,000 inhabitants. In the early 900s, villagers to the north, on the Zimbabwean plateau, began to mine gold, which for the next four centuries was the major export item from Swahili cities to the Middle East and India. Workshops for the manufacture of ivory and gold figurines in the Limpopo towns testify to the emergence of an indigenous demand for the products of specialized craftspeople. When Mapungubwe arose as an urban-centered kingdom, the southern African interior not only was integrated into the Swahili Indian Ocean trade but also possessed the crucial urban and royal mark of an urban craftspeople class who did not practice agriculture and cattle herding.

Golden Rhinoceros. This golden rhinoceros was found among the items of the royal dynasty of Mapungubwe, signifying the power and magic of the kings. The kingdom was organized around the mining and trading of gold with the Swahili cities and, from there, with the Islamic Middle East.

Excavations in Mapungubwe and ethnographic studies have yielded important insights into the institution of southern African kingship. The king resided on what had been previously a hill for chiefly rain-making ceremonies. He was in ritual seclusion from the commoners, who lived in the town at the foot of the hill. The hill also contained residences for a few senior wives. The remainder of the wives resided in villages outside Mapungubwe, where they were married to allies and clients of the kings. The graves of the royal cemetery contained large numbers of gold and glass beads, a bowl made of gold leaf, as well as shards of Chinese dishes. Seclusion and an elaborate set of regalia thus marked the king of Mapungubwe.

Court rituals also emphasized the exalted position of the king. The king was in charge of rain-making ceremonies and harvest feasts, but the actual rituals were conducted by the diviner. Of forager descent and often itinerant, diviners were experts in spirituality, experienced in handling the realm of the benevolent and evil spirits. Although royal power was associated with spiritual authority, there was an institutional division between the king's power over life and death and the

Great Zimbabwe, Passageway. The boy, visible at the end of the curve, provides an idea of the massive urban structures erected under the kings. The stone masons were highly specialized craftspeople, who constructed walls that have outlasted the demise of the Zimbabwe kingdom in the middle of the fifteenth century.

diviner's authority to summon the spirits. Thus, African kingship shared the pattern of rulership development encountered also in Eurasia and the Americas: Royal power was legitimate only if combined with spiritual or divine authority.

The Kingdom of Great Zimbabwe   The kingdom of Great Zimbabwe (1250–1505) ("the great house built of stone boulders" [Shona, *ziimba remabwe* or *ziimba rebwe*]) represents the culmination of the southern African kingdoms (see Map 14.4). Initially a tributary state of Mapungubwe, Great Zimbabwe emerged as a kingdom in its own right when the cooling and drying trend in the climate, which in Eurasia signaled the end of the early medieval agricultural expansion, made agriculture in the relatively dry Limpopo valley more difficult. Inhabitants abandoned Mapungubwe in the second half of the 1200s, with evidence of some royalty migrating north to Great Zimbabwe, which was more humid.

The capital city was located at the southern end of the arc of rock surfaces on the Zimbabwean plateau where gold was found. Granite for the construction of stone walls could be

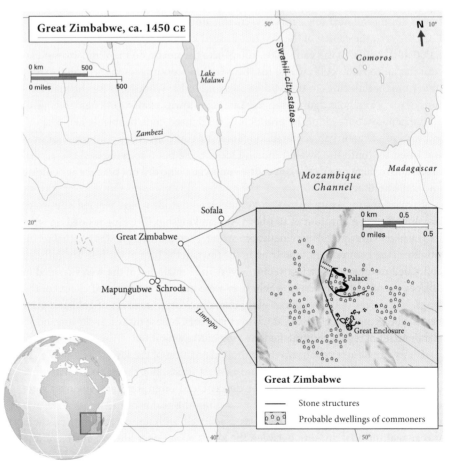

MAP 14.4 Great Zimbabwe, ca. 1450.

quarried easily, using heat from fires to split off layers of rock. Regular building blocks could be dressed with less effort from these layers than in Mapungubwe. At its height, the capital encompassed 18,000 inhabitants and was the seat of a kingdom extending northward across the Zimbabwean plateau. Most settlements in the kingdom were dedicated to gold mining and trading, but a few practiced different trades, such as iron mining and salt panning. The primary sources of income, however, were cattle and grain.

Today, three main archaeological complexes remain of the capital. The first is a hill with a walled palace, accessible through a staircase. Two other complexes at a distance of half a mile to the south are the Western and Central Valley Walled Enclosures. The best-known structure is the so-called Great Enclosure within the Western Enclosure complex, an imposing 36-feet-high circular wall built of closely fitting blocks of granite. The royal palace precinct contained buildings similar to those in Mapungubwe. In the enclosures, some of the better-preserved ruins indicate that they once were buildings with solid stone walls, with plastered and perhaps even painted surfaces inside. Some residences were connected with walls which formed courtyards or narrow passageways. All enclosures were once densely packed with houses, presumably occupied by the kings and/or the ruling classes. Commoners lived perhaps in simple thatched huts built with timber and plastered with clay in the space between the hill and around the two enclosures.

The kingdom of Great Zimbabwe ended around 1505 when Swahili merchants replaced the initial southern Limpopo trade route with the shorter northern Zambezi route. A Chinese porcelain dish bearing this date was found in a burned and collapsed structure in the compound, though it appears that portions of Great Zimbabwe were still inhabited for some time. Thus, there was some overlap between the decline of Zimbabwe and the rise of the new trade route.

Central African Chiefdoms and Kingdoms

The central African rain forest and savanna, although more sparsely settled than the other parts of Africa during 600–1450, nevertheless participated in the general pattern of increased agricultural production and population expansion. In a number of places, especially the Congo Basin, favorable agricultural conditions supported the formation of chiefdoms which evolved into kingdoms. One savanna site, the Lake Upemba depression in the south of today's Democratic Republic of the Congo, was the home of the Luba people, who founded a kingdom based on a diversified agriculture and regional trade sometime in the period between 1000 and 1300 (see Map 14.5).

Luba Origins   Archaeologists date the earliest evidence for the existence of permanent agricultural and fishing settlements around Lake Upemba to the period around 800. They found

MAP **14.5** **The Luba Kingdom, ca. 1400.**

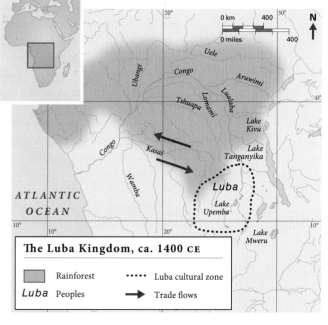

The Luba Kingdom, ca. 1400 CE

- Rainforest
- *Luba* Peoples
- ••••• Luba cultural zone
- → Trade flows

these settlements between the lakes, marshes, and rivers of one of the tributaries of the Congo River. Apart from fish, the villagers also relied on sorghum, millet, chickens, goats, and sheep for their livelihood. Locally produced iron and salt added to the resources. Hunting groups cut across the village lineages and formed the nucleus, around 1000, for the emergence of chiefs who were recognizable in their graves through copper ornaments. Copper had to be acquired through regional trade with the west, and its value made it into the metal preferred for jewelry, as in many other parts of Africa.

Luba oral tradition reaches back to the period between 1000 and 1300. The founding myth appears to refer to a process whereby two chiefs, each claiming his own source of legitimacy, were competing for the unification of the villages. As in many other African foundation stories, the true founder is conceived of as a suffering, disadvantaged hero who has to endure trials before becoming a successful founder king. In the traditions of Africa, as in those of many other parts of the world, exalted kingship was acceptable only if rooted in humble beginnings.

As in Zimbabwe, Luba kings possessed magic powers, which entitled only descendants from his bloodline to succeed to the throne. The chieftains of other clans, although holding court offices and meeting in council to assist in the administration, were excluded from the succession. The royal clan maintained a small military force, sufficient to collect tributes from outlying villages but not large enough to destroy any of the chieftainships. A stable balance was established between the king and the chieftains, making Luba the model for subsequent kingdoms in the savanna of central Africa. The Luba kingdom itself survived until the arrival of Belgian colonialism at the end of the nineteenth century.

Cultural Encounters: West African Traditions and Islam

A pattern of regional trade, urbanization, and chiefdom formation was also characteristic for the Sahel and savanna of West Africa from the middle of the first millennium CE onward. Around 600, chiefs became kings when they unified their clans, conquered some neighbors from whom they collected tributes, and arranged alliances with others. Like their later African colleagues in the eastern half of Africa, they claimed to possess magic powers and adopted royal customs of seclusion. Two kingdoms, ancient Ghana and Mali, followed each other in the period 600–1450. Their royal–military ruling clans benefited from trans-Saharan trade with Islamic civilization and gradually converted to Islam, while the general population of herders, farmers, miners, smiths, and other craftspeople remained faithful to their animist traditions.

The Kingdom of Ancient Ghana

Ancient Ghana emerged in the 600s as the strongest group of chiefdoms in the Sahel and savanna between the Niger inland delta in the east and the Senegal valley in the west. It advanced to the status of a kingdom after 750, when it became the center for trade across the Sahara with the North African Islamic states. Thanks to this trade, the kingdom was dominant in the Sahel for half a millennium. In the 1100s, however, drought and provincial unrest weakened Ghana. The kingdom gave way in 1240 to Mali, an empire which began its rise in the upper Niger rain forest and savanna.

Formation of Ancient Ghana

As discussed in Chapter 6, a long period of progressive desertification (3000–300 BCE) had driven the inhabitants of the southern Sahara southward into what became the Sahel, a belt of steppe, grassland, and marginal agriculture. They had domesticated millet and bred cattle herds in Saharan villages shortly before the desiccation began. During the period 600 BCE–600 CE, the climate stabilized and millet agriculture, cattle herding, and village formation expanded across the Sahel and northern savanna from the Senegal valley in the west to Lake Chad in the east. In some places, as in the inland delta of the Niger, where irrigation was possible, villages were clustering. Jenné-jeno emerged around 300 as a city surrounded by a collection of villages. The city was a center of regional trade for iron and gold from the upper Niger and Senegal valleys and copper from the Sahara, in return for urban manufactures, such as textiles, leather goods, metal implements, and utensils. The people who populated the Sahel were ethnically Soninke, speaking a Bantu language, like the majority of West Africans.

After 300, the regional trade became a long-distance trade. Thanks to the arrival of the Arabian camel among the Berbers of North Africa and the northern Sahara, it became possible to travel through the desert. Long-distance merchants from the cities of Roman North Africa made contact with Soninke merchants in the Sahel, some 3 months away by camel caravan. They exchanged Roman manufactures, such as glassware, cloth, and ceramics, plus Saharan copper and salt for gold. Berber miners in the central Sahara quarried salt from deposits left by dried-up prehistoric lakes. Cowrie shells, imported by Rome from the Indian Ocean and exported to West Africa, document trade connections even farther than the Mediterranean.

It took some time, however, for the initially infrequent trans-Saharan exchanges to intensify and become regular. Only after the loss of their gold mines in northwestern Iberia to Germanic tribal migrants did the Romans regularize the trans-Saharan trade, beginning in the mid-500s. The regularization had a profound effect in the Sahel. In the 600s, Soninke chiefs on the western outskirts of the inland Niger delta, enriched by the profits from the Saharan trade, equipped their followers with arms, such as swords and lances. Riding on small West African horses immune to the diseases carried by the tsetse fly, they subjugated more distantly related Soninke groups in the Sahel between the Niger and Senegal valleys. In the mid-700s, one of the chiefs proclaimed himself king in Wagadu, a city in the Sahel northwest of the inland delta, and founded the kingdom of ancient Ghana (as distinguished from the modern state of Ghana).

As told in the founding myth at the beginning of this chapter, Dinga was the first mythical king. His kingdom, so it was foretold, was destined to rule the Sahel, dominate the gold trade, and benefit from abundant rain as long as its subjects sacrificed a virgin and a colt every year to its well-dwelling patron snake. Modern scholars would say that ancient Ghana lasted through the wet period of the first millennium (300–1100) and eventually succumbed to its successor Mali when it could not adapt in the Sahel to the emerging dry period (1100–1500).

From Roman to Islamic Trade

Ancient Ghana received its gold from Bambuk, a region in the rain forest at the western edge of the kingdom. Villagers on a left-bank tributary of the middle Senegal River panned and mined the metal during the dry season, and Soninke merchants transported it by donkey and bullock some 500 miles east to Wagadu. The Bambuk gold fields occupied a no-man's-land between the kingdom of ancient Ghana and the chiefdom of Takrur on the lower Senegal. The two polities left the villagers to their own devices since neither possessed the technical and administrative means to organize or even control the panning and mining operations. Soninke merchants went no farther than nearby towns, from where they conducted their trading activities with the villagers.

Romanized Berbers gave way to Islamized Berbers in the trans-Saharan trade after about 750. As was the case in Swahili East Africa, Khariji merchants pushed by the emerging Islamic empire into the outer provinces were the first Muslims to travel to the African interior. According to an eleventh-century Arabic source, Wagadu was a twin city, with its merchant and royal halves several miles apart. If Wagadu can be identified with the partially excavated ruins of Koumbi-Saleh on the southern border of today's Mauritania—an identification still disputed among scholars—the merchant city had a dozen mosques, a market place, and residences.

The royal city consisted of a domed palace and other domed buildings, including a courthouse and the homes of the king's treasurer, translator, and other ministers. A grove surrounded the palace area, containing the royal prison and the dwellings of the priests and diviners, as well as the tombs of ancestral kings. In contrast to their Swahili colleagues, the kings of Ghana avoided a combination of traditional kingship with Islam. Even though they benefited from including Muslims in their administration, they were not about to surrender their exalted, magical royal authority over life and death to the supremacy of Islamic law.

From Animism to Islam in the Ruling Class

While the kings of Ghana had reasons to hold on to traditional African animist spirituality, the Soninke merchants gradually converted to Islam. Business with the North African and Middle Eastern merchants was easier to transact if everyone adhered to the same ethics and laws. By the early 1000s, the merchants in the trading towns near the Bambuk villages were Muslims, and the adjacent state of Takrur had also become Islamic. The sectarian Khariji Islam gave way to mainstream Sunnism, which rose to dominance in the Islamic world after 1050. In North Africa, the proponents of Sunnism were the Almoravids, southern Moroccan Berbers who spearheaded a movement that evolved into a short-lived empire in Morocco, the western Sahara, and Islamic Spain (see Chapter 10).

Perhaps under pressure of the Almoravids, in the early 1100s the kings of Ghana followed their merchants by also converting to Islam. The Sahel and savanna villagers, however, remained wedded to their African spirituality. As a result, Ghana now resembled the states on the Swahili coast and their hinterlands, where only the rulers and merchants were Islamic. In addition to the villagers, a number of allied Soninke chiefs remained faithful to traditional spirituality; and during the second half of the 1100s the cohesion of the kingdom began to soften. In 1180, the founding clan of ancient Ghana ceded power to another clan, which established a new dynasty in Wagadu and adopted a policy of conquest of the southern savanna. For the next half-century Ghana was an imperial power, trading gold not only from the Senegal River in the west but also from newly developed fields in the rain forest on the upper Niger and Black Volta Rivers (see Map 14.6).

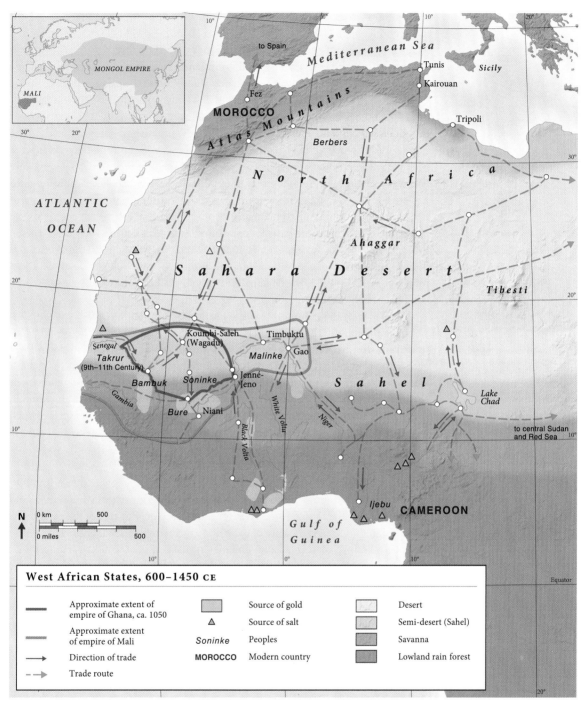

MAP **14.6** **West African States, 600–1450.**

The Empire of Mali

The opening of new gold fields in the rain forest exposed hitherto marginal peoples to the influence of long-distance trade, royal rule, and Islam. One of these peoples, the Malinke, followed the by now familiar pattern of rallying around an inspiring chief who, as a conqueror, built the foundations for an expanding polity. By uniting both savanna and Sahel peoples, the Malinke built the empire of Mali, a polity of many ethnic, linguistic, and religious groups. At its height, Mali stretched from the Atlantic to the Niger bend and from the Sahara to the rain forest.

Mali was the beneficiary of a significantly increased demand for gold in Islamic civilization on the other side of the Sahara. In addition to the existing Islamic mints, Christian mints began to stamp gold coins. The king of Castile in Spain was the first, in 1173; and by the mid-1200s Italian city-states had followed suit. In response to this increased demand, merchants encouraged the opening of new gold fields in the rain forest. The people in the savanna of the upper Niger and its tributaries were Malinke villagers who spoke a language related to that of the Soninke but who were ethnically distinct. In the course of the 1000s, these villagers had acculturated to ancient Ghana, which they recognized as overlord. Although composed of dozens of chiefdoms, the Malinke also encompassed hunter associations, which cut across the chiefdoms and formed the basis for ambitious leaders seeking to unify the Malinke. When the new dynasty of Ghana conquered much of the Malinke lands at the end of the 1100s, resistance led by the hunters against the new rulers rose quickly. In a rebellion in 1230–1235, the Malinke not only liberated themselves but went on to conquer ancient Ghana.

The leader of the conquest was the inspiring hero Sundiata (also spelled Sunjata or Sundjata, ca. 1217–1255). He and his adventures were at the center of an **oral tradition**, with traveling bards telling stories which they handed down from generation to generation and told and retold publicly in villages. In the nineteenth and twentieth centuries, anthropologists recorded these traditions and made them available in translation. At the head of a cavalry force borrowed from a chiefdom in the Sahel, Sundiata defeated ancient Ghana in 1235 and founded the empire of Mali, with its capital, Niani, on an upper Niger tributary in modern Guinea.

Oral traditions: Myths, tales, stories (e.g., the foundation myth of Wagadu) handed down from generation to generation.

The Malian Empire

Mali was the first enduring empire in sub-Saharan Africa, lasting officially for over four centuries (1235–1645). At its height in the early 1300s, Mali encompassed most of the West African Sahel, large parts of the savanna, and the gold fields in the rain forest—a territory surpassed only by that of the contemporary Mongol Empire. At the core of the empire were privileged Malinke clans whose kings and chiefs formed an alliance and met in an assembly (Malinike *gbara*), under the emperors who assumed the title of *mansa*. We do not know how frequently or long this assembly met. Oral tradition records the laws, customs, and traditions of which it was the guardian and according to which the empire was governed. As in Mesopotamia, Vedic India, Greece, and Rome, Mali preserved traditions of chiefly assemblies from pre-royal forms of social organization.

Similar to ancient Ghana, Mali's power rested on a large, horseborne army recruited from the Soninke clans that could move swiftly and overwhelm its opponents with surprise attacks. From the 1300s onward Mali began to import tall Middle Eastern and North African horses in larger numbers and to form cavalry units equipped with chain mail, lances, and swords. But this cavalry was probably not numerous enough to become the elite force characteristic of the Middle East and Europe prior to the introduction of firearms. Infantry, using bow and arrow and moving about on small horses, continued to form the backbone of the military.

Also like their royal predecessors in ancient Ghana, the Malian emperors relied on a small central administration primarily concerned with finances and justice and run by Muslims as well as by slaves. The empire financed itself by tributes from vassal kingdoms in the Sahel and river chiefdoms with villagers and fishermen, as well as taxes on the commerce of gold, iron, copper, salt, textiles (both local and foreign), leather goods, and other manufactures. Since the new gold fields and the capital of Niani were located on a tributary of the Niger, the rulers relied on water transport down river to the cities of Jenné-jeno, Timbuktu (founded in 1100), and Gao. In the mid-1300s, these three cities replaced Wagadu as the main transshipment centers of goods for the Saharan caravans. Thus, with the rise of Mali, the trans-Saharan trade shifted eastward.

In 1324, the most famous ruler of Mali, Mansa Musa (r. ca. 1312–1337), annexed the city of Timbuktu from its Touareg Berber founders. There he founded a college (Arabic *madrasa*) and library, part of the Sankoré Mosque. Timbuktu became a center of learning, focused on Islamic law but also offering geometry, algebra, geography, and astronomy as ancillary fields of study, which judges and independent scholars were required to know. The independent scholars were often well-off members of merchant families. Many kept private libraries in their residences, where they and their descendants accumulated masses of manuscripts over the centuries, estimated today to number in the hundreds of thousands. In the mid-1400s, with some 100,000 inhabitants, the commercial and scholarly hub of Timbuktu was one of the larger cities in the world.

The Decline of Mali　Timbuktu flourished even while its imperial overlord, Mali, declined in the later 1300s. Weak rulers arrived on the throne and dynastic disputes broke out. Outside groups that had adapted to Mali influences—rainforest groups with newly acquired horses and Touareg nomads from the desert—attacked from the south and north. As a result, some of the subjugated provinces in the Sahel began to break away and establish independent kingdoms. More generally, even though Mali had exploited the weakening of ancient Ghana at the onset of the dry period after 1100, the deepening of the drought conditions eventually caught up with Mali as well. By 1450, Mali had shrunk to the size of a kingdom in the savanna.

The Sankoré Mosque of Timbuktu, Mali. The mosque evolved in the fourteenth century into a large university with a library housing hundreds of thousands of manuscripts. A preservation program under United Nations' auspices seeks to restore and preserve these manuscripts today.

Patterns Up Close | The Sculptures of Ife

Sculptures, figures, and figurines in Africa followed a pattern that was shared early on with Eurasia and, during the periods of 600 BCE–600 CE and 600–1450 CE, also with Australia, the Pacific, and parts of the Americas. Broadly speaking, forager, village, and pastoral societies developing in the direction of chiefdoms, but not yet kingdoms, preserved traditional ancestor cults within their animist spirituality.

As lineages evolved, the memory of the generations between the founder and oneself blurred so that the in-between ancestors became an anonymous collective. The spirits of the ancestors in the invisible world, therefore, were conceived as being collectively present, to be consulted, nourished through sacrifices, cajoled, etc. One could "trap" them in sculptures, figures, and figurines, which emphasized the head, believed to be the seat of the spirit, at the expense of the torso and limbs, which were indicated in rudimentary fashion. Even the heads were generally fashioned in abstract, geometrically simplified ways, corresponding to the collective nature of the ancestors. These artifacts, therefore, were not "primitive," even though they are still today often described as such. Their style was generic because the collective of the ancestors was generic.

When societies reached levels of wealth and complexity that led to the emergence of kingdoms, kings became exceptional persons, endowed with ancestral magic (in Africa) or a transcendent divine mandate (in Eurasia) to exercise power, not merely chiefly authority. Generic ancestor "traps" would not do: Artists had to apply the techniques of naturalistic representation so that the kings would recognize

(a) Guardian Figure, Bakota Area, Gabon, Nineteenth–Twentieth Century. The abstract Bakota figure, above, with its generic geometrical elements, represents the collective lineage spirit; the much more realistic Nigerian figure on the right represents royalty who wished to be remembered individually.

Rain-Forest Kingdoms

As discussed in earlier chapters, the West African rain forest was a 200-mile-wide strip of tropical vegetation stretching from modern Guinea above the southwestern corner of West Africa to Cameroon on the bend to central Africa, where it transits to the Congo rain forest. In the earlier period of 600 BCE to 600 CE, savanna peoples with iron implements had entered the rain forest and founded villages in clearings, farming yam and oil palm kernels. The banana, arriving from East Africa around 800, was an important addition, helping in the increase of agricultural productivity. As elsewhere in Africa, the result was a pattern of political formation which included village clusters, chiefdoms, and kingdoms with urban centers and sophisticated crafts, such as bronze casting in Nigeria.

The Kingdom of Ife The earliest village cluster to urbanize was that of Ife [EE-fay], west of the Niger delta in 500 CE, the spiritual center of the Yoruba ethnic group and its oral traditions. By 1000 it was a kingdom with a walled capital, which enclosed a palace, groves, shrines, stone-built residences, and craft workshops for pottery, textiles, and glassware (especially beads). Courtyards and passageways in the city were paved with terra-cotta, to remain passable during the rainy season. One highly developed art was sculpting, in terra-cotta, copper, or bronze.

themselves in them. Of course, after a while sculptures turned into generic like-nesses again, as they did in Mesopotamia and Egypt, since kingship became an ordinary institution with undistinguished kings not worth remembering (*a*).

The Ife terra-cotta, copper, and bronze royal heads stem from that short, experimental, and highly innovative time period of about 200 years (1100–1300) when kingship was new in Ife. The naturalism of these figures is striking, especially when one takes into consideration that western European figurative art during the same period was still "primitive," in the sense of being iconic. (It typically represented standardized ideas about how biblical figures should look so that their God-pleasing nature was immediately recognizable.) The stripes on the faces of some Ife figures (*b*) are believed to represent *scarifications*, or scars marking the passage from youth to adulthood or distinguishing one lineage from another, as practiced in parts of Africa.

(*b*) Ife Shrine Head, Terra-Cotta, Nigeria, ca. 1200.

Questions

- How does the history of African sculpture, such as those from Ife, provide evidence for studying the patterns of state building in this period?

- Why does material culture play such an important dimension in understanding the African past?

Sungbo's Eredo   Ife set the example for several further chiefdoms to advance to the threshold of kingdoms between 1000 and 1450. One of them toward the north was Oyo, which (thanks to the adoption of a cavalry force) expanded from the rain forest northward toward the edge of the savanna. It arose as a trade center for the exchange of palm oil kernels and kola nuts (a mild narcotic containing caffeine) in return for Mediterranean manufactures and Sahel horses, through first Ghanaian and then Malian merchants. In the other chiefdoms, leaders mobilized villagers for the construction of earthworks, which astound even today by their size and scope. One of these chiefdoms, Ijebu, encompassed a capital and villages on a territory of 22 square miles, surrounded by a moat and rampart combination up to 70 feet deep/high and 100 miles long. In nearby Benin, smaller earthworks around villages collectively added up to 10,000 miles and became the nucleus for an important kingdom in 1440. In both Ijebu and Benin, the moats and ramparts cut through the hard, iron-saturated soil, rivers, and swamps, requiring centuries of hard labor with nothing more than iron shovels.

Scholars are still undecided over the purpose of these constructions: Did they protect against enemies and elephants, were they boundary markers for ancestral lands and their spirits, or did they facilitate the collection of tolls? Perhaps they were intended for all three. Equally difficult is the explanation for the phenomenon of collective labor: How were chiefs able to motivate workers to contribute their voluntary efforts? Evidently they were, as they were also in the Americas and Pacific, where followers built huge temples or rolled heavy stone sculptures across distances. Authority without power, buttressed by ancestral pedigree and spirituality, can thus be seen as a powerful motivator to take on great tasks and validate the institutions it represents.

Putting It All Together

Africa in the period 600–1450 displayed patterns of political and cultural development that included creative adaptation of animism to the monotheisms of Christianity and Islam and indigenous kingdom formation. Depending on regional conditions and the degree of integration into Eurasian long-distance trade, peoples in the different parts of sub-Saharan Africa mixed the two cultural heritages of Christianity and Islam in a variety of ways. The Nile valley and northeastern highlands, long adapted to the Mediterranean prior to 600, incorporated Christianity into their local traditions. They adopted the Christian institutional division between kingship and church, in which kingship was a sacred office but subject to law and Christian ethics. The church, for its part, was an autonomous, hierarchical body. As in post-1000 Christian western Europe, the Nubian and Ethiopian churches were subject to a distant religious authority.

Coastal East and West Africa adopted Islam, which arrived through merchants, not missionaries. In eastern Africa, Islam took root among the coastal people and did not penetrate inland. In western Africa, only merchants and kings converted but did so across the interior. Thus, Africans adapted to Christianity and Islam during 600–1450 in very different ways.

In the same period, African kingship was a new institution with roots in the traditions of chieftainship in villages and village clusters. The kings emphasized their royal powers over life and death but also continued to claim the traditional chiefly powers of spirituality and magic. As Christians or Muslims, they at least paid lip service to the divine laws to which they were subject. In southern and central Africa, kingship arose from its African context without modification by Christian or Islamic law, and it is important to emphasize that Africa needed neither Christianity nor Islam to embark on its own distinctive pattern of kingdom formation.

During 600–1450, however, this pattern clearly remained an exception amid the sub-Saharan population, the majority of which remained "stateless," to use an expression in common use among historians of Africa. This population, organized in farming villages or pastoral camps, possessed chiefs and hunting or youth societies cutting across village and camp boundaries but did not unite into larger polities or trade farther away than regionally for locally unavailable metals and salt. It had specialized craftspeople, such as smiths and miners, who were also farmers. The unique position of this silent majority of stateless Africans should always be kept in mind, alongside the kingdoms and empires, in seeking to understand Africa's significance in world history during this period.

▶ For additional resources, including maps, primary sources, visuals, and quizzes, please go to www.oup.com/us/vonsivers. Please see the Further Resources section at the back of the book for additional readings and suggested websites.

Thinking Through Patterns

▶ **What patterns of adaptation did the Christian kingdoms of northeast Africa demonstrate in their interactions with the civilizations of the Middle East and eastern Mediterranean?**

In the period 600–1450, the northeast of sub-Saharan Africa was firmly drawn into the orbit of eastern Christian and Islamic civilizations, without, however, fully adapting their formative patterns. Perhaps the closest adaptation occurred in the sphere of trade, where the Christian kingdoms became the providers of luxury goods, such as ivory, skins, and hardwoods from tropical Africa to the Middle East and eastern Mediterranean, in return for manufactures, Indian spices, and Chinese silks. Beginning in 1250 in the Nilotic kingdom of Nubia, the expansionist regime of the Muslim Mamluks in Egypt put the African Christians on the defensive. By 1450 the middle Nile region was Islamized. In contrast, an expansionist Christian Ethiopia put Muslims on the coast of the Red Sea on the defensive and Christianized the pagan southern highlands.

The inclusion of the East African coast and sub-Saharan West Africa into the Muslim Indian Ocean and Mediterranean trading zone resulted in the rise of small coastal Swahili states and two large West African polities: the kingdom of ancient Ghana and the empire of Mali. Muslim mariners and merchants interacted with Islamized local African rulers and merchants to exchange Middle Eastern textiles, leather goods, and metal wares for ivory, gold, slaves, skins, and hardwoods. African rulers and merchants obtained their African goods from pagan miners and hunters in the African interior outside their states. Adaptation to Islamic religious civilization was a phenomenon limited to the ruling classes and associated merchant circles.

▶ **What were the responses of Africans to Muslim merchants who connected them with the trading zone of the Indian Ocean and Mediterranean? As these Africans adapted to Islam, which forms of political organization did they adopt?**

▶ **In what ways did the economic and political transformations on the east African coast and West Africa affect developments in the interior?**

The adaptation of coastal East Africa to Islamic religious civilization had an indirect effect on the interior in the region of southern Africa. Here, chiefs in Zimbabwe attached themselves to the Swahili trade network and used the wealth from this trade for the transformation of their chiefdoms into kingdoms. Impressive masonry constructions serving as centers for incipient administrative structures testify to the ability of kings to transform chiefly authority into royal military power. The East and West African expansion of trade under the impact of Islam may have also indirectly led to a population increase in the interior of Africa. Such an increase became noticeable toward the 1300s, especially in the Congo basin, where the Luba kingdom was the first to emerge.

Chapter 15   600-1550 CE
The Rise of Empires in the Americas

ATLANTIC
OCEAN

Caribbean Sea

Meso-
america

PACIFIC
OCEAN

Andes

Just outside Lima, in a sandy and dry ravine 3 miles to the east, is the shantytown of Túpac Amaru, named after the last Inca ruler, who died in 1572. People fleeing the Maoist-Marxist "Shining Path" guerillas in the highlands southeast of Lima settled here during the 1980s. Archaeologists had known for years that the site was an ancient burial place called "Puruchuco" (in Quechua "Feathered Helmet") but could not prevent the influx of settlers. By the late 1990s, the temporary shantytown had become an established settlement with masonry houses, streets, and a school. Dwellers were anxious to acquire title to their properties, introduce urban services and utilities, and clean up ground contaminated in many places by raw sewage. However, residents realized that archaeologists had to be called in before the shantytown could be officially recognized. Túpac Amaru was facing an increasingly familiar dilemma in the developing world, pitting modern needs against the wish to know the past through discovering and (if possible) preserving its last traces.

During emergency excavations from 1999 to 2001, the archaeologist Guillermo Cock, together with Túpac Amaru residents hired as field assistants, unearthed one of the most astounding treasures in the history of American archaeology. The team discovered some 2,200 mummies, most

ABOVE: One of 2,200 mummies from the Inca period (1438–1533) excavated in Túpac Amaru, Peru.

of them bundled up in blankets and perfectly preserved with their hair, skin, eyes, and genitals intact. Many bundles also contained rich burial gifts, including jewelry, corn, potatoes, peanuts, peppers, and coca leaves. Forty bundles had false heads made of cotton cloth, some topped with wigs, making the bundles look like oversized persons.

Scholars hope that in a few years, when all of the mummies will be unwrapped, answers can be given as to the social characteristics of the buried people. Were they members of an Inca colony planted into one of the empire's provinces? Or were they locals under their own lord, recognizing Inca overlordship? Were they specialized laborers, such as weavers, who produced cloth tributes for the Incas? Were children and women sacrificed to accompany the cotton king in his journey to the afterlife? Had assimilation between the conquerors and conquered begun? These questions are difficult to answer as so much about the Inca Empire that ruled the Andes from 1438 to 1533 remains unknown. Yet, the questions are exciting precisely because they could not have been posed prior to the discovery of these mummies.

The Inca Empire and its contemporary, the Aztec Empire (1427–1521), both grew out of political, economic, and cultural patterns that began to form around 600 CE in Mesoamerica and the Andes (see Chapter 5). At that time, kingdoms had emerged out of chiefdoms in two small areas of Mesoamerica, the southern Yucatán Peninsula and the Valley of Mexico. After 600, kingdom formation became more general across Mesoamerica and arose for the first time in the Andes. These kingdoms were states with military ruling classes that used new types of weapons and could conquer larger territories than was possible prior to the 600s. Military competition prepared the way for the origin of empires—multireligious, multilinguistic, and multiethnic states encompassing many thousands of miles. Even though empires arrived later in the Americas than in Eurasia, they demonstrate that humans, once they had adopted agriculture, evolved in remarkably similar patterns of social and political formation across the world.

The Legacy of Teotihuacán and the Toltecs in Mesoamerica

As discussed in Chapter 5, the city-state of Teotihuacán had dominated northern Mesoamerica from 200 BCE to the late 500s CE. It fell into ruin probably as the result of an internal uprising against an overbearing ruling class. After its collapse, the surrounding towns and villages, as well as half a dozen other cities in and around the Valley of Mexico, perpetuated the cultural legacy of Teotihuacán for centuries. Employing this legacy, the conquering state of the Toltecs unified a major part of the region for a short period from 900 to 1180. At the same time, after an internal crisis,

▶ Within the patterns of state formation basic to the Americas, which types of states emerged in Mesoamerica and the Andes during the period 600–1550? What characterized these states?

▶ Why did the Tiwanaku and Wari states have ruling classes but no dynasties and central bureaucracies? How were these patterns expressed in the territorial organization of these states?

▶ What patterns of urban life characterized the cities of Tenochtitlán and Cuzco, the capitals of the Aztec and Inca Empires? In which ways were these cities similar to those of Eurasia and Africa?

the southern Maya kingdoms on the Yucatán Peninsula reached their late flowering, together with the northern state of Chichén Itzá.

Militarism in the Valley of Mexico

After the ruling class of Teotihuacán disintegrated at the end of the sixth century, the newly independent local lords and their supporters in the small successor states of Mesoamerica continued Teotihuacán's cultural heritage. This heritage was defined by Teotihuacán's temple style, ceramics, textiles, and religious customs, especially the cult of the feathered serpent god Quetzalcoatl [Ketz-al-CO-wa]. The Toltecs, migrants from the north, militarized the Teotihuacán legacy and transformed it into a program of conquest.

Ceremonial Centers and Chiefdoms   In the three centuries after the end of the city-state of Teotihuacán, the local population declined from some 200,000 to about 30,000. Although largely ruined, the ceremonial center continued to attract pilgrims, but other places around the Valley of Mexico and beyond rose in importance. The semiarid region to the northwest of the valley had an extensive mining industry, with many mine shafts extending a mile or more into the mountains. It produced gemstones, such as greenstone, turquoise, hematite, and cinnabar. Independent after 600, inhabitants built ceremonial centers and small states of their own, trading their gemstones to their neighbors in all directions.

To the north were the Pueblo cultures in today's southwestern United States. These cultures were based on sophisticated irrigated farming systems and are known for their distinctive painted pottery styles. They flourished between 700 and 1500 in the canyons of what are today the states of New Mexico, Arizona, southwestern Colorado, and southeastern Utah. In turn, these cultures might have been in contact with the Mississippi cultures, among which the ceremonial center and city of Cahokia (650–1400) near modern St. Louis is the best known. An obsidian scraper from the Pachuco region north of the Valley of Mexico found in Spiro Mounds, Oklahoma, attests to at least occasional contacts between Mesoamerica and the Mississippi culture (see Map 15.1).

In western Mesoamerica, ceremonial centers and chiefdoms flourished on the basis of metallurgy, which arrived through Ecuadoran seaborne merchants ca. 600–800. The Ecuadorans received their copper from Peru, in return for seashells found in the warm waters off their coast as well as farther north. Copper, too soft for agricultural implements or military weapons, served mostly in households and as jewelry for the rich.

In the south, a number of small, fortified hilltop states flourished in the post-Teotihuacán period. Their inhabitants built moats and ramparts to protect these states. More than in other Mesoamerican states, the southern ruling classes were embroiled in fierce wars during 600–900, images of which are depicted in the stone reliefs of gruesome battle scenes.

The Toltec Conquering State   Early after the collapse of Teotihuacán, crafts-people and farmers migrated some 60 miles north to Tula, a place on a ridge in the highlands watered by two tributaries of a river flowing into the Gulf of Mexico. They founded a small ceremonial center and town with workshops known for the high quality of the scrapers, knives, and spear points fabricated from the local Pachuca

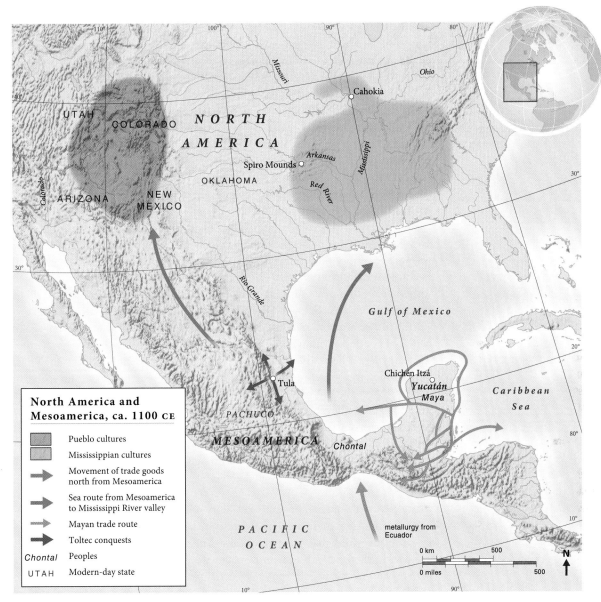

MAP **15.1** **North America and Mesoamerica, ca. 1100.**

obsidian. Around 900, new migrants arrived from northwest Mexico as well as the Gulf coast. The northerners spoke Nahuatl [NA-hua], the language of the later Aztecs, who considered Tula their ancestral city.

The integration of the new arrivals was apparently not peaceful since it resulted in the abandonment of the temple and the departure of a defeated party of Tulans.

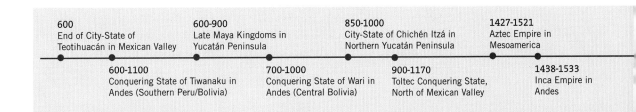

600	600-900	850-1000	1427-1521
End of City-State of Teotihuacán in Mexican Valley	Late Maya Kingdoms in Yucatán Peninsula	City-State of Chichén Itzá in Northern Yucatán Peninsula	Aztec Empire in Mesoamerica

600-1100	700-1000	900-1170	1438-1533
Conquering State of Tiwanaku in Andes (Southern Peru/Bolivia)	Conquering State of Wari in Andes (Central Bolivia)	Toltec Conquering State, North of Mexican Valley	Inca Empire in Andes

This abandonment may well have been enshrined in the myth of Tolpiltzin, a priest-king of the feathered serpent god Quetzalcoatl, who after his departure to the east would one day return to restore the cult to its rightful center. The myth later played a fateful part in the establishment of Spanish rule in the Americas.

The new Tula of 900 developed quickly into a large city with a new temple, 60,000 urban dwellers, and perhaps another 60,000 farmers on surrounding lands. It was the first city-centered state to give prominence to the sacrifice of captured warriors. As it evolved, Tula became the capital of the conquering state of the Toltecs, which imprinted its warrior culture on large parts of Mesoamerica from around 900 to 1180 (see Map 15.1).

The Toltecs introduced two innovations in weaponry that improved the effectiveness of hand-to-hand combat. First, there was the new weapon of the short (1.5-foot) sword made of hardwood with inlaid obsidian edges, which could slash as well as crush, in contrast to the obsidian-spiked clubs that had been primary weapons in earlier times. Second, warriors wore obsidian daggers with wooden handles inside a band on the left arm, replacing simpler obsidian blades, which were difficult to use as they had no handles. Traditional dart throwers and slings for stone projectiles completed the offensive armament of the warriors.

The Toltec army of 13,000–26,000 soldiers was sufficiently large to engage in battles of conquest within an area of 4 days' march (roughly 40 miles) away from Tula. Any target beyond this range was beyond their capabilities, given the logistics of armor, weapons, food rations, narrow dirt roads, and uneven terrain—and, of course, Toltecs did not have the benefit of wheeled vehicles. Thus, the only way of projecting power beyond the range of 40 miles was to establish colonies and to have troops accompany traders, each of which could then supply himself by foraging or through trade along the way. As a result, the Toltec state projected its power by the prestige of its large military, rather than through a full-scale imperial program with the imposition of governors, tributes, and taxes.

Trade   Apart from demonstrating military might, the Toltecs pursued the establishment of a large trade network. Merchants parlayed Tula's obsidian production into a trade network that radiated southward into the cacao, vanilla, and bird feather production centers of Chiapas and Guatemala; to the north into gemstone mining regions; and westward into centers of metal mining. Metallurgy advanced around 1200 with the development of the technology of bronze casting. Bronze axes were stronger and more useful for working with wood than copper axes. Bronze bells produced a greater variety of sounds than those of copper. As ornamental objects, both were trade goods highly prized by the elites in Tula.

The Late Toltec Era   Toltec military power declined in the course of the twelfth century when the taxable grain yield diminished, because of either prolonged droughts or a depletion of the topsoil on the terraces, or a combination of the two. Sometime around 1180, a new wave of foraging peoples from the northwest invaded, attacking with bows and arrows and using hit-and-run tactics against Toltec communication lines. The disruptions caused an internal revolt, which brought down the ceremonial center and its palaces. By 1200, Tula was a city with a burned-out center, like Teotihuacán six centuries earlier; and Mesoamerica relapsed into a period of small-state coexistence characteristic of the pre-600 period.

Late Maya States in Yucatán

Teotihuacán's demise at the end of the sixth century was paralleled by a realignment of the balance of power among the Maya kingdoms in the southern Yucatán lowlands of Mesoamerica. This realignment, accompanied by extensive warfare, was resolved by around 650. A period of late flowering spanned the next two centuries, followed by a shift of power from the southern to the northern part of the peninsula.

The Southern Kingdoms At its height during the fourth and fifth centuries, Teotihuacán in the Valley of Mexico had interjected itself into the delicate balance of power existing among the Maya kingdoms of southern Yucatán. Alliances among the states shifted, and prolonged wars of conquest racked the lowlands, destroying several older states. A dozen new kingdoms emerged and established a new balance of power among themselves. After a lengthy hiatus, Maya culture entered its final period (650–900).

The most striking phenomenon of the final period in the southern, rain forest–covered lowlands and adjacent highlands were massive new programs of agricultural expansion and ceremonial monument construction. Agriculture was expanded again through cutting down the rain forest on hillsides and terracing the hills for soil retention. The largest kingdoms grew to 50,000–60,000 inhabitants and reached astounding rural population densities of about 1,000 persons per square mile. (In comparison, England's most densely populated counties just prior to its agricultural expansion after 1700 were Middlesex and Surrey, with 221 and 207 persons per square mile, respectively.) Although the late Maya states were geographically small, they were administratively the most centralized polities ever created in indigenous American history.

The late Maya states did not last long. In spite of all efforts, the usually torrential downpours of the rainy season gradually washed the topsoil from the newly built hillside terraces. The topsoil, accumulating as alluvium in the flatlands, was initially quite fertile; but from around 800 onward it became more and more depleted of nutrients. In addition, in many wetlands, farmers found it difficult to prevent clay from forming over the alluvium and hardening in the process. Malnutrition resulting from the receding agricultural surface began to reduce the labor force. Ruling classes had to make do with fewer workers and smaller agricultural surpluses. In the end, even the ruling classes suffered, with members killing each other for what remained of these surpluses. By about 900, the Maya kingdoms in southern Yucatán had shriveled to the size of chiefdoms with small towns and villages.

Chichén Itzá in the North A few small Maya states on the periphery survived. The most prominent among them was Chichén Itzá [Chee-CHEN Eat-SA] in the northern lowlands, which flourished from about 850 to 1000. At first glance the region would appear to be less than hospitable for a successful state. The climate in the north was much drier than that in the south. The surface was rocky or covered with thin topsoil, supporting mostly grass, scrub vegetation, and isolated forests. In many places, where the soil was too saline, agriculture was impossible and the production of salt was the only source of income. There were no rivers, but many sinkholes in the porous limestone underneath the soil held water. Countless cisterns to hold additional amounts of water for year-round use were cut into the limestone and plastered to prevent seepage. This water, carried in jars to the surface, supported an intensive garden agriculture, productive enough to sustain entire towns and city-states.

Chichén Itzá, El Caracol ("The Snail") Observatory. This domed building was aligned with the northern extreme of the path of Venus. Here, astronomers made the lengthy and systematic observations necessary to coordinate the three different calendars in use in Mesoamerica from about 500 BCE (see Chapter 6).

Chichén Itzá was founded during the phase of renewed urbanization in 650. It was built near two major sinkholes and several salt flats. The population was composed of local Maya as well as the Maya-speaking Chontal from the Gulf coast farther west. Groups among these people engaged in long-distance trade, both overland and in boats along the coast. Since trade in the most lucrative goods (such as cacao, vanilla, jade, copper, bronze, turquoise, and obsidian) required contact with people well outside even the farthest political reach of either Teotihuacán or Tula, merchants (*pochtecas* [potsh-TAY-cas]) traveled in armed caravans. These merchant groups enjoyed considerable freedom and even sponsorship by the ruling classes of the states of Mesoamerica.

Chontal traders adopted Toltec culture, and when they based themselves in Chichén Itzá around 850 they superimposed their adopted culture over that of the original Maya. How the city was ruled is only vaguely understood, but there is some evidence that there were two partially integrated ruling factions, possibly descended from the Chontal and local Maya, sharing in the governance of the city. At the very end of the period of Teotihuacán, Maya, and Toltec cultural expansion, the three cultural traditions finally merged on the Yucatán Peninsula in only one geographically marginal region. This merger, however, did not last long; already at around 1000 the ruling-class factions left the city-state for unknown reasons. As a result, the city-state diminished in size and power to town level.

The Legacy of Tiwanaku and Wari in the Andes

Mesoamerica and the Andes, from the time of chiefdom formation in 2500 BCE in Caral-Supé onward, shared the tradition of regional temple pilgrimages. In the Andes, the chiefdoms remained mostly coastal, with some inland extensions along valleys of the Andes. Around 600 CE, the two conquering states of Tiwanaku in the highlands of what are today southern Peru and Bolivia, and Wari, in central Peru, emerged. Both states encompassed several tens of thousands of inhabitants and represented a major step in the formation of larger, militarily organized polities.

The Conquering State of Tiwanaku

Tiwanaku was a political and cultural power center in the south-central Andes during the period 600–1100. It began as a ceremonial center with surrounding villages and gradually developed into a state dominating the region around Lake Titicaca. At its apogee it was an expanding state, planting colonies in regions far from the lake and conveying its culture through trade to peoples even beyond the colonies.

Agriculture on the High Plain   The Andes consist of two parallel mountain chains stretching along the west coast of South America. For the most part, these chains are close together, divided by small plains, valleys, and lower mountains. In

southeastern Peru and western Bolivia an intermoun-
tain plain, 12,500 feet above sea level, extends as wide
as 125 miles. At its northern end lies Lake Titicaca,
subdivided into a larger and deeper northern valley
and a smaller, shallower, swampy, and reed-covered
southern valley. Five major and 20 smaller rivers coming from the eastern Andes chain feed the lake, which
has one outlet at its southern end, a river flowing into
Lake Poopó [Po-POH], a salt lake 150 miles south.
The Lake Titicaca region, located above the tree line,
receives winter rains sufficient for agriculture and pasture, whereas the southern plain around Lake Poopó
is too dry to sustain more than steppes.

Tiwanaku, Kalassaya Gate.
Within the Temple of the Sun,
this gate is aligned with the
sun's equinoxes and was used
for festive rituals. Note the
precise stone work, which the
Incas later developed further.

In spite of its elevation, the region around Lake
Titicaca offered everything necessary for an advanced
urbanization process. The lake's freshwater supported
fish and resources such as reeds from the swamps, which served for the construction
of boats and roofs. Corn flourished only in the lower elevations of the Andes and
had to be imported, together with the corn-derived *chicha*, a beer-like drink. Instead
of corn, food staples were potatoes and quinoa. The grasslands of the upper hills
served as pastures for llama and alpaca herds. Llamas were used as transportation
animals, and alpacas provided wool. The meat of both animals—preserved for winter through drying—was a major protein source. Although frost was an ever-present
danger in Tiwanaku, nutrition was quite diversified.

Farmers grew their crops on hillside terraces, where runoff water could be channeled, or on raised fields close to the lake. The raised-field system, which farmers
had adopted through interaction with the peoples of the Maya lowlands, consisted
of a grid of narrow strips of earth, separated from each other by channels. Mud from
the channels, heaped onto the strips, replenished their fertility. A wooden foot plow
with perhaps a bronze blade seems to have been the main farming implement, although hard archaeological proof is still elusive. By 500, the combined sustenance
from fishing, hunting, farming, and herding supported dozens of villages and, by
700, the city of Tiwanaku and its 20,000 inhabitants.

Coordinated with the calendar as well as life-cycle events (such as initiation
rituals), ceremonial feasts brought together elite lineages and clients, or ordinary
craftspeople and villagers. Elites and clients cohered through **reciprocity**, that is,
communal labor for the construction of the ceremonial centers and elaborate feasting, in which elite wealth was expended for the ceremonial leveling of status differences. Until shortly before the end of the state it does not appear that this reciprocity
gave way to more forcible ways of allocating labor through conscription or taxation.

Reciprocity: In its
basic form, an informal
agreement among people
according to which a
gift or an invitation has
to be returned after
a reasonable amount
of time; in the pre-
Columbian Americas,
an arrangement of feasts
instead of taxes between
ruling classes and
subjects in a state.

Expansion and Conquest   Like Tiwanaku, the core region around the southern arm of Lake Titicaca housed a set of related but competing elite–client hierarchies. Ruling clans with intermediate leaders and ordinary farmers in the villages
comprised a state capable of imposing military power beyond the center. But coun-
terbalancing clans at the head of similar hierarchies prevented the rise of dynasties that would command permanent, unified central administrations and military
forces. The projection of power over the northern lake, therefore, was not primarily

of a military nature. Whatever the military expeditions by ruling clans outside the city, the primary form of Tiwanaku authority was the unrivaled prestige of its ceremonial center. This center attracted pilgrims not merely from the northern lake but also from more distant regions. Pilgrims partaking in Tiwanaku feasting ceremonies can be considered as extensions of the reciprocity and clientage system of the ruling classes and, hence, of Tiwanaku power.

More direct expressions of Tiwanaku influence beyond Lake Titicaca were armed trading caravans and the foundation of colonies in the western valleys of the Andes. Merchants accompanied by warriors and llama drivers crossed multiple polities in order to exchange textiles and ceramics for basalt cores in the south, metal ingots and obsidian cores in the north, and coca leaves and other psychotropic substances in the east, often hundreds of miles away. Colonies were more tangible forms of power projection, especially those established in the Moquegua [Mow-KAY-gah] valley 200 miles or 10–12 days of walking to the west. Here, at some 2,800 feet above sea level, Tiwanaku emigrants established villages, which sent their corn or beer to the capital in return for salt, as well as stone and obsidian tools. Although overall less militarily inclined than the Mesoamerican states of the same time period, Tiwanaku wielded a visible influence over southern Peru (see Map 15.2).

The Expanding City-State of Wari

Little is known about early settlements in central Peru, some 450 miles or 3–4 weeks of foot travel north from Tiwanaku. The state of Wari emerged around 600

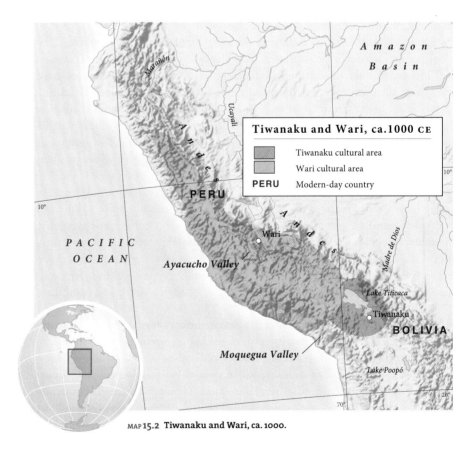

MAP 15.2 **Tiwanaku and Wari, ca. 1000.**

from a number of small polities organized around ceremonial centers. Expansion to the south put Wari into direct contact with Tiwanaku. The two states came to some form of mutual accommodation, and it appears that neither embarked on an outright conquest of the other. Their military postures remained limited to their regional spheres of influence.

Origins and Expansion

Wari was centered on the Ayacucho valley, a narrow plain in the highlands of northern Peru. Here, the land between the two chains of the Andes is mountainous, interspersed with valleys and rivers flowing to the Pacific or the Amazon. The elevation of 8,000 feet in the Ayacucho valley allowed for the cultivation of potatoes as well as corn and cotton. In the course of the seventh century, Wari grew into a city of 30,000 inhabitants and brought a number of neighboring cities under its control. It also pushed for an enlargement of the agricultural base through the expansion of terrace farming. Like Tiwanaku, Wari eventually became the center of a developed urbanism and a diversified agriculture.

In addition to maintaining control over the cities in its vicinity, Wari employed architects who constructed new towns. These planned centers included plazas, housing for laborers, and halls for feasting. Outside the core area, Wari elites established colonies, some of which appeared—even if only briefly around 800—in northern Peru as far as 450 miles away. It appears that Wari exercised much stronger political control over the elites of its core region than Tiwanaku and was more active in founding colonies.

The Wari–Tiwanaku Frontier

Early on, Wari established a colony upstream in the Moquegua valley on southern Peru's west coast, some 100 miles away. The settlers built extensive terraces and canals together with protective walls and settlements on mountain peaks. This building activity coincided with the Tiwanaku establishment of downstream farming colonies. It is possible that there was considerable tension with Tiwanaku during the initial period (650–800) over the division of water between the two colonies. But during 800–1000 the two agricultural communities developed closer ties, with indications that the two local elites engaged in a peaceful sharing of the water resources and common feasting activities. Very likely, the Moquegua valley was politically so far on the periphery of both states that neither had the means to impose itself on the other.

At its origins, Wari was an expanding state very similar to Tiwanaku. Both were governed by elite clans under leaders who derived their strength from reciprocal patron–client organizations binding leaders to farmers and craftspeople. Extensive feasts strengthened the bond. Something must have happened to erode this bond, however, since there is evidence of increased internal tension after 950 in the two states. Groups arose which defaced sculptures, destroyed portals, and burned down edifices. Somehow, crowds previously happy to uphold elite control in return for participation in the lavish feasts (provided by the elites) must have become angry at these elites, their ceremonies, and the temple sculptures. Scholars have argued that it was perhaps the fragility of power based on an increasingly unequal reciprocity that caused the rift between elites and subjects.

Why would elites allow reciprocity to be weakened to such a degree that it became a sham? Previous generations of scholars argued that climatic change deprived the elites of the wherewithal to throw large feasts. In the case of Tiwanaku there is evidence that a drought hit the high plain beginning in 1040, but this date is clearly a century too late for an explanation. A more convincing explanation suggests environmental degradation as the result of agricultural expansion. Land that was only marginally suitable for agriculture was exhausted and could no longer sustain a vastly increased population, as with the late Maya kingdoms. Unfortunately, there is still too little evidence to extend the environmental argument from the Maya kingdoms to the Andes highland and sierra. An ultimate explanation for the disintegration of the expanding states of Tiwanaku and Wari thus remains elusive.

American Empires: Aztec and Inca Origins and Dominance

Expanding and conquering states in the Andes and Mesoamerica gave way in the early fifteenth century to empires. At this time, demographic growth and the evolution of militarism in the Americas reached a point of transition to the pattern of imperial political formation. Conquering states had been cities with ceremonial centers, which dominated agricultural hinterlands and projected their prestige or power across regions. By contrast, the Aztec (1427–1521) and Inca (1438–1533) Empires in Mesoamerica and the Andes were states with capitals and ceremonial centers, vastly larger tributary hinterlands, and armies capable of engaging in campaigns at distances twice (or more) as far away than previous states. As in Eurasia, they were centralized multireligious, multiethnic, and multilinguistic polities: empires in every sense of the word.

The Aztec Empire of Mesoamerica

Hailing from the mountainous semidesert regions of northwest Mexico, the ancestors of the Aztecs entered history as migrants in search of a better life. They found this life as conquerors of the Valley of Mexico, the site of today's Mexico City (after the drainage of most of the valley). In the course of the fifteenth century they conquered an empire that eventually encompassed Mesoamerica from the Pacific to the Gulf of Mexico and from the middle of modern northern Mexico to the Isthmus of Panama.

Settlement in the Mexican Valley
The Aztecs traced their origins back to a founding myth. According to this myth, the first Aztec was one of seven brothers born on an island in a lake or in a mountain cave, "150 leagues" (450 miles) northwest of the Valley of Mexico. The distance, recorded by Spaniards in the sixteenth century, can be interpreted as corresponding to a mountain in the modern state of Guanajuato [Goo-wa-na-hoo-WA-to]. This Aztec ancestor and his descendants left their mythical homeland as foragers dressed in skins and lacking agriculture and urban civilization. Their hunter–warrior patron god Huitzilpochtli [Hoo-it-zil-POSHT-lee] promised to guide them to a promised land of plenty.

After settling for a while in Tula (claimed later as a place of heritage), their god urged the foragers to move on to the Valley of Mexico. Here, an eagle perched on a cactus commanded the Aztecs to settle and build a temple to their god. In this temple, they were to nourish him with the sacrificial blood of humans captured in war. Like many peoples in Eurasia as well as the contemporary Incas, the Aztecs contrasted their later empire and its glory with a myth of humble beginnings and long periods of wandering toward an eventual promised land.

The historical record in the Valley of Mexico becomes clearer in the fourteenth century. In the course of this period, the Aztecs appeared as clients of two Toltec-descended overlords in states on the southwestern shore. Here, they created the two islands of Tenochtitlán [Te-notsh-tit-LAN] and Tlatelolco [Tla-te-LOL-co], founded a city with a ceremonial center on Tenochtitlán, engaged in farming, and rendered military service to their overlords. Thanks to successes on the battlefield, Aztec leaders were able to marry into the elites of the neighboring city-states and gained the right to have their own ruler ("speaker," *tlatloani* [Tla-tlo-AH-nee]) presiding over a council of leading members of the elite and priests. Toward the end of the fourteenth century, an emerging Aztec elite was firmly integrated with the ruling classes of many of the two dozen or so city-states in and around the valley.

The Rise of the Empire After a successful rebellion in 1428 of a triple alliance among the Aztec city-state of Tenochtitlán and two other vassal states against the reigning city-state in the Valley of Mexico, the Aztec leader Itzcóatl [Its-CO-aw] (r. 1428–1440) emerged as the dominant figure. Itzcóatl and his three successors, together with the rulers of the two allied states, expanded their city-states on the two islands and the shore through conquests into a full-fledged empire. Tenochtitlán, on one of the islands, became the capital, growing into an empire that consisted of a set of six "inner provinces" in the Valley of Mexico. Local elites were left in place, but they were required to attend ceremonies in Tenochtitlán, bring and receive gifts, leave their sons as hostages, and intermarry with the elites of the triple alliance. Commoner farmers outside the cities had to provide tributes in the form of foodstuffs and labor services, making the imperial core self-sufficient.

After the middle of the fifteenth century, the triple alliance conquered a set of 55 city-states outside the valley as "outer provinces." It created an imperial polity from the Pacific to the Gulf, from Tarasco, 200 miles to the northwest, to Oaxaca, over 500 miles to the south (see Map 15.3). This state was now far more centralized than the preceding Teotihuacán and Toltec city-states. In this empire, local ruling families with their ceremonial centers and gods were generally left in place, but commoners had to produce tributes in the form of raw materials or lightweight processed and manufactured goods.

In some provinces, Aztec governors replaced the rulers; in most others, Aztec tribute collectors (supported by troops) held local rulers in check and supervised the transportation of the tributes by porters to the valley. Reciprocity, once of central

List of Tributes Owed to the Aztecs. The list includes quantities of cotton and wool textiles, clothes, headgear with feathers, and basketry. The Aztecs did not continue the complex syllabic script of the Maya but used instead images, including persons with speech bubbles, for communication. Spanish administrators and monks who copied the Aztec manuscripts added their own explanations to keep track of Native American tributes.

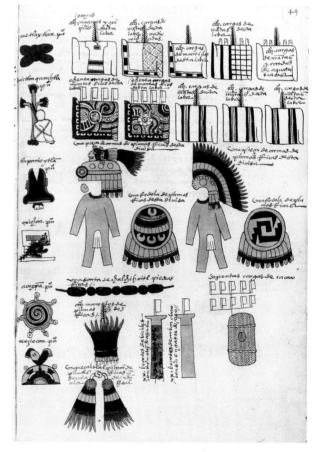

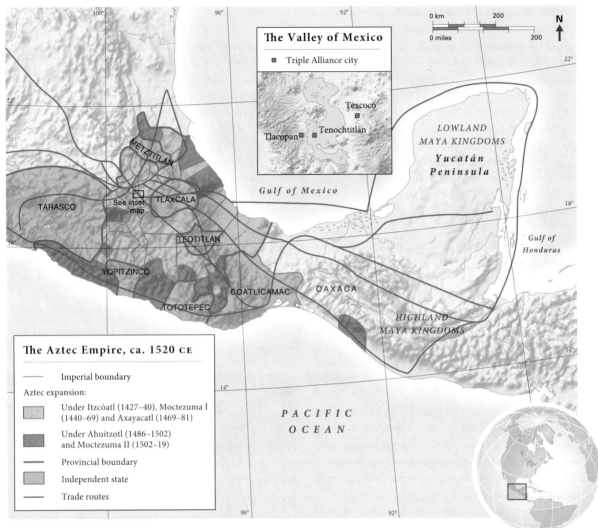

The Valley of Mexico
■ Triple Alliance city

Texcoco

Tlacopan ■   ■ Tenochtitlán

LOWLAND
MAYA KINGDOMS
*Yucatán
Peninsula*

Gulf of Mexico

METZTITLAN

TARASCO   See inset
map   TLAXCALA

*Gulf of
Honduras*

TEOTITLAN

YOPITZINCO

COATLICAMAC   OAXACA

TOTOTEPEC

*HIGHLAND
MAYA KINGDOMS*

The Aztec Empire, ca. 1520 CE

───── Imperial boundary

Aztec expansion:

Under Itzcóatl (1427–40), Moctezuma I
(1440–69) and Axayacatl (1469–81)

Under Ahuitzotl (1486–1502)
and Moctezuma II (1502–19)

───── Provincial boundary

Independent state

───── Trade routes

*PACIFIC
OCEAN*

MAP 15.3 **The Aztec Empire, ca. 1520.**

importance in Mesoamerica, continued on a grand scale but was now clearly subordinate to military considerations.

The resulting multiethnic, multireligious, and multilinguistic empire of eventually some 19 million inhabitants was still a work in progress in the early sixteenth century when the Spanish arrived. Right in the middle of the empire, just 50 miles east of the Valley of Mexico, the large state of Tlaxcala [Tlash-KAH-lah], Nahuatl-speaking like the Aztecs, held out in opposition, together with multiple enemy states on the periphery. Although the ruling elites of the triple alliance did everything to expand, including even inviting enemy rulers to their festivities in order to secure their loyalty through gestures of reciprocity, pockets of anti-Aztec states survived and eventually became crucial allies of the Spanish, providing the latter's tiny military forces with a critical mass of fighters.

Some outer provinces possessed strategic importance, with Aztec colonies implanted to prepare for eventual conquest of remaining enemies outside the empire.

The most relentlessly pursued policy of continued expansion of Aztec central control was the threat of warfare, for the purpose of capturing rebels or enemies as prisoners of war to be sacrificed to the gods in the ceremonial centers. This fear-inducing tactic—or "power propaganda"—was an integral innovation in the imperialism of the Aztecs.

Aztec Weapons. Aztec weapons were well-crafted hardwood implements with serrated obsidian edges, capable of cutting through metal, including iron. As slashing weapons they were highly effective in close combat.

The Military Forces   The triple alliance ruled a Nahuatl-speaking population of some 1.5 million inhabitants in the core provinces of the Valley of Mexico. This number yielded a maximum of a quarter of a million potential soldiers, taking into consideration that most soldiers were farmers with agricultural obligations. From this large number of adult males, the Aztecs assembled units of 8,000 troops each, which they increased as the need arose. Initially, the army was recruited from among the elite of the Aztecs and their allies. But toward the middle of the fifteenth century, Aztec rulers set up a military school system for the sons of the elite plus those commoners who were to become priests. A parallel school system for the sons of commoners, aged 15–20 years, also included military training. After graduation, recruits began as porters, carrying supplies for the combat troops—an Aztec innovation which considerably enlarged the marching range of armies on campaign. Soldiers rose in the army hierarchy on the basis of merit, particularly their success in the capture of enemies for future sacrifice.

The Aztecs inherited the weaponry and armor of the Toltecs but also made some important innovations. The bow and arrow, which arrived from northwest Mexico at the end of Toltec rule, became a standard weapon in Aztec armies. In addition, perhaps as late as the fifteenth century, the Aztecs developed the three-foot obsidian-spiked broadsword, derived from the Toltec short sword, in order to enhance the latter's slashing force. As a result, clubs, maces, and axes declined in importance in the Aztec arsenal. Thrusting spears, dart throwers, and slings continued to be used as standard weapons. Body armor, consisting of quilted, sleeveless cotton shirts, thick cotton helmets, and round wooden or cane shields, was adopted from the Toltecs. With the arrival of the Aztecs, the Americas had acquired the heaviest infantry weaponry in their history, reflective of the intensity of militarism reached in their society—a militarism which was also typical of the earlier empires of the beginning Iron Age in the Middle East.

The Inca Empire of the Andes

After the disintegration of Tiwanaku and Wari around 1100, the central Andes returned to the traditional politics of local chiefdoms in small city-states with ceremonial centers and agricultural hinterlands. The best-known city-state was Chimú on the Peruvian coast, with its capital of Chan Chan numbering 30,000 inhabitants. Tiwanaku cultural traditions, however, remained dominant and were expressed in religious ceremonies, textile motifs, and ceramic styles.

Given the fierce competition among the pilgrimage centers, insecurity was rampant during the period 1100–1400, with particular influence granted to charismatic military leaders who could project military force and pacify the land. After a gestation period during the fourteenth century, the southern Peruvian city-state of Cuzco with its Inca elite emerged in the early fifteenth century at the head of a highly militaristic, conquering polity. Within another century, the Incas had established an empire, called "Tawantinsuyu" [Ta-wan-tin-SOO-yuh] (Quechua, "Four Regions"), symbolizing its geographical expanse. It stretched from Ecuador in the north to central Chile in the south, with extensions into the tropical upper Amazon region and western Argentinean steppes (see Map 15.4).

As in the case of the Aztecs, the founding myth of the Incas involves a cave, an island, and a promised land of rich agriculture. In one version, the creator god Viracocha [Vee-rah-KOT-shah] summoned four brothers and four sisters from caves "seven leagues" (21 miles) from Cuzco to the south, pairing them as couples and promising them a land of plenty. They would find this land when a golden rod, to be used on their wanderings, would get stuck in the soil. Alternatively, the sun god Inti [IN-tee] did the pairing of the couples on an island in Lake Titicaca and thereby bestowed the glory of Tiwanaku on them, before sending them with the golden rod to their promised land. Cuzco, where the rod plunged into the fertile soil, was settled land however; and a war ensued in which the Incas drove out the previous farmers.

In the fourteenth century, Cuzco became a serious contender in the city-state competition. Like Wari, Cuzco was located at a highland elevation of 11,300 feet between the two Andes chains of southern Peru, roughly one-third of the way from Lake Titicaca north to Wari. Eight rulers (*curacas* [koo-RA-kas]) are said to have succeeded each other in the consolidation of Cuzco as a regional power. Although their names are recorded, events are hazy and dates are missing altogether. Firm historical terrain is reached with the ninth ruler, Pachacuti (r. 1438–1471), who overthrew his father and might have appropriated some of the latter's political accomplishments. The history of the Incas after 1438 is known much better, primarily because of the memories of the grandchildren of the original Inca conquerors, recorded by the Spanish who defeated them in turn.

Imperial Expansion   The system of reciprocity that characterized earlier Mesoamerican and Andean history continued under the Incas but was also, as in the case of Aztecs, decisively cast in the mold of power-enforced unilateralism. *Ayllu* [AY-yoo], the Quechua term for a household with an ancestral lineage, implied mutual obligations among groups of households, neighborhoods, villages, and city-states. To negotiate these obligations, society—from households to city-states—was divided into halves with roughly equal reciprocities. On the elite level, there were two sets of reciprocities, the first within two main branches of the elite and the second between the two branches of the elite and the subjects. The most important social expression of reciprocity remained the feast. In the Incan Empire, the state collected considerably more from the subject *ayllus* than Tiwanaku and Wari had done, but whether it returned comparable amounts through feasts and celebrations was a matter of contention, often leading to armed rebellion.

The earliest conquests under Pachacuti were toward the near south around Lake Titicaca, as well as the agriculturally rich lands north of the former Wari state. Thereafter, in the later fifteenth century, the Incas expanded 1,300 miles northward to southern Ecuador and 1,500 miles southward to Chile. The final provinces, added in the early sixteenth century, were in northern Ecuador as well as on the eastern slopes of the Andes, from the upper Amazon to western Argentina. The capital, Cuzco, which counted some 100,000 inhabitants in the early sixteenth century, was laid out in a cross-shaped grid of four streets leading out into the suburbs. Symbolically, the capital reached out to the four regions of the empire—coast, north, south, and Amazon rain forest.

Administration   Ethnic Inca governors administered the four regions, which were subdivided into a total of some 80 provinces, each again with an Inca subgovernor. Most provinces were composites of former city-states, which remained under their local elites but had to accept a unique decimal system of population organization imposed by the Inca rulers. According to this system, members of the local elites commanded 10,000, 1,000, 100, and 10 household or *ayllu* heads for the purpose of recruiting the manpower responsible for the *mit'a* [MIT-ah] ("to take a turn," in reference to service obligations rotating among the subjects). The services, which subjects owed the empire as equivalents of taxes, were in farming, herding, manufacturing, military service, and portage. In its structure it was not unlike the Ming and Qing Chinese systems of local organization called *baojia*.

The mit'a was perhaps the single most important innovation the Incas contributed to the history of the Americas. In contrast to the Aztecs, who shipped taxes in kind to their capital by boat, the Incas had no efficient means of transportation for long distances. The only way to make use of the taxes in kind was to store them locally as provisions for visiting administrators and soldiers, apart from the traditional feasting in the villages. The Incas built tens of thousands of storehouses everywhere in their empire, requiring subjects to deliver a portion of their harvests, animal products, and domestically produced goods under mit'a obligations to the nearest storehouse in their vicinity. These supplies were available to officials and troops and enabled the Incas to conduct military campaigns far from Cuzco without the need for foraging among local farmers. In addition, it was through the mit'a that quotas of laborers were raised for the construction of inns, roads, ceremonial centers, palaces, terraces, and irrigation canals, often far away from the urban center. Finally, mit'a provided laborers for mines, quarries, state and temple farms, and colonies. No form of labor or service went untaxed.

To keep track of mit'a obligations, officials passed bundles of knotted cord (**khipu** [KEE-poo]) upward from level to level in the imperial administration. The

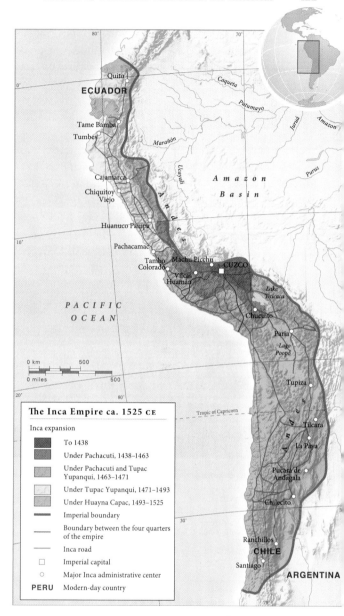

MAP 15.4 **The Inca Empire, ca. 1525.**

The Inca Empire ca. 1525 CE

Inca expansion

- To 1438
- Under Pachacuti, 1438–1463
- Under Pachacuti and Tupac Yupanqui, 1463–1471
- Under Tupac Yupanqui, 1471–1493
- Under Huayna Capac, 1493–1525
- Imperial boundary
- Boundary between the four quarters of the empire
- Inca road
- □ Imperial capital
- ○ Major Inca administrative center
- **PERU** Modern-day country

Khipu: Bundles of knotted cords used by Andean peoples for record keeping.

Inca Roads. Inca roads were paths reserved for runners and the military. They were built on beds of rocks and rubble and connected strategic points in the most direct line possible.

numbers of knots on each cord in the bundles contained information on population figures and service obligations. As discussed in Chapter 5, the use of khipus was widespread in the Andes long before the Inca and can be considered as the Andean equivalent of a communication system. The only innovation contributed by the Incas seems to have been the massive scale on which these cord bundles were generated and employed. Unfortunately, all modern attempts to decipher them have so far failed, and thus, it is impossible to accurately outline the full picture of Inca service allocations.

Military Organization   Perhaps the most important mit'a obligation which subject households owed to the Inca in the conquest phase of the empire was the service of young, able-bodied men in the military. Married men 25–30 years old were foot soldiers, often accompanied by wives and children; unmarried men 18–25 years of age served as porters or messengers. As in the Aztec Empire, administrators made sure that enough laborers remained in the villages to take care of their other obligations of farming, herding, transporting, and manufacturing. Sources report armies in the range of 35,000–140,000. Intermediate commanders came from the local and regional elites, and the top commanders were members of the upper and lower Inca ruling elites.

Inca weaponry was comparable to that of the Aztecs, consisting of bows and arrows, dart throwers, slings, clubs with spiked bronze heads, wooden broadswords, bronze axes, and bronze-tipped javelins. Using Bolivian tin, Inca smiths were able to make a much harder and more widely useful bronze than was possible with earlier techniques. The Incas lacked the Aztec obsidian-serrated swords but used a snare (which the Aztecs did not possess) with attached stone or bronze weights to entangle the enemy's legs. Protective armor consisted of quilted cotton shirts, copper breastplates, cane helmets, and shields. These types of weapons and armor were widely found among the Incas and their enemies. The advantage enjoyed by the Incas resulted from the sheer massiveness of their weapons and supplies, procured from craftspeople through the mit'a and stored in strategically located armories.

During the second half of the fifteenth century the Incas turned from conquest to consolidation. Faced at that time with a number of rebellions, they deemphasized the decimal draft and recruited longer-serving troops from among a smaller number of select, trusted peoples. These troops garrisoned the forts distributed throughout the empire. They also were part of the settler colonies implanted in rebellious provinces and in border regions. The fiercest resistance came from the people of the former Tiwanaku state and from the northeast Peruvian provinces, areas with long state traditions of their own. Since elite infighting also became more pronounced toward the end of the fifteenth century, personal guards recruited from non-Inca populations and numbering up to 7,000 soldiers accompanied many leading ruling-class members. The professionalization of the Inca army, however, lagged behind that of the Aztecs since the Incas did not have military academies open to subjects.

Communications   Although they lacked the military professionalization of the Aztecs, the Incas created an imperial communication and logistics structure that was unparalleled in the Americas. Early on, the Incas systematically improved on the road network that they inherited from Tiwanaku, Wari, and other states. Two parallel trunk roads extended from Cuzco nearly the entire length of the empire in both southerly and northerly directions. One followed the coast and western slopes of the western Andes chain; the other led through the mountain lands, valleys, and high plains between the western and eastern Andes chain. In numerous places, additional highways connected the two trunk roads. Suspension bridges made of thick ropes crossed gorges, while rafts were used for crossing rivers. The roads, 3–12 feet wide, crossed the terrain as directly as possible, often requiring extensive grounding, paving, staircasing, and tunneling. In many places, the 25,000-mile road network still exists today, attesting to the engineering prowess of the Incas.

The roads were reserved for troops, officials, and runners carrying messages. For their convenience, every 15 miles, or at the end of a slow 1-day journey, an inn provided accommodation. Larger armies stopped at barracks-like constructions or pitched tents on select campgrounds. Like the Romans, and despite the fact that they did not have wheeled transport, the Incas were well aware how crucial paved and well-supplied roads were for infantry soldiers.

Imperial Society and Culture

As Mesoamerica and the Andes entered their imperial age, cosmopolitan capitals with monumental ceremonial centers and palaces emerged. The sizes of both capitals and monuments were visual expressions of the exalted power that the rulers claimed. Almost daily ceremonies and rituals, accompanied by feasts, further underscore the power claims of rulers. These ceremonies and rituals expressed the shamanic and polytheistic heritage but were modified to impress on enemies and subjects alike the irresistible might of the empires.

Imperial Capitals: Tenochtitlán and Cuzco

In the fifteenth century, the Aztec and Inca capitals were among the largest cities of the world, encompassing between 100,000 and 200,000 inhabitants. Both cities maintained their high degree of urbanism through a complex command system of labor, services, and goods. Although their monumental architecture followed different artistic traditions, both emphasized platforms and sanctuaries atop large pyramid-like structures as symbols of elevated power as well as closeness to the astral gods, especially those associated with the sun and Venus.

Aqueduct from the Western Hills to Tenochtitlán. This aqueduct, still standing today, provided fresh water to the palace and mansions of the center of the island, to be used as drinking water and for washing.

Tenochtitlán as an Urban Metropolis   More than half of the approximately 1.5 million people living during the fifteenth century in the Valley of Mexico were urban dwellers, including elites, priests, administrators, military officers, merchants, traders, craftspeople, messengers, servants, and laborers. Tenochtitlán was among the 10 largest world cities of the fifteenth century. Such an extraordinary concentration of urban citizens was unique in the agrarian world prior to the industrialization of Europe (beginning around 1800), when cities usually held no more than 10 percent of the total population (see Map 15.5).

The center of Tenochtitlán, on the southern island, was a large platform where the Aztec settlers had driven pilings into marshy ground and heaped rocks and rubble. In an enclosure on this platform were the main pyramid, with temples to the Aztec gods on top, and a series of smaller ceremonial centers. Adjacent to this on the platform were a food market and a series of palaces of the ruling elite, which included guest quarters, administrative offices, storage facilities for tributes, kitchens, the high court for the elite and the court of appeals for commoners, the low court for civil cases, workshops for craftspeople, the prison, and councils for teachers and the military. Large numbers of Aztecs and visitors assembled each day to pay respect to the ruler and to trade in the market in preparation for assemblies and feasts.

MAP **15.5** Tenochtitlán and the Valley of Mexico.

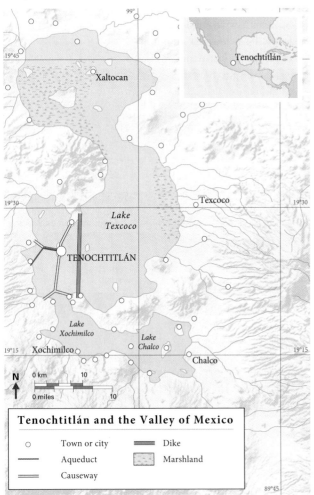

Tenochtitlán and the Valley of Mexico

○	Town or city	▬	Dike
—	Aqueduct	▦	Marshland
═	Causeway		

In 1473, the southern island was merged with the northern island, to form a single unit. At the center of the northern island was a platform that contained the principal market of the combined islands. This daily market attracted as many as 40,000 farmers, craftspeople, traders, porters, and laborers on the main market day. The sophistication of the market was comparable to that of any market in Eurasia during the fifteenth century.

A number of causeways crossed the capital and linked it with the lakeshore. People also traveled inside the city on a number of main and branch canals. Dikes with sluices on the east side regulated both the water level and the salinity of the lake water around the islands. The runoff during the summer rainy season from the southwestern mountains provided freshwater to lighten the lake's salinity, and the eastern dikes kept out salt water from the rest of the lake. Potable water arrived from the shore via an aqueduct on one of the western causeways. This aqueduct served mostly the ceremonial center and palace precinct, but branches brought potable water to a number of elite residences nearby as well. Professional water carriers took freshwater to commoners in the various quarters of the city; professional waste removers collected human waste from urban residences and took it to farmers for fertilizer. In short, Tenochtitlán possessed a fully developed urban infrastructure comparable to the best amenities found elsewhere in the world at that time.

The two city centers—the pyramid and palaces in the south and the market in the north—were surrounded by dozens of residential city quarters. Built on a layer of firm ground, many of these quarters were inhabited by craftspeople of a shared profession, who practiced their crafts in their residences. As discussed earlier in this chapter, merchants occupied a privileged position between the elite and the commoners. As militarily trained organizers of large caravans of porters, the merchants also provided the Aztec capital with luxury goods. Depending on their social rank, craftspeople occupied residences of larger or smaller size, usually grouped into compounds of related families. The rooms of the houses surrounded a central patio on which most of the household activities took place—an architectural preference common to Mesoamerica and the Andes, as well as the Middle East and Mediterranean.

Residents of quarters farther away from the center were farmers. In these quarters, making up nearly two-thirds of Tenochtitlán's surface, families engaged in intensive farming. Here, a grid of canals encased small, rectangular islands devoted to housing compounds and/or farming. People moved within these barrios by boat. Since the Valley of Mexico received year-round rains that were often insufficient for dry farming, a raised-field system prevailed, whereby farmers dredged the canals, heaped the fertile mud on top of the rectangular islands, and added waste from their households or brought by boat from the urban neighborhoods. In contrast to the luxurious palaces of the elite, housing for farmers consisted of plastered huts made of cane, wood, and reeds. As in all agrarian societies, farmers—subject to high taxes or rents—were among the poorest folk.

On the surface of the raised beds, or **chinampas**, farmers grew corn, beans, squash, amaranth, and peppers. These seed plants were supplemented by maguey [mag-AY], a large cactus related to the agave. This evergreen plant grew in poor soils; had a large root system, which helped in stabilizing the ground; and produced fiber useful for weaving and pulp useful for making *pulque* [POOL-key], a fermented drink. To plant these crops in the soft soil, a digging stick, slightly broadened at one end, was sufficient. Regular watering made multicropping of seed plants possible. Trees, planted at the edges, firmed up the islands against water erosion.

Ownership of the *chinampas* was vested in clans, which, under neighborhood leaders, were responsible for the adjudication of land allocations and disputes as well as the payment of taxes in kind to the elite. But there were also members of the elite who, as absentee owners, possessed estates and employed managers to collect rents from the farmers. Whether there was a trend from taxes to rents (that is, a central tax system to a decentralized landowner class) is unknown. Given the high productivity of raised-field farming, which was similar to that of the Eurasian agrarian–urban centers, such a trend would not have been surprising.

Chinampas: Mesoamerican agricultural practice by which farmers grew crops upon small, human-made islands in Lake Texcoco.

Cuzco as a Ceremonial-Administrative City The site of the Inca city of Cuzco was an elongated triangle formed by the confluence of two rivers. At one end, opposite the confluence, was a hill with a number of structures, including the imperial armory, and a temple dedicated to the sun god. Enormous, zigzagging walls followed the contours of the hill. The walls were built with stone blocks weighing up to 100 tons and cut so precisely that no mortar was needed, a technique which the Incas adopted from Tiwanaku.

Cuzco Stone Masonry. Inspired by the masonry of the people of Tiwanaku, the Inca built imposing structures with much larger blocks of limestone or granite. To cut the blocks, masons used copper and bronze chisels, making use of natural fissures in the stone.

Below, on the plain leading to the confluence, the city was laid out in a grid pattern. The residents of the city, all belonging to the upper and lower Inca ruling class, lived in adobe houses arranged in a block and courtyard pattern similar to that of Wari. Several squares and temples within the city served as ceremonial centers. One plaza contained a platform, with the imperial throne and a pillar, placed symbolically atop what the Incas considered the earth's center or navel. The Coricancha [Co-ri-CAN-tsha], the city's main temple, stood near the confluence of the rivers. This temple was a walled compound comprised of six buildings set around a courtyard. Chambers in these buildings contained the Inca gods and goddesses as well as the divine statues or sacred objects confiscated from the provinces. Each year priests of the empire's ceremonial centers sent one such sacred object to the Coricancha, to document their obedience to the central Inca temple (see Map 15.6).

Across the rivers, in separate suburbs, were settlements for commoners with markets and storehouses. They were surrounded by fields, terraces, and irrigation canals. In the fields, interspersed stone pillars and shrines were aligned on sight lines radiating from the Coricancha, tying the countryside closely to the urban center. These alignments were reminiscent of the Nazca lines drawn half a millennium earlier in southern Peru (Chapter 9). Farther away were imperial estates with unfree laborers from outside the *mit'a* system and its feasting reciprocities. In contrast to the Aztec elite, which allowed meritorious generals to rise in the hierarchy, the Inca elite remained exclusionary, allowing no commoners to reside in Cuzco.

Power and Its Cultural Expressions

Ruling elites, as repeatedly emphasized in this chapter, put a strong emphasis on the display of their power during the period 600–1500. This was particularly true with the Aztecs and Incas during the fifteenth century. Among these displays were human sacrifices, mausoleums, and mummy burials. Although all three involved changes in social relations, these changes were accommodated in the existing overall religious culture.

Inca Ruling Class Gender Relations   The ruling classes in the Inca Empire displayed their power in several ways. Among the examples were the "Houses of Chosen Women" in Cuzco and provincial colonies. The greatest honor for Inca girls was to enter, at age 10–12, into the service of these houses. An inspector from Cuzco made regular visits to the villages of the empire to select attractive young girls for the service. The girls were marched to the capital or the colonies, where they were divided according to beauty, skills, and social standing. These houses had female instructors who provided the girls with a 4-year education in cooking, beer making, weaving, and officiating in the rituals and ceremonies of the Inca religion. After their graduation, the young women became virgin temple priestesses, were given in marriage to non-Incas honored for service to the ruler, or became palace servants, musicians, or concubines of the Inca elite. The collection of the girl tribute was separate from the reciprocity system. As such, it was an act of assigning gender roles in an emerging social hierarchy defined by power inequalities.

MAP 15.6 **Cuzco.**

Traditionally, gender roles were less strictly divided than in Eurasia. The horticultural form of agriculture in Mesoamerica and the Andes gave males fewer opportunities to accumulate wealth and power than plow agriculture did in Eurasia. Hoes and foot plows distinguished men and women less from each other than plows and teams of oxen or horses did. Nevertheless, it comes as no surprise that the gradual agrarian–urban diversification of society, even if it was slower in the Americas than in Eurasia, proceeded along similar paths of increasing male power concentration in villages, ceremonial centers, temple cities, conquering states, and empires. Emphasizing gender differences, therefore, should be viewed as a characteristic phenomenon arising in imperial contexts.

Inca Mummy Veneration   Other houses in Cuzco were ghostly residences in which scores of attendants and servants catered to what were perceived as the earthly needs of deceased, mummified Inca emperors and their principal wives. During the mummification process attendants removed the cadaver's internal organs, placed them in special containers, and desiccated the bodies until they were completely mummified. Servants dressed the mummies (*mallquis* [MAY-kees]) in their finest clothing and placed them back into their residences amid their possessions, as if they had never died. The mummies received daily meals, and their

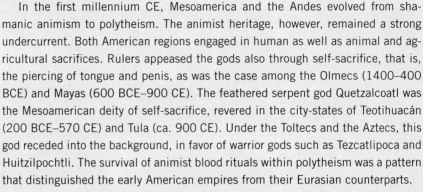

Patterns Up Close | Human Sacrifice and Propaganda

In the first millennium CE, Mesoamerica and the Andes evolved from shamanic animism to polytheism. The animist heritage, however, remained a strong undercurrent. Both American regions engaged in human as well as animal and agricultural sacrifices. Rulers appeased the gods also through self-sacrifice, that is, the piercing of tongue and penis, as was the case among the Olmecs (1400–400 BCE) and Mayas (600 BCE–900 CE). The feathered serpent god Quetzalcoatl was the Mesoamerican deity of self-sacrifice, revered in the city-states of Teotihuacán (200 BCE–570 CE) and Tula (ca. 900 CE). Under the Toltecs and the Aztecs, this god receded into the background, in favor of warrior gods such as Tezcatlipoca and Huitzilpochtli. The survival of animist blood rituals within polytheism was a pattern that distinguished the early American empires from their Eurasian counterparts.

Whether human sacrifices were prolific under Aztec and Inca imperialism is questionable. About the same number of human victims were excavated at the Feathered Serpent Temple of Teotihuacán and at the Templo Mayor of Tenochtitlán: 137 versus 126. These numbers are minuscule in comparison to the impression

Human Sacrifice. Human sacrifice among the pre-Columbian Mesoamericans and Andeans was based on the animist concept of a shared life spirit or mind, symbolized by the life substance of blood. In the American animist-polytheistic conceptualization, the gods sacrificed their blood, or themselves altogether, during creation; rulers pierced their earlobes, tongues, or penises for blood sacrifices; and war captives lost their lives when their hearts were sacrificed.

retinues carried them around for visits to their mummified relatives. On special occasions, mummies were lined up according to rank on Cuzco's main plaza to participate in ceremonies and processions. In this way, they remained fully integrated in the daily life of the elite.

"Ghost residences" with mummies can be considered an outgrowth of the old Andean custom of mummification. This custom was widely practiced among the elites of the ceremonial centers, who, however, generally placed their ancestors in temple tombs, shrines, or caves. Mummies were also buried in cemeteries, sometimes collectively in bundles with "false heads" made of cotton. Preserving the living spaces of the deceased obviously required considerable wealth—wealth provided only by imperial regimes.

As a general phenomenon in Andean society, of course, mummies were a crucial ingredient in the religious heritage, in which strong shamanic elements survived underneath the polytheistic overlay of astral gods. In the shamanic tradition, body and spirit cohabit more or less loosely. In a trance, a shaman's mind can travel, enter the minds of other people and animals, or make room for other people's minds. Similarly, in death a person's spirit, while no longer in the body, remains nearby and therefore still needs daily nourishment in order not to be driven away. Hence, even though non-Incan Andean societies removed the dead from their daily living spaces, descendants had to visit tombs regularly with food and beer or provide buried mummies with ample victuals.

created by the Spanish conquerors and encourage doubts about the magnitude of human sacrifices in temple ceremonies. It appears that even though the Aztec and Inca ruling classes were focused on war, the ritual of human sacrifice was not as pervasive as has been widely assumed.

Could it be that there was no significant increase in human sacrifice under the Aztecs and Incas, as the self-serving Spanish conquerors alleged? Were there perhaps, instead, imperial propaganda machines in the Aztec and Inca Empires, employed in the service of conquest and consolidation—similar to those of the Assyrians and Mongols in Eurasia who sought to intimidate their enemies? In this case, the Aztec and Inca Empires would not be exceptional barbaric aberrations in world history but two typical examples of the general world-historical pattern of competitive militaristic states during the early agrarian era, using propaganda to further their imperial power.

Questions

- In examining the question of whether empires such as the Inca and the Aztec employed human sacrifice for propaganda purposes, can this practice be considered an adaptation that evolved out of earlier rituals, such as royal bloodletting?

- If the Aztec and the Inca did indeed employ human sacrifice for propaganda purposes, what does this say about the ability of these two empires to use cultural and religious practices to consolidate their power?

The expenses for the upkeep of the mummy households were the responsibility of the deceased emperor's bloodline, headed by a surviving brother. As heirs of the emperor's estate, the members of the bloodline formed a powerful clan within the ruling class. The new emperor was excluded from this estate and had to acquire his own new one in the course of his rule, a mechanism evidently designed to intensify his imperial ambitions for conquest. In the early sixteenth century, however, when it became logistically difficult to expand much beyond the enormous territory already accumulated in the Andes, this ingenious mechanism of keeping the upper and lower rungs of the ruling class united became counterproductive. Emperors lacking resources had to contend with brothers richly endowed with inherited wealth and ready to engage in dynastic warfare—as actually occurred shortly before the arrival of the Spanish (1529–1532).

Putting It All Together

During the short time of their existence, the Aztec and Inca Empires unleashed extraordinary creative energies. Sculptors, painters, and (after the arrival of the Spanish) writers recorded the traditions as well as the innovations of the fifteenth century. Aztec painters produced codices, or illustrated manuscripts, that present the divine pantheons, myths, calendars, ceremonial activities, chants, poetry, and administrative activities of their societies in exquisite and colorful detail. They fashioned these codices, using bark paper, smoothing it with plaster, and connecting the pages accordion-style. Today, only a handful of these codices survive, preserved in Mexican and European libraries.

The Aztec and Inca Empires were polities that illustrate how humans not in contact with the rest of the world and living within an environment that was different from Eurasia and Africa in many respects developed patterns of innovation that were remarkably similar. On the basis of an agriculture that eventually produced ample surpluses, humans made the same choices as their cousins in Eurasia and Africa. Specifically, in the period 600–1500, they created temple-centered city-states, just like their Sumerian and Hindu counterparts. Their military states were not unlike the Chinese warring states. And, finally, their empires—although just beginning to flourish in the Bronze Age—were comparable to those of the New Kingdom Egyptians or Assyrians. The Americas had their own unique variations of these larger historical patterns, to be sure; but they nevertheless displayed the same humanity as found elsewhere.

▶ For additional resources, including maps, primary sources, visuals, and quizzes, please go to www.oup.com/us/vonsivers. Please see the Further Resources section at the back of the book for additional readings and suggested websites.

Thinking Through Patterns

▶ **Within the patterns of states formation basic to the Americas, which types of states emerged in Mesoamerica and the Andes during the period 600–1550? What characterized these states?**

The basic pattern of state formation in the Americas was similar to that of Eurasia and Africa. Historically, it began with the transition from foraging to agriculture and settled village life. As the population increased, villages under elders became chiefdoms, which in turn became city-states with temples. As in Eurasia and Africa, American city-states often became conquering states, beginning with the Maya kingdoms and Teotihuacán. Both, however, remained small. Military states, in which ruling classes sought to expand regions, such as Tula and, to a lesser degree, Tiwanaku and Wari, were characteristic for the early part of the period 600–1550. The successors of these—the Aztec and Inca Empires—were multiethnic, multilinguistic, and multireligious polities that dominated Mesoamerica and the Andes for about a century, before the Spanish conquest brought them to a premature end.

The states of Tiwanaku and Wari had more or less cohesive ruling classes but no dynasties of rulers and centralized bureaucracies. These ruling classes and their subjects—corn and potato farmers—were integrated with each other through systems of reciprocity, that is, military protection in return for foodstuffs. They customarily rejuvenated the bonds of reciprocity in common feasts. After one or two centuries, however, tensions arose, either between stronger and weaker branches of the ruling classes or between rulers and subjects over questions of obligations and justice. When these tensions erupted into internal warfare, the states disintegrated, often in conjunction with environmental degradation and climate change.

▶ **Why did the Tiwanaku and Wari states have ruling classes but no dynasties and central bureaucracies? How were these patterns expressed in the territorial organization of these states?**

▶ **What patterns of urban life characterized the cities of Tenochtitlán and Cuzco, the capitals of the Aztec and Inca Empires? In which ways were these cities similar to those of Eurasia and Africa?**

Tenochtitlán and Cuzco, the capitals of the Aztec and Inca Empires, were two urban centers organized around temples and associated residences of the ruling dynasties and their priestly classes. They also contained large city quarters inhabited by craftspeople, specializing in the production of woven textiles, pottery, leather goods, and weapons. Large central markets provided for the exchange of foodstuffs, crafts, and imported luxury goods. Armed caravans of merchants and porters transported the luxury goods, such as cacao, feathers, obsidian, and turquoise, across hundreds of miles. Tenochtitlán had an aqueduct for the supply of drinking water, and Cuzco was traversed by a river. Both capitals had agricultural suburbs in which farmers used irrigation for the production of the basic food staples.

PART FOUR

Interactions Across the Globe

1450–1750

S tarting around 1450, important changes can be detected in the patterns of world history. The religious civilizations that emerged in the period after 600 CE continued to evolve, but the competing states that constituted these civilizations began to give way to new empires, such as the Mughals, the Ottomans, the Safavids, and the Habsburgs. China, historically an empire, had already reconstituted itself under the Ming after the collapse of the Mongol superempire that had straddled Eurasia. Finally, on the Atlantic coast, smaller European countries, such as Portugal, Spain, the Netherlands, England, and France, were creating the first global seaborne empires. Large or small, land-based or maritime, however, all of these empires employed the vitally important innovation of firearms. In addition, many reorganized themselves as *fiscal–military states* based on money economies, centralizing bureaucracies, and professional armies. Locked into far-flung competition for resources, markets, and ideological influence, they interacted with each other with increasing intensity.

While this renewal of the drive for empire among these civilizations was a significant turning point in world history, two new phenomena appeared during the three centuries in question that would have far-reaching implications. Indeed, they would ultimately provide the basis on which our modern society would be built: the New Science (or Scientific Revolution) and the Enlightenment. Attempts to found an understanding of the universe on mathematics and experimentation would lead to the primacy of science as the chief mode of interpreting the physical realm. Attempts to apply the principles of science to understanding and improving human societies would lead to the concepts of individual rights, natural law, and popular sovereignty that would become the modern legacy of the Enlightenment. The combination of these two trends would create the foundations of the *scientific–industrial society* that now dominates our modern global culture.

The process by which this took place was, of course, extremely complex, and it is impossible for us to do more than suggest some of the larger components of it here. Moreover, because of the long-standing argument in Western historiography for European "exceptionalism"—that there was something unique in the European historical experience that preordained it to rise to dominance—we must be careful to explore the various aspects of this process without sliding into easy assumptions

1440–1897
Benin Kingdom, West Africa

1492
Spanish Conquest of Granada, Expulsion of Jews, and Discovery of the Americas

ca. 1500
Beginning of Columbian Exchange

1514
Nicolaus Copernicus Formulates the Heliocentric System

1453
Ottoman Capture of Constantinople

1498
Vasco da Gama's Circumnavigation of Africa and Journey to India

1511
First African Slaves Land in Hispaniola

1517
Beginning of Martin Luther's Reformation

about their inevitability. For example, one question that suggests itself is, To what extent did the societies of western Europe (what we have termed the "religious civilization" of western Christianity) part ways with the other religious civilizations of the world? Here, the aspects of the question are tantalizingly complex and, thus, have recently been the subject of considerable debate:

- On the one hand, there appears to have been no movement comparable to that of the European Renaissance or Reformation arising during this time in the other parts of the world to create a new culture similar to that of Europe. The Middle East, India, and China for the most part continued ongoing cultural patterns, although often on considerably higher levels of refinement and sophistication. Recent scholarship on neglected cultural developments in these areas from 1450 to 1750 has provided ample proof for the continuing vitality of Islamic, Hindu, Buddhist, Confucian, and Daoist cultural traditions. Thus, former assumptions of stagnation or decline no longer seem supportable.

- On the other hand, Europe, like much of the rest of the world, remained rooted in agrarian–urban patterns until the effects of the Industrial Revolution began to be felt some time after 1800. The centuries-old patterns in which the majority of the population being in agriculture in support of cities continued unchanged. Furthermore, through nearly this entire period, China and India were more populous and at least as wealthy and diversified in their economies and social structures as their European counterparts. The "great divergence," as scholars currently refer to it, happened only *after* the Western constitutional and industrial revolutions. Nonetheless, the overall wealth of European countries involved in the conquest and exploitation of the resources of the Americas and the development of global trading systems advanced immensely—as did knowledge of the globe as a whole. Thus, while India and China had possessed these resources partially or completely already for a long time, European countries were now utilizing them at an accelerating rate. This wealth and the patterns of its acquisition and distribution would soon have far-reaching consequences.

It is important to emphasize that these developments we deem crucial today were not immediately apparent to the people living at the time. Indeed, for the great majority of people, even in 1750, much seemed to go on as before. Everywhere in the world empires continued to grow and decline, religious tensions continued to erupt into warfare, and rulers continued to ground their authority not in their peoples but in the divine. Thus, for a full understanding of world history during 1450–1750 one has to carefully balance cultural, political, social, and economic factors and constantly keep in mind that although change was certainly occurring, it was often too imperceptible for contemporaries to detect.

Thinking Like a World Historian

▶ What new and different patterns characterized the development of states and empires in the period 1450–1750?

▶ How did the emergence of fiscal–military states lead to more intensive and frequent interactions among empires in the period 1450–1750? What were the consequences of this far-flung competition for new resources and markets?

▶ How did the New Science and the Enlightenment lay the foundation for the scientific–industrial society that dominates our global culture today?

▶ To what extent did the societies of western Europe part ways with the other civilizations of the world in the period 1450–1750? Why is the notion of "exceptionalism" a problematic way to examine this question?

1521, 1533
Spanish Conquest of the Aztec and Inca Empires

1577
Matteo Ricci, First Jesuit Missionary to Arrive in China

1607
Founding of Jamestown, Virginia

1720
Edo, Capital of Japan, Becomes the World's Largest City

1542–1605
Akbar, the Most Innovative of the Mughal Rulers (India)

1604
Galileo Galilei Formulates the Mathematical Law of Falling Bodies

1687
Isaac Newton Unifies Physics and Astronomy

1736–1795
Reign of Qianlong Emperor, China

Chapter 16 1450-1650

The Ottoman–Habsburg Struggle and Western European Overseas Expansion

Al-Hasan Ibn Muhammad al-Wazzan (ca. 1494–1550) was born into a family of bureaucrats in Muslim Granada soon after the Christian conquest of this kingdom in southern Iberia in 1492. Unwilling to convert to Christianity, Hasan's family emigrated to Muslim Morocco around 1499–1500 and settled in the city of Fez. Here, Hasan received a good education in religion, law, logic, and the sciences. After completing his studies, he entered the administration of the Moroccan sultan, traveling to Sub-Saharan Africa and the Middle East on diplomatic missions.

In 1517, as he was returning home from a mission to Istanbul, Christian **corsairs** kidnapped him from his ship. Like their Muslim counterparts, these corsairs roamed the Mediterranean to capture unsuspecting travelers, whom they then held for ransom or sold into slavery. For a handsome sum of money, they turned the cultivated Hasan over to Pope Leo X (1513–1521), who

ABOVE: An officer in the army of Charles V buys the freedom of two Christian women from their Muslim captor. Painting by Jan Cornelisz Vermeyen (c.1500–1559).

ordered Hasan to convert to Christianity and baptized him with his own family name, Giovanni Leone di Medici. Hasan became known in Rome as Leo Africanus ("Leo the African"), in reference to his travels in sub-Saharan Africa. He stayed for 10 years in Italy, initially at the papal court, later as an independent scholar in Rome. During this time, he taught Arabic to Roman clergymen, compiled an Arabic–Hebrew–Latin dictionary, and wrote an essay on famous Arabs. His most memorable and enduring work was a travelogue, first composed in Arabic and later translated into Italian, *Description of Africa*, which was for many years the sole source of information about sub-Saharan Africa in the western Christian world.

After 1527, however, life became difficult in Rome. In this year, Charles V (r. 1516–1558), king of Spain and emperor of the Holy Roman Empire of Germany, invaded Italy and sacked the city. Hasan survived the sack of Rome but departed for Tunis sometime after 1531, seeking a better life in Muslim North Africa. Unfortunately, all traces of Hasan after his departure from Rome are lost. It is possible that he perished in 1535 when Charles V attacked and occupied Tunis (1535-1574), although it is generally assumed that he lived there until around 1550. Around 1531, Leo traveled to Tunis, where he perhaps lived until around 1550.

The world in which Hasan lived and traveled was a Muslim–Christian world composed of the Middle East, North Africa, and Europe. Muslims on the Iberian Peninsula and in the Balkans formed a bracket around this world, with the western Christians in the center. Although Muslims and Christians traveled in much of this world more or less freely—as merchants, mapmakers, adventurers, mercenaries, or **corsairs**—the two religious civilizations were locked in a pattern of fierce competition. During 750–1050, the Muslims justified their conquests as holy wars (*jihads*) and during 1050–1300 the Christians retaliated with their crusades and the reconquest of Iberia.

By the fifteenth century, the Christians saw the liberation of Iberia and North Africa from Muslim rule and circumventing the Muslims in the Mediterranean as stepping stones toward rebuilding the crusader kingdom of Jerusalem, which had been lost to the Muslims in 1291. Searching for a route that would take them around Africa, they hoped to defeat the Muslims in Jerusalem with an attack from the east. Driven at least in part by this search, the Christians discovered the continents of the Americas. For their part, the Muslims sought to conquer eastern and central Europe (the Balkans, Hungary, and Austria), while simultaneously shoring up their defense of North Africa and seeking to drive the Portuguese out of the Indian Ocean. After a hiatus of several centuries—when commonwealths of states characterized western Christian and Islamic civilizations—imperial polities reemerged, in the form of the Ottoman and Habsburg Empires vying for world rule.

The Muslim–Christian Competition

Seeing Patterns

▶ What patterns characterized Christian and Muslim competition in the period 1300–1600? Which elements distinguished them from each other, and which elements were similar? How did the pattern change over time?

▶ How did the fiscal–military state in the Middle East and Europe function in the period 1450–1600? How did economics, military power, and imperial objectives interact to create the fiscal–military state?

▶ Which patterns did cultural expressions follow in the Habsburg and Ottoman Empires? Why did the ruling classes of these empires sponsor these expressions?

Corsairs: In the context of this chapter, Muslim or Christian pirates who boarded ships, confiscated the cargoes, and held the crews and travelers for ransom; nominally under the authority of the Ottoman sultan or the pope in Rome, but they operated independently.

in the East and West, 1450–1600

After a long period during which the Christian kings in Iberia found tributes by the Muslim emirs more profitable than war, in the second half of the fifteenth century the kings resumed the Reconquista. During the same time period, the small principality of the Ottomans took advantage of Mongol and Byzantine weakness to conquer lands in both Anatolia and the Balkans. After the Muslim conquest of Constantinople in 1453 and the western Christian conquest of Granada in 1492, the path was open for the emergence of the Ottoman and Habsburg Empires.

Iberian Christian Expansion, 1415–1498

During a revival of anti-Muslim Crusade passions in the course of the fourteenth century, Portugal resumed its Reconquista policies by expanding to North Africa in 1415. Looking for a way to circumvent the Muslims, collect West African gold along the way, and reach the Indian spice coast, Portuguese sailors and traders established fortified harbors along the African coastline. Castile and Aragon, not to be left behind, conquered Granada in 1492, occupied ports in North Africa, and sent Columbus on his way to discover an alternate route to what the Portuguese were seeking. Columbus' discovery of America did not yield Indian spices but delivered a new continent to the rulers of Castile and Aragon (see Map 16.1).

Maritime Explorations   Portugal's resumption of the Reconquista had its roots in its mastery of Atlantic seafaring. In 1277–1281, mariners of the Italian city-state of Genoa pioneered commerce by sea between the Mediterranean and northwestern Europe. One port on the route was Lisbon, where Portuguese shipwrights and their Genoese teachers teamed up to develop new ships suited for the stormy Atlantic seas. In the course of the early fifteenth century, they developed the *caravel*, a small ship with high, upward-extending fore and aft boards; a stern rudder; and square as well as triangular lateen sails. With their new ships, the Portuguese became important traders between England and the Mediterranean countries.

The sea trade now stimulated an exploration of the eastern Atlantic. By the early fifteenth century, the Portuguese had discovered the uninhabited islands of the Azores and Madeira, while the Castilians, building their own caravels, began a century-long conquest of the Canary Islands. Here, the indigenous, still Neolithic Berber inhabitants, the Guanches, put up a fierce resistance. But settlers, with the backing of Venetian investors, carved out colonies on conquered parcels of land, on which they enslaved the Guanches to work in sugarcane plantations. They thus adopted the slave labor and sugarcane plantation system from the eastern Mediterranean, where it had Byzantine and Crusader roots on the island of Cyprus, as discussed in greater detail in Chapter 18.

Apocalyptic Expectations   Parallel with the Atlantic explorations, Iberian Christians began to rethink their relationship with the Muslims on the peninsula. The loss of the crusader kingdom in Palestine to the Muslim Mamluks in 1291 was an event that stirred deep feelings of guilt among the western Christians. Efforts to organize military expeditions to reconquer Jerusalem failed to get off the ground, however, mostly because rulers in Europe were now more interested in warring against each other for territorial gain. The failure did not dampen spiritual revivals,

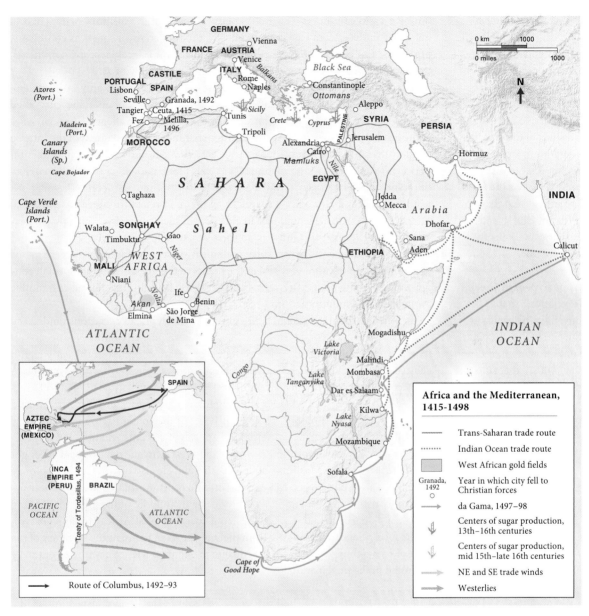

MAP 16.1 **Africa and the Mediterranean, 1415–1498.**

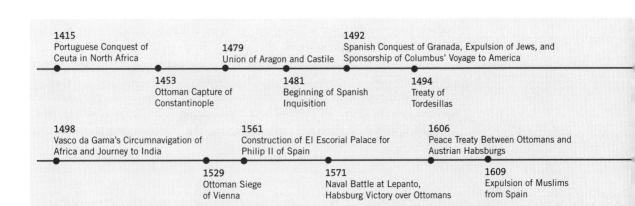

Military orders: Ever since the early 1100s, the papacy encouraged the formation of monastic fighting orders, such as the Hospitalers and Templars, to combat the Muslims in the crusader kingdom of Jerusalem; similar Reconquista orders, such as the Order of Santiago and the Order of Christ, emerged in Iberia to eliminate Muslim rule.

Apocalypse: In Greek, "revelation," that is, unveiling the events at the end of history, before God's judgment; during the 1400s, expectation of the imminence of Christ's Second Coming, with precursors paving the way.

however, especially among the monks of the Franciscan and **military orders** of Iberia. These monks, often well connected with the Iberian royal courts as confessors, preachers, and educators, were believers in revelation (Greek *apocalypsis*), that is, the imminent end of the world and the Second Coming of Christ.

According to the **Apocalypse**, Christ's return could happen only in Jerusalem, which, therefore, made it urgent for the Christians to reconquer the city. They widely believed that they would be aided by Prester John, an alleged Christian ruler at the head of an immense army from Ethiopia or India. In the context of the intense religious fervor of the period, Christians as well as Muslims saw no contradiction between religion and military conquest. A providential God, so they believed, justified the conquest of lands and the enslavement of the conquered. The religious justification of military action, therefore, was not a pretext for more base material interests (though these would be a likely effect of such conquests) but a proud declaration by believers that God was on their side to help them convert and conquer the non-Christian world. Even today such ideas still can be found in many religious traditions; that they were very real in the minds of the Portuguese and Spanish conquistadores of the period between 1400 and 1500 is well-documented as a motive for political and military action.

In Portugal, political claims in the guise of apocalyptic expectations guided the military orders in "reconquering" Ceuta, a northern port city of the Moroccan sultans. The orders argued that prior to the Berber–Arab conquest of the early eighth century CE, Ceuta had been Christian and that it was therefore lawful to undertake its Reconquista. Accordingly, a fleet under Henry the Navigator (1394–1460) succeeded in taking Ceuta in 1415, capturing there a huge stock of West African gold ready to be minted as money. Henry, a brother of the ruling Portuguese king, saw himself as a precursor in the unfolding of apocalyptic events and invested huge resources into the search for the *Rio de oro*, the West African "river of gold" thought to be the place where Muslims obtained their gold. He also instructed the explorers to look for a sea bay alleged to be in the middle of Africa that would give them access to Christian Ethiopia and Prester John. By the middle of the fifteenth century, Portuguese mariners had reached the "gold coast" of West Africa (today's Ghana), where local rulers imported gold from the interior Akan fields, near a tributary of the Niger River—the "gold river" of the Muslim merchants. The sea bay turned out to be a figment of the imagination.

Reforms in Castile   The Portuguese renewal of the Reconquista stimulated a similar revival in Castile. For a century and a half, Castile had collected tributes from Granada instead of completing the reconquest of the peninsula. The revival occurred after the dynastic union of Castile and Aragon–Catalonia under their respective monarchs Queen Isabella (r. 1474–1504) and King Ferdinand II (r. 1479–1516). The two monarchs, now joined by marriage, embarked on a political and religious reform program designed to strengthen their central administrations and used the reconquest ideology as a convenient vehicle to speed up the reforms.

Among the political reforms was the recruitment of urban militias and judges, both under royal supervision, to check the military and judicial powers of the aristocracy. Religious reform focused on improved education for the clergy and stricter enforcement of Christian doctrine in the population at large. The new institution entrusted with the enforcement of doctrine was the Spanish Inquisition, a body of clergy first appointed by Isabella and Ferdinand in 1481 to ferret out any beliefs and practices among people that were deemed to violate Christian theology and church law. With their religious innovations, the monarchs regained the initiative from the popes and laid the foundations for increased state power.

The Conquest of Granada   The Reconquista culminated in a 10-year campaign (1482–1492), now fought on both sides with cannons. In the end, Granada fell into Christian hands because the Ottomans, still consolidating their power in the Balkans, sent only a naval commander who stationed himself in North Africa and harassed Iberian ships. The Mamluks of Egypt, less powerful than the Ottomans, sent an embassy to Granada that merely made a feeble threat of retribution against Christians in Egypt and Syria. Abandoned by the Muslim powers, the last emir of Granada negotiated terms for an honorable surrender. According to these terms, Muslims who chose to stay as subjects of the Castilian crown were permitted to do so, practicing their faith in their own mosques.

The treaty did not apply to the Jews of Granada, however, who were forced either to convert to Christianity or to emigrate. In the 1300s, anti-Jewish preaching by the Catholic clergy and riots by Christians against Jews

St. James the Moor-Slayer.
As the twin impulses of Reconquista and Crusade surged in fifteenth-century Spain and Portugal, devotion to warrior cults increased among the Christian faithful. The cult of St. James the Moor-Slayer gained particular prominence among crusading knights during this time as the saint's miraculous appearance was believed to have helped a vastly outnumbered Christian army defeat Muslim forces in 844. Devotion to the saint (*Santiago Matatmoros*) remains high in Spain today. In 2004, authorities reversed an earlier decision to relocate an enormous statue of St. James the Moor-Slayer from the cathedral of Santiago de Compostela in northwest Spain after a storm of protest.

in Seville had substantially reduced the Jewish population of some 300,000 at its peak ca. 1050 to a mere 80,000 in 1492. Of this remainder, a majority emigrated in 1492 to Portugal and the Ottoman Empire, strengthening the urban population of the latter with their commercial and crafts skills. Thus, the nearly millennium and a half–long Jewish presence in "Sefarad," as Spain was called in Hebrew, ended, with an expulsion designed to strengthen the Christian unity of Iberia.

After the expulsion of the Jews, it did not take long for the Christians to violate the Muslim treaty of surrender. The church engaged in forced conversions, the burning of Arabic books, and transformations of mosques into churches, triggering an uprising of Muslims in Granada (1499–1500). Christian troops crushed the rising, and Isabella and Ferdinand took it as an excuse to abrogate the treaty of surrender. In one province after another during the early sixteenth century, Muslims were forced to either convert or emigrate. Like the family of al-Hasan al-Wazzan described at the beginning of this chapter, thousands of Muslims left for North Africa rather than convert to Christianity. The number of remaining Muslims, however, exceeded the ability of the Inquisition to enforce the conversion process. In practical terms, baptized Muslims—called *moriscos* ("Moor-like")—continued to practice Islam, even if discreetly.

Columbus' Journey to the Caribbean   At the peak of their royal power in early 1492, Isabella and Ferdinand seized a golden opportunity to catch up quickly with the Portuguese in the Atlantic. They authorized the seasoned mariner Christopher Columbus (1451–1506), the son of a Genoese wool weaver, to build two caravels and a larger carrack and sail westward across the Atlantic. Columbus promised to reach India ahead of the Portuguese, who were attempting to find a route to India by sailing around Africa. The two monarchs pledged him money for the construction of ships from Castilian and Aragonese Crusade levies collected against the Ottomans. In September, Columbus and his mariners departed from the Castilian Canary Islands, catching the favorable south Atlantic easterlies. After a voyage of a little over a month, Columbus landed on one of the Bahaman islands. From there he explored a number of Caribbean islands, mistakenly assuming that he was close to the Indian subcontinent. After a stay of 3 months, he left a small colony of settlers behind and returned to Iberia with seven captured Caribbean islanders and a small quantity of gold.

Columbus was a self-educated explorer. Through voracious but indiscriminate reading, he had accumulated substantial knowledge of such diverse subjects as geography, cartography, the Crusades, and the Apocalypse. On the basis of this reading (and his own faulty calculations), he insisted that the ocean stretching between western Europe and eastern Asia was relatively narrow. Furthermore, he fervently believed that God had made him the forerunner of an Iberian apocalyptic world ruler who would recapture Jerusalem from the Muslims just prior to the Second Coming of Christ. For many years, Columbus had peddled his idea about reaching Jerusalem from the east at the Portuguese court. The Portuguese, however, while sharing Columbus' apocalyptic fervor, dismissed his Atlantic Ocean calculations as fantasies. Even in Castile, where Columbus went after his rejection in Portugal, it took many years and the victory over Granada before Queen Isabella finally listened to him. Significantly, it was at the height of their success at Granada in 1492 that Isabella and Ferdinand seized their chance to beat the Portuguese to Asia.

Although disappointed by the meager returns of Columbus' first and subsequent voyages, Isabella and Ferdinand were delighted to have acquired new islands in the Caribbean, in addition to those of the Canaries. In one blow they had drawn even with Portugal.

Vasco da Gama's Journey to India   Portugal redoubled its efforts after 1492 to discover the way to India around Africa. In 1498, the king appointed an important court official and member of the crusading Order of Santiago, Vasco da Gama (ca. 1469–1524), to command four caravels for the journey to India. Da Gama, an experienced mariner, made good use of the accumulated Portuguese knowledge of seafaring in the Atlantic and guidance by Arab sailors in the Indian Ocean. After a journey of 6 months, the ships arrived in Calicut, the main spice trade center on the Indian west coast.

The first Portuguese sent ashore in Calicut encountered two Iberian Muslims, who addressed him in Castilian Spanish and Italian: "The Devil take you! What brought you here?" The Portuguese replied: "We came to seek Christians and spices." When da Gama went inland to see the ruler of Calicut, he was optimistic that he had indeed found what he had come for. Ignorant of Hinduism, he mistook the Indian religion for the Christianity of Prester John. Similarly ignorant of the conventions of the India trade, he offered woolen textiles and metal goods in exchange for pepper, cinnamon, and cloves. The Muslim and Hindu merchants were uninterested in these goods designed for the African market and demanded gold or silver, which the Portuguese had only in small amounts. Rumors spread about the Muslims plotting with the Hindus against the apparently penniless Christian intruders. Prudently, da Gama lifted anchor and returned home with small quantities of spices.

After these modest beginnings, however, within a short time Portugal had mastered the India trade. The Portuguese crown organized regular journeys around Africa, and when Portuguese mariners on one such journey discovered northeast Brazil they claimed it for their expanding commercial network. During the early sixteenth century, the Portuguese India fleets brought considerable amounts of spices from India back to Portugal, threatening the profits of the Egyptian and Venetian merchants who had hitherto dominated the trade. Prester John, of course, was never found; and the project of retaking Jerusalem receded into the background.

Rise of the Ottomans and Struggle with the Habsburgs for Dominance, 1300–1609

While Muslim rule disappeared in the late fifteenth century from the Iberian Peninsula, the opposite happened in the Balkans. Here, the Ottoman Turks spearheaded the expansion of Islamic rule, initially over Eastern Orthodox Christians, and eventually over western Christians. By the late sixteenth century, when the East–West conflict between the Habsburgs and Ottomans reached its peak, entire generations of Croats, Germans, and Italians lived in mortal fear of the "terrible Turk" who might conquer all of Christian Europe.

Late Byzantium and Ottoman Origins   The rise of the Ottomans was closely related to the decline of Byzantium. The emperors of Byzantium had been able to reclaim their "empire" in 1261 from its Latin rulers and Venetian troops by allying themselves with the Genoese. This empire, which during the early fourteenth century included Greece and a few domains in western Anatolia, was no more than a mid-size kingdom with modest agricultural resources. But it was still a valuable trading hub, thanks to Constantinople's strategic position as a market linking the Mediterranean with Slavic kingdoms in the Balkans and the Ukrainian–Russian principality of Kiev. Thanks to its commercial wealth, Byzantium experienced a cultural revival, which at its height featured the lively scholarly debate over Plato and Aristotle that exerted a profound influence on the western Renaissance in Italy.

Inevitably, however, both Balkan Slavs and Anatolian Turks appropriated Byzantine provinces in the late thirteenth century, further reducing the empire. One of the lost provinces was Bithynia, across the Bosporus in Anatolia. Here, in 1299, the Turkish warlord Osman (1299–1326) gathered his clan as well as a motley assembly of Islamic holy warriors (Turkish *ghazis*), including a local saint and his followers, and declared himself an independent ruler. Osman and a number of other Turkish lords in the region were nominally subject to the Seljuks, the Turkish dynasty which had conquered Anatolia from the Byzantines two centuries earlier but by the early 1300s had disintegrated.

During the first half of the fourteenth century, Osman and his successors emerged as the most powerful emirs by conquering further Anatolian provinces from Byzantium. The Moroccan Abu Abdallah Ibn Battuta (1304–1369), famous for his journeys through the Islamic world, Africa, and China, passed through western Anatolia and Constantinople during the 1330s, visiting several Turkish principalities. He was duly impressed by the rising power of the Ottomans, noting approvingly that

Patterns Up Close | Shipbuilding

With the appearance of empires during the Iron Age, four regional but interconnected traditions—Mediterranean, Indian Ocean, Chinese Sea, and North Sea—emerged.

In the Mediterranean, around 500 BCE, shipwrights began to use nailed planks for their war galleys as well as cargo transports, as evidenced by shipwrecks of the period. In the Roman Empire (ca. 200 BCE–500 CE), nailed planking allowed the development of the roundship (photo a), a large transport of 120 feet length and 400 tons of cargo transporting grain from Egypt to Italy. The roundship and its variations had double planking, multiple masts, and multiple square sails. After 100 BCE, the triangular ("lateen") sail allowed for zigzagging ("tacking") against the wind, greatly expanding shipping during a summer sailing season.

The Celtic North Sea tradition adapted to the Mediterranean patterns of the Romans. When the Roman Empire receded during the 300s CE, shipwrights in Celtic regions continued with their own innovations, shifting to frame-first construction for small boats in the 300s. At the same time Norsemen, or Vikings, innovated by introducing overlapping ("clinkered") plank joining for their eminently seagoing boats. The North Sea innovations, arriving as they did at the end of the western Roman Empire, remained local for nearly half a millennium.

The evolution of China into an empire resulted in major Chinese contributions to ship construction. In the Han period (206 BCE–220 CE) there is evidence from clay models of riverboats for the use of nailed planks. One model, dating to the first century CE, shows a central steering rudder at the end of the boat. At the same time, similar stern rudders appeared in the Roman Empire. Who adapted to whom, if at all, is still an unanswered question.

Patterns of Shipbuilding. Left to right: (a) Hellenistic-Roman roundship, (b) Chinese junk, (c) Indian Ocean dhow.

they manned nearly 100 forts and castles and maintained pressure on the eastern Christian infidels. In 1354, the Ottomans gained their first European foothold on a peninsula about 100 miles southwest of Constantinople. Thereafter, it seemed only a question of time before the Ottomans would conquer Constantinople.

Through a skillful mixture of military defense, tribute payments, and dynastic marriages of princesses with Osman's descendants, however, the Byzantine emperors extended their rule for another century. They were also helped by Timur the

Shipbuilding innovations continued after 600 CE. In Tang China, junks with multiple watertight compartments ("bulkheads") and multiple layers of planks appeared. The average junk was 140 feet long, had a cargo capacity of 600 tons, and could carry on its three or four decks several hundred mariners and passengers (see photo *b*). Junks had multiple masts and trapezoid ("lug") and square sails made of matted fibers and strengthened ("battened") with poles sewed to the surface. The less innovative Middle Eastern, eastern African, and Indian *dhow* was built with sewed or nailed planks and sailed with lateen and square sails, traveling as far as southern China (see photo *c*).

In western Europe, the patterns of Mediterranean and North Sea shipbuilding merged during the thirteenth century. At that time, northern shipwrights developed the cog as the main transport for Baltic grain to ports around the North Sea. The cog was a ship of some 60 feet in length and 30 tons in cargo capacity, with square sails, flush-planking below, and clinkered planking above the water line. Northern European Crusaders traveled during 1150–1300 on cogs via the Atlantic to the Mediterranean. Builders adapted the cog's clinker technique to the roundship tradition that Muslims as well as eastern and western Christians had modified in the previous centuries. Genoese clinkered roundships pioneered the Mediterranean–North Sea trade in the early fourteenth century (see photo *d*).

Lisbon shipwrights in Portugal, learning from Genoese masters, borrowed from local shipbuilding traditions and Genoese roundship construction patterns for the development of the caravel around 1430. The caravel was a small and slender 60-foot-long ship with a 50-ton freight capacity, a stern rudder, square and lateen sails, and a magnetic compass (of Chinese origin). The caravel and, after 1500, the similarly built but much larger galleon were the main vessels the Portuguese, Spanish, Dutch, and English used during their oceanic voyages from the mid-fifteenth to mid-eighteenth centuries (see photo *e*).

Patterns of Shipbuilding. From top: (*d*) Baltic cog, and (*e*) Iberian caravel. These ships illustrate the varieties of shipbuilding traditions that developed over thousands of years.

Questions

- How does the history of shipbuilding demonstrate the ways in which innovations spread from one place to another?
- Do the adaptations in shipbuilding that flowed between cultures that were nominally in conflict with each other provide a different perspective on the way these cultures interacted?

Great (r. 1370–1405), a Turkish-descended ruler from central Asia who sought to rebuild the Mongol Empire. He surprised the Ottomans, who were distracted by their ongoing conquests in the Balkans, and defeated them decisively in 1402. Timur and his successors were unsuccessful with their dream of neo-Mongol world rule, but the Ottomans needed nearly two decades (1402–1421) to recover from their collapse and reconstitute their empire in the Balkans and Anatolia. Under

Siege of Constantinople, 1453. Note the soldiers on the left pulling boats on rollers and wheels over the Galata hillside. With this maneuver, Sultan Mehmet II was able to circumvent the chain spanned across the entrance to the Golden Horn (in place of the anachronistic bridge in the image). This allowed him to speed up his conquest of Constantinople by forcing the defenders to spread their forces thinly over the entire length of the walls.

Mehmet II, the Conqueror (r. 1451–1481), they finally assembled all their resources to lay siege to the Byzantine capital.

From Istanbul to the Adriatic Sea   Similar to Isabella and Ferdinand's siege of Granada, Mehmet's siege and conquest of Constantinople (April 5–May 29, 1453) was one of the stirring events of world history. The Byzantines were severely undermanned and short of gunpowder, unable to defend the full length of the imposing land walls that protected the city. Although they had some help from Genoese, papal, and Aragonese forces, it was not nearly enough to make a difference. With a superiority of 11 to 1 in manpower, the Ottomans besieged and bombarded Constantinople's walls with heavy cannons. The weakest part of the Byzantine defenses was the central section of the western walls where it was relatively easy to tunnel into the soil underneath. Here, Mehmet stationed his heaviest guns to bombard the masonry and have his sappers undermine the foundations of the walls.

Another weak section was on the north side, along the harbor in the Golden Horn, where the walls were low. Here, the Byzantines had blocked off the entrance to the Golden Horn with a huge chain. In a brilliant tactical move, Mehmet circumvented the chain. He had troops drag ships on rollers over a hillside into the harbor. The soldiers massed on these ships were ready to disembark and assault the walls with the help of ladders. On the first sign of cracks in the northern walls, the Ottoman besiegers stormed the city. The last Byzantine emperor, Constantine XI, perished in the general massacre and pillage which followed the Ottoman occupation of the city.

Mehmet quickly repopulated Constantinople ("Istanbul" in Turkish, from Gr. "to the city," *istin polin*) and appointed a new patriarch at the head of the eastern Christians, to whom he promised full protection as his subjects. In quick succession, he ordered the construction of the Topkapı Palace (1459), the transfer of the administration from Edirne (which had been the capital since 1365) to Istanbul, and the resumption of expansion in the Balkans, where he succeeded in forcing the majority of rulers into submitting to vassal status. One of the Balkan lords resisting the sultan was Vlad III Dracul of Wallachia, who in 1461–1462 impaled a contingent of Ottoman troops sent against him on sharpened tree trunks. Mehmet replaced Dracul with his more compliant brother, but the memory of the impalements lived on to inspire vampire folktales and, eventually, in 1897, the famous Gothic horror novel *Dracula*.

Mehmet's ongoing conquests eventually brought him to the Adriatic Sea, where one of his generals occupied Otranto on the heel of the Italian peninsula. The Ottomans were poised to launch from Otranto a full-scale invasion of Italy, when the sultan died unexpectedly. His successor evacuated Otranto, preferring to consolidate the Ottoman Empire in the Middle East, North Africa, and the Balkans before reconsidering an invasion of central and western Europe.

Imperial Apogee   Between 1500 and 1600 the Ottoman sultans succeeded magnificently in the consolidation of their empire. In 1514, with superior cavalry and infantry forces, cannons, and muskets, the Ottomans defeated the Persian Safavids in Iran, who had risen in 1501 to form a rival Shiite empire in opposition to the Sunni Ottomans. In the southern Middle East, intermittent tensions between the Ottomans and the Mamluk Turks in Egypt, Syria, and eastern Arabia gave way to open war in 1517. The Ottomans, again due to superior firepower, defeated the Mamluks and took control of western Arabia, including the holy pilgrimage city of Mecca. A year later, in 1518, Sultan Süleyman I, the Magnificent (r. 1520–1566), appointed a naval commander to drive the Spanish from a series of fortifications and cities in North Africa, which the latter had conquered in the name of the Reconquista in the 1490s and early 1500s.

In the Balkans, the Ottomans completed their conquests of Serbia and Hungary with the annexation of Belgrade and Buda (of Budapest) as well as a brief siege of Vienna in 1529, begun too late in the year and eventually stopped by the approaching winter. By the second half of the sixteenth century, when the submission of most of Hungary had been secured, the Ottoman Empire was a vast multiethnic and multireligious state of some 15 million inhabitants extending from Algeria in the Maghreb to Yemen in Arabia and from Upper Egypt to the Balkans and the northern shores of the Black Sea (see Map 16.2).

Vlad Dracul next to Impaled Ottoman Soldiers. The woodcut depicts the alleged impalement of 1,000 Ottoman soldiers sent against Vlad Dracul, prior to Sultan Mehmet II leading a victorious campaign into Wallachia and removing Dracul from power. Dracul's cannibalism, as suggested in the image, is not confirmed by historical sources.

Morocco and Persia   In the early modern period 1450–1600, the two large empires of the Ottomans and Indian Mughals dominated Islamic civilization. Two smaller and more short-lived realms existed in Morocco and Persia, ruled by the Saadian (1509–1659) and Safavid (1501–1722) dynasties, respectively. The Saadian sultans defended themselves successfully against the Ottoman expansion and liberated themselves from the Portuguese occupation of Morocco's Atlantic ports which had followed the conquest of Ceuta in 1415. In 1591, after their liberation,

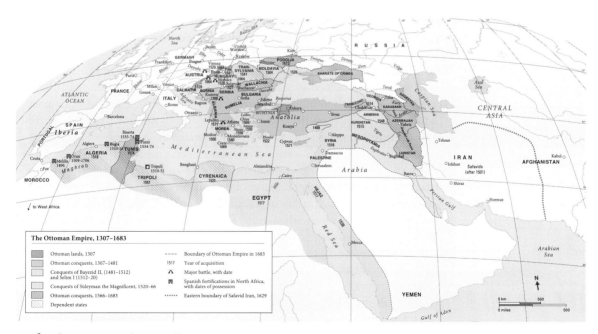

MAP **16.2** The Ottoman Empire, 1307–1683.

the Saadians sent a firearm-equipped army to West Africa in order to revive the gold trade, which had dwindled to a trickle after the Portuguese arrival in Ghana. The army succeeded in destroying the West African empire of Songhay but failed to revive the gold trade. Moroccan army officers assumed power in Timbuktu, and their descendants, the Ruma, became provincial lords independent of Morocco. The Saadians, unable to improve their finances, split into provincial realms. The still-reigning Alaouite dynasty of Moroccan kings replaced them in 1659.

The Safavids grew in the mid-1400s from a Turkish mystical brotherhood in northwestern Iran into a Shiite *ghazi* organization (similar to the Sunni one participating in the early Ottoman expansion) that carried out raids against Christians in the Caucasus. In 1501, the leadership of the brotherhood put forward the 14-year-old Ismail as the Hidden Twelfth Imam. According to Shiite doctrine, the Hidden Imam, or Messiah, was expected to arrive and establish a Muslim apocalyptic realm of justice at the end of time, before God's Last Judgment. This realm would replace the "unjust" Sunni Ottoman Empire. The Ottomans countered the Safavid challenge in 1514 with the Battle of Chaldiran, where they crushed the underprepared Safavids with their superior cannon and musket firepower. After his humiliating defeat, Ismail dropped his claim to apocalyptic status and his successors assumed the more modest title of "king" (Persian *shah*) as the head of state, quite similar in many respects to that of the Ottomans.

Learning from their defeat, the Safavids recruited a standing firearm-equipped army from among young Christians on lands conquered in the Caucasus. They held fast to Shiism, thereby continuing their opposition to the Sunni Ottomans, and supported the formation of a clerical hierarchy, which made this form of Islam dominant in Iran. As sponsors of construction projects, the Safavids greatly improved urbanism in the country. After moving the capital from Tabriz to the centrally located Isfahan in 1590, they built an imposing palace, administration, and mosque complex in the city. In a suburb they settled a large colony of Armenians, who held the monopoly in the production of Caspian Sea silk, a high-quality export product which the Dutch—successors of the Portuguese in the Indian Ocean trade—distributed in Europe.

As patrons of the arts, the shahs revived the ancient traditions of Persian culture to such heights that even the archrival Ottomans felt compelled to adopt Persian manners, literature, and architectural styles. Persian royal culture similarly radiated to the Mughals in India. Not everyone accepted Shiism, however. An attempt to force the religion on the Afghanis backfired badly when enraged Sunni tribes formed a coalition, defeated the Safavids, and ended their regime in 1722.

Rise of the Habsburgs

Parallel to the rise and development of the Safavid state, Castile–Aragon on the Iberian Peninsula evolved into the center of a vast empire of its own. A daughter of Isabella and Ferdinand married a member of the Habsburg dynastic family, which ruled Flanders, Burgundy, Naples, Sicily, and Austria, as well as Germany (the "Holy Roman Empire of the German Nation," as this collection of principalities was called). Their son, Charles V (r. 1516–1558), not only inherited Castile–Aragon, now merged and called "Spain," and the Habsburg territories, but also became the ruler of the Aztec and Inca Empires in the Americas, which Spanish adventurers had conquered in his name between 1521 and 1536. In both Austria and the western Mediterranean the Habsburgs were direct neighbors of the Ottomans (see Map 16.3).

MAP **16.3** Europe and the Mediterranean, ca. 1560.

After a victorious battle against France in 1519, Charles V also won the title of emperor, which made him the overlord of all German principalities and supreme among the monarchs of western Christianity. Although this title did not mean much in terms of power and financial gain in either the German principalities or western Christianity as a whole, it made him the titular political head of western Christianity and thereby the direct counterpart of Sultan Süleyman in the struggle for dominance in the Christian–Muslim world of Europe, the Middle East and northern Africa. Both the Habsburgs and the Ottomans renewed the traditional Arab/Islamic–Christian imperialism which had characterized the period 600–950 and which had been replaced by the Muslim and Christian commonwealths of 950–1450.

Habsburg Distractions   Charles V faced a daunting task in his effort to prevent the Ottomans from advancing against the Christians in the Balkans and

Mediterranean. Multiple problems in his European territories diverted his attention and forced him to spend far less time than he wanted on what Christians in most parts of Europe perceived as a pervasive Ottoman–Muslim threat. During the first three decades of the sixteenth century, revolts in Iberia, the Protestant Reformation in the German states, and renewed war with France for control of Burgundy and Italy commanded Charles' attention.

The emperor's distractions increased further in 1534 when, in an attempt to drive the Habsburgs out of Italy, France forged an alliance with the Ottomans. This alliance horrified western Europe. It demonstrated, however, that the Ottomans, on account of their military advances against the Christians in eastern Europe and the western Mediterranean, had become a crucial player in European politics. As fierce as the struggle between Muslims and Christians for dominance was, when the French king found himself squeezed on both sides of his kingdom by his archrival Charles V, the Ottomans became his natural allies.

Habsburg and Ottoman Losses   All these diversions seriously strained Habsburg resources against the Ottomans, who pressed relentlessly ahead on the two fronts of the Balkans and North Africa. Although Charles V deputized his younger brother Ferdinand I to the duchy of Austria in 1521 to shore up the Balkan defenses, he was able to send him significant troops only once. After a series of dramatic defeats, Austria had to pay the Ottomans tribute and, eventually, even sign a humiliating truce (1562). On the western Mediterranean front, the Habsburgs did not do well either. Even though Charles V campaigned several times in person, most garrisons on the coast of Algeria, Tunisia, and Tripoli were too exposed to withstand the Ottoman onslaught by sea and by land. In 1556, at the end of Charles V's reign, only two of eight Habsburg garrisons had survived.

A third frontier of the Muslim–Christian struggle for dominance was the Indian Ocean. After Vasco da Gama had returned from India in 1498, the Portuguese kings invested major resources into breaking into the Muslim-dominated Indian Ocean trade. In response, the Ottomans made great efforts to protect existing Muslim commercial interests in the Indian Ocean. They blocked Portuguese military support for Ethiopia and strengthened their ally and main pepper producer, the sultan of Aceh on the Indonesian island of Sumatra, by providing him with troops and weapons. War on land and on sea, directly and by proxy, raged in the Indian Ocean through most of the sixteenth century. In the long run, the Portuguese were successful at destroying the Ottoman fleets sent against them, but smaller convoys of Ottoman galleys continued to harass Portuguese shipping interests. As new research on the Ottoman "age of exploration" in the Indian Ocean has demonstrated, by 1570 the Muslims traded again as much via the Red Sea route to the Mediterranean as the Portuguese did by circumnavigating Africa. In addition, the Ottomans benefited from the trade of a new commodity—coffee, produced in Ethiopia and Yemen. Portugal (under Spanish rule 1580–1640) reduced its unsustainably large military presence in the Indian Ocean, followed by the Ottomans, which allowed the Netherlands in the early seventeenth century to overtake both Portugal and the Ottoman Empire in the Indian Ocean spice trade (see Map 16.4).

Habsburg–Ottoman Balance   In the 1550s, Charles V despaired of his ability to ever master the many challenges posed by the Ottomans as well as by France and

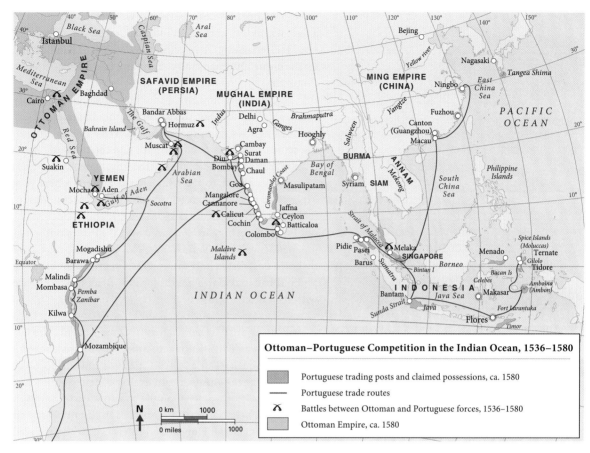

MAP **16.4** **Ottoman–Portuguese Competition in the Indian Ocean, 1536–1580.**

the Protestants. He decided that the only way to ensure the continuation of Habsburg power would be a division of his western and eastern territories. Accordingly, he bestowed Spain, Naples, the Netherlands, and the Americas on his son Philip II (r. 1556–1598). Further, Charles V had his brother Ferdinand I (r. 1558–1564) crowned Holy Roman Emperor by the pope, thereby making him overlord of the German principalities as well as ruler of the direct Habsburg possessions of Austria, Bohemia, and the remnant of Hungary not lost to the Ottomans. Together, Charles hoped, his son and his brother would cooperate and help each other militarily against the Ottomans.

When Philip took over the Spanish throne, he realized, to his concern, that most of the Habsburg military was stationed outside Spain, leaving that country vulnerable to attack. As the Ottomans had recently conquered most Spanish strongholds in North Africa, a Muslim invasion of Spain was a distinct possibility. Fearful of morisco support for an Ottoman invasion of Spain, Philip's administration and the Inquisition renewed their decrees of conversion which had lain dormant for half a century. This sparked a massive revolt among the moriscos of Granada in 1568–1570, supported by Ottoman soldiers and Moroccan arms. Philip was able to suppress the revolt only after recourse to troops and firearms from Italy. To break up the dangerously large concentrations of Granadan moriscos in the south of Spain, Philip ordered them to be dispersed throughout the peninsula. At the same time, to alleviate the Ottoman naval threat, Philip, the pope, Venice, and Genoa formed

Paolo Veronese, The Battle of Lepanto (ca. 1572), altar painting with four saints beseeching the Virgin Mary to grant victory to the Christians. In the sixteenth century, the entire Mediterranean, from Gibraltar to Cyprus, was a naval battleground between Christians and Muslims. The Battle of Lepanto was the first major sea battle in world history to be decided by firepower: Even though Christian forces had slightly fewer ships, they had more, and heavier, artillery pieces. At the end of the battle "the sea was entirely covered, not just with masts, spars, oars, and broken wood, but with an innumerable quantity of blood that turned the water as red as blood."

the Holy Christian League. Its task was the construction of a fleet which was to destroy Ottoman sea power in the eastern Mediterranean. The fleet succeeded in 1571 in bottling up the entire Ottoman navy at Lepanto, in Ottoman Greece, destroying it in the ensuing firefight.

The Ottomans, however, had enough resources not only to rebuild their navy but also to capture the strategic port city of Tunis in 1574 from the Spaniards. With this evening of the scores, the two sides decided to end their unsustainable naval war in the Mediterranean. The Ottomans turned their attention eastward, to the rival Safavid Empire, where they exploited a period of dynastic instability for the conquest of territories in the Caucasus (1578–1590). The staunch Catholic Philip II, on his part, was faced with the Protestant war of independence in the Netherlands. This war was so expensive that, in a desperate effort to straighten out his state finances, Philip II had to declare bankruptcy (1575) and sue for peace with the Ottomans (1580).

The Limits of Ottoman Power   After their victory over the Safavids, the Ottomans looked again to the west. While the peace with Spain was too recent to be broken, a long peace with Ferdinand I in Austria (since 1562) was ready to collapse. A series of raids and counterraids at the Austrian and Transylvanian borders had inflamed tempers, and in 1593 the Ottomans went on the attack. Austria, however, was no longer the weak state it had been a generation earlier. Had it not been for a lack of support from the Transylvanian and Hungarian Protestants, who preferred the sultan to the Catholic emperor as overlord, the Austrians might have actually prevailed over the Ottomans. However, thanks to the Protestants' support, the Ottomans drew even on the battlefield with the Austrians. In 1606, the Ottomans and Austrian Habsburgs made peace again. With minor modifications in favor of the Austrians, the two sides returned to their earlier borders. The Austrians made one more tribute payment and then let their obligation lapse. Officially, the Ottomans conceded nothing, but in practical terms Austria was no longer a vassal state.

Expulsion of the Moriscos   In the western Mediterranean, the peace between the Ottomans and Spanish Habsburgs held. But Philip and his successors remained aware of the possibility of renewed Ottoman aid to the moriscos. Even though they had been scattered after 1570, the moriscos continued to resist conversion. Among Castilians, an intense debate began about the apparent impossibility of assimilating them to Catholicism in order to create a religiously unified state. The church advocated the expulsion of the moriscos, arguing that the allegedly high Muslim birth rate in a population of 7.5 million (mostly rural) Spaniards was a serious threat. Fierce resistance against the proposed expulsion, however, rose among the Christian landowners in the southeastern province of Valencia. These landowners benefited greatly from the farming skills of the estimated 250,000 morisco tenant farmers who worked their irrigated rice and sugarcane estates. Weighing the potential Ottoman threat against the possibility of economic damage, the government decided in 1580 in favor of expulsion. Clearly, they valued Christian unity against the Ottomans more than the prosperity of a few hundred landowners in Valencia.

It took until 1609, however, before a compensation deal with the landowners in Valencia was worked out. In the following 5 years, some 300,000 moriscos were forcibly expelled from Spain, under often appalling circumstances: They had to leave all their possessions behind, including money and jewelry, taking only whatever clothes and household utensils they could carry. As in the case of the Jews a century earlier, Spain's loss was the Ottoman Empire's gain, this time mostly in the form of skilled irrigation farmers.

Fiscal–Military State: Origins and Interactions

The major technological change that occurred in the Middle East and Europe during 1250–1350 was the growing use of firearms. It took until the mid-1400s, however, before cannons and muskets were technically effective and reliable enough to make a difference in warfare. At this time, a pattern emerged whereby rulers created centralized, **fiscal–military states** to finance their strategic shift to firearm-bearing infantries. They resumed the policy of imperialism, which had lain dormant during the preceding period, when the religious civilizations of Islam and Christianity had evolved into commonwealths of many competing realms. Both the Ottomans and the Habsburgs raised immense amounts of cash in silver and gold to spend on cannons, muskets, and ships for achieving world rule.

Fiscal–military state: Early modern conquering polity, such as the Ottoman, Habsburg, and Safavid Empires, and the French, English, and Swedish kingdoms, in which the rulers raised their revenues in the form of cash and employed firearm-equipped foot soldiers for pay.

State Transformation, Money, and Firearms

In the early stages of their realms, the kings of Iberia (1150–1400) and the Ottoman sultans (1300–1400), with little cash on hand, compensated military commanders for their service in battle with parcels of conquered land, or land grants (*timars*). That land, farmed by villagers, generated rental income for the officers. Once the Iberian and Ottoman rulers had conquered cities and gained control over long-distance trade, however, patterns changed. Rulers began collecting taxes in cash, with which they paid regiments of personal guards to supplement the army of land-grant officers and their retainers. They created the fiscal–military state, forerunner of the absolutist state of the early seventeenth century.

The Land-Grant System
When the Ottoman *beys*, or chieftains, embarked on their conquests in the early 1300s, they created personal domains on the choice lands they had conquered. Here, they took rents in kind from the resident villagers to finance their small dynastic households. Their comrades in arms, such as members of their clan or adherents (many of whom were holy warriors and/or adventurers), received other conquered lands, from which they also collected rents. As the Ottomans conquered Byzantine cities, first in Anatolia and, in the second half of the 1300s, in the Balkans, they gained access to the **money economy**. They collected taxes in coins from the markets and tollbooths at city gates where foods and crafts goods were exchanged, as well as from the Christians and Jews responsible for the head tax (Turkish *cizye*). The taxes helped in adding luxuries to the household of the Ottoman emirs, which became a palace.

As a consequence of the full conquest of the southern Balkans by the Ottoman Empire in the fifteenth and sixteenth centuries, both the land-grant system and the money economy expanded exponentially. An entire military ruling class of grant holders

Money economy: Form of economic organization in which mutual obligations are settled in the form of monetary exchanges; in contrast, a system of land grants obliges the landholders to provide military service, without payment, to the grantee (sultan or king).

Boy Levy (*devşirme*) in a Christian Village. This miniature graphically depicts the trauma of conscription, including the wailing of the village women and the assembly of boys waiting to be taken away by implacable representatives of the sultan.

Janissaries: Centrally paid infantry soldiers recruited among the Christian population of the Ottoman Empire.

Devşirme: The levy on boys in the Ottoman Empire; that is, the obligation of the Christian population to contribute adolescent males to the military and administrative classes.

emerged, forming the backbone of the early Ottoman army and administration. The grant holders were cavalrymen who lived with their households of retainers in the villages and towns of the interior of Anatolia and the Balkans. Most of the time, they were away on campaign with the sultans, leaving managers in charge of the collection of rents from the villagers on their lands. At the conclusion of the rapid growth period of the Ottoman Empire toward the end of the fifteenth century, the landed ruling class of cavalrymen numbered some 80,000, constituting a vast reserve of warriors for the mobilization of troops each summer.

The Janissaries   An early indicator of the significance of the money economy in the Ottoman Empire was the military institution of the **Janissaries**—troops which received salaries from the central treasury. This institution probably appeared during the second half of the fourteenth century and is first documented for 1395. It was based on a practice (called ***devşirme*** [dev-SHIR-me]) of conscripting young boys, which palace officers carried out irregularly every few years among the empire's Christian population. For this purpose, the palace officers traveled to Christian villages, towns, and cities in the Balkans, Greece, and Anatolia. At each occasion, they selected hundreds of boys between the ages of 6 and 16 and marched them off to Istanbul, where they were converted to Islam and trained as future soldiers and administrators. The boys and young men then entered the central system of "palace slaves" under the direct orders of the sultan and his viziers or ministers.

The devşirme contradicted Islamic law, which forbade the enslavement of "peoples of the Book" (Jews, Christians, and Zoroastrians). Its existence, therefore, documents the extent to which the sultans reasserted the Roman–Sasanian–Arab imperial traditions of the ruler making doctrine and law. Ruling by divine grace, the Ottomans were makers of their own law, called *kanun* (from Greek *kanon*). Muslim religious scholars, who had assumed the role of guardians of law and doctrine during the preceding commonwealth period of Islamic civilization (950–1300), had no choice but to accept sultanic imperialism and seek to adapt it to the sharia as best they could.

Toward the first half of the fifteenth century, the sultans equipped their Janissaries with cannons and matchlock muskets. According to reports in Arabic chronicles, firearms first appeared around 1250 in the Middle East, probably coming from China. When the Janissaries received them, firearms had therefore undergone some 150 years of experimentation and development in the Middle East and North Africa. Even though the cannons and muskets were still far from being decisive in battle, they had become sophisticated enough to make a difference. By the mid-1400s, gigantic siege cannons and slow but reliable matchlock muskets were the standard equipment of Ottoman and other armies. The sultans relied on large numbers of indigenous, rather than European, gunsmiths, as new research in Ottoman archives has revealed.

Revenues and Money   The maintenance of a salaried standing army of infantry soldiers and a central administration to provide the fiscal foundation would have been impossible without precious metals. Therefore, the Ottoman imperial expansion was guided by the need to acquire mineral deposits. During the fifteenth century the Ottomans captured the rich silver, lead, and iron mines of Serbia and Bosnia. Together with Anatolian copper, iron, and silver mines occupied earlier, the Balkan mines made the Ottomans the owners of the largest precious metal production centers prior to the Habsburg acquisition of the Mexican and Andean mines in the mid-1500s.

The sultans left the mining and smelting operations in the hands of preconquest Christian entrepreneurs from the autonomous Adriatic coastal city-states of Ragusa and Dubrovnik. These entrepreneurs were integrated into the Ottoman imperial money economy as tax farmers obliged to buy their right of operation from the government in return for reimbursing themselves from the mining and smelting profits. **Tax-farming** was the preferred method of producing cash revenues for the central administration. The holders of tax farms delivered the profits from the production of metals, salt, saltpeter, and other minerals to the state, minus the commission they were entitled to subtract for themselves. They also collected the head tax—payable in money—from the Jews and Christians and the profits from the sale of the agricultural dues from state domains. Thus, tax farmers were crucial members of the ruling class, responsible for the cash flow in the fiscal–military state.

The right to mint silver into the basic coin of the empire, the *akçe* [ak-TSHAY], was similarly part of the tax-farm regime, as were the market, city gate, and port duties. The tax-farm regime, of course, was crucially dependent on a strong sultan or chief minister, the grand vizier. Without close supervision, this regime could easily deteriorate into a state of decentralization, something which indeed eventually happened in the Ottoman Empire on a large scale, although not before the eighteenth century.

Süleyman's Central State

The centralized fiscal–military state of the Ottomans reached its apogee under Sultan Süleyman I, the Magnificent. At the beginning of the sultan's reign, the amount of money available for expenditures was twice that of half a century earlier. By the end of his reign, this amount had again doubled. With this money, the sultan financed a massive expansion of the military and bureaucracy. Palace, military, and bureaucracy formed a centralized state, the purpose of which was to project power and cultural splendor toward its predominantly rural subjects in the interior as well as Christian enemies outside the empire.

The bureaucrats were recruited from two population groups. Most top ministers and officers in the fifteenth and sixteenth centuries came from the *devşirme* among the Christians. The conscripted boys learned Turkish, received an Islamic education, and underwent intensive horsemanship or firearm training, in preparation for salaried service in the Janissary army or administration. The empire's other recruits came from colleges in Istanbul and provincial cities to which the Muslim population of the empire had access. Colleges were institutions through which ambitious villagers far from major urban centers could gain upward mobility. Graduates with law degrees found

Ottoman Siege of a Christian Fortress. By the middle of the fifteenth century, cannons had revolutionized warfare. Niccolò Machiavelli, ever attuned to new developments, noted in 1519 that "no wall exists, however thick, that artillery cannot destroy in a few days." Machiavelli could have been commenting on the Ottomans, who were masters of siege warfare. Sultan Mehmet II, the conqueror of Constantinople in 1453, founded the Imperial Cannon Foundry shortly thereafter; and it would go on to make some of the biggest cannons of the period.

Tax-farming: Governmental auction of the right to collect taxes in a district. The tax farmer advanced these taxes to the treasury and retained a commission.

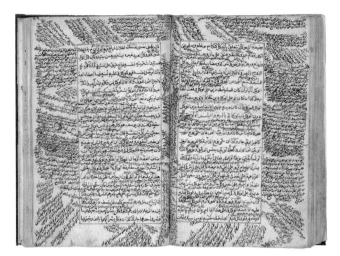

Ottoman Law Book. Covering the entire range of human activity—from spiritual matters, family relations, and inheritances to business transactions and crimes— the *Multaka al-abbur (The Confluence of the Currents)* was completed in 1517 and remained for hundreds of years the authoritative source for many of the laws in the Ottoman Empire. Written in Arabic script by the legal scholar Ibrahim al-Halabi, later commentators added annotations in the margins and within the body of the text itself.

employment as clerical employees in the bureaucracy or as judges in the villages, towns, and cities. Only the judges in the upper ranks of jurisdiction, however, such as the chief judges of Anatolia and the Balkans and the supreme judge of the empire, occupied positions of influence in the administration. Muslims of Christian parentage made up the top layer of the elite, while Muslims of Islamic descent occupied the middle ranks.

Under Süleyman, the Janissaries comprised about 18,000 soldiers, divided into 11,000 musket-equipped troopers, a cavalry of 5,000, and 2,000 gunners who formed the artillery regiments. Most were stationed in barracks in and near the Topkapı Palace in Istanbul, ready to go on campaign at the sultan's command. Other Janissaries provided service in provincial cities and border fortresses. For his campaigns, the sultan added levies from among the cavalry troops in the towns and villages of the empire. Typical campaigns involved 70,000 soldiers and required sophisticated logistics. All wages, gunpowder, and weapons and the majority of the foodstuffs were carried on wagons and barges since soldiers were not permitted to provision themselves from the belongings of the villagers, whether friend or foe. Although the fiscal–military state collected heavy taxes, it had a strong interest in not destroying the productivity of the villagers.

Charles V's Central State   The fiscal–military state began in Iberia with the political and fiscal reforms of Isabella and Ferdinand and reached the mature phase of centralization under Charles V. From the late fifteenth century onward, Castile and Aragon shared many fiscal characteristics with those of the Ottomans. The Spanish monarchs derived cash advances from tax farmers, who organized the production and sale of minerals and salt. From other tax farmers, they received advances on the taxes collected in money from the movement of goods in and out of ports, cities, and markets, as well as on taxes collected in kind from independent farmers and converted through sale on urban markets. In addition, Muslims paid head taxes in cash. Most of the money taxes were also enforced in Flanders, Burgundy, Naples, Sicily, and Austria, after Iberia's incorporation into the Habsburg domain in 1516. Together, these taxes were more substantial than those of Spain, especially in the highly urbanized Flanders, where the percentage of the urban population was about twice that of Spain.

From 1521 to 1536, the Spanish crown enlarged its money income by the one-fifth share to which it was entitled from looted Aztec and Inca gold and silver treasures. Charles V used these treasures to finance his expedition against Tunis. Thereafter, he collected a one-quarter share from the silver mines in the Americas that were brought into production beginning in 1545. Full production in the mines did not set in until the second half of the sixteenth century, but already under Charles V Habsburg imperial revenues doubled, reaching about the same level as those of the Ottomans. Thus, at the height of their struggle for dominance in the Muslim–Christian world, the Habsburgs and the Ottomans expended roughly the same amounts of resources to hurl against each other in the form of troops, cannons, muskets, and war galleys.

In one significant respect, however, the two empires differed. The cavalry ruling class of the Ottoman Empire was nonhereditary. Although land-grant holdings went in practice from father to son and then grandson, their holders had no recourse to the law if the sultans decided to replace them. By contrast, ever since the first half of the thirteenth century, when the Iberian kings were still lacking appreciable monetary resources, their landholders possessed a legal right to inheritance. The landholders met more or less regularly in parliaments (Spanish *cortes*), where they could enforce their property rights against the kings through majority decisions. When Isabella and Ferdinand embarked on state centralization, they had to wrestle with a powerful, landed aristocracy that had taken over royal jurisdiction and tax prerogatives (especially market taxes) on their often vast lands, including cities as well as towns and villages. The two monarchs took back much of the jurisdiction but were unable to do much about the taxes, thus failing in one crucial respect with their centralization effort. Although Habsburg Spain was a fully evolved fiscal–military state, it was in the end less centralized than that of the Ottomans.

The Habsburgs sought to overcome their lack of power over the aristocracy and the weakness of their Spanish tax base by squeezing as much as they could out of the Italian and Flemish cities and the American colonies. But in the long run their finances remained precarious, plentiful in some years but sparse in others. Relatively few Spanish aristocrats bothered to fulfill their traditional obligation to unpaid military service, and if they did, they forced the kings to pay them like mercenaries. As a result, in the administration and especially in the military, the kings hired as many Italians, Flemings, and Germans as possible. At times, they even had to deploy them to Spain in order to maintain peace there. Most of these foreigners were foot soldiers, equipped with muskets.

The Ottoman and Habsburg patterns of fiscal–military state formation bore similarities to patterns in the Roman and Arab Empires half a millennium earlier. At that time, however, the scale was more modest, given that the precious metals from West Africa and the Americas were not yet part of the trade network. In addition, earlier empires did not yet possess firearms, requiring an expensive infrastructure of charcoal and metal production, gunsmithing, saltpeter mining, and gunpowder manufacture. Thanks to firearms, the fiscal–military states of the period after 1450 were much more potent enterprises. They were established states, evolving into absolutist and eventually national states.

Imperial Courts, Urban Festivities, and the Arts

Habsburg kings and Ottoman sultans set aside a portion of revenues to project the splendor and glory of their states to subjects at home as well as enemies abroad. They commissioned the building of palaces, mosques, and churches and sponsored public festivities. Since the administrators, nobility, tax farmers, and merchants had considerable funds, they also patronized writers, artists, and architects. Although Christian and Muslim artists and artisans belonged to different religious and cultural traditions and expressed themselves through different media, their artistic achievements were inspired by the same impulse: to glorify their states through religious expression.

The Spanish Habsburg Empire: Popular Festivities and the Arts

The centrality of Catholicism gave the culture of the Habsburg Empire a strongly religious coloration. Both state-sponsored spectacles and popular festivities displayed devotion to the Catholic faith. More secular tendencies, however, began to appear as well, if only because new forms of literature and theater emerged outside the religious sphere as a result of the Renaissance. Originating in Italy and the Netherlands, Renaissance aesthetics emphasized pre-Christian Greek and Roman heritages, which had not been available to medieval Christian artists.

Capital and Palace   The Habsburgs focused relatively late on the typical symbols of state power and splendor, that is, a capital city and a palace. Most Spaniards lived in the northern third and along the southern and eastern rims of the Iberian Peninsula, leaving the inhospitable central high plateau, the Meseta, thinly inhabited. Catholicism was the majority religion by the sixteenth century and a powerful unifying force, but there were strong linguistic differences among the provinces of the Iberian Peninsula. Charles V resided for a while in a palace in Granada next door to the formerly Muslim Alhambra palace. Built in an Italian Renaissance-derived style and appearing overwhelming and bombastic in comparison to the outwardly unprepossessing Alhambra, Granada was too Moorish and, geographically, too far away in the south for more than a few Spanish subjects to be properly awed.

The Escorial Palace of King Philip II. Note the austere façade and the long horizontal lines of this building, representative of the Renaissance interpretation of the classical Greek-Roman architectural heritage.

Passion play: Dramatic representation of the trial, suffering, and death of Jesus Christ; passion plays are still an integral part of Holy Week in many Catholic countries today.

Only a few places in the river valleys traversing the Meseta were suited for the location of a central palace and administration. Philip II eventually found such a place near the city of Madrid (built on Roman-Visigothic foundations) that in the early sixteenth century had some 12,000 inhabitants. There, he had his royal architect in chief and sculptor Juan Bautista de Toledo (ca. 1515–1567), a student of Michelangelo, build the imposing Renaissance-styled palace and monastery complex of El Escorial (1563–1584). As a result, Madrid became the seat of the administration and later of the court. A large central square and broad avenue were cut across the narrow alleys of the old city, which had once been a Muslim provincial capital. People of all classes gathered in the square and avenue, to participate in public festivities and learn the latest news "about the intentions of the Grand Turk, revolutions in the Netherlands, the state of things in Italy, and the latest discoveries made in the Indies."

Like its Italian paradigm, architecture of the Spanish Renaissance emphasized the Roman imperial style—itself derived from the Greeks—with long friezes, round arches, freestanding columns, and rotunda-based domes. With this style, Spanish architects departed from the preceding Gothic, stressing horizontal extension rather than height and plain rather than relief or ornament-filled surfaces.

Christian State Festivities   Given the close association between the state and the Church, the Spanish crown expressed its glory through the observance of feast days of the Christian calendar. Christmas, Easter, Pentecost, Trinity Sunday, Corpus Christi, and the birthdays of numerous saints were the occasion for processions and/or **passion plays**, during which urban residents affirmed the purity of their

Catholic faith. Throngs lined the streets or marched in procession, praying, singing, weeping, and exclaiming. During Holy Week preceding Easter, Catholics—wearing white robes, tall white or black pointed hats, and veils over their faces—marched through the streets, carrying heavy crosses or shouldering large floats with statues of Jesus and Mary. A variety of religious lay groups or confraternities competed to build the most elaborately decorated floats. Members of flagellant confraternities whipped themselves. The physical rigors of the Holy Week processions were collective reenactments of Jesus' suffering on the Cross.

By contrast, the Corpus Christi (Latin, meaning "body of Christ") processions that took place on the Sunday after Trinity Sunday (several weeks after Easter) were joyous celebrations. Central to these processions was a float with a canopy covering the consecrated host (bread believed to have been transfigured into the body of Jesus). Marchers dressed as giants, serpents, dragons, devils, angels, patriarchs, and saints participated in jostling and pushing contests. Others wore masks, played music, performed dances, and enacted scenes from the Bible. Being part of the crowd in the Corpus Christi processions meant partaking in a joyful anticipation of salvation.

The Auto-da-Fé   The investigation or proceeding of faith (Portuguese *auto-da-fé*, "act of faith") was a show trial in which the state, through the Spanish Inquisition, judged a person's commitment to Catholicism. Inquisitional trials were intended to display the all-important unity and purity of Counter-Reformation Catholicism. The Inquisition employed thousands of state-appointed Church officials to investigate anonymous denunciations of individuals failing to conform to the prescribed doctrines and liturgy of the Catholic faith.

Suspected offenders, such as Jewish or Muslim converts to Catholicism or perceived deviants from Catholicism, had to appear before one of the 15 tribunals distributed over the country. In secret trials, officials determined the degree of the offense and the appropriate punishment. These trials often employed torture, such as stretching the accused on the rack, suspending them with weights, crushing hands and feet in an apparatus called "the boot," and burning them with firebrands. In contrast to the wide perception of the Inquisition as marked by pervasive cruelties, however, scholarship has emphasized that in the great majority of cases the punishments were minor or investigations did not lead to convictions.

Popular Festivities   *Jousts* (mock combats between contestants mounted on horseback) were secular, primarily aristocratic events, also frequently connected with dynastic occurrences. The contestants, colorfully costumed as "Muslims," "Turks," and Christians, rode their horses into the city square accompanied by trumpets and drums and led their Arabian thoroughbreds or Lusitanian warmbloods through a precise and complex series of movements. At the height of the spectacle, contestants divided into groups of three or four at each end of the square. At a signal, they galloped at full speed past each other, hurling their javelins at one another while protecting themselves with their shields. The joust evolved eventually into exhibitions of dressage ("training"), cultivated by the Austrian Habsburgs, who in 1572 founded the Spanish Court Riding School in Vienna.

Bullfights, also fought on horseback, often followed the jousts. Fighting wild animals, including bulls, in spectacles was originally a Roman custom that had evolved from older bovine sacrifices in temples around the Mediterranean. During

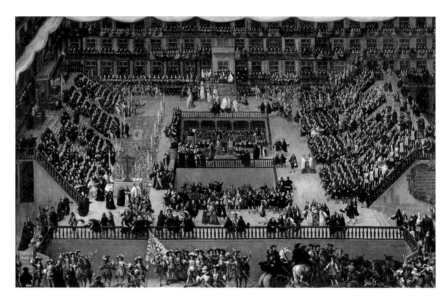

Auto-da-Fé, Madrid. This detail from a painting showing a huge assembly in Plaza Mayor, Madrid, in 1683, captures the drama and spectacle of the auto-da-fé. In the center, below a raised platform, the accused stand in the docket waiting for their convictions to be pronounced; ecclesiastical and civil authorities follow the proceedings from huge grandstands set up for the event. On the left, an outdoor altar is visible—the celebration of mass was a common feature of the auto-da-fé, which would often last for several hours.

the Middle Ages, bullfights were aristocratic occupations that drew spectators from local estates. Bullfighters, armed with detachable metal points on 3-foot-long spears, tackled several bulls in a town square, together with footmen who sought to distract the bulls by waving red capes at them. The bullfighter who stuck the largest number of points into the shoulders of the bull was the winner.

Theater and Literature   The dramatic enactments of biblical scenes in the passion plays and Corpus Christi processions were the origin of a new phenomenon in Spain, the secular theater. During earlier centuries, traveling troupes had often performed on wagons after processions. Stationary theaters with stages, main floors, balconies, and boxes appeared in the main cities of Spain during the sixteenth century. A performance typically began with a musical prelude and a prologue describing the piece, followed by the three acts of a drama or comedy. Brief sketches, humorous or earnest, filled the breaks. Plays dealt with betrayed or unrequited love, honor, justice, or peasant–nobility conflicts. Many were hugely successful, enjoying the attendance or even sponsorship of courtiers, magistrates, and merchants.

An important writer of the period was Miguel de Cervantes (1547–1616), who wrote his masterpiece, *Don Quixote*, in the new literary form of the novel. *Don Quixote* describes the adventures of a poverty-stricken knight and his attendant, the peasant Sancho Panza, as they wander around Spain searching for the life of bygone Reconquista chivalry. Their journey includes many hilarious escapades during which they run into the reality of the early modern fiscal–military state dominated by monetary concerns. Cervantes confronts the vanished virtues of knighthood with the novel values of the life with money.

Cervantes' personal life was full of struggle. The son of a poor surgeon, he received a literary education before enlisting in the military. In the battle of Lepanto in 1571, an injury incapacitated his left arm. In 1575, Muslim corsairs from North Africa captured and imprisoned him in Algiers. Like Leo Africanus, discussed in the vignette at the beginning of this chapter, he was one of tens of thousands of kidnap victims on both the Christian and Muslim sides during the 1500s. Cervantes regained his freedom 5 years later when a Catholic religious order seeking release for captives in North Africa paid his ransom. Cervantes' early publications attracted little attention, and several times he was imprisoned for unpaid debts. Not until late in life did he receive recognition for his literary works.

Painters   The outstanding painter of Spain during Philip II's reign was El Greco (Domenikos Theotokopoulos, ca. 1546–1614), a native of the island of Crete. After early training in Crete as a painter of eastern Christian icons, El Greco went to Venice for further studies. In 1577, the Catholic hierarchy hired him to paint the altarpieces of a church in Toledo, the city in central Spain that was one of the residences of the kings prior to the construction of El Escorial in Madrid. El Greco's works reflect the spirit of Spanish Catholicism, with its emphasis on strict obedience to traditional faith and fervent personal piety. His characteristic style features elongated, pale figures surrounded by vibrant colors and represents a variation of the so-called mannerist style (with its perspective exaggerations), which succeeded the Renaissance style in Venice during the later sixteenth century.

El Greco, **View of Toledo,** *ca.* **1610–1614.** The painting, now in the Metropolitan Museum, New York, illustrates El Greco's predilection for color contrasts and dramatic motion. Baroque and Mannerist painters rarely depicted landscapes and this particular landscape is represented in eerie green, gray, and blue colors giving the impression of a city enveloped in a mysterious natural or perhaps spiritual force.

The Ottoman Empire: Palaces, Festivities, and the Arts

Similar to the Habsburgs, the Ottomans built palaces and celebrated public feasts to demonstrate their imperial power and wealth. In Ottoman Islamic civilization, however, there were no traditions of official public art. The exception was architecture, where a veritable explosion of mosque construction occurred during the sixteenth century. High-quality pictorial artistry, in the form of portraits, book illustrations and miniatures, was found only inside the privacy of the Ottoman palace and wealthy administrative households. As in Habsburg Spain, theater and music enjoyed much support on the popular level, in defiance of official religious restrictions against these forms of entertainment.

The Topkapı Palace   When the Ottoman sultans conquered the Byzantine capital Constantinople in 1453, they took over one of the great cities of the world. Although richly endowed with Roman monuments and churches, it was dilapidated and depopulated when the Ottomans took over. The sultans initiated large construction projects, such as covered markets, and populated them with craftspeople and traders drawn from both Asian and European sides of their empire. By 1600 Istanbul was again an imposing metropolis with close to half a million inhabitants, easily the largest city in Europe at that time.

One of the construction projects was a new palace for the sultans, the Topkapı Sarayı or "Palace of the Gun Gate," begun in 1463. The Topkapı was a veritable minicity, with three courtyards, formal gardens, and forested hunting grounds. It also included the main administrative school for the training of imperial bureaucrats, barracks for the standing troops of the Janissaries, an armory, a hospital, and—most

Imperial Hall, Topkapı Palace.
The Ottomans never forgot
their nomadic roots. Topkapı
Palace, completed in 1479 and
expanded and redecorated
several times, resembles in
many ways a vast encampment,
with a series of enclosed
courtyards. At the center of the
palace complex were the harem
and the private apartments of
the sultan, which included the
Imperial Hall, where the sultan
would receive members of his
family and closest advisors.

important—the living quarters, or harem, for the
ruling family. Subjects were permitted access only
through the first courtyard—reserved for imperial
festivities—to submit their petitions to the sultan's
council of ministers.

The institution of the harem rose to prominence
toward the end of the reign of Süleyman. At that
time, sultans no longer pursued marriage alliances
with neighboring Islamic rulers. Instead, they chose
slave concubines for the procreation of children,
preferably boys. Concubines were usually from the
Caucasus or other frontier regions, often Christian, and, since they were slaves, deprived of family
attachments. A concubine who bore a son to the
reigning sultan acquired privileges, such as influence
on decisions taken by the central administration. The head eunuch of the harem
guard evolved into a powerful intermediary for all manner of small and large diplomatic and military decisions between a sultan's mother, who was confined to the
harem, and the ministers or generals she sought to influence. In addition, the sultan's
mother arranged marriages of her daughters to members of the council of ministers
and other high-ranking officials. In the strong patriarchal order of the Ottoman Empire, it might come as a surprise to see women exercise such power, but this power
evidently had its roots in the tutelage exercised by mothers over sons who were potential future sultans.

Public Festivities   As in Habsburg Spain, feasts and celebrations were events
that displayed the state's largesse and benevolence. Typical festivities were the Feast
of Breaking the Fast, which came at the end of the fasting month of Ramadan, and
the Feast of Sacrifice, which took place a month and a half later at the end of the Meccan pilgrimage. Festive processions and fairs welcomed the return of the Meccan
pilgrimage caravan. Other feasts were connected with the birthday of the Prophet
Muhammad and his journey to heaven and hell. Muslims believed that the Prophet's
birth was accompanied by miracles and that the angel Gabriel accompanied him
on his journey, showing him the joys of heaven and the horrors of hell. Processions
with banners, music, and communal meals commemorated the birthdays of local
Muslim saints in many cities and towns. As in Christian Spain, these feasts attracted
large crowds.

Wrestlers, ram handlers, and horsemen performed in the Hippodrome, the stadium for public festivities. Elimination matches in wrestling determined the eventual champion. Ram handlers spurred their animals to gore one another with their
horns. Horsemen stood upright on horses, galloping toward a mound, which they
had to hit with a javelin. At the harbor of the Golden Horn, tightrope artists stood
high above the water, balancing themselves on cables stretched between the masts
of ships, as they performed juggling feats. Fireworks—producing a variety of effects, noises, and colors—completed the circumcision festival in the evening. Court
painters recorded the procession and performance scenes in picture albums. The
sultans incorporated these albums into their libraries, together with history books
recording in word and image their battle victories against the Habsburgs.

Popular Theater   The evenings of the fasting month of Ramadan were filled with festive meals and a special form of entertainment, the Karagöz ("Blackeye") shadow theater. This form of theater came from Egypt, although it probably had Javanese–Chinese roots. The actors in the Karagöz theater used figures cut from thin, transparent leather, painted in primary colors, and fashioned with movable jaws and limbs. With brightly burning lamps behind them, actors manipulated the figures against a cloth screen. The audience was seated on the other side of the screen, following the plays with rapt attention (or not).

Among boys, a performance of the Karagöz theater accompanied the ritual of circumcision, a rite of passage from the ancient Near East adopted in Islamic civilization. It called for boys between the ages of 6 and 12 to be circumcised. Circumcision signified the passage from the nurturing care of the mother to the educational discipline of the father. Groups of newly circumcised boys were placed in beds from which they watched the Karagöz plays.

Mosque Architecture   During the sixteenth century, the extraordinarily prolific architect Sinan (ca. 1492–1588) filled Istanbul and the earlier Ottoman capital Edirne with a number of imperial mosques, defined by their characteristic slender minarets. According to his autobiography, Sinan designed more than 300 religious and secular buildings, from mosques, colleges, and hospitals to aqueducts and bridges. Sultan Süleyman, wealthy officials, and private donors provided

Ottoman Festivities, 1720. The sultan watches from a kiosk on the shore of the Golden Horn as artists perform high-wire acts, musicians and dancers perform from rowboats offshore, and high officials and foreign dignitaries view the festivities from a galleon.

Selimiye and Hagia Sophia. The architect Sinan elegantly melded the eight, comparatively thin columns, inside the mosque (*a*) with the surrounding walls and allows for a maximum of light to enter the building. In addition, light enters through the dome (*b*). Compare this mosque with the much more heavily built, late Roman-founded Hagia Sophia (*c*).

the funds. Sinan was able to hire as many as 25,000 laborers, enabling him to build most of his mosques in six years or less.

Sinan was a Christian-born Janissary from a Greek village in northwestern Anatolia. He entered the palace school at the comparatively late age of 19, and it was only after many years of service in the army corps of engineers before he received his first commission for a mosque in 1538. Sinan himself describes the Shehzade and Süleymaniye mosques in Istanbul and the Selimiye mosque in Edirne as his apprentice, journeyman, and master achievements. All three followed the central dome-over-a-square concept of the Hagia Sophia, which in turn is built in the tradition of Persian and Roman dome architecture. His primary, and most original, contribution to the history of architecture was the replacement of the highly visible and massive four exterior buttresses, which marked the square ground plan of the Hagia Sophia, with up to eight slender pillars as hidden internal supports of the dome. His intention with each of these mosques was not massive monumentality but elegant spaciousness, giving the skylines of Istanbul and Edirne their unmistakable identity.

Putting It All Together

The Ottoman–Habsburg struggle can be seen as another chapter in the long history of competition that began when the Achaemenid Persian Empire expanded into the Mediterranean and was resisted by the Greeks in the middle of the first millennium BCE. Although India and China were frequently subjected to incursions from central Asia, neither of the two had to compete for long with any of its neighbors. Sooner or later the central Asians either retreated or were absorbed by their victims. The Ottomans' brief experience with Timur was on the same order. But the Middle East and Europe were always connected, and this chapter, once more, draws attention to this connectedness.

There were obvious religious and cultural differences between the Islamic and western Christian civilizations as they encountered each other during the Ottoman–Habsburg period. But their commonalities are equally, if not more, interesting. Most importantly, both Ottomans and Habsburgs were representatives of the return to imperialism, and in the pursuit of their imperial goals, both adopted the fiscal–military state with its firearm infantries and pervasive urban money economy. Both found it crucial to their existence to project their glory to the population at large and to sponsor artistic expression. In the long run, however, the imperial ambitions of the Ottomans and Habsburgs exceeded their ability to raise cash. Although firearms and a monetized urban economy made them different from previous empires, they were as unstable as all their imperial predecessors. Eventually, around 1600, they reached the limits of their conquests.

▶ For additional resources, including maps, primary sources, visuals, and quizzes, please go to www.oup.com/us/vonsivers. Please see the Further Resources section at the back of the book for additional readings and suggested websites.

Thinking Through Patterns

▶ **What patterns characterized the Christian and Muslim imperial competition in the period 1300–1600? Which elements distinguished them from each other, and which elements were similar? How did the pattern change over time?**

In 1300, the Ottomans renewed the Arab-Islamic tradition of jihad against the eastern Christian empire of Byzantium, conquering the Balkans and eventually defeating the empire with the conquest of Constantinople 1453. They also carried the war into the western Mediterranean and Indian Ocean. In western Christian Iberia, the rekindling of the reconquest after the lull of the thirteenth and fourteenth centuries was more successful. Invigorated by a merging of the concepts of the Crusade and the Reconquista, the Iberians expanded overseas to circumvent the Muslims and trade Indian spices directly. The so-called Age of Exploration, during which western Christians traveled to and settled in overseas lands, is deeply rooted in the Western traditions of war against Islamic civilization.

In the mid-1400s, the Middle East and Europe returned to the pattern of imperial state formation after a lull of several centuries, during which states had competed against each other within their respective commonwealths. The element which fueled this return was gunpowder weaponry. The use of cannons and handheld firearms became widespread during this time but required major financial outlays on the part of the states. The Ottomans and Habsburgs were the states with the most resources, and the Ottomans even built the first standing armies. To pay the musket-equipped soldiers, huge amounts of silver were necessary. The two empires became centralized fiscal–military states based on a money economy: Bureaucracies maintained centralized departments that regulated the collection of taxes and the payroll of soldiers.

▶ **How did the fiscal–military state in the Middle East and Europe function in the period 1450–1600? How did economics, military power, and imperial objectives interact to create the fiscal-military state?**

▶ **Which patterns did cultural expressions follow in the Habsburg and Ottoman Empires? Why did the ruling classes of these empires sponsor these expressions?**

The rulers of these empires were concerned to portray themselves, their military, and their bureaucracies as highly successful and just. The state had to be as visible and benevolent as possible. Rulers, therefore, were builders of palaces, churches, or mosques. They celebrated religious and secular festivities with great pomp and encouraged ministers and the nobility to do likewise. In the imperial capitals, they patronized architects, artists, and writers, resulting in a veritable explosion of intellectual and artistic creativity. In this regard, the Ottomans and the Habsburgs followed similar patterns of cultural expression.

Chapter 17 1450-1750

Renaissance, Reformation, and the New Science in Europe

URBAN POPULATION
OF EUROPE IN 1700

■ Over 30%
■ 25-30%
■ 10-15%
■ 5-10%
■ 1-5%
□ 0-1%
• city with population
over 200,000

T hough less celebrated than her male contemporaries, one of the most remarkable scientific minds of the seventeenth century was that of Maria Cunitz (ca. 1607–1664). Under the tutorship of her father, a physician, she became accomplished in six languages (Hebrew, Greek, Latin, Italian, French, and Polish), the humanities, and the sciences. For a number of years while the Thirty Years' War (1618–1648) raged in Germany and her home province of Silesia, Cunitz and her Protestant family sought refuge in a Cistercian monastery in neighboring Catholic Poland. There, under difficult living conditions, she wrote *Urania propitia* (*Companion to Urania*), in praise of the Greek muse and patron of astronomy. When the family returned to Silesia after the war, Cunitz lost her scientific papers and instruments to a fire; but she continued to devote her life to the New Science through her careful astronomical observations.

Cunitz's book is a popularization of the astronomical tables of Johannes Kepler (1571–1630), the major scientific innovator remembered today for his discovery of the elliptical trajectories of the planets. Cunitz's book makes corrections in Kepler's tables and offers simplified calculations of star positions. Written in both Latin and German, she published it privately in 1650. It was generally well received, although there were a few

ABOVE: Telescopic drawing of the moon by Galileo Galilei (1564–1642), showing the moon as a solid body—an observation that led him to argue that the Earth was not unique.

detractors who found it hard to believe that a woman could succeed in the sciences. Whatever injustice was done to her during her lifetime, today the scientific community has made amends. A crater on Venus has been named after her, and a statue of her stands in her Silesian hometown.

Cunitz lived in a time when western Christianity had entered the age of early global interaction, from 1450 until 1750. During most of this time, Europe remained institutionally similar to the other parts of the world, especially the Middle East, India, China, and Japan. Rulers throughout Eurasia governed by divine grace. All large states followed patterns of fiscal–military organization. Their urban populations were nowhere more than ca. 40 percent, and their economies depended on the prosperity of agriculture. As research on China, the Middle East, and India during 1450–1750 has shown, the "great divergence" in the patterns of political organization, social formation, and economic production between western Christianity and the other religious civilizations, whatever the characteristics that made each unique in other ways, did not take place until around 1800.

Culturally, however, northwestern Europe began to move in a different direction from Islamic, Hindu, Neo-Confucian, and Buddhist civilizations. The New Science and the Enlightenment of England, France, the Netherlands, and parts of Germany initiated new cultural patterns for which there was no equivalent in the other parts of Eurasia, including southern Europe. As significant as these patterns were, for almost the entire three centuries of 1450–1750 the New Science and the Enlightenment remained limited to a few hundred and later to a few thousand educated persons, largely outside the ruling classes. Their ideas and outlooks diverged substantially from those represented by the Catholic and Protestant ruling classes and resulted frequently in tensions or, in a few cases, even repression of New Scientists by the authorities. The new scientific and intellectual culture broadened into a mass movement only after 1750. The subsequent Industrial Revolution was rooted in this movement.

———

This chapter begins with a focus on the political pattern of fiscal–military state formation which coincided with the Protestant Reformation. The combustible mix of large armies of firearm-bearing mercenaries and fiery anti- and pro-Catholic polemics exploded in a series of religious wars lasting for a century and a half. When the religious fervor eventually died down, Europe separated into Catholic and Protestant fiscal–military states, now called "absolutist," which struggled with the challenges of economic viability. Accompanying the political–religious struggle was a pattern of rapid cultural transformations, explored in the second half of this chapter. The European Renaissance, Baroque, and New Science formed a sequence that was discontinuous with the western Christian

Seeing Patterns

▶ What were the patterns of fiscal–military state formation and transformation in the period 1450–1750? How did the Protestant Reformation and religious wars modify these patterns?

▶ What are the reasons for the cultural change that began in Europe around 1750? In which ways were the patterns of cultural change during 1450–1750 different from those in the other religious civilizations of Eurasia?

▶ When and how did the New Science begin, and how did it gain popularity in northwestern Europe? Why is the popularization of the New Science important for understanding the period 1450–1750?

Middle Ages and signified the search for a new cultural consensus. Cultural discontinuity, a rapid succession of different styles of cultural expression, and the absence of a consensus typified western Christianity, in contrast to the Middle East, India, and China, where cultural continuity reigned until the 1800s.

Fiscal–Military States and Religious Upheavals

The pattern of the fiscal–military state transforming the institutional structures of society was a characteristic not only in the Ottoman and Habsburg Empires during 1450–1750 but also in other countries of Europe, the Middle East, and India. The financial requirements for sustaining a fiscal–military state required everywhere a reorganization of the relationship between rulers, ruling classes, and regional as well as local forces. The Protestant Reformation and religious wars slowed the pattern of fiscal–military state formation, but once the religious fervor was spent, two types of states emerged: the French, Russian, and Prussian landed fiscal–military state and the Dutch and English naval fiscal–military state.

The Rise of Fiscal–Military Kingdoms

The shift from feudal mounted and armored knights to firearm-equipped professional infantries led to the emergence of the fiscal–military state. Rulers sought to centralize state power, collect higher taxes to subsidize their infantries, and curb the decentralizing forces of the nobility, cities, and other local institutions. Not all autonomous units (such as city-states, city-leagues, and religious orders dating to the previous period, 600–1450) were able to survive the military challenges of the rulers. A winnowing process occurred during 1450–1550, which left a few territorially coherent fiscal–military kingdoms in control of European politics.

The Demographic Curve   Following the demographic disaster of the Black Death in 1348 and its many subsequent cycles, the population of Europe expanded again after 1470. It reached its pre-1348 levels around 1550, with some 85 million inhabitants (not counting the Spanish Habsburg and Ottoman Empires). The population continued to grow until about 1600 (90 million), when it entered a half-century of stagnation during the coldest and wettest period in recorded history, the "Little Ice Age" (1550–1750).

During 1650–1750, the population rose slowly at a moderate rate from 105 to 140 million. In 1750, France (28 million) and Russia (21 million) were the most populous countries, followed by Germany (18 million), Italy (15 million), Poland (13 million), England (7 million), and the Netherlands and Sweden (2 million each). While the population figures of the individual countries for the most part bore little resemblance to their political importance during 1450–1750, as we shall see, the overall figures for Europe demonstrate that western Christianity had risen by 1750 to a status of demographic comparability vis-à-vis the other two major religious civilizations of India (155 million) and China (225 million).

Political Realignments   Bracketed between the two empires of the Ottomans and Habsburgs at either geographical end, western Christian Europe during the second half of the fifteenth century was a quilt of numerous independent or autonomous units, including the nascent fiscal–military kingdoms of France and England, the Hanseatic League of trading cities, the Catholic crusading order of Teutonic knights, and the small kingdoms of Denmark, Sweden, Norway, Poland–Lithuania, Bohemia, and Hungary. It furthermore comprised the principalities and cities of Germany, the duchy of Burgundy, the Alpine republic of Switzerland, and the city-states of Italy. At the northeastern periphery was the Grand Duchy of Moscow, representing eastern Christianity after the fall of Byzantium to the Ottomans in 1453. In this quilt, the majority of units competed vigorously with each other, seeking either to exploit the new possibilities which armies of mercenaries with firearms gave them or to survive as best as possible with just a handful.

By the first half of the sixteenth century, the competition had produced a number of winners and losers. Burgundy's dream for an independent kingdom came to an end with its defeat by and incorporation into France in 1477. France's further territorial expansion at the expense of the Italian city-states, beginning with Milan and Naples in 1499–1501, initially looked promising but eventually failed against Spain's similar aims. By the middle of the 1500s only Venice remained independent from Spain. The biggest winner was the Habsburg King Charles V of Spain (r. 1516–1558), who ended the imperial ambitions of King Francis I (r. 1515–1547) of France when the pope, handsomely bribed with Habsburg loans, bestowed the crown of the Holy Roman Empire (Germany, Austria, and the Netherlands) on Charles. Habsburg rounded off its territories in 1526 with the acquisition of Bohemia and the non-Ottoman portion of Hungary. But its lack of territorial cohesion limited its fiscal–military effectiveness.

In northern and eastern Europe, a similar sorting out occurred. England lost Calais, its last toehold on the European continent, to France in 1558. Militarily uninvolved on the Continent and with no need for a standing army, it fell behind in its evolution toward a fiscal–military state. The rising territorial kingdom of Poland–Lithuania (an elective kingdom after 1569) assumed control over a number of Baltic cities of the Hanseatic League and absorbed the lands of the Teutonic Order in 1525 as the duchy of Prussia. When united with Brandenburg in 1618, Prussia evolved into a potent fiscal–military kingdom independent from Poland. On the other side of the Baltic Sea, the union of the Scandinavian countries broke apart when Sweden, with the invasion of Danish Stockholm in 1526, declared its fiscal–military ambitions. On the eastern periphery, the Russian ruler Ivan IV, the Terrible (r. 1533–1584), took the title of emperor (*tsar*, from Latin for "caesar") in 1547 and embarked on a program of conquest which later made Russia a full-fledged fiscal–military rival of the Ottoman Empire.

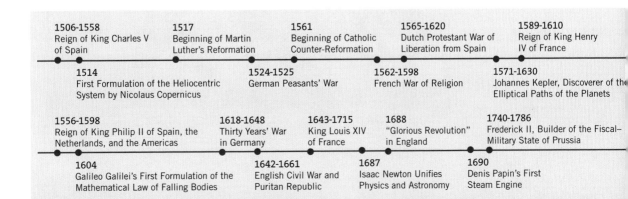

Military and Administrative Capacities   The fiscal–military kingdoms which arose in the sixteenth century remained at the forefront of military innovation. In the course of the century, some kingdoms turned their mercenary troops into standing armies and stationed them in star-shaped forts, a fifteenth-century Italian innovation that made walls more resistant to artillery fire and trapped attackers in cross fires. Sweden introduced the line infantry in the mid-seventeenth century. In this strategy, three-deep lines of musketeers advanced on a broad front toward the enemy, with the front line firing, stepping back to reload, and making room for the next two lines to step forward and repeat the action. These forces underwent extensive peacetime drills and maneuvers. They wore uniforms and soon fired bayonet-equipped flintlock muskets, both introduced in the late seventeenth century in France. Pikemen, equipped with thrusting spears-cum-battle-axes for the protection of musketeers in hand-to-hand combat, were phased out with the appearance of the bayonet. By 1750, armies in the larger European countries were both more uniform and more numerous, increasing from a few thousand to hundreds of thousands of soldiers (see Map 17.1).

The military forces devoured copious amounts of tax money. Accordingly, taxes expanded substantially during the period 1450–1550. But rulers could not raise land, head, and commerce taxes without the formal (in assemblies) or informal (based on customs and traditions) assent of the ruling classes and cities. Similarly, villagers voted with their feet when taxes became too oppressive. The taxation limits were reached in most European countries in the mid-sixteenth century, and for the next two centuries rulers could raise additional finances only to the detriment of their previously acquired central powers, such as by borrowing from merchants and selling offices. The Netherlands was an exception. Only there did the urban population rise from 10 to 40 percent, willing to pay higher taxes on expanded urban manufactures and commercial suburban farming. The Dutch government also derived substantial revenues from charters granted to armed overseas trading companies. Given the severe limits on revenue-raising measures in most of Europe, the eighteenth century saw a general deterioration of state finances, which eventually became a major contributing factor to the American and French Revolutions.

Musketeers. These pictures from an English illustrated drill manual demonstrate the steps by which a seventeenth-century musketeer "makes ready" his weapon, typically in less than 30 seconds. In battle, a sergeant would stand alongside each company of musketeers, organizing its movements and volley fire. Once a rank of musketeers had discharged its weapons it would move out of the way for another rank to fire. If combat was joined at close quarters, the musketeers would use their rifle butts as clubs.

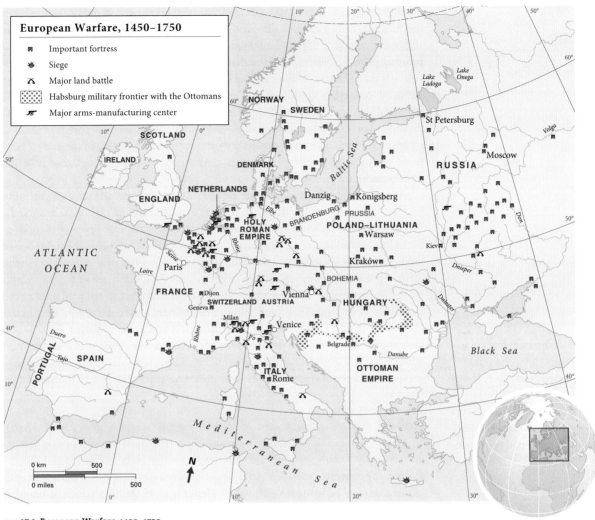

MAP **17.1** European Warfare, 1450–1750.

The Protestant Reformation, State Churches, and Independent Congregations

Parallel to the growing centralism of the kings, the popes restored the central role of the Vatican in the Church hierarchy, after the devastating Great Schism of competing papal lines (1305–1415). Outwardly, the popes displayed this restoration through expensive Vatican construction projects that aroused considerable criticism outside Rome, especially in Germany where the leading clergy under a weak emperor was more strongly identified with Rome than elsewhere. Growing literacy and lay religiosity helped in the growth of a profound theological dissatisfaction which exploded in the **Protestant Reformation**. The Reformation began as an antipapal movement of reform in the early sixteenth century that demanded a return to the simplicity of early Christianity. The movement quickly engulfed the fiscal–military kingdoms and divided their ruling classes and populations alike. Vicious religious wars were the consequence. Although these wars eventually subsided, the divisions were never healed completely and mark the culture of many areas in Europe even today.

Protestant Reformation: Broad movement to reform the Roman Catholic Church, the beginnings of which are usually associated with Martin Luther.

Background to the Reformation   Several religious and political changes in the fifteenth century led to the Protestant Reformation. One important religious shift was the growth of popular religiosity, a consequence of the introduction of the printing press (1454/55) and the distribution of printed materials. A flood of devotional tracts catered to the spiritual interests of ordinary people. Many Christians attended mass daily, confessed, and did penance for their sins. Wealthy Christians endowed saint cults, charitable institutions, or confraternities devoted to the organization of processions and passion plays. Poor people formed lay groups or studied scripture on their own and devoted themselves to the simple life of the early Christians. More Europeans than in previous centuries had a basic, though mostly literal, understanding of Christianity.

An important political change in the fifteenth century was an increasing inability for the popes, powerful in Rome, to appoint archbishops and bishops outside Italy. The kings of France, Spain, England, and Sweden were busy transforming their kingdoms into centralized fiscal–military states, in which they reduced the influence of the popes. Only in Germany, where the powers of the emperor and the rulers in the various principalities canceled each other out, was the influence of the popes still strong. What remained to the popes was the right to collect a variety of dues in the kingdoms of Europe. They used these dues to finance their expensive and, in the eyes of many, luxuriously worldly administration and court in Rome, from which they engaged in European politics. One of the dues was the sale of **indulgences**, which, in popular understanding, were tickets to heaven. Many contemporary observers found the discrepancy between declining papal power and the remaining financial privileges disturbing and demanded reforms.

Indulgence: Partial remission of sins after payment of a fine. The payment would mean the forgiveness of sins by the Church, but the sinner still remained responsible for his or her sins before God.

Luther's Reformation   One such observer was Martin Luther (1483–1546), an Augustinian monk, ordained priest, and New Testament professor in northeastern Germany. Luther was imbued with deep personal piety and confessed his sins daily, doing extensive penance. After a particularly egregious sale of indulgences in his area, in 1517 he wrote his archbishop a letter with 95 theses in which he branded the indulgences and other matters as contrary to scripture. Friends translated the theses from Latin into German and made them public. What was to become the Protestant Reformation had begun.

News of Luther's public protest traveled quickly across Europe. Sales of indulgences fell off sharply. In a series of writings, Luther spelled out the details of the church reform he envisaged. One reform proposal was the elevation of original New Testament scripture over tradition, that is, over canon law and papal decisions. Salvation was to be by faith alone; good works were irrelevant. Another reform was the declaration of the priesthood of all Christians, doing away with the privileged position of the clergy as mediators between God and believers who could forgive sins. A third reform was a call to German princes to begin church reform in their own lands through their power over clerical appointments, even if the Habsburg emperor was opposed. Finally, by translating the Bible into German, Luther made the full sacred text available to all who, by reading or listening, wanted to rely solely on scripture as the source of their faith. Luther's Bible was a monument of the emerging literary German language. A forceful and clear writer in his translation and own publications, Luther fully explicated the basics of Protestantism.

Reaction to Luther's Demands   Both emperor and pope failed in their efforts to arrest Luther and suppress his call for church reform. The duke of Saxony was successful in protecting the reformer from seizure. Emperor Charles V, a devout Catholic, considered Castile's successful church reform of half a century earlier to be fully sufficient. In his mind, Luther's demands for church reform were to be resisted. Two other pressing concerns, however, diverted the emperor's attention. First, the Ottoman-led Islamic threat, in eastern Europe and the western Mediterranean, had to be met with decisive action. Second, his rivalry with the French king precluded the formation of a common Catholic front against Luther. Enthusiastic villagers and townspeople in Germany exploited Charles' divided attention and abandoned both Catholicism and secular obedience. A savage civil war, called the "Peasants' War," engulfed Germany from 1524 to 1525, killing perhaps as many as 100,000 people.

Luther and other prominent reformers were horrified by the carnage. They drew up church ordinances that regulated preaching, church services, administrative councils, education, charity, and consistories for handling disciplinary matters. In Saxony, the duke endorsed this order in 1528. He thereby created the model of Lutheran Protestantism as a state religion, in which the rulers were protectors and supervisors of the churches in their territories. A decade later, Saxony was fully Lutheran.

A minority of about half a dozen German princes and the kings of Denmark and Sweden followed suit. In England, Protestants gained strength in the wake of Henry VIII's (r. 1509–1547) break with Rome and assumption of church leadership in his kingdom (1534). Although remaining Catholic, he surrounded himself with religious reformers and proclaimed an Anglican state church whose creed and rites combined elements of Catholicism and Protestantism. A similar pattern was followed in other states in northern Europe (except for France), where upon breaking with Catholicism they established state churches (see Map 17.2).

Calvinism in France   In France, as in England, the king controlled all church appointments. King Francis I, however, did not take the final step toward the creation of an independent state church. Since he competed with Charles V for dominance over the papacy in Italy, he had to appear especially loyal and devout. When a few Protestants in France went public with their demands for church reform, Francis I gave them the stark choice of exile or burning at the stake. One reformer who chose exile was the French lawyer John Calvin (1509–1564, Jean Cauvin). Calvin went to republican Switzerland, where, in the absence of a central state authority, magistrates implemented the Protestant Reformation in a number of cities.

In Geneva, the magistrates called on Calvin to help them devise a strict Protestant moral code, which they introduced in 1541. The city was under the nominal rule of the duke of Savoy (himself under the nominal rule of the Habsburgs) and not yet part of Switzerland. As expressed in Calvin's central work, *Institutes of the Christian Religion* (1536), and numerous other writings, a crucial doctrine of Calvin's was *predestination*. According to this doctrine, God has "predestined" each

Anti-Catholic Propaganda. This anonymous woodcut of 1520 by a German satirist depicts the devil (complete with wings and clawed feet) sitting on a letter of indulgence and holding a money collection box. The devil's mouth is filled with sinners who presumably bought letters of indulgence in good faith, thinking they had been absolved from their sins.

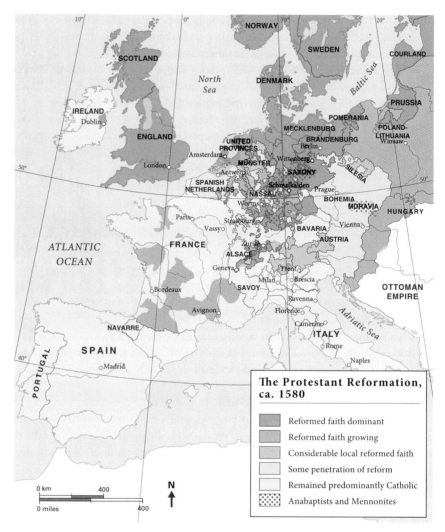

MAP **17.2 The Protestant Reformation, ca. 1580.**

human prior to birth for heaven or hell. Believers could only hope, through faith alone, that sometime during a life of moral living they would receive a glimpse of their fate. In contrast to Luther, however, Calvin made the enforcement of morality through a formal code, administered by local authorities, part of his version of Protestantism. Calvin died in his Genevan exile, but Geneva-trained Calvinist preachers went to France and the Netherlands in the mid-1500s. Under the protection of local magistrates, they organized the first clandestine independent Calvinist congregations. Calvinist religious self-organization by independent congregations thus became a viable alternative to Lutheran state religion.

The Counter-Reformation   The rivalry between Spain and France made it initially difficult for the popes to tackle the problem of Catholic reforms in order to meet the Protestant challenge. When they finally called together the Council of Trent (1545–1563), they abolished payment for indulgences and phased out other church practices considered to be corrupt. These actions launched the

Counter-Reformation, an effort to gain back lapsed Catholics. Supported by the kings of Spain and France, however, the popes reaffirmed the doctrines of faith together with good works, priestly mediation between believer and God, and monasticism. They even tightened church control through the revival of the papal Inquisition and a new Index of Prohibited Books. To counterbalance these punitive institutions, the popes furthered the work of the Basque priest Ignatius Loyola (1491–1556). At the head of the new order of the Society of Jesus, or "Jesuits," Loyola devoted himself tirelessly to the education of the clergy, establishment of a network of Catholic schools and colleges, and conversion of Protestants as well as non-Christians by missionaries to the Americas and eastern Asia. Thanks to Jesuit discipline, Catholics regained a semblance of self-assurance.

Counter-Reformation: Reaffirmation of the Catholic papal supremacy and the doctrine of faith together with works as preparatory to salvation; such practices as absenteeism (bishops in Rome instead of their bishoprics) and pluralism (bishops and abbots holding multiple appointments) were abolished.

Religious Wars and Political Restoration

The growth of Calvinism led to a civil war in France and to a war of liberation from Spanish Catholic rule in the Netherlands in the later sixteenth century. In England, the slow pace of reform in the Anglican Church, with which neither Calvinists nor Catholics could identify, erupted in the early seventeenth century into a civil war. In Germany, the Catholic–Protestant struggle turned into the devastating Thirty Years' War (1618–1648), which France and Sweden won at the expense of the Habsburgs. On the religious level, western Christians grudgingly accepted denominational toleration; on the political level, the fiscal–military states evolved into polities based on a combination between absolutist and decentralized administrative practices.

Civil War in France   During the mid-1500s, Calvinism in France grew to about 1,200 congregations, mostly in the western cities of the kingdom, where literate merchants and craftspeople catering to trade overseas were receptive to Protestant publications. Calvinism was essentially an urban denomination, and peasants did not join in large numbers. Some 2 million, or 10 percent of the total population of 18.5 million, were "Huguenots," as the Protestants were called in France. They continued to be persecuted, but given their numbers, it was impossible for the government to imprison and execute them all. In 1571, they even met in a kingdom-wide

Wars of Religion. The massacre of 74 Huguenots (as the Calvinists were called in France) in the town of Vassy east of Paris in 1562 was the opening salvo in the French wars of religion. The Huguenots were holding religious services in a barn when followers of Francis, Duke of Guise, fell into a quarrel with the unarmed Calvinists. The Duke was hit by a stone, inciting a bloody revenge.

synod, where they ratified their congregational church order. They posed a formidable challenge to French Catholicism.

In many cities, relations between Huguenots and Catholics were uneasy. From time to time, groups of agitators crashed each other's church services. The arrival of a child king to the French throne in 1560 was an open invitation to escalate hostilities. In vain, the queen mother, Catherine de' Medici (1519–1589), who acted as the king's regent, sought to reign in the passions. The first three rounds of war ended with the victorious Huguenots achieving full freedom of religious practice and self-government in four western cities. In this new situation, she arranged in 1572 for the marriage of her daughter to King Henry III of Navarre (later King Henry IV of France, 1589–1610), a Protestant of the Bourbon family in southwestern France. Henry had risen to the leadership of the Huguenots a few years earlier, but he detested the fanaticism that surrounded him.

The prospect of a Huguenot king drove the Catholic aristocracy into a renewed frenzy of religious persecution. On St. Bartholomew's Day (August 24, 1572), just 6 days after the wedding of the future Henry IV, they perpetrated a wholesale slaughter of thousands of Huguenots. This massacre, in response to the assassination of a French admiral, occurred with the apparent connivance of the queen. For over a decade and a half, civil war raged, in which Spain aided the Catholics and Henry enrolled German and Swiss Protestant mercenaries.

A turning point came only in 1589 when Henry of Navarre became King Henry IV. Surviving nearly three dozen plots against his life, the new king needed 9 years and two conversions to Catholicism—"Paris is well worth a Mass," he is supposed to have quipped—before he was able to calm the religious fanaticism among the majority of French people. With the Edict of Nantes in 1598, he decreed freedom of religion for Protestants. A number of staunch Catholic adherents were deeply offended by the edict as well as the alleged antipapal policies of Henry IV. The king fell victim to an assassin in 1610. Catholic resentment continued until 1685, when King Louis XIV revoked the edict and triggered a large-scale emigration of Huguenots to the Netherlands, Germany, and England. At last, France was Catholic again.

Dutch War of Independence   In the Netherlands, the Counter-Reformation Spanish overlords were even more determined to keep the country Catholic than the French monarchs prior to Henry IV. When Charles V resigned in 1556 (effective 1558), his son Philip II (r. 1556–1598) became king of Spain and the Netherlands, consisting of the French-speaking regions of Wallonia in the south and the Dutch-speaking regions of Flanders and Holland in the north. Like his father, Philip was a staunch supporter of the Counter-Reformation. He asked the Jesuits and the Inquisition to aggressively persecute the Calvinists. For better effect, Philip subdivided the bishoprics into smaller units and recruited clergymen in place of members of the nobility. In response, in 1565 the nobility and Calvinist congregations rose in revolt. They dismantled the bishoprics and cleansed the churches of images and sculptures, thereby triggering what was to become a Protestant war of Dutch liberation from Catholic Spanish overlordship (1565–1620). Philip retaliated by sending in an army that succeeded in suppressing the liberation movement, reimposing Catholicism, and executing thousands of rebels, many of them members of the Dutch aristocracy.

Remnants of the rebellion struggled on and, in 1579, renewed the war of liberation in three of the 17 northern provinces making up the Netherlands. Later joined by four more provinces, the people in these breakaway regions called themselves members of the "United Provinces of the Dutch Republic." Spain refused to recognize the republic and kept fighting until acute Spanish financial difficulties prompted the truce of 1609–1621. But the truce collapsed at the outbreak of the Thirty Years' War, and the Netherlands were drawn into the European conflagration. Spain eventually relinquished its claims only in 1648, when the European powers ended the Thirty Years' War with the peace settlement of Westphalia.

At the head of the Dutch republic was a governor (*stadhouder*) from the House of Orange-Nassau, one of the leading aristocratic families of the Netherlands. The representative body, with which the stadhouder governed, was the States-General and the privileged religious body was the Calvinist Dutch Reformed Church. In the Netherlands, about 20 percent of the population of 1 million was Calvinist, double the percentage in France and England. But there were also sizeable groups of Catholics and other Protestants. Among the latter, the Anabaptists and Mennonites (characterized by the doctrines of adult baptism and pacifism, respectively) were prominent. The Netherlands was also a haven for Jews, who had originally arrived there after their expulsion from Spain and Portugal in 1492–1498. Gradually, the Dutch accepted each other's doctrinal differences and the Netherlands became a model of religious tolerance.

Civil War in England   As in the Netherlands, the dominant form of Protestantism in England was Calvinism. During the sixteenth century, the Calvinists numbered about 10 percent in a kingdom in which the Anglican Church encompassed the majority of subjects in a total population of 7 million. English Catholics, who refused to recognize the king as the head of the Anglican Church, numbered 3 percent. The percentage of Calvinists was the same as in France, but the partially reformed Anglican Church was able to hold them in check. The Calvinists were, furthermore, a fractious group, encompassing moderate and radical tendencies that neutralized each other. Among the radicals were the Puritans, who demanded the abolition of the Anglican clerical hierarchy and a new church order of independent congregations. Other radicals, such as the Diggers, demanded distribution of land from the commons. In the early seventeenth century, when Anglican Church reform slowed under the Catholic successors of Elizabeth I (r. 1558–1603), the Puritan cause began to acquire traction. Realizing that these Stuart successors and their bishops were immovable, some Puritans emigrated to North America rather than continue to chafe under the Anglican yoke. Other Puritans began to agitate openly.

Along with their efforts to restrain would-be reformers, the Stuart kings were busy building their version of the fiscal–military state. They collected taxes without the approval of Parliament. Many members resented being bypassed since Parliament was the constitutional cosovereign of the kingdom. A slight majority in the House of Commons was Puritan, and the stalled church reform added to their resentment. Eventually, when all tax resources were exhausted, the king, Charles I (r. 1625–1649), had to call Parliament back together. Mutual resentment was so deep, however, that the two sides were unable to make any decisions on either financial or religious matters. The standoff erupted into civil war, which cost the king his life and ended the monarchy.

Despite the brutal fate of Charles I, the English civil war of 1642–1651 was generally less vicious than that in France. Nevertheless, because of widespread pillage and destruction of crops and houses, the indirect effects of the war were severe for the population of thousands of villages. The New Model Army, a professional body of 22,000 troops raised by the Puritan-dominated Parliament against the king, caused further upheavals by cleansing villages of their "frivolous" seasonal festivals, deeply rooted in local pagan traditions and featuring pranks, games, dances, drunkenness, and free-wheeling behavior. A republican theocracy emerged, with preachers enforcing Calvinist morality in the population.

Republic, Restoration, and Revolution   The ruler of this theocracy, Oliver Cromwell (r. 1649–1658), was a Puritan member of the lower nobility (the gentry) and a commander in the New Model Army. After dissolving Parliament, Cromwell handpicked a new parliament but ruled for the most part without its consent. Since both Scotland and Ireland had opposed the Puritans in the civil war, Cromwell waged a brutal war of submission against the Scottish Presbyterians (Calvinists organized in a state church) and Irish Catholics. The Dutch and Spanish, also opponents of the Puritans in the civil war, were defeated in naval wars that substantially improved English shipping power in the Atlantic. But the rising fear among the gentry in Parliament of a permanent fiscal–military state led Cromwell's parliament to refuse further funds. After Cromwell's death in 1658, it took just 3 years for the restoration of the Stuart monarchy and the Anglican state church to their previous places.

The recalled kings in the Restoration of 1661–1688 resumed the policies of fiscal–military centralism and Catholicism. As before, the kings called Parliament together only sparingly and raised funds without its authorization. Their standing army of 30,000, partially stationed near London, was intended more to intimidate the parliamentarians than to actually wage war. In the "Glorious Revolution" of 1688 the defiant Parliament, dominated since the Restoration by mostly Anglican gentry, deposed the Catholic king, James II (r. 1685–1688). It feared that the recent birth of a royal son threatened the succession of the king's daughter by his first marriage, Mary, a Protestant married to William of Nassau-Orange, the *stadhouder* of the Netherlands. It offered the throne to William and Mary as joint monarchs, and the Stuarts went into exile in France.

Outbreak of the Thirty Years' War   As religious tensions were mounting in England during the early seventeenth century, they erupted into a full-blown war in Germany, the second such conflagration in a century. As we saw earlier, Lutheran Protestantism had become the state religion in a majority of the two dozen largest and most powerful princely German states. Lutheran minorities were generally free to practice their religion in the Catholic German states. Not all rulers, however, were satisfied with the status quo among the princes. One of these rulers was the Jesuit-educated Ferdinand II (r. 1619–1637), ruler of the Holy Roman Empire, who resented the century-old religious freedoms enjoyed in Bohemia by Protestants. As newly elected king of Bohemia (and before becoming emperor), he began to exclude members of the Protestant aristocracy from administrative offices in re-Catholicized cities of the Bohemian kingdom. In response, Protestant leaders in 1618 unceremoniously threw two Habsburg emissaries out of a window of the Prague castle (the "Defenestration of Prague") and made the Calvinist prince of Palatinate in the Rhineland their new king. With these events in Bohemia, open hostilities between religious groups began in Germany.

Ferdinand and the Catholic princes suppressed the Bohemian rebellion in 1619, confiscated the properties of the Protestant aristocracy, and officially converted the kingdom to Catholicism. An imperial army of over 100,000 men chased the Calvinist prince not only from Prague but also from Palatinate and advanced toward northern Germany, capturing further territories for reconversion to Catholicism. When the Danish king intervened in favor of Lutheranism, he was crushed and the Protestant cause seemed to be doomed.

Outside Powers and the Peace of Westphalia

In 1630, however, the Lutheran king Gustavus II Adolphus (r. 1611–1632) of Sweden decided to intervene. The king's main goal was the completion of a Swedish-Lutheran fiscal–military state around the Baltic Sea, a project begun before the Thirty Years' War. By aiding the German Lutherans, he hoped to consolidate or even enlarge his predominance in the region. Louis XIII (r. 1610–1643) of France granted Sweden financial subsidies since he was concerned that Ferdinand's victories would further strengthen the Habsburg Spanish–Flemish–Austrian–German–Italian grip around France. For the French, the fact that Gustavus Aldolphus was a Protestant was secondary to the intra-Catholic rivalry between the Habsburgs and France. With the politically motivated alliance between Sweden and France, the German Catholic-Protestant war turned into a war for state dominance in Europe.

At first, Swedish troops turned the situation in favor of the Protestants. Gustavus Adolphus advanced victoriously as far as Bavaria in the south. On the verge of a final victory, however, the king fell in battle and the Swedes withdrew to northern Germany. In a position of renewed strength but fearful of a French entry into the war, Ferdinand II decided to compromise with the Protestant princes of Germany. In the peace of 1635, the two sides agreed to a return to the prewar territorial division between Catholic and Protestant princes in northern Germany.

Since the French were determined to break the Habsburg grip, they now entered the war. During the next 13 years, French armies sought to cut the Habsburg supply lines from Italy to the Netherlands by occupying Habsburg Alsace. Swedish armies, exploiting the French successes against the Habsburgs, fought their way back into Germany. In the end, the Austrian–German Habsburgs, pressured on two sides, agreed in October 1648 to the Peace of Westphalia. They allowed religious freedom in Germany and ceded territories in Alsace to France and the southern side of the Baltic Sea to Sweden. The Spanish Habsburgs, however, continued their war against France until 1659, when they also bowed to superior French strength, giving up parts of Flanders and northeastern Spain. France now emerged as the strongest power in Europe (see Map 17.3).

Fiscal–Military States at War. German imperial troops besiege Swedish troops in the northern German city of Stralsund in 1628. The etching shows typical features of the fiscal–military state, from top to bottom: galleon-style warships (successors of the caravel); a star-shaped fort (an Italian innovation) designed to withstand artillery barrages; the medieval walls of the city; musket-equipped infantry troops; field cannons; and the colorful Baroque uniforms worn by the musketeers of the period.

MAP **17.3** Europe in 1648.

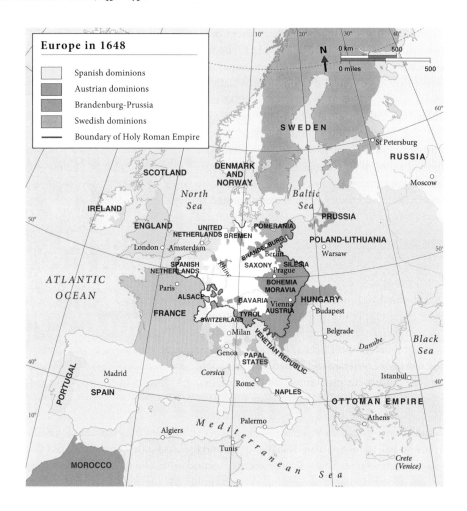

Europe in 1648

- Spanish dominions
- Austrian dominions
- Brandenburg-Prussia
- Swedish dominions
- —— Boundary of Holy Roman Empire

Absolutism in France?   During its period of greatest political dominance, France came under the rule of its longest reigning monarch, King Louis XIV (1643–1715). He was of small stature—for which he compensated with high-heeled shoes—but his hardy constitution and strong self-discipline helped him to dominate even the most grueling meetings with his advisors. He enjoyed pomp and circumstance and built Versailles—his gigantic palace and gardens near Paris, populated with 10,000 courtiers, attendants, and servants—into a site of almost continuous feasting, entertainment, and intrigue. It was here that Louis, the "Sun King," beamed benevolently with his "absolute" divine mandate upon his aristocracy and commoners alike. Versailles played an important role in Louis's efforts to undercut the power of the nobility. Anyone with any aspirations of attracting the king's attention had to come to the palace to attend him. By keeping both friends and potential enemies close by and forcing them to spend lavishly to stay abreast of the fashions inspired by the king and vie for his attention, he was able, like the Tokugawa shoguns in Edo, Japan, to bypass them administratively and rule through central bureaucratic institutions.

Absolutism: Theory of the state in which the unlimited power of the king, ruling under God's divine mandate, is emphasized.

In practice, the French **absolutism** of Louis XIV and his eighteenth-century successors, as well as practitioners in other European countries, was a complex mixture of centralized and decentralized forces. On the one hand, after the end of the religious wars in 1648, mercenary armies under autonomous dukes and counts disappeared from the European scene, replaced by permanent armies or navies under the central command of fiscal–military royal or princely dynasties. The kings also no longer called their respective assemblies of nobles and notables together to have new taxes approved (in France from 1614 to 1789), and thus, many of the nobility's tax privileges disappeared.

On the other hand, the kings of the seventeenth century were acutely aware that true absolutism was possible only if centrally salaried employees collected taxes. It was physically impossible to transport tax revenues, in the form of silver money and grain, from the provinces to the capital, pay the central bureaucrats, and then cart the remaining revenues back to the provinces to pay salaried tax collectors there. A centrally paid bureaucracy would have required a central bank with provincial branches, using paper money. The failed experiment with such a bank in Paris from 1714 to 1720 demonstrates one such effort to find a solution to the central salary problem. But the bank's short life demonstrates that absolute central control was beyond the powers of the kings and princes.

Instead, the kings had to rely on subcontracting most offices and the collection of most taxes out to the highest bidders, who then helped themselves to the collection of their incomes. Under Louis XIV, a total of 46,000 administrative jobs were available for purchase in Paris and the provinces. Anyone who had money, or borrowed it from financiers, was encouraged to buy an office—from the old aristocracy of the "sword," receiving rents from the farmers on their rural estates, to ordinary merchant sons with law degrees, borrowing money from their fathers. Once in office, the government often forced these officers to grant additional loans to the crown. To retain their loyalty, the government rewarded them with first picks for retaining their offices within the family, buying landed estates, or acquiring titles of nobility to the secondary (and less prestigious) tier of the "nobility of the robe" (as opposed to the first-tier "nobility of the sword," which by the seventeenth century was demilitarized).

About the only way for Louis XIV to keep the semblance of a watchful eye on the honesty of the officeholders was to send salaried, itinerant *intendants* around the provinces to ensure that collecting taxes, rendering justice, and policing functioned

Versailles. Built between 1676 and 1708 on the outskirts of Paris, Versailles emphatically demonstrated the new centralized power of the French monarchy. The main building is a former hunting lodge that Louis XIV decorated with mythological scenes that showed him as the "Sun King." The outer wings housed government offices. Behind the palace, elaborate entertainments were held in the gardens.

properly within the allowable limits of "the venality of office," as the subcontracting system was called. Louis XIV had roughly one intendant for each province. About half of the provinces had *parlements*—appointed assemblies for the ratification of decrees from Paris—whose officeholders, drawn from the local noble, clerical, and commoner classes, frequently resisted the intendants. The Paris *parlement* even refused to accept royal writs carried by the intendants. In later years, when Louis XIV was less successful in his many wars against the rival Habsburgs and Protestant Dutch, the crown overspent and had to borrow heavily with little regard for the future. Louis's successors in the first half of the eighteenth century were saddled with crippling debts. French-inspired European "absolutism" was thus in practice a careful (or not so careful) balancing act between the forces of centralization and decentralization in the fiscal–military states of Europe.

The Rise of Russia   Although France's absolutism was more theory than practice, its glorious ideological embodiment by the Versailles of Louis XIV spawned adaptations across Europe. These adaptations were most visible in eastern Europe, which was populated more thinly and had far fewer towns and cities. Since rulers in those areas did not have a large reservoir of urban commoners to aid them as administrators in adopting the fiscal–military state, they had to make do with the landowning aristocracy. As a result, the villagers who in agrarian society bore the brunt of taxation were more exposed to the absolutist aspirations of the rulers and their administrators than in western Europe.

In Russia, Tsar Peter I, the Great (r. 1682–1725), of the eastern Christian Romanov dynasty, was a towering figure who singlehandedly sought to establish the fiscal–military state during his lifetime. At nearly 7 feet tall, Peter was an imposing, energetic ruler, controllable only by his second wife (and former mistress) Catherine, a warmhearted woman and beloved tsarina. Peter invited western European soldiers, mariners, administrators, craftspeople, scholars, and artists into his service and succeeded within just a few years in building a disciplined army and imposing navy. He built ports on the Baltic Sea and established the new capital of St. Petersburg, distinguished by many very beautiful palaces and official buildings. A typical

A World Turned Upside Down. In this popular satirical woodcut of 1766, based on a similar woodcut from the early 1700s, the mice are capturing and burying the cat: In other words, Peter the Great has turned the world upside down with his reforms.

example among thousands invited to Russia by the tsar was Peter von Sivers, a Danish mariner (and ancestor of one of the coauthors of the book) who rose to the position of admiral in the Baltic fleet that broke Swedish dominance in northern Europe. Since the tsar was not able to pay these advisors salaries (any more than Louis XIV could pay salaries to advisors to the French court), he gave many western guests estates with serfs in the Baltic provinces and Finland, conquered from Sweden, and made them aristocrats in his retinue.

The Russian military was completely reorganized by the tsar. After a rebellion early on, Peter savagely decimated the inherited firearm regiments and made them part of a new army recruited from the traditional Russian landed nobility. Both classes of soldiers received education at military schools and academies and were required to provide lifelong service. In order to make his soldiers look more urban, Peter decreed that they shave their traditional beards and wear European uniforms or clothes. Every twentieth peasant household had to deliver one foot soldier to conscription. A census was taken to facilitate the shift from the inherited household tax on the villagers to a new capitation tax collected by military officers. In the process, many free farmers outside the estate system of the aristocracy found themselves classified and taxed as serfs, unfree to leave their villages. The result of Peter's reforms was a powerful, expansionary fiscal–military state that played an increasingly important role among European kingdoms during the eighteenth century (see Map 17.4).

The Rise of Prussia   Similar to Russia, the principality of Prussia-Brandenburg was underurbanized. It had furthermore suffered destruction and depopulation during the Thirty Years' War. When the Lutheran Hohenzollern dynasty embarked on the construction of a fiscal–military state in the later seventeenth century, they first broke the tax privileges of the landowning aristocracy in the estates-general and raised taxes themselves. As in Russia, farmers who worked on estates held by landlords were serfs. Since there were few urban middle-class merchants and professionals, the kings enrolled members of the landlord aristocracy in the army and civilian administration.

Elevated by the Habsburg Holy Roman emperor to the status of kings in 1701, the Hohenzollern rulers systematically enlarged the army, employing it during peacetime for drainage and canal projects as well as palace construction in Berlin, the capital. Under Frederick II, the Great (1740–1786), Prussia pursued an aggressive foreign policy, capturing Silesia from the Habsburgs in a military campaign. Frederick also expended major efforts into attracting immigrants, intensifying agriculture, and establishing manufacturing enterprises. Prussia emerged as a serious competitor of the Habsburgs in the Holy Roman Empire of Germany.

Prussian Military Discipline. The Prussian line infantry made full use in the mid-1700s of flintlock muskets, bayonets, and drilling. Most of the drilling concerned the rotation of the front line with the rear lines after salvos, for the purpose of reloading. The introduction of the bayonet made pikemen—infantry with long thrusting spears employed to protect the musketeers from hand-to-hand combat—obsolete.

English Constitutionalism   In contrast to Prussia, France, Spain, Austria, and other European states, England had since 1450 a political system ruled by a king or a queen, with a parliament composed of the

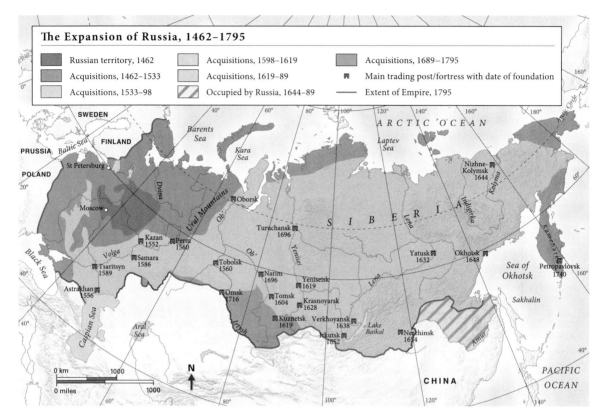

MAP **17.4** **The Expansion of Russia, 1462–1795.**

aristocracy as well as representatives of towns and cities. Only in England did the interests of the nobility and the urban merchants gradually converge. Rulers on the European continent financed their early fiscal–military states through raising indirect taxes on sales, commerce, imports, and exports, affecting cities more than noble estates. In England, the cities allied with the aristocracy in resisting indirect tax increases and forcing the throne to use the less ample revenues of its royal estates to pay soldiers. Efforts of the Stuart kings to create a fiscal–military state based on firearm infantries failed. Instead, the ruling class preferred to build a naval fiscal–military state. After the Glorious Revolution of 1688, this state achieved dominance on the world's oceans.

After its victory over the Stuart kings, Parliament consolidated its fiscal–military powers through the creation of the Bank of England in 1694, two decades before a similar but ill-fated attempt in France. When first Mary and then William died without children, England continued in 1701 with a distantly related dynasty from the principality of Hannover in Germany. Under a new monarch, England and Scotland united in 1707, creating the "United Kingdom." Parliament collected higher taxes than France and, through its bank, was able to keep its debt service low. The navy grew twice as large as that of France and was staffed by a well-salaried, disciplined military, while the few land troops, deemed superfluous, were mostly low-paid Hessian-German mercenaries. A rudimentary two-party system of two aristocracy–merchant alliances came into being. The two parties were known as the Whigs and the Tories, the former more parliamentarian and the latter more royalist, with the Whigs in power for most of the first half of the eighteenth century.

Cultural Transformations: Renaissance, New Science, and Early Enlightenment

The rise of the fiscal–military state coincided with the **Renaissance**, a period of cultural formation which in the fifteenth century followed the scholastic Middle Ages in western Christianity. With state profits, rulers, courts, and merchants sponsored much of the arts and sciences that flourished during the Renaissance. In many ways, the Renaissance was an outgrowth of scholasticism, but its thinkers and artists saw themselves as people who had broken away from its precepts. They considered their period as a time of "rebirth" (which is the literal meaning of "renaissance" in French), during which they were powerfully influenced by the writings of Greek and Hellenistic-Roman authors who had been unknown during the scholastic age. In the sixteenth century, the Renaissance gave way to the Baroque in the arts and the **New Science** in astronomy and physics, which in turn produced the Enlightenment. Thus, the Renaissance was just the first of further periods of cultural formation following each other in rapid succession.

The Renaissance and Baroque Arts

Beginning around 1400 in Italy and spreading later through northwestern Europe, an outpouring of learning, scholarship, and art came from theologians, philosophers, writers, painters, architects, and musical composers. These thinkers and artists benefited from Greek and Hellenistic-Roman texts which scholars had discovered recently in mostly eastern Christian archives in Byzantium. In addition, in the early fifteenth century Byzantine scholars from Constantinople arrived in Italy with new texts, which exerted a profound impact. The emerging cultures of the Renaissance and Baroque were creative adaptations of those Greek and Hellenistic-Roman writings to the cultural heritage of western Christianity. Out of this vibrant mixture arose the overarching concept of **humanism**.

New Manuscripts and Printing
Byzantium experienced a cultural revival between its recovery in 1261 from the Latin interlude and its collapse in 1453 when the Ottomans conquered Constantinople. During this revival, for example, scholars engaged in a vigorous debate about the compatibility of Plato and Aristotle with each other. The debate made Italian scholars fully aware of how much of Greek literature was still absent from western Christianity; at the time, they possessed just two of Plato's 44 dialogues. Italians invited about a dozen eastern scholars, who brought manuscripts to Florence, Rome, and Venice to translate and to teach. Their students became fluent in Greek and translated Hesiod and Homer, some Greek tragedies and comedies, Plato and the Neo-Platonists, the remaining works of Aristotle, Hellenistic scientific texts, and the Greek Church fathers. Western Christianity had finally absorbed the ancient heritage.

The work of translation was helped by the development of a more rounded, simplified Latin script, which replaced the angled, dense Gothic script used since the 1150s. In addition, the costly vellum (scraped leather) writing material on which many manuscripts had been laboriously written was replaced by cheaper paper, introduced from Islamic Spain in the early twelfth century and common in the rest of Europe by 1400, which allowed for more space on each page. Experimentation

Renaissance: "Rebirth" of culture in its full sense, based on large-scale publications and translations of Greek, Hellenistic, and Roman authors whose writings were previously unknown in the West.

New Science: Changes in the practice of science inherited from the Middle Ages; the discovery of the Americas inspired Copernicus to abandon the Aristotelian theory of elements and adopt heliocentrism; Galileo then replaced Aristotelian descriptive science with mathematized science, through the law of falling bodies.

Humanism: Intellectual movement focusing on human culture, in such fields as philosophy, philology, and literature, as based on the corpus of Greek and Roman texts.

Bookseller. By 1600, the increase in literacy levels combined with widespread printing of books, pamphlets, and tracts had made images like this itinerant bookseller in Italy a commonplace sight throughout much of Europe.

in the 1430s with movable metal typeface, arranged in frames and combined with traditional wooden presses for grape or olive crushing, resulted in the innovation of the printing press. A half-century later, with more than 1,000 printers all over Europe and more than 8 million books in the hands of readers, a veritable printing revolution had taken place in Europe.

Philology and Political Theory   The flood of new manuscripts and the renewed examination of existing manuscripts in libraries encouraged the study of Greek, Latin, and Hebrew philology. Scholars trained in these languages edited definitive texts based on multiple manuscripts and exposed inauthentic texts. The best known among these philologists was the Dutchman Desiderius Erasmus (1466–1536), who published an edition of the Greek and Latin New Testaments in 1516. The most infamous fake text to be exposed was the so-called Donation of Constantine, which the Italian Lorenzo Valla (1407–1457) proved through textual criticism to have been a self-serving forgery favoring the papal claims to supreme authority in the Middle Ages. Critical textual research, which became central to all subsequent scholarship, can trace its foundations to the Renaissance.

Biting criticism also emerged as a central element in political thought. In *The Prince*, Niccolò Machiavelli (1469–1527) reflected on the ruthless political competition among the princes of Europe for dominance over his hopelessly disunited native Italy. What Italy needed, Machiavelli argued, was a unifier who practiced what Aristotle enumerated in Book 5 of his *Politics*, that is, an intuitive ability to take proper action when survival in power was at stake. He called this ability *virtù*, by which he meant the power instinct of a ruler to take any appropriate measure, forceful or subtle, in order to remain in control of the vicissitudes—or, in his words, the *fortuna*—of politics. The New Scientists rejected Aristotle and the majority of humanists preferred Plato over Aristotle, but Machiavelli remained faithful to Aristotle, the superior political realist—an Aristotle held in high esteem centuries later by the American founding fathers.

The Renaissance Arts   In Italy, the reception of the new texts of the fifteenth century was paralleled by a new artistic way of looking at the Roman past and the natural world. The first to adopt this perspective were the sculptor Donatello (ca. 1386–1466) and the architect Filippo Brunelleschi (1377–1446), who received their inspiration from Roman imperial statues and ruins. The artistic triumvirate of the high Italian Renaissance included Leonardo da Vinci (1452–1519), Michelangelo (1475–1564), and Raphael (1483–1520). Inspired by the Italian creative outburst, the Renaissance flourished also in Germany, the Netherlands, and France. With a bit of exaggeration one could conclude that sponsorship of the arts by the ruling classes became almost as competitive as victory in battle.

The earliest musical composers of the Renaissance in the first half of the fifteenth century were Platonists, who considered music a part of a well-rounded education. The difficulty, however, was that the music of the Greeks or Romans was completely unknown. A partial solution for this difficulty was found through emphasizing the relationship between the word—that is, rhetoric—and music, which coincided in

the sixteenth century with the Protestant and Catholic de-mand for liturgical music. During this century, a huge output of hymns and masses in church music and *madrigals* (verses sung by unaccompanied voices) in secular music attests to this emphasis. The works of the Italian composer Giovanni Pierluigi da Palestrina (ca. 1525–1594) represent Renaissance music at its most exquisite.

The theater was a relatively late expression of the Renaissance. The popular mystery, passion, and morality plays from the centuries prior to 1400 continued in Catholic countries. In Italy, in the course of the fifteenth century, a secular popu-lar theater, the *commedia dell'arte* emerged, often using masks and staging plays of forbidden love, jealousy, and adultery. In England during the sixteenth century the popular traveling theater troupes became stationary and professional, attracting playwrights who composed more elaborate plays. Sponsored by the aristocracy and the Elizabethan court, playwrights wrote hundreds of scripts—some 600 are still extant—beginning in the 1580s. The best known among these playwrights was Wil-liam Shakespeare (1564–1616), who also acted in his tragedies and comedies.

Renaissance Art. Brunelleschi's cupola for the cathedral of Florence, completed in 1436, was one of the greatest achievements of the early Renaissance (*a*). Raphael's *School of Athens* (1509–1510) depicts some 50 philosophers and scientists, with Plato (in red tunic) and Aristotle (blue) in the center of the painting (*b*). Peter Bruegel's *The Harvesters* (1565) shows peasants taking a lunch break (*c*).

The Baroque Arts

The Renaissance gave way around 1600 to the Baroque, which dominated the arts until about 1750. Two factors influenced its emergence. First, the Protestant Reformation, Catholic Counter-Reformation, and religious wars changed the nature of patronage, on which architects, painters, and musicians depended. Many Protestant churches, opposed to imagery as incompatible with their view of early Christianity, did not sponsor artists for the adornment of their buildings with religious art. Wealthy urban merchants, often Protestant, stepped into the breach but avoided paintings with religious themes, preferring instead secu-lar portraits, still lives, village scenes, and landscapes.

Second, the predilection for Renaissance measurement, balance, and restraint gave way in both Catholic and Protestant regions to greater spontaneity and dramatic effect. Even more pronounced was the parallel shift in church and palace architecture to a "baroque" voluptuousness of forms and decorations, exemplified by Bavarian and Austrian Catholic churches, the Versailles Palace, and St. Paul's Cathedral in London, all completed between 1670 and 1750. Baroque music, benefitting from ample church and palace patronage, experienced a veritable explosion of unrestrained exploration.

The Pioneers of the New Science

Eastern Christian scholars invited from Byzantium to Florence in Italy during the first half of the fifteenth century brought with them full sets of Platonic manuscripts, which stirred much interest among western Christian scholars. It did not take long for these scholars to realize that Plato was not fully compatible with Aristotle, whose writings had dominated the debates since the thirteenth century. Scholars also began to pay attention to other Greek authors outside the Aristotelian tradition, such as the scientist Archimedes. Eventually, three great scientific pioneers—Copernicus, Galileo, and Newton—overturned the *descriptive* science of Aristotle in the sixteenth and seventeenth centuries and replaced it with the *mathematical* New Science, which many centuries later became the basis of modern scientific–industrial society.

Copernicus Questions Aristotle

According to the scholastic heritage, based on Aristotle's physics, all objects in nature were composed of the four elements (in ascending order of lightness) of earth, water, fire, and air. In astronomy, based on Aristotle and Ptolemy, earth was in the center of the planetary universe, with planets composed of the fifth element of ether traveling around the earth in concentric circles. Both of these theories collapsed during the Renaissance, when a chorus of critics of Aristotle arose. One of the critics was Nicolaus Copernicus (1473–1543) from Torun, a German-founded city which had come under Polish rule a few years before his birth. Copernicus began his studies at the University of Kraków, the only eastern European school to offer courses in astronomy. During the years 1495–1504, he continued his studies—of canon law, medicine, astronomy, and astrology—at Italian universities. In 1500 he briefly taught mathematics in Rome and perhaps read Greek astronomical texts translated from Arabic in the library of the Vatican. Eventually, Copernicus graduated with a degree in canon law and took up an administrative position at the cathedral of Torun, which allowed him time to pursue astronomical research.

Sometime between 1507 and 1514 Copernicus became aware of the scientific significance of Columbus's discovery of the Americas. Spanish and Portuguese mariners sailing north and south from the Caribbean a few years after 1492 had realized that the Americas, with their long coastlines, were not at all islands off the coast of India, as Columbus had thought. As a result, in 1507 the German cartographer Martin Waldseemüller (ca. 1470–1520) published an early map and an accompanying updated version of Ptolemy's geography, both showing the east coast of the Americas. He was, thus, the first to describe the Americas as continents in their own right.

Copernicus saw the map soon after its publication and realized that, rather than a deep ocean, the Americas on the other side of the globe formed an entire "inhabited world" (Gr. *oikumene*). With this realization it became impossible for Copernicus to think that earth was the heaviest element: Too much earth in the form of continents

was protruding from the oceans. Consequently, Copernicus rejected Aristotle's descriptive science of five elements and with it the idea that the earth was in the center of the planetary universe. He exchanged the places of the earth and sun, which described similar circles in the Ptolemaic system, and concluded that nothing much needed to be modified in the trigonometry of this system to accommodate that exchange. A century later, Johannes Kepler corrected the circles into concentric ellipses.

Galileo's Mathematical Physics   During the near-century between the births of Copernicus and Galileo Galilei (1564–1642), mathematics—with its two branches of Greek geometry and Arabic algebra—improved considerably. Euclid's *Elements*, badly translated from Arabic in the late twelfth century with a garbled definition of proportions, was retranslated correctly from the Greek in 1543. In physics, the new translation in 1544 of a text on floating and descending bodies by the Hellenistic thinker Archimedes (287–212 BCE) attracted enthusiastic attention. The text, unknown to the Arabs, had been translated from the Greek already in the thirteenth century but subsequently remained unappreciated, on account of its incompatibility with the then-prevailing Aristotelianism. All that was needed was for an anti-Aristotelian genius to bring together geometry, algebra, and Archimedian physics. In 1604, that genius came forward in the person of Galileo, who formulated his mathematical law of descending bodies.

Running Afoul of the Church   Galileo was also a first-rate astronomer, one of the first to use a telescope, which had been recently invented in Flanders. On the basis of his astronomical discoveries, in 1610 he received a richly endowed appointment as chief mathematician and philosopher at the court of the Medici, rulers of Florence. But his increasing fame also attracted the enmity of the Catholic Church. As a proponent of Copernican heliocentrism, Galileo seemed to contradict the

Waldseemüller's 1507 World Map. Although most of its features would have appeared on any Ptolemaic map of the era, this influential map is notable for one major mistake. The German map maker, Martin Waldseemüller (1470–1520), lacked any first-hand knowledge of the places he depicted on his map and was unable to access the newly developed nautical charts of the world. Instead, he relied upon secondhand sources, including the misleading accounts of the Italian navigator, Amerigo Vespucci (1454–1512) who claimed that he, not the Portuguese, discovered the Atlantic seaboard of Brazil. As a result, instead of putting the original Portuguese name on the coast (Land of the True Cross), he placed the name of Amerigo (America). Waldseemüller soon realized his mistake, for the name America never reappeared on any of his subsequent maps.

Patterns Up Close | The Mathematization of Science, 1500–Present

According to Archimedes (and contrary to Aristotle), stones sink in water at the same speed, regardless of their weight. Galileo was able to prove that Archimedes was correct and that bodies descend with the same acceleration if one disregards the medium. To create the experiment, he had a craftsperson build him a 6.5-foot inclined, grooved beam, propped up at an angle, down which brass balls could be rolled. For timing, Galileo used the swings of a pendulum. After many experiments and false starts, he decided to divide the time of the ball's accelerating descent down the beam into eight equal segments. For the passing of each time segment he placed markers on the incline and carefully measured the resulting unequal distances.

As he compared these distances, he realized that their increasing lengths roughly followed the progression of the odd integers 1, 3, 5, 7, 9, 11, 13, 15, etc. On the basis of Euclid's mathematics of ratios, Galileo concluded that these distances, added together, corresponded to squares of time ($1 + 3 = 2^2$, $1 + 3 + 5 = 3^2$, $1 + 3 + 5 + 7 = 4^2$, and so forth). (Today, this lengthy number sequence is expressed in the short equation $s = t^2$, where s is distance and t is time.) Galileo concluded that, contrary to Aristotle, earthly motion—such as the accelerating motion of a body rolling down in the groove of a beam or falling from a tower—could be mathematized.

Galileo's math of ratios strikes us today as elementary. Several New Scientists after him, such as Descartes, Pascal, Leibniz, and Newton, created new fields of higher mathematics that enabled Newton to unify Copernican–Keplerian astronomy and Galilean physics into a single theory of a fully determined mechanical universe. Newton's concepts of atoms, forces, and planetary bodies dominated the sciences from the early eighteenth century to the early twentieth century. They became such

passage in the Hebrew Bible where God stopped the motion of the sun for a day, to allow the Israelites to win a battle (Joshua 10:12–13). In contrast to the more tolerant pope at the time of Copernicus, the Counter-Reformation Inquisition favored a strictly literal interpretation of this passage, which implied that God once had halted the sun's motion. In 1632 Galileo found himself condemned to house arrest and forced to make a public repudiation of heliocentrism.

The condemnation of Galileo had a chilling effect on scientists in the southern European countries where the Catholic Counter-Reformation reigned. Wealthy patrons reduced their stipends to scientists, and scientific research declined. During the seventeenth century, interest in the New Science shifted increasingly to France, Germany, the Netherlands, and England. There, no single church authority dominated, of either the Catholic or the Protestant variety, to enforce the literal understanding of scripture, as much as each would have wanted. These countries produced numerous mathematicians, physicists, and inventors, both Catholics as well as Protestants. The New Scientists in northern Europe had a certain liberty that their southern colleagues lacked. It was this intellectual freedom, not any great sympathy impressively powerful tools that mathematically untrained philosophers like Auguste Comte (1798–1857) and Karl Marx (1818–1883) drew the conclusion that not only nature but also history were mechanically determined and that one could predict the future of social developments in the same way scientists predicted ballistic trajectories or astronomical constellations.

In the early twentieth century, Albert Einstein (1879–1955) formulated the theory of relativity as a replacement of Newtonianism. At the speed of light and across vast distances, space and time are no longer absolute but relative to each other, forming a single curved space–time, which in turn can be related to mass, energy, and momentum with the help of Einsteinian field equations. Newtonian planetary motions are for Einstein straight movements that appear curved because of space–time. Between 1920 and 1930, scientists such as Nils Bohr (1885–1962) pushed scientific abstraction even further and developed quantum theory. Here, in the very small, subatomic realm of physics, scientists discovered that energy waves and subatomic particles form an indivisible duality. Quantum theorists assume an invisible subatomic continuum of particle waves that underlies the Einsteinian universe of space–time where relativity theory applies. The mathematics of particle waves, however, have withstood so far all efforts of unification with the mathematics of space–time, and scientists in the twenty-first century are still on the elusive hunt for what they call a "theory of everything."

Acceleration Experiment. This nineteenth-century reconstruction of Galileo's inclined plane is located in the Museum for the History of Science in Florence, Italy. The metal gates, spaced along the grooved inclines according to Galileo's ratio of uneven integers, held bells, which helped him to measure the elapsed time segments as the balls passed through.

Questions

- How do Galileo's experiments with falling bodies demonstrate the shift away from descriptive science to mathematical science?

- Why did the New Science lead to conflicts between thinkers like Galileo and the Church?

on the part of religious authorities for the New Science, which allowed the latter to flourish, especially in the Netherlands and England.

Isaac Newton's Mechanics   In the middle of the English dispute over the dominance of Protestant or Catholic authority, Isaac Newton (1643–1727) completed the New Science of Copernicus and Galileo. As a professor at the University of Cambridge, he worked in the fields of mathematics, optics, astronomy, physics, alchemy, and theology. His main early contribution to the New Science was calculus, a new field in mathematics, which he developed at the same time as the German philosopher Gottfried Wilhelm Leibniz (1646–1716). Later in his career, Newton unified the fields of physics and astronomy, establishing the so-called Newtonian synthesis. His *Mathematical Principles of Natural Philosophy*, published in 1687, one year before the English settled their religious and constitutional disputes with the compromise of the Glorious Revolution, was the towering achievement of the New Science. It established a deterministic universe following mathematical rules and formed the basis of science until the early twentieth century.

The New Science and Its Social Impact

Scientists in the seventeenth century were in close communication with each other. They met in scientific societies or residential salons. Popularizers introduced an increasingly large public to the New Science. Scientists carried out experiments with constantly improved scientific instruments, such as telescopes, microscopes, thermometers, and barometers. Experience with barometers led technically versatile scientists and engineers to experiment with vacuum chambers and cylinders operating with condensing steam. Experimentation culminated with the invention of the steam engine in England in 1712.

New Science Societies   When the Counter-Reformation drove the New Science to northwestern Europe, the Italian-style academies gave way to chartered scientific societies, such as the Royal Society of London (1660) and the Paris Academy of Sciences (1666). Other countries, like Prussia, Russia, and Sweden, soon followed. These societies employed staffs of administrators, co-opted scientists as fellows, held regular discussion meetings, challenged their fellows to answer scientific questions, awarded prizes, and organized field trips and expeditions. They also published transactions, correspondences, and manuscripts. Many societies attracted thousands of members—famous pioneers, obscure amateurs, technically proficient tinkerers, theoretical mathematicians, daring experimenters, and flighty dreamers—representing an important cross section of the upper strata of seventeenth-century urban society in northwest Europe (see Map 17.5).

Other popularizers were textbook authors and itinerant lecturers who addressed audiences of middle-class amateurs, instrument makers, and specialized craftspeople, especially in England and the Netherlands. Many lecturers toured coffeehouses, urban residences, country estates, and provincial schools. Coffeehouses allowed the literate urban public to meet, read the daily newspapers (first published in the early seventeenth century), and exchange ideas. Coffee, introduced from Ethiopia and Yemen via the Ottoman Empire in the sixteenth century, was the preferred nonalcoholic social drink before the arrival of tea in the later eighteenth century. Male urban literacy is estimated to have exceeded 50 percent in England and the Netherlands during this period, although it remained considerably lower in France, Germany, and Italy.

Some lecturers were veritable entrepreneurs of the speaking circuit, teaching a kind of "Newtonianism-lite" for ladies and gentlemen with little time or patience for serious study. Other lecturers set up subscriptions for month-long courses. Wealthy businessmen endowed public lectures and supported increasingly elaborate experiments and expensive laboratory equipment. In the first half of the eighteenth century, the New Science triumphed in northwestern Europe among a large, scientifically and technically interested public of experimenters, engineers, instrument makers, artisans, business people, and lay folk.

Women and the New Science   Women formed a significant part of this public. In the fields of mathematics and astronomy, Sophie Brahe (1556–1643), sister of the Danish astronomer Tycho Brahe (1546–1601), and Maria Cunitz (see chapter-opening vignette) were the first to make contributions to the new astronomy of Copernicus and Kepler. According to estimates, in the second half of the seventeenth century some 14 percent of German astronomers were women. A dozen particularly

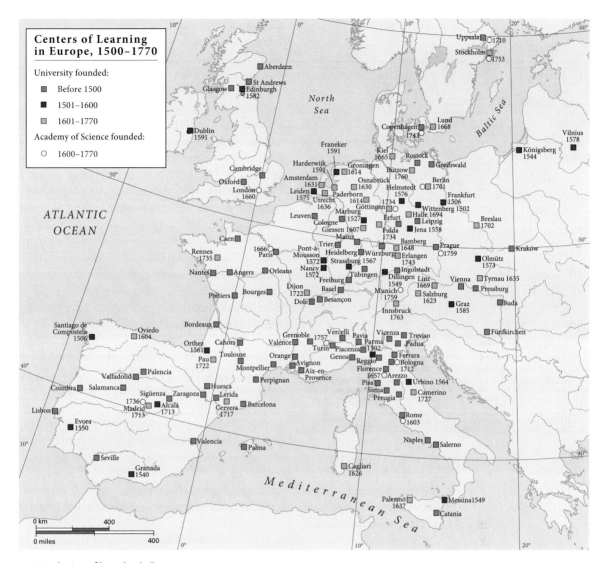

Centers of Learning in Europe, 1500–1770

University founded:
- ■ Before 1500
- ■ 1501–1600
- ■ 1601–1770

Academy of Science founded:
- ○ 1600–1770

MAP **17.5 Centers of Learning in Europe, 1500–1770.**

prominent female astronomers practiced their science privately in Germany, Poland, the Netherlands, France, and England.

Social Salons   Another institution which helped in the popularization of the New Science was the salon. As the well-furnished, elegant living room of an urban residence, the salon was both a domestic chamber and a semipublic meeting place for the urban social elite to engage in conversations, presentations, and experiments. The culture of the salon emerged first in Paris sometime after the closure of the court-centered Palace Academy in the 1580s. Since the Catholic French universities remained committed to Aristotelianism, the emerging stratum of educated urban aristocrats and middle-class professionals turned to the salons as places to inform themselves about new scientific developments. Furthermore, French universities as well as scientific academies refused to admit women, in contrast to Italian and

New Scientist. Maria Cunitz is honored today with a sculpture in Ratusz, Poland.

German institutions. The French salon, therefore, became a bastion of well-placed and respected female scholars.

One outstanding example of French salon science was Gabrielle-Emilie du Châtelet (1706–1749). In her youth, Châtelet fulfilled her marital duties to her husband, the Marquis of Châtelet. She had three children before turning to the sciences. In one of the Paris salons she met François Marie Arouet, known as Voltaire (1694–1778), the eighteenth-century Enlightenment writer, skeptic, satirist, and amateur Newtonian. Châtelet and Voltaire became intimate companions under the benevolent eyes of the Marquis at the family estate in Lorraine in northwestern France. Although Voltaire published prolifically, Châtelet eventually outstripped him both in research and scientific understanding. Her lasting achievement was the translation of Newton's *Principles* into French, published in 1759.

Discovery of the Vacuum Among the important scientific instruments of the day were telescopes, microscopes, and thermometers. It was the barometer, however, that was the crucial instrument for the exploration of the properties of the vacuum and condensing steam, eventually leading to the invention of the steam engine. The scientist laying the groundwork for the construction of this instrument was Evangelista Torricelli (1608–1647), mathematician and assistant of Galileo. In collaboration with Florentine engineers, he experimented with mercury-filled glass tubes, demonstrating the existence of atmospheric pressure in the air and of vacuums in the tubes.

Four years later, the French mathematician and philosopher Blaise Pascal (1623–1662) had his brother-in-law haul a mercury barometer up a mountain to experiment with demonstrations of lower air pressures at higher altitudes. Soon thereafter, scientists discovered the connection between changing atmospheric pressures and the weather, laying the foundations for weather forecasting. The discovery of the vacuum, the existence of which Aristotle had held to be impossible, made a deep impression on the scientific community in the seventeenth century and was an important step toward the practical application of the New Science to mechanical engineering in the eighteenth century.

The Steam Engine The French Huguenot scientist and engineer Denis Papin (ca. 1647–1712) took the first crucial step from the vacuum chamber to the steam engine. Papin began his career as an assistant in English scientific laboratories, where he familiarized himself with the phenomenon of steam contracting its volume when cooled in a chamber, creating a vacuum in the process. In 1690, when he was a court engineer and professor in Germany, Papin constructed a cylinder with a piston. Weights, via a cord and two pulleys, held the piston at the top of the cylinder. When

Vacuum Power. In 1672, the New Scientist and mayor of Magdeburg, Otto von Guericke, demonstrated the experiment that made him a pioneer in the understanding of the physical properties of the vacuum. In the presence of German emperor Ferdinand III, two teams of horses were unable to pull the two sealed hemispheres apart. Guericke had created a vacuum by pumping out the air from the two sealed copper spheres.

heated, water in the bottom of the cylinder turned into steam. When subsequently cooled through the injection of water, the steam condensed, forcing the piston down and lifting the weights up. Papin spent his last years (1707–1712) in London where the Royal Society of London held discussions of his papers, thereby alerting engineers, craftspeople, and entrepreneurs in England to the steam engine as a labor-saving machine. In 1712, the mechanic Thomas Newcomen built the first steam engine to pump water from coal mine shafts.

Altogether, it took a little over a century, from 1604 (Galileo) to 1712 (Newcomen), for Europeans to apply the New Science to the development of the steam engine. Had it not been for the New Science, this engine—based on contracting steam—would not have been invented. (Hero of Alexandria, who invented steam-driven machines in the first century CE, made use of the expanding force of steam.) Prior to 1600, mechanical inventions—such as the wheel, the compass, the stern rudder, and the firearm—were constructed by anonymous tinkerers with a good commonsense understanding of nature. With the arrival of the New Science, Aristotelian common sense was no longer a virtue. It became a hindrance for the building of mechanical machinery. In 1700, engineers had to have at least a basic understanding of mathematics and such abstract physical phenomena as inertia, gravity, vacuums, and condensing steam if they wanted to build a steam engine or other complex machinery.

The Early Enlightenment in Northwestern Europe

The New Science engendered a pattern of radically new intellectual and religious thinking, which evolved in the course of the seventeenth and early eighteenth centuries. This thought, called the "Enlightenment," was deemed to be incompatible with the inherited medieval scholasticism. It eventually evolved into a powerful instrument of critique of Christian doctrine and the constitutional order of the fiscal–military states. Initially, the Enlightenment was confined to a few thinkers, but with the Glorious Revolution of 1688 in England it became a potent social force.

Descartes and Bacon   After the replacement of descriptive physics with mathematical physics, brought about by Galileo with his law of descending bodies, the question arose whether Aristotelian philosophy and Catholic theology were still adequate for the understanding of reality. New Scientists perceived the need to start philosophizing and theologizing from scratch. The first major New Scientist who, in his own judgment, started a radical reconsideration of philosophy from the ground up was the Frenchman René Descartes (1596–1650). He earned a degree in law, traveling widely after graduation. In the service of the Dutch and Bavarian courts, he bore witness to the beginning of the Thirty Years' War and its atrocities committed in the name of religious doctrines. During the war, he spent two decades in the Netherlands, studying and teaching the New Sciences. His principal innovation in mathematics was the discovery that geometry could be converted through algebra into analytic geometry.

Descartes was shocked by the condemnation of Galileo and decided to abandon all traditional propositions and doctrines of the Church as well as Aristotelianism. Realizing that his common sense (that is, the five senses of seeing, hearing, touching, smelling, and tasting) were unreliable, he determined that the only reliable body of knowledge was thought, especially mathematical thought. As a person capable of thought, he concluded—bypassing his unreliable senses—that he existed: "I think, therefore I am" (*cogito ergo sum*). A further conclusion from this argument was that he was composed of two radically different substances, a material substance consisting of his senses and another immaterial substance consisting of thought. According to Descartes, body and mind, although joined through consciousness, belong to two different realms of reality.

The Philosophy of the New Science

Descartes's distinctions between body, mind, and consciousness stimulated a lively debate not only among the New Scientists but also among the growing circle of philosophers of the New Science. The Englishmen Thomas Hobbes (1588–1679) and John Locke (1632–1704) were among the latter. Hobbes, interested in the New Science since his student days, described himself as a philosopher. Locke had a basic medical education but made his contributions to the field of philosophy. Both applied Descartes's New Science philosophy to constitutional theory, making crucial contributions to the formation of constitutional nationalism in the United States, France, and Haiti at the end of the 1700s. Constitutional nationalism and its later rival, ethnic nationalism, are today the main political forces driving the patterns of world politics.

Thomas Hobbes

As a nonscientist outside the field of mathematics, astronomy, and physics—the most advanced mathematical sciences in the seventeenth and eighteenth centuries—Hobbes had little interest in Galileo's and Descartes' concept of the mind as pure mathematical thought. Therefore, it escaped him that for Descartes (as also, before him, Plato and Galileo) mathematics was the new divine: God was equivalent to mathematics; and the Mind, insofar as it could conceive of mathematics, was pure, transcendent thought.

The nonmathematician Hobbes paid attention only to consciousness; that is, the personal mind in a living body, subject to the law of motion. And since bodies are made up of corpuscles (later scientists and philosophers would speak of atoms), so, Hobbes concluded, reality is entirely material and determined by the law of motion. With Hobbes, the philosophy of materialism was born, according to which nothing but matter exists and anything mathematical, intellectual, or spiritual is dependent on matter.

Once Hobbes decided that materialism was the only possible new philosophy, the extension of materialism to political philosophy followed easily. If people are nothing but bodies, they are equal to each other with their basic bodily functions, such as their emotions and passions. Foremost among the passions, so Hobbes concluded, is selfishness. Therefore, in the natural state of humanity, which is defined as millions of atoms in motion, clashing with each other, there is "war of every man against every man."

In this general war, fear of death—another major passion—drives humans to give up their sovereignty, their "absolute" personal liberty to wage war. They do so either because they are forced by a single sovereign to do so or because they transfer their sovereignty voluntarily to a sovereign or a collective representative assembly that possesses sovereignty. Hobbes, well aware of the horrors of the recent English religious wars, preferred the alternative of the single sovereign. Thus, we can conclude that it is on the grounds of materialist philosophical thinking that Hobbes arrived at the principles of equality, rule by law, and the constitutional state. It was from the philosophy of the New Science, and specifically the concept of materialism, that the theory of democracy arrived on the world historical scene.

The Social Contract. Hobbes believed that the "war of all against all" could only be avoided when human beings entered into a contract in which they agreed to be ruled by an absolute sovereign. The title page from his most famous work, *Leviathan*, depicts the ruler as an absolute monarch, but one whose body incorporates the many individuals of society who have consented to live in a commonwealth under his authority.

John Locke   Locke also outlined a philosophy derived from the New Science that eliminates the mind and makes consciousness rigorously dependent on matter. According to Locke, the mind is a blank slate at birth on which sense perception impresses all categories of thought and reflection. Matter, in the form of atoms, impresses itself on the mind and creates consciousness. Through trial and error we overcome what Descartes considered to be the deception by the senses. Locke, in the Anglo-American philosophical tradition, became the principal figure of Enlightenment materialism.

In the political realm, Locke also took the passions as his starting point. But, for him, the basic passion was the desire of ownership—of oneself, one's labor, and property—which he considered to be inalienable rights. Self-possession excluded slavery, ownership of one's labor meant self-employment, and ownership of property included land and portable wealth. When this passion could no longer be satisfied, war would break out. But once the passions of war subsided, reason would lead humans to the establishment of a peaceful or civil government. In so doing, however, humans would not give up their liberty, as argued by Hobbes. They would merely empower the government to protect private property. Therefore, also in contrast to Hobbes, citizens retained the right to rise against an unjust government. Ironically, by default, Locke allowed for the kind of general war to which Hobbes was opposed.

The early Enlightenment was a curious mixture of a flawed philosophy of materialism and base human passions and an eventually highly successful political theory of democracy. Forgetting that Descartes held fast to the Platonic–Galilean notion of the divine as mathematics and the mind as pure mathematical thought, they developed a philosophy of consciousness as the concrete individual consciousness in a moving body determined by passions. A split occurred between the New Science, in which mathematics functioned as the new equivalent of religion, and the

Transcendence: Realm in reality that is as real as matter; the transcendent realm is both separate and mingled with the realm of matter; the difficulty of thinking of the two as both separate and mingled has caused much confusion, beginning with Hobbes and Locke.

Enlightenment philosophy of materialism, in which no religion was needed, even if philosophers remained nominally Christian. This division is still unhealed today, with both scientists and the general public unaware that the equivalent of the divine in the modern age is the **transcendence** of mathematics.

Putting It All Together

Prior to 1500, all religious civilizations possessed sophisticated mathematics and practiced variations of descriptive science, such as astronomy, astrology, geography, alchemy, and medicine. Only after 1550 did astronomy and physics in western Christianity transform themselves into mathematical science. This transformation, however, had no practical consequences prior to the invention of the steam engine in the 1700s and the subsequent industrialization of England in the 1800s. Furthermore, the mathematization of astronomy and physics did little to influence the continued prevalence of description as the chief underlying pattern of the other sciences. Astrology, alchemy, and medicine continued with what we regard today as mistaken descriptive theories well into the nineteenth century.

Most importantly, the rise of the New Science and Enlightenment should not be confused with the vast political, social, economic, and cultural changes, called "modernity" after 1750, which propelled the West on its trajectory of world dominance. Although the West began to acquire its specific scientific and philosophical identity with the introduction of mathematical science in the one hundred-year span between Copernicus and Galileo, its impact on the world became felt only after it applied science to industry. Once this process got underway, in the nineteenth century, Asia and Africa had no choice but to adapt to modern science and industrialization.

▶ For additional resources, including maps, primary sources, visuals, and quizzes, please go to www.oup.com/us/vonsivers. Please see the Further Resources section at the back of the book for additional readings and suggested websites.

Thinking Through Patterns

▶ **What were the patterns of fiscal–military state formation and transformation in the period 1450–1750? How did the Protestant Reformation and religious wars modify these patterns?**

European kingdoms, such as France, Sweden, and Prussia, expanded their powers of taxation to the detriment of the nobility. With the accumulated funds, they hired and salaried mercenary infantries equipped with firearms, using them to conquer land from their neighbors. The religious wars of the 1500s and 1600s strengthened centralization efforts and hastened the demise of the nobility as obstacles to the fiscal–military state. In England, Parliament blocked the Stuart kings from building an infantry fiscal–military state and instead pursued the construction of a naval state, which succeeded a similar one built by the Netherlands in 1688.

Located far from the traditional agrarian–urban centers of Eurasia, western Christianity repeatedly adapted its culture (particularly theological, philosophical, scientific, and artistic forms of expression) in response to outside stimuli coming from Islamic and eastern Christian civilizations. Without these stimuli, the Renaissance, Baroque, New Science, and Enlightenment would not have developed. In contrast, the Middle East, Byzantium, India, and China, originating firmly within the traditional agrarian–urban centers, received far fewer outside stimuli prior to the scientific–industrial age.

▶ **What are the reasons for the cultural change that began in Europe around 1750? In which ways were the patterns of cultural changes during 1450–1750 different from those in the other religious civilizations of Eurasia?**

▶ **When and how did the New Science begin, and how did it gain popularity in northwestern European society? Why is the popularization of the New Science important for understanding the period 1450–1750?**

The discovery of the two new continents of the Americas prompted Nicolaus Copernicus to reject Aristotle's astronomical theory of spheres and to posit a sun-centered planetary system. It continued with Galileo Galilei's discovery of the mathematical law of falling bodies in physics and was completed with Isaac Newton unifying physics and astronomy. The New Science became popular among educated urban circles in northwestern Europe, where Catholic and Protestant church authorities were largely divided. In southern Europe, where the Catholic Counter-Reformation was powerful and rejected the New Science, no such popularization occurred. The New Science possessed practical applicability: After discovering the properties of the vacuum and condensing steam, scientists began experimenting with steam engines, which served as the principal catalyst for the launching of the scientific–industrial age.

Chapter 18 1500-1800

New Patterns in New Worlds

COLONIALISM AND INDIGENOUS RESPONSES IN THE AMERICAS

Alonso Ortíz was a deadbeat. He fled from his creditors in Zafra, Estremadura, in southwestern Spain, in the early 1770s to find a new life in the Americas. In Mexico City, with the help of borrowed money, he set up shop as a tanner. His business flourished and, with a partner, Ortíz expanded into two rented buildings. Eight Native American employees, whom he had trained, did the actual labor of stomping the hides in the vats filled with tanning acids. A black slave, belonging to his partner, was the supervisor. Happy that he no longer had to take his shoes off to work, Ortíz concentrated on giving instructions and hustling up business.

Ortíz's situation in Mexico City was not entirely legal, however. He had left his wife, Eleanor González, and children alone in Zafra, though the law required that families should be united. The authorities rarely enforced this law, but that was no guarantee for Ortíz. Furthermore, he had not yet sent his family any remittances, leaving Eleanor to rely on the largesse of her two brothers back home for survival. And then, there was still the debt. Ortíz had reasons to be afraid of the law.

To avoid prosecution, Ortíz wrote a letter to Eleanor. In this letter, he proudly described the comfortable position he had achieved. He announced that his kind business partner was sending her a sum of money sufficient to begin preparations for her departure from Spain. To his creditors, Ortíz

ATLANTIC OCEAN

PACIFIC OCEAN

THE AMERICAS IN 1750

- Spanish
- Portuguese
- British
- French
- Dutch

ABOVE: The meeting of Moctezuma and Cortés, from *The History of the Conquest of Mexico by the Spaniards*, by Spanish historian Antonio de Solís (1610–1686).

promised to send 100 tanned hides within a year. "Your arrival would bring me great joy," he wrote to Eleanor, reneging on an original promise to be already back home in Spain. Evidently aware of her reluctance to join him in Mexico, Ortíz closed his letter with a request to grant him 4 more years abroad and to do so with a notarized document from her hand. Unfortunately, we do not know her answer.

The Ortíz family drama gives a human face to European emigration and colonialism from Europe to the Americas. Like Alonso Ortíz, some 300,000 other Spaniards emigrated between 1500 and 1800. They came alone or with family, temporarily or for good, and either failed or succeeded in their new lives. A few hundred letters by emigrants exist, giving us glimpses of their lives in Mexico, Peru, and other parts of the Americas conquered by the Spanish and Portuguese in the sixteenth century. As these relatively privileged immigrants settled, they hoped to build successful enterprises using the labor of Native Americans as well as black slaves imported from Africa. As the example of Ortíz documents, even in the socially not very prestigious craft of tanning a man could achieve a measure of comfort by having people of even lower status working for him.

Seeing Patterns

▶ What is the significance of western Europeans acquiring the Americas as a warm-weather extension of their northern continent?

▶ What was the main pattern of social development in colonial America during the period 1500–1800?

▶ Why and how did European settlers in South and North America strive for self-government, and how successful were they in achieving their goals?

Beginning in the sixteenth century, Americas became an extension of Europe. European settlers extracted mineral and agricultural resources from these new lands. In Europe these resources had become increasingly expensive and impractical to produce (if they could be produced at all). A pattern emerged in which gold and silver, as well as agricultural products that could not be grown in Europe's cooler climate, were intensively exploited. In their role as supplementary subtropical and tropical extensions of Europe, the Americas became a crucial factor for Europe's changing position in the world. First, Europe acquired large quantities of precious metals, which its two largest competitors, India and China, lacked. Second, with its new access to warm-weather agricultural products, Europe rose to a position of agrarian autonomy similar to that of India and China. In terms of resources, compared with the principal religious civilizations of India and China, Europe grew between 1550 and 1800 from a position of inferiority to one of near parity.

The Colonial Americas: Europe's Warm-Weather Extension

The European extension into the subtropical and tropical Americas followed Columbus's pursuit of a sea route to India and its spices that would circumvent the Mediterranean and its dominance by Muslim traders. The Spaniards justified the conquest of these new continents and their Native American inhabitants with Christ's command to convert the heathen in the Spanish Habsburg world empire, the glorious final empire before Christ's return. They financed their imperial expansion as well as their wars against Ottoman and European rivals with American gold and silver, leaving little for domestic investment in productive enterprises. A pattern evolved in which Iberian settlers transformed the Americas into mineral-extracting and agrarian colonies based on either cheap or forced labor.

The Conquest of Mexico and Peru

The Spanish conquerors of the Aztec and Inca Empires, although small in number, succeeded by exploiting internal weaknesses in the empires. They swiftly eliminated the top of the power structures, paralyzing the decision-making apparatuses long enough for their conquests to succeed. Soon after the conquests, the Old World disease of smallpox—to which New World inhabitants had never been exposed and, therefore, had never developed immunity—ravaged the Native American population and dramatically reduced the indigenous labor force. To make up for this reduction, colonial authorities imported black slaves from Africa for employment in mines and in agriculture. Black Africans, who had long been in contact with Eurasia, were, similar to Europeans, less susceptible to smallpox. A three-tiered society of European immigrants, Native Americans, and black slaves emerged in the Spanish and Portuguese Americas.

From Trade Posts to Conquest   Columbus had discovered the Caribbean islands under a royal commission, which entitled him to build fortified posts and to trade with the indigenous Taínos. The Portuguese had pioneered the use of fortified trade posts in their explorations along the costs of West Africa. Friendly trade relations with the Taínos, however, quickly deteriorated into outright exploitation, with the Spaniards usurping the traditional entitlements of the Taíno chiefs to the labor of their tribesmen, who panned gold in rivers or mined it in shallow shafts. With the help of **land-labor grants** (Spanish *encomiendas*), the Spanish took over from the Taíno chiefs and, through forced labor, amassed sizeable quantities of gold. What had begun as trade post settlement turned into full-blown conquest.

The Spaniards conquered the Caribbean islands not only through force. Much more severe in its consequences was the indirect conquest through disease. The Old World disease of smallpox quickly wiped out an estimated 250,000 to 1 million Taínos on the larger northern islands as well as the less numerous Caribs on the smaller southern Caribbean islands. Isolated for more than 10,000 years from the rest of humankind, Native Americans possessed no immunity against smallpox and were similarly ravaged by other introduced diseases such as measles, diphtheria, mumps, plague, influenza, typhoid, malaria, and yellow fever.

Protests, mostly among members of the clergy, arose against both the brutal labor exploitation by the conquerors and the helplessness of the Taínos dying of disease. Unfortunately, the protesters remained a small minority, even within the clergy. The best-known among several was Bartolomé de las Casas (1474–1566), from a family of merchants in Seville. Las Casas had practiced law before emigrating to Hispaniola, where he received an *encomienda*. After becoming a priest in 1510 and later a Dominican monk, however, he became a bitter opponent of the labor grant system. He demanded nothing less than the end of this institution, something that did not come until after 1542 with the introduction of the *repartimiento* system.

Land-labor grant (*encomienda*): Land grant by the government to an entrepreneur entitling him to use forced indigenous or imported slave labor on this land for the exploitation of agricultural and mineral resources.

First Mainland Conquests Another early settler on Hispaniola was Hernán Cortés (1485–1547). His father was a lower-level nobleman in Estremadura, a rough, formerly Islamic frontier region in southwestern Iberia. Chosen by his parents for a career in law, Cortés learned Latin but left the university before graduation. After his arrival in the New World in 1504, he advanced quickly from governmental scribe in Hispaniola to mayor of Santiago in Cuba. Thanks to several labor grants, he became rich. When the Cuban governor asked him in the fall of 1518 to equip and lead a small preparatory expedition for trade and exploration to the Yucatán Peninsula in southeastern Mexico, Cortés enthusiastically agreed. Within a month he assembled 300 men, considerably exceeding his contract. The governor tried to stop him, but Cortés departed quickly for the American mainland.

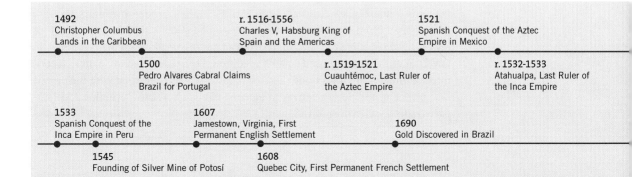

Cultural Intermediary. The Tabascans gave Malinche, or Doña Marina, to Hernán Cortés as a form of tribute after they were defeated by the Spanish. Malinche served Cortés as a translator and mistress, filling a central role in Cortés's eventual victory over the Aztecs. She was in many respects the principal face of the Spanish and is always depicted center stage in Native American visual accounts of the conquest.

As the Cuban governor had feared, Cortés did not bother with trade posts in Yucatán. The Spanish had previously learned of the existence of the Aztec Empire, with its immense silver and gold treasures. In a first encounter, Cortés's motley force—numbering by now about 530 Spanish men—defeated a vastly superior indigenous force at Tabasco, mostly thanks to the Spaniards' pikes, swords, daggers, plate armor, and a few matchlock muskets and horses. Their steel weapons and armor proved superior in hand-to-hand combat to the obsidian-spiked lances, wooden swords, and quilted cotton vests of the defenders. Among the gifts of submission presented by the defeated Native Americans in Tabasco was Malinche, a Nahuatl [NA-hu-wah]-speaking woman whose father, an Aztec lord, had given her as a teenager to the Tabascans. Malinche quickly learned Spanish and became the consort of Cortés, teaching him about the subtleties of Aztec culture. In her role as translator, Malinche was nearly as decisive as Cortés in shaping events. Indeed, Aztecs often used the name of Malinche when addressing Cortés, forgetting that her voice was not that of Cortés. With Tabasco conquered, Cortés quickly moved on; he was afraid that the Cuban governor, who was in pursuit, would otherwise force him to return to Cuba.

Conquest of the Aztec Empire On the southeast coast of Mexico, Cortés founded the city of Veracruz as a base from which to move inland. In the city, he had his followers elect a town council, which made Cortés their head and chief justice, allowing Cortés to claim legitimacy for his march inland. To prevent opponents in his camp from notifying the Cuban governor of his usurpation of authority, Cortés had all ships stripped of their gear and the hulls sunk. Marching inland, the Spaniards ran

1492		r. 1516-1556		1521	
Christopher Columbus Lands in the Caribbean		Charles V, Habsburg King of Spain and the Americas		Spanish Conquest of the Aztec Empire in Mexico	
	1500 Pedro Alvares Cabral Claims Brazil for Portugal		r. 1519-1521 Cuauhtémoc, Last Ruler of the Aztec Empire		r. 1532-1533 Atahualpa, Last Ruler of the Inca Empire
1533 Spanish Conquest of the Inca Empire in Peru		1607 Jamestown, Virginia, First Permanent English Settlement		1690 Gold Discovered in Brazil	
	1545 Founding of Silver Mine of Potosí		1608 Quebec City, First Permanent French Settlement		

into resistance from indigenous people, suffering their first losses of horses and men. Although bloodied, they continued their march with thousands of Native American allies, most notably the Tlaxcalans, traditional enemies of the Aztecs. The support from these indigenous peoples made a crucial difference when Cortés and his army reached the court of the Aztecs.

When Cortés arrived at the city of Tenochtitlán on November 2, 1519, the Emperor Moctezuma II (r. 1502–1519) was in a quandary over how to deal with these invaders whose depredations neither his tributaries nor his enemies had been able to stop. To gain some time for deliberating about how to deal with Cortés, Moctezuma greeted the Spaniard in person on one of the causeways leading to the city and invited him to his palace. Cortés and his company, now numbering some 600 Spaniards, took up quarters in the palace precincts. After a week of gradually deteriorating discussions, Cortés suddenly put the incredulous emperor under house arrest and made him swear allegiance to Charles V.

Before being able to contemplate his next move, however, Cortés was diverted by the need to march back east, where troops from Cuba had arrived to arrest him. After defeating those troops, he enrolled the straggling Cuban soldiers into his own service and marched back to Tenochtitlán. During his absence, the Spaniards who had remained in Moctezuma's palace had massacred a number of unarmed Aztec nobles participating in a religious ceremony. An infuriated crowd of Tenochtitlán's inhabitants invaded the palace. In the melee, Moctezuma and some 200 Spaniards died. The rest of the Spanish fled for their lives, retreating east to their Tlaxcalan allies, who, fortunately, remained loyal. Here, after his return, the indomitable Cortés devised a new plan for capturing Tenochtitlán.

After 10 months of preparations, the Spaniards returned to the Aztec capital. Numbering now about 2,000 Spanish soldiers and assisted by some 50,000 Native American troops, Cortés laid siege to the city, bombarding it from ships he had built in the lake and razing buildings during forays onto land. After nearly 3 months, much of the city was in ruins, fresh water and food became scarce, and smallpox began to decimate the population of some 3–4 million inhabitants in the Valley of Mexico and 25 million in the Aztec Empire. On August 21, 1521, the Spaniards and their allies stormed the city and looted its gold treasury. They captured the fiercely resisting last emperor, Cuauhtémoc [Cu-aw-TAY-moc], a few days later and executed him in captivity in 1525, thus ending the Aztec Empire (see Map 18.1).

Conquest of the Inca Empire   At about the same time, a relative of Cortés, Francisco Pizarro (ca. 1475–1541), conceived a plan to conquer the Andean empire of the Incas (which, in 1492, comprised some 9–12 million inhabitants). Pizarro, like Cortés born in Estremadura, was an illegitimate son of an infantry captain from the lower nobility. Illiterate and without education, he had come to Hispaniola as part of an expedition in 1513 that discovered Panama and the Pacific. He became mayor of Panama City, acquired some wealth, and began to hear rumors about an empire of gold and silver to the south. After a failed initial expedition, he and 13 followers captured some precious metal from an oceangoing Inca sailing raft. Since the governor of Panama opposed a new expedition, Pizarro traveled to Spain to receive direct authorization for a trade post from Charles V. He returned with his permit, four brothers, and other relatives to Panama City and, in late December 1530, departed south with a host of 183 men.

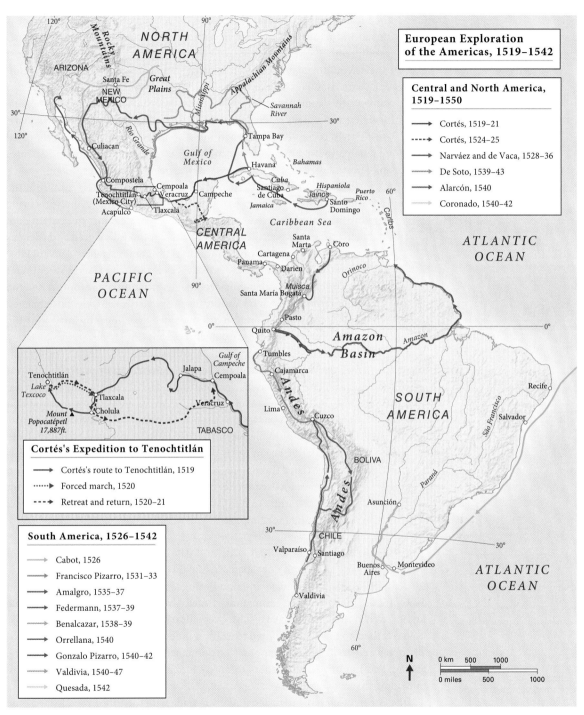

**European Exploration
of the Americas, 1519-1542**

**Central and North America,
1519-1550**

→	Cortés, 1519–21
‑‑‑▶	Cortés, 1524–25
→	Narváez and de Vaca, 1528–36
→	De Soto, 1539–43
→	Alarcón, 1540
→	Coronado, 1540–42

Cortés's Expedition to Tenochtitlán

→	Cortés's route to Tenochtitlán, 1519
‧‧‧‧▶	Forced march, 1520
‑‑‑▶	Retreat and return, 1520–21

South America, 1526–1542

→	Cabot, 1526
→	Francisco Pizarro, 1531–33
→	Amalgro, 1535–37
→	Federmann, 1537–39
→	Benalcazar, 1538–39
→	Orrellana, 1540
→	Gonzalo Pizarro, 1540–42
→	Valdivia, 1540–47
→	Quesada, 1542

MAP **18.1 The European
Exploration of the Americas,
1519–1542.**

In a grimly fortuitous bit of luck for Pizarro, smallpox had preceded him in his expedition. In the later 1520s, the disease had ravaged the Inca Empire, killing the emperor and his heir apparent. A brutal and protracted war of succession between two surviving sons broke out. Atahualpa, in the north, sent his army south to the capital, Cuzco, where it defeated his half-brother, Huascar. When Pizarro entered

ATAHUALLPA. INCA XIII.

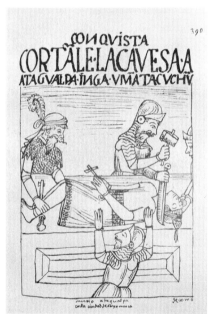

Conquest by Surprise. The Spanish conqueror Francisco Pizarro captured Emperor Atahualpa (top) in an ambush. Atahualpa promised a roomful of gold in return for his release, but the Spaniards collected the gold and murdered Atahualpa (bottom) before generals of the Inca army could organize an armed resistance.

the Inca Empire, Atahualpa was encamped with an army of 40,000 men near the northern town of Cajamarca, on his way south to Cuzco to install himself as emperor.

Arriving at Cajamarca, Pizarro succeeded in arranging an unarmed audience with Atahualpa in the town square. On November 16, 1532, Atahualpa came to this audience, surrounded by several thousand unarmed retainers, while Pizarro hid his soldiers in and behind the buildings around the square. At a signal, these soldiers rushed into the square. Some soldiers captured Atahualpa to hold him hostage. In the ensuing bloodbath, not one Spanish soldier was killed. The whole massacre was over in less than an hour.

With his ambush, Pizarro succeeded in paralyzing the Inca Empire at the very top. Without their emperor Atahualpa, none of the generals in Cuzco dared to seize the initiative. Instead of ordering his captors to liberate him, Atahualpa sought to pacify their greed with a room full of gold and silver as ransom. In the following 2 months, Inca administrators delivered immense quantities of precious metals to Pizarro. Inevitably, resentment arose among the Spaniards over the distribution of the loot. When the time came to march on Cuzco, those Spaniards who felt shortchanged by the unequal distribution of loot cooled their anger by instigating the execution of the hapless Atahualpa on July 26, 1533.

The Spaniards took Cuzco 3 months later. They did so against minimal resistance, massacring the inhabitants and stripping the city of its immense gold and silver treasures. Pizarro did not stay long in the now worthless, isolated capital in the Andes. In 1535 Pizarro founded a new capital, Lima, which was more conveniently located on the coast and about halfway between Cajamarca and Cuzco. As the immensity of their defeat began to sink in, the hitherto paralyzed Inca generals finally bestirred themselves. Learning from past mistakes, they avoided mass battles, focused on deadly guerilla strikes, and rebuilt a kingdom that held out until 1572. It was only then that the Spanish gained full control of the Inca Empire.

The Portuguese Conquest of Brazil The Portuguese were not far behind the Spaniards in their pursuit of conquest. Navigators of three fleets, two Spanish and one Portuguese, sighted the Brazilian coast in 1499/1500. The Portuguese commander Pedro Alvares Cabral, on his way to India, immediately notified his king of his discovery. Brazil's indigenous population at that time is estimated to have amounted to nearly 5 million. The great majority were tribally organized and lived in temporary or permanent villages based on agriculture, fishing, and hunting. Only a small minority in remote areas of the Amazon were pure foragers.

The Portuguese were interested initially in trade with the tribes, mostly for a type of hardwood called "brazilwood," which was ground into sawdust and used as a red dye. When French traders showed up, ignoring the Portuguese commercial treaties with the tribes, the Portuguese crown shifted from simple trade agreements to trade post settlements. This involved giving land grants to commoners and lower noblemen with the obligation to build fortified coastal villages for settlers and to engage in agriculture and friendly trade. By the mid-sixteenth century, a handful of these villages became successful, their inhabitants intermarrying with the surrounding indigenous chieftain families and establishing sugarcane plantations.

Explanations for the Spanish Success   The slow progression of the Portuguese in tribal Brazil is readily understood. But the stupendous victories of handfuls of Spaniards over huge empires with millions of inhabitants and large cities defy easy explanation. Five factors invite consideration.

First, and most important, the conquistadors went straight to the top of the imperial pyramid. The emperors and their courts expected diplomatic deference by inferiors, among whom they included the minuscule band of Spaniards. Confronted, instead, with a calculated combination of arrogance and brutality, the Spaniards threw the emperors and courts off balance. Exploiting their opportunity, the conquistadors struck with deadly determination. Most important, as the emperors were removed from the top level, their administration immediately below fell into paralysis, unable to seize the initiative and respond in a timely fashion.

Second, both the Aztec and Inca Empires were relatively recent creations in which there were individuals and groups who contested the hierarchical power structure. The conquistadors either found allies among the subject populations or encountered a divided leadership. In either case, they were able to exploit divisions in the empires.

Third, European-introduced diseases, traveling faster than the conquerors, took a devastating toll. In both empires, smallpox hit at critical moments during or right before the Spanish invasions, causing major disruptions.

Fourth, thanks to horses and superior European steel weapons and armor, primarily pikes, swords, and breast plates, small numbers of Spaniards were able to hold large numbers of attacking Aztecs and Incas at bay in hand-to-hand combat. Contrary to widespread belief, cannons and matchlock muskets were less important since they were useless in close encounters. Firearms were still too slow and inaccurate to be decisive.

In contrast to a popular view, a fifth factor, indigenous religion, was probably of least significance. According to this interpretation, Moctezuma was immobilized by his belief in the prophecy of having to relinquish his power to the savior Quetzalcoatl returning from his mythical city of Tlapallan on the east coast (see Chapter 15). Modern scholarship provides convincing reasons, however, to declare this prophecy a postconquest legend, circulated by Cortés both to flatter Charles V and to aggrandize himself as a savior.

Spanish Steel. The Lienzo de Tlaxcala, from the middle part of the sixteenth century, is our best visual source for the conquest of Mexico. In this scene, Malinche, protected by a shield, directs the battle on the causeway leading to Tenochtitlán. The two Spanish soldiers behind her, one fully armored, brandish steel swords, which were more effective than the obsidian blades carried by the Aztec defenders (one of whom is dressed in leopard skins), shown on the left.

The Establishment of Colonial Institutions

The Spanish crown established administrative hierarchies in the Americas, similar to those of the Aztecs and Incas, with governors at the top of the hierarchy and descending through lower ranks of functionaries. A small degree of settler autonomy was permitted through town and city councils, but the crown was determined to make the Americas a territorial extension of the European pattern of fiscal–military state formation. Several hundred thousand settlers (including Alonso Ortíz) found

Creoles: American-born descendants of European, primarily Iberian, immigrants.

a new life in the Americas, mostly as urban craftspeople, administrators, and professionals. By the early seventeenth century, a powerful elite of Spanish who had been born in America, called **Creoles** (Spanish *criollos*, Portuguese *crioules*, natives) was in place, first to assist and later to replace most of the administrators sent from Spain in the governance of the Americas (see Map 18.2).

From Conquest to Colonialism   The unimaginable riches of Cortés and Pizarro inspired numerous further expeditions. Adventurers struck out with small bands of followers into Central and North America, Chile, and the Amazon. Their expeditions, however, yielded only modest amounts of gold and earned more from selling captured Native Americans into slavery. Only the fortified village chiefdoms of the 1 million Muisca, in what is today Colombia, yielded significant quantities of gold to their conquerors, in 1537. In the north, expeditions penetrated as far as Arizona, New Mexico, Texas, Oklahoma, Kansas, and Florida but encountered only villagers and the relatively poor Pueblo towns. No new golden kingdoms (the mythical El Dorado, or "golden city") beyond the Aztec and Inca Empires were discovered in the Americas.

In the mid-sixteenth century, easy looting was replaced by a search for the mines from where the precious metals came. In northern Mexico, Native Americans led a group of soldiers and missionaries in 1547 to a number of rich silver mines. In addition, explorers discovered silver in Bolivia (1545) and northern Mexico (1556), gold in Chile (1552), and mercury in Peru (1563). The conquistadors shifted from looting to the exploitation of Native American labor in mines and in agriculture.

Bureaucratic Efficiency   During the first two generations after the conquest, Spain maintained an efficient colonial administration, which delivered between 50 and 60 percent of the colonies' revenues to Spain. These revenues contributed as much as one-quarter to the Spanish crown budget. In addition, the viceroyalty of New Spain in Mexico remitted another 25 percent of its revenues to the Philippines, the Pacific province for which it was administratively responsible from 1571 onward. As in Spain, settlers in New Spain had to pay up to 40 different taxes and dues, levied on imports and exports, internal trade, mining, and sales. The only income tax was the tithe to the church, which the administration collected and, at times, used for its own budgetary purposes. Altogether, however, for the settlers the tax level was lower in the New World than in Spain, and the same was true for the English and French colonies in North America.

Labor assignment (*repartimiento*): Obligation by villagers to send stipulated numbers of people as laborers to a contractor, who had the right to exploit a mine or other labor-intensive enterprise; the contractors paid the laborers minimal wages and bound them through debt peonage to their businesses.

In the 1540s the government introduced rotating **labor assignments** (*repartimientos*) to phase out the encomiendas that powerful owners sought to perpetuate within their families. This institution of rotating labor assignments was a continuation of the mit'a system, which the Incas had devised as a form of taxation, in the absence of money and easy transportation of crops in their empire (see Chapter 15). Rotating labor assignments meant that for fixed times a certain percentage of villagers had to provide labor to the state at low pay for road building, drainage, transportation, and mining. Private entrepreneurs could also contract for indigenous labor assignments, especially in mining regions.

In Mexico the repartimiento fell out of use in the first half of the seventeenth century as a result of the continuing Native American population decline due to recurring smallpox epidemics. It is estimated that the indigenous population in the

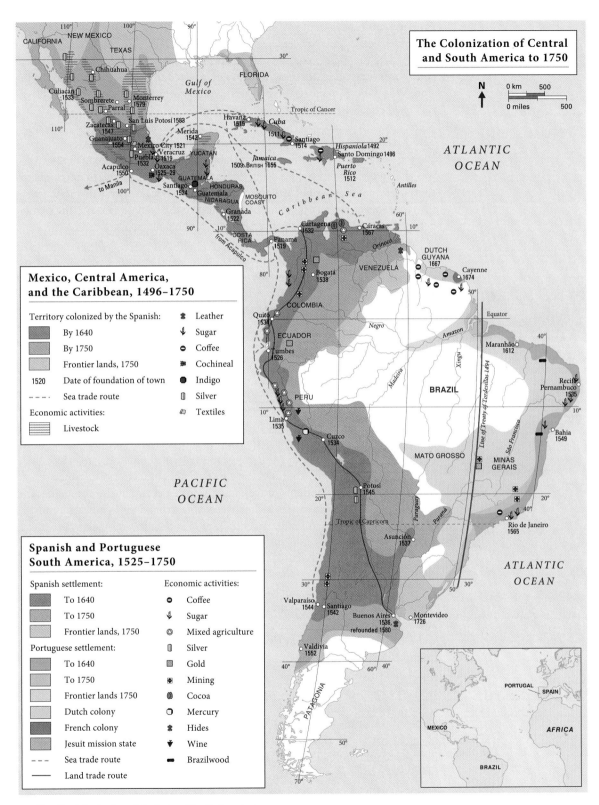

The Colonization of Central and South America to 1750

N

| 0 km | 500 |
| 0 miles | 500 |

Mexico, Central America, and the Caribbean, 1496–1750

Territory colonized by the Spanish:
- By 1640
- By 1750
- Frontier lands, 1750
- 1520 Date of foundation of town
- - - - Sea trade route

Economic activities:
- Livestock

- ✦ Leather
- ⇂ Sugar
- ● Coffee
- ✿ Cochineal
- ● Indigo
- ▯ Silver
- ▱ Textiles

Spanish and Portuguese South America, 1525–1750

Spanish settlement:
- To 1640
- To 1750
- Frontier lands, 1750

Portuguese settlement:
- To 1640
- To 1750
- Frontier lands 1750
- Dutch colony
- French colony
- Jesuit mission state
- - - - Sea trade route
- —— Land trade route

Economic activities:
- ● Coffee
- ⇂ Sugar
- ◎ Mixed agriculture
- ▯ Silver
- ▪ Gold
- ✥ Mining
- ◍ Cocoa
- ◔ Mercury
- ✦ Hides
- ▼ Wine
- ▬ Brazilwood

MAP **18.2 The Colonization of Central and South America to 1750.**

Americas, from a height of 54 million in 1550, declined to 10 million by 1700 before recovering again. The replacement for the lost workers was wage labor. In highland Peru, where the indigenous population was less densely settled and the effects of smallpox less ravaging, the assignment system lasted to the end of the colonial period. Wage labor expanded there as well. Wages for Native Americans and blacks remained everywhere lower than for those for Creoles.

The Rise of the Creoles   Administrative and fiscal efficiency, however, did not last very long. The wars of the Spanish Habsburg Empire cost more than the crown was able to collect in revenues. King Philip II (r. 1556–1598) had to declare bankruptcy four times between 1557 and 1596. In order to make up the financial deficit, the crown began to sell offices in the Americas to the highest bidders. The first offices put on the block were elective positions in the municipal councils. By the end of the century, Creoles had purchased life appointments in city councils as well as positions as scribes, local judges, police chiefs, directors of processions and festivities, and other sinecures. In these positions, they collected fees and rents for their services. Local oligarchies emerged, effectively ending whatever elective, participatory politics existed in Spanish colonial America.

Over the course of the seventeenth century a majority of administrative positions became available for purchase. The effects of the change from recruitment by merit to recruitment by wealth on the functioning of the bureaucracy were far-reaching. Creoles advanced on a broad front in the administrative positions, while fewer Spaniards found it attractive to buy their American positions from overseas. The only opportunities which European Spaniards still found enticing were the nearly 300 positions of governors and inspectors since these jobs gave their owners the right to subject the Native Americans to forced purchases of goods, yielding huge profits. For the most part, wealthy Spanish merchants delegated junior partners into these highly lucrative activities. By 1700, the consequences of the Spanish crown selling most of its American administrative offices were a decline in the competence of office holders, the emergence of a Creole elite able to bend the Spanish administration increasingly to its will, and a decentralization of the decision-making processes.

Northwest European Interference   As Spain's administrative grip on the Americas weakened during the seventeenth century, the need to defend the continents militarily against European interlopers arose. At the beginning, there were European privateers, holding royal charters, who harassed Spanish silver shipments and ports in the Caribbean. In the early seventeenth century, the French, English, and Dutch governments sent ships to occupy the smaller Caribbean islands not claimed by Spain. Privateer and contraband traders stationed on these islands engaged in further raiding and pillaging, severely damaging Spain's monopoly of shipping between Europe and the Caribbean.

Conquests of Spanish islands followed in the second half of the century. England captured Jamaica in 1655, and France colonized western Hispaniola in 1665, making it one of their most profitable sugar-producing colonies. Along the Pacific coast, depredations continued into the middle of the eighteenth century. Here, the galleons of the annual Acapulco–Manila fleet carrying silver from Mexico to China and returning with Chinese silks, porcelain, and lacquerware were the targets of English privateers. Over the course of the seventeenth century, Spain allocated one-half to two-thirds of its American revenues to the defense of its annual treasure fleets and Caribbean possessions, which continued despite limited losses to pirates and storms. Only the defense of the many islands eventually proved too difficult for the thinly stretched Spanish forces to maintain.

Bourbon Reforms   The last of the Spanish Habsburg rulers produced no heirs, and after the demise of the dynasty in 1700, the new French-descended dynasty of the Bourbons made major efforts to regain control over their American possessions. They had to begin from a discouragingly weak position as nearly 90 percent of all goods traded from Europe to the Americas were of non-Spanish origin. Fortunately, population increases among the settlers as well as the Native Americans (after having overcome their horrific losses to the epidemics) offered opportunities to Spanish manufacturers and merchants. After several false starts, in the middle of the eighteenth century the Bourbon reform program began to show results.

The reforms aimed at improved naval connections and administrative control between the mother country and the colonies. The monopolistic annual armed silver fleet was greatly reduced. Instead, the government authorized more frequent single sailings at different times of the year. Newly formed Spanish companies, receiving exclusive rights at specific ports, succeeded in reducing contraband trade. Elections took place again for municipal councils. Spanish-born salaried officials replaced scores of Creole tax and office farmers. The original two viceroyalties were subdivided into four, to improve administrative control. The sale of tobacco and brandy became state monopolies. Silver mining and cotton textile manufacturing were expanded. By the second half of the eighteenth century, Spain had regained a measure of control over its colonies.

As a result, tax receipts rose substantially. Government revenues increased more than twofold, even taking into account the inflation of the late eighteenth century. In the end, however, the reforms remained incomplete. Since the Spanish economy was not also reformed, in terms of expanding crafts production and urbanization, the changes did not diminish the English and French dominance of the import market by much. Spain failed to produce textiles, metalwares, and household goods at competitive prices for the colonies; thus English and French exports to the Americas remained high.

Early Portuguese Colonialism   In contrast to the Spanish Americas, the Portuguese overseas province of Brazil remained initially confined to a broad coastal strip, which developed only slowly during the sixteenth century. The first governor-general, whose rank was equivalent to a Spanish viceroy, arrived in 1549. He and his successors were members of the high aristocracy, but their positions were salaried and subject to term limits. As the colony grew, the crown created a council in the capital of Lisbon for all Brazilian appointments and established a high court for all judicial affairs in Bahia, northern Brazil. Commoners with law degrees from the Portuguese university of Coimbra filled the nonmilitary colonial positions. In the early seventeenth century, however, offices became as open to purchase as in the Spanish colonies, although not on the city council level, where a complex indirect electoral process survived.

Jesuits converted the Native Americans, whom they transported to villages that the Jesuits administered. Colonial cities and Jesuits repeatedly clashed over the slave

Mine Workers. The discovery of gold and diamonds in Minas Gerais led to a boom, but did little to contribute to the long-term health of the Brazilian economy. With the Native American population decimated by disease, African slaves performed the back-breaking work.

raids of the "pioneers" (*bandeirantes*) in village territories. The bandeirantes came mostly from São Paulo in the south and roamed the interior in search of human prey. Native American slaves were in demand on the wheat farms and cattle ranches of São Paulo as well as the sugar plantations of the northeast. Although the Portuguese crown and church had, like the Spanish, forbidden the enslavement of Native Americans, the bandeirantes exploited a loophole. The law was interpreted as allowing the enslavement of Native Americans who resisted conversion to Christianity. For a long time, Lisbon and the Jesuits were powerless against this flagrantly self-interested interpretation.

Expansion into the Interior   In the middle of the seventeenth century, the Jesuits and Native Americans finally succeeded in pushing many bandeirantes west and north, where they switched from slave raiding to prospecting for gold. In the far north, however, the raids continued until 1680, when the Portuguese administration finally prevailed and imposed an end to Native American slavery, almost a century and a half after Spain. Ironically, it was mostly thanks to the "pioneer" raids for slaves that Brazil expanded westward, to assume the borders it has today.

As a result of gold discoveries in Minas Gerais in 1690 by bandeirantes, the European immigrant population increased rapidly, from 1 to 2 million during the 1700s. Minas Gerais, located north of Rio de Janeiro, was the first inland region of the colony to attract settlers. By contrast, as a result of smallpox epidemics beginning in the 1650s in the Brazilian interior, the Native American population declined massively, not to expand again until the end of the eighteenth century. To replace the loss of labor, Brazilians imported slaves from Africa, at first to work in the sugar plantations and, after 1690, in the mines, where their numbers increased to two-thirds of the labor force. In contrast to Spanish mines, Brazilian mines were surface operations requiring only minimal equipment outlays. Most blacks worked with pickaxes and shovels. The peak of the gold boom came in the 1750s, when the importance of gold was second only to that of sugar on the list of Brazilian exports to Europe.

Early in the gold boom, the crown created a new Ministry of the Navy and Overseas Territories, which greatly expanded the administrative structure in Brazil. It established 14 regions and a second high court in Rio de Janeiro, which replaced Bahia as the capital in 1736. The ministry in Lisbon ended the sale of offices, increased the efficiency of tax collection, and encouraged Brazilian textile manufacturing to render the province more independent from English imports. By the mid-1700s, Brazil was a flourishing overseas colony of Portugal, producing brazilwood, sugar, gold, tobacco, cacao, and vanilla for export.

North American Settlements   Efforts at settlement in the less hospitable North America in the sixteenth century were unsuccessful. Only in the early part of the seventeenth century did French, English, and Dutch merchant investors succeed on the northeastern coast in establishing small communities of settlers, who grew their own food on land purchased from the local Native American villagers. These settlements were Jamestown (founded in 1607 in today's Virginia), Quebec (1608, Canada), Plymouth and Boston (1620 and 1630, respectively, New England), and New Amsterdam (1625, New York). Subsistence agriculture and fur, however, were meager ingredients for the settlements to prosper. The northerly settlements struggled through the seventeenth century, sustained either by Catholic missionary efforts or by the Protestant enthusiasm of the Puritans who had escaped persecution in England. Southern places like Jamestown survived because they adopted tobacco, a warm-weather plant, as a cash crop for export to Europe. In contrast to Mexico and Peru, the North American settlements were not followed—at least not at first—by territorial conquests (see Map 18.3).

Native Americans   Once they had established themselves agriculturally, the European arrivals in North America began supplementing agriculture with trade. They exchanged metal and glass wares, beads and seashells for furs, especially beaver pelts, with the Native American tribal groups of the interior. The more these tribal groups came into contact with the European traders, however, the more dramatic the demographic impact of the trade on them was: Smallpox, already a menace during the 1500s in North America, became devastating as contacts intensified. In New England, for example, of the ca. 144,000 estimated Native Americans in 1600, fewer than 15,000 remained in 1620. The introduction of guns contributed an additional lethal factor to trading arrangements: English, French, and Dutch traders provided their favorite Native American trading partners with flintlocks, in order to increase the yield of furs. As a result, in the course of the 1600s the Iroquois in the northeast were able to organize themselves into a heavily armed and independent-minded federation, capable of inflicting heavy losses on rival groups as well as on European traders and settlers.

Further south, in Virginia, the Jamestown settlers encountered the Powhatan confederacy. These Native Americans, living in some 200 well-fortified, palisaded villages, dominated the region between the Chesapeake Bay and the Appalachian Mountains. Initially, the Powhatan supplied Jamestown with foodstuffs and sought to integrate the settlement into their confederation. When this invitation to integration failed, however, benevolence turned to hostility and the confederacy raided Jamestown twice in an attempt to rid their region of foreign settlers. But the latter were able to turn the tables and defeat the Powhatan in 1646, thereafter occupying their lands and reducing them to small scattered remnants. Pocahontas, daughter of the Powhatan chief at the time of the foundation of Jamestown, was captured during one of the raids, converted to Christianity, and lived in England as the wife of a returning settler for a number of years. The decline of the Powhatan in the later 1600s opened the way for English settlers to move westward, in contrast to New England where the Iroquois, although allied with the English against the French, de facto blocked any western expansion.

The Iroquois were fiercely determined to maintain their dominance of the fur trade and wrought havoc among the Native American groups living between New

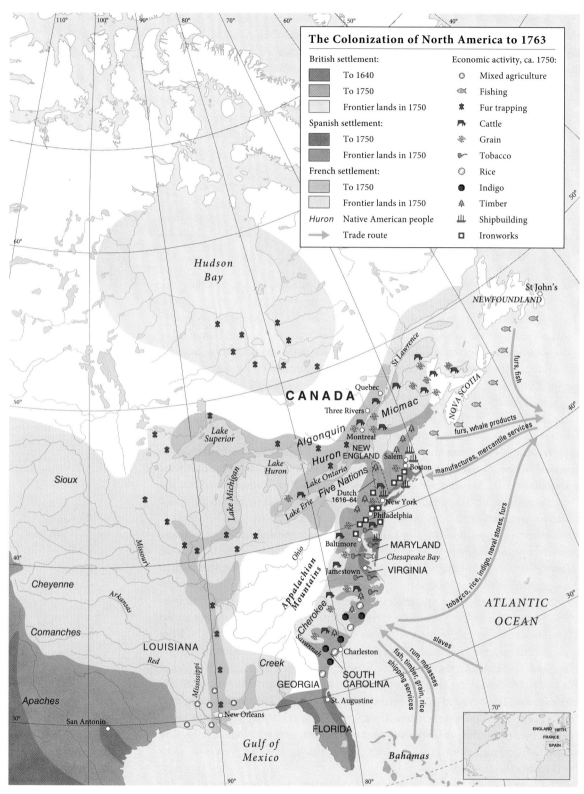

MAP **18.3** The Colonization of North America to 1763.

England and the Great Lakes. In the course of the second half of the 1600s they drove many smaller tribal groups westward into the Great Lakes region and Mississippi plains. Here, these groups settled as refugees. French officials and Jesuit missionaries sought to create some sort of alliance with the refugee tribes, to counterbalance the powerful Iroquois to the east. Many Native Americans converted to Christianity, creating for themselves a Creole Christianity similar to that of the Africans of Kongo and the Mexicans after the Spanish conquest of the Aztecs.

Major population movements also occurred further west on the Great Plains, where the Apaches arrived from the southwest on horses. They had captured horses which had escaped during the Pueblo uprising of 1680–1695 against Spain. The Comanches, who also arrived on horses at the same time from the Great Basin in the Rockies, had, in addition, acquired firearms. The Sioux from the northern forests and the Cheyenne from the Great Basin added to the mix of tribal federations on the Great Plains in the early 1700s. At this time, the great transformation of the Native Americans in the center of North America into horse breeders and horsemen warriors began. Smallpox epidemics did not reach the Plains until the mid 1700s while in the east the ravages of this epidemic had weakened the Iroquois so much that they concluded a peace with the French in 1701.

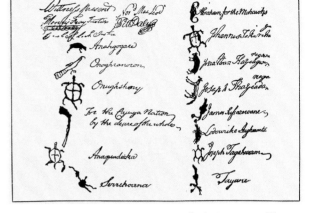

Land Sale. Signatures of the Iroquois federation leaders to a treaty with Thomas and Richard Penn in 1736. By the terms of this treaty the Iroquois sold land to the founders of the English colony of Pennsylvania. The leaders of the six nations that made up the Iroquois federation (Mohawk, Oneida, Onondaga, Cayuga, Seneca, and Tuscarora) signed with their pictograms. The names were added later.

French Canada   The involvement of the French in the Great Lakes region with refugees fleeing from the Iroquois was part and parcel of an expansion program into the center of North America, begun in 1663. The governor of Quebec had dispatched explorers, fur traders, and missionaries not only into the Great Lakes region but also the Mississippi valley and the Mississippi delta. The French government then sent farmers, craftspeople, and young single women from France with government-issued agricultural implements and livestock to establish settlements. The most successful settlement was in the subtropical district of the delta, called "La Louisianie," where some 300 settlers with 4,000 African slaves founded sugar plantations. Immigration was restricted to French subjects and excluded Protestants. Given these restrictions, Louisiana received only some 30,000 settlers by 1750, in contrast to English North America, with nearly 1.2 million settlers by the same time.

From English to British Colonies   As immigration to New England picked up, the merchant companies in Europe, which had financed the journeys of the settlers, were initially responsible for the administration of about a dozen settlement colonies. The first settlers to demand participation in the colonial administration were Virginian tobacco growers with interests in the European trade. In 1619 they deputized delegates from their villages to meet as the House of Burgesses. They thereby created an early popular assembly in North America, assisting their governor in running the colony. Using this example of self-administration as a model, the other English colonies soon followed suit, with the creation of their own assemblies. In contrast to Spain and Portugal, England—wracked by its internal Anglican–Puritan conflict—was initially uninvolved in the governance of the overseas territories.

When England eventually stepped in and took the governance of the colonies away from the charter merchants and companies in the second half of the seventeenth century, it faced entrenched settler assemblies, especially in New England. Only in New Amsterdam, conquered from the Dutch in 1664–1674 and renamed "New York," did the governor initially rule without an assembly. Many governors were deputies of wealthy aristocrats who never traveled to America but stayed in London. They were powerless to prevent the assemblies from appropriating rights to levy taxes and making appointments. The assemblies thus modeled themselves after Parliament in London. As in England, these assemblies were highly select bodies that excluded poorer settlers, who did not meet the property requirements to vote or stand for elections.

Steady immigration, also from the European mainland, encouraged land speculators in the British colonies to cast their sights beyond the Appalachian Mountains. (According to historical convention, the English are called "British" after the English–Scottish union in 1707.) In 1749, the Ohio Company of Virginia received a royal permit to develop land, together with a protective fort, south of the Ohio River. The French, however, also claimed the Ohio valley, considering it a part of their Canada–Mississippi–Louisiana territory. A few years later, tensions over the valley erupted into open hostility. Initially, the local encounters went badly for the Virginian militia and British army. In 1755, however, the British and French broadened their clash into a worldwide war for dominance in the colonies and Europe, the Seven Years' War of 1756–1763.

The Seven Years' War   Both France and Great Britain borrowed heavily to pour resources into the war. England had the superior navy and France, the superior army. Since the British navy succeeded in choking off French supplies to its increasingly isolated land troops, Britain won the war overseas. In Europe, Britain's failure to supply the troops of its ally Prussia against the Austrian–French alliance caused the war on that front to end in a draw. Overseas, the British gained most of the French holdings in India, several islands in the Caribbean, all of Canada, and all the land east of the Mississippi. The war costs and land swaps, however, proved to be unmanageable for both the vanquished and the victor. The unpaid debts became the root cause of the American, French, and Haitian constitutional revolutions that began 13 years later. Those revolutions, along with the emerging industrialization of Great Britain, signaled the beginning of the modern scientific–industrial age in world history.

The Making of American Societies: Origins and Transformations

The pattern of transforming the Americas into an extension of Europe evolved unevenly. The exploitation of both mineral resources and tropical agricultural resources, powered largely by the forced labor of Native American and black slaves, developed along different lines in the Spanish, Portuguese, French, and English colonies. Before we examine these differences, it is worth pausing for a moment to consider that the creation of new societies and economies in the Americas was made possible by the **Columbian Exchange**. The transfer of plants, animals, and diseases from the Old World to the New and from the New World to the Old marks a major turning point in human history. Without this exchange of biota the European exploitation of the Americas cannot be fully appreciated (see "Patterns Up Close").

Columbian Exchange: Exchange of plants, animals, and diseases between the Americas and the rest of the world.

Exploitation of Mineral and Tropical Resources

The pattern of European expansion into subtropical and tropical lands began with the Spanish colonization of the Caribbean islands. When the Spanish crown ran out of gold in the Caribbean, it exported silver from Mexico and Peru in great quantities to finance a fiscal–military state that could compete with the Ottomans and European kings. By contrast, Portugal's colony of Brazil did not at first mine for precious metals, and consequently, the Portuguese crown pioneered the growing of sugar on plantations. Mining would be developed later. The North American colonies of England and France had, in comparison, little native industry at first. By moving farther south, however, they adopted the plantation system for indigo and rice and, thus, joined their Spanish and Portuguese predecessors in exploiting the subtropical–tropical agricultural potential of the Americas.

Silver Mines   When the interest of the Spaniards turned from looting to the exploitation of mineral resources, two main mining centers emerged: Potosí in southeastern Peru (today Bolivia) and Zacatecas and Guanajuato in northern Mexico. For the first 200 years after its founding in 1545, Potosí produced over half of the silver of Spanish America. In the eighteenth century, Zacatecas and Guanajuato jumped ahead of Potosí, churning out almost three times more of the precious metal. During the same century, gold-mining in Colombia and Chile rose to importance as well, making the mining of precious metals the most important economic activity in the Americas.

Innovations, such as the "patio" method, which facilitated the extraction process through the use of mercury, and the unrestrained exploitation of indigenous labor, made American silver highly competitive in the world market. Conditions among the Native Americans and blacks employed as labor were truly abominable. Few laborers lasted through more than two forced recruitment (*repartimiento*) cycles before they were incapacitated or dead.

Given gaps in bookkeeping and high degrees of smuggling, scholars have found it extremely difficult to estimate the total production of the American mines from 1550 to 1750. The best current estimate is that Spanish America produced 150,000 tons of silver (including gold converted into silver weight). This quantity corresponded to roughly 85 percent of world production. The

The Silver Mountain of Potosí. Note the patios in the left foreground and the water-driven crushing mill in the center, which ground the silver-bearing ore into a fine sand that then was moistened, caked, and eventually amalgamated with mercury. The mine workers' insect-like shapes reinforce the dehumanizing effects of their labor.

Patterns Up Close | The Columbian Exchange

Few of us can imagine an Italian kitchen without tomatoes or an Irish meal without potatoes or Chinese or Indian cuisine without the piquant presence of chilies, but until fairly recently each of these foods was unknown to the Old World. Likewise, the expression, "as American as apple pie" obscures the fact that for millennia apples, as well as many other frequently consumed fruits, such as peaches, pears, plums, cherries, bananas, oranges, and lemons, were absent from the New World. It was not until the sixteenth century, when plants, animals, and microbes began to flow from one end of the planet to another, that new patterns of ecology and biology changed the course of millions of years of divergent evolution.

When historians catalog the long list of life-forms that moved across the oceans in the Columbian Exchange, pride of place is usually reserved for the bigger, better-known migrants like cattle, sheep, pigs, and horses. However, the impact of European weeds and grasses on American grasslands, which made it possible for the North American prairie and the South American pampas to support livestock, should not be overlooked. By binding the soil together with their long, tough roots, these "empires of the dandelion" provided the conditions for the grazing of sheep, cattle, and horses, as well as the planting of crops like wheat.

The other, silent invader that accompanied the conquistadors was, of course, disease. Thousands of years of mutual isolation between the Americas and Afro-Eurasia rendered the immune systems of Native Americans vulnerable to the scourges that European colonists unwittingly brought with them. Smallpox, influenza, diphtheria, whooping cough, typhoid, chicken pox, measles, and meningitis wiped out millions of Native Americans—by some estimates, the Indian populations of Mesoamerica and the Andes plummeted by 90 percent in the period 1500–1700. In comparison, the contagion the New World was able to reciprocate upon the Old World—syphilis and tuberculosis—did not unleash nearly the same virulence, and the New World origin of these diseases is still debated.

It is therefore obvious that the big winner in the Columbian Exchange was western Europe, though the effects of the New World bounty took centuries to be fully discerned. While Asia and Africa also benefited from the Columbian Exchange in the forms of new foods that enriched diets, the Europeans got a continent endowed with a warm climate in which they could create new and improved versions of their homelands. Undoubtedly, Native Americans were the biggest losers: They

figures underline the extraordinary role of American silver for the money economies of Spain, Europe, the Middle East, and Asia, especially China.

Since the exploitation of the mines was of such central importance, for the first century and a half of New World colonization the Spanish crown organized its other provinces around the needs of the mining centers. Hispaniola and Cuba in the Caribbean were islands which had produced foodstuffs, sugar, and tobacco from the time of Columbus but only in small quantities. Their main function was to feed and protect Havana, the collection point for the Mexican and Peruvian

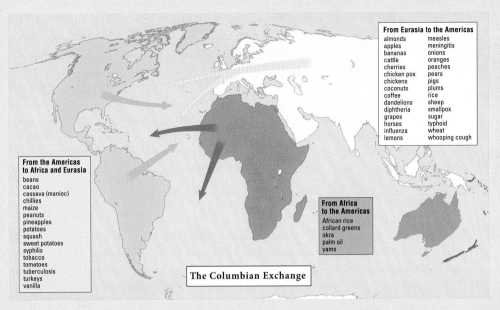

From Eurasia to the Americas

almonds	measles
apples	meningitis
bananas	onions
cattle	oranges
cherries	peaches
chicken pox	pears
chickens	pigs
coconuts	plums
coffee	rice
dandelions	sheep
diphtheria	smallpox
grapes	sugar
horses	typhoid
influenza	wheat
lemons	whooping cough

From the Americas to Africa and Eurasia

beans
cacao
cassava (manioc)
chillies
maize
peanuts
pineapples
potatoes
squash
sweet potatoes
syphilis
tobacco
tomatoes
tuberculosis
turkeys
vanilla

From Africa to the Americas

African rice
collard greens
okra
palm oil
yams

The Columbian Exchange

MAP 18.4 **The Columbian Exchange.**

were nearly wiped out by disease, their lands appropriated, and the survivors either enslaved or marginalized. Africans were losers as well. The precipitous drop in the population of Native Americans, combined with the tropical and semitropical climate of much of the Americas, created the necessary conditions for the Atlantic slave trade. Even though the introduction of corn and manioc from the Americas fueled population growth across Africa and more than offset population loss from slaving, overall, the traffic in slaves negatively affected African societies.

Questions

• Can the Columbian Exchange be considered one of the origins of the modern world? How? Why? How does the Columbian Exchange demonstrate the origins, interactions, and adaptations model that is used throughout this book?

• Weigh the positive and negative outcomes of the Columbian Exchange. Is it possible to determine whether the effects of the Columbian Exchange on human society and the natural environment were for the better or for the worse?

silver and the port from where the annual Spanish fleet shipped the American silver across the Atlantic.

A second region, Argentina and Paraguay, was colonized as a bulwark to prevent the Portuguese and Dutch from cutting across the southern end of the continent and to access Peruvian silver. Once established, the two colonies produced wheat, cattle, mules, horses, cotton, textiles, and tallow to feed and supply the miners in Potosí. The subtropical crop of cotton, produced by small farmers, played a role in Europe's extension into warm-weather agriculture only toward the end of the colonial period.

A third colonial region, Venezuela, began as a grain and cattle supply base for Cartagena, the port for the shipment of Colombian gold, and Panama and Porto-belo, ports for the transshipment of Peruvian silver from the Pacific to Havana. Its cocoa and tobacco exports flourished only after the Dutch established themselves in 1624 in the southern Caribbean and provided the shipping. Thus, three major regions of the Spanish overseas empire in the Americas were mostly peripheral as agricultural producers during the sixteenth century. Only after the middle of the century did they begin to specialize in tropical agricultural goods, and they were ex-porters only in the eighteenth century. By that time, the Dutch and English provided more and more shipping in the place of the Spanish.

Wheat Farming and Cattle Ranching

To support the mining centers and administrative cities, the Spanish colonial government encouraged the development of agricultural estates (*haciendas*). These estates first emerged when conquistadors used their *encomienda* rights to round up Native American labor to produce subsis-tence crops. Native American tenant farmers were forced to grow wheat and raise cattle, pigs, sheep, and goats for the conquerors, who were now agricultural entre-preneurs. In the latter part of the sixteenth century, the land grants gave way to rotat-ing forced labor as well as wage labor. Owners established their residences and built dwellings for tenant farmers on their estates. A landowner class emerged.

Like the conquistadors before, a majority of landowners produced wheat and an-imals for sale to urban and mining centers. Cities purchased wheat and maintained granaries in order to provide for urban dwellers in times of harvest failure. Entrepre-neurs received commissions to provide slaughterhouses with regular supplies of ani-mals. As the Native American population declined in the seventeenth century and the church helped in consolidating the remaining population in large villages, ad-ditional land became available for the establishment of estates. From 1631 onward, authorities granted Spanish settler families the right to maintain their estates undi-vided from generation to generation. Through donations, the Church also acquired considerable agricultural lands. Secular and clerical landowning interests supported a powerful upper social stratum of Creoles from the eighteenth century onward.

Plantations and Gold Mining in Brazil

Brazil's agricultural industry began with brazilwood, followed by sugar plantations, before gold mining rose to promi-nence in the eighteenth century. A crisis hit sugar production in 1680–1700, mostly as a result of the Dutch beginning production of sugar in the Antilles. It was at that time that the gold of Minas Gerais, in the interior of Brazil, were discovered.

Gold-mining operations in Brazil during the eighteenth century were consid-erably less capital-intensive than the silver mines in Spanish America. Most min-ers were relatively small operators with sieves, pickaxes, and a few black slaves as unskilled laborers. Many entrepreneurs were indebted for their slaves to absentee capitalists, with whom they shared the profits. Since prospecting took place on the land of Native Americans, bloody encounters were frequent. Most entrepreneurs were ruthless frontiersmen who exploited their slaves and took no chances with the indigenous people. Brazil produced a total of 1,000 tons of gold in the eighteenth century, a welcome bonanza for Portugal at a time of low agricultural prices. Overall, minerals were just as valuable for the Portuguese as they were for the Spanish.

Plantations in Spanish and English America   The expansion of plantation farming in the Spanish colonies was a result of the Bourbon reforms. Although sugar, tobacco, and rice had been introduced early into the Caribbean and southern Mexico, it was only in the expanded plantation system of the eighteenth century that these crops (plus cactuses for cochineal, and indigo, and cacao) were produced on a large scale for export to Europe. The owners of plantations did not need expensive machinery and invested instead in African slave labor, with the result that the slave trade hit its full stride, beginning around 1750.

English North American settlements in Virginia and Carolina exported tobacco and rice beginning in the 1660s. Georgia was the thirteenth British colony, beginning in 1733 as a bulwark against Spanish Florida and a haven for poor Europeans. In 1750 it joined southern Carolina as a major plantation colony and rice and indigo producer. In the eighteenth century, even New England finally had its own export crop, in the form of timber for shipbuilding and charcoal production in Great Britain, at the amazing rate of 250 million board feet from about 1 million acres per year by the start of the nineteenth century. These timber exports illustrate an important new factor appearing in the Americas in the eighteenth century. Apart from the cheap production of precious metals and warm-weather crops, the American extension of Europe became increasingly important as a replacement for dwindling fuel resources across much of northern Europe. Altogether, it was thanks to the Americas that cold and rainy Europe rose successfully into the ranks of the wealthy, climatically balanced, and populated Indian and Chinese empires.

Social Strata, Castes, and Ethnic Groups

The population of settlers in the New World consisted primarily of Europeans who came from a continent that had barely emerged from its population losses to the Black Death. Although population numbers were rising again in the sixteenth century, Europe did not have masses of emigrants to the Americas to spare. Given the small settler population of the Americas, the temptation to develop a system of forced labor in agriculture and mining was irresistible. Since the Native Americans and African slaves pressed into labor were ethnically so completely different from the Europeans, however, a social system evolved in which the latter two not only were economically underprivileged but also populated the ethnically nonintegrated lowest rungs of the social ladder. A pattern of legal and customary discrimination evolved which, even though partially vitiated by the rise of ethnically mixed groups, prevented the integration of American ethnicities into settler society.

The Social Elite   The heirs of the Spanish conquistadors and estate owners—mixed farmers, ranchers, and planters—maintained city residences and employed managers on their agricultural properties. In Brazil, cities emerged more slowly, and for a long time estate owners maintained their manor houses as small urban islands. Estate owners mixed with the Madrid- and Lisbon-appointed administrators and, during the seventeenth century, intermarried with them, creating the top tier of settler society known as Creoles. This tier, the "respectable people" (Spanish *gentes decentes*), encompassed about 4 percent of the total population. In a wider sense, the tier included also merchants, professionals, clerks, militia officers, and the clergy. They formed a relatively closed society in which descent, intermarriage, landed property, and a government position counted more than money and education.

The great majority of estate owners were mixed farmers and ranchers. In the seventeenth and eighteenth centuries, they farmed predominantly with Native American forced labor. The estates produced grain and/or cattle, legumes, cattle, sheep, and pigs for local urban markets or mining towns. In contrast to the black slave plantation estates of the Caribbean and coastal regions of Spanish and Portuguese America, the mixed farming estates did not export their goods to Europe. Madrid and Lisbon, furthermore, discouraged these mixed estates from producing olive oil, wine, or silk, to protect their home production. Nevertheless, there were Mexicans who produced silk in the second half of the sixteenth century and Peruvian and Chilean vintners who produced wine by the seventeenth century and brandy by the following century, albeit for American consumption only.

As local producers with little competition, mixed farming and ranching estate owners did not feel market pressures. Since for the most part they lived in the cities, they exploited their estates with minimal investments and usually drew profits of less than 5 percent of annual revenues. They were often heavily indebted, and as a result, there was often more glitter than substance among the *gentes decentes*.

Lower Creoles   The second tier of Creole society consisted of people like Alonzo Ortíz, the tanner introduced at the beginning of this chapter. Even though of second rank, these "popular people" (*gentes de pueblo*) were privileged European settlers who, as craftspeople and traders, theoretically worked with their hands. In practice, many of them were owner-operators who employed Native Americans and/or black slaves as apprentices and journeymen. Many invested in small plots of land in the vicinity of their cities. As in Spain, they were organized in guilds, which controlled prices and quality standards.

Textile Production. Immigrants from Spain, like Alonso Ortíz discussed at the beginning of the chapter, established workshops (*obrajes*) as tanners, weavers, carpenters, or wheelwrights. As craftspeople producing simple but affordable goods for the poor, they remained competitive throughout the colonial period, in spite of increasingly large textile, utensil, and furniture imports from Europe. At the same time, indigenous textile production by native women continued as in the preconquest period, albeit under the constraints of labor services imposed by officials or clergy, as shown in these examples.

Wealthy weavers ran textile manufactures (*obrajes*), mostly concentrated in the cities of Mexico, Peru, Paraguay, and Argentina. In some of these manufactures, up to 300 Native American and black workers produced cheap, coarse woolens and a variety of cottons on dozens of looms. Men were the weavers and women, the spinners—in contrast to the pre-Columbian period, when textile manufacture was entirely a woman's job. These textiles were alternatives to the higher-quality European imports, unaffordable to most. On a smaller scale, manufactures also existed for pottery and leather goods. On the whole, the urban manufacturing activities of the popular people, serving local markets, remained vibrant until well into the nineteenth century, in spite of massive European imports.

Mestizos and Mulattoes

The mixed European–Native American and European–African population had the collective name of "caste" (*casta*), or ethnic group. The term originated in the desire of the Iberian and Creole settlers to draw distinctions among degrees of mixture in order to counterbalance as much as possible the masses of Native Americans and Africans, especially from the eighteenth century onward. The two most important castes were the *mestizos* (Spanish) or *mestiços* (Portuguese), who had Iberian fathers and Native American mothers, and *mulatos*, who had Iberian fathers and black mothers. By 1800 the castas formed the third largest population category in Latin America as a whole (20 percent), after Native Americans (40 percent) and Creoles (30 percent). In Brazil, mulattoes and black freedmen were even with Creoles (28 percent each), after black slaves (38 percent) and before Native Americans (6 percent in the settled provinces outside Amazonia). In both Spanish and Portuguese America, there was also a small percentage of people descended from Native American and black unions. Thus, most of the intermediate population groups were sizeable, playing important neutralizing roles in colonial society, as they had one foot each in the Creole and subordinate social strata (see Figure 18.1).

As such neutralizing elements, mestizos and mulattoes filled lower levels of the bureaucracy and the lay hierarchy in the church. They held skilled and supervisory positions in mines and on estates. In addition, in the armed forces mulattoes dominated the ranks of enlisted men; in the defense militias, they even held officer ranks. In Brazil, many mulattoes and black freedmen were farmers. Much of the craft production was in their hands. A wide array of laws existed to keep mestizos and mulattoes in their peculiarly intermediate social and political positions.

Women

The roles played by women depended strongly on their social position. Well-appointed elite Creole households followed the Mediterranean tradition of secluding women from men. Within their confines of the household, elite women were persons of means and influence. They were the owners of substantial dowries and legally stipulated grooms' gifts. Often, they actively managed the investment

Race, Class, and Gender in Colonial Mexico. An outraged mulatta defends herself against an aggressive Creole, with a fearful child clinging to the woman's skirt.

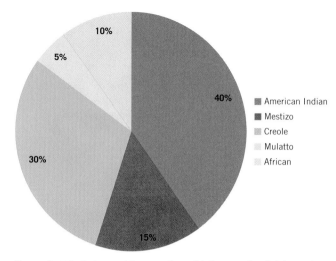

10%

5%

40%

30%

15%

■ American Indian
■ Mestizo
■ Creole
■ Mulatto
■ African

Figure 18.1 Ethnic Composition of Latin America, ca. 1800.

of their assets. Outside their confines, however, even elite women lost all protection. Crimes of passion, committed by honor-obsessed fathers or husbands, went unpunished. Husbands and fathers who did not resort to violence nevertheless did not need witnesses to obtain court judgments to banish daughters or wives to convents for alleged lapses in chastity. Thus, even elite women obeyed definite limits set by a patriarchal society.

On the lower rungs of society, be it popular Creole, mestizo, mulatto, or Native American, gender separation was much less prevalent. After all, everyone in the family had to work in order to make ends meet. Men, women, and children shared labor in the fields and workshops. Girls or wives took in clothes to wash or went out to work as domestics in wealthy households. Older women dominated retail in market stalls. As in elite society, wives tended to outlive husbands. In addition, working families with few assets suffered abandonment by males. Women headed one-third of all households in Mexico City, according to an 1811 census. Among black slaves in the region of São Paulo, 70 percent of women were without formal ties to the men who fathered their children. Thus, the most pronounced division in colonial society was that of a patriarchy among the Creoles and a slave society dominated by women, with frequently absent men—an unbridgeable division that persists today.

Native Americans   In the immediate aftermath of the conquest, Native Americans could be found at all levels of the social scale. Some were completely marginalized in remote corners of the American continents. Others acculturated into the ranks of the working poor in the silver mines or textile manufactures. A few even formed an educated Aztec or Inca propertied upper class, exercising administrative

Illustration from an Indian Land Record. The Spaniards almost completely wiped out the Aztec archives after the conquest of Mexico; surviving examples of Indian manuscripts are thus extremely rare. Although the example shown here, made from the bark of a fig tree, claims to date from the early 1500s, it is part of the so-called "Techialoyan" land records created in the seventeenth century to substantiate native land claims. These "*titulos primordiales*," as they were called, were essentially municipal histories that documented in text and pictures local accounts of important events and territorial boundaries.

functions in Spanish civil service. Social distinctions, however, disappeared rapidly during the first 150 years of Spanish colonialism. Smallpox reduced the Native American population by nearly 80 percent. Diseases were more virulent in humid, tropical parts of the continent than in deserts; and the epidemics took a far greater toll on dense, settled populations than they did on dispersed forager bands in dry regions. In the Caribbean and on the Brazilian coast, Native Americans disappeared altogether; in central and southern Mexico, their population shrank by two-thirds. It was only in the twentieth century that population figures reached the preconquest level again in most parts of Latin America.

Apart from European diseases, the native forager and agrarian Native Americans in the Amazon, Orinoco, and Meracaíbo rain forests were the least affected by European colonials during the period 1500–1800. Not only were their lands economically least promising, but they also defended those lands successfully with blowguns, poison darts, and bow and arrow. In many cold and hot arid or semiarid regions, such as Patagonia, southern Chile, the Argentine grasslands (*pampas*), the Paraguayan salt marshes and deserts, and northern Mexican mountains and steppes, the situation was similar. In many of these lands, the seminomadic Native Americans quickly adopted the European horse and became highly mobile warrior people in defense of their mostly independent territories. Ironically, their successful assimilation of this European import allowed them to delay their ultimate full surrender (and adaptation) to the European colonizers.

The villagers of Mexico, Yucatán, Guatemala, Colombia, Ecuador, and Peru had fewer choices. When smallpox reduced their numbers in the second half of the sixteenth century, state and church authorities razed many villages and concentrated the survivors in *pueblos de indios*. Initially, the Native Americans put up strong resistance against these resettlements, by repeatedly returning to their destroyed old settlements. From the middle of the seventeenth century, however, the pueblos were fully functional, self-administering units, with councils (*cabildos*), churches, schools, communal lands, and family parcels.

The councils were important institutions of legal training and social mobility for ordinary Native Americans. Initially, the traditional, "noble" chiefly families descending from the preconquest Aztec and Inca ruling classes were in control as administrators. The many village functions, however, for which the *cabildos* were responsible, allowed commoners to move up into auxiliary roles. In some of these roles, they had opportunities to learn the system and acquire modest wealth. Settlers constantly complained about insubordinate Native Americans pursuing lawsuits in the courts. Native American villages were closed to settlers, and the only outsiders admitted were Catholic priests. Contact with the Spanish world remained minimal, and acculturation went little beyond official conversion to Catholicism. Village notaries and scribes were instrumental in preserving the native Nahuatl in Mexico and Quechua in Peru, making them into functional, written languages. Thus, even in the heartlands of Spanish America, Native American adaptation to the rulers remained limited.

Unfortunately, however, tremendous demographic losses made the Native Americans in the pueblos vulnerable to the loss of their land. Estate owners expanded their holdings, legally and illegally, in spite of the heroic litigation efforts of the villages opposed to this expansion. When the population rebounded, many estates had grown to immense sizes. Villages began to run out of land for their inhabitants.

Increasing numbers of Native Americans had to rent land from estate owners or find work on estates as farmhands. They became estranged from their villages, fell into debt peonage, and entered the ranks of the working poor in countryside or city, bearing the full brunt of colonial inequities.

In the territory of today's Arizona, the pueblo Native Americans remained in their traditional farming villages, but estate owners subjected them first to the *encomienda* and later the *repartimiento* on their ranches. Estate farming and Native American conversion to Catholicism proceeded more slowly in this sparsely populated part of the Spanish colony. Among the indigenous people, the adaptation process to Spanish culture reached a critical point in the 1660s when priests outlawed the local masked *kachina* dances and sought to destroy masks. Tensions over these measures built, with public hangings and whippings of Native Americans convicted of sorcery. During 1680–1695, the indigenous villagers were in full revolt, killing priests, burning churches, and chasing estate owners from their lands. Spanish forces eventually suppressed this extraordinary Native American rebellion in their American colonies but ended the repartimiento system as a measure of pacification.

New England Society   For a long time in the early modern period, the small family farm where everyone had to work to eke out a precarious living remained the norm for the majority of New England's population. Family members specializing in construction, carpentry, spinning, weaving, or iron works continued to be restricted to small perimeters around their villages and towns. An acute lack of money and cheap means of transportation hampered the development of market networks in the interior well into the 1770s. The situation was better in the agriculturally more favored colonies in the Mid-Atlantic, especially in Pennsylvania. Here, farmers were able to produce marketable quantities of wheat and legumes for urban markets. The number of plantations in the south rose steadily, demanding increasing numbers of slaves (from 28,000 in 1700 to 575,000 in 1776), although world market fluctuations left planters vulnerable. Except for boom periods in the plantation sector, the rural areas remained largely poor.

Real changes occurred during the early eighteenth century in the urban regions. Large port cities emerged which shipped in textiles and ironwares from Europe in return for timber at relatively cheap rates. The most important were Philadelphia (28,000 inhabitants), New York (25,000), Boston (16,000), and Newport, Rhode Island (11,000). A wealthy merchant class formed, spawning urban service strata of professionals (such as lawyers, teachers, and newspaper journalists). Primary school education was provided by municipal public schools as well as some churches, and evening schools for craftspeople existed in some measure. By the middle of the eighteenth century a majority of men could read and write, although female literacy was minimal. Finally, in contrast to Latin America, social ranks in New England were less elaborate.

The Adaptation of the Americas to European Culture

European settlers brought two distinct cultures to the Americas. In the Mid-Atlantic, Caribbean, and Central and South America, they brought with them the Counter-Reformation Catholicism of southern Europe, a culture and perspective that resisted the New Science of Galileo and the Enlightenment thought of Locke until the late eighteenth century. In the northeast, colonists implanted dissident

Protestantism as well as the Anglicanism of Great Britain. The rising number of adherents of the New Science and Enlightenment in northwestern Europe had also a parallel in North America. Settlers and their locally born offspring were proud of their respective cultures, which, even though provincial, were dominant in what they prejudicially viewed as a less civilized, if not barbaric, Native American environment.

Catholic Missionary Work   From the beginning, Spanish and Portuguese monarchs relied heavily on the Catholic Church for their rule in the new American provinces. The pope granted them patronage over the organization and all appointments on the new continents. A strong motive driving many in the Church as well as society at large was the belief in the imminent Second Coming of Jesus. This belief was one inspiration for the original Atlantic expansion (see Chapter 16). When the Aztec and Inca Empires fell, members of the Franciscan order, the main proponents of the belief in the imminence of the return, reinterpreted its meaning as imposing the urgent duty to convert the Native Americans to Christianity. If Jesus' kingdom was soon to come, according to this interpretation, all humans in the Americas should be Christians.

Thousands of Franciscan, Dominican, and other preaching monks, later followed by the Jesuits, fanned out among the Native Americans. They baptized them, introduced the sacraments (Eucharist, baptism, confession, confirmation, marriage, last rites, and priesthood), and taught them basic theological concepts of Christianity. The missionaries learned native languages, translated the catechism and New Testament into those languages, and taught the children of the ruling native families how to read and write. Thanks to their genuine efforts to understand the Native Americans on their own terms, a good deal of preconquest Native American culture was recorded without too much distortion.

The role and function of saints as mediators between humans and God formed one element of Catholic Christianity to which Native Americans acculturated early. Good works as God-pleasing human efforts to gain salvation in the afterlife formed another. The veneration of images of the Virgin Mary and pilgrimages to the chapels and churches where they were kept constituted a third element. The best-known example of the last element is Our Lady of Guadalupe, near Mexico City, who in 1531 appeared in a vision to a Native American in the place where the native goddess Tonantzin used to be venerated. On the other hand, the Spanish Inquisition also operated in the Spanish and Portuguese colonies, seeking to limit the degree to which Catholicism, animism, and polytheism mingled. The church tread a fine line between enforcement of doctrine and leniency toward what it determined were lax or heretical believers.

Education and the Arts   The Counter-Reformation expressed itself also in the organization of education. The Franciscans and Dominicans had offered general education to the children of settlers early on and, in colleges, trained graduates

Virgin of Guadalupe. There is perhaps no more potent symbol of the new patterns of religious belief that emerged out of the Spanish conquest of Mexico than the Virgin of Guadalupe. Missionary sources, written years after the fact, tell of an indigenous inhabitant of Mexico City, Juan Diego, who in 1531 had visions of the Virgin Mary on the hill of Tepeyac, which Aztec traditions associated with the mother goddess Tonantzin. By the eighteenth century, the hill attracted pilgrims throughout Mexico and the Church created books, images, and organizations devoted to her cult. To this day, the Virgin of Guadalupe remains one of the most powerful and revered symbols of Mexico.

Spanish Cruelty to Incas.
Felipe Guamán Poma de Ayala, a Peruvian claiming noble Inca descent, was a colonial administrator, well educated, and an ardent Christian. He is remembered today as a biting critic of the colonial administration and the clergy, whom he accused of mistreating and exploiting the Andean population, as in this colored wood print..

for missionary work. The first New World universities, such as Santo Domingo (1538), Mexico City, and Lima (both 1553) taught theology, church law, and Indian languages. Under the impact of the Jesuits, universities broadened the curriculum, offering degrees also in secular law, Aristotelian philosophy, the natural sciences, and medicine. In the seventeenth and eighteenth centuries, the number of universities grew to 26. By contrast, Brazil did not offer higher education prior to 1800. In spite of this greater breadth, however, the Counter-Reformation universities did not admit the New Sciences and Enlightenment of northwestern Europe into their curriculum prior to the independence of the colonies.

Missionary monks collected and recorded Native American manuscripts and oral traditions, such as the Aztec *Anales de Tula* and the Maya *Popol Vuh*. Others wrote histories and ethnographies of the Taíno, Aztec, Maya, Inca, and Tupí peoples. Bartolomé de las Casas, Toribio Motolonía de Benavente, Bernardino de Sahagún, Diego de Landa, Bernabé Cobo, and Manoel de Nóbrega are merely a handful of noteworthy authors who wrote about the Native Americans. Many labored for years, worked with legions of informers, and produced monumental tomes.

A number of Native American and mestizo chroniclers, historians, and commentators on the early modern state and society are similarly noteworthy. Muñoz Camargo was a Tlazcaltecan; Fernando de Alva Ixtlixóchitl and Fernando Alvarado Tezózomoc were Mexican mestizos; and Juan de Santa Cruz Pachacuti Yamqui and Felipe Inca Garcilaso de la Vega were Peruvian mestizos, all writing on their native regions. Felipe Guamán Poma de Ayala (ca. 1535–1616), a native Peruvian, is of particular interest. He accompanied his 800-page manuscript, entitled *The First New Chronicle and Good Government*, with some 400 drawings of daily-life activities in the Peruvian villages. These drawings provide us with invaluable cultural details, which would be difficult to render in writing. Unfortunately, King Philip II of Spain, a relentless proponent of the Counter-Reformation, took a dim view of authors writing on Native American society and history. In 1577 he forbade the publication of all manuscripts dealing with what he called idolatry and superstition. Many manuscripts lay hidden in archives and did not see the light of day until modern times.

Protestantism in New England From the start, religious diversity was a defining cultural trait of English settlements in North America. The spectrum of Christian denominations ranged from a host of English and continental European versions of Protestantism to Anglicanism and a minority of Catholics. As if this spectrum had not been sufficiently broad, dissenters frequently split from the existing denominations, moved into new territory, and founded new settlements. Religiosity was a major characteristic of the early settlers.

An early example for religious splintering was the rise of an antinomian ("anti-law") group within Puritan-dominated Massachusetts. The Puritans dominant in this colony generally recognized the authority of the Anglican Church but strove to move it toward Protestantism from within. The preachers and settlers represented in the General Court, as their assembly was called, were committed to the Calvinist balance between "inner" personal grace obtained from God and "outer" works according to the law. The antinomian group, however, digging deep into early traditions in Christianity, advocated an exclusive commitment to inner grace through spiritual perfection. Their leader was Anne Hutchinson, an early and tireless proponent of women's rights and an inspiring preacher. She was accused of arguing that she could recognize those believers in Calvinist Protestantism who were predestined for salvation and that these believers would be saved even if they had sinned. After a power struggle with the deeply misogynistic magistrates opposed to influential women, the General Court prevailed and forced the Antinomians to move to Rhode Island in 1636.

The example is noteworthy because it led to the founding of Harvard College in 1626 by the General Court. Harvard was the first institution of higher learning in North America, devoted to teaching the "correct" balanced Calvinist Protestantism. A few years later, the college became a university and functioned as the main center for training the colony's ministers in Puritan theology and morality. In spite of its primary function as a seminary, however, Harvard became an early outpost of the New Science.

The New Science in the New World. This painting by Samuel Collings, *The Magnetic Dispensary* (1790), shows how men and women, of lay background, participated in scientific experiments in the English colonies of North America, similar to educated middle-class people in western Europe at the same time.

New Science Research   As discussed in Chapter 17, the New Science had found its most hospitable home in northwestern Europe by default. The rivalry between Protestantism and Catholicism had left enough of an authority-free space for the New Science to flourish. Under similar circumstances—intense rivalry among denominations—English North America also proved hospitable to the New Science. An early practitioner was Benjamin Franklin (1706–1790), who began his career as a printer, journalist, and newspaper editor. Franklin founded the University of Pennsylvania (1740), the first secular university in North America, and the American Philosophical Society (1743), the first scientific society. This hospitality to the New Science in North America was quite in contrast to Latin America, where a uniform Catholic Counter-Reformation prevented its rise.

Under the impact of the New Science, seventeenth-century northern European philosophers had begun the task of replacing Aristotelianism, the dominant medieval form of philosophy, with new forms of thought. Among the early New Science–influenced philosophers in England were James Harrington (1611–1677) and John Locke (1632–1704). Both wrote constitutional treatises influenced by the experience of the New World. Harrington's *Oceanea* (1656) and Locke's political thought, later published as *Two Treatises on Civil Government* (1690), inspired the founders of Carolina (1664) and Pennsylvania (1681) in their experiments of colonialism. Thus, the tradition of American secular intellectual as well as political constitutionalism was born and evolved parallel to the traditions of Protestant political self-organization in the colonies.

Secular American constitutionalism, as represented later by the founding fathers, relied on Harrington's innovative concept of a **civil theology**. The myriad religious denominations competing in English North America, so secular constitutionalists

Civil theology: Form of thought according to which the state supports basic religious principles, without espousing a particular denomination.

argued, had in common a basic set of essential theological agreements about God, providence, and the moral order on which society is built. Hence, any commonwealth based on the will of the people was a polity in which everyone had to agree on a minimum of religious doctrines but was otherwise free to add his or her own specific religious obligations in the congregations to which he or she belonged. Today, of course, civil theology is understood to be the notion of a political order that relies on neither the acceptance of God nor providence but on a universal moral order that is shared by the members of all religious civilizations and formulated concretely in the Preamble of the United Nations Charter.

Witch Hunts and Revivalism   The level of religious competitiveness and intensity remained high throughout the seventeenth century. In the last decade of the century, religious fervor was at the root of a witchcraft frenzy which seized New England. The belief in witchcraft was a survival of the animist concept of a shared mind or spirit that allows initiates to influence other people, either positively or negatively. Witches, male and female, were persons exerting a negative influence, or black magic, on their victims. Legislation against black magic and sorcery is as ancient as Hammurabi's law in the Middle East (1700 BCE) and continued in religious civilizations from India to China. In animist Africa, as discussed in the example of Dona Beatriz's early training in Angola (see Chapter 19), the distinction between benevolent and evil magic was fundamental, as it was in Native American society.

In Europe, the phenomenon of witchcraft had expanded rapidly during the time of extreme hardship that accompanied the religious wars and the harsh climate of the Little Ice Age (1550–1750) when harvests frequently failed. The similarly harsh environment of the early New England colonies was also a fertile breeding ground for the terror of witchcraft. The one case where it erupted into hysteria and which therefore has attracted most attention was that of Salem, Massachusetts. Here, the excitement erupted in 1692 with Tituba, a Native American slave from Barbados who worked in the household of a pastor. Tituba practiced voodoo, the central African–originated, part-African, and part-Christian religious practice of influencing others. When a young daughter and niece in the pastor's household suffered from convulsions, mass rioting broke out, in which 20 women accused of being witches were executed, although Tituba, ironically, survived. A new governor finally calmed the passions and restored order.

Religious fervor expressed itself also in periodic Protestant renewal movements, among which the "Great Awakening" of the 1730s and 1740s was the most important. The main impulse for this revivalist movement came from the brothers John and Charles Wesley, two Methodist preachers in England who toured Georgia in 1735. Preachers from other denominations joined, all exhorting Protestants to literally "start anew" in their relationship with God. Fire-and-brimstone sermons rained down on the pews, reminding the faithful of the absolute sovereignty of God, the depravity of humans, predestination to hell and heaven, the

Witch Trial. In the course of the 1600s, in the relatively autonomous English colonies of North America more witches were accused, tried, and convicted than anywhere else. Of the 140 persons coming to trial between 1620 and 1725, 86 percent were women. Three witch panics are recorded: Bermuda, 1651; Hartford, Connecticut, 1652–1665; and Salem, Massachusetts, 1692–1693. This anonymous American woodcut of the early 1600s shows one method to try someone for witchcraft: swim if innocent, or sink if guilty.

inner experience of election, and salvation by God's grace alone. Thus, revivalism, recurring with great regularity to the present, became a potent force in Protestant America, at opposing purposes with the civil theology of founding father constitutionalism. Even today, the United States is torn between religious commitment, with its emotional engagement for the specifics of religious practice, and the more detached view of civil theology, with its much more universal principles of faith and morality.

Putting It All Together

During the period 1500–1800 the contours of a new pattern in which the Americas formed a resource-rich and warm-weather extension of Europe took shape. During this time, China and India continued to be the most populous and wealthiest agrarian–urban regions of the world. Scholars have estimated China's share of the world economy during this period as comprising 40 percent. India probably did not lag much behind. In 1500, Europe was barely an upstart, forced to defend itself against the push of the Ottoman Empire into eastern Europe and the western Mediterranean. But its successful conquest of Iberia from the Muslims led to the discovery of the Americas. Possession of the Americas made Europe similar to China and India in that it now encompassed, in addition to its northerly cold climates, subtropical and tropical regions which produced rich cash crops as well as precious metals. Over the course of 300 years with the help of its American extension, Europe narrowed the gap between itself and China and India, although it was only after the beginning of industrialization, around 1800, that it eventually was able to close this gap.

Narrowing the gap, of course, was not a conscious policy in Europe. Quite the contrary, because of fierce competition both with the Ottoman Empire and within itself, much of the wealth Europe gained in the Americas, especially silver, was wasted on warfare. The fiscal–military state, created in part to support war, ran into insurmountable budgetary barriers, which forced Spain into several state bankruptcies. Even mercantilism, a logical extension of the fiscal–military state, had limited effects. Its centerpiece, state support for the export of manufactures to the American colonies through shipping monopolies in return for primary goods (minerals and warm-weather cash crops), functioned unevenly. The Spanish and Portuguese governments, with weak urban infrastructures and low manufacturing capabilities, especially in textiles, were unable to enforce this state-supported trade until the eighteenth century and even then only in very limited ways. France and especially England practiced mercantilism more successfully but were able to do so in the Americas only from the late seventeenth century onward, when their plantation systems began to take shape. Although the American extension of Europe had the potential of making Europe self-sufficient, this potential was realized only partially during the colonial period.

A fierce debate has raged over the question of the degree of wealth the Americas added to that of Europe. On the one hand, considerable quantitative research has established that the British slave trade for sugar plantations added at best 1 percent to the British gross domestic product (GDP). The profits from the production of sugar on the English island of Jamaica may have added another 4 percent to the British GDP. Without doubt, individual slave-trading and sugar-producing enterprises were at times immensely profitable to individuals and groups, not to mention the mining of silver through forced labor. In the larger picture, however, these profits were considerably smaller if one takes into account the immense waste of revenues on military ventures—hence, the doubts raised by scholars today about large gains made by Europe through its American colonial acquisitions.

On the other hand, the European extension to the Americas was clearly a momentous event in world history. It might have produced dubious profits for Europe, but it definitely encouraged the parting of ways between Europe and Asia and Africa, once a new scientific–industrial society began to emerge around 1800.

> For additional resources, including maps, primary sources, visuals, and quizzes, please go to www.oup.com/us/vonsivers. Please see the Further Resources section at the back of the book for additional readings and suggested websites.

Thinking Through Patterns

▶ **What is the significance of western Europeans acquiring the Americas as a warm-weather extension of their northern continent?**

In their role as supplementary subtropical and tropical extensions of Europe, the Americas exerted considerable impact on Europe's changing position in the world. First, Europe acquired large quantities of precious metals, which its two largest competitors, India and China, lacked. Second, with its new access to warm-weather agricultural products, Europe rose to a position of agrarian autonomy similar to that of India and China. In terms of resources, compared with the principal religious civilizations of India and China, Europe grew between 1550 and 1800 from a position of inferiority to one of near parity.

Because the numbers of Europeans who emigrated to the Americas was low for most of the colonial period—just 300,000 Spaniards left for the New World between 1500–1800—they never exceeded the numbers of Native Americans or African slaves. The result was a highly privileged settler society that held superior positions on the top rung of the social hierarchy. In principle, given an initially large indigenous population, labor was cheap and should have become more expensive as diseases reduced the Native Americans. In fact, labor always remained cheap, in part because of the politically supported institution of forced labor and in part because of racial prejudice.

▶ **What was the main pattern of social development in colonial America during the period 1500–1800?**

▶ **Why and how did European settlers in South and North America strive for self-government, and how successful were they in achieving their goals?**

Two contrasting patterns characterized the way in which European colonies were governed. The Spanish and Portuguese crowns, primarily interested in extracting minerals and warm-weather products from the colonies, had a strong interest in exercising as much centralized control over their possessions in the Americas as they could. In contrast, the British crown granted self-government to the North American colonies from the start, in part because the colonies were initially economically far less important and in part because of a long tradition of self-rule at home. Nevertheless, even though Latin American settlers achieved only partial self-rule in their towns and cities, they destroyed central rule indirectly through the purchase of offices. After financial reforms, Spain and Portugal reestablished a degree of central rule through the appointment of officers from the home countries.

Further Resources

Chapter 1

Burroughs, William J. *Climate Change in Prehistory: The End of the Reign of Chaos*. Cambridge: Cambridge University Press, 2005. Very well-researched and up-to-date discussion of climate and human evolution.

Conard, Nicholas J. "Cultural Modernity: Consensus or Conundrum?" *Proceedings of the National Academy of Sciences of the United States of America* 107, no. 17 (2010): 6721–6722, http://www.pnas.org/content/107/17/7621.full. Thoughtful critique, with references, of the out-of-Africa hypothesis of anatomically and culturally modern humans by the archaeologist of Vogelherd in southwestern Germany.

Flood, Josephine. *Archaeology of the Dreamtime: The Story of Prehistoric Australia and Its People*. New Haven, CT: Yale University Press, 1989. Overview of the Australian archaeological record; short on discussion of Aboriginal Dreamtime and myths.

Johanson, Donald, and Kate Wong. *Lucy: The Quest for Human Origins*. New York: Three Rivers, 2009.

McBrearty, Sally, and Allison S. Brooks. "The Revolution that Wasn't: A New Interpretation of the Origin of Modern Human Behavior." *Journal of Human Evolution* 39 (2000): 453–463. Crucial, pioneering article in which the authors grounded anatomically and intellectually fully evolved *H. sapiens* in Africa.

Stringer, Chris, and Peter Andrews. *The Complete World of Human Evolution*. London: Thames and Hudson, 2005. Clearly organized and richly illustrated summary.

WEBSITES

http://iho.asu.edu/. Arizona State University, Institute of Human Origins, runs the popular but scholarly well-founded website Becoming Human (http://www.becominghuman.org/).

http://www.bradshawfoundation.com/. The Bradshaw Foundation has a large website on human evolution and rock art, with many images, and a link to Stephen Oppenheimer's, The Journey of Mankind—The Peopling of the World, an important overview of *Homo sapiens'* migrations.

Chapter 2

Assmann, Jan. *The Search for God in Ancient Egypt*. Ithaca, NY: Cornell University Press, 2001. Reflective investigation of the dimensions of Egyptian polytheism by a leading Egyptologist.

Bottéro, Jean. *Mesopotamia: Writing, Reasoning, and the Gods*. Chicago: University of Chicago Press, 1992. Classic intellectual history of ancient Mesopotamia.

Drews, Robert. *The End of the Bronze Age: Changes in Warfare and the Catastrophe ca. 1200 B.C.* Princeton, NJ: Princeton University Press, 1993. Closely argued essay on the destruction of Mycenaean culture and its consequences for the eastern Mediterranean.

Finkelstein, Israel. *The Archaeology of the Israelite Settlement*. Jerusalem: Israel Exploration Society, 1988. Authoritative presentation of the archaeology of the earliest period of Israelite social formation.

Kuhrt, Amélie. *The Ancient Near East, c. 3000–330 BCE*, 2 vols. London: Routledge, 1994. Comprehensive handbook surveying all regions of the Middle East.

Mithen, Steven. *After the Ice: A Global Human History, 20,000–5000 B.C.* Cambridge, MA: Harvard University Press, 2003. Engagingly written story of humans settling, becoming farmers, and founding villages and towns, as seen through the eyes of a modern time traveler.

Van de Mieroop, Marc. *The Ancient Mesopotamian City*. Oxford: Clarendon Press, 1997. Full examination of Mesopotamian urban institutions, including city assemblies.

WEBSITES

http://mesopotamia.lib.uchicago.edu/. "Ancient Mesopotamia," Website of the Oriental Institute, University of Chicago. A user-friendly portal to the world-renowned Mesopotamia collection of the Oriental Institute.

http://www.ancientegypt.co.uk/menu.html. "Ancient Egypt," website of the British Museum. Pictorial introduction, with short texts.

http://www.livius.org/babylonia.html. "Livius, Articles on Ancient History." A large collection of translated texts and references to philological articles, with portals on Mesopotamia, Egypt, Anatolia, and Greece.

Chapter 3

Bryant, Edwin. *The Quest for the Origins of Vedic Culture: The Indo-Aryan Migration Debate*. Oxford: Oxford University Press, 2001. A scholarly yet readable attempt to address the linguistic and archaeological evidence surrounding the thesis of Aryan migration versus the more recent theory of indigenous Vedic development.

Embree, Ainslee T., ed. *Sources of Indian Tradition*, vol. 1, 2nd ed. New York: Columbia University Press, 1988. Though the language is dated in places, this is still the most comprehensive sourcebook of Indian thought available. Recent additions on women and gender make it even more so. Sophisticated yet readable introductions, glosses, and commentary.

Eraly, Abraham. *Gem in the Lotus: The Seeding of Indian Civilization*. London: Weidenfeld & Nicholson, 2004. Readable, comprehensive survey of recent scholarship from prehistory to the reign of Ashoka during the Mauryan dynasty of the fourth and third centuries BCE. Emphasis on transitional period of sixth-century religious innovations, particularly Buddhism.

Fairservis, Walter A. *The Roots of Ancient India. The Archaeology of Early Indian Civilization*. New York: Macmillan, 1971. Classic, well-detailed, and well-documented treatment of Indian archaeology and history to 500 BCE. Particularly well done on the so-called Vedic dark ages to 800 BCE. More useful in general for experienced students.

Kenoyer, Jonathan Mark. *Ancient Cities of the Indus Valley Civilization*. New York: Oxford University Press, 1998. Comprehensive work by team leader of Harappan Research Project. Particularly good on Lothal.

Kinsley, David R. *Hinduism. A Cultural Perspective*. Englewood Cliffs, NJ: Prentice Hall, 1993. Short, highly accessible overview of the major traditions within the constellation of belief systems called by outsiders "Hinduism." Sound treatment of the formative Vedic and Upanishadic periods.

Possehl, Gregory L., ed. *Harappan Civilization: A Recent Perspective*, 2nd ed. New Delhi: Oxford University Press, 1993. Sound and extensive treatment of recent work and issues in Indus valley archaeology by one of the leading on-site researchers and a former student of Fairservis. Used to best advantage by experienced students.

Trautmann, Thomas. *India: Brief History of a Civilization*. New York: Oxford University Press, 2011. A succinct and lucid account of 4,000 years of Indian history, with particular emphasis on early developments.

Wolpert, Stanley. *A New History of India*, 5th ed. New York: Oxford University Press, 2004. Another extremely useful, readable, one-volume history from Neolithic times to the present. Excellent first work for serious students.

WEBSITES

www.columbia.edu/cu/lweb/indiv/southasia/cuvl/history.html. Run by Columbia University, this site contains links to "WWW.Virtual Library: Indian History"; "Regnal Chronologies"; "Internet Indian History Sourcebook"; and "Medical History of British India."

http://www.harappa.com. Contains a wealth of images of artifacts and other archaeological treasures from the Indus Valley.

Chapter 4

Chang, Kwang-chih. *The Archaeology of Ancient China*, 4th ed. New Haven, CT: Yale University Press, 1986. Sophisticated treatment of archaeology of Shang China. Prime exponent of the view of overlapping periods and territories for the Sandai period. Erudite, yet accessible for experienced students.

Ebrey, Patricia Buckley, ed. *Chinese Civilization: A Sourcebook*, 2nd ed. New York: Free Press, 1993. Wonderful supplement to the preceding volume. Some different classical sources and considerable material on women and social history. Time frame of this work extends to the modern era.

Keightly, David N., ed. *The Origins of Chinese Civilization*. Berkeley: University of California Press, 1983. Symposium volume on a variety of Sandai topics by leading scholars. Some exposure to early Chinese history and archaeology is necessary in order to best appreciate these essays.

Keightly, David N., ed. *Sources of Shang History: The Oracle-Bone Inscriptions of Bronze Age China*. Berkeley: University of California Press, 1978 (2nd ed. 1985). Benchmark in the authoritative interpretation and contextualization of ritual inscriptions. Some grounding in ancient Chinese history helpful.

Lowe, Michael, and Edward L. Shaughnessy, eds. *The Cambridge History of Ancient China. From the Origins of Civilization to 221 B.C.* Cambridge: Cambridge University Press, 1999. The opening volume of the Cambridge History of China series, this is the most complete multiessay volume on all aspects of recent Chinese ancient historical and archaeological work. The place to start for the serious student contemplating in-depth research.

Schirokauer, Conrad. *A Brief History of Chinese Civilization*. New York: Harcourt, Brace Jovanovich, 1991. Readable one-volume text on Chinese history up to the present. More thorough treatment of Sandai period than is generally the case with one-volume texts.

Thorp, Robert L. *China in the Early Bronze Age: Shang Civilization*. Philadelphia: University of Pennsylvania Press, 2006. Comprehensive yet accessible survey of recent archaeological work on the period 2070–1046 BCE, including traditional Xia and Shang periods under the heading of China's "bronze age."

Wang, Aihe. *Cosmology and Political Culture in Early China*. Cambridge: Cambridge University Press, 2000. Part of the Cambridge Studies in Chinese History, Literature, and Institutions series. Wang argues that control of *cosmology*—how the world and universe operate—was a vital key to the wielding of power among the Shang and Zhou rulers. Recommended for serious students.

Watson, Burton, trans. *The Tso Chuan. Selections from China's Oldest Narrative History*. New York: Columbia University Press, 1989. Elegant translation by one of the most prolific of scholars working today. Excellent introduction to Zhou period and politics. Appropriate for beginning students, though more useful for those with some prior introduction to the period.

WEBSITES

http://lucian.uchicago.edu/blogs/earlychina/ssec/. This is the site of the Society for the Study of Early China. The site is for scholars, and the organization also publishes its own journal, *Early China*, as well as scholarly books.

www.ancientchina.co.uk. This site provides access to the British Museum's ancient Chinese collections and is highly useful for students seeking illustrations of assorted artifacts in a user-friendly environment.

Chapter 5

The Americas

Benson, Sonia, and Deborah J. Baker. *Early Civilizations in the Americas Reference Library*. Farmington Hills, MI: Gale UXL, 2009. Extensive three-volume encyclopedia available as a download or in hard copy. Contains an almanac of historical information and one of biographies and primary sources. Recommended for beginning and experienced students.

Bruhns, Karen Olsen, and Karen E. Stothert. *Women in Ancient America*. Norman: University of Oklahoma Press, 1999. A comprehensive account of women's roles in daily life, religion, politics, and war in foraging and farming as well as urban societies in the Americas.

Burger, Richard L. *Chavín and the Origins of Andean Civilization*. London: Thames and Hudson, 1992. Though somewhat outdated with the work being done on Caral-Supé, this richly illustrated discussion of Andean civilization still has considerable import.

Fiedel, Stuart J., *Prehistory of the Americas*, 2nd ed. Cambridge: Cambridge University Press, 1992. Accessible, detailed survey of the archaeology of the Americas by a leading American scholar.

Thomas, David Hurst. *Exploring Native North America*. Oxford: Oxford University Press, 2000. Selected chapters are useful on the major early North American sites, particularly Adena and Hopewell.

Trigger, Bruce G., Wilcomb E. Washburn, Richard E. W. Adams, Murdo J. MacLeod, Frank Salomon, and Stuart B. Schwartz, eds. *Cambridge History of the Native Peoples of the Americas*, 3 vols. Cambridge: Cambridge University Press, 1996–2000. As with all of the Cambridge histories this is a highly useful set for beginner and accomplished scholar alike. Useful bibliographies with the article entries.

von Hagen, Adriana, and Craig Morris. *The Cities of the Ancient Andes*. Thames and Hudson, 1999. While more geared to later periods, still a useful overview, with illustrations, by specialists on Andean cultures.

Oceania

Bellwood, Peter S. *Man's Conquest of the Pacific: The Prehistory of Southeast Asia and Oceania*. New York: Oxford University Press, 1979. Along with Bellwood's later volume, *The Polynesians*, traces the migrations of succeeding groups through the archipelagoes of the Pacific. Balanced treatment of controversies over gradual versus episodic migrations of Lapita cultures. For advanced students.

Fagan, Brian M., ed. *The Oxford Companion to Archaeology*. New York: Oxford University Press, 1996. Perhaps the best place to start for students interested in archaeological and historical overviews of the peopling of the Pacific. Extensive coverage of Lapita culture and expansion into Micronesia and Polynesia.

Kirch, Patrick V., *The Lapita Peoples: Ancestors of the Oceanic World*. Cambridge, MA.: Blackwell, 1997. Basic introduction by one of the pioneers of Polynesian research.

WEBSITE

http://novaonline.nvcc.edu. Reputable site containing links to online lectures on subjects including "Civilizations in America," "History of the American Indians," "Mesoamerican Civilization," and "Ancient Meso-American Civilizations."

Chapter 6

Sub-Saharan Africa

Collins, Robert O., and James M. Burns. *A History of Sub-Saharan Africa*. Cambridge: Cambridge University Press, 2007. Balanced, well-informed textbook with nearly half of its pages on the pre-1450 period.

McIntosh, Roderick J. *Ancient Middle Niger: Urbanism and the Self-Organizing Landscape*. Cambridge: Cambridge University Press, 2005. Important revisionist work on the origins of urbanism and kingship in West Africa.

Vansina, Jan. *Paths in the Rainforests: Toward a History of Political Tradition in Equatorial Africa*. Madison: University of Wisconsin Press, 1990. Magisterial presentation of the Bantu dispersal and village life in the rain forest.

Mesoamerica and the Andes

Aveni, Anthony F. *Skywatchers*, rev. ed. Austin: University of Texas Press, 2001. Classic study on astronomy and calendars of pre-Columbian Americans, including a discussion of the Nazca lines.

Evans, Susan Tobey. *Ancient Mexico and Central America: Archaeology and Culture History*. London: Thames and Hudson, 2004. Densely but clearly written and detailed, with many sidebars on special topics.

Grube, Nikolai, ed. *Maya: Divine Kings of the Rain Forest*. Cologne, Germany: Könemann, 2001. Lavishly illustrated book with short contributions by many hands.

Schele, Linda, and David Freidel. *A Forest of Kings: The Untold Story of the Ancient Maya*. New York: Quill-William Morrow, 1990. Classic study summarizing the results of the Maya glyph decipherment, by two pioneers.

WEBSITES

http://www-sul.stanford.edu/depts/ssrg/africa/history.html.   Africa south of the Sahara: A large, resource-filled website based at Stanford University.

http://www.allempires.com/article/index.php?q=americas_history. Americas: World-historical site with interesting overviews of Pre-Columbian History.

Chapter 7

Boatwright, Mary, Daniel J. Gargola, and Richard J. A. Talbert. *The Romans: From Village to Empire*. New York: Oxford University Press, 2004. Clearly written, comprehensive introduction to Roman history.

Boyce, Mary. *A History of Zoroastrianism*, vol. 1. *The Early Period*. Handbuch der Orientalistik, second impression, with corrections. Leiden, the Netherlands: E. J. Brill, 1989. Standard work by the leading scholar on the subject.

Briant, Pierre. *From Cyrus to Alexander: A History of the Persian Empire*. Warsaw, Poland: Eisenbrauns, 2000. Monumental work, the most detailed and authoritative study of the topic to date.

Burstein, Stanley M. "The Hellenistic Period in World History." American Historical Association Pamphlets, August 1997, http://www.historians.org/pubs/Free/BURSTEIN.HTM. Comprehensive overview of recent scholarship in Hellenistic studies.

Cameron, Averil. *The Mediterranean World in Late Antiquity, AD 395–600*. London: Routledge, 1993. New perspective on the strengths and weaknesses of the late empire.

Dignas, Beate, and Engelbert Winter. *Rome and Persia in Late Antiquity: Neighbours and Rivals*. Cambridge: Cambridge University Press, 2007. Detailed historical investigation of the rivalry between Rome and Persia.

Shaked, Shaul. *Dualism in Transformation: Varieties of Religion in Sasanian Iran*. London: School of Oriental and African Studies, 1994. Short history of the different religions in Sasanid Persia.

Smith, Mark S. *The Early History of God: Yahweh and the Other Deities in Ancient Israel*. San Francisco: Harper & Row, 1990. Very readable introduction to the problem of early monotheism among Israelites.

WEBSITES

http://www.perseus.tufts.edu/hopper/. Perseus Digital Library, probably the largest website on Greece and Rome, with immense resources, located at Tufts University.

http://darmc.harvard.edu/icb/icb.do?keyword=k40248&pageid=icb.page188868. The University of Harvard allows students to tailor searches in order to access specific geo-political and spatial cartographical representations of the Roman and medieval worlds.

http://www.ancientgreece.co.uk/menu.html. Open the door to the compelling world of Ancient Greece. The British Museum has compiled a collection of images and information on various aspects of Greek History such as the Acropolis, Athens, daily life, festivals and games, Sparta, war, and gods.

Chapter 8

Auboyer, Jeannine. *Daily Life in Ancient India*. London: Phoenix Press, 2002. Overview consisting of sections on social structures/religious principles; individual/collective existence; and royal and administrative existence. Multidisciplinary approach appropriate for most undergraduates.

Chakravarti, Uma. *The Social Dimensions of Early Buddhism*. New Delhi: Oxford University Press, 1987. Thorough analysis, with extensive glossary, of the influence of the north Indian economic transition to peasant market farming on the social milieu of early Buddhism.

Embree, Ainslee T. *Sources of Indian Tradition*, 2nd ed., 2 vols. New York: Columbia University Press, 1988. The latest edition contains a number of new selections useful for the study of social relations in addition to the older religious material. As with all of the works in this series, the level of writing is sophisticated, though accessible; the overviews are masterly; and the works are ably translated.

Keay, John. *India. A History*. New York: Grove Press, 2000. Lively, highly detailed narrative history, with a number of highly useful charts and genealogies of ruling houses. Sympathetic treatment of controversial matters.

Knott, Kim. *Hinduism: A Very Short Introduction*. New York: Oxford University Press, 1998. Sound, brief discussion of modern Hinduism and its formative influences. Asks provocative questions such as "What is a religion?" and "Is Hinduism something more than the Western conception of religion?"

Nikam, N. A., and Richard McKeon, eds. and trans. *The Edicts of Asoka*. Chicago: University of Chicago Press, 1959. Slim but useful volume for those interested in reading the entire collection of Ashoka's Pillar, Cave, and Rock Edicts. Short, accessible introduction.

Pelikan, Jaroslav, ed. *Buddhism: The Dhammapada*. Translated by John Ross Carter and Mahinda Palihawadana. Sacred Writings, vol. 6. New York: Quality Paperback Book Club, 1992. Erudite but accessible translation of one of the key texts in the Buddhist corpus. Students with some exposure to the introductory ideas of Buddhism will find it very useful in its step-by-step elucidation of a number of central concepts.

Willis, Michael. *The Archaeology of Hindu Ritual*. Cambridge: Cambridge University Press, 2009. Best utilized by experienced students, this book uses site archaeology, Sanskrit documents, and studies of ancient astronomy to plot the development of Hinduism under the Guptas and their use of it in statecraft as they created their vision of a universal empire.

Wolpert, Stanley. *A New History of India*, 6th ed. Oxford, New York: Oxford University Press, 2000. The standard introductory work to the long sweep of Indian history. Evenly divided between the period up to and including the Mughals and the modern era. Good coverage of geography, environment, as well as social and gender issues. Good select bibliography arranged by chapter; highly useful glossary of Indian terms.

WEBSITE

www.dli.ernet.in. Digital Library of India. This online resource, hosted by the Indian Institute of Science at Bangalore, contains primary and secondary sources for not only history but also culture, economics, literature, and a host of other subjects.

Chapter 9

Ebrey, Patricia Buckley, ed. *Chinese Civilization: A Sourcebook*, 2nd ed. New York: Free Press, 1993. Varied primary sources with an accent on social history material: letters, diary excerpts, etc. Particularly strong on women's history sources.

Hinsch, Bret. *Women in Early Imperial China.* Lanham, MD: Rowman and Littlefield, 2002. Broad examination of the place and transition of the place of women during the crucial early Chinese dynasties.

Huang, Ray. *China: A Macro History.* Armonk, NY: M.E. Sharpe, 1997. Readable, entertaining, and highly useful one-volume history. Particularly good on the complex politics of the post-Han and Song-Yuan periods.

Lewis, Mark Edward. *The Early Chinese Empires: Qin and Han.* Cambridge, MA: Harvard University Press, 2007. Detailed exploration of the rise and adaptations of China's initial empires. Better for advanced students.

Loewe, Michael. *Everyday Life in Early Imperial China During the Han Period, 202 B.C.–A.D. 220.* New York: Harper and Row, 1968. Short, highly useful one-volume survey of Han social history by a preeminent scholar. Especially good on details of peasant and elite daily existence.

Snow, Philip. *The Star Raft: China's Encounter with Africa.* Ithaca, NY: Cornell University Press, 1988. Important, accessible study of the little known area of China's maritime trade with Africa from Han times to the epic fifteenth-century voyages of Zheng He and beyond.

WEBSITES

http://afe.easia.columbia.edu/cosmos/ort/daoism.htm. Defining "Daoism": A Complex History, looks at Daoism as a term, its use and its practice in terms of morality, society, nature, and the self.

http://newton.uor.edu/departments&programs/asianstudiesdept/. *East and Southeast Asia: An Annotated Directory of Internet Resources.* "China," "History." One of the most complete guides to websites dealing with all manner of Chinese history and society.

Chapter 10

al-Khalili, Jim. *The House of Wisdom.* New York: Penguin, 2010. Elegant and accessible introduction to the golden age of Arabic science.

The Arabian Nights. Translated by Husain Haddawy. New York: Norton, 1990. Translation of the new edition by Muhsin Mahdi, which reconstitutes the original, thirteenth-century text.

Chaudhuri, K. N. *Trade and Civilization in the Indian Ocean.* Cambridge: Cambridge University Press, 1985. Discusses the historical evolution of the trade and its various aspects (sea route, ships, commodities, and capital investments).

Fryde, Edmund. *The Early Palaeologan Renaissance (1261–c. 1360).* Leiden, the Netherlands: Brill, 2000. Detailed presentation of the main philosophical and scientific figures of Byzantium after the recovery from the Latin interruption.

Laiou, Angeliki E., and Cécile Morrisson. *The Byzantine Economy.* Cambridge: Cambridge University Press, 2007. Comprehensive and well-researched study of ups and downs in the demography, productive capacity, and long-distance trade of Byzantium.

Lapidus, Ira. *Muslim Cities in the Later Middle Ages.* Cambridge: Cambridge University Press, 1984. Seminal work and still the only study of Muslim urban society, although it should be supplemented by Shlomo D. Goitein's monumental study of Jews, *A Mediterranean Society* (1967–1988).

Rippin, Andrew. *Muslims: Their Religious Beliefs and Practices,* 2nd ed. London: Routledge, 2001. One of the best and most accessible introductions to the basic beliefs and practices in Islam, based on the reevaluation of Islamic origins also presented in this chapter.

Tyerman, Christopher. *God's War: A New History of the Crusades.* Cambridge, MA: Belknap Press, 2006. Persuasive revisionist history by a leading Crusade historian.

Whittow, Mark. *The Making of Byzantium, 600–1025.* Berkeley: California University Press, 1996. Revisionist study of the Byzantine struggle for survival in the early years.

WEBSITES

Applied History Research Group, University of Calgary. *The Islamic World to 1600,* http://www.ucalgary.ca/applied_history/tutor/islam/. A multimedia tutorial by a university research group.

Asia Topics in World History. http://afe.easia.columbia.edu/mongols/. With a timeline spanning 1000-1500 C.E., The Mongols in World History delivers a concise and colorful history of the Mongol's impact on global history.

Chapter 11

Bartlett, Robert. *The Making of Europe: Conquest, Colonization and Cultural Change, 950–1350.* Princeton, NJ: Princeton University Press, 1993. Analyzes the expansion of Europe from a cultural perspective.

Brown, Peter. *The Rise of Western Christendom: Triumph and Diversity, A.D. 200–1000,* 2nd ed. Oxford: Wiley-Blackwell, 2003. Traces the development of Christian Europe from the perspective of the Church.

Grant, Edward. *The Foundation of Modern Science in the Middle Ages.* Cambridge: Cambridge University Press, 1996. Seminal study of the contributions of medieval science to the scientific revolution of the seventeenth century.

Lawrence, C. H. *Medieval Monasticism: Forms of Religious Life in Western Europe in the Middle Ages,* 2nd ed. New York: Longman, 1984. Thorough survey of the development of the Western monastic tradition.

McKitterick, Rosamond. *Charlemagne: The Formation of a European Identity.* Cambridge: Cambridge University Press, 2008. An examination of how Charlemagne's policies contributed to the idea of Europe.

Platt, Colin. *King Death: The Black Death and Its Aftermath in Late-Medieval England.* Toronto: University of Toronto Press, 1997. Riveting analysis of the effects of the Black Death on all aspects of society.

Reynolds, Susan. *Fiefs and Vassals: The Medieval Evidence Reinterpreted.* Oxford: Oxford University Press, 1994. Important revisionist study of medieval feudal institutions.

Riley-Smith, Jonathan, ed. *The Oxford Illustrated History of the Crusades.* New York: Oxford University Press, 1995. A very useful and readable history of the crusading movement.

WEBSITES

http://www.bc.edu/bc_org/avp/cas/fnart/arch/gothic_arch.html. Boston College's Digital Archive of Architecture has a quick index reference guide, which opens up links to images from both early and high Gothic architecture.

http://www.bl.uk/treasures/magnacarta/virtual_curator/vc9.html. An excellent website that makes available a digitized version of the Magna Carta. Audio files answer many FAQ's about the manuscript and its significance.

Chapter 12

DeBary, William T., ed. *Sources of Chinese Tradition,* vol. 1. New York: Columbia University Press, 1960. Excellent introduction to major Chinese philosophical schools. Extensive coverage of Buddhism and Neo-Confucianism with accessible, highly informative introductions to the documents themselves.

Ebrey, Patricia Buckley, ed. *Chinese Civilization: A Sourcebook,* 2nd ed. New York: Free Press, 1993. More varied than DeBary with more social history material: letters, diary excerpts, etc. Particularly strong on women's history sources.

Ebrey, Patricia Buckley, ed. *The Inner Quarters.* Berkeley and Los Angeles: University of California Press, 1993. Perhaps the best scholarly exploration of the roles of women in Song China.

Hansen, Valerie. *The Open Empire: A History of China to 1600.* New York: W. W. Norton, 2000. A fresh and accessible synthesis of pre-modern Chinese history.

Levathes, Louise. *When China Ruled the Seas*. London: Oxford University Press, 1994. Delightful coverage of the voyages of Zheng He from 1405 to 1433. Particularly good on the aftermath of the voyages.

Mujeeb, M. *The Indian Muslims*. London: Allen Unwin, 1967. Thorough historical overview from the eighth century to the twentieth. Especially useful on political and administrative systems of the early and middle periods of Muslim hegemony in north India.

Singh, Patwant. *The Sikhs*. London: John Murray, 1999. Readable popular history of the Sikh experience to the present by an adherent. Especially useful on the years from Guru Nanak to the changes of the early eighteenth century and the transition to a more militant faith.

Chapter 13

General

Mann, Susan. *East Asia (China, Korea, Japan)*. Washington, DC: American Historical Association, 1999. The second volume in the Women's and Gender History in Global Perspective series. Short, informative volume with historiographic overviews and cross-cultural comparisons among the three title countries. Critical annotated bibliographies on the use of standard texts in integrating women and gender into Asian studies.

Murphey, Rhoads. *East Asia. A New History*. New York: Longman, 1997. One of the few one-volume histories that includes material on China, Japan, Korea, Vietnam, and southeast Asia. Written by a leading scholar of modern China and east Asia. Appropriate for beginning students but more useful for those with some background on the area.

Ramusack, Barbara N., and Sharon Sievers. *Women in Asia*. Bloomington: Indiana

University Press, 1999. Part of the series Restoring Women to History. Far-ranging book divided into parts on "Women in South and Southeast Asia" and "Women in East Asia." Coverage of individual countries, extensive chronologies, valuable bibliographies. Most useful for advanced undergraduates.

Korea

DeBary, William T., ed. *Sources of Korean Tradition*, vol. 1. New York: Columbia University Press, 1997. The latest in the renowned Columbia series on the great traditions of east Asia. Perhaps the most complete body of accessible sources for undergraduates.

Korean Overseas Information Service. *A Handbook of Korea*. Seoul: KOIS, 1993. Wonderfully complete history, geography, guidebook, and sociology text. Excellent source, but students should keep in mind its provenance and treat some of its historical claims to uniqueness accordingly.

Japan

DeBary, William T., ed. *Sources of Japanese Tradition*, vol. 1. New York: Columbia University Press, 2002. Like the volume above on Korea, and the others of this series on India and China, the sources are well selected, the glossaries are sound, and the overviews of the material are masterful. As with the other east Asia volumes, the complexities of the various Buddhist schools are especially well drawn. As with the others in the series, students with some previous experience will derive the most benefit from this volume.

Reischauer, Edwin O., and Albert Craig. *Japan. Tradition and Transformation*. Boston: Houghton Mifflin, 1989, and subsequent editions. The companion volume to J. K. Fairbank's *China*, by the leading American scholar of and former US ambassador to Japan. A one-volume history but more emphasis on the modern than ancient periods.

Totman, Conrad. *A History of Japan*. Oxford: Blackwell, 2000. One of Blackwell's History of the World series. A larger, more balanced, and comprehensive history than the Reischauer volume. More than half

of the material is on the pre-1867 period, with extensive coverage of social history and demographics.

Vietnam

Steinberg, Joel David, ed. *In Search of Southeast Asia*, rev. ed. Honolulu: University of Hawaii Press, 1987. Extensive coverage of Vietnam within the context of an area study of southeast Asia. Though weighted toward the modern period, very good coverage of agricultural and religious life in the opening chapters.

Taylor, Keith W. *The Birth of Vietnam*. Berkeley: University of California Press, 1983. Comprehensive, magisterial volume on early Vietnamese history and historical identity amid the long Chinese occupation. Best for students with some background in southeast Asian and Chinese history.

WEBSITES

http://www.britishmuseum.org/the_museum/departments/prints_and_drawings.aspx. Department of Prints and Drawings, British Museum. A comprehensive source for all manner of interests related to Asian studies.

http://digicol.library.wisc.edu/PAIR. Portal to Asian Internet Resources. Extensive list of Internet sources for Asian studies.

Chapter 14

Birmingham, David, and Phyllis M. Martin, eds. *History of Central Africa*, vol. 1. London: Longman, 1983. The first chapter, by Birmingham, provides an excellent summary of the history of Luba prior to 1450.

Crummey, David. *Land and Society in the Christian Kingdom of Ethiopia: From the Thirteenth to the Twentieth Century*. Urbana: University of Illinois Press, 2000. The first book in which the rich land records of the church have been used for a reconstruction of agriculture and land tenure.

Horton, Mark, and John Middleton. *The Swahili: The Social Landscape of a Mercantile Society*. Oxford: Blackwell, 2000. A study that gives full attention to the larger context of East Africa, in which the Swahilis flourished. Middleton is the author of another important study, *The World of the Swahili: An African Mercantile Civilization* (1992, Yale University Press).

Huffman, Thomas N. *Mapungubwe: Ancient African Civilization on the Limpopo*. Johannesburg, South Africa: Witwatersrand University Press, 2005. Short but illuminating summary of the archaeological record by a leading South African expert, although his interpretation of Zimbabwe in an earlier work (*Snakes and Crocodiles*, 1996, Witwatersrand University Press) is controversial.

Levtzion, Nehemia. *Ancient Ghana and Mali*. New York: Africana Publishing, 1980. Originally published London: Methuen, 1973. Standard history of ancient Ghana, Mali, and Songhay based on a thorough knowledge of the Arabic sources; a revision by David Conrad, Paulo Farias, Roderick J. McIntosh, and Susan McIntosh has been announced but has yet to appear.

Robinson, David. *Muslim Societies in African History*. Cambridge: Cambridge University Press, 2004. Advertised as part of a series of new approaches, this book, nevertheless, presents a conventional view of Islam, albeit in its African context.

Trigger, Bruce. *History and Settlement in Lower Nubia*. Yale University Publications in Anthropology 69. New Haven, CT: Yale University Press, 1965. Chapter 9 is still the best overview of Nubian history, by a scholar with a broad understanding of early civilizations.

WEBSITES

http://www.metmuseum.org/toah/hd/ife/hd_ife.htm. "Heilbrunn Timeline of Art History," "Ife (from ca. 350 B.C.)." An excellent introductory we site can be found at the Metropolitan Museum of Art. It contains many links and presents clear overviews.

For a website by Patrick Darling, the principal archaeological investigator of the Nigerian earthworks see http://cohesion.rice.edu/CentersAndInst/SAFA/emplibrary/49_ch09.pdf for a copy of a 1998 article.

Chapter 15

Bruhns, Karen Olsen, and Karen E. Stothert. *Women in Ancient America*. Norman: University of Oklahoma Press, 1999. Comprehensive account of women's role in the daily life, religion, politics, and war in hunter–gatherer and agrarian–urban societies.

Brumfield, Elizabeth M., and Gary F. Feinman, eds. *The Aztec World*. New York: Abrams, 2008. Collection of expert short chapters on a variety of topics, richly illustrated.

Carrasco, Davíd. *Daily Life of the Aztecs: People of the Sun and Earth*. With Scott Sessions. Westport, CT: Greenwood Press, 1998. Clear, straightforward account by a specialist.

D'Altroy, Terence. *The Incas*. Malden, MA: Blackwell, 2002. Well-organized, comprehensive, and up to-date overview.

Hassig, Ross. *War and Society in Ancient Mesoamerica*. Berkeley: University of California Press, 1992. Best study of the rising importance of militarism in Mesoamerican city-states, up to the Aztec Empire.

Malpass, Michael A. *Daily Life in the Inca Empire*, 2nd ed. Westport, CT: Greenwood Press, 2009. Clear, straightforward, and readable account of ordinary people's lives by a specialist.

WEBSITE

http://www.aztec-history.com/. Aztec-History.com. Introductory website, easily maneuverable, with links.

Chapter 16

Agoston, Gábor. *Guns for the Sultan: Military Power and the Weapons Industry in the Ottoman Empire*. Cambridge: Cambridge University Press, 2005. Thorough study, which is based on newly accessible Ottoman archival materials and emphasizes the technological prowess of Ottoman gunsmiths.

Casale, Giancarlo. *The Ottoman Age of Exploration*. New York: Oxford University Press, 2010. Detailed correction, based on Ottoman and Portuguese archives, of the traditional characterization of the Ottoman Empire as a land-oriented power.

Casey, James. *Early Modern Spain: A Social History*. London: Routledge, 1999. Detailed, well-documented analysis of rural–urban and royal–nobility tensions.

Elliott, John Huxtable. *Spain, Europe, and the Wider World: 1500–1800*. New Haven, CT: Yale University Press, 2009. A comprehensive overview, particularly strong on culture during the 1500s.

Glete, Jan. *War and the State in Early Modern Europe: Spain, the Dutch Republic, and Sweden as Fiscal–Military States, 1500–1660*. London: Routledge, 2002. A complex but persuasive construction of the forerunner model to the absolute state. Unfortunately leaves out the Ottoman Empire.

Murphy, Rhoads. *Ottoman Warfare, 1500–1700*. New Brunswick, NJ: Rutgers University Press, 1999. Author presents a vivid picture of the Janissaries, their discipline, organization, campaigns, and voracious demands for salary increases.

Pamuk, Sevket. *A Monetary History of the Ottoman Empire*. Cambridge: Cambridge University Press, 2000. Superb analysis of Ottoman archival resources on the role and function of American silver in the money economy of the Ottomans.

Ruiz, Teofilo R. *Spanish Society, 1400–1600*. London: Longman, 2001. Richly detailed social studies rewarding anyone interested in changing class structures, rural–urban movement, and extension of the money market into the countryside.

Subrahmanyam, Sanjay. *The Career and Legend of Vasco da Gama*. Cambridge: Cambridge University Press, 1997. Focuses on the religious motivations in Vasco da Gama and the commercial impact of his journey to India.

WEBSITES

http://www.pbs.org/wgbh/pages/frontline/shows/apocalypse/. *Frontline*, "Apocalypse! The Evolution of Apocalyptic Belief and How It Shaped the Western World," PBS, 1995. The contribution by Bernard McGinn, University of Chicago, under the heading of "Apocalypticism," is of particular relevance for the understanding of Christopher Columbus viewing himself as a precursor of Christ's Second Coming.

http://www.pbs.org/empires/islam/timeline.html. Comprehensive and informative, PBS website on the Ottoman Empire examines the various facets of this Islamic culture such as scientific innovations, faith and its leaders.

Chapter 17

Black, Jeremy. *Kings, Nobles, and Commoners: States and Societies in Early Modern Europe—A Revisionist History*. London: Tauris, 2004. Available also electronically on ebrary; persuasive thesis, largely accepted by scholars, of a continuity of institutional practices in Europe across the sixteenth and seventeenth centuries, casting doubt on absolutism as being more than a theory.

Geanakoplos, Deno John. *Constantinople and the West: Essays on the Late Byzantine (Paleologan) and Italian Renaissances and the Byzantine and Roman Churches*. Madison: University of Wisconsin Press, 1989. Fundamental discussion of the extensive transfer of texts and scholars during the 1400s.

Jacob, Margaret C. *Scientific Culture and the Making of the Industrial West*. Oxford: Oxford University Press, 1997. Widely cited short book emphasizing the connections between New Science, scientific societies, and the steam engine.

Margolis, Howard. *It Started with Copernicus: How Turning the World Inside Out Led to the Scientific Revolution*. New York: McGraw-Hill, 2002. Important scholarly study of the connection between the discovery of the Americas and Copernicus' formulation of a sun-centered planetary system.

Nexon, Daniel H. *The Struggle for Power in Early Modern Europe: Religious Conflict, Dynastic Empires & International Change*. Princeton, NJ: Princeton University Press, 2009. Charles Tilly–inspired reevaluation of the changes occurring in sixteenth- and seventeenth-century Europe.

Rublack, Ulinka. *Reformation Europe*. Cambridge: Cambridge University Press, 2006. Cultural history approach to the effects of Luther and Calvin on western Christians.

Schiebinger, Londa. *The Mind Has No Sex? Women in the Origins of Modern Science*. Cambridge, MA: Harvard University Press, 1989. A pioneering study presenting biographies and summaries of scientific contributions. Discusses the importance of Marie Cunitz.

WEBSITES

http://www.earlymodernweb.org.uk/emr/ (http://sharonhoward.org/). "Early Modern Resources." Website with many links on the full range of institutional and cultural change.

http://kepler.nasa.gov/Mission/JohannesKepler/. NASA's website looks at the life and views of Johannes Kepler. It examines his discoveries, contemporaries, and the events that shaped modern science.

Chapter 18

Alchon, Suzanne A. *A Pest in the Land: New World Epidemics in a Global Perspective*. Albuquerque: University of New Mexico Press, 2003. A broad overview, making medical history comprehensible.

Behringer, Wolfgang. *Witches and Witch-Hunts: A Global History*. Cambridge: Polity Press, 2004. A well-grounded overview of the phenomenon of the fear of witches, summarizing the scholarship of the past decades.

Bulmer-Thomas, Victor, John S. Coatsworth, and Roberto Cortés Conde, eds. *The Cambridge Economic History of Latin America*. Vol. 1, *The Colonial Era and the Short Nineteenth Century*. Cambridge: Cambridge University Press, 2006. Collection of specialized summary articles on aspects of Iberian colonialism.

Burkholder, Mark A., and Lyman L. Johnson. *Colonial Latin America*, 6th ed. Oxford: Oxford University Press, 2008. A well-established text, updated multiple times.

Ekberg, Carl J. *French Roots in the Illinois Country: The Mississippi Frontier in Colonial Times*. Urbana: University of Illinois Press, 1998. Detailed, deeply researched historical account.

Socolow, Susan M. *The Women of Latin America*. Cambridge: Cambridge University Press, 2000. Surveys the patriarchal order and the function of women within it.

Stein, Stanley J., and Barbara H. Stein. *Silver, Trade and War: Spain and America in the Making of Early Modern Europe*. Baltimore: Johns Hopkins University Press, 2000. Covers the significance of American silver reaching as far as China.

Taylor, Alan. *American Colonies*. London: Penguin, 2001. History of the English colonies in New England, written from a broad Atlantic perspective.

Wood, Michael. *Conquistadors*. Berkeley: University of California Press, 2000. Accessible, richly illustrated history of the conquest period.

WEBSITE

http://www.pbs.org/conquistadors/. Wonderful interactive website that allows you to track the journy's made by the Conquistadors such as Cortés, Pizzaro, Orellana, and Cabeza De Vaca. Learn more about their conquests in the Americas and the legacy they left behind them.

Chapter 19

Carney, Judith A. *Black Rice: The African Origins of Rice Cultivation in the Americas*. Cambridge, MA: Harvard University Press, 2001. Study which goes a long way toward correcting the stereotype that black slaves were unskilled laborers and carefully documents the transfer of rice-growing culture from West Africa to the Americas.

Dubois, Laurent, and Julius S. Scott. *Origins of the Black Atlantic: Rewriting Histories*. New York: Routledge, 2009. Book that focuses on African slaves in the Americas as they had to arrange themselves in their new lives.

Gray, Richard, and David Birmingham, eds. *Pre-Colonial African Trade*. London: Oxford University Press, 1970. Collective work in which contributors emphasize the growth and intensification of trade in the centuries of 1500–1800.

Hall, Gwendolyn Midlo. *Slavery and African Ethnicities in the Americas: Restoring the Links*. Chapel Hill: University of North Carolina Press, 2005. Study that focuses on slaves in the Americas according to their regions of origin in Africa.

Heywood, Linda M., and John K. Thornton. *Central Africans, Atlantic Creoles, and the Foundation of the Americas*. Cambridge: Cambridge University Press, 2007. Pathbreaking investigation of the creation and role of Creole culture in Africa and the Americas.

Iliffe, John. *Africans: The History of a Continent*. Cambridge: Cambridge University Press, 1995. Standard historical summary by an established African historian.

Kriger, Colleen E. *Cloth in West African History*. Lanham, MD: Altamira, 2006. Detailed investigation of the sophisticated indigenous West African cloth industry.

Oliver, Roland, and Anthony Atmore. *Medieval Africa, 1250–1800*. Cambridge: Cambridge University Press, 2001. Revised and updated historical overview, divided into regions and providing detailed regional histories on the emerging kingdoms.

Thornton, John. *The Kongolese Saint Anthony: Dona Beatriz Kimpa Vita and the Antonian Movement, 1684–1706*. Cambridge: Cambridge University Press, 1998. Detailed biography of Dona Beatriz, from which the vignette at the beginning of the chapter is borrowed; includes a general overview of the history of Kongo during the civil war.

WEBSITES

http://www.slavevoyages.org/tast/index.faces. Atlantic Slave Trade Database. A large electronic website based at Emory University and sponsored by a number of American universities, presenting up-to-date demographic tables.

www.britishmuseum.org/PDF/british_museum_benin_art.pdf. In addition to offering a brief historical backdrop to the art of the Benin Kingdom, The British Museum's PDF also depicts various artifacts taken by the British from the Royal Palace.

Chapter 20

Bernier, Francois. *Travels in the Mogul Empire, A.D. 1656–1668*. Translated by Archibald Constable. Delhi: S. Chand, 1968. One of many fascinating travel accounts by European diplomats, merchants, and missionaries.

Eaton, Richard M. *Essays on Islam and Indian History*. New York: Oxford University Press, 2002. A compendium of the new scholarly consensus on, among other things, the differences between the clerical view of Islamic observance and its actual impact in rural India. Contains both historiography and material on civilizational and cultural issues.

Nizami, Khaliq A. *Akbar and Religion*. Delhi: IAD, 1989. Extensive treatment of Akbar's evolving move toward devising his Din-i-Ilahi movement, by leading scholar of Indian religious and intellectual history.

Richards, John F. *The Mughal Empire*. Cambridge: Cambridge University Press, 1993. Comprehensive volume in the New Cambridge History of India. Sophisticated treatment; best suited to advanced students. Extensive glossary and useful bibliographic essay.

Schimmel, Annemarie. *The Empire of the Great Mughals: History, Art, and Culture*. London: Reaktion Books, 2004. Revised edition of a volume published in German in 2000. Lavish illustrations, wonderfully drawn portraits of key individuals, and extensive treatment of social, family, and gender relations at the Mughal court.

WEBSITES

http://www.aasianist.org/EAA and http://www.aasianist.org/links/index.htm. As with other Asian topics, two of the most reliable websites are sponsored by the Association for Asian Studies.

http://www.bbc.co.uk/religion/religions/islam/history/mughalempire_1.shtml. The Mughal Empire ruled most of India and Pakistan in the sixteenth and seventeenth centuries. Learn more about the religious divides and governance of Muslim Mughals in a country with a majority of Hindi populace.

Chapter 21

China

DeBary, William T., and Irene Bloom. *Sources of Chinese Tradition*, vols. 1 and 2, 2nd ed. New York: Columbia University Press, 1999. Thoroughgoing update of classic sourcebook for Chinese literature and philosophy, with a considerable amount of social, family, and women's works now included.

Fairbank, John K., and Edwin O. Reischauer. *China: Tradition and Transformation*. Boston: Houghton Mifflin, 1989. A complete textbook on Chinese history, with the majority of the material geared toward the modern era. Emphasis on the "change within tradition" model of Chinese history.

Pomeranz, Kenneth. *The Great Divergence. China, Europe, and the Making of the Modern World Economy*. Princeton, NJ: Princeton University Press, 2001. Pathbreaking work mounting the strongest argument yet in favor of the balance of economic power remaining in east Asia until the Industrial Revolution was well under way.

Spence, Jonathan. *The Memory Palace of Matteo Ricci*. New York: Penguin, 1984. Highly original treatment of Ricci and the beginning of the Jesuit interlude in late Ming and early Qing China. Attempts to penetrate Ricci's world through the missionary's own memory techniques.

Japan

DeBary, William T., ed. *Sources of Japanese Tradition*, vols. 1 and 2. New York: Columbia University Press, 1964. The Tokugawa era spans volumes 1 and 2, with its inception and political and philosophical foundations thoroughly covered in volume 1, while the Shinto revival of national learning, the later Mito school, and various partisans of national unity in the face of foreign intrusion covered in the beginning of volume 2.

Duus, Peter. *Feudalism in Japan*, 3rd ed. New York: McGraw-Hill, 1993. Updated version of short, handy volume spanning all of Japanese history to 1867, with special emphasis on the shogunates. Good introduction on the uses and limitations of the term "feudalism" with reference to Japan within a comparative framework.

Gordon, Andrew. *A Modern History of Japan from Tokugawa Times to the Present*. New York: Oxford University Press, 2009. One of the few treatments of Japanese history that spans both the Tokugawa and the modern eras, rather than making the usual break in either 1853 or 1867/68. Both the continuity of the past and the novelty of the new era are therefore juxtaposed and highlighted. Most useful for students with a background at least equivalent to that supplied by this text.

WEBSITE

http://ngm.nationalgeographic.com/ngm/0507/feature2/map.html. Track the voyages made by Zheng He to Southeast Asia, India, Arabia and Africa.

Chapter 22

Israel, Jonathan I. *A Revolution of the Mind: Radical Enlightenment and the Origins of Modern Democracy*. Princeton, NJ: Princeton University Press, 2010. Israel is a pioneer of the contemporary renewal of intellectual history, and his investigations of the Enlightenment tradition are pathbreaking.

Kaiser, Thomas E., and Dale K. Van Kley, eds. *From Deficit to Deluge: The Origins of the French Revolution*. Stanford, CA: Stanford University Press, 2011. Thoughtful reevaluation of the scholarly field that takes into account the latest interpretations.

Kitchen, Martin. *A History of Modern Germany: 1800 to the Present*. Hoboken, NJ: Wiley-Blackwell, 2011. A broadly conceived historical overview, ranging from politics and economics to culture.

Rakove, Jack. *Revolutionaries: A New History of the Invention of America*. Boston: Houghton Mifflin, 2010. A new narrative history focusing on the principal figures in the revolution.

Riall, Lucy. *Risorgimento: The History of Italy from Napoleon to Nation-State*. New York: Palgrave Macmillan, 2009. Historical summary, incorporating the research of the past half-century, presented in a clear overview.

Wood, Gordon S. *The American Revolution: A History*. New York: Modern Library, 2002. A short, readable summary reflective of many decades of revisionism in the discussion of the American Revolution.

WEBSITES

http://www.nationalismproject.org/what.htm. Nationalism Project. A large website with links to bibliographies, essays, new books, and book reviews.

http://chnm.gmu.edu/revolution/. This website boasts 250 images, 350 text documents, 13 songs, 13 maps, and a timeline all focused on the French Revolution.

Chapter 23

Allen, Robert C. *The British Industrial Revolution in Global Perspective*. Cambridge: Cambridge University Press, 2009. An in-depth analysis, well supported by economic data, of not only why the Industrial Revolution occurred first in Britain but also how new British technologies carried industrialism around the world.

Dublin, Thomas, ed. *Farm to Factory: Women's Letters, 1830–1860*. New York: Columbia University Press, 1981. A fascinating collection of correspondence written by women who describe their experiences in moving from rural areas of New England to urban centers in search of work in textile factories.

Headrick, Daniel R. *The Tools of Empire: Technology and European Imperialism in the Nineteenth Century*. Oxford: Oxford University Press, 1981. A fascinating and clearly written analysis of the connections between the development of new technologies and their role in European imperialism.

Hobsbawm, Eric. *The Age of Revolution: 1789–1848*. London: Vintage Books, 1996. A sophisticated analysis of the Industrial Revolution (one element of the "dual revolution," the other being the French Revolution) that examines the effects of industrialism on social and cultural developments from a Marxist perspective.

Mokyr, Joel. "Accounting for the Industrial Revolution." In *The Cambridge Economic History of Modern Britain*, vol. 1. Edited by Roderick Floud and Paul Johnson. Cambridge: Cambridge University Press, 2004. An analysis of the industrial movement that emphasizes its intellectual sources, embraced in the term "Industrial Enlightenment."

More, Charles. *Understanding the Industrial Revolution*. London: Routledge, 2000. A comprehensive explanation of how theories of economic growth account for the development of the industrial movement in Britain.

Stearns, Peter N. *The Industrial Revolution in World History*. Boulder: University of Colorado Press, 1993. A comprehensive study of the origin, spread, and influence of the European industrial revolution and its impact on globalization.

WEBSITES

http://www.thomasedison.org/. Remarkable website that explores Thomas Edison's impact on modernity through his innovations and inventions. This site also reproduces all of Edison's scientific sketches which are available to download as PDF files.

http://www.monetpainting.net/. A visually beautiful website which reproduces many of Monet's masterpieces, this site also includes an extensive biographical account of the famous painter's life and works. It also includes information about his wife Camille, his gardens at Giverny, and a chronology.

http://darwin-online.org.uk/. This website has reproduced, in full, the works of Charles Darwin. In addition to providing digitized facsimiles of his works, private papers and manuscripts it has also added a concise biographical account and numerous images of Darwin throughout his life.

http://www.alberteinstein.info/. Fantastic and informative website that houses digitized manuscripts of Einstein's work. Also includes a gallery of images.

Chapter 24

China

Cohen, Paul. *Discovering History in China*. New York: Columbia University Press, 1984.

Fairbank, John K., and Su-yu Teng. *China's Response to the West*. Cambridge, MA: Harvard University Press, 1954.

Kang, David C. *East Asia Before the West: Five Centuries of Trade and Tribute*. New York: Columbia University Press, 2010.

Spence, Jonathan D. *The Search for Modern China*. New York: Norton, 1990.

Spence, Jonathan D. *God's Chinese Son*. New York: Norton, 1996.

Japan

Beasley, W. G. *The Meiji Restoration*. Stanford, CA: Stanford University Press, 1972.

Reischauer, Edwin O., and Albert M. Craig. *Japan: Tradition and Transformation*. Boston: Houghton Mifflin, 1989.

Totman, Conrad. *Japan Before Perry*. Berkeley: University of California Press, 1981.

Totman, Conrad. *A History of Japan*. Oxford: Blackwell, 2000.

WEBSITES

http://www.asian-studies.org/eaa/. Education About Asia. This site provides the best online sources for modern Chinese and Japanese history.

http://www.asian-studies.org/ This is the site of the Association for Asian Studies, the home page of which has links to sources more suited to advanced term papers and seminar projects.

http://sinojapanesewar.com/. Packed with maps, photographs and movies depicting the conflict between Japan and China at the end of the nineteenth century, students can learn more about causes and consequences of the Sino-Japanese war.

Chapter 25

Gaudin, Corinne. *Ruling Peasants: Village and State in Later Imperial Russia*. DeKalb: Northern Illinois University Press, 2007. A close and sympathetic analysis of rural Russia.

Inalcik, Halil, and Donald Quataert, eds. *An Economic and Social History of the Ottoman Empire*. Vol. 2, *1600–1914*. Cambridge: Cambridge University Press, 1994. A pioneering work with contributions by leading Ottoman historians on rural structures, monetary developments, and industrialization efforts.

Kasaba, Resat, ed. *The Cambridge History of Turkey*. Vol. 5, *Turkey in the Modern World*. Cambridge: Cambridge University Press, 2008. An ambitious effort to assemble the leading authorities on the Ottoman Empire and provide a comprehensive overview.

Lieven, Dominic. *Empire: The Russian Empire and Its Rivals*. New Haven, CT: Yale University Press, 2002. Broad, comparative history of the Russian Empire, in the context of the Habsburg, Ottoman, and British Empires.

Nikitenko, Aleksandr. *Up from Serfdom: My Childhood and Youth in Russia, 1804–1824*. Translated by Helen Saltz Jacobson. New Haven, CT: Yale University Press, 2001. Touching autobiography summarized at the beginning of the chapter.

Poe, Marshall T. *Russia's Moment in World History*. Princeton, NJ: Princeton University Press, 2003. A superb scholarly overview of Russian history, written from a broad perspective and taking into account a good number of Western stereotypes about Russia, especially in the nineteenth century.

Quataert, Donald. *Manufacturing in the Ottoman Empire and Turkey, 1500–1950*. Albany: State University of New York Press, 1994. The author is still the leading American historian on workers and the early industrialization of the Ottoman Empire.

Riasanovsky, Nicholas, and Mark Steinberg. *A History of Russia*, 8th ed., 2 vols. New York: Oxford University Press, 2011. A comprehensive, fully revised history, ranging from politics and economics to literature and the arts.

Uyar, Mesut, and Edward J. Erickson. *A Military History of the Ottomans: From Osman to Atatürk*. Santa Barbara, CA: Praeger Security International, 2009. A detailed, well-documented history of the Ottoman Empire from the perspective of its imperial designs and military forces, by two military officers in academic positions.

WEBSITE

http://www.russianlegacy.com/en/go_to/history/russian_empire.htm. Russian Legacy, a website devoted to the Russian Empire, organized as a timeline with links.

Chapter 26

Belich, James. *Replenishing the Earth: The Settler Revolution and the Rise of the Anglo-World, 1783–1939*. Oxford: Oxford University Press, 2009. Important study by an Australian historian, focusing on the British settler colonies.

Burbank, Jane, and Frederick Cooper. *Empires in World History: Power and Politics of Difference*. Princeton, NJ: Princeton University Press, 2010. Well-written and remarkably comprehensive comparative work.

Ferguson, Niall. *Empire: The Rise and Demise of the British World Order and the Lessons for Global Power*. New York: Perseus, 2002. Controversial but widely acknowledged analysis of the question of whether imperialism deserves its negative reputation.

Fieldhouse, David K. *Economics and Empire, 1830–1914*. New York: Macmillan, 1984. A classic, profoundly influential study of the economic costs of imperialism, coming to the conclusion that it was not cost-effective.

Hobsbawm, Eric. *The Age of Empire, 1875–1914*. New York: Vintage, 1989. Immensely well-informed investigation of the climactic period of the new imperialism at the end of the nineteenth century.

Jefferies, Matthew. *Contesting the German Empire, 1871–1918*. Malden, MA: Blackwell, 2008. Up-to-date summary of the German historical debate on the colonial period.

Ricklefs, Merle Calvin. *A History of Modern Indonesia Since c. 1200*, 3rd ed. Stanford, CA: Stanford University Press, 2001. Standard history with relevant chapters on Dutch imperialism and colonialism.

Singer, Barnett, John Langdon, and John W. Langdon. *Cultured Force: Makers and Defenders of the French Empire*. Madison: University of Wisconsin Press, 2004. Study of the principal (military) figures who helped create the French nineteenth-century empire.

WEBSITE

http://www.allempires.com/. All Empires Online History Community. Website dedicated to assembling materials on all historical empires, including those of the nineteenth century.

Chapter 27

Bulmer-Thomas, Victor. *The Economic History of Latin America Since Independence*, 2nd ed. Cambridge: Cambridge University Press, 2003. A highly analytical and sympathetic investigation of the Latin American export and self-sufficiency economies, calling into question the long dominant dependency theories of Latin America.

Burkholder, Mark, and Lyman Johnson. *Colonial Latin America*, 6th ed. New York: Oxford University Press, 2008. Overview, with focus on social and cultural history.

Dawson, Alexander. *Latin America Since Independence: A History with Primary Sources*. New York: Routledge, 2011. Selection of topics with documentary base; for the nineteenth century on the topics of the nation-state, caudillo politics, race, and the policy of growth through commodity exports.

Drake, Paul W. *Between Tyranny and Anarchy: A History of Democracy in Latin America*. Palo Alto, CA: Stanford University Press, 2009. The author traces the concepts of constitutionalism, autocracy, and voting rights since independence in clear and persuasive strokes.

Eakin, Marshall Craig. *The History of Latin America: Collision of Cultures*. New York: Palgrave Macmillan, 2007. A Brazilianist with a special eye on the ethnic and social class system of Latin America.

Meade, Teresa A. *A History of Modern Latin America: 1800 to the Present*. Chichester, UK: Wiley-Blackwell, 2010. The nineteenth-century portion of this study presents a comprehensive political, social, and economic survey, going more deeply into the details of many aspects discussed in this chapter.

Prados de la Escosura, Leandro. "The Economic Consequences of Independence in Latin America." In: *The Cambridge Economic History of Latin America*. Vol. 1, *The Colonial Era and the Short Nineteenth*

Century. Edited by Victor Bulmer-Thomas, John H. Coatsworth, and Roberto Cortés Conde, pp. 463–504. Cambridge: Cambridge University Press, 2006. Superb analysis of the main factors characteristic for Latin America's special path toward economic development without industrialization.

Thurner, Mark, and Andrés Guerrero, eds. *After Spanish Rule: Postcolonial Predicaments of the Americas.* Durham, NC: Duke University Press, 2003. Collection of articles by different authors on the multiple cultural and social challenges which Latin Americans faced after independence.

Wasserman, Mark, and Cheryl English Martin. *Latin America and Its People*, 2nd ed. New York: Pearson Longman, 2007. Thematic approach, drawing general conclusions by comparing and contrasting the individual countries of Latin America.

WEBSITES

http://www.casahistoria.net/latin_american_history19.html. Casahistoria.net. Website on nineteenth-century Latin America, for students.

http://www.suite101.com/latinamericanhistory. Suite101.com. A website featuring a long list of short essays on Latin American topics.

Chapter 28

Berend, Ivan T. *An Economic History of Twentieth-Century Europe: Economic Regimes from Laissez-Faire to Globalization.* Cambridge: Cambridge University Press, 2006. Includes Europe-wide, comparative chapters on laissez-faire and state-directed economies, including deficit spending.

Bose-Sugata, and Ayesha Jalal. *Modern South Asia: History, Culture, Political Economy.* New York: Routledge, 2004. Well-informed analyses by two of the foremost South Asia specialists.

Fritzsche, Peter. *Life and Death in the Third Reich.* Cambridge, MA: Harvard University Press, 2008. Book that seeks to understand the German nation's choice of arranging itself to Nazi rule.

Gelvin, James L. *The Modern Middle East: A History*, 3rd ed. Oxford: Oxford University Press, 2011. Contains chapters on Arab nationalism, British and French colonialism, as well as Turkey and Iran in the interwar period.

Gordon, Andrew. *A Modern History of Japan: From Tokugawa Times to the Present*, 2nd ed. Oxford: Oxford University Press, 2009. Detailed overview of Japan's interwar period in the middle chapters.

Grasso, June M., J. P. Corrin, and Michael Kort. *Modernization and Revolution in Modern China: From the Opium Wars to the Olympics*, 4th ed. Armonk, NY: M. E. Sharpe, 2009. General overview with a focus on modernization, in relation to the strong survival of tradition.

Lombardo, Paul A., ed. *A Century of Eugenics in America: From the Indiana Experiment to the Human Genome Era.* Bloomington: Indiana University Press, 2011. Study of a dark chapter in US history.

Martel, Gordon, ed. *A Companion to Europe 1900–1945.* Malden, MA: Wiley-Blackwell, 2010. Collective work covering a large variety of cultural, social, and political European topics in the interwar period.

Meade, Teresa A. *A History of Modern Latin America: 1800 to the Present.* Malden, MA: Wiley-Routledge, 2010. Topical discussion of the major issues in Latin American history, with chapters on the first half of the twentieth century.

Snyder, Timothy. *Bloodlands: Europe Between Hitler and Stalin.* New York: Basic Books, 2010. Book that chronicles the horrific destruction left behind by these two dictators.

WEBSITES

http://www.ushistory.org/us/. Maintained by Independence Hall Association in Philadelphia, it contains many links to topics discussed in this chapter.

http://www.bbc.co.uk/history/worldwars/wwone/ and http://www.bbc.co.uk/history/worldwars/wwtwo/. The BBC's treatment of the causes, course and consequences for both WWI and WWII from an Allied position.

http://www.marxists.org/subject/bolsheviks/index.htm. A complete review of the Bolshevik party members including biographies and links to archives which contain their works.

http://www.ushmm.org/wlc/en/article.php?ModuleId=10005151. The US Holocaust Memorial Museum looks back on one of the darkest times in western history. http://www.nanking-massacre.com/Home.html. A disturbing collection of pictures and articles tell the gruesome history of the Raping of Nanking.

Chapter 29

Baret, Roby Carol. *The Greater Middle East and the Cold War: US Foreign Policy Under Eisenhower and Kennedy.* London: Tauris, 2007. Thoroughly researched analysis of American policies in the Middle East, North Africa, and south Asia.

Birmingham, David. *Kwame Nkrumah: Father of African Nationalism.* Athens: University of Ohio Press, 1998. Short biography by a leading modern African historian.

Conniff, Michael L. *Populism in Latin America.* Tuscaloosa: University of Alabama Press, 1999. The author is a well-published scholar on modern Latin America.

Damrosch, David, David Lawrence Pike, Djelal Kadir, and Ursula K. Heise, eds. *The Longman Anthology of World Literature.* Vol. F, *The Twentieth Century.* New York: Longman/Pearson, 2008. A rich, diverse selection of texts. Alternatively, Norton published a similar, somewhat larger anthology of world literature in 2003.

De Witte, Ludo. *The Assassination of Lumumba.* Translated by Ann Wright and Renée Fenby. London: Verso, 2002. An admirably researched study of the machinations of the Belgian government in protecting its mining interests, with the connivance of CIA director Allen Dulles and President Dwight D. Eisenhower.

Goscha, Christopher E., and Christian F. Ostermann. *Connecting Histories: Decolonization and the Cold War in Southeast Asia, 1945–1962.* Stanford, CA: Stanford University Press, 2009.

Guha, Ramachandra. *India After Gandhi. A History of the World's Largest Democracy.* New York: Harper Collins, 2007. Highly readable, popular history with well-sketched biographical treatments of leading individuals, more obscure cultural figures, and ordinary people. Accessible to even beginning students.

Hasegawa, Tsuyoshi. *The Cold War in East Asia, 1945–1991.* Stanford, CA: Stanford University Press, 2011. A new summary, based on archival research by a leading Japanese historian teaching in the United States. New insights on the Soviet entry into WWII against Japan.

WEBSITES

http://www.economist.com/node/7218678. The Economist Magazine looks back on 'An Affair to Remember, the Suez Crisis and its implications.

http://www.nasa.gov/mission_pages/shuttle/sts1/gagarin_anniversary.html. In addition to providing information and video footage regarding Yuri Gagarin's orbit of the earth, students will also find information on America's space history.

http://www.newseum.org/berlinwall/. The Newseum's interactive website looks at what life was like on both sides of the Berlin Wall.

Chapter 30

Duara, Prasenjit. *Decolonization: Perspectives from Now and Then.* London: Routledge, 2004. A leading scholar of China and postcolonial studies edits essays in this offering in the Rewriting Histories series on the fall of the colonial empires by scholars such as Michael Adas and John Voll and activists and leaders such as Frantz Fanon and Kwame Nkrumah.

Fanon, Frantz. *The Wretched of the Earth*. New York: Grove Press, 1961. One of the most provocative and influential treatments of theoretical and practical issues surrounding decolonization. Fanon champions violence as an essential part of the decolonization process and advocates a modified Marxist approach that takes into consideration the nuances of race and the legacies of colonialism.

Frieden, Jeffrey. *Global Capitalism: Its Fall and Rise in the Twentieth Century*. New York: W. W. Norton, 2006. Despite the title, a comprehensive history of global networks from the days of mercantilism to the twenty-first century. Predominant emphasis on twentieth century; highly readable, though the material is best suited for the nonbeginning student.

Gaddis, John Lewis. *The Cold War: A New History*. New York: Penguin, 2005. Though criticized by some scholars for his pro-American positions, America's foremost historian of the Cold War produces here a vivid, at times counterintuitive, view of the Cold War and its global impact. Readable even for beginning students.

Gitlin, Todd. *The Sixties: Years of Hope, Days of Rage*, rev. ed. New York: Bantam, 1993. Lively, provocative account of this pivotal decade by the former radical, now sociologist. Especially effective at depicting the personalities of the pivotal period 1967–1969.

Liang Heng and Judith Shapiro. *After the Nightmare: A Survivor of the Cultural Revolution Reports on China Today*. New York: Knopf, 1986. Highly readable, poignant, first-person accounts of people's experiences during the trauma of China's Cultural Revolution by a former husband and wife team. Especially interesting because China was at the beginning of its Four Modernizations and the wounds of the Cultural Revolution were still fresh.

Smith, Bonnie. *Global Feminisms Since 1945*. London: Routledge, 2000. Part of the Rewriting Histories series, this work brings together under the editorship of Smith a host of essays by writers such as Sara Evans, Mary Ann Tetreault, and Miriam Ching Yoon Louie on feminism in Asia, Africa, Latin America, as well as Europe and the United States. Sections are thematically arranged under such topics as "Nation-building," "Sources of activism," "Women's liberation," and "New waves in the 1980s and 1990s." Comprehensive and readable, though some background in women's history is recommended.

WEBSITES

www.wilsoncenter.org/program/cold-war-international-history-project. Cold War International History Project of the Woodrow Wilson International Center for Scholars. Rich archival materials including collections on the end of the Cold War, Soviet invasion of Afghanistan, Cuban Missile Crisis, and Chinese foreign policy documents.

Codlibrary.org. College of DuPage Library. Typing in the "search" box "Research guide to 1960s websites" yields a wide-ranging set of relevant topics.

Chau, Adam Yuet, ed. *Religion in Contemporary China*. New York: Routledge, 2011. Collection of fascinating chapters on the revival of Daoist, Confucian, and Buddhist traditions and their adaption to middle-class modernity, with their proponents operating often in a gray zone between official recognition and suppression.

Daniels, Robert V. *The Rise and Fall of Communism in the Soviet Union*. New Haven, CT: Yale University Press, 2010. A magisterial summary of the communist period by a specialist.

Dillon, Michael. *Contemporary China: An Introduction*. New York: Routledge, 2009. Concise yet quite specific overview of the economy, society, and politics of the country.

Eichengreen, Barry. *Exorbitant Privilege: The Rise and Fall of the Dollar and the Future of the Monetary System*. New York: Oxford University Press, 2011. The author is an academic specialist on US monetary policies, writing in an accessible style and presenting a fascinating picture of the role of something as prosaic as greenbacks.

Meade, Teresa A. *A History of Modern Latin America: 1800 to the Present*. Malden, MA: Wiley-Blackwell, 2010. The book is an excellent, comprehensive analysis and has a strong final chapter on recent Latin America.

Saxonberg, Steven. *The Fall: A Comparative Study of the End of Communism in Czechoslovakia, East Germany, Hungary, and Poland*. Amsterdam: Harwood Academic, 2001. A well-informed overview of the different trajectories by an academic teaching in Prague.

Speth, James Gustav. *The Bridge at the Edge of the World: Capitalism, the Environment, and Crossing from Crisis to Sustainability*. New Haven, CT: Yale University Press, 2008. A strong plea to change our capitalist system.

Swanimathan, Jayshankar M. *Indian Economic Superpower: Fact or Fiction?* Singapore: World Scientific Publishing, 2009. A thoughtful evaluation of the pros and cons, in concise overviews.

Wapner, Kevin. *Living through the End of Nature: The Future of American Environmentalism*. Cambridge, MA: MIT Press, 2010. A specialist's look at the vast transformation of nature which is taking place according to the best evidence science can marshal.

WEBSITES

http://sierraclub.org/. Balanced and informative environmental websites.

http://www.epa.gov/climatechange/. The US Environmental Protection Agency's website reviews the threat to the world's climate and the implications of consistent abuse. The site also looks at various initiatives to help reverse some of the damage already done.

http://www.bbc.co.uk/news/world-africa-12305154. The BBC News looks back at the life and career of Nelson Mandela.

Chapter 31

Béja, Jean-Philippe, ed. *The Impact of China's 1989 Tiananmen Massacre*. New York: Routledge, 2011. Highly diverse contributions on this watershed event and the devastating effect it had on middle-class self-evaluation.

Credits

Chapter 1: pg. 4 © Christoph Hormann; pg. 8 Morton Beebe / Corbis; pg. 10 (left) Réunion des Musées Nationaux / Art Resource, NY; pg. 10 (top right) akg-images / CDA / Guillemot; pg. 10 (bottom right) National Museum of Tanzania, Dar es Salaam, (c) 1985 David L. Brill; pg. 14 © Kenneth Garrett Photography; pg. 18 Photograph by Chris O'Connell, Bradshaw Foundation, Geneva; pg. 19 (top) „Lion-man," statuette carved of mammouth-tusk, H 296 mm Site: Hohlenstein-Stadel-cave, community Asselfingen, Baden-Württemberg, Germany Upper Paleolithic period (Aurignacien), approx. 32 000 BP. Inv. Ulmer Museum Prä Slg. Wetzel Ho-St. 39/88.1 Photo Thomas Stephan, © Ulmer Museum; pg. 19 (bottom) Foto: Hilde Jensen, copyright University Tübingen; pg. 20 (top) © Walter Geiersperger/Corbis; pg. 20 (bottom) © Charles & Josette Lenars / CORBIS; pg. 24 Francesco d'Errico; pg. 27 ASSOCIATED PRESS

Chapter 2: pg. 30 The Trustees of The British Museum / Art Resource, NY; pg. 33 Courtesy of the Peabody Museum of Archaeology and Ethnology, Harvard University, 61-23-60/N10296.0 (digital file #98790058); pg. 37 adapted from Gianni Tortoli / Photo Researchers, Inc; pg. 39 Erich Lessing / Art Resource, N.Y.; pg. 41 © Copyright Alfred Molon pg. 42 Réunion des Musées Nationaux / Art Resource, NY; pg. 45 Nimatallah / Art Resource, NY; pg. 48 Werner Forman / Art Resource, NY; pg. 54 © Nathan Benn / Alamy; pg. 57 (right) akg-images / John Hios; pg. 57 (left) Scala / Art Resource, NY

Chapter 3: pg. 60 © DeA Picture Library / Art Resource, NY; pg. 64 © Diego Lezama Orezzoli / CORBIS; pg. 67 (top) Photo courtesy of National Museum of Pakistan, Karachi; pg. 67 (bottom) © Harappa; pg. 68 © Harappa; pg. 75 bpk, Berlin / Museum fuer Asiatische Kunst, Staatliche Museen / Iris Papadopoulos / Art Resource, NY; pg. 79 Firmin Didot, ~ 1810, Copyright: ImagesofAsia.com; pg. 80 © Doranne Jacobson; pg. 81 © Doranne Jacobson

Chapter 4: pg. 84 © Xiaoyang Liu/Corbis; pg. 89 Photo ChinaStock; pg. 90 © Asian Art & Archaeology, Inc. / CORBIS; pg. 93 V&A Images, London / Art Resource, NY; pg. 95 photo by Gary Lee Todd; pg. 103 Photo ChinaStock; pg. 104 © Lowell Georgia/CORBIS; pg. 105 © Asian Art & Archaeology, Inc. / CORBIS

Chapter 5: pg. 110 ERNESTO BENAVIDES/AFP/Getty Images/ Newscom; pg. 118 (top) © David Muench / CORBIS; pg. 118 (bottom) © Ricardo Azoury / CORBIS; pg. 120 National Geographic; pg. 123 © Sean Sprague / The Image Works pg. 124 © Charles & Josette Lenars / CORBIS; pg. 125 Image copyright © The Metropolitan Museum of Art. Image source: Art Resource, NY; pg. 126 © Charles & Josette Lenars / CORBIS; pg. 129 Science © 2006; pg. 133 © Caroline Penn / Impact / HIP / The Image Works; pg. 134 © ImageSpan

Chapter 6: pg. 140 © Kazuyoshi Nomachi/Corbis; pg. 147 Werner Forman / Art Resource, NY; pg. 152 Werner Forman / Art Resource, NY; pg. 155 Richard Maschmeyer; pg. 159 bpk, Berlin / Ethnologisches Museum, Staatliche Museen / Art Resource, NY; pg. 160 Photograph K2803© Justin Kerr; pg. 163 DEA / G. DAGLI ORTI; pg. 164 © Gianni Dagli Orti / CORBIS; pg. 165 © Keren Su/CORBIS

Chapter 7: pg. 168 Vanni / Art Resource, NY; pg. 172 SEF / Art Resource, NY; pg. 176 Louis and Nancy Hatch Dupree Collection, Williams Afghan Media Project Archive; pg. 178 Vanni / Art Resource, NY; pg. 188 © Wolfgang Kaehler/Corbis; pg. 191 Photo © Zev Radovan; pg. 194 akg-images / Gerard Degeorge; pg. 195 Image copyright © The Metropolitan Museum of Art / Art Resource, NY; pg. 196 (bottom) Erich Lessing / Art Resource, NY

Chapter 8: pg. 200 Courtesy of the Library of Congress; pg. 205 Borromeo / Art Resource, NY; pg. 206 © Clive Friend; pg. 209 © Lindsay Hebberd/CORBIS; pg. 211 R. u. S. Michaud / akg-images; pg. 214 akg-images / A.F.Kersting; pg. 216 Image copyright © The Metropolitan Museum of Art; pg. 220 © The Trustees of the British Museum; pg. 223 Image copyright © The Metropolitan Museum of Art.

Chapter 9: pg. 228 © The Trustees of the British Museum; pg. 232 © Glow Asia RF / Alamy; pg. 236 akg-images / Laurent Lecat/; pg. 237 HIP / Art Resource, NY; pg. 240 photo by Gary Lee Todd; pg. 242 Courtesy of ChinaStock; pg. 245 Courtesy of ChinaStock; pg. 250 Courtesy of the Museum of Fine Arts, Boston. Francis Bartlett Donation of 1912; pg. 251 (top) Image copyright © The Metropolitan Museum of Art; pg. 251 (bottom) Courtesy of the National Archive and Records Administration.

Chapter 10: pg. 256 Courtesy of the Library of Congress; pg. 260 © Kazuyoshi Nomachi/Corbis; pg. 261 © The Trustees of the British Museum / Art Resource, NY; pg. 265 ALIMDI.NET / Fabian von Poser; pg. 269 (left) © Bruno Morandi / SOPA / Corbis; pg. 269 (right) © Jon Hicks / Corbis; pg. 270 © Steven Vidler / Eurasia Press / Corbis; pg. 275 © British Library Board. All Rights Reserved; pg. 276 Scala / White Images / Art Resource, NY; pg. 280 bpk, Berlin / Bibliotheque Nationale / Gérard Le Gall / Art Resource, NY; pg. 281 With kind permission of the University of Edinburgh; pg. 284 (top) The Metropolitan Museum of Art / Art Resource, NY; pg. 284 (bottom) V&A Images, London / Art Resource, NY.

Chapter 11: pg. 288 Erich Lessing / Art Resource, NY; pg. 292 bpk, Berlin / Cathedral (Palatine Chapel), Aachen, Germany / Stefan Diller / Art Resource, NY; pg. 301 bpk, Berlin / Bodleian Library / Hermann Buresch / Art Resource, NY; pg. 302 bpk, Berlin / Hamburger Kunsthalle / Elke Walford / Art Resource, NY; pg. 304 (left) Alinari; pg. 304 (right) akg-images / Henning Bock; pg. 308 bpk, Berlin / Kupferstichkabinett, Staatliche Museen, Berlin, Germany / Joerg P. Anders / Art Resource, NY; pg. 310 Peter Willi; pg. 311 (left) Anthony Scibilia / Art Resource, NY; pg. 311 (right) Anthony Scibilia / Art Resource, NY; pg. 313 akg-images / VISIOARS

Chapter 12: pg. 322 akg-images; pg. 325 Image by © Michael S. Yamashita/CORBIS; pg. 327 akg-images / Gerard Degeorge; pg. 331 National Museum of China / China Stock; pg. 337 The Art Archive at Art Resource, NY; pg. 338 (top) © All rights reserved by Seoul Korea; pg. 338 (bottom) The Art Archive at Art Resource, NY; pg. 344 Courtesy of ChinaStock; pg. 345 © CORBIS; pg. 347 Freer Gallery of Art, Smithsonian Institution, Washington, D.C.: Purchase, F1959.6.

Chapter 13: pg. 350 Photo © AISA; pg. 355 © Carmen Redondo / CORBIS; pg. 359 from A Handbook of Korea. Korean Overseas Information Service. Seoul, 1993. pg 50; pg. 360 © Atlantide Phototravel / Corbis; pg. 361 Image copyright © The Metropolitan Museum of Art / Art Resource, NY; pg. 365 Plan of Heiankyo. Transcribed by Mori Koan in 1750. National Archives of Japan; pg. 367 Image copyright © The Metropolitan Museum of Art / Art Resource, NY; pg. 370 Image copyright © The Metropolitan Museum of Art / Art

Resource, NY; pg. 376 © Luca Tettoni/Robert Harding World Imagery / Corbis.

Chapter 14: pg. 380 Detail from the Catalan Atlas, 1375 (vellum) (detail of 151844), Cresques, Abraham (1325-87) / Bibliotheque Nationale, Paris, France / The Bridgeman Art Library; pg. 386 © Franck Guiziou / Hemis / Corbis; pg. 392 © Nigel Pavitt / JAI / Corbis; pg. 393 Mapungubwe Museum, Department of UP Arts, at the University of Pretoria; pg. 394 © South African Railways & Amp Harbors / National Geographic Society / Corbis; pg. 401 © Sandro Vannini / CORBIS; pg. 402 akg-images / André Held; pg. 403 Image courtesy of The Minneapolis Institute of Arts.

Chapter 15: pg. 406 © Margaret Sidlosky; pg. 412 © Michael Freeman / CORBIS; pg. 413 © Christophe Boisvieux / Corbis; pg. 417 The Art Archive / Bodleian Library Oxford; pg. 419 Gianni Dagli Orti / The Art Archive at Art Resource, NY; pg. 422 (top) Robert Cortright, Bridge Ink; pg. 422 (bottom) © RICKEY ROGERS / Reuters / Corbis; pg. 423 © Ellisphotos / Alamy; pg. 426 © Kelly-Mooney Photography / Corbis; pg. 429 © Bettmann / CORBIS.

Chapter 16: pg. 434 Erich Lessing / Art Resource, NY; pg. 439 The Art Archive / Real Monasterio del Escorial Spain / Granger Collection; pg. 442 (left) © DeA Picture Library / Art Resource, NY; pg. 442 (center) The Art Archive / Eileen Tweedy; pg. 442 (right) © John Warburton-Lee Photography / Alamy; pg. 443 (left) AP Photo/Thomas Haentzschel; pg. 443 (right) s70 / ZUMA Press / Newscom; pg. 444 © The Granger Collection, New York; pg. 445 ullstein - Archiv Gerstenberg/akg; pg. 450 Cameraphoto Arte, Venice / Art Resource, NY; pg. 452 Topkapi Palace Museum, Istanbul, Turkey / The Bridgeman Art Library; pg. 453 Bridgeman-Giraudon / Art Resource, NY; pg. 454 Courtesy of the Library of Congress; pg. 456 Erich Lessing / Art Resource, NY; pg. 458 Erich Lessing / Art Resource, NY; pg. 459 The Metropolitan Museum of Art / Art Resource, NY; pg. 460 © Bob Krist/Corbis; pg. 461 (top) The Art Archive / Topkapi Museum Istanbul / Gianni Dagli Orti; pg. 461 (a) Art Resource, NY; pg. 461 (b) Vanni / Art Resource, NY; pg. 461 (c) © Simon Harris / Robert Harding World Imagery / Corbis.

Chapter 17: pg. 464 Courtesy of the Library of Congress; pg. 468 Peter Newark Military Pictures; pg. 471 © DHM; pg. 473 akg-images; pg. 477 veröffentlicht in den Hogenbergschen Geschichtsblättern; pg. 479 Réunion des Musées Nationaux / Art Resource, NY; pg. 480 akg-images / RIA Nowosti; pg. 481 akg-images; pg. 484 Courtesy of the Library of Congress; pg. 485 (a) Alinari / Art Resource, NY; pg. 485 (b) Réunion des Musées Nationaux / Art Resource, NY; pg. 485 (c) Image copyright © The Metropolitan Museum of Art. Image source: Art Resource, NY; pg. 487 Courtesy of the Library of Congress; pg. 489 Museo Galileo. Florence–Photo Franca Principe; pg. 492 © Witold Skrypczak / Lonely Planet Image; pg. 493 akg-images/.

Chapter 18: pg. 498 Courtesy of the Library of Congress; pg. 501 Archives Charmet; pg. 504 (top) bpk, Berlin / Ethnologisches Museum, Staatliche Museen /Dietrich Graf / Art Resource, NY; pg. 504 (bottom) Biblioteca del ICI, Madrid, Spain / Index / The Bridgeman Art Library International; pg. 505 Courtesy of the Library of Congress; pg. 510 The Art Archive / Biblioteca National do Rio de Janiero Brazil / Gianni Dagli Orti; pg. 513 © Lebrecht Music & Arts/Corbis; pg. 515 Courtesy of The Hispanic Society of America, New York; pg. 520 Snark / Art Resource, NY; pg. 521 Museo de America, Madrid, Spain / The Bridgeman Art Library International; pg. 522 Courtesy of the Library of Congress; pg. 525 Giraudon; pg. 526 The Granger Collection, NYC—All rights reserved; pg. 527 The Library Company of Philadelphia; pg. 528 The Stapleton Collection.

Chapter 19: pg. 532 Courtesy of Michele Araldi; pg. 540 Erich Lessing / Art Resource, NY; pg. 541 (a) © CORBIS; pg. 541 (b) Werner Forman / Art Resource, NY; pg. 542 Werner Forman / Art Resource, NY; pg. 544 Image copyright © The Metropolitan Museum of Art. Image source: Art Resource, NY; pg. 545 Art Resource; pg. 548 HIP / Art Resource, NY; pg. 553 Art Resource; pg. 556 © Michael Graham-Stewart; pg. 557 Abby Aldrich Rockefeller Fold Art Museum, The colonial Williamsburg Foundation, Williamsburg, Va; pg. 558 © Robert Holmes/CORBIS; pg. 559 Collection of Herbert M. and Shelley Cole. Photo by Don Cole; pg. 560 Archives Charmet.

Chapter 20: pg. 564 © dbimages / Alamy; pg. 568 (c) The British Library Board, J. 1,2; pg. 569 V&A Images / The Art Resource, NY; pg. 570 (top) Erich Lessing / Art Resource, NY; pg. 570 (bottom left) Werner Forman / Art Resource, NY; pg. 570 (bottom right) Image copyright © The Metropolitan Museum of Art. Image source: Art Resource, NY; pg. 572 © Arthur Thévenart / CORBIS; pg. 574 Courtesy of The Chester Beatty Library; pg. 578 Rijksmuseum, Amsterdam; pg. 580 © The Trustees of the Chester Beatty Library, Dublin / The Bridgeman Art Library International; pg. 583 Digital Image © [year] Museum Associates / LACMA. Licensed by Art Resource, NY; pg. 586 © Historical Picture Archive / CORBIS.

Chapter 21: pg. 593 John C Weber Collection. Photo: John Bigelow Taylor; pg. 597 © Hulton-Deutsch Collection/CORBIS; pg. 598 The Metropolitan Museum of Art / Art Resource, NY; pg. 599 The Metropolitan Museum of Art / Art Resource, NY; pg. 600 © CHINASTOCK/QI WEN; pg. 602 © Bettmann/CORBIS; pg. 604 Roy Miles Fine Paintings; pg. 608 Réunion des Musées Nationaux / Art Resource, NY; pg. 610 © The Granger Collection, New York; pg. 613 Courtesy of the Library of Conrgess; pg. 614 University of British Columbia Library, Rare Books and Special Collections; pg. 616 akg-images; pg. 619 V&A Images, London / Art Resource, NY.

Chapter 22: pg. 624 © Trustees of the British Museum; pg. 628 Stock Sales WGBH / Scala / Art Resource, NY; pg. 632 (top left) © Bettmann / CORBIS; pg. 632 (top right) © Gianni Dagli Orti / CORBIS; pg. 632 (bottom) © Gianni Dagli Orti / CORBIS; pg. 634 © Gianni Dagli Orti / CORBIS; pg. 635 Courtesy of the Library of Congress; pg. 637 Musée de l'Armée / Dist. Réunion des Musées Nationaux / Art Resource, NY; pg. 638 SSPL / Science Museum / Art Resource, NY; pg. 641 bpk, Berlin / Art Resource, NY; pg. 644 © Lebrecht Music & Arts / Corbis; pg. 646 © The Print Collector / Corbis; pg. 650 National Folklore Collection, University College Dublin; pg. 652 (top) National Gallery, London / Art Resource, NY; pg. 652 (bottom) Erich Lessing / Art Resource, NY; pg. 653 © Hulton-Deutsch Collection / CORBIS.

Chapter 23: pg. 656 Courtesy of the Library of Congress; pg. 664 SSPL via Getty Images; pg. 669 © Bettmann/CORBIS; pg. 673 The Stapleton Collection; pg. 676 Archives Charmet; pg. 677 IAM / akg-images; pg. 678 Peter Newark Pictures; pg. 680 Natural History Museum, London, UK / The Bridgeman Art Library International; pg. 683 Giraudon.

Chapter 24: pg. 686 © Philadelphia Museum of Art / CORBIS; pg. 690 (right) The Art Archive at Art Resource, NY; pg. 690 (left) Courtesy of the Library of Congress; pg. 692 Eileen Tweedy / The Art Archive at Art Resource; pg. 695 (top) National Palace Museum; pg. 695 (bottom) © The Print Collector / Heritage / The Image Works; pg. 696 (top) akg-images / British Library; pg. 696 (a) Peter Newark Pictures / The Bridgeman Art Library International; pg. 698 (b) © Philadelphia Museum of Art / CORBIS; pg. 699 © Mary Evans Picture Library / The Image Works; pg. 700 Tz'U-Hsi (1835-1908) Empress Dowager of

China with ladies of the court, 1903 (b/w photo), Chinese School, (20th century) / Private Collection / The Bridgeman Art Library International; pg. 701 IAM / akg / NA; pg. 706 John Thomson; pg. 710 Courtesy of the Library of Congress.

Chapter 25: pg. 716 Auction of Serfs, 1910 (w/c on paper), Lebedev, Klavdiy Vasilievich (1852-1916) / Arkhangelsk Museum, Russia / The Bridgeman Art Library International; pg. 722 (a) Réunion des Musées Nationaux / Art Resource, NY; pg. 722 (b) akg-images / British Library; pg. 726 Courtesy of the Library of Congress; pg. 728 © Bettmann / CORBIS; pg. 731 © Roger-Viollet / The Image Works; pg. 732 (a) © Tibor Bognar / Corbis; pg. 732 (b) © Paule Seux / Hemis / Corbis; pg. 732 (c) © Diego Lezama Orezzoli / CORBIS; pg. 738 © Heritage Images / Corbis; pg. 741 © Reproduced by permission of The State Hermitage Museum, St. Petersburg, Russia / CORBIS; pg. 744 RIA Novosti.

Chapter 26: pg. 748 Kharbine Tapabor; pg. 751 (a) © National Portrait Gallery, London; pg. 751 (b) (c) The British Library Board, Add. Or.3079; pg. 753 Eileen Tweedy / The Art Archive at Art Resource, NY; pg. 758 Réunion des Musées Nationaux / Art Resource, NY; pg. 759 (top) Archives Charmet; pg. 759 (bottom) Dorling Kindersley; pg. 761 National Library of Australia; pg. 765 © Hulton-Deutsch Collection / CORBIS; pg. 769 (top) Getty Images; pg. 769 (bottom) © Bojan Brecelj / CORBIS; pg. 770 ullstein bild / The Granger Collection , New York; pg. 776 Courtesy of the Library of Congress; pg. 777 Courtesy of the Library of Congress.

Chapter 27: pg. 780 Battle on Santo Domingo, a painting by January Suchodolski; pg. 784 Schalkwijk / Art Resource, NY; pg. 789 Erich Lessing / Art Resource, NY; pg. 790 Ralph Arnold Collection, Huntington Library, San Marino, California; pg. 791 © CORBIS; pg. 798 The Granger Collection, New York; pg. 807 Courtesy of the Library of Congress; pg. 808 © akg-images / The Image Works.

Chapter 28: pg. 814 Courtesy of the Library of Congress; pg. 816 © Hulton-Deutsch Collection / CORBIS; pg. 818 Popperfoto / Getty Images; pg. 822 Courtesy of the Library of Congress; pg. 824 Getty Images; pg. 828 The Granger Collection, NYC—All rights reserved; pg. 829 (a) Digital Image © The Museum of Modern Art/Licensed by SCALA / Art Resource, NY; pg. 829 (b) © 2007 Artists Rights Society (ARS), New York / VEGAP, Madrid; pg. 831 Getty Images; pg. 832 Getty Images; pg. 836 © Bettmann / CORBIS; pg. 839 Courtesy of the Library of Congress; pg. 841 © Hulton-Deutsch Collection / CORBIS; pg. 844 Courtesy of the Library of Congress; pg. 849 Getty Images; pg. 850 © Bettmann / CORBIS.

Chapter 29: pg. 854 Getty Images; pg. 856 Time & Life Pictures / Getty Images; pg. 859 Associated Press; pg. 861 © Bettmann/CORBIS; pg. 864 © CORBIS; pg. 865 SSPL via Getty Images; pg. 866 (a & b) © The Museum of Modern Art/Licensed by SCALA / Art Resource, NY; pg. 868 Chris Brown; pg. 872 Courtesy of the Library of Congress; pg. 873 AFP/Getty Images; pg. 878 © Volkmar K. Wentzel / National Geographic Society / Corbis.

Chapter 30: pg. 886 © Alain DeJean / Sygma / CORBIS; pg. 889 © CORBIS; pg. 891 © Robert Maass / CORBIS; pg. 895 © Bettmann/ CORBIS; pg. 897 © Henry Diltz / CORBIS; pg. 901 © Bettmann / CORBIS; pg. 904 (a) © Jacques Langevin / Sygma / Corbis; pg. 904 (b) © Reuters/CORBIS; pg. 906 (a) © Bettmann / CORBIS; pg. 906 (b) © Geneviève Chauvel / Sygma / Corbis; pg. 909 © Bettmann / CORBIS; pg. 910 Courtesy of the Library of Congress.

Chapter 31: pg. 916 Getty Images Europe; pg. 923 © Hubert Boesl / dpa / Corbis; pg. 927 (a) © Lee Frost / Robert Harding World Imagery / Corbis; pg. 927 (b) Getty Images; pg. 928 (a) ASSOCIATED PRESS; pg. 928 (b) AP Images; pg. 935 © Samuel Aranda / Corbis; pg. 937 Associated Press; pg. 938 Associated Press; pg. 941 © Louise Gubb / CORBIS SABA; pg. 943 AFP / Getty Images.

Index

The letter f or m following a page number denotes a figure or map.